WHAT THE EXPERTS ARE SAYING . . .
ABOUT NEOCONNED

"This trenchant collection of articles about the U.S. war in the Middle East is a fulfillment of my dearest wish: seeing the left-wing and the right-wing, religious and non-religious, Christian and Muslim opposition to the war united in one front against one mutual enemy. It will be the cornerstone of every future realignment of anti-war forces in the U.S. and elsewhere. Read it, buy it, steal it, take it to your heart . . . !"

—Israel Adam Shamir
Journalist and author of *Flowers of Galilee*, Jaffa, Israel

"Jude Wanniski's analysis is superb, yet highly sobering. Citing authorities from the U.S. and abroad, Wanniski documents over two decades of lies, distortions and half-truths about Saddam Hussein and Iraq. From our self-serving interference in the 80s, through to the present, deadly quagmire in Iraq, Wanniski makes clear that *our* government was the real warmonger in the Persian Gulf region, not Baghdad's. Many supporters of the war will claim that the recent failure to find WMD in Iraq represents only an unfortunate detail in an otherwise justifiable invasion and occupation. Sadly, it appears we have been duped all along."

—Mark Gery
Clinical therapist and Iraq Analyst & Researcher, Education
for Peace in Iraq Center

"*Neo-CONNED!* is a first-of-a-kind compilation of essays that dissects from every vantage point – left, right, and center – the disastrous war in Iraq. It is essential reading for anyone who still lacks just the right argument to convince that pro-war uncle of yours. And for those who understand the importance for moving our nation from its present disastrous path of empire-building to one of a democracy that respects international law, *Neo-CONNED!* will give you a heaping plate of food for thought and ideas for action."

—Medea Benjamin
Co-Founder, Iraq Occupation Watch

"The subject of this book is extremely important and urgent. The range of opinions represented is impressive."

—Uri Avnery
Israeli journalist, writer, peace activist, and founding member,
Gush Shalom (Peace Bloc), Independent Peace Movement

"At last, a truly universal critique of the war in Iraq. As an Australian I always ask myself the question: why did we Australians join in? After reading *Neo-CONNED!* and *Neo-CONNED! Again* I find myself even more convinced that we were never given an adequate answer to that question."

—Anthony Cappello
Researcher, Victoria University, Australia; Director, Freedom
Publishing; and National Secretary, Thomas More Centre

"Although one need not agree with everything in these volumes, they show that there are orthodox Catholics who do follow the just-war doctrine of the Catholic Church, who are not knee-jerk super patriots. Germans Catholics have been blasted for not doing enough to oppose Hitler's wars, and Pope Pius XII has been implicated, rightly or wrongly. Let it be known, then, that not only did Pope John Paul II oppose the invasion of Iraq, but so did a good number of American orthodox Catholics. Posterity must know."

—Dale Vree
Editor, *New Oxford Review*

"Shakespeare has Hamlet remark that "Tis dangerous when the baser nature comes Between the pass and fell incensed points Of mighty opposites.' How much more dangerous when mighty opposites stop dueling each other and turn their sights on a common target. The essays in these volumes, ranging from the best minds of the liberal left to the great wisdom of the orthodox right, take on the war in Iraq, closely examining the ideas and motives of its planners, promoters, and defenders. Here is genuine intellectual diversity and hard analysis – fascinating and required reading."

—David Allen White, Ph.D.
Professor of English, U.S. Naval Academy

"Forged in the fires of urgent necessity, this magnificent compilation of essays from assorted thinkers, warrior and peacemaker alike, shall stand for generations to come as a lighthouse upon the shoals which threaten to destroy whatever is left of both our Christian civilization and even of any merely human ideals of justice and decency in the conduct of the domestic and international affairs of states. A thorough reading and understanding of this book will crystallize for the confused or unconvinced reader the knowledge that practically all-modern warfare (particularly the American war of Imperium against Iraq) is not only criminal but also contrary *in toto* to both Christian morality and to the *ratio recta* of the natural man. As a Catholic and an American I am profoundly grateful to Light in the Darkness Publications for the timely publication of this polemical masterpiece."

—Doug Bersaw
Educator, Publisher and President of Loreto Publications,
and Prefect of the Third Order of the Slaves of the
Immaculate Heart of Mary

"Having served in the army throughout WW2, half of the time as a Japanese POW, I have known some of the suffering involved in war, and its even sadder residue of hatred. From the beginning of the Gulf War, never for a moment has it seemed to me that it was in fact a just war. And if it was not a just war, it was an *unjust* war. These books support that judgment, and I wish them every success."

—Fr. Hugh Simon-Thwaites, S.J.
Onetime POW in Changi, Singapore

"IHS Press does a tremendous good work by its efforts to disseminate the riches of the social teachings of the Catholic Church. Of course, that wisdom is not limited to economics. It is essential to fidelity to our common patrimony within Western civilization, our citizenship in the United States, and our duty to God and His Church to be informed about the issues of our day. Regardless of one's position on the so-called "war on terrorism" and its prosecution in Afghanistan, Iraq, and the streets of

America, this collection of essays published by IHS's imprint, Light in the Darkness Publications, should offer anyone in pursuit of intellectual honesty an opportunity to weigh the arguments so seldom heard in the media, from politicians, and at the coffee counter."

—Fr. Lawrence C. Smith
Catholic priest

"'Might is not Right' is the saucy, Chestertonian title of Fr. J. C. Iscara's essay against 'preventive' war. What an awesome burden for the modern-day statesmen to carry, determining when it is licit, even imperative, to go to war, and still observing both international law *and* the higher moral law, which is also that of God. Warmly recommended!"

—Fr. Stephen Somerville, S.T.L.
Chaplain, *Regina Mundi* Retreat Centre,
Queensville, ON, Canada

"It's a monumental collection; fascinating reading."

—Judge (ret.) Albert C. Walsh
Author and Editor, *Christian Political Action Newsletter*

"From a remarkable array of different perspectives, a remarkably singular message: this war is illegal, ill-conceived, immoral, wrong. The reasons why – political, moral, and religious – are cogently spelled out in this powerful set of essays. Taken together, they are a cause for hope and a sign of peace. May these volumes be disseminated far and wide."

—Michael J. Baxter, C.S.C., Ph.D.
Professor of Theology, University of Notre Dame and
National Secretary, Catholic Peace Fellowship

"An excellent guide for students and all who are concerned with the current state of affairs. Too many books, essays, and articles offer one approach – either political, historical, or theological. This volume brings together the most recent news about the lies told regarding the reasons to go to war with Iraq, an astute history of the region, and a comprehensive just-war theology – the first I've seen that is used to argue against a war! A thoroughly religious book, with no smack of piety. Brilliant! The widest representation of voices against this war I have seen. Strong, very strong."

—Sheila McCarthy
Assistant Editor, *The Catholic Worker* and author,
The Veneer of Normalcy

"These often-profound and challenging essays meet an urgent need for analyses inspiring resistance to a moral catastrophe that can otherwise last years or decades."

—Daniel Ellsberg
Political activist and Senior Research Associate,
Massachusetts Institute of Technology's Center for
International Studies

"War should always be the last option; however, the fight to prevent war must be on-going and everlasting. *Neo-CONNED!* is a must read."

—Danny K. Davis
U.S. Congressman (D-Il., 7th District)

"Like many, I fear that the impact on the interests, well-being, and safety of the American people as a result of the ill-conceived, poorly executed and baseless devastation of Iraq will be highly negative, pervasive and of long duration. While it is too late to prevent the invasion, steps to reduce the length and savagery of the occupation can be taken. A public correctly informed on the political, economic, moral, and military issues involved will be far better able to play a role in ending the catastrophe – or at least limiting its effects. These volumes, filled with valuable insights from knowledgeable experts, can make a major contribution to achieving those desirable goals."

—Ambassador Edward L. Peck (ret.)
Former Chief of Mission in Iraq and Deputy Director,
Cabinet Task Force on Terrorism, Reagan White House

"Pope John Paul II warned President George W. Bush that his intended war in Iraq would violate the ancient Church doctrine of just war. American Catholics, torn between the teachings of their faith and loyalty to their elected president, prayed that post-war Iraq would somehow justify the blood their sons and daughters in uniform were about to shed. Those prayers will not be answered. Christian faith insists that accurate moral calculation is not beyond human capability. As *Neo-CONNED!* demonstrates, the flawed moral and political basis for this war was knowable and known by lay and religious experts long before the Iraq Survey Group admitted in 2004 that Iraq had destroyed its WMD arsenal thirteen years before. Light in the Darkness Publications has compiled a remarkable resource for every believer. The 84 distinguished contributors document in compelling detail that failure to meet the moral standards for just war are devastating for the interests of the victimizers as well as the victims. No reader of this crucial book will ever again mistake political loyalty for moral duty."

—John Brady Kiesling
Foreign Service Officer (ret.)

"What has happened to this once good and great nation? Where are the champions of liberty and human dignity? Where are the cries of moral outrage from the pulpits? Where are the thundering editorials lamenting the intrusions on civil liberties? Where are the voices of tenured academics calling our government to task for launching imperialist doctrines? *Largely absent.* It is for this reason that these two volumes are so welcome – because they champion Truth and Justice, and unite men and women of diverse political and religious beliefs in a crusade to end the killing of Iraqis and Americans in an unjust and unwinnable war."

—Paul Findley
Former U.S. Congressman (R-Il., 20th District)

"American Christians will find much food for thought in *Neo-CONNED!* Theologians explain Christian just-war doctrine while laymen – politicians, academics, military and intelligence officers, journalists, international lawyers and ordinary citizens – examine the policies, beliefs and misrepresentations of the neoconservatives who led our country to invade Iraq. Sobering stuff for those who inhabit this 'one nation under God' and believe that it can do no wrong."

—David MacMichael, Ph.D.
Former Analyst and Estimates Officer, CIA National
Intelligence Council

"This eclectic collection fills a large gap in the literature about the Iraq War by focusing squarely on the themes of religion and morality. The thoughtful and heartfelt commentaries it contains should offer great insight and inspiration to the millions of Americans who seek ethical answers to contemporary questions of war and peace."

—Greg Thielmann
Foreign Service Officer (ret.); former Director, Strategic,
Proliferation, and Military Affairs Office, State Department
Intelligence Bureau; and member, President's Advisory
Council, Wesley Theological Seminary

"This volume is an unwelcome but necessary dose of reality to the euphoria of Washington fantasies. Rather than content themselves with White House spin and propaganda these authors take an objective look at the facts surrounding the misadventure in Iraq and offer invaluable, incisive analysis. Read at your own risk."

—Larry Johnson
Former Deputy Director, U.S. State Department's Office of
Counter Terrorism and former Central Intelligence Agency
analyst and professional, Directorates of Operations and
Intelligence

"A magnificent achievement. This book provides unimpeachable arguments against the Iraq war, written by the most authoritative and most knowledgeable experts on the political, moral and religious dimensions of the issue."

—John Laughland, Ph.D.
British lecturer, author, and journalist

"These books really uncover the vested interests behind this war, and thus deserve a wide readership."

—Gearoid Mag Eochadha
Journalist, *Irish Family*, Ireland

"The world is a complicated place, and simple solutions rarely work. This is especially true where war is concerned. The rights and wrongs of warfare, self-defense, humanitarian intervention, and preemptive action, the way in which war is actually waged and on whose authority, do not lead to simple answers. These two volumes cover the ground, offering wide and differing perspectives, from numerous ideological, theological, and philosophical points of view. It is perhaps impressive that whichever route they take, they all tend to come to a similar conclusion to mine: that the Bush attack on Iraq was illegal, immoral – and what's more – stupid. A comprehensive collection of arguments that should be read by anyone who wants to pontificate on Iraq – but maybe a little too long and heavy for some talk show hosts to read."

—Ian Williams
UN correspondent, *The Nation*, and author, *The UN for Beginners*

"*Neo-CONNED!* says it all. This is a fascinating guidebook to the strange world of a handful of intriguers and the lies and deceits they utilized so skillfully and so ruthlessly in order to set the stage for the senseless and shameful no-win war in Iraq that will haunt America for generations."

—Michael Collins Piper
Author of *Final Judgment* and *The High Priests of War*;
veteran journalist on America's Israel policy; and
correspondent, *American Free Press*

"*Neo-CONNED!* is made up of a host of Catholic theologians and intellectuals who offer a deep insight into the Church's teachings on matters of war; metaphysical and moral problems linked to the Just War Doctrine; Higher Law; Conscience; and the stance of the Catholic and Roman Church towards the present war against Iraq in particular. Collectively they condemn the immorality of the neocon notion of "preventive war" in the light of the Church's teachings."

> —Susanne Scheidt
> Journalist, *Arab Monitor*

"These collections are an extremely valuable contribution both to the debate on the real causes of the Iraq War, and to the literature on the theory and practice of just war in history and in the world today."

> —Anatol Lieven, Ph.D.
> Senior Associate, Carnegie Endowment for International
> Peace, Washington, D.C.

"Any person seriously interested in peace should read this book. It provides a major and much-needed intellectual counterweight to the voices that recklessly plunged our world into the war on Iraq. The just-war doctrine was twisted and misinterpreted by the proponents of invading Iraq. If the just-war doctrine is to survive as a set of real analytical and moral principles, this book will help."

> —Bill Quigley, Ph.D.
> Professor of Law, Loyola University New Orleans and Editor,
> *Blueprint for Social Justice*

"What do the editors of *The Wanderer* and of the *Houston Catholic Worker* have in common? And Noam Chomsky and Patrick Buchanan? They with dozens of others oppose Bush's war in Iraq, seeing the country conned by his neoconservative advisers and their compatriots in the press and think tanks. These disparate essays are held together by the book's focus on traditional just-war theory. Some of the essays are gems and others not. The writers are weighted to the conservative side, but the book as a whole should provide a body blow to the pretensions of the neoconservative war hawks that are now dominant in the country."

> —Charles K Wilber, Ph.D.
> Emeritus Professor, Department of Economics, Notre Dame;
> Fellow, Kellogg Institute for International Studies; and Fellow,
> Kroc Institute for International Peace Studies

"Here at last are the voices of Christendom, of constitutional government, and of common sense that so far have been sadly missing from American public discourse on the aggression in Iraq."

> —Clyde Wilson, Ph.D.
> Professor of History, University of South Carolina and Director
> of Programs and Publications, League of the South Institute

"*Neo-CONNED!* is a welcome addition to the debate surrounding American policy in Iraq. In part, the book provides a particular Catholic theological perspective on the morality of the Iraq war. Just-war theory regarding the resort to, and the conduct of war emanated from the writings of St. Augustine, St. Thomas Aquinas, and more recently from the Catholic Bishops of America regarding the morality of nuclear strategy based on the threat to conduct total nuclear war. In a similar but more direct and incisive fashion, this book provides a critique of Washington's Iraq policy from a Catholic moral tradition. Was this war necessary? Is the use of military force proportionate to the situation on the ground? Does U.S. bombing discriminate adequately between combatants and civilians? Contributors to the book examine various dimensions of the Iraq crisis that led the Bush Administration to wander so far from its initial objective of bringing regional stability and democratic justice to the Middle East, into what now appears to be an immoral military and social quagmire."

—George C. Thomas, Ph.D.
Allis Chalmers Distinguished Professor of International Affairs, Marquette University, Milwaukee

"President Bush claims that his re-election demonstrates that there is no need to hold administration officials accountable for mistakes or misjudgements in connection with Iraq. The more than 80 essays and interviews contained in *Neo-CONNED!* and *Neo-CONNED! Again* present overwhelming evidence that this statement is as wrongheaded as the administration's earlier assertion that we know where the weapons are or its premature claim of mission accomplished. These two remarkably comprehensive volumes make it clear that no election can erase the fact that the war in Iraq is a moral disgrace and a strategic blunder. An unwillingness to hold both members of the administration and ourselves accountable for it will simply set the stage for a similar tragedy in the future."

—George W. Downs, Ph.D.
Dean of Social Science and Professor of Politics, New York University

"*Neo-CONNED!* is the most thorough compendium of writing from the left and the right, to date, on the principles and stratagems which led us into the Iraq war, and which threaten to keep us there for years to come. What is most useful to those of us working within the field of Catholic higher education is the project's emphasis on the application of Catholic social teachings on war and peace, and the application of same to the Iraqi situation. This is an invaluable reader and would make for an excellent textbook, as well."

—Gerard O'Sullivan, Ph.D.
Dean of Arts and Sciences and Associate Professor of English and Religious Studies, Felician College, New Jersey and co-author with Edward S. Herman, *The "Terrorism" Industry: The Experts and Institutions that Shape Our View of Terror*

"This volume shows the continued vitality of the just-war tradition as a source of theological and moral criticism of current American involvement in Iraq. Insofar as religious America is in great need of liberation from the political-religious hypocrisy of neoconservative thought, this volume provides just the right antidote."

—Hayward R. Alker, Ph.D.
John A. McCone Professor of International Relations, University of Southern California

"*Neo-CONNED!* brilliantly exposes the illegality, immorality, and danger of Bush's new 'preventive war' doctrine."

—Marjorie Cohn, J.D.
Professor of Law, Thomas Jefferson School of Law;
Executive Vice President, National Lawyers Guild; and U.S.
representative to the American Association of Jurists

"*Neo-CONNED!* is hardly a good foot soldier in the neoconservative battle for America's soul. On the one hand, this readable study turns neoconservative politics against itself, using conservative political principles to undermine the Bush Administration's struggle for world democracy. On the other hand, it draws from the rich tradition of Christian just-war theory to expose the immorality of the less-than-holy crusade that the neoconservatives have disingenuously launched in Iraq. In short, this lively book is an intellectually engaging exercise in political and religious iconoclasm."

—Michael G. Long, Ph.D.
Assistant Professor of Peace Studies and Assistant Professor
of Religious Studies, Elizabethtown College, Pennsylvania

"Anyone who continues to harbor the illusion that Bush's war in Iraq is morally legitimate will be shaken by the essays in this volume. They demonstrate conclusively that the criteria for just war, notably those derived from Roman Catholic doctrine, have been violated in every instance by the actions of Bush, Cheney, Rumsfeld, Powell and their lieutenants. A few of the earlier chapters minimize Saddam's responsibility for successive aggressions against Iran and Kuwait, and attribute the Iraq operation to a conspiracy hatched by a small coterie of neoconservatives committed to protecting Israel and spreading democracy in the Middle East. Like most conspiracy theories, it credits the neocons with considerably more influence than they actually possess. The important contribution of this book is its series of learned essays on just war and the failure of America's invasion of Iraq to comply with its requirements."

—Milton J. Esman, Ph.D.
John S. Knight Professor Emeritus, International Studies,
Cornell University

"The little-known statements by Bishop (Eparch) Botean deserve to be highlighted. They express a principled opposition to service in the Iraq war. Many another American bishop (certainly not all) would wish to state something similar, were it not so difficult to avoid misinterpretation and unwarranted crises of conscience on the part of members of the armed forces who find themselves now in a tough defensive position."

—Paul Misner, Ph.D.
Professor of Theology, Marquette University and
author, *Social Catholicism in Europe: From the Onset of
Industrialization to the First World War*

"This volume is a true goldmine of critical analysis of current U.S. foreign policy that focuses on the illegality of the armed military intervention in Iraq. It includes numerous excellent essays that draw upon the long theological/philosophical traditions of the Roman Catholic Church to challenge the legitimacy and legality of the invasion. Perhaps the most original contribution is the long interview with Jude Wanniski who challenges, with much supporting documentation, many of the negative assertions about Saddam Hussein and his foreign and domestic policies. The overall result is a volume that is at one and the same time depressing – because it lays out so clearly the duplicity of the U.S. government – and impressive in documenting the weaknesses underlying U.S. policy."

—Roger E. Kanet, Ph.D.
Professor of Political Science and Political Developments in
Central & Eastern Europe, University of Miami

"Was, and is, U.S. armed intervention in Iraq legal, prudent, and moral? Profound and wide-ranging analyses of these intertwined questions are presented in this thought-provoking volume by outstanding intellectuals, academics, theologians, and military professionals. An intriguing collection of essays that is timely and bound to be read widely."

—Saul Mendlovitz, Ph.D.
Dag Hammarskjold Professor of Peace and World Order
Studies Emeritus, Rutgers Law School

"*Neo-CONNED!* is a beacon of light at a time when religious faith is being used to justify the worst forms of nationalism, parochialism, and intolerance. It brings together a diverse group of noted academics, journalists, and religious leaders united by their opposition to American policy in Iraq. Emphasizing the unjust character of an increasingly barbaric war, insisting upon the need for resistance, this collection blends humanist values with the best elements of the Catholic tradition."

—Stephen Eric Bronner, Ph.D.
Professor of Political Science, Rutgers University

"The just-war tradition has always sought to be a practical guide to statecraft, not just a set of 'nice ideas.' These volumes confront the Iraq war from the standpoint of just-war theory and raise a serious challenge to common justifications for that war."

—Timothy J. McKeown, Ph.D.
Professor of Political Science, University of North Carolina,
Chapel Hill and Editorial Board, *American Journal of
Political Science*

"Here is a book that finally tells the truth about the Iraq War. It is written by thoughtful conservatives who reject the liberal messianic agenda of the Republican Party machine, whose only goal is the pursuit of power – both at home and abroad. This book will surely open a much needed debate on the war and other social issues that will determine America's future."

—Tobias Lanz, Ph.D.
Professor of Political Science, University of South Carolina

"The invasion and occupation of Iraq is the most massive U.S. intervention since the Vietnam War. Illegal and immoral, it has resulted in a predictable disaster for the peoples of Iraq and of the United States, undermined international law, militarized world politics, and threatened global peace and security. Now comes *Neo-CONNED!*, the most extensive collection anywhere of essays by leading commentators and analysts from faith-based communities, the policy world, the military, the media, and academia. These indispensable volumes provide readers with the background and context for understanding the war in Iraq. They unmask the lies and deceit upon which it was justified, analyze the interests behind it, the distinct players, the implications and possible outcomes. A must read for all who wish to become informed on the most urgent issue of our time."

—William I. Robinson, Ph.D.
Author and Professor of Sociology, Global and International Studies, and Latin American Studies, University of California, Santa Barbara

"In *Neo-CONNED!*, prominent paleo-conservative, libertarian and liberal commentators, journalists and clergy present a very compelling case that the invasion of Iraq was a moral, practical and strategic failure, which has cost the United States dearly in credibility, blood, treasure, and perhaps even its future as a constitutionally limited republic. It is an indispensable resource; I only hope that conservatives who are tempted to support these interventionist foreign policies will take this book seriously."

—Scott Horton
Host, *The Weekend Interview Show*, Republic Broadcasting Network

"Questions of what is and what is not a just war are more complex and urgent than ever after recent events in Iraq. Born of a passion for true justice, this collection deals with these questions with clarity, courage and compassion. Not all will agree with the conclusions, but none can evade the issues raised so starkly by these voices."

—Mark Coleridge
Auxiliary Catholic Bishop of Melbourne, Australia

"I found the distinction between pre-emptive and preventive war very interesting. It makes a huge difference in the case of a military action conducted in 'self-defense'. Even when 'self-defense' is used in its widest sense, there is still a 'burden of proof' which must be met, and which has not been in the case of Iraq."

—Giorgio Acquaviva
Editor for Religious Affairs, *Il Giorno*, Milan; *Il Resto del Carlino*, Bologna; and *La Nazione*, Florence, Italy

"From the first moment it became evident that the Bush/Blair transatlantic alliance was going to plunge us all into a morally unjustifiable 'preventive war,' *The Universe* campaigned relentlessly against the Iraq war. As a lone and isolated voice of doubt in the British media establishment we attracted considerable approbation for questioning openly the moral legitimacy of military action. Three years on, there are even more ominous signs that the Iraq paradigm is fast becoming a model for the imposition of so-called Western liberal democratic politics on other ancient cultures. This should concern all Catholics deeply, as it has everything to do with oppression, and very little to do with justice as we understand it. The Catholic Church is uniquely positioned to represent the oppressed, the vulnerable and the marginalized, and a coherent response is needed urgently to counteract Western militarist ambitions. The most remarkable thing I discovered in reading this powerful and overwhelmingly rational collection of essays is that other Catholic voices have been there all along. I'm just so grateful that the threads of rational, ethical discernment have been drawn together at last, in what is an astonishingly potent and timely critique of post-modern Western militarist aspirations."

—Joseph Kelly
Editorial Director, *The Universe*, England

"'Supply side' economists and 'neoconservative' think tankers are a marginalized minority within their academic professions because they prefer the security of ideology over the reality of experience. Nonetheless, they have been embraced by conservative politicians who prefer to be told what they want to hear instead of what they need to know. They have achieved a stranglehold on the thinking of our head of state and by so doing, put our body politic in grave danger. Shedding light on this subject, *Neo-CONNED!* offers a detailed description as to how this foreign policy paradigm shift has led us to war in Iraq and seriously compromised our security at home."

—James P. Moran
U.S. Congressman (D-Va., 8th District)

"*Neo-CONNED! Just War Principles: A Condemnation of War in Iraq* is both a thorough introduction to just-war theory and an excellent application of its principles. While the scholars who contributed to this volume come from a variety of confessional backgrounds, they all share a deep and abiding commitment to this important legacy of what used to be called Christendom. Any man of good faith who does not understand why Pope Benedict XVI declared that America's war in Iraq "has no moral justification" needs to read this book."

—Scott P. Richert
Executive Editor, *Chronicles: A Magazine of American Culture*

NEOCONNED

*Jus belli est odiosum, et poena ejus gravissima;
ergo restringenda est quoad fieri potest.*

THE RIGHT OF WAR IS HATEFUL, and its
punishment is most grave; therefore it is to be
restricted as far as can be.

—Francisco Suárez, S.J., *Doctor Eximius*
De Caritate, XIII, 7, 4

Ad Reginam Pacis

*To Samuel Francis and Jude Wanniski, who both
died unexpectedly while this book was being prepared.
May it be a fitting tribute to their journalistic combat
against the evils of so-called neoconservatism.*

*And to Pope Benedict XVI, with the prayerful hope that
Your Holiness will vigorously defend the Church's traditional
doctrine on matters of war and peace, and vindicate the
rights of Truth and Justice over brute force and egotism.*

*In doing so may Your Holiness follow in the path of Your illustrious
Predecessor, Benedict XV, whose efforts for peace were of such renown
that a Muslim Committee of Paris, on behalf of all Muslims of Egypt,
lamented His death with the following tribute: " . . . the grevious loss
of His Holiness Benedict XV, that soul of an apostle of the peace of the
world. If his statue set up at Constantinople, the capital of Islam, gives
us the consolation of making him present to us, his devout soul, his
efforts for worldwide peace, his deep respect of the peoples' right to
freedom will remain an undying page in the
history of the whole world."*

*And, may the inscription that the Turks placed upon the statue
in His honor provide Your Holiness with fitting inspiration:*

To the great Pope of the world's tragic hour

BENEDICT XV

Benefactor of the people
Without discrimination of nationality or religion
A token of gratitude from the Orient

*T*O THE READER

The two volumes of *Neo-CONNED!* have one purpose: to bring together the best minds on the Iraq War and everything pertaining to it. We have, in consequence, assembled an eclectic group, spanning the political, religious, and professional spectrum. We submit that the result is a tremendous intellectual and analytical dynamic, hitherto unavailable in the vitally important debate over war and peace.

The appearance of a contributor in either of our two volumes implies *no endorsement* by that contributor of anything beyond the words attributed to him or her; it particularly does not imply endorsement of any other contributor's work, either in these pages or in other fora. Whether the various contributors agree, in whole or part, with any of the pieces contained in this work beyond their own is a matter for each contributor; it should certainly not be assumed. The fact that our authors come from widely divergent philosophical, political, and religious backgrounds ought to make this obvious.

As for our own views, they do not, strictly speaking, appear in this volume. In compiling and editing the *Neo-CONNED!* texts, we have, of course, sought to produce a coherently integrated whole. Nevertheless, our authors speak for *themselves* throughout. While most grateful for their participation, and feeling, of course, a general sympathy for what they have contributed, we do not necessarily subscribe to their each and every view as expressed either in these volumes or in their writings in other places, on other subjects. No doubt the contributors would feel the same about our own view of things.

These works are about *Iraq*, and Iraq alone. We believe that they vindicate the principles of the Catholic just-war tradition, which convict the war in Iraq of manifest injustice. We pray that these volumes serve the cause of Truth, for it is in that spirit that they are presented.

The Editors

neo-CONNED!

Just War Principles: A Condemnation of War in Iraq

Asserting the traditional, Christian just war doctrine against the
neoconservative caricature that masks violence and aggression.

D. L. O'Huallachain & J. Forrest Sharpe • Editors

Vienna, Virginia • 2005

Footnotes to the contributions are their authors' except where indicated. Information from periodicals available through the Internet is referenced as "online" (or identified by the web-based source title) in lieu of page numbers or URLs. References to scholarly works have been standardized by the editors across contributions. Reprinted works (Appendicies II and III) have been reproduced with original formatting, spelling, punctuation, and footnoted references, aside from minor editorial corrections. Notes to Appendix III are the author's or the translator's except where indicated.

ISBN-10: 1-932528-04-0
ISBN-13: 978-1-932528-04-6

Library of Congress Cataloging-in-Publication Data

Neo-conned! : just war principles : a condemnation of war in Iraq / editors, D.L.
    O'Huallachain and J. Forrest Sharpe ; foreword by Hilarion Capucci ; introduction
    by George Lopez.
        p. cm.
    "Asserting the traditional, Christian just war doctrine against the neoconservative
caricature that masks violence and aggression."
    ISBN 1-932528-04-0 (alk. paper)
    1. Iraq War, 2003-   --Moral and ethical aspects. 2. Just war doctrine. 3.
United States--Military policy. 4. Conservatism--United States. 5. Aggression
(International law)   I. O'Huallachain, D. L. II. Sharpe, J. Forrest.
    DS79.76.N464 2005
    956.7044'31--dc22

                                                                    2005016043

Printed in the United States of America.

Light in the Darkness Publications is an imprint of IHS Press.
IHS Press is the only publisher dedicated exclusively to the
Social Teachings of the Catholic Church. For information on
current or future titles, contact IHS Press at:

        toll-free phone/fax: 877.447.7737 (877-IHS-PRES)
            e-mail: info@ihspress.com
            e-mail: info@lidpubs.com

CONTENTS

VI. SPEAKING WITH AUTHORITY:
THE TRUE JUST-WAR DOCTRINE AS A LIGHT FOR OUR TIME

There also exists a theory of "preventive war," according to which the State has a right to attack on preventive grounds another State which is still inoffensive and peaceful, but which may be led at a future date, on becoming aware of its increasing strength, to commit an unjust aggression . . . .

THE DOCTRINE IS INDEFENSIBLE, *since it would leave the way open to arbitrariness and thus legitimize every kind of abuse.*

A PREVENTIVE WAR AGAINST A POSSIBLE AGGRESSOR IS INIQUITOUS OF ITS VERY NATURE. *A ruler who would claim to regulate his policy according to a still uncertain future could allow himself every kind of surmise and would have no difficulty in imagining a distant menace which would give a plausible pretext to his ambitious or rapacious aims. Peace and international order would soon disappear under a regime which allowed recourse to "offensive-defensive" war for the most imaginary grievances.*

Only a very real and imminent menace – such as a systematically aggressive policy, an unusual concentration of troops, and the like – can authorize a State, which considers that it is menaced thereby, to demand the cessation of these suspicious activities, and, in case of refusal, to impose it by force.

—International Catholic Union of Social
Sciences, Malines, Belgium
Jozef-Ernest Cardinal van Roey, Primate of
Belgium, President
Code of International Ethics, 1949

Foreword

A PEOPLE THAT HAS suffered 14 years of cruel sanctions, terrifying bombardments, radioactive contamination from depleted uranium weapons, military invasion and permanent war – after more than 50 years have elapsed since the ratification of the United Nations Charter and dozens of Conventions and Treaties – is the proof that nothing, unfortunately, has changed. One does not export freedom, peace, and democracy through the use of bombs and violence. As the late Holy Father, John Paul II, reminded us on March 16, 2003: "War is never inevitable; it is always a defeat for humanity."

The basis and the *raison d'être* of the Christian is Charity, Love, to the point where the Master of Peace and Love, Jesus Christ, urged us even to love our enemy. Confronted by injustice, this is a difficult but essential undertaking for those who wish to define their existence as Christian.

To send bombers to destroy an entire country and to sow death amidst a people already in agony, in the name of God, is the greatest offense committed against Jesus Christ, and the most terrible curse laid against the Peace and Love of Christ. This is because Peace, for us Christians, is a Person, the Person of Christ. Jesus Christ is the Victory of Peace and Love. The unbearable sight of the suffering Iraqi people is Christ on the Cross. And it goes beyond that: the youth raised under sanctions in a country destroyed by bombs have minds suffocated with hatred, and have nothing more to lose, and are ready for every kind of vengeance. In an Arab country where mutual harmony between Christians and Muslims was a model, today bombs are placed in churches and tens of thousands of Christians are fleeing abroad; even the children of Iraqi Christians are being kidnapped. Before the invasion of Iraq, the peaceful co-existence between Christians and Muslims was a model; it has been replaced by a nightmare. The war against Iraq has destroyed years of dialogue with Islam, has given new pretexts to Islamic extremists, and has fed discord between the Arab world and the West.

When I offer the Holy Mass, at a certain point in the Liturgy, I invite the faithful to exchange a sign of peace. It is well and good to exchange a sign of peace between Christians, but in the light of what is taking place in Iraq, it is better still to exchange a sign of peace between Christians and Muslims. Before it becomes too late.

Bishop Hilarion Capucci
Greek-Melkite Patriarchal Vicar of
Jerusalem in Exile
February 2005

Introduction

THE CHAPTERS AND essays of this volume could not be more important in their timing and content. The former is critical because, as this book goes to press, the U.S. body politic has settled into a new stage in its moral relativism regarding the U.S. invasion and occupation of Iraq. Flush with a "successful" election in January 2005 to bolster its case for the legitimacy of continued actions – some would call it occupation – the Bush administration has yet again remained a step ahead of those whose ethical sensibilities should call them to more critical political commentary. The continuing anarchic security conditions in the country and the apparent show of progress via the election has either silenced moral critique, or relegated it to a begrudging agreement with the continued U.S. role.

In fact, the state of the non-debate in ethics circles has grown quite narrow and defeatist. Many of those who argued that the war in Iraq was illegal under international law, or who claimed that the administration failed to make a case about where and how the war failed to meet just-war criteria on ethical terms, now treat this as a judgment distinct – in both a moral and a historic sense – from how to judge U.S. actions in early 2005. Relying on what they claim is the same just-war thinking that led them to declare the war unjust in the first place, they zero in on the *jus ad bellum* criteria that a nation which has chosen to pursue war must, as victor, guarantee that greater peace and justice (in the broadest sense) result from the war. Their claim is that whatever the wrongs of going into Iraq, the only ethical choice now is to ensure political stability and a brighter future for all Iraqis.

Somehow, these ethicists reason, the two decisional phases – and seemingly the two political realities of pre-war and post-war Iraq – operate in totally distinct moral and real-life universes. It is as if the security conditions now operative "on the ground" in Iraq have no connection, much less a causal one, to the invasion itself. So that one can condemn the invasion but – in the form of an ethical consolation prize – uphold just-war norms by clinging to the narrow *jus ad bellum* notion that the people of Iraq will supposedly be better off after the war than they were before providing we hold the U.S. to its responsibilities as a belligerent occupier under international law.

Never mind that even if the U.S. *were* to meet those responsibilities there would still be a whole host of just-war criteria that were not met in the run-up to the war and which therefore condemn the war as unjust and immoral. Furthermore, never mind further that this popular idea that the U.S. must leave Iraq "better off" in order to meet its obligations under just-war theory is in fact a *misrepresentation* of the *jus ad bellum* criteria. These stipulate that the good resulting from war must outweigh the evil that war brings with it. In other words, whatever good may ultimately be done by the U.S. invasion must admittedly outweigh the evil that is caused. This is a tall order in light of the dead and wounded – civilian and military – on both sides, along with the near total destruction of Iraqi social and economic infrastructure.

If we leave these concerns aside, though, and accept the interpretation of the "just leave Iraq better off" school, the burden the U.S. faces to meet even this criterion is a heavy one. Reflecting upon what would be required in order to measure up to this notion of greater justice resulting from the invasion, a few points come quickly to mind:

1. Saddam Hussein and other well-known Iraqi officials should have been formally charged with war crimes and crimes against humanity, and an international court proceeding held to bring their cases to justice in the fullest sense of that term. But unfortunately, both the capture of the infamous "deck of cards" leaders and their holding has been used for intelligence and political purposes only, the latter indicated through frequent manipulation by the interim government of news statements of impending trials.

2. There would be proper stewardship of resources, most especially, in this case, of the natural resources of the Iraqi population, particularly their oil. Many administration supporters in Congress and their related pundits have engaged in a frontal assault on the UN "Oil-for-Food" Program as a source by which Saddam allegedly manipulated this humanitarian relief operation to sell oil for his own profit. At the extreme there are claims that the UN was a co-participant in depriving the Iraqi people of their resources and the revenues to be derived therefrom. Now, two years after the invasion, a just-war-stewardship perspective would invite equal scrutiny of U.S. and Coalition Provisional Authority (CPA) management

of Iraqi oil resources in the time under its aegis. As this book goes to press, the Government Accountability Office and other entities are scrutinizing what appears to be a situation of billions of unaccounted for oil revenues, possibly including the $372 million the UN turned over to the CPA in November 2003.

3. There would be attempts to continue to address the security situation with an eye toward increasing respect for Iraqi civilian lives and casualties. This has been the "elephant in the living room" since the start of the Iraq war. Journalists and others have simply not investigated what we *know* is happening in Iraq: that innocent civilians – already indiscriminately targeted by insurgents and jihadists – are now dying in larger numbers at the hands of U.S. forces, most notably from aerial bombing and our use of heavy attack weapons. At the war's outset the Pentagon announced that it had no obligation to provide information on the number of Iraqi soldiers killed or wounded. The policy adopted regarding civilians mirrored that of the first Gulf War: "we don't do body counts." So the major assault on Fallujah proceeded with virtually no documentation or imperative about doing so regarding its resident civilians.

4. There would be no "selfish gains" as a result of the war. Space and information limitations constrain us in looking at U.S. companies' practice here, but when the long history of this Iraq war is written, the exposure of profits garnered by U.S. companies and their share-holders will not be the result of a leftist critique or research. Rather, it will be publicly available information that will lead directly to the conclusion that this just-war criteria was hardly considered seriously. And the most pronounced – in a legal and political sense – "selfish gain" lies in the development of several large, permanent military bases in the country.

5. There would be every attempt to protect the safety and security of Iraq's future so that nation's people, having been involved in a devastating war against Iran in the 1980s and against an international coalition in 1991, and now deprived of its professional military as a result of the CPA decision to disband it, should not be subject to hostile neighbors. Recent events in the Israeli-Palestinian conflict *may* create a more positive regional environment in which Iraq can exist in peace and safety, but less favorable trends exist with direct neighbors Iran and Syria. Here, the U.S. refusal to engage these two states directly as regional partners for stability impacts Iraqi security in a negative manner. This is worsened by the sword-wielding diplomacy towards these two states that has characterized the rhetoric of President Bush's second term.

The tenuousness of the United States' ability to guarantee any of these conditions at this time – nearly two years after the toppling of Saddam Hussein – makes this first volume of *Neo-CONNED!* so important. Assembling an array of first-rate yet diverse essayists, the editors provide the important substance that permits a systematic re-examination of the multiple ethical boundaries crossed by the decision to initiate the Iraq war. Such a reassessment is especially important because those who so strongly pushed for war (as necessary and indicative of the supposedly new era of "pre-emption" ethics) now seem to be lying fairly low in the public square. In the absence of a robust ethical exchange (which at least characterized the pre-war period), those who still argue for the war's morality on just-war grounds have gone silent.

This volume's strong voice counters this trend. It contains the best collection of critical analyses of Church positions I have seen to date, and will serve as a primer for those who engage in teaching, social comment, and the broader effort of remaining true to just-war traditions.

People of politics, principle, and action should take heart that despite the daily debacle we continue to witness in Iraq, this volume preserves the arguments that must not be lost about why this war was and is illegal and immoral. And no amount of U.S. tax dollars, manipulated press accounts, demonstration elections, or political debate can change that basic fact.

Prof. George A. Lopez, Ph.D.
Notre Dame, Indiana
March 2005

With gladness We have learned from you that, in the United States of America, learned men, under the patronage of a group whose influence with the people is very great, are busily engaged in making studies the purpose of which is the preservation of the benefits of peace for all nations. To compose differences, to restrain the outbreak of hostilities, to prevent the dangers of war, to remove even the anxieties of so-called armed peace is, indeed, most praiseworthy, and any effort in this cause, even though it may not immediately or wholly accomplish its purpose, manifests, nevertheless, a zeal which cannot but redound to the credit of its authors and be of benefit to the States.

This is especially true at the present day, when vast armies, instrumentalities most destructive to human life, and the advanced state of military science portend wars which must be a source of fear even to the most powerful rulers.

Wherefore, We most heartily commend the work already begun, which should be approved by all good men and especially by Us, holding as We do, the supreme pontificate of the Church and representing Him Who is both the God and the Prince of Peace; and We most gladly lend the weight of Our authority to those who are striving to realize this most beneficent purpose.

As for the remaining aspects of the matter, We recall to mind the example of so many of Our illustrious Predecessors, who, when the condition of the times permitted, rendered, in this very matter also, the most signal service to the cause of humanity and to the stability of governments; but since the present age allows Us to aid in this cause only by pious prayers to God, We, therefore, most earnestly pray God, Who knows the hearts of men and inclines them as He wills, that He may be gracious to those who are furthering peace among the peoples, and may grant to the nations which, with united purposes, are laboring to this end, that the destruction of war and its disasters being averted, they may at length find repose in the beauty of peace . . . .

—Pope St. Pius X
Letter of June 11, 1911, to Archbishop Falconio,
Apostolic Delegate to the United States, on the
occasion of the founding of the Carnegie Endowment
for International Peace, Washington, D.C.

There is something immoral or amoral in the constant statement: I think it would be wrong, morally wrong, stupid, foolish for us to get into the war, but if we should get in, then it's the duty of all of us to rally behind the President. National unity before all else! National unity, even in the prosecution of an unjust war?

If a war is unjust, then IT MUST BE OPPOSED BEFORE THE OUTBREAK OF HOSTILITIES AND AFTER. *If a war is unjust,* I MUST REFUSE TO BE A PARTY TO THE INJUSTICE AFTER THE DECLARATION OF WAR, *as well as before. It is only when nationalism is put before conscience that leaders can do what they will with a country, and a country's wealth, and a country's blood. If leaders knew that the people would not follow them into an unjust war, if leaders knew that in an unjust declaration of war, they would have to build prisons and concentration camps to house thousands upon thousands of conscientious objectors, leaders would not lead us to war. A sit-down strike even on the barbed wire of a concentration camp is the only answer to an unjust participation in war.*

—Fr. John P. Delaney, S.J.
The Catholic World, April, 1941

THE STATESMEN SPEAK:
A WAR BOTH UNNECESSARY AND VAIN

THE EDITORS' GLOSS: As many know but perhaps insufficiently reflect upon, the linchpin of the just-war doctrine is the notion of a "just cause." While a nation's right to repel an ongoing, unjustified attack is self-evident and recognized, a nation's right to initiate a war in other circumstances cannot be based simply on a vague sense that "it might be a reasonable course of action." It must be based upon a morally certain, vital threat to the nation's life or existence, or to the exercise of rights necessary to that life or existence.

Regardless of what one thinks of the exact nature of the charges made against Saddam Hussein's Iraq, it cannot be denied, in view of the evidence and argument provided by Jude Wanniski, that those charges were *at the very least questionable.* While various commissions and investigations have already vindicated the truth of much of what Wanniski says, the point to note is that, in spite of the so-called massive intelligence failure (in our opinion, a convenient but rather dishonest "out"), the charges against Iraq were questionable (if not wholly bogus) even *before* the "intelligence" disaster was confirmed by our singular failure to find the notorious "WMD."

As for those who maintain that the WMD and al-Qaeda charges may very well have been questionable but Saddam's "human rights abuses" were not, Wanniski's comments raise serious doubts about even those charges – notwithstanding the fact that the war was sold to the American public as a necessary means of dealing with the threat of WMD, not as retribution for Saddam's decade-old (and alleged) crimes against Kurds and Shiites.

In view of the unquestionable fact that just-war teaching does not allow the initiation of a war based on doubtful suppositions (see Appendix I by Fr. Francis Stratmann on this point), Wanniski's comments point to one clear conclusion: the 2003 war against Iraq was unjust, and was known to have been such even before it was launched.

1

The (Bogus) Case Against Saddam
• • • • • • • • • •

An Interview with Jude Wanniski

> " . . . why could we all be so wrong?"
> —David Kay

> "We were almost all wrong."
> —Charles A. Duelfer

> " . . . the Intelligence Community was dead wrong in almost all of
> its pre-war judgments about Iraq's weapons of mass destruction."
> —The Commission on the Intelligence Capabilities
> of the United States Regarding Weapons of Mass Destruction

THE INVASION OF *Iraq in 2003 by the United States and Britain
was based primarily on the claim that Saddam Hussein possessed
weapons of mass destruction, theoretically being manufactured to
threaten other countries. How much truth was there in that assertion?*

JW: None at all. The U.S. Armed Forces only considers nuclear weapons to be weapons of mass destruction. Iraq had neither nuclear weapons nor chemical or biological weapons. The only thing it may have possessed were some of the ingredients necessary to develop chemical or biological weapons. In fact, there were several attempts by France, Russia, and China to declare Iraq in compliance with the resolutions some years before Gulf War II, but each time they were vetoed by the United States and the U.K. For example on November 20, 1997, a Russian-Iraqi Press communiqué was released in which Moscow pledged "to promote energetically the speedy lifting of sanctions against Iraq on the basis of its compliance with the corresponding UN resolutions." On July 30, 1998, the New York Times reported that "Russia tried and failed to get Security Council action today on a resolution declaring that Iraq had complied with demands to destroy its nuclear weapons program and was ready to move away from intrusive inspections to long-term monitoring." These are just a couple of the many examples that could be cited.

WMD

The presentation of the Duelfer Report on October 6, 2004 – and the confirmation of its conclusions by both the report of the "Commission on the Intelligence Capabilities of the United States Regarding of Weapons of Mass Destruction" (delivered on March 31, 2005) and the Duelfer addendum, released on April 25 of this year and officially declaring "exhausted" the search for WMD in Iraq – is the final proof of this fact. No WMDs were found; no facilities to produce such weapons were found. The conclusion was that the Hussein government had, indeed, complied with the relevant UN resolutions in the wake of the first Gulf War – exactly as countless experts had said *prior to Gulf War II.*

LID: What do you mean by "countless experts"? Surely it is well known that up to their departure in 1998, the UN inspectors were uncovering hidden WMDs almost on a daily basis?

JW: What I mean is that the people in the best position to know the true extent of Iraq's WMDs – both real and alleged – were the inspectors sent in by the UN after the end of the first Gulf War. Those experts concluded years ago that in practical terms the weapons and the production facilities for such weapons had been destroyed. As for being "well-known," I think that it is truer to say that the "impression" was given that WMDs were being found on a daily basis, though the truth of the matter was not being reported.

LID: Could you be more specific since this will be news to a lot of people?

JW: Many of us pointed out that Iraq was always being put in the position of having to "prove a negative." From the end of 1992 onward, Iraq insisted it did not possess WMDs any longer. We now know that they were telling the truth, but the U.S. government – both the Clinton and Bush administrations – insisted they were not telling the truth and had to prove to us that they had nothing hidden. By 1995, we now know Iraq did not possess the facilities to recreate the arsenal that it originally had, but how could it prove this fact at the time? How could it take us to a hidden cache somewhere in the hills or mountains if no such cache existed? Yes, the Iraqis seemed to be acting suspiciously at times, at least in U.S. press accounts that described a "cat and mouse" game with UN inspectors. But the bottom line is what counts at the time the decisions were being made to go to war, and by 2001, with George W. Bush a newly minted President, the former UN weapons inspector, Scott Ritter, was asserting: "There is absolutely no reason to believe that Iraq could have meaningfully reconstituted any element of its WMD capabilities in the past 18 months."

The period to which Ritter referred was when the UNSCOM inspectors were pulled out of Iraq at the insistence of the Clinton administration, which decided on its own that Iraq had to be punished for its "cat-and-mouse" behavior. It proceeded to bomb Iraq and did not want any inspectors killed in the process. As you point out in your question, very few Americans to this day are aware of the specific cause of action that led to the bombing, although the press corps only needed to ask Scott Ritter, who had resigned in dismay that the U.S. State Department had provoked Iraq by demanding massive entry into the political headquarters of the Ba'ath Party in Baghdad to look for WMD evidence. It was because of the "irregularities" of U.S. behavior that the UN later folded the UNSCOM inspection process, which permitted the U.S. to name and finance inspection teams on its own, replacing it with an UNMOVIC inspection process, entirely under the control of the UN Security Council in its appointment and payment of inspectors.

LID: Why was there a cat-and-mouse game to begin with?

JW: Knowing they had fully complied with the UN resolutions, the Iraqis came to believe that the inspection teams were laced with CIA operatives, looking not for WMD but for ordinary military operations that could be pinpointed in subsequent bombing raids. There were also realistic suspicions that the operatives were trying to locate Saddam's whereabouts so they could take him out. At one point, as I recall, the chief foreign correspondent of the *New York Times,* Thomas L. Friedman, wrote a column entitled "Head Shot," in which he recommended that the U.S. seriously consider a covert operation to assassinate Saddam Hussein. The Iraqis can read, you know.

LID: On April 13, 1999, you wrote to Tim Weiner at the New York Times *about the then recently published book of Scott Ritter entitled* Endgame. *Can you tell us about that?*

JW: You must remember that in this period, soon after Ritter quit UNSCOM and came home, he was celebrated as a hero for seeming to justify the harsh actions taken against the Baghdad regime. Weiner criticized the hastily-written book for its inconsistencies, and I wrote what I thought could explain those inconsistencies, although I had never met Ritter, and still have not.

I suggested to Tim that the 240-page book demonstrated "Ritter's frustration in spending seven years looking under rocks and behind trees for WMDs and not finding any." The fact is that the propaganda surrounding our effort to starve more than 20 million Iraqis into submission to cover up the botched job of our political establishment in that sorry land has been among the most effective of the twentieth century. After several years of living with what I knew to be stacks of baloney in the news media, I decided, in 1998, to arrange a meeting with Nizar Hamdoon, then Iraq's Ambassador to the UN I knew that would draw the ire of some in the American establishment, especially when it became known that successive governments had forbidden our Ambassadors to the UN even to speak to their Iraqi counterparts. I consider this a childish and counterproductive approach to diplomacy.

In the event, I told Hamdoon that I had come to believe our government was lying through its teeth, Democrats and Republicans, because there was nobody around with the guts to tell it to stop. I told him flat out I would act as "devil's advocate" for Iraq, but only on the condition that whatever he told me in regard to the weapons issue had to be *verifiable* as truthful, otherwise I would look like a dope *and* a traitor!

LID: You mean, like Reagan, you would trust, but verify? How could you verify?

JW: Let me explain. When Hamdoon agreed, I first asked him when had been the last time that UNSCOM – the UN Inspectorate set up after the conclusion of the first Gulf War – had destroyed any weapons of mass destruction. He said: "November 1991." I found that hard to believe, indeed incredible. I repeated my question and again he insisted that in the previous six and half years UNSCOM had not destroyed any WMDs. Not one lousy, crummy nuclear, chemical, or biological weapon. Shocked, yet still skeptical, I then asked him how many WMDs had been found and destroyed by UNSCOM inspectors *without the help* of the Iraqi government in the seven months between the end of the first Gulf War in early 1991 and November 1991. He looked me in the eye and said "none." Every WMD that had been destroyed in that period was the result of UNSCOM *being taken* to a WMD site and shown the stuff, either stuff that had already been destroyed, or stuff awaiting destruction. I suspected Hamdoon was playing verbal tricks with me, but he was so fervent I decided I would risk going forward.

A few days later, in Washington, I met Senate Majority Leader Trent Lott, who I had known for decades, and I told him what I had heard from Hamdoon and I saw the disbelief in his eyes. He said – I'm paraphrasing here now – "No way, Jude boy, you have got to be wrong. The UNSCOM inspectors are finding WMDs every day of the week, except Sundays which they observe as a Day of Rest."

I then went and told the story to my good friend, Jack Kemp, at *Empower America* – someone who normally believes everything I tell him. His response was that everyone knew the inspectors were digging up WMDs all the time, in all the secret places Saddam had located in Iraq which would be many and varied since it is 10,000 square miles larger than California. Still, he sent one of his people, a young lawyer, over to the UN offices in Washington to look into the matter. After poring over the UNSCOM documents for two days, Kemp was informed: the record shows that *no* WMDs had been found *without* the help of Baghdad, and *none* had been destroyed since November 1991!

LID: Can you say what came of all this?

JW: Well, for one thing, Kemp became a believer, enough so that I could first arrange for his chief-of-staff at Empower America, Larry Hunter, to meet with me and Hamdoon in New York City for dinner, with Hunter taking Hamdoon's measure. I then arranged a meeting of Kemp and Hamdoon in New York City – as Hamdoon was not allowed to leave the UN environs without special permission. Hamdoon is no longer with us. He died of cancer last year, but Kemp would tell you if you asked, I'm sure, that he then met with UN General Secretary Kofi Annan to try to head off what seemed to be imminent U.S. action against Iraq. This was in early 1998. As a result of back-and-forth discussions, Iraq agreed to alter the modality of inspections to permit UNSCOM to look anywhere they wished for WMD, including the presidential palaces. The neocons who wanted war with Iraq back then, under Clinton auspices, were totally frustrated and have been out to get Kofi Annan ever since. In the several months that followed, UNSCOM inspectors under the direction of Richard Butler – an Australian diplomat who owed his appointment to the U.S. State Department – prowled all over, and finding nothing were led to provoke the Iraqi government into the Ba'ath Party incident I described earlier.

LID: So at this point Saddam did not kick the inspectors out of Iraq?

JW: No, Iraq did *not* expel the inspectors. The U.S. State Department *instructed the inspectors to leave,* because the inspections incident was deemed sufficient for the U.S. to conduct its unprovoked, unauthorized military action that became known as "Desert Fox." It is also important to note that on January 6, 1999, the *Washington Post* confirmed publicly that the weapons inspection had been used by the CIA as a cover for military espionage, and Scott Ritter mentioned on the NBC *Today* show on December 17, 1998, that "Washington perverted the UN weapons process by using it as a tool to justify military actions, falsely so. . . . The U.S. was using the inspection process as a trigger for war." Once again we see that it was the Iraqis, not the Americans, telling the truth.

LID: Was none of this known to President Bush?

JW: I really don't think it was known to President Clinton. The CIA certainly must have known all about it, for goodness sakes, because Ritter wrote another book about it in the spring of 2002 with William Rivers Pitt, *War on Iraq: What Team Bush Doesn't Want You to Know.* If George Tenet of the CIA didn't read it or know about it, he should be ashamed of himself. It takes only an hour or two to read and you can buy it used on Amazon these days for less than $1.

Yet, when President George W. Bush appeared before the UN General Assembly in September 2002, he produced a raft of unsubstantiated accusations to justify forceful action by the United Nations – and failing that, unilateral action by the United States. Upon hearing all this, the then Iraqi Ambassador to the UN, Mohammed Aldouri, a man of integrity and respect to the best of my knowledge, told the *New York Times* that the list of charges against his government contained more untruths than any he had heard in any similar speech in his experience. After reeling off pages of charges against the Iraqi government that began with the pre-invasion period before the first Gulf War and ran up to 2002, Bush had said: "The history, the logic, and the facts lead to one conclusion: Saddam Hussein's regime is a grave and gathering danger."

Was it really a serious and imminent threat to anyone, especially the United States? Subsequent events have shown that there was no substance to this "threat" at all, and they have also shown that men like Hamdoon and Aldouri – indeed the Iraqi government – were telling the truth all along. That may be hard for some Americans to accept, but that is the reality. And it is a reality that was known by the experts long before the second

Gulf War was launched unilaterally. Scott Ritter wrote in *Arms Control Today* in June 2000:

> What is often overlooked in the debate over how to proceed with Iraq's disarmament is the fact that from 1994 to 1998 Iraq was subjected to a strenuous program of ongoing monitoring of industrial and research facilities that could be used to reconstitute proscribed activities. This monitoring provided weapons inspectors with detailed insight into the capabilities, both present and future, of Iraq's industrial infrastructure. It allowed UNSCOM to ascertain, with a high level of confidence, that Iraq was not rebuilding its prohibited weapons programs and it lacked the means to do so without an infusion of advanced technology and a significant investment of time and money. Given the comprehensive nature of the monitoring put in place by UNSCOM, which included a strict export-import control regime, it was possible as early as 1997 to determine that, from a qualitative standpoint, Iraq had been disarmed. Iraq no longer possessed any meaningful quantities of chemical or biological agent, if it possessed any at all, and the industrial means to produce these agents had either been eliminated or were subject to stringent monitoring. The same was true of Iraq's nuclear and ballistic missile capabilities. As long as monitoring inspections remained in place, Iraq presented a WMD-based threat to no one.

Let me go further. I wrote a letter to President Bush on September 23, 2003, in which I recapitulated a lot of these points, points which were obviously known among the highest levels of the American government and bureaucracy. I wrote:

> You could see with your own eyes and hear with your own ears that the Security Council Resolution 1441 was working like a charm. This was at a time when the French were pointing out that UNMOVIC inspectors [the successors to UNSCOM and headed by Hans Blix] were crawling all over Iraq. They had gone to several hundred places where they were most likely to find illegal activities and found not a scrap of evidence that could hold up even to casual questioning. Mohammed ElBaradei, chief of the IAEA, said emphatically that Iraq had no nukes and could not acquire them without being discovered. Hans Blix said his team was interviewing Iraqi scientists in private and that all that remained was to clear up some of the discrepancies in how Iraq disposed of chemical and biological weapons in 1991. Blix said this would take perhaps two more months at most and that Iraq was co-operating to expedite the process! Because of constant hints from your team that UNMOVIC was not quick enough to spot WMDs, Iraq invited you to send CIA teams into the country to swoop down at a moment's notice on sites they suspect. How much clearer could it be that multi-national diplomatic action by the UN was working?

LID: Did President Bush respond?

JW: No, no. I have no idea whether he saw my letter, which I posted openly on my website and sent to the personal email addresses of some of his top advisors. At this point Saddam seemed willing enough to stand on his head and spit nickels to satisfy U.S. concerns . . . and of course via the UN Ambassador I was advising Baghdad to do just that. Remember the Hussein government cooperated to the point of allowing the destruction – in the weeks leading up to the unilateral attack by the U.K. and the U.S. – of dozens of al-Samoud missiles in spite of the fact they were perfectly legal and *not* covered by any UN resolution.

It should also be added that the "discrepancies" that Blix referred to were a consequence of the eagerness and energy of the Iraqi government in the immediate aftermath of the first Gulf War to have the sanctions lifted – they started the destruction themselves but did not keep very good accounts. That's it. We are in a war because of simple accounting errors by the Iraqis, but there is a much more serious question laying at the door of the President's office. In going to Congress and seeking authorization for military action, it was necessary to promise that he would work through the UN and that it was based solely upon the alleged specific threat posed by Iraqi WMDs. If the war had been proposed on any other basis, Public Law 107-243 would not have been passed. That's not merely my opinion. Paul Wolfowitz, the former Deputy Defense Secretary, and one of the main architects of the current Iraq war, said that much in an interview in *Vanity Fair*, even suggesting that Bush would not even have had the support of his Cabinet. In a nutshell, the President acted entirely outside the law.

LID: And here you're referring to domestic *law, right?*

JW: Right. In order for him to get the support of the U.S. Senate on PL 107-243, he had to promise he would exhaust all diplomatic remedies, which he clearly did not.

LID: So, in the light of all this, what is "well-known" seems much closer to a fairy story than to the facts.

JW: Sadly. But it's not through want of me trying to enlighten people. I wrote up all this and sent it around to various powerful people, including Senator Helms of the Foreign Relations Committee, and I sent the stuff around to the newspapers and magazines. Nobody paid any attention to me because it was too inconvenient. You just have to accept the fact that the good old U.S. of A. engages in propaganda at many levels, and the Press Corps goes along with it, because to do otherwise would be bad for careers. I am not alone in this. John MacArthur, the publisher of *Harper's Magazine* and the author of *Second Front: Censorship and Propaganda in the Gulf War* – he is referring to Gulf War I – says that considering the number of senior officials shared by both Bush administrations, the American public should bear in mind the lessons of Gulf War propaganda. He adds: "These are all the same people who were running it more than 10 years ago. They will make up just about anything . . . to get their way." Or listen to Lee Hamilton, a former Democratic representative who spent 34 years as a lawmaker, who served on numerous foreign affairs and intelligence committees, and is now Director of the Woodrow Wilson International Center for Scholars in Washington. Speaking to Scott Peterson of the *Christian Science Monitor* in September 2002, he said that the Bush team "understands that it has not yet carried the burden of persuasion [about an imminent Iraqi threat], so they will look for any kind of evidence to support their premise. . . . My concern in these situations, always, is that the intelligence that you get is driven by the policy, rather than the policy being driven by the intelligence. . . . I'm always skeptical about intelligence. It is not as pure as the driven snow."

LID: Even if Iraq had no nuclear weapons program, surely they could have started one as soon as the UN inspectors left, and then built a nuclear weapon within six months to a year.

JW: In the 1980s, Iraq had a clandestine nuclear program, in violation of its agreement not to seek nuclear weapons under the Non-Proliferation Treaty. It could do so because it could import the materials needed to build a nuke and assemble them in places unknown to the International Atomic Energy Agency. The IAEA in 1998 closed this loophole, which means that all materials that could conceivably be used to build a nuke or make fissile material have to be cleared through a Nuclear Suppliers Group. Even after the IAEA inspection team had completed its work under UN Resolution 1441, it would have retained the right to repeat inspections of Iraq at will, under new protocols developed by the agency to make the process airtight. If Saddam were still in power today, he would be under such strict constraints that he would not waste a moment's time thinking about how to acquire WMD.

LID: Here's a very specific question on the alleged hiding of WMDs by Iraq. Many people will no doubt remember the assertion, made many times by the Bush administration, that the WMDs were being hidden in underground tunnels and caves in Baghdad. Did Duelfer's Iraq Survey Group look into this? What did they report? Or was it simply a lie from start to finish?

JW: At a Press Conference in December 2002, Donald Rumsfeld spoke of "the enormous miles and miles and miles of underground tunneling. . . . 'I don't know how inspectors on the surface of the earth can even know what's going on in the underground facilities that the Iraqis have.'" Secretary of State Colin Powell thought enough of the accusation to refer to "the extensive system of underground tunnels and bunkers" in his (now famously fraudulent) address to the UN Security Council in February 2003. He claimed that Iraq was probably using the tunnels for mobile biological weapons factories: "They can produce enough dry biological agent in a single month to kill thousands upon thousands of people."

What is the truth of the matter? Saddam Hussein launched a multibillion dollar subway project in 1983 to alleviate the traffic congestion of Baghdad, and he employed a California company, Parson Corporation, to draw up the designs for him. According to the proposed project, the Parson design envisaged two underground lines: one branch would link the eastern district of Masbah to the western district, Aadhamiya; the other would connect the urban center to al-Thawra, better known as Saddam City, and which is dominated by Shiites. In other words, Saddam's dastardly aim was to provide cheap transport for poor Shiites.

In the mid-80s, the project was cancelled and the crew of international contractors was laid off. The reason was simple. Iraq's war with Iran was costing a fortune, and the country simply could not afford the luxury of an underground system at that time. It is a story that countless Western countries have experienced on different occasions: insufficient money for "luxury" projects in a time of austerity.

The source of the accusation was an Iraqi defector, Dr. Hussein al-Shahristani, a former head of the Iraqi Atomic Energy Commission who left the country in 1991. In February 2003 he appeared on an episode of CBS's *60 Minutes* entitled "Saddam's Deadly Subway Scheming." In this interview, he said that he had knowledge – at second-hand only – that there were nearly 60 miles of subway tunnels and that Saddam had decided to use this network to store his WMDs. One or two points about al-Shahristani need to be made here. Firstly, in a document leaked from the State Department in May 2004, his name appeared as one of the leading candidates to be Iraq's Prime Minister, but that job went to former CIA operative, Iyad Allawi, when al-Shahristani turned it down. Secondly, al-Shahristani is one of the main people who drew up the so-called national list of Shiite parties for the January 2005 elections, under the guidance of the suspect Grand Ayatollah al-Sistani. It is interesting, too, to note that the Iraqi National Congress leader, Ahmad Chalabi, described by his critics in a December 3, 2004, *New York Times* piece by Edward Wong as "a slippery charlatan," produced a number of defectors in 2001who claimed that Saddam was using a network of underground tunnels for storing documents related to WMDs, and that Chalabi is now bosom buddies with the al-Shahristani/al-Sistani setup.

The Duelfer Report runs to 1,000 pages but the Baghdad Metro is not mentioned; nor does the word "subway" appear. The two references to "tunnel" in the report are merely concerned with a railway tunnel at al-Mansuriyah.

At the end of the day, one wag called the tunnels full of WMDs "a turban myth," while the investigative journalist Brian McWilliams wrote that before Operation Iraqi Freedom "one of the most compelling symbols of the depravity and danger of Saddam Hussein was the uncompleted Baghdad Metro." It is also perhaps pertinent to remember that in early 2004 a Dutch newspaper, *De Telegraaf*, reported that Iraq's WMDs were being "hidden in tunnels throughout Syria" – a snippet of news dished up to the American public by Fox News. Perhaps this lie will live again?

LID: What you say is very interesting, even compelling, but you do not say why the United States indulged in such propaganda. For instance, on March 9, 2003, Dr. Edward Luttwak of the Center for Strategic and International Studies in Washington wrote in a piece entitled, "Saddam's Street Fighters will be No Match for Allies Elite," that "Even now, Saddam Hussein could avoid the war that could destroy his regime. . . . He does not even have to surrender every one of his forbidden weapons. If he would just admit the UN inspectors to a persuasive number of warehouses, bunkers and caves containing biological, chemical and nuclear materials, political support for the war would evaporate even among the Bush administration's Republican faithful and certainly among Americans at large." If Saddam was really cooperating with the inspectors and had really destroyed all his banned weapons, how is it that until the last moment senior spokesmen for the government's position were arguing that all Saddam had to do was cooperate with inspectors and reveal his stockpiles of weapons? Could they really have misunderstood the facts all this time, or was there another agenda?

JW: But I have answered this in part already. First of all, how do you show people something that you do not have? We now know conclusively that Saddam possessed no such materials. Luttwak makes the unwarranted assumption that these materials were there. But the idea that the Bush administration, if given access to the much discussed WMDs, would have dropped their clamor for war is simply disingenuous. The answer to

Luttwak's point is also the answer to your question of why the propaganda. It is because United States's policy was "regime change" – in simple terms, eliminating Saddam Hussein – and had been ever since the first Gulf War.

LID: Can you substantiate that statement?

JW: Of course I can. On May 20, 1991, President George H. W. Bush announced: "At this juncture, my view is we don't want to lift these sanctions as long as Saddam Hussein is in power." His Secretary of State, James Baker, followed the same line: "We are not interested in seeing a relaxation of sanctions as long as Saddam Hussein is in power." On January 15, 1993, incoming President Bill Clinton, having come under attack from the *New York Times* in particular because it was being suggested that he might seek to lift the sanctions against Iraq and even normalize relations with Saddam, told the *Boston Globe:* "There is no difference between my policy and the policy of the present administration. . . . I have no intention of normalizing relations with him."

On March 26, 1997, Madeline Albright, in her first major foreign policy address as Secretary of State said: "Our view, which is unshakeable, is that Iraq must prove its peaceful intentions. It can only do that by complying with all of the Security Council resolutions to which it is subjected. Is it possible to conceive of such a government under Saddam Hussein?" She continued: "The overwhelming evidence is that Saddam Hussein's intentions will never be peaceful." On October 5, 1998, the House passed, by 360 to 38, the "Iraqi Liberation Act," which, among other things, instructed the Pentagon to channel up to $97 million in overt military aid to alleged Iraqi rebel groups to bring down the government of Saddam. That law was simply the codification of the American policy of removing Saddam Hussein from power.

If that's not enough for you, President Clinton also put this on record: "Sanctions will be there until the end of time, or as long as he [Saddam] lasts." Is it any wonder that Iraqi Deputy Prime Minister, Tariq Aziz, stated on November 7, 1997: "The American government says, openly, clearly, that it is not going to endorse lifting the sanctions on Iraq unless the leadership of Iraq is changed." Is it really any surprise that the Ba'athist government sought on the one hand to fulfill its obligations to UN resolutions, while simultaneously being truculent with American authorities that sought more than the resolutions provided for? So you see the talk of "regime change" is not something new, but has a long pedigree spanning the Bush

I, Clinton, and Bush II presidencies, and stemming from the likes of Paul Wolfowitz and Richard Perle at the Defense Policy Board as well as entities like the "Project for the New American Century." In one of his last books, former President Nixon also urged his followers – who are numerous in the Republican Party and U.S. bureaucracy – to oppose the lifting of the sanctions as long as Saddam remained in power.

LID: What do you mean when you say the U.S. "sought more than the resolutions provided for?"

JW: I mean that while the UN resolutions declared that all sites and facilities that could house, manufacture, or in any way assist in the development and production of WMDs had to be made available to UN inspectors, the U.S. government sought more. Saddam's palaces, installations concerning purely national security and the administration of the country, were not included in the original UN resolutions of 1991 that created the first inspection regime.

In 1998, though, faced with threats of bombings by the Clinton administration, Iraq opened all "sensitive sites," including the palaces, to UNSCOM inspectors, as long as certain modalities were followed. As I said earlier, it was when the inspectors asked to inspect the Ba'ath Party headquarters in Baghdad for evidence of WMDs, without regard to the agreed-upon modalities, that Iraq refused entry. In 1998 Washington also demanded to have access to the Iraqi government's personnel files, the basis of its power structure; not unreasonably it refused to cooperate because it was not obliged by the UN resolutions to do so. Saddam essentially believed by this time that all that was happening was that Anglo-American demands were forever increasing, and Iraq was getting precisely nothing in return. No government with any self-respect would accept such a situation. Saddam's government also said that it would not cooperate with the inspections because many of the inspectors were American spies. It is important to note that they refused co-operation because of their doubts about the inspection team's composition and aims.

Saddam "Gassed His Own People" and "Threatened His Neighbors"

LID: OK, let's accept that you have a point. But a Devil's Advocate might suggest the following: perhaps the American government has been right to deal with Saddam in a, shall we say, oblique manner. Let's face it, Saddam is a wily character. Worse, he has a proven record of unsavory behavior. He invaded Kuwait illegally and without provocation. He massed his troops on the border of Saudi Arabia and was about to pounce when the international coalition came together to face him down. In the aftermath of the first Gulf War, he massacred God only knows how many southern Shiites who had rebelled. He used chemical weapons at Halabja in which many thousands of Kurds were killed, and in the Anfal campaign he murdered by one means or another anywhere between 100,000 and 180,000 Kurds. So, let's accept that various U.S. governments cut corners or were perhaps less than truthful at times, yet it still remains that Saddam is a monster who needed to be dealt with.

JW: Well, that's a long question with many constituent elements to it. Let's break it down into the following subjects:

A. The invasion of Kuwait.
B. The implied invasion of Saudi Arabia.
C. The accusation of genocide at Halabja.
D. The Anfal Campaign.
E. Atrocities such as the suppression of the Shiites in Basra.

The First Gulf War

A. The first thing that needs to be grasped is that the Iraqi invasion of Kuwait is directly and inextricably linked to the Iran-Iraq War that lasted eight years and took tens of thousands of lives. We often hear from all kinds of people, including some anti-war folks, that Saddam was "a friend" of the United States during the Iran-Iraq war. That may be true to some extent, but it is not the whole truth, especially when you consider that the U.S. and Iraq only renewed official relations in 1984. The United States supported Saddam in his war with the Islamic fundamentalists because it suited *our* purposes. There was every risk that Iraq, with a population of about 23 million people, would be overwhelmed by an Iran with almost three times that number. The revolutionary fervor of the mullahs and their open demand to overthrow the secular government of Baghdad was not merely a threat to the Ba'ath Party, but a threat to the entire region – and consequently to *our* sources of oil. American self-interest was at work here and little else. We did everything to encourage Iraqis to fight to the last man in that war.

You probably don't need to be reminded that when Saddam, after the war, tried to dig himself out of the mountain of war debts that were smothering his economy – reckoned to be $40 billion *excluding* aid extended by other Arab states during the war – his efforts were thwarted by the greed of the Emir of Kuwait. How? By producing several hundred thousand barrels of oil per day above Kuwait's OPEC-agreed quota. Furthermore, Kuwait was stealing oil – to the tune of several billion dollars – from Iraqi territory through slant drilling, and the oil fields in question – the Rumaylah oil fields – were part of disputed territory, some of which had originally belonged to Iraq until the British assigned it to "Kuwait" following the collapse of the Ottoman Empire during WWI.

The collective effect was to drive down the price of oil to $10 or $11 per barrel from the standard $20 or so per barrel that had prevailed. This meant a huge reduction in Iraq's budget of between $6 and $7 billion annually. In other words, the life of Iraq was being threatened by the greed of the Emir. This was well known at the time. Neither the Saudis nor the Egyptians were bothered about Saddam's invasion of the emirate because they knew that Kuwait had been cheating all the oil countries in order to finance al-Sabah's harem and high living in Paris. Indeed the record shows that King Fahd of Saudi Arabia had supported Saddam during the early stages of the crisis.

Getting no satisfaction from the Kuwaitis, and with the Iraqi economy suffering terribly because of Kuwaiti duplicity, Saddam turned to the United States – in the form of the U.S. Ambassador to Iraq, April Glaspie – to see if there would be any problems with America if Iraq decided to sort out the question militarily, if so required. The reply of Glaspie was that inter-Arab disputes were not the business of the U.S. Thereafter, Saddam made a final attempt to get reparations from the Emir, but the Emir snubbed him and flew off to Paris. The rest is history.

LID: So you are saying that in 1990 the United States advised Saddam Hussein that his issues with Kuwait were a local matter, and that America had no diplomatic obligation to defend Kuwait if attacked by Iraq?

JW: Yes. The U.S. State Department testified before congressional committees to that effect. At the time, Saddam Hussein was merely weighing his options with Kuwait.

LID: Is it true that Saddam Hussein personally assured the United States Ambassador to Baghdad that he would take no military action against Kuwait if the Emir of Kuwait – in a meeting scheduled to take place in July 1990 – agreed to end its "economic warfare" against Iraq?

JW: Yes. The Ambassador, April Glaspie, was assured by that, and left on vacation. But the Emir of Kuwait decided not to show up at the meeting in Riyadh; and he had assurance from the Pentagon that it would defend Kuwait (without an agreement to do so). Thus, Saddam invaded.

LID: If what you are saying is true, it means that the U.S. government lied to Saddam Hussein through Ambassador Glaspie, and that we gave a guarantee of military protection to Kuwait for ulterior motives.

JW: Well, there were a couple of voices emanating from the U.S. government: a diplomatic voice from State and a belligerent voice from the Pentagon. Yes, it is a serious business. So why not look at the official record to see what it says? On July 25, 1990, Saddam Hussein summoned April Glaspie to his office for a meeting that was to be the last high level contact between Iraq and America before the Iraqi invasion of Kuwait on August 2. The *New York Times* published excerpts from an Iraqi document about the meeting between Saddam and the U.S. envoy on September 23, 1990. The *NYT* had received a copy of the Iraqi transcript from *ABC News* which had translated the Arabic, and it is interesting that the State Department refused to comment on its accuracy. *Why?*

The meeting was quite lengthy and covered a number of related subjects, so I can only give a few highlights to demonstrate what the Iraqi attitude was, and how the U.S. responded to this.

SADDAM: "Iraq came out of the war burdened with $40 billion of debts, excluding the aid given by Arab states, some of whom consider that too to be a debt although they knew – and you knew too – that without Iraq they would not have had these sums and the future of the region would have been entirely different.... We began to face the policy of the drop in price of oil. We then saw the United States, which always talks about democracy, but which has no time for the other point of view.... When planned and deliberate policy forces the price of oil down without good commercial reasons, then that means another war against Iraq. Because military war kills people by bleeding them, and economic war kills their humanity by depriving them of their chance to have a good standard of living. As you know, we gave rivers of blood ... but we did not lose our humanity. Iraqis have a right to live proudly. We do not accept that anyone can injure Iraqi pride or the Iraqi right to have high standards of living.... Kuwait and the United Arab Emirates were at the front of this policy.... We do not accept threats from anyone because we do not threaten anyone. But we say clearly that we hope the U.S. will not entertain too many illusions and will seek new friends rather than increase the number of its enemies.... Of course, it is the right of everyone to choose their friends. We can have no objections. But you know you are not the ones who protected your friends during the war with Iran. I assure you, had the Iranians overrun the region, the America troops would not have stopped them, except by the use of nuclear weapons...."

We are not the kind of people who will relinquish their rights. There is no historic right, or legitimacy, or need, for the UAE and Kuwait to deprive us of our rights. If they are needy, we too are needy. . . . The United States wants to secure the flow of oil. This is understandable and known. But it must not deploy methods which the U.S. says it disapproves of. . . . If you use pressure, we will deploy pressure and force. We know that you can harm us although we do not threaten you. You can come to Iraq with aircraft and missiles but do not push us to the point where we cease to care. And when we feel that you want to injure our pride and take away the Iraqis chance of a high standard of living, then we will cease to care and death will be the choice for us. Then we would not care if you fired 100 missiles for each missile we fired. Because without pride life would have no value. It is not reasonable to ask our people to bleed rivers of blood for eight years and then to tell them 'Now you have to accept aggression from Kuwait, the UAE, or from the United States, or from Israel.' . . . We do not place America among the enemies. We place it where we want our friends to be, and we try to be friends. But repeated American statements last year make it apparent that America did not regard us as friends."

GLASPIE: "The President directed the U.S. administration to reject the suggestion of implementing trade sanctions. . . . I have a direct instruction from the President to seek better relations with Iraq. . . . President Bush not only wanted better and deeper relations with Iraq, but he also wants an Iraqi contribution to peace and prosperity in the Middle East. President Bush is an intelligent man. He is not going to declare an economic war against Iraq. . . . It is true what you say that we do not want higher prices for oil. But I would ask you to examine the possibility of not charging too high a price for oil."

SADDAM: "We do not want too high prices for oil. I remind you that in 1974 I gave Tariq Aziz the idea for an article he wrote which criticized the policy of keeping oil prices high. It was the first Arab article which expressed this view."

GLASPIE: "I think I understand this. I admire your extraordinary efforts to rebuild your country. I know you need funds. We understand that and our opinion is that you should have the opportunity to rebuild your country. But we have no opinion on the Arab-Arab conflicts, like your border disagreement with Kuwait. . . . I was in the U.S. Embassy in Kuwait during the late 1960s. The instruction we had during this period was that we should express no opinion on this issue and that the issue is not associated with America. James Baker has directed our official spokesmen to emphasize this instruction. We hope that you can solve this problem using any suitable methods. . . . Normally that would not be any of our business, but when we see the Iraqi point of view that the measures taken by the UAE and Kuwait is, in the final analysis, parallel to military aggression against Iraq, then it would be reasonable for me to be concerned."

SADDAM: "We do not ask people not to be concerned when peace is at issue. This is a noble human feeling which we all feel. It is natural for you as a superpower to be concerned. But what we ask is not to express your concern in a way that would make an aggressor believe that he is getting support for his aggression. We want to find a just solution which will give us our rights but not deprive others of their rights. . . . We asked the Servant of the Two Shrines – King Fahd – to hold a four member summit, but he suggested a meeting between the Oil Ministers. We agreed, and the meeting took place in Jeddah. They reached an agreement which did not express what we wanted, but we agreed. Only two days after the meeting, the Kuwaiti Oil Minister made a statement that contradicted the agreement. . . . We agreed with President Mubarak that the Prime Minister of Kuwait would meet with the Deputy Chairman of the Revolution Command Council in Saudi Arabia because the Saudis initiated contact with us. . . . Mubarak just telephoned me a short while ago to say the Kuwaitis have agreed to that suggestion. Brother Mubarak told me they were scared. They said troops were only 20 kilometers north of the Arab League line. I said to him that regardless of what is there, whether they are police, border guards or army, and regardless of how many are there, and what they are doing, assure the Kuwaitis and give them our word that we are not going to do anything until we meet with them. When we meet and when we see that there is hope, then nothing will happen."

These are just a few excerpts from a long transcript, but they do not bear out the notion that Saddam was intent on war with Kuwait. They do not demonstrate the man to be irrational or crazed. They show a man concerned for his war-battered country and the need to rebuild the economy. They show a willingness to be friendly with the U.S. and with Kuwait, but insist that they will not be humiliated nor deprived of their rights. They also show that the U.S. was not being straight with him. It is also interesting to remember that the Glaspie interview with Saddam was filmed, and during which time the telephone call from Mubarak to Saddam about the meeting in Saudi Arabia occurred. The change in Saddam's expression, from serious and concerned to happy and relieved, is palpable. It speaks volumes about his sincerity. And it is also available, in part, to the public.[1]

LID: OK, let's admit that the U.S. suckered Iraq into invading Kuwait. Nonetheless, it doesn't change the fact that the Iraqis carried out terrible atrocities in the process. After all, who can forget the defenseless Kuwaiti children being removed from their incubators and left to die?

JW: I'm surprised you bring that up. That "atrocity" was proven to be false years ago, but let's briefly run over it.[2] In the fall of 1990, members

---

1. See www.benjaminforiraq.org for a copy of the video to which Wanniski refers.—Ed.

2. See also the essay by Sheldon Rampton and John Stauber, "The Mother of All Clients,"

of Congress and the American public were swayed towards war with Iraq by the tearful testimony of a 15-year-old girl known only as Nayirah. In the girl's testimony before a Congressional caucus – which is well-documented in MacArthur's book, *Second Front* – she described how, as a volunteer in a Kuwaiti maternity ward, she had seen Iraqi troops storm the hospital, steal the incubators, and leave 312 babies "on the cold floor to die." During the debate no less than seven U.S. Senators referred to this story, a debate which resulted in war by a mere five votes. In the weeks after Nayirah spoke, President Bush, Sr., invoked the incident five times, saying that such "ghastly atrocities" were like "Hitler revisited." But just weeks before the U.S. bombing campaign began in January 1991, questions began to be raised about the veracity of the incubator tale. It was later learned that Nayirah had no connection with the hospital that she referred to, but was, in fact, the daughter of the Kuwaiti Ambassador to America! She had been coached – along with a handful of others who would "corroborate" the story – by senior executives of Hill & Knowlton, the largest PR firm in the world at that time, and who had a contract worth more than $10 million with the Kuwaitis "to make the case for war." In 1995 Brent Scowcroft, Bush Sr.'s National Security Adviser, gave an interview to the London *Guardian* in which he claimed, referring to Nayirah's story, that "we didn't know it wasn't true at the time," but added that "it was useful in mobilizing public opinion." One suspects that even if they had known it was a lie, it would not have prevented war.

LID: OK, what about your point B? Didn't the Iraqi army position itself on the border of Saudi Arabia and threaten an invasion?

JW: No. I was present at a Saudi Embassy press briefing just before the war along with Jeanne Kirkpatrick, the former UN Ambassador. The briefing was conducted by Prince Bandar – he is still at the embassy – and its purpose was to explain why King Fahd had suddenly decided that Saddam was a threat to Saudi Arabia and to the peace of the region.

The U.S. government informed King Fahd that Iraq was poised to invade Saudi Arabia. Fahd sent out scouts to check and they could find no sign of the Iraqi army. According to Bandar he was shown photographs taken by "Naval Intelligence" at a Pentagon briefing. The Pentagon aerial photographs purported to show Saddam's army on the Kingdom's border, and so King Fahd quickly agreed to join the coalition. A few days later, September 11 to be precise, at a joint session of Congress, President Bush declared that

---

on pp. 831–839 of the companion volume, *Neo-CONNED! Again.*—Ed.

"following negotiations and promises by Iraqi dictator Saddam Hussein not to use force, a powerful army invaded its trusting and much weaker neighbor, Kuwait. Within three days, 120,000 troops with 850 tanks had poured into Kuwait and moved south to threaten Saudi Arabia. It was then I decided to act to check that aggression."

The first inkling that the photographs were not what they were purported to be showed up in the *St. Petersburg Times* (Florida) on January 6, 1991. *Times* journalist Jean Heller, in a piece entitled "Public Doesn't Get Picture With Gulf Satellite Photos," wrote – and I quote *in extenso:*

> Satellite photographs taken by the Soviet Union on the precise day Bush addressed Congress failed to show any evidence of Iraqi troops in Kuwait or massing along the Kuwait-Saudi Arabian border. While the Pentagon was claiming as many as 250,000 Iraqi troops in Kuwait, it refused to provide evidence that would contradict the Soviet satellite photographs. U.S. forces, encampments, aircraft, camouflaged equipment dumps, staging areas, and tracks across the desert can easily be seen. But as Peter Zimmerman, formerly of the U.S. Arms Control and Disarmament Agency in the Reagan administration, and a former image specialist for the DIA, who analyzed the photographs said: "We didn't find anything of that sort [i.e., comparable to the U.S. build up] anywhere in Kuwait. We don't see any tent cities, we don't see concentrations of tanks, we cannot see troop concentrations, and the main Kuwaiti airbase appears deserted. It is five weeks after the invasion, and from what we can see, the Iraqi air force hadn't flown a single fighter to the most strategic airbase in Kuwait. There is no infrastructure to support large numbers of people. They have to use toilets, or the functional equivalent. They have to have food . . . but where is it?"
>
> On September 18, 1990, only a week after the Soviet photos were taken, the Pentagon was telling the American public that Iraqi forces in Kuwait had grown to 360,000 men and 2,800 tanks. But the photos of Kuwait do not show any tank tracks in southern Kuwait. They clearly do show tracks left by vehicles which serviced a large oil field, but no tank tracks. In other words there was no proof at all of any Iraqi military build up that suggested an imminent invasion of Saudi Arabia. But photographs taken by Soviet commercial satellites tell a very convincing story. On August 8, 1990, photographs of southern Kuwait – six days after the initial invasion and right at the moment Bush was telling the world of an impending invasion of Saudi Arabia – show light sand drifts over patches of roads leading from Kuwait City to the Saudi border. The photos taken on September 11, 1990, show exactly the same sand drifts but now larger and deeper, suggesting that they had built up naturally without the disturbance of traffic for a month. Roads in northern Saudi Arabia during this same period, in contrast, show no sand drifts at all, having been swept clean by the heavy traffic of supply convoys. Zimmerman added: "The roads could be passable by tank but not by personnel or supply vehicles. Yet there is no sign that tanks have used those roads. And there is no evidence of new roads being cut. By contrast, none of the roads in Saudi Arabia has any sand cover at all. They have all been swept clean.

In early January of 1991, Heller's newspaper asked the Defense Department to show them evidence that would support the official U.S. estimate of the Iraqi build-up. Spokesman Bob Hall turned down the request, although he had been supplied with the results of the Zimmerman analysis. He said that the Iraqi numbers were "based on various intelligence resources and those are the numbers we stand by." But it is important to know that the mystery first arose because *ABC News* had purchased several photographs from Soyuz-Karta, a Soviet commercial satellite agency that sells pictures worldwide for such purposes as geological studies and energy exploration, at a cost of $1,500 per photograph.

Of course it might be argued that the Soviet satellite photographs were not to be trusted, even though they were commercial, not military, satellites. Zimmerman considered the idea that the Soviets deliberately or accidentally supplied a false image, but he contends that "we have to take on faith that the image is what the Soviets say it is. I think that is a reasonable assumption, because they would not have a motive to misrepresent it, and if they did misrepresent it and the word got out, they would never sell another picture to anybody." It is telling that satellite photographs at the same time showed the presence of U.S. forces at Dhahran Airport in Saudi Arabia in quite clear detail – but Iraqis are nowhere to be seen. When confronted with all of this Bob Hall said: "There is no mystery as far as we are concerned. They – the Iraqi troops – are there. We would like it to remain a mystery what our intelligence capabilities are. We are not going to make our intelligence public." Jean Heller recalls her newspaper asking Dick Cheney three times to confirm or deny the story, but no dice. To this day the story and photographs remain buried in top secret Pentagon files.

But the fact remains there was never *any* chance at all that Iraq would invade Saudi Arabia, whatever your take on the satellite photographs story. Why? Because Saddam was as happy as a clam with the Saudis for having forgiven Baghdad its multi-billion dollar war debt. Who attacks someone who has just made your life immeasurably easier, and who provides a positive example for others to follow?

LID: True enough. And you have also argued that, after Iraq invaded Kuwait in August 1990, Saddam immediately offered to negotiate a withdrawal in response to the UN demand that it do so. Please elucidate.

JW: Yes. In fact, although there was no formal "surrender" before Operation Desert Storm, two days before the operation started, Soviet President Mikhail Gorbachev informed President Bush that Saddam had agreed to leave Kuwait *without* conditions, and in fact, Radio Baghdad reported its troops would be returning. As U.S. ground troops moved into Kuwait from Saudi Arabia, the Iraqi Republican Guard was already moving back into Iraq. When Colin Powell said the plan was to encircle the Republican Guard and "kill it," he did not know – or so we are led to believe – the elite troops were already gone.

LID: But we were told at the time that the real reason the United States and its coalition allies only lost 143 troops in the Gulf War was not because the Republican Guard was already retreating, but because the Iraqi army was ill-equipped and demoralized, and did not put up a fight. What about that?

JW: The Iraqi army had been ordered to withdraw and it only provided a cover for retreat. Its conscripts suffered heavy casualties as the coalition forces fired upon the retreating army in what became known as "the turkey shoot." Journalist Seymour Hersh wrote an article on it for *The New Yorker* that was published in May of 2000, about how then Major General Barry McCaffrey's troops massacred a retreating Republican Guard tank division. Though the political and military "establishment" never seemed to take the charges that Hersh publicized very seriously – at least not in public – commentator Robert Novak had one source, a retired Army officer, confirm to him that "Hersh [got] it about 85 percent right. Everybody knows that. The old boys network has just circled the wagons."

Halabja

LID: OK, let's take C. It is alleged that in March 1988 Saddam Hussein committed genocide by killing thousands of Iraqi Kurds at Halabja with poison gas. This is the most often-cited instance of when Saddam "gassed his own people." Surely this is true?

JW: No, it is very far from being true. Firstly we need to get some background information in place in order to explain logically why it is not a credible story even though it has been repeated *ad nauseum*. Indeed President Bush used it in his State of the Union address in January 2003 as part of the "justification" for attacking Iraq, given that the smoking-gun evidence for Iraq's alleged weapons programs was wholly lacking. He stated the following in order to bolster his "moral" case: "The dictator [Saddam] who is assembling the world's most dangerous weapons has already used them on whole villages, leaving thousands of his own citizens dead, blind, or disfigured" – a very clear allusion to Halabja.

The Iran-Iraq war began at the end of 1980. With Iran possessing a population almost three times that of Iraq, it was largely expected that the former would win, but Saddam proved wholly superior to Ayatollah Khomeini in organizing resources. It is now generally agreed by historians that by the end of 1987 the advantage had shifted to Iraq. The Iranians had, in desperation, thrown "human waves" of soldiers against Iraq, and Iraq had used mustard gas to turn the tide. In early 1988, Iraq was using Scud missiles to hit Teheran, and the Iranian government was reeling.

It was at this point that Halabja broke into the news. A relatively small unit of the Iranian army broke into the town from a point only a few miles from the border. It overwhelmed the Iraqi garrison, but two days later it was driven out as Iraqi reinforcements arrived from a number of other points in the vicinity.

The first question to ask – and one that is almost never asked – is: why Halabja? Well, it could have been simply luck or an accident, but it is rare to find armies striking out in a particular direction without any clear-cut reason for doing so. Now, while we are constantly reminded by the news media that Iraq has, perhaps, the world's largest reserves of oil, known and potential, it may be more important to know that Iraq has the most extensive river system in the Middle East – a fact of regional and perhaps even geopolitical importance. In addition to the Tigris and Euphrates, there are the Greater Zab and Lesser Zab rivers in the north of the country. It is no coincidence, then, that Iraq had been covered with irrigation works by the sixth century A.D. and was the granary of the region.

Before the first Gulf War, Iraq had built an impressive system of dams and river control projects (you know, the kind of thing routinely built by crazed, blood-lusting dictators), the largest being the Darbandikhan dam in the Kurdish region. It was this dam that the Iranians were aiming to take control of when they seized Halabja – because water is life.

The Iranians attacked Halabja, a town of around 30,000 people, on March 16, 1988. It has been alleged that Jalal Talabani, leader of the Patriotic Union of Kurdistan, facilitated the entry of the Iranians into the town, though that is not something wholly certain. What is certain is that both Talabani and Masood Barzani, leader of the Kurdish Democratic Party – both of Marxist origin – had, despite occasional opportunistic shifts of allegiance, allied themselves with Iran during the war, though together they never represented more than a significant *minority* of the Kurdish people. It was something that Saddam would, not unnaturally, not forget.

What happened during the attack on Halabja? The most authoritative source on this subject is Dr. Stephen Pelletière, who was the CIA's senior political analyst on Iraq during the Iran-Iraq war, and was afterwards a Professor at the Army War College in Pennsylvania from 1988 to 2000, when he retired. Along with two other people, LTC Douglas V. Johnson and Leif Rosenberger, he headed a 1990 Army investigation into how the Iraqis would fight a war against the U.S.; the result was published in an Army War College Strategic Studies Institute publication entitled, "Iraqi Power and U.S. Security in the Middle East." He says, "I was privy to much of the classified material that flowed through Washington. . . . The classified version of the report went into great detail on the Halabja affair."

Let us quote him extensively so that his position is ultra-clear:

> This much about the gassings at Halabja we undoubtedly know: it came about in the course of a battle between Iraqis and Iranians. Iraq used chemical weapons to try and kill Iranians who had seized the town. The Kurdish civilians who died had the misfortune to be caught up in that exchange. But they were not Iraq's main target.
>
> The story gets murkier. Immediately after the battle, the U.S. Defense Intelligence Agency investigated and produced a classified report, which it circulated within the intelligence community on a need-to-know basis. That study asserted that it was Iranian gas that killed the Kurds, not Iraqi gas.
>
> The agency did find that each side used gas against each other in the battle around Halabja. The condition of the dead Kurds' bodies, however, indicated that they had been killed with a blood agent – that is, a cyanide-based gas – which Iran was known to use. The Iraqis, who are thought to have used mustard gas in the battle, are not known to have possessed blood agents at the time.
>
> These facts have long been in the public domain but, extraordinarily, as often as the Halabja affair is cited, they are rarely mentioned. A much-discussed article in *The New Yorker* in March 2002 did not make reference to the DIA report, or consider that Iranian gas might have killed the Kurds. On the rare occasions the report is brought up, there is usually speculation, *with no proof,* that it was skewed out of American political favoritism towards Iraq in its war against Iran.
>
> I am not trying to rehabilitate the character of Saddam Hussein. . . . But accusing him of gassing his own people at Halabja as an act of genocide is not correct, because as far as the information we have goes, all of the cases where gas was used involved battles. These were tragedies of war. There may be justification for invading Iraq, but Halabja is not one of them.

One interesting point to put into the equation is the fact that when Secretary of State James Baker met the Iraqi Deputy Prime Minister, Tariq Aziz, in Geneva in 1990, in the run up to the first Gulf War, he told Aziz that he did not believe the story of Iraq gassing the Kurds.

What is even more interesting is that there is perhaps one area where Dr. Pelletière *may* not be wholly correct, based upon my correspondence with Dr. Mohammed al-Obaidi, a University Professor in the U.K. who was born and educated in the al-Adhamiyah district of Baghdad. His perspective questions the idea that both sides used gas. Dr. al-Obaidi's brother was a colonel in the Iraqi Army in 1988 (he eventually became a General), and he was sent to Halabja when news came through of the impending Iranian attack on the town. The doctor passed on his brother's recollections to me. I should point out, though, that Dr. al-Obaidi is no fan of Saddam and managed to leave Iraq for London only after years of obstruction. He is also a Shiite Muslim and thus cannot be accused of being a voice for the Sunni minority.

His brother relates that he was based near Mosul when the news came through about the Halabja attack. He says that when his regiment arrived, two days later, the whole thing was over. When he arrived, he found that the Deputy Chief-of-Staff of the Iraqi Army, General Nezar al-Khazraji, was in the area, and had met with all of the commanders. The General was both shocked and surprised by what happened to the Kurds, because he was not aware of any use of gas by the Iraqi forces. Something else that his brother related was that no Iraqi aircraft or any other Iraqi military assets had started the fire before the Iranians attacked them. That being the case, he thinks, one should ask (1) why the Iraqis didn't gas the Iranians in advance, if they did in fact use gas, since they had advance warning that the Iranians were headed to Halabja, and (2) why didn't Saddam order a much more sweeping use of chemical weapons against Iran, since the war was costing Iraq thousands of young, university-educated men, and Iran could have been brought to its knees with the widespread use of this kind of weaponry.

It so happens that some years later, General al-Khazraji fell out with Saddam and had to be spirited out of the country. He was aided in this by the Kurds. Is it really credible that the man who would have authorized the use of gas to kill civilian Kurds would have been aided by Kurdish leaders? I think not. Not to mention that when al-Khazraji finally settled in Denmark, a Danish court – at the instigation of some members of the Danish parliament who had heard of the issue – tried to make trouble for al-Khazraji over the alleged gassing of Kurds. The general invited the court to contact the leaders of the Kurdish parties who had hosted him for a time during his evacuation from Iraq, and ask them if he was guilty. On the contrary, the Kurds who were contacted confirmed his innocence, the court dropped its charges, and the general was living quietly in Denmark until just before the war.

In April 2002 Dr. al-Obaidi wrote something else to me, which I think is also of interest.

> Let me start by telling a little bit about the attitude and behaviour of the Ba'ath regime when it comes to defending themselves against a mistake they have committed or were about to commit. They initially prepare all their media by injecting them with false information regarding any particular act they did or were about to do, and once they committed that action, they release their media to defend the regime. In addition, all party members will be served with strict information of how to deny the action that took place and how to convince people that the Iraqi regime did not commit that mistake. In other words, the party members plus the media are ready.
>
> What surprised the Iraqi people after the gassing of the Kurds at Halabja was that the Iraqi regime was not prepared at all to defend itself against the allegations that they were behind these gassings at a time when they were able to do so. It seems that they were taken by surprise as the only thing they could do was to show on national TV the result of that failed offensive by the Iranians at Halabja. However, the opposition to the regime in Iraq, and in particular the Shiites supported and supplied by Iran, turned the story around so as to be an act by the Iraqi regime against the Kurds.

From day one, the Iraqi government insisted that it had nothing to do with any poison gas being used on its own nationals, not even accidentally in attacks on its Iranian adversaries. The Defense Ministry said it would be ridiculous for them to use poison gas in the town when their own forces were going in the direction of the Iranian retreat, which began within hours of the latter's attack on the town.

With this kind of information we can come to a serious understanding of the alleged genocide of Halabja. According to the CIA – and this is confirmed in a relatively new report issued by them in October 2002 – "hundreds" – at most – of Iraqi Kurds died at Halabja, though the event has taken on a life of its own with the figures of "victims" ranging from anywhere between 2,000 and 10,000 according to which "source" is telling the story. In June 2004, for example, the *New York Times* published two articles which mentioned the affair in passing, and although published only days apart the figures were variously given as 2,000 and 5,000. In serious journalism, one cannot afford to be so cavalier with such information, since the line between truth and propaganda becomes irrevocably blurred. Yet the U.S. government concluded in 1990 that the Kurds who died were victims of a cyanide-based gas, which the Iranians possessed, but which the Iraqi army did not. This pathetic story has been rolled out on countless occasions, yet even in a journalistic work such as *Instant Empire* by Simon Henderson, published in 1991, it is made clear that Saddam was innocent, with Henderson stating "the Iranians arrived first with television cameras and exploited the opportunity to censure Iraq."

Even the late Dr. Edward Said had his doubts about the "Saddam gassed his own people" line, and interestingly he based his doubt partially on Pelletière's 1990 study, which everyone else was more or less (intentionally?) ignoring. Said wrote, in a March 7, 1991, piece for the *London Review of Books*: "The claim that Iraq gassed its own citizens has often been repeated. At best, this is uncertain. There is at least one War College report, done while Iraq was a U.S. ally, which claims that the gassing of the Kurds in Halabja was done by Iran. Few people mention such reports in the media today."

LID: So did Saddam's forces ever use gas?

JW: Yes, they did, and they admitted to it openly. The fact is that Iraq, in the person of Tariq Aziz, the deputy prime minister, acknowledged in July 1988 that the Iraqi Republic had used gas during the Iran-Iraq war, but that it had been only in response to a first strike by Iran. Dr. Stephen Pelletière points out in his comprehensive work, *Iraq and the International Oil System: Why America Went to War in the Gulf,* published in 2001 by Praeger, that the Iraqis were not very effective in using gas, a curb in its use in itself. Pelletière writes:

> The first known and fairly well-credited use of gas by the Iraqis was at Haj Umran in 1983. There, the Iranians, with the co-operation of the Barzani Kurds, had invaded the northern Kurdish territories, and the Iraqis, to dislodge them, used gas [mustard gas]. The attempt was a fiasco, as the Iraqis dropped the gas on peaks held by the Kurds and the Iranians, only to have it drift down into the valleys, where the Iraqi forces were set up, which disoriented Iraq's attacks."

The October 2002 CIA report, along with other credible sources, cites 10 "documented" Iraqi uses of chemical weapons, most against the Iranians, with three against Kurds and Iranians, but always within the context of the Iran-Iraq war. The report indicates merely "hundreds" of casualties resulting from the last of these 10 incidents, namely the Halabja incident, so it would seem that the CIA as well has accepted the judgment of Dr. Pelletière and his colleagues. Long after the CIA report was published and readily available at the agency's website, a triumphant Defense Secretary Rumsfeld visited Halabja and mourned the thousands of Saddam's victims buried in mass graves there, although none have yet been unearthed. Cemeteries yes, mass graves no.

[29]

The "Anfal" Campaign

LID: How about your point D: the so-called Anfal campaign of roughly 1987 to 1989, when Saddam allegedly tried to annihilate the Kurds by gassing, deportations, and the machine-gunning of a hundred thousand or more Iraqi Kurds?

JW: This subject is so convoluted that it's almost impossible to evaluate what the *charges* are, let alone respond to them – which should be the first cause for a "red flag" to go up. The various sources that continue to promulgate these accusations – such as Human Rights Watch, Physicians for Human Rights, the American press, and of course the U.S. officials who staffed the CPA – cannot even get their story straight as to what Saddam is accused of doing and how many supposedly perished under his regime.

Let's try to sort it out, though, because this is serious stuff. And since two of the three major justifications for the war – the Iraq/al-Qaeda connection and the stockpiles of WMD – have turned out, as I suspected they would, to be bogus, the last argument Uncle Sam will have for having gone after Saddam is that he committed large-scale atrocities, murdering tens if not hundreds of thousands of "his own people."

The claim that Saddam initiated an intentional program to commit genocide against the Kurds in the north began as an accusation from the U.S. State Department and its Secretary in the late 1980s, George Schultz, that the Iraqis were using gas against the Kurds in the north as a means of suppressing the rebellion that had developed towards the end of the Iran-Iraq war. Never mind that according to Pelletière's 1990 study (and as is well known) "significant numbers of the Kurds had launched a revolt against Baghdad and in the process teamed up with Tehran," Iraq's enemy at that point for almost a decade. Evidently it was a convenient time, at the end of the Iran-Iraq war, for our government to join Israel in making Iraq an enemy. Here's the story, from Dr. Pelletière's recent book:

> [O]n September 7, 1988, America's Secretary of State George Shultz invited Iraq's junior foreign minister, Sadoun Hammadi, to Foggy Bottom, ostensibly to discuss how the negotiations could be speeded up. Hammadi appeared on September 8, unaware that he was about to be ambushed. For, in a routine press briefing before television cameras, Shultz, without warning, leveled the charge that, once again (as at Halabja) Iraq was using gas against its Kurdish citizens.
>
> In fact, the Iraqis were at the moment carrying out operations to recapture the north from rebel Kurds concentrated in an area called Amadiyah, close to the Turkish border. However, the Iraqi Minister denied, vehemently, that gas was

being used. He demanded that Shultz reveal his evidence, and Shultz said that he was not at liberty to do that, as this would compromise intelligence sources.

Well, then, said Hammadi, where are the victims? Here was a problem. *Where were the victims?* Rebel Kurds were pouring across the borders into Turkey and Iran, desperate to escape the Iraqi onslaught. *Peshmergas* [i.e., Kurdish armed fighters—Ed.] were everywhere in evidence, but reporters who rushed to interview them all reported they were seemingly fit; there was not a sign of gassing.

Indeed, Turkish doctors asked by the reporters to confirm that Kurds had been victimized denied this to be the case, or at least they said that they could not confirm that any such attacks had occurred because they had not seen any gassing victims. The UN High Commission for Refugees (UNHCR), which also had representatives in the area, confirmed this view, as did the Red Cross and the Red Crescent Societies and a doctor from *Medicins du Monde.*

Momentarily, it appeared that the Iraqis were exonerated. It was not to be, however, because of what happened next.

If the ambush interview arranged by Shultz caused controversy, what followed certainly augmented it. Within 24 hours after Shultz's public accusation of Iraq, the Senate voted sanctions on the basis of his charges. The vote was nearly unanimous, and, as the *Washington Post* reported, it put a heavy burden on the Iraqis, since they would now have enormous difficulties trying to roll over their $69 billion debt. . . .

To be sure, the Senate's action was not the final word on the matter; the House had yet to act. But in the meantime, the Senate Foreign Relations Committee sent two of its staffers to the region to report personally on what might have occurred.

Within a week the two were back, claiming that the Iraqis had gassed not only the rebel guerrillas but some hundreds of thousands of other Kurds, killing in the process possibly as many as 100,000.

The Iraqis were naturally upset by this allegation. When newsmen confronted their defense minister, he denied that this had occurred and further claimed that Iraq had no need of gas. Indeed, in that terrain, he said, gas would have been a liability. [In pursuit of the smaller Iranian force, the Iraqi army would have been spraying gas in its own path.]

This essentially is correct. Gas is an extremely tricky weapon to use and, except under certain circumstances, is not particularly lethal. It is interesting that although this feature of chemical warfare is well known throughout the military community, no one in the Western media (to the author's knowledge) ever confirmed it.

As the controversy escalated, the Iraqis became as incensed as the Americans. They demanded that the Arab League take a stand, and the League did, branding the outcry against Iraq as contrived. Like the Iraqis, the League asserted that the Americans lacked proof of their allegations.

The Senate staffers claimed to have "overwhelming" proof that the attacks had occurred. However, this turned out to be anecdotal evidence – the Kurds *told* them that they had been gassed. The staffers also claimed to have seen obvious gassing victims and to have taken photographs of them. But no photographs were ever produced, and the alleged victims never were identified. As for the claim of 100,000 dead, this would appear to have been speculation. At the same time, however, it was quite a serious charge, implying "genocide."

LID: A serious charge indeed. Then what?

JW: Well, the leader of the 1988 Senate Foreign Relations Committee staff mission to Iraqi Kurdistan, Peter Galbraith – son of the famed economist John Kenneth, and senior advisor to the Committee from 1979 to 1993 – maintains to this day that he received authentic testimony from the Kurds as to the campaign supposedly conducted against them. But his position is not confirmed by contemporaries who also either visited the area or studied the events.

Milton Viorst, a *Washington Post* reporter, went to Kurdistan a few days after Schultz made his charge. He didn't hear the same testimony; in fact his experience was the opposite. His October 7, 1988, article appeared in the *International Herald Tribune,* and said:

> The Kurds compose a fifth of the Iraqi population, and they are a tightly knit community. If there had been large-scale killing, it is likely they would know and tell the world. But neither I nor any Westerner I encountered heard such allegations.
>
> Nor did Kurdish society show discernible signs of tension. The northern cities, where the men wear Kurdish turbans and baggy pants, were as bustling as I had ever seen them. I talked to armed Kurds near the border, members of Iraqi military units mobilized against the rebels.
>
> On the other hand, Iraq probably used gas of some kind in air attacks on rebel positions. Journalists visiting the Turkish camps saw refugees with blistered skin and irritated eyes, symptoms of gassing. But doctors sent by France, the United Nations and the Red Cross have said these symptoms could have been produced by a powerful but non-lethal tear gas.
>
> Citing national security, Mr. Shultz has declined to submit the U.S. data to scrutiny, even by America's NATO allies, though State Department sources say it is the sort of information that the United States routinely shares with them. American officials acknowledge that Mr. Shultz's evidence, chiefly radio intercepts, may be subject to conflicting interpretations.

And Dr. Pelletière's 1990 report dismissed the allegations outright:

> Having looked at all of the evidence that was available to us, we find it impossible to confirm the State Department's claim that gas was used in this instance. To begin with there were never any victims produced. International relief organizations who examined the Kurds – in Turkey where they had gone

for asylum – failed to discover any. Nor were there ever any found inside Iraq. The claim rests solely on the testimony of the Kurds who had crossed the border into Turkey, where they were interviewed by staffers of the Senate Foreign Relations Committee.

Finally, remember that these charges refer to alleged uses of gas *after* Halabja, and the CIA report of late 2002 confirmed only 10 documented cases of Iraqi use of chemical weapons, and the *last* of these is, in fact, Halabja, of March 1988.

LID: So between the Pelletière study and the testimony from people like Viorst who visited Iraqi Kurdistan, that was that, right?

JW: Hardly. The story faded for a time, but resurfaced when Iraq invaded Kuwait in 1990. In the years since, it has been amplified again and again by the Washington organization, *Human Rights Watch*. Its resident expert, Joost Hiltermann, an Arabic-speaking law professor at Johns Hopkins School for International Studies, has been chiefly responsible for this amplification. Since 1990, HRW has produced a series of reports on the issue, from the earliest, in 1991 (which asserted that "Halabja was not the first time Iraq had turned its chemical arsenal on the Kurds. Thousands – and most likely tens of thousands – of civilians were killed during chemical and conventional bombardments stretching from the spring of 1987 through the fall of 1988. The attacks were part of a long-standing campaign that destroyed almost every Kurdish village in Iraq"), to later, more bulky reports from 1992 and 1993, culminating in one from 1994 entitled, "Iraq's Crime of Genocide: the Anfal Campaign against the Kurds." Claims made in these various reports range from repeated chemical weapons attacks to the destruction of villages and the exaggeration of the number of deaths at Halabja (from 3,200 to 7,000), all resulting in anywhere from 50,000 to 100,000 alleged deaths. Kenneth Pollock, a member of Clinton's National Security team and in recent years an Iraqi "expert" used as a commentator on Fox News, repeatedly used 200,000 as the number of Kurds murdered by Saddam. As recently as the summer of 2004, Pat Roberts of Kansas, the Republican chairman of the Senate Intelligence Committee, used 500,000 as the number of Saddam's genocide victims. It was all hearsay magnified.

LID: That all sounds pretty damning. Maybe that's what Shultz was referring to. Was there something to it after all?

JW: The problem with these allegations is that they don't stand up to scrutiny. My belief is that all this "genocide" reporting was mostly a propaganda effort to "demonize" Saddam after Iraq invaded Kuwait, because initially there was little support for the United States to commit itself to kicking Saddam out of Kuwait. The accusations made by Shultz had not been taken seriously by the U.S. government until this period coinciding with the crisis that led to the first Gulf War. At which point the "gassing" of the Kurds was convenient and at hand. What is also likely is that when Iraq won the war with Iran, the surprised Israeli supporters in the United States decided Saddam was no longer an ally, but the victorious power in the region, a man who would be a threat to Israel's survival. This too would have provided an impetus for Iraq's demonization.

LID: So you really think that these allegations are mere propaganda, and that the idea that Saddam committed genocide is not credible?

JW: Let me review the charges for you, first, and then give you some background you need to understand the circumstances that were really extant during the period in question. Then I'll tell you why I think the charges aren't persuasive.

A *Radio Free Europe* dispatch of July 7, 2003, put it like this: "Rights groups that have been cataloguing the abuses of the regime estimate the toll of missing at close to 300,000. There are no confirmed numbers, but they are expected to be high, says Mona Rishmawi, senior adviser to the UN High Commissioner for Human Rights in Baghdad." It's hard to tell where these totals come from, but what is clear is that the standard 50,000–100,000 come from the "Anfal" campaign (which Barbara Crossette referred to in a *New York Times* piece from December 11, 2000, entitled "Iraq is Forcing Kurds From Their Homes"; she wrote: "in 1987 and 1988 50,000 to 100,000 Kurds were gassed to death with chemical agent by Mr. Hussein's government, American officials say"). These numbers are sometimes used by Human Rights Watch also to identify the number of victims of a machine-gunning massacre in southern Iraq that supposedly took place in the late 1980s or early 1990s. Another number of thousands alone are supposedly to have died at Halabja in 1988, which is or isn't part of the anti-Kurdish "Anfal" campaign, depending upon who the accuser is. (An April 27, 2003, *Associated Press* story out of New York claimed, for instance, that Halabja was "part of a scorched-earth campaign to wipe out a Kurdish rebellion in northern Iraq.") Then there are Kurds and Shiites killed during the suppression of rebellions at the end of both the Iran-Iraq and Gulf Wars – again in some cases considered to be part of "Anfal" – along with numerous refugees in the Kurdish north who are lumped in with the "missing." So you have, at the end of the day, some number of thousands that are supposed to have perished at Saddam's hands. But as you can see it's all pretty vague.

LID: How can one respond to these kinds of charges when it's not even clear what they are?

JW: Yes, that's a good point. But let me go on with the "background" that you should have about what was going on in Iraqi Kurdistan during the 1980s, because this really puts the allegations into perspective, I think.

The relationship between the central government of Saddam Hussein and the Iraqi Kurds in the north is not one that lends itself to easy categorization or generalization. According to something that Dr. al-Obaidi wrote to me recently, Saddam considers them to be an integral part of Iraq: "neither Saddam nor his party were considering the Kurds as 'guests' in Iraq, but they were recognised as a . . . minority part of the Iraqi Nation." Thus you will find that Saddam opposes the Kurds when they threaten the territorial integrity of Iraq and when they act to undermine the central government in Baghdad, and he relaxes his opposition when they attempt to integrate themselves into Iraq. Let me back this up with examples.

Saddam proposed offering a degree of autonomy to the Kurds as early as 1970, although he was an influential Minister, not Head of State, at the time. In an interesting though little-known 1992 book called *Saddam Hussein*, by the American journalist Nita Renfrew, the proposal is discussed in these terms, on pages 55 and 56:

> In 1970, Saddam proposed a plan for Kurdish autonomy, meant to take effect as law in March 1974. The plan included provisions for the administration of Kurdish territory to pass into Kurdish hands and for a Kurdish parliament to be elected. Also, Iraq would have a mandatory Kurdish Vice President. Unlike Turkey and Iran, where the Kurds have not been allowed to speak their own language, Iraq ensured that Kurdish would be the first language in the local Kurdish government, schools and universities. However, at the instigation of the Shah of Iran, the CIA, and Israel, the Kurds rejected the terms and unleashed a bloody civil war. Within a year there were 60,000 casualties, among them 16,000 Iraqi soldiers. It was only after Iraq agreed to the terms of the Algiers Accord in 1975, signed by Saddam and the Shah, that the civil war came to an end. In the agreement, both countries [Iraq and Iran] agreed to refrain from interfering in the internal affairs of the other. This meant that no more weapons could reach the Kurds through Iran.

In case one would be inclined to doubt Renfrew's objectivity, the historical soundness of her account is confirmed by a 1993 research paper produced for the Industrial College of the Armed Forces, part of the U.S.

National Defense University, by Clifton W. Flowers. He writes that in 1970 "Saddam Hussein agreed to Kurdish leaders' demands for a great measure of autonomy. The agreement was to be completely implemented over a period of four years." While this was going on, Flowers reports, the U.S. was conducting an admitted covert operation to "contain" Iraq by funneling assistance to the Kurds (in terms of a President Nixon-authorized $16 million worth of weapons and supplies, according to a September 11, 1996, *New York Times* article by Tim Weiner). This assistance was *in addition to,* Flowers writes, *that which Iran and Israel were already providing to the Kurds.* Jim Hoagland of the *Washington Post,* writing on August 4, 1992, confirms that the arms and cash were an encouragement to the Kurds to "rebel against Baghdad." The bitterness of Masood Barzani (mentioned before, as one of the two principal leaders of the Iraqi Kurds) over having been "let down" by the U.S. after being encouraged to act against Baghdad is proof positive that American intentions – at least those stated to Barzani – were to have the Kurds rebel. Weiner's piece even quotes the memo that the Kurds sent to the CIA immediately following the Iran-Iraq deal that undercut Iranian support for the Kurds: "Intervene according to your promises." And a later, 1996, study by Dr. Pelletière for the Army War College, "Managing Strains in the Coalition: What to Do About Saddam?" also confirms that Barzani felt betrayed by the Americans – or at least by Henry Kissinger.

LID: No doubt, then, with that level of intrigue that the offer of autonomy from Baghdad didn't work out.

JW: Right. Saddam was exasperated that Iran was working to bolster the Kurdish opposition – and one might speculate that he was especially annoyed that this was going on while he was trying to settle the Kurdish issue by granting them what Flowers calls "a great measure of autonomy." Is it reasonable to expect that Saddam would have negotiated indefinitely with *these* Kurds while they were being manipulated by the CIA, Henry Kissinger, and Tehran?

LID: Not really.

JW: Now during the Iran-Iraq war, the Kurds were effectively caught in the middle, from a geographical perspective, though there is no doubt that the two main players in the war – Barzani and Talabani – at one time or another, when they weren't opposing each other, were more or less supportive of Iran with their bands of Kurdish fighters. Pelletière's 1996 study makes it clear that the Iranians tried to make a "second front" against Iraq using both leaders' tribes. It is, in fact, in this context that the CIA's October 2002 report notes the Iraqi use of chemical weapons against Iranians and Kurds, since much of the fighting in the Iran-Iraq war was done both by Iranians and Iranian Kurds, and in Kurdish areas.

Several years after the end of the war – in fact immediately after the First Gulf War – history seems to have repeated itself. In January of 1991, Tim Weiner's *New York Times* piece reports, "as the Gulf War began, the C.I.A. began aiming propaganda at the Kurds in Iraq. The Kurds listened to President Bush's call to 'force Saddam Hussein the dictator to step aside.'" The resultant Kurdish rebellion was quite successful initially, until Saddam's forces had finished dealing with a Shiite rebellion in the south, when they went North to deal with the rebellion there. In other words, the legitimate government was going to put down a rebellion that had actually gone to the point of collaborating with a foreign enemy during a time of war, a couple of years before, and was inspired by a third-party government. There are few governments in history that have not responded in the same way – including the United States during its war against the Confederacy (in which over 250,000 of the "rebels" were killed). As in the early 1970s, the Kurds claimed in this case that they were motivated in their rebellion by the Americans, counted on American support, and were "shocked" when it did not come. This is the contention of the Flowers paper, and it is confirmed in an email I received from Dr. al-Obaidi in the U.K., who wrote the following:

> I am also absolutely sure from my sources that the Iraqis knew very well that the uprising was orchestrated not by initiatives from their leadership but by a well-planned scenario set for them by the CIA and the Mossad. In fact, part of this scenario was to drive the Kurds out of their homes and villages when the Kurd leaderships were told that Saddam was preparing to use WMD against them, whereas the main reason for this was to show the world how brutal Saddam was.

LID: So now we come back to the use of WMD?

JW: The connection will become clear in a minute. Meanwhile, in spite of the behaviour of the Kurds, Saddam made another offer of autonomy to them in May 1991. This is stated in Pelletière's "Managing Strains in the Coalition," referencing *Washington Post, New York Times,* and *Middle East International* articles. The Flowers paper confirms that at one point both Kurdish chiefs were confident an agreement would be made. But the talks stalled, and the U.S. didn't seem to mind. "During the negotiations with Baghdad," Pelletière says, "Washington and London behaved as if they disapproved of the talks, and afterwards both appeared relieved the deal was not consummated." Flowers quotes a May 1991 *Congressional Research Report* which explains why: "Saddam may actually be strengthened by a settlement." And that's not something that American policy has intended to permit for many years.

LID: It's surprising that Saddam would make such an offer, given that he is portrayed as such a horrible tyrant.

JW: It only sounds unbelievable if you believe everything that you read – or cannot read because of suppression – in our deplorable press. The Kurds are not a united people, and they are not wholly or uniformly anti-Saddam. Saddam is the same, not wholly anti-Kurd or wholly pro-Kurd. He was simply, throughout his reign, wholly pro-Iraq, and it seems to me that he did what he did with that single purpose in mind.

Consider this report, for instance, from the French Press Agency (AFP) on October 6, 2004:

> A Kurdish tribal leader with links to former Iraqi President Saddam Hussein was assassinated Wednesday in the main northern city of Mosul, police said. "Khaled Abdel Ghafur al-Dubardani was in his car in the Sayyidati al-Jamila neighbourhood when four men opened fire on his vehicle," Muzahem Abdullah al-Shummari told AFP. Sheikh Dubardani was one of the most prominent tribal leaders in northern Iraq and had led a unit of Kurdish volunteers loyal to Saddam Hussein.

Not just a Kurd, but a prominent tribal leader; and not the only one, but merely "one of the most prominent." How is it that there can be such a prominent tribal leader of the Kurds loyal to Saddam if there is, by definition, this natural and implacable antagonism between Saddam and the Kurds? Another relevant fact is the support that Talabani gave to Saddam for at least a time during the Iran-Iraq war; as Flowers writes, "In 1984, led by Talabani from Damascus, PUK forces joined with Iraqi troops in the north, and fought Massoud Barzani-led KDP soldiers attacking from, and supported by, Iran." Now how could this be if the main, driving force behind the Kurds is their glaring hatred of Saddam?

LID: Good point.

JW: Which is not to say that either the Talabani or Barzani people were necessarily "loyal" to Baghdad or had any desire to be; but if you study the facts it becomes clear that both of them simply deal with whomever they think will be the most advantageous for their aims at the moment. The Flowers paper notes that, in the mid-1970s when the Kurds and Baghdad were attempting to work out a deal for Kurdish autonomy, Barzani had invested three years worth of efforts to see the deal through, and it was pressure from other Kurdish factions that soured him on the deal. He was accused of putting the interests of his tribe ahead of those of the greater "Kurdish nation," even though such a thing never really existed. It sounds to me like pressure from those who were already dealing with Iran and the CIA. A further point illustrating this is from the 1992, Jim Hoagland, *Washington Post* article we mentioned earlier: before coming to the U.S. in August 1992, following the 1991 Kurdish rebellion in Iraq, Barzani had met with Saddam and tried to work out an acceptable arrangement. The U.S. was his second choice.

LID: So what do you conclude from all this?

JW: That effectively Barzani and Talabani, and the people they represent, are opportunists. They simply take whatever offer, from whoever is offering, that seems best capable of securing their aims. No doubt money drives much of this. The aid that went into Kurdistan wasn't much, according to Pelletière's 1996 paper, but it was enough to support Barzani and Talabani, and it effectively forced those who wanted an income to become mercenaries for one of the two. And any loyalty that the two commanded was driven the same way, at least according to Pelletière:

> Barzani and Talabani are, effectively, warlords who dominate their respective regions, but this mainly came about because of their close ties to Washington and London. In fact, within both areas there are a number of powerful agas, Kurdish chiefs, who acquiesced in following Barzani and Talabani only because they were handsomely recompensed.

LID: So the upshot is that in his dealings with the Kurds – at least the ones with the Washington connections – Saddam was attempting to work out what was by all accounts a sincere and generous autonomy with people who, in response, acted like they were for sale to the highest bidder, allowing themselves to be manipulated by the Americans, among others, against Baghdad, if they felt it was to their advantage.

JW: Exactly.

LID: No wonder he was suspicious of their loyalty to the Iraqi State.

JW: No wonder indeed, and that's when we come to the two efforts that Saddam made to deal with their mischief definitively, at the end of both the Iran-Iraq and the Gulf Wars. Remember, this is a problem Saddam was dealing with even *during* the Iran-Iraq war, when Kurds were used by the Iranians against Iraq. Now you have another series of anti-Baghdad efforts by the Barzani and Talabani forces, and Saddam responded with characteristic decisiveness.

Of the first episode, Dr. Pelletière's 1990 report states, "as soon as the war with Iran ended, Iraq announced its determination to crush the Kurdish insurrection, and it sent Republican Guards to the Kurdish areas." The reporter Milton Viorst writes in his 1994 book, *Sandcastles:*

> Saddam, after the cease-fire, sent in his army to stamp out the Kurdish insurgency once and for all. He ordered his troops to go as far as the Iranian border and depopulate a swath of territory eight or ten miles deep, neutralizing for all time an area that had served the rebels as sanctuary.
>
> Saddam's objectives were understandable; his tactics were characteristically brutal. The army dynamited dozens of villages into rubble and dispatched thousands of inhabitants from their ancestral homes to newly built "resettlement villages" far in the interior. In the process, sixty thousand Kurds crossed the border into Turkey, where they told journalists they were fleeing from attacks of gas.

Referring to the second Kurdish uprising, Clifton Flowers writes in his paper:

> On the fourth of March, 1991, four days after the end of the Gulf War, the Kurds began another uprising against Saddam. . . .
>
> The Kurdish rebellion enjoyed tremendous success initially, taking control of most of the traditionally Kurdish regions. However, once the Iraqi army had crushed the simultaneous Shiite rebellion in the South, they turned their full attention to the North. Iraqi helicopter gunships proved particularly effective in the rough terrain. Without external assistance, the Kurdish fighters were soon overwhelmed, and recalling the poison gas attacks of the 1980s, Kurdish civilians began a mass exodus towards the Turkish and Iranian borders.

LID: So you think that this alleged extermination of the Kurds that Human Rights Watch reports are really references to the suppression of these two Kurdish rebellions?

JW: I do.

LID: Then what of the so-called documentation that proves a campaign of "genocide" against the Kurds? Isn't there proof of atrocities during the late 1980s, which would have been separate from the conventional military responses to the two Kurdish rebellions, in 1988 and 1991?

JW: No, I don't think there is. First, you should bear in mind that the same people who were giving Saddam trouble through the 1970s, 80s, and early 90s – this faction of Kurds and their American sponsors – in order to destabilize his country and his government, are the same people who have come up with the charges that have created a campaign of "genocide" out of what could just as easily been seen as a legitimate – if harsh – response to a group of fighters aiding an enemy in wartime and then staging outright rebellions several years later. There is no doubt that Saddam responded to these threats; the question is how these actions are spun by those who are – and were, through the whole period, going back to 1972 – on the opposite side.

LID: What do you mean?

JW: Well, remember I just mentioned that in his 1994 book, *Sandcastles*, Viorst says that after Saddam cleared a strip of land between Iran and Iraq, after the war, " . . . sixty thousand Kurds crossed the border into Turkey, where they told journalists they were fleeing from attacks of gas." He also says this: "The Iraqis angrily denied the charge, but Secretary of State Shultz claimed it was true, and the Senate Foreign Relations Committee, without investigating, proposed a bill to impose heavy sanctions on Iraq." Why were some of our leaders so eager to jump on the anti-Saddam band-wagon? Viorst's comment is simply this: "With the pro-Israeli lobby fanning the fire, the bill nearly passed."

Dr. al-Obaidi says, furthermore, that it is a known fact "that key Kurdish leaders aided by the CIA and the Israeli Mossad have used a wide network of public relations companies and media outlets in the West to manipulate and twist the truth of what happened in Kurdish Halabja in 1988 in favour of the Kurdish political parties." If this strains credibility, it should be remembered that all the stories about the "genocide" originated from Saddam's Iraqi opponents in exile – and his troublesome Kurdish opponents like Barzani and Talabani – all the same folks who assured us he was hiding weapons of mass destruction and was in league with Osama bin Laden and al-Qaeda.

It's worthwhile to hear a little more from Dr. al-Obaidi on this point, because it explains a lot:

> In 1993, an organisation was established in Israel called "The Kurdish Israeli Friendship League" founded by a Jewish Kurd called Moti Zaken, who originally immigrated from Zakho, Iraq, and worked closely with the American Zionist lobby in the U.S.

His efforts ended in 1996 in the establishment of the Washington Kurdish Institute, an organisation founded with the financial help and supervision of the Zionist Mike Amitay.

Mike Amitay is the son of Morris Amitay, a long-time legislative assistant in Congress and lobbyist for the influential American Israeli Public Affairs Committee.

Amitay senior is an adviser to Frank Gaffney's Centre for Security Policy and the former Vice-Chairman of the Jewish Institute for National Security Affairs (JINSA), a U.S.-based pro-Israeli Likud advocacy outfit that specialises in connecting U.S. military brass to their counterparts in the Israeli armed forces.

JINSA associates include Dick Cheney, John Bolton, Douglas Feith, and Richard Perle. A group of Kurdish figures known for their connection with the Israeli Mossad manage the Washington Kurdish Institute. These are: Najmaldin Karim, Omar Halmat, Birusk Tugan, Osman Baban, Asad Khailany, Kendal Nezan, Asfandiar Shukri and Mohammad Khoshnaw.

Such organisations have devoted themselves to championing the claims that the Iraqi army bombed Kurdish villages with chemical agents throughout 1988.

I might point out that this isn't a fairy tale invented by the good doctor. Stories along these lines – that there has been an overt and covert effort to undermine what was the legitimate government of Iraq through activities in the north of Iraq, sponsored by the U.S. – are confirmed publicly, in places such as the *New York Times.* The Tim Weiner article of September 11, 1996, which we've already mentioned, said:

> The C.I.A. has tried for more than five years to create political and paramilitary organizations that could supplant Mr. Hussein. Covert operations to undermine his 17-year regime are still under way, Government officials said. . . .
>
> [T]he agency . . . ran a separate, small paramilitary program largely staffed by Iraqi military defectors. . . .
>
> In that operation, the Iraqi National Accord, a resistance group based in Jordan, used $6 million from the C.I.A. and a handful of high-ranking Iraqi military defectors in an effort to breed dissent within Mr. Hussein's armed forces. It trained and armed small cells of rebels. . . .
>
> Meanwhile, at a small base in northern Iraq, a handful of C.I.A. officers worked with members of the Iraqi National Congress, a political coalition with offices in the protected zone. They gathered intelligence, coordinated propaganda broadcasts and provided safe passage for Iraqi military defectors and political dissidents, some of whom joined the C.I.A.-backed armed resistance.

In the paragraph immediately following the last one above, Weiner refers to "the Iraqis and Kurds who worked with them." This means that the Americans were still exploiting Kurdish opposition to the Baghdad government – and egging them on to acts of armed rebellion – 5 years after Saddam attempted to deal with the problem militarily.

LID: That's incredible history. Essentially the Americans, through the CIA, the Iranians, and certain of the Kurdish tribes, have been making trouble in Iraqi Kurdistan – encouraging sedition, from Saddam's point of view – for at least a quarter of a century, and the upshot of it has been for these trouble-makers to convict Saddam publicly of charges – highly exaggerated, if not altogether bogus – dealing with how he has responded to that sedition.

JW: That's right.

LID: OK, but the facts of the charges are still there, and they command a lot of attention. How do you respond to them?

JW: There are several kinds of problems with the accusations. First, the claims aren't consistent. Human Rights Watch claims, as we have said, 50,000 to 100,000 dead. The Kurds claim that 182,000 have vanished or been exterminated. A comment in 2003 from a CPA person, Sandy Hodgkinson, claimed 300,000, as did Senator Joe Biden on CNN on December 14, 2003. The Iraqi ambassador to the U.S., Rend al-Rahim, has upped the number to 400,000, while, as I noted earlier, Senator Pat Roberts made it 500,000 on a weekend talk show in July 2004.

How can this be taken seriously when no one knows what the numbers really are?

LID: Well what about the detailed anecdotal evidence that Human Rights Watch claims to possess? Even if the numbers don't match they still tell some disturbing stories.

JW: No doubt the stories as they are told are disturbing. The problem is that contrary testimony is simply ignored. Some of those who perpetuate the claims even admit that they ignore arguments from the other side. When Jeffrey Goldberg wrote of "genocide" in *The New Yorker* in 2002, he didn't even think to contact anyone who disputes the standard line. "I didn't give it much thought, because [the other side of the story] was dismissed by so many people I consider to be experts," he said in a later interview with Roger Trilling in the *Village Voice* (May 1-7, 2002, issue). "Very quickly into this story," Goldberg continued, "I decided that I support the mainstream view – of Human Rights Watch, Physicians for Human Rights, the State Department, the UN, and various Kurdish groups – that the Iraqis were responsible for Halabja. In the same way, I didn't give any merit to the Iraqi denials."

"Implying that the Pentagon, the DIA, and the CIA are no more reliable than the Iraqis seems a bit extreme," Trilling commented. And intentionally ignoring the claims made by the other side for a piece of "objective" journalism is extreme too.

Sadly, this seems to be the approach taken by the few talkative groups who perpetuate the "genocide" claims. They rarely admit that there is testimony to the contrary that they need to deal with, and when they do admit it they don't refute it.

Speaking of the article by Trilling, it's worth noting that at least he was able to point out that, at the time, people evaluated arguments on both sides of the "Saddam committed genocide" debate, and many seemed to understand the issue wasn't as black and white as many today have made it out to be:

> On May 3, 1990, referring to yet another study [besides Dr. Pelletière's War College report], *The Washington Post* stated: "A Defense Department reconstruction of the final stages of the Iran-Iraq war has assembled what analysts say is conclusive intelligence that one of the worst civilian massacres of the war, in the Iraqi Kurdish city of Halabja, was caused by repeated chemical bombardments from both belligerent armies."
>
> In response to the orthodoxy already established around the event, the *Post*'s Patrick Tyler went on to note that the reconstruction "calls into question the widely reported assertion of human rights organizations and Kurdish groups that Iraq bore the greatest responsibility for the deaths of hundreds of Iraqi Kurds – women, infants and elderly – who died at Halabja."
>
> Articles asserting Iranian complicity also ran in *The New York Times* ("Years Later, No Clear Culprit in Gassing of Kurds"), *Newsday*, *The New York Review of Books*, and elsewhere.
>
> But that's all forgotten now. Since the 1991 Gulf War, the demonization of Saddam has become a linchpin of U.S. foreign policy, and his solo turn as Killer of Kurds has passed beyond question.

There's also a 1993 yearbook from the Stockholm International Peace Research Institute, called *World Armaments and Disarmament,* that noted (on page 324) that "there have been numerous allegations that Iraq used chemical weapons in the 1980-88 Iran-Iraq war, but only a few of these allegations have been proved."

There is also Milton Viorst's testimony, from his October 7, 1988, *International Herald Tribune* article, which he followed up with this comment from his book, *Sandcastles:*

> On returning home, I interviewed academic experts; none unequivocally ruled out the use of gas, but the most reliable among them were doubtful. It was only Washington, and particularly Congress – although, conspicuously, not the U.S. Embassy in Baghdad, which was in the best position to know – that stuck stubbornly to the original story, and this persistence bewildered the Iraqis. . . .

[I]n the Turkish refugee camps, international teams of doctors were more skeptical of the refugees' claims, saying their examinations did not confirm the use of gas at all.

As we have seen, the October 2002 CIA report doesn't note any mass gassing or genocide. The sources in Dr. Pelletière's book are incredulous as well: the Turkish doctors, the UN High Commission for Refugees (UNHCR), the Red Cross, the Red Crescent Societies, and a doctor from *Medicins du Monde.*

LID: It sounds like the line that the "genocide" crowd takes isn't as clear cut as they make it out to be.

JW: It's not. The 1993 paper we've been referring to by Clifton Flowers doesn't mention the "genocide" assertion, though he specifically mentions Iraq's use of chemical agents during the Iran-Iraq war. Dr. Pelletière has elsewhere pointed out that common sense itself challenges the standard story, because the gas that the Iraqis had at the time simply was not effective for wholesale killing. In comments reported by a *Globe-Intel* dispatch of October 10, 2002, Pelletière stated:

> The Iraqis did fire mustard gas into Halabja, after the Iranians had attacked and occupied the town, but despite its fearsome reputation mustard gas is an incapacitating agent, rather than an efficient killer. Slightly more than two percent of those exposed to mustard gas attack can be expected to die.

In the same dispatch, Pelletière is also quoted as revealing that the military had looked into the claims made by a British journalist, Gwynne Roberts, made in late 1988. Of course you never hear about the other side – only that Roberts's findings further prove Saddam's guilt.

> According to Pelletière, U.S. military had closely studied eyewitness testimony collected from Kurdish refugees in Iran by the veteran British journalist Gwynne Roberts and shown on Channel 4 on November 23,1988.
> Survivors described a massacre at Bassay Gorge, in northern Iraq, on August 29, 1988, in which something between 1,500 and 4,000 people, mainly women and children, were supposedly killed by what appears to have been a mixture of various nerve gasses while trying to reach the Turkish border.
> Their bodies were allegedly piled up and burnt by Iraqi troops wearing gas masks the following morning.
> Roberts claimed to have entered Iraq clandestinely and brought back fragments of an exploded shell with samples of the surrounding soil, which were later confirmed by a British laboratory as containing traces of mustard gas.
> "This report meant nothing," Pelletière said. "We all know that refugees lie."

"We all understand the physics of chemical warfare and the difficulties involved in disposing of 4,000 dead bodies.

"Roberts wouldn't – or couldn't – tell us where he got the shell fragments from."

One other point of interest on this topic is a short New York Associated
Press report that appeared on April 27, 2003, written by Scheherezade
Faramarzi. It reported that numerous Kurds and Arabs had never heard
of the alleged gassing of the Kurds in 1988, and that even fewer Arabs believed it. It's worth quoting in detail from the story. Even though the writer
incredibly attributes to Saddam's repressive censorship the ignorance and
incredulity of the people he spoke to, is it likely that the Iraqi Kurds, the so-
called "tightly knit community," would have been ignorant of a campaign
to eradicate them, and which successfully, we are told, eliminated 100,000,
if not 200,000 or 300,000 of them?

> Arabs who heard rumors of the slaughter in the northern city of Halabja say
> they did not believe them at the time. Some remain unconvinced today. . . .
>
> [V]ery few people in the village of Manqouba, 155 miles west of Halabja, had
> heard of the chemical massacre there. And even fewer believed it.
>
> Iraqi Arabs in other towns in northern Iraq's oil-producing province of
> Kirkuk showed similar disbelief, even though Kurds, Arabs and Turkmen live
> side by side in the region. In fact, until Iraqi security documents were seized
> during the Kurdish uprising of 1991, even many Kurds of northern Iraq had
> not heard of the Halabja attack or didn't know details of it.
>
> Nafeh Mohammed Saleh, 42, and his brother Adel, 40, were soldiers in the
> Iraqi army during the Iran-Iraq war in the 1980s. Adel was serving in Panjwain,
> in northern Iraq, close to Halabja.
>
> "We heard there had been a chemical attack but we didn't know where in the
> north or the south or the central sector," Adel said.
>
> Nafeh said he had seen a video of the dead that his Kurdish friends had shown
> him, with children and women lying dead in the streets.
>
> "We still have our doubts."
>
> But Salem Mohammed al-Hamdani, 45, insisted that the attack could not
> have occurred. He said he was in Halabja recently.
>
> "Impossible, impossible," he said, using his index finger to stress his point.

LID: We're starting to see your point. What else?

JW: There are other inconsistencies in the story as well. Let me mention
just two. First of all, Ali Hassan Majeed, nicknamed "Chemical Ali" by the
same propagandists at the Pentagon who made him the King of Spades in
its deck of cards, supposedly gave the order to the Iraqi Air Force to drop
chemical bombs on Halabja. Numerous reports are made, by the same
people, that Halabja was "bombed" by the Iraqis. But Col. W. Patrick Lang,

who was the senior analyst for the Defense Intelligence Agency in that period and who concurs with Pelletière on the facts in evidence, tells me the armies exchanged gas by mortars and no aircraft were used. I've repeatedly suggested to senior journalists that they ask Lang about this, as I have, but there seems to be no interest in opening this can of worms.

Secondly, you probably know that in the months immediately preceding the "green light" given by our Ambassador, April Glaspie, to Saddam for his invasion of Kuwait, a number of senators, including Bob Dole, had traveled to Baghdad, met with Saddam, and found him to be a head of state worthy of support. Even Senator Howard Metzenbaum, an Ohio Democrat, Jewish liberal, and *staunch* supporter of Israel, gave him a seal of approval.

LID: Maybe they didn't know of the accusations.

JW: Nonsense. The meetings occurred *after* the Senate Foreign Relations Committee, following Secretary Shultz, had accused Iraq of using poison gas against its own people, i.e., the Kurds. Would Metzenbaum have given Saddam an "OK" if there was such overwhelming proof that he did what he is accused of?

LID: Not likely. Go on.

JW: In my estimation, the most important criticism of the case against Saddam for having "gassed his own people" is the lack of hard, physical evidence. As Dr. Pelletière has said, "The only satisfactory procedure for the United States would be either to say where the 100,000 alleged gassing victims repose (which it should be able to do with all of its satellite and infra-red imagining equipment), or to give a convincing explanation of how the Iraqis could have gassed 100,000 people in a two week period and disposed of them without a trace."

LID: And they haven't done either?

JW: Well, they have tried – or I should say that Human Rights Watch has tried, but the explanations strike me as a little too convenient.

LID: In what way?

JW: Well, the nature of the offense and the location of the evidence seems to shift with circumstances. At one point thousands of Kurds are gassed at Halabja as part of the "Anfal" campaign, and then when Dr. Pelletière seriously challenges the Halabja story, it is jettisoned – at least as evidence of "genocide" (Dr. Joost Hiltermann confirmed to me in an email of May 21,

2002, that "Human Rights Watch never said the Halabja attack constituted genocide") – and the 50,000 to 100,000 dead as a result of Anfal become the main focus. If you ask for physical evidence, you get either a few "mass" graves with somewhere on the order of a couple to a dozen corpses being found. Never mind that as the CIA's chief analyst during the Iran-Iraq war, Dr. Pelletière, points out that there are such graves all over Iraq dating back to the late 1960s. Alternatively you are told that the "real" mass graves could not be found, at the time, because the bodies were taken out of Kurdistan and buried in areas that were at that time under Iraqi control (this was again noted in the May 21, 2002, email from Dr. Hiltermann: "the graves of those who died during the Anfal campaign have not and cannot now be examined by forensic experts because they continue to be in areas under Iraqi government control; they are not in the Kurdish areas. The mass graves found and examined in the Kurdish areas are of people executed for primarily political offenses. . . . They would not contain more than a few hundred people, as far as I know."). This, of course, implicitly acknowledges that they did not die of gassing in the north, as it would not be credible that they were piled onto trucks for shipment and burial south.

LID: What happened to the bodies, then?

JW: Well, the current line is as stated in an August 12, 2002, letter to the *New York Times* from Hanny Megally, Executive Director of HRW's Middle East and North Africa Division. It's worth quoting in its entirety:

> Your Aug. 11 report of the Kurds' suffering under Saddam Hussein describes Kurdish accounts that in 1988 thousands of Kurdish men were arrested and never seen again.
>
> In fact, we know what happened to these men (and boys). Human Rights Watch conducted an extensive investigation in northern Iraq, including interviews with survivors, exhumation of mass graves and the taking of soil samples to reveal chemical weapons use.
>
> This investigation showed conclusively that Iraqi troops used chemical weapons at least 40 times to flush Kurds from the northern Iraqi highlands. Some 100,000 Kurdish men and boys were then rounded up, trucked to remote areas and machine-gunned to death, their bodies bulldozed into mass graves.

LID: But this too concedes the gassing point, right? Because if they were "flushed" with gas out of the mountains, then they weren't gassed "to death." The gas couldn't have been lethal – as Dr. Pelletière said – if they were "rounded up"?

JW: You're catching on.

LID: So what HRW would have to do to prove its point would be to indicate where the bodies are of those that were machine gunned ... presumably in grave sites that are now accessible because Iraq is now open for inspection, being under Coalition control.

JW: Right, that's what they'd have to do.

LID: Well?

JW: As of August 6, 2003, they were working on it. "They [HRW] haven't published anything on it yet," Dr. Hiltermann wrote to me, "as those graves are yet to be exhumed and the evidence gathered. The task in Iraq is overwhelming."

As of December 7, 2003, Associated Press was reporting the existence of six "major suspected mass grave sites," which were reported to have from 45 to 5000 bodies either already exhumed or waiting to be exhumed. What the report did *not* do – and what so many of even HRW's reports do not do – is distinguish the grave sites of people executed for political crimes from people who have died in wartime (i.e., the Iran-Iraq war or Gulf I), from those who were victims of a perhaps harsh but quite possibly legal response to an insurrection, from those who are victims of so-called "genocide."

The final episode in what seems like a tragic farce is, as I wrote November 5, 2004, the November 2004 Human Rights Watch report called, "Iraq: State of the Evidence." Pay close attention to this one. It turns out that in 19 months, HRW's experts have not been able to find the missing 100,000 bodies it said were of Kurds who had been rounded up and trucked south, machine-gunned to death, and buried in mass graves. In fact, it now blames the U.S. coalition for not securing those mass graves containing smaller numbers of Iraqis or keeping looters from carrying off official Iraqi records of the genocide and the mass graves. Here's the thrust of their report:

> In the case of both documents and mass graves, U.S.-led coalition forces failed to secure the relevant sites at the time of the overthrow of the former government. They subsequently failed to put in place the professional expertise and assistance necessary to ensure proper classification and exhumation procedures, with the result that key evidentiary materials have been lost or tainted....
>
> The extent of the negligence with which key documentary and forensic evidence has been treated to date is surprising, given that the U.S.-led coalition and Iraqi authorities alike knew that trials of Hussein and key Ba'ath government officials would be important landmarks in Iraq's political recovery, that

successful trials require solid evidence, and that, as international experience has shown, preserving such trial-ready evidence is a difficult task.

Dr. Pelletière's characteristic remark on this final report pretty much sums it up:

> This claim of HRW that they haven't got evidence that will stand up because the graves have been compromised, overlooks one key fact: they were claiming that the Ba'ath killed hundreds of thousands. If these graves really contained all the bodies they're supposed to contain, the numbers of dead alone would convict the Ba'ath. If you read the report, they say over and over again they "believe" such-and-such a grave actually contains thousands of bodies; but all they've been able to find is a few score (at best). I think that's what gives the scam away. They can't produce the hundreds of thousands, or even the tens of thousands they promised they would.

LID: So there's no evidence?

JW: Nothing beyond word of mouth. Hilterman in his email to me speaks of "the few survivors of the Anfal campaign" who provide "their testimonies." The HRW reports themselves are based upon interviews with "survivors." The press coverage adds testimony from "defectors" and "exiles." Absent thousands upon thousands of bodies, it all amounts to very professionally presented hearsay.

LID: And if you consider the source, it's hearsay from people who, for the most part, had been in opposition to the legitimate government of Iraq and were working to obtain support and favors from the U.S., with the hopes of working to destabilize or undermine the Baghdad government of Saddam. Their background in this kind of activity is and was well-known, and – as you've pointed out earlier – has been thoroughly reported. And they also happen to be the very people who have been providing testimony against Saddam of his alleged atrocities.

JW: In the absence of any real physical evidence, that testimony can and should at least be considered alongside the no less credible testimony of journalists and American government people who say that there was no campaign of genocide. Even if it's just a "wash" it's certainly not something to start a war over. Especially a war in which the most recent estimates of the dead total at least 100,000 Iraqi civilians and 60,000 to 80,000 Iraqi military, plus over 1800 Americans.

As for the credibility of the word-of-mouth evidence on the side of the "genocide" allegations, there are two points to bear in mind. The first is that the testimony gathered by Human Rights Watch should be taken with a grain of salt. A freelance journalist, Robin C. Miller, wrote an article dated February 8, 2003, called "Claims of Saddam's Genocide Far from Proven." It didn't receive huge circulation, but it's the best effort I know of to vet the forensics, and it makes some interesting observations about the credibility of the testimony regarding the alleged "genocide." I won't go into detail (it's 4300 words and should be read in its entirety), but will simply mention a couple of his serious questions, namely the fact that the testimony was obtained 5 years after the fact, and that it was obtained in a politically charged environment (the Kurds certainly had a motive to help HRW inflate the charges against Saddam, with the hope that U.S. action would be prompted as a result).

Our own sources raise some of the same questions. The Senate Intelligence Committee report on pre-Iraq war intelligence says, on page 400, under the heading, "1. Information sources," that the "human rights abuses" reports came from opposition figures and couldn't be verified:

> According to comments from IC analysts who spoke to Committee staff, a large part of the information available to the IC concerning human rights abuses was from refugees, defectors and opposition groups. The IC also depended on the Foreign Broadcast Information Service (FBIS). In all cases, verification of the reporting on human rights abuses was difficult. . . . Unfortunately, the immigrant/refugee reporting usually could not be verified on the ground in Iraq.

On page 402 it elaborates that "the environment was a denied and hostile area that thwarted most intelligence collection by organizations following human rights issues," meaning that word-of-mouth from defectors, exiles, and others was *most* of what these organizations had to go on. Furthermore, the CIA report of October 2002 confirms that "human rights organizations" learned by word-of-mouth of alleged chemical attacks from "Kurdish villagers." No matter how professionally assembled, it's simply hearsay, the credibility of which is undermined by a number of factors, not the least of which is the fact that the accusers and those who were interviewed for evidence had a motive to collaborate against the regime of Saddam.

Bearing this in mind, I think that without hard evidence it's more than a "wash" – i.e., more than a question of "he said/she said." Since the thousands upon thousands of dead in mass graves have not been found, I have to conclude that the assertions of genocide that President Bush cited again and again to justify war are as false as the assertions about hidden weapons of mass destruction.

Let me make one other point. In a May 2002 letter to *The Village Voice*, Joost Hiltermann, the HRW official championing the genocide claim, wrote "I, too, find it distasteful that the Bush administration is using this atrocity as a justification for a new attack on Iraq, but this should not be allowed to stand in the way of a dispassionate analysis of the available facts." Now it is at least partly, if not substantially, as a result of the HRW assertions that the Bush administration justified its use of force to replace the duly constituted government in Baghdad. How is it that Hiltermann can claim to take these reports so seriously and then pretend that they don't provide a rationale for war? It doesn't make sense to me. Either Saddam's a butcher and we were justified all along, since the mid-1970s, and certainly since 1991, in opposing him, or he's not and any antagonistic action on our part is unjustified. I cannot see how you can have it both ways.

LID: True, it doesn't seem to make much sense. One more question on this score. Is there any way to account for the 100,000 Kurds that have "disappeared" according to Human Rights Watch, or is the number just meaningless?

JW: No, it means something. Most people do not seem to be aware that at the end of the war with Iran, Baghdad ordered a strip of land cleared all along the border with Iran. This meant that the villages along the border had to be razed and their residents "relocated' to locations 50 miles from the border. That is, the "disappeared" were not buried in mass graves but placed in new locations, some in high-rise apartment buildings. The "tons" of documents that supposedly show men, women and children "arrested" by the Army and sent off to extermination may actually be lists of those relocated. The foreign press was invited in at the time to witness the process and there were many accounts of the relocation. Human Rights Watch now seems to think these were the Kurds who were exterminated. Don't forget that Viorst offers a recollection of the episode in his book, *Sandcastles*, that we've already noted, and Dr. Pelletière confirms this event as well. And there's the mass exodus of Kurds towards the Iranian and Turkish borders to remember, too, following the suppression of the 1991 rebellion, as discussed by the 1993 Flowers paper on the Kurds.

LID: Well, at the very least it seems safe to say that these facts don't fit with what is popularly believed about Saddam, for instance, how – according to the May 13, 2002, edition of the Christian Science Monitor *– he issued an order to kill every Iraqi Kurdish male between the ages of 18 and 55 in the summer of 1988.*

JW: Why would he do such a thing? The Iraqi Kurds of the Barzani and Talabani tribes never amounted to more than a substantial minority – about 15% – of Iraqi Kurds, many of whom felt quite comfortable as part of the Iraqi nation, as Dr. al-Obaidi said. These Kurdish Iraqis were represented in the Iraqi military in proportion to their numbers in Iraqi society as a whole, and they fought on the side of Iraq. This is consistent with Saddam's equitable treatment of the Kurds – when they weren't trying to overthrow his government – which was recognized by Clifton Flowers in a telling comment in his 1993 paper: "Ironically [indeed!], Iraq has recognized Kurdish rights more so than other countries in the region."

The bottom line? There is no report in the history of the world of a political leader using poison gas against his own people in an open field for no reason. It's nonsense. I would simply say that there is no possibility that Saddam gassed his own people and no evidence that he did. None.

LID: Before moving to other subjects, two more questions relating to the Kurds and the so-called "gassing." On April 28, 1998, Richard Butler, Executive Chairman of UNSCOM, announced that his inspectors had recently discovered in Iraq significant quantities of shells filled with mustard gas of the highest purity. Does this not show, firstly, returning to an earlier subject, that Saddam's government had reconstituted, at least in part, its weapons program; and, secondly, that they had in fact manufactured and used this gas in war time?

JW: The answer to both parts of your question is no. It is probably best answered by the Press Release issued in New York on April 30, 1998, by the Permanent Mission of the Republic of Iraq to the United Nations. Ambassador Hamdoon said:

> The facts on these shells are as follows: in 1991, the Iraqi side declared a quantity of chemical ammunitions in the al-Oukhaydir site in the southern desert of Iraq. The bunkers containing this ammunition were partially damaged during the U.S.-led bombing of Iraq in 1991. An UNSCOM team inspected the site and its bunkers thoroughly in 1991 and tagged all the equipment in the site. The team, upon their own decision, did not extract the shells from the bunker for analysis due to safety concerns. The team requested the Iraqi side to keep the site as is without any changes. Later, many inspection teams visited the site and checked the tags on the shells. The site remained under the control of UNSCOM until the recent visit of an inspection team that concluded an analysis of four shells from the site.
>
> The results of the analysis, though we think it needs to be complemented by a thorough analysis of all the quantity of mustard gas in the shells, does not indicate any shortcomings from the Iraqi side, nor can they be qualified as a "discovery." The only conclusion to be made from Mr. Butler's "discovery" is

that it is a distortion of the facts aimed at prolonging the inhumane sanctions imposed on the people of Iraq.

I wrote on June 25, 1998, to Bill Cohen, the then Secretary of Defense, on the subject of this "discovery" of VX gas. I said to him that this is one more deceptive maneuver by our side to prevent the lifting of sanctions. It saddens me to have to believe Saddam Hussein's government over Uncle Sam, but the record I've observed since 1994 has persuaded me that we have been acting in bad faith from 1991 onwards. My guess is that the material presented to the American labs had been salted with traces of VX so that the scientists at Aberdeen would be able to confirm VX without having to perjure themselves down the line, if it came to that. Iraqi Ambassador Nizar Hamdoon is correct to point out that his government cannot trust a government that openly admits it will do anything in its power to overthrow it. The CIA usually operates clandestinely in such maneuvers, but in this case it has been overt in admitting its failed attempts to destabilize the regime and foment civil uprisings.

The VX story does not add up. Iraq admits it attempted to produce weapons grade VX at the time of its war with Iran, but that it failed. Nobody anywhere asserts that they ever used VX gas. This new allegation derives from UNSCOM's return to a site that Iraq itself had identified in 1991! Now, with the United States alarmed that Iraq has gained sympathy around the world as it has become clear we are not acting in good faith, and have no intention in lifting the sanctions, UNSCOM insists on returning to the site of the missile fragments, digging up some shells, transporting them to a laboratory in Maryland, and wouldn't you know it? Traces of VX are found! The story got front page play, but when Iraq asked for an independent opinion, other shards from the site were examined in a Swiss laboratory that reported no trace of VX.

LID: The second question on the Kurds is to ask what relation the "No-Fly" zones in Northern and Southern Iraq, set up in 1992 by American and British air forces, and supposedly authorized by the United Nations precisely to protect the Iraqi Kurds in the north and the Iraqi Shiites in the South, have to the history we've just been discussing?

JW: I think the best way to answer this question is to quote you a few paragraphs from a letter that I wrote to Representative Henry Hyde, chairman of the House Foreign Affairs Committee, on October 2, 2001.

Almost every politician I know believes our bombers are blowing up stuff in Iraq under one United Nations resolution or another. I hope you know that we are making those bombing runs with the Brits when the Pentagon gets a hankering for target practice. Yes, we are blasting various buildings that *might* be housing military stuff, but in the process we have killed thousands of civilians over the years. *And it is all illegal.* The only reason we get away with this civilized form of political terrorism is because we are the most powerful nation in the history of the world. The fig leaf for the "no-fly" zone was the joint decision of the U.S., British and French to launch operation "Provide Comfort," providing humanitarian aid to Kurds in the north and Shiite Muslims in the south. The operation banned Iraqi aircraft and helicopters in the two, which have been widened in the years since, long after their supposed reason for existence ended. France pulled out in 1998 when it said the operation had changed to military from humanitarian. The bombs have kept falling even though there never has been a UN resolution giving them any grounding in international law. We rarely hear of any results of the raids, but the Islamic/Arab world totes up the deaths and chalks them up to American imperialism.

The most outrageous use of the "fig leaf" of "Provide Comfort" was President Clinton's decision to kick off his 1996 re-election campaign by bombing Iraq for its "violation of the no-fly zone" in the northern Kurdish area of Iraq. It was, at least to me, a clear violation on Clinton's part of the War Powers Act, which required him to inform Congress of military action. Instead he simply gave a green light to the Pentagon to bomb. Did you know, Henry, that Saddam did not violate the illegal no-fly zone? All he did was send ground troops into the province at the request of the duly-elected provincial government, composed exclusively of Iraqi Kurds. They were fearful Iranian Kurds were going to overthrow them. . . . Of the nation's press only the *Christian Science Monitor* regularly notes that there is no UN authorization for this bombing and none by the U.S. Congress either.

Persecution of the Shiites

LID: And does Saddam also get a clean bill of health on point E, his alleged persecution of the Shiites?

JW: I think that the evidence of persecution is pretty thin, as with so much else written about Saddam. Does he like Shiites? Perhaps, perhaps not. But it certainly did not prevent him from having them in high-level positions in both the Iraqi military and in the Ba'ath Party. It is a logical position for him as his whole political career, based on Ba'athist ideology, insisted that the Arab nations could only progress once they were united *internally* and *externally*. If you take out the now famous Bush "Deck of Cards," you will find – perhaps to your surprise – that some of them are Shiites, and at important levels.

I think that it is far more credible to believe that Saddam took the same attitude to Shiites as he took to the Kurds. Those who were loyal to Iraq and worked with the Ba'ath Party were treated as partners, those who refused such loyalty and worked with foreign powers – Israel and Iran, in particular – were treated as a fifth column in the country.

Most of the "persecution" of Shiites can actually be reduced to two major "events." The first is simple and straightforward enough. At the end of the first Gulf War, President George H. W. Bush broadcast regularly to the Shiites in southern Iraq urging them to rise up against Saddam, and he made it clear that he would be prepared to help them with weapons and assistance if they did so. Believing that the Americans were telling the truth, the Shiites in Basra – or at least some of them – revolted. Seeing this as an insurrection, Saddam sent in the Republican Guard to put it down. It was a bloody affair and resulted in some thousands of deaths, depending on which source you believe. Needless to say, President Bush did nothing to help them in spite of his public utterances. So, who really is responsible for this loss of life: Bush or Hussein? The fact that the U.S. urged the Shiites to revolt during the second Gulf War, pouring down masses of leaflets in Arabic on major Shiite urban centers, and that there was no response from the Shiites other than violently combating American and British forces, tells its own story.

The other basis for the "persecution" of the Shiites stems from the "murder" of Ayatollah Mohammed Bakr al-Sadr, whose son, Moqtada al-Sadr, is the leader of the Madhi Army which fought ferociously against the U.S. in Najaf in 2004. The murder is taken to be a sign of Saddam's supposed hatred of the Shiites.

Let's go back in time to see the roots of this particular allegation. On March 15, 1980, Ayatollah Khomeini urged Iraqis in a radio broadcast to rise up against Saddam, the same broadcast which declared that Bahrain, Kuwait, and the southern part of Iraq were part of the Islamic Republic of Iran. At the same time that the sons of Barzani, the Kurdish leader, were invited to Teheran to meet Khomeini, the Iranian government was pouring money into a Shiite political group called al-Dawa. This was the prelude to the Iran-Iraq war.

Let Nita Renfrew, in her book, *Saddam Hussein*, tell the rest of the story.

> A turning point came on April 1, when a member of the al-Dawa party attempted to assassinate Tariq Aziz, Saddam's Deputy Prime Minister. When Aziz began his speech at the Mustansiriyya University in Baghdad, a bomb was thrown at the podium. Aziz managed to get to the ground before it exploded, escaping injury. But a number of students were killed and injured. The police immediately arrested the al-Dawa party's number two man, a mullah

named Mohammed Bakr al-Sadr. The following day, Saddam turned up at the site of the assassination attempt in the pouring rain, drawing crowds of angry students around him. In a passionate speech, the rain pouring down his face, he vowed, "By God, the innocent blood that was shed at Mustaniriyya will not go unavenged."

On April 5, al-Dawa struck again. This time a bomb was thrown from an Iranian religious school into the funeral cortege of the students killed in the university attempt. More students were killed and injured. Bakr al-Sadr was executed along with several family members, and some 30,000 Shiites presumed to be of Iranian descent living in the holy cities were expelled from Iraq. This created a great deal of hostility because many Iraqi Arabs were included in the roundup. Very soon there was an attempt on the Minister of Information's life. . . . There were rumors that there was also an attempt on Saddam's life.

Can this really be called a "persecution of Shiites"? Is there any reason to believe that if Sunnis, or Christians, or Turkomen had carried out this kind of murderous activity they would have received a different kind of treatment? If they had carried out such actions, and if Saddam had reacted in the same way as he did with the al-Sadr clan, would that have made Saddam anti-Sunni, anti-Christian, or anti-Turkoman? It seems clear to me that Saddam was doing what any government would have done: defend itself and deal with the culprits. Insofar as he made an error, it was in not being more discerning in his expulsion of the Shiites he believed involved.

Finally, we have all heard for some time now that Grand Ayatollah al-Sistani, allegedly the most revered Shiite leader in Iraq, was kept under close surveillance by Saddam's government. How many have heard, however, that al-Sistani is of Iranian descent too? And how many read the piece by Maggie Michael, for the Associated Press, on December 1, 2004, that 38 Shiite parties had broken off negotiations with al-Sistani's aides, "claiming that a candidate list under discussion was dominated by religious extremists." Hussein al-Mousawi, a spokesman for the Shiite Political Council, said: "We don't want to be an extension of Iran inside Iraq. We found out that the top 10 names in the list are extremist Shiite Islamists who believe in the rule of religious clerics." It transpires that one of the extremist groups was none other than al-Dawa! Though the Shiites more or less united for the election, the deep cracks in their electoral alliance that cannot simply be papered over. All of this seems to confirm what Dr. Mohammed al-Obaidi wrote to me on March 15, 2002: "As a Muslim Shiite, I assure you that a very small percentage of the Shiites in Iraq are against the regime, and in general no Iraqi would like to see a government imposed on its people by the U.S. or the U.K."

LID: This discussion of al-Dawa brings up an article by Colin Freeman that appeared in the British Daily Telegraph *on February 20, 2005, entitled "Saddam's Brother to Face Early Trial for Revenge Massacre in [Shiite] Village." According to which, residents of this village, Dujayl, "plan to testify that their village was singled out for slaughter by Saddam's half-brother, Barzan al-Tikriti" in retribution for a 1982 assassination attempt against Saddam that occurred there, led by members of al-Dawa. Allegedly more than 900 people were rounded up and tortured, and the survivors are (interestingly) claiming that what went on in the village is "the forgotten Halabja."*

JW: Yes, I read the story and concluded it was yet another example of Shiite political factions, aligned with the Iranian fundamentalists in the war period, trying to bring down Saddam and the government. And Saddam and the government responded. I have no doubt that his regime acted brutally when threatened, and maybe this is one of those instances. But as I read the story the thought that occurred to me was that it was fed to the *Telegraph* – a pro-war British paper – by the folks in the Green Zone who are gearing up to try Saddam and his Cabinet for war crimes.

LID: Because maybe some of the other charges aren't going to stick?

JW: I do suspect that the interim government in Baghdad may already be concerned that the charges of Saddam's "war crimes" may not be able to stand up to close scrutiny. They are probably preparing back-up allegations.

LID: How valid would one like this be?

JW: I don't doubt that *something* occurred at Dujayl, but it's hard to call it a war crime if Saddam was responding to an assassination attempt by al-Dawa. Of course, if there were 400 deaths, as Freeman reports, it would *look* like retribution, wiping out a whole village in response to an assassination attempt. But the town has a population of 70,000! (The reporter would never have called Dujayl a "settlement" or "village" if he had been there.) Not to mention that once again the numbers of dead vary widely. While Freeman has 400, Hal Bernton's January 2, 2004, *Seattle Times* piece reports that "hundreds of men" were rounded up. And a year-old report in the *Middle East Intelligence Bulletin* (Vol. 5, No. 6, June, 2003) I came across says that about 150 people died in the "fierce gunfight" that took place between Saddam's security forces and al-Dawa insurgents.

At any rate, even if there had been 400 deaths, they could easily have been the result of the clashes between insurgents and government forces that took place there – along with innocent bystanders. That's the nature of civil war. The bottom line as far as I can tell – and I'm only one fellow who has tried to get to the bottom of these charges of genocide and revenge killings by Saddam – is that none of them would stand up to scrutiny in a U.S. court of law.

LID: Besides, isn't it more than a little hypocritical that people who tried to kill Saddam should then be part of the process that meets out justice to those who responded militarily to that attempt? Freeman's article notes that "villagers speak proudly of the attempt on Saddam's life and are eager to help convict his half-brother." No surprise that they're after this conviction, when they've been trying to get Saddam and Co. for decades. But is it therefore a crime for Saddam and Co. to fight back?

JW: It's one thing for these people to have opposed Saddam's rule. But it's another to ignore their lawlessness in the face of a legitimately constituted government, and to solely pick on Saddam's justified, if extremely brutal, response to it. We claim to be fighting this war to oppose and end "terror," but it was al-Dawa that staged what the *Middle East Intelligence Bulletin* I mentioned earlier called the "first modern suicide bombing." Here's the full passage:

> Al-Dawa's military wing, now named Shahid al-Sadr (The Martyr al-Sadr), steadily increased the frequency and lethality of its assassinations and sabotage operations throughout the 1980s – both inside and outside Iraq. It staged a suicide bomb attack against the Iraqi embassy in Beirut in December 1981 that claimed the lives of 27 people. This attack has been described as the first major modern suicide bombing. In July 1982, it carried out a daring attempt to kill Saddam Hussein near the town of Dujayl, resulting in fierce gun battles between Ba'athist security personnel and al-Dawa fighters that left 150 dead. The following month, al-Dawa bombed the Ministry of Planning, causing extensive damage and casualties. In November 1983, al-Dawa suicide bombers struck the Defense Ministry and the headquarters of the Mukhaberat (secret police) in the Mansour district of Baghdad. In April 1987, scores of al-Dawa gunmen ambushed Saddam's motorcade in Mosul, claiming the lives of several senior bodyguards of the former Iraqi leader. In December 1996, al-Dawa assassins nearly succeeded in killing Saddam's eldest son, Uday.

So even if Saddam was "brutal," it's a stretch to turn him into a monster simply for effectively dealing with opponents who were employing the same kinds of tactics in Iraq that we ourselves are now deploring. Sadly, it's just the same old hypocrisy. Ba'athist fighters who oppose the American occupation are referred to as "terrorist death squads." But when a question is raised about the al-Dawa association of the current Transitional Prime Minister of Iraq, Ibrahim al-Jaafari, we simply paint him as a "freedom fighter" against Saddam. Condi Rice said as much to Tim Russert on a recent *Meet the Press.* Did you see it? After Russert rightly asked the Secretary *twice* about whether al-Jaafari's association with al-Dawa, and his having been a terrorist, were problematic, Rice simply said that "a lot of people in that period of time who were fighters against Saddam Hussein were branded with various labels." What's important, she noted, is that al-Jaafari is devoted to "an Iraq which will be a fighter in the war on terrorism."

LID: But what she really meant is a fighter in the war on the terrorism that we oppose.

JW: Just so. At the end of the day, this "persecution" of the Shiites by the Ba'ath Party was more often than not just a Ba'athist attempt – if brutal – to keep order and defend itself from the terror and treason associated with outfits like al-Dawa.[1]

Look, when I think of "religious persecution," what comes to mind are popular references to the Spanish Inquisition. Everything I know about Iraq is through talking to lots of Iraqis and reading lots of books about it over the last 15 years. This doesn't make me an expert, by any means, but I do know that a chief aim of the Ba'ath Party was to rid Iraq of sectarian *politics.* Saddam even had laws passed forbidding the use of surnames that included sectarian identification, and under him Iraq had become a thoroughly secular society. Women had relative equality with males and could wear Western garb. There were liquor stores operating freely. And there was no religious persecution, even of Jews, despite reports to the contrary in the Western press. There was of course great hostility to Israel, but that's true throughout the Arab and Muslim world.

Suffering Iraqis

LID: Changing the subject just a bit, there seems to be some discrepancy concerning the number of civilian deaths in Iraq due to the economic sanctions, particularly with respect to children. Is it possible to make a judgment accurately on this?

---

1. Another example of the rise to power of former anti-Iraqi agitators is the career of Hadi al-Amri, the leader of the Shiite Badr Brigade – supposedly a "political" organization now, following the January 2005 election – formerly (many say it remains so) the military wing of SCIRI, the Supreme Council for Islamic Revolution in Iraq. See the brief discussion of al-Amri's career in the piece by Mark Gery in the companion to the present volume, *Neo-CONNED! Again,* pp. 761–795.—Ed.

JW: The UN had the number of children's deaths at 500,000 in 1996. By 2002, Baghdad would claim over 600,000. Certain neoconservatives attempted to whittle down the number of children killed to "more than 100,000." That may be right, and I have not personally been over to do a body count. When you get to this level of child deaths because of the embargo of calories and chemicals needed for water and sewer sanitation, though, I do not think the time spent kicking these dead children around serves any good purpose. In any case, the number of Iraqi civilians who have died since the Gulf War, under five or over five years of age, is enormous. It has been the result of U.S. policy to make the Iraqi people suffer so much that they would overthrow Saddam Hussein.

Our political establishment and the major media that does its bidding has known and supported this evil policy all along. In the end, the exact number of dead children is unimportant when set against Madeleine Albright's stupid remark on Lesley Stahl's *60 Minutes* about it being worth the deaths of 500,000 children to contain Saddam. Once that went into global circulation, it is a waste of time for reporters to fuss about the exact number. The reporting on Iraq by our press corps has been scandalous and as a result of its incompetence, 9/11 was the price we have paid. *So far.*

At any rate, the United States has been responsible for raising the barriers for compliance to prevent lifting of the sanctions. The Arab/Islamic world knows full well that the 1.5 million innocent Iraqi civilians who have died of disease and starvation since 1991 were the result of American policy – a policy specifically designed to increase the level of suffering of the Iraqi people to a point where they would overthrow the regime. The U.S. government never intended the sanctions to be lifted, no matter what level of compliance Iraq achieved. This policy has been voiced repeatedly over the years by officials of the U.S. government, for instance, in 1991 by then Secretary of State James Baker III, and in 1998 by then Secretary of State Madeleine Albright.

LID: Couldn't Saddam have done anything to get rid of these sanctions? After all, the United Nations resolved in 1991 that the economic embargo on Iraq could be lifted if Iraq destroyed its chemical, biological and nuclear weapons programs within six months.

JW: Right, and Iraq *spent* the next six months destroying all the nuclear, chemical and biological programs that it had been working on in the 1980s. When the UN inspectors arrived, they complained that Iraq should not have destroyed the weapons, but should have waited for the inspectors to verify their existence and supervise their destruction. Several of the "gaps" in the inspection process that UNMOVIC said needed to be cleared up in the run up to Gulf War II were really a result of Iraq's desire to cooperate.

LID: But it's still Saddam's fault that there were and are so many deaths in Iraq, isn't it? Surely he could have fed his people instead of buying weapons and building palaces?

JW: The idea that Saddam is responsible for the death of so many Iraqis is grotesque. Any government can only do what it can within the limit of its means and circumstances and, unfortunately, most of the Western world, and especially America, simply doesn't know what has been done in their name.

Denis Halliday is an Irishman who was one of the United Nations' humanitarian co-ordinators in Iraq. In October 1998 he resigned his position and went public, lamenting the fact that the UN sanctions – which were never intended to go on so long, and which were being artificially maintained at the insistence of the U.S. and U.K. governments for political reasons – were killing tremendous numbers of innocent people. If the sanctions were intended to remove Saddam – and remember they were instituted by the UN *not* for this purpose but to disarm Iraq – they were not having any effect. Going public made Halliday a pariah among American officials overnight.

Speaking to Jeff Stein of *Salon.com* in January 1999, he said:

> You know, the coalition forces did a good job. They destroyed the sewage and water system throughout the country. So you've now got raw sewage in the water, in the street. It's a total disaster. It was tremendously effective bombing, but it's killing a lot of kids, because the water is carrying typhoid and other communicable diseases that are hard to deal with, and which kill infants very quickly.

The media coverage of his testimony was sparse, to put it charitably.

Halliday is no liberal, he is simply a man with a conscience. As is Pat Buchanan who slammed the sanctions as immoral. As are the people in the group *Voices in the Wilderness* who began marching to draw attention to the punishing effects of the sanctions on ordinary Iraqis, effects that were never intended by most of the countries that voted for the sanctions at the end of the first Gulf War. It is symptomatic of the amoral mentality found in too many government bureaucrats that *Voices in the Wilderness* was fined $160,000 by the U.S. Treasury Department for sending *medicine*

and toys to people in Iraq. It is a perfect example of what Halliday meant
when he told Stein:

> Washington has successfully demonized Saddam Hussein, but they've de-
> monized the entire Iraqi population too. And the American people cannot
> identify with the Iraqis as people like themselves, with families, with kids, with
> gardens and cars. So they're dying? Nobody cares. When Madeline Albright
> can go on *60 Minutes* and justify 5,000 children dying a month, which is what
> she did, that is quite revolting.

Unfortunately, other revelations – that have barely seen the light of day
– indicate that this catastrophe was *deliberately* sought by the U.S. administration. Writing in November 2001, Rahul Mahajan highlighted the work
of Thomas Nagy of Georgetown University. Professor Nagy discovered a
Defense Intelligence Agency document entitled "Iraq Water Treatment
Vulnerabilities," a document that was circulated to all major allied commands just *one day after* the first Gulf War started. The document analyzed the weaknesses of the Iraqi water treatment system, the effects of
sanctions on a damaged system, and the health effects of untreated water
on the Iraqi populace. Pointing out that chlorine, so necessary for water
treatment and purification, is embargoed under the sanctions, the DIA
document speculates that "Iraq could try convincing the UN or individual
countries to exempt water treatment supplies from sanctions for humanitarian reasons." The U.S. government steadfastly opposed this for years.

During the first Gulf War nearly every large water treatment plant in
Iraq was attacked, and seven out of the eight dams damaged. This suggests
that there was a deliberate targeting of the Iraqi water supply for "post-war
leverage," a suggestion that received its confirmation when U.S. government officials admitted in the *Washington Post* on June 23, 1991, that such
attacks had been part of the military planning.

Professor Nagy subsequently unearthed other documents which suggest that the plan to destroy water treatment, then to restrict chlorine
and other necessary water treatment supplies was, according to Mahajan,
"done with full knowledge of the explosion of water-borne disease that
would result."

Combined with this blocking of water treatment essentials was the
arbitrary restriction placed on medicines – including vaccines for common infectious diseases – and the destruction of Iraq's vaccine facilities.
Ludicrously, these were placed on the so-called "1051 List" of substances,
as though vaccines or essential medicines were linked to Iraq's WMDs.
Mahajan concludes:

Deliberately creating the conditions for disease and then withholding the treatment is little different morally from deliberately introducing a disease-causing organism like anthrax – but no major U.S. paper seems to have editorialized against the U.S. engaging in biological warfare, or even a run a news article reporting Nagy's evidence that it had done so.

Perhaps the best way to picture this whole, sick scenario is to look at what Jon Basil Utley wrote in "The Seven Big Lies" about Iraq in March 2001. He says:

> Nearly all oil sales money has been allocated through United Nations inspectors, subject to nearly 40% reduction for reparations and UN expenses, and subject to Washington's veto and foot dragging – usually months for even the simplest decision.... For nearly ten years it blockaded chlorine to sanitize the water, and any equipment to rebuild the electricity grid, sanitation, and irrigation facilities. Even pencils for school children were prohibited.... Finally, the Europeans rebelled at the cruelty and shamed Washington into allowing such imports, according to the *New York Times* in June 2000. Until oil prices increased in 2000, sales ran at about $4 billion annually minus about 35% withheld by the UN, leaving $2.6 billion divided by a population of 20 million – equivalent to $130 per year, per person – that is, 36 cents per day per person for food and medicine.... Obviously, Iraq needed to rebuild its agriculture and transport infrastructure to feed itself, but this was prevented by Washington.

In the light of this, and so much more for which we have no space, can any reasonable person believe that Saddam Hussein is really responsible for the catastrophe in Iraq? Does not so much of the burden of guilt lie with our government?

If you think that that is a cheap shot, take a look at a piece written by Karl Vick in the *Washington Post* on November 21, 2004. Writing from Baghdad, he says: "Acute malnutrition among young children in Iraq has nearly doubled *since the U.S. led an invasion* [my emphasis] of the country 20 months ago, according to surveys by the United Nations, aid agencies, and the interim Iraqi government." He continues:

> After the rate of acute malnutrition among children younger than 5 steadily declined to 4% two years ago, it shot up to 7.7% this year, according to a study conducted by Iraq's Health Ministry in co-operation with Norway's Institute for Applied International Studies and the UN Development Program. The new figure translates to roughly 400,000 Iraqi children suffering from "wasting," a condition characterized by chronic diarrhea and dangerous deficiencies of protein.

Now read this paragraph later in the report and wonder. "Iraqi health officials like to surprise visitors by pointing out that the nutrition issue facing young Iraqis a generation ago was obesity. Malnutrition, they say, appeared in the early 1990s with UN trade sanctions championed by Washington."

How do we explain these paragraphs? Firstly, under Saddam the people ate very well, to the point of it being a problem. Secondly, the real problem begins with the American-led campaign for brutal sanctions, provoking a huge crisis of malnutrition. Thirdly, once the sanctions are somewhat relaxed under European pressure, Saddam's government gets into action and the malnutrition crisis starts to be tackled efficiently.

Now things are even worse than before. *Things are worse under American control.* What excuses has the U.S. administration? Saddam is no longer in power. There are no sanctions, and America is the richest country on the planet. How is it that Saddam did better under the sanctions than America without the sanctions?

An assessment from the Washington-based Center for Strategic and International Studies says that the health care situation is worsening. An administrator at Baghdad's Central Teaching Hospital for Pediatrics said: "Believe me, we thought a magic thing would happen with the fall of Hussein and the start of the U.S.-led occupation. So we're surprised that nothing has been done. And people talk now about how the days of Saddam were very nice."

Karl Vick concludes his piece with this telling paragraph: "Iraqis say such conditions carry political implications. Baghdad residents often point out to reporters that after the 1991 Persian Gulf War left much of the capital a shambles, Hussein's government restored electricity and kerosene supplies in two months." Add to the foregoing a report from the UN, noted by *BBC News* on March 30 of this year, that malnutrition among children under 5 as of the end of last year has *doubled* (from four to eight percent) under the American occupation and then ask yourself: is it any wonder that there is a growing and vibrant insurgency against the U.S. occupation? I think not.

LID: But if Saddam was faithfully directing whatever money there was to the needs of his people, what is the Oil-for-Food scandal all about?

JW: Frankly, I think it's a transparent scheme of the neocons to smear UN General Secretary Kofi Annan over what are purely allegations. I am happy that for the moment it appears that the President is not one of the pack after Kofi's scalp. Kofi appears safe, but the neocons are still intent on weakening the UN as much as they can, as I made clear in the commentary I wrote in late November 2004, at the English-language website of *Aljazeera.*

LID: Could you elaborate; the "Oil-for-Food" scandal is simply a neocon "scheme"?

JW: I think so. The intent of the neocons was "regime change" in Iraq, to fit their plans for an American empire, with a permanent outpost in Baghdad. To do this, they had to clear out all the obstacles in their path – which meant open assaults on the international institutions that had been developed to prevent war, through diplomacy backed by the threat of sanctions.

This meant demeaning the United Nations, the UN Monitoring, Verification and Inspection Commission (UNMOVIC) inspectors of chemical and biological weapons under Hans Blix, and the International Atomic Energy Agency under Muhammad ElBaradei. France, Germany, Russia and China had become obstacles to regime change in Baghdad, either at the UN Security Council or at NATO, or both.

To neutralize them with American public opinion, the neocons used their contacts in the news media to broadcast the argument that these countries were pursuing selfish interests related to Iraq's oil. Out of this soup came the "Oil-for-Food scandal." It's clear enough the neocons and the news outlets that do their bidding are behind the story.

On the surface, there has yet to be found a single person with his hand in the UN cookie jar. All that has appeared to date are assertions that various people associated with the management of the "Oil-for-Food" Program in Iraq and the UN benefited financially through shady transactions.

It is further alleged that UN officials looked the other way as Saddam Hussein arranged kickbacks that went into foreign bank accounts, with inferences that he was using the cash to finance his military machine and international terrorism, build palaces to aggrandize himself, all the while diverting money from the intended recipients – the poor Iraqi people.

Interestingly enough, we were initially led to believe that Saddam made off with $26 billion – that's $26,000,000,000 – most recently we've been advised that the audits show $1.5 million in questionable transactions. That's $1,500,000! I've yet to see a news report pointing out that this kind of misplaced pocket change can be identified by the Government Accountability Office for practically any administration bureaucracy, down to the tiniest.

To put all this in perspective, remember that Saddam was the duly constituted head of state in Iraq, his government not only officially recognized by the US during the Iran-Iraq war, but also was given palpable support in the war. Why he invaded Kuwait in 1990 is another story, as we discussed, but it is now absolutely clear his dispute was only with the emir of Kuwait and not any other country in the Middle East. He was not a threat to his neighbors. It is also clear that Iraq had met the conditions of the UN Security Council post-Gulf War resolution that demanded he destroy his unconventional weapons before economic sanctions could be lifted and the Iraqi government could resume the sale of oil.

From this vantage point, *it was the UN that took possession of the oil resources of Iraq.*

By rough reckoning: if the sanctions had been lifted in 1991 (when they should have been lifted), Iraq would have earned enormous amounts of money from the sale of their oil. At an average of $10 a barrel over 14 years, they would have collected $126 billion. At a more reasonable average over the period of $15 to $20 a barrel, the Iraqi government would have been able to pay all its creditors and at the same time enable the Iraqi people to return to the high living standards they enjoyed before the Iran-Iraq war (during which, I repeat, the US supported Iraq).[1]

Remember that it was because of the UN economic sanctions that persisted, thanks to U.S./British insistence, that the "Oil-for-Food" Program came into existence in 1996. This was partly the result of UN reports that 1.5 million Iraqi civilians had died because of the malnutrition and disease engendered by the sanctions. More directly, it was because President Clinton bombed Iraq in early September 1996 during his re-election campaign that year, on the information that Baghdad had violated the "no-fly zone" over Iraqi Kurdistan. It turned out Saddam did not violate the "no-fly zone," but had sent troops on the ground to Kurdistan at the request of the provincial government, which had come under attack by Iranian-backed Kurds.

The reason? Economic distress, with the region suffering from the same malnutrition and disease afflicting all of Iraq.

The Kurds are the friends of the neoconservatives. They had to be helped out of this distress. Hence, the "Oil-for-Food" Program, designed to relieve all Iraqi citizens, but mostly Kurds, who would get the lion's share of the relief from the oil revenues.

I'm not sure about all the details of how the program was managed in the years since. But when the neocons raised the corruption issue at the UN through their friends in the news media, Annan finally saw he had to respond. He said he would investigate the allegations and persuaded former Federal Reserve chairman Paul Volcker – arguably the most respected, squeaky-clean political figure in America – to undertake the investigation and make a report, which is expected sometime late in 2005.

---

1. See the postscripts to the present chapter for more on the "Oil-for-Food" issue.—Ed.

My guess is that the game plan would be to force Volcker to issue a report that smears the UN and threatens it with a cut-off of U.S. funds unless there is a house cleaning. But what if Volcker finds that the only "wrong" was committed by the Baghdad government in selling Iraq's own oil to its neighbors, particularly to Turkey and Jordan, and that the revenues were deposited in state bank accounts and used for legitimate state reasons?

We also know the oil that went through the hands of the UN agency set up to make sure the revenues went to the people, not to the Iraqi government, also had to have the cooperation of Baghdad in lifting the oil and delivering it. A 2.5% "kickback," as it has been termed by the neocon press corps, can be more properly be termed a "fee" for facilitating this process. If these fees were paid into the government, not to numbered bank accounts, the regime would have to be judged clean on that count by Volcker. He is in a tight spot.

And remember the report of Charles Duelfer and his Iraqi Survey Group, which announced in October of 2004 that Saddam Hussein destroyed all of his weapons of mass destruction and their programs in 1991? In his report, he also brought up the "Oil-for-Food" Program, which was never part of his mission when he was appointed by Bush to check further into Iraq's WMD intentions. Duelfer clearly used the "Oil-for-Food" Program to distract attention from his central finding. His report gratuitously contained the thesis that if Saddam someday wanted to rebuild his WMD capabilities, he could be using the program to that end, with the complicity of the French, Russians, Chinese, United Nations and major oil companies.

Logic should tell you, though, that the neocons have been behind this hoax from the start, that they never intended to lift the sanctions on Iraq even while knowing back in 1991 that Saddam almost certainly had complied with that first UN resolution.

And of course the Iraqis who are in a position to clear all this up and demonstrate that while certain transactions might appear suspicious on the surface, but can be fully explained, are not available for testimony.

At any rate, the interim reports released by Volcker, on February 3, March 29, and August 9, have produced little in the way of serious financial misconduct, have merely indicated some improprieties and conflicts of interest within the UN bureaucracy, and have omitted to charge either Saddam or Kofi Annan with grave wrongdoing. Eventually Volcker's final report to the UN will be made public, and ultimate judgments can then be made. It may be there is no scandal at all. Just another trick of the neoconservatives to blow away anyone who gets in the way of their plans for a global empire.

LID: Which is pretty much what George Galloway, the British MP, told them when he appeared on May 17, before the Permanent Investigations Subcommittee of the Senate Committee on Homeland Security and Governmental Affairs, right? He said the "Oil-for-Food" investigation was the "mother of all smokescreens"!

Senator Norm Coleman of Minnesota – the Subcommittee chairman – is a young Republican who clearly has dreams of riding the so-called "Oil-for-Food scandal" to the White House, a la Richard Nixon's prosecution of Alger Hiss as a Communist spy. From what I've seen so far, Coleman's background as a prosecutor may make him smarter than his colleagues in understanding the Minnesota penal code, but otherwise he is as dumb as a post. At least in the sense that he still doesn't realize he has been chosen by the neocons and their friends in the pro-war conservative press to smear the UN, Kofi Annan, and, ultimately all the agencies of the UN that are likely to get in their way of an imperial America. In return, they are telling him he is, by gosh, presidential timber!

Senator Coleman seems to think that as long as the stuff he is getting from the neocons is winning him the plaudits of the *Wall Street Journal* editorial page and Rupert Murdoch's news empire, he can not only take it to the Sunday talk shows, but also attack members of the British Parliament who have different views on the subject.

As you say, instead of slinking away into the London fog, Galloway showed up in Washington *after* having won, in December 2004, 150,000 British pounds in libel damages from the *Daily Telegraph* over its separate claims that he had received money from Saddam's regime.

So after Coleman laid out a series of charges against him, Galloway made a robust reply, building upon that December victory, which you have to see to believe.[1] It turned out to be Senator Coleman slinking away into the fog.

Avoiding War

LID: Well, if Saddam isn't as guilty as he was made out to be by our government and the press, what, if anything, did he do to prevent America's preemptive war?

JW: In the months leading up to the American attack, there were frantic attempts by Baghdad to cut a deal with the Bush administration, giv-

---

1. See the webcast of Galloway's testimony, at http://hsgac.senate.gov/audio_video/051705video.ram.—Ed.

ing it everything it wanted and more in order to avert further bloodshed. Everything, that is, but "regime change," i.e. the departure of Saddam and his government. The *New York Times*, in November 2003, reported a back-channel attempt by Baghdad in December 2002 to negotiate a deal, which apparently included an offer to hold real democratic elections; but the Pentagon was not interested. The President had long ago made up his mind to make his mark in history by having his war, with little regard for the consequences. He would not have pulled the trigger, of course, if he knew for sure that Saddam would accept retirement at a villa in France or Lower Slobovia. Mohammed Aldouri, Iraq's ambassador to the United Nations, wrote a very brief article at the eleventh hour, named, "Ten Points on Iraq," which is worth reading, showing clearly the position of the Iraqi administration on the brink of war.

What's worth noting, however, is that this type of situation – nations trying to regularize their status with America – is more common than we think. For example, Libya and Qathafi have been trying to reach a diplomatic solution to their differences with the U.S. for years – ever since it became clear the cold war was ending with their patrons in Moscow on the losing side. The same is true not only of Iraq, but with Iran, North Korea, and even Cuba as well. The problem has always been what President Eisenhower loosely called "the military-industrial complex." That is, if the U.S. comes to terms with all the "rogue states" of the world who were aligned with Moscow or Beijing in the cold war, there would be no enemies to guard against or to defeat if they were deemed imminent threats. Public support for defense spending would dry up and the Pentagon would wind up living on crumbs, as it was in the 1930s.

LID: Do you think the situation in Iraq is due to a larger problem of American foreign policy in general?

JW: I have been of the opinion that our government has put us all in jeopardy with a foreign policy that generated the kind of frustration abroad, especially in Islamic countries, which results in the kind of political terrorism that was directed at the World Trade Center. Pat Buchanan has often called for a lifting of all economic embargoes which the United States now places on 61 different countries of the world – including the embargoes on Cuba, Iran, Iraq, Libya, the Sudan, and North Korea. It is my belief that this kind of "Moral Foreign Policy" is the only kind that can extinguish the outrage that is at the heart of political terror. The President of the United States cannot list his "enemies" without offering a reasonable method by which they can be removed from the list, or they will have no choice but to make his life even more miserable.

There are basically two approaches to solving the problem of terrorism. One is that you understand the mind of the terrorist in order to establish defenses against it. The other is that you kill all the terrorists and all the potential terrorists. Richard Perle and company would certainly not flinch at that latter possibility, although I'm sure he would think we would only have to kill a significant fraction of the 1.25 billion Muslims before the rest "got the message."

In 1998, I recommended to the then Chairman of Senate Foreign Relations, Jesse Helms, that he hold hearings on the Arab/Islamic world. If our government would simply announce a willingness to hear the petitions of Arabs and Muslims, to hear out their grievances, the incidence of terrorism and the threat of terrorism would drop sharply here and around the world. I *publicly* warned that unless we did so, the forces that attempted to bring down the World Trade Center in 1993 would return and finish the job. Senator Helms at first responded with an openness to the idea of such hearings, but the Perle neocon network closed that idea down, and of course the forces I worried about returned to bring the twin towers down.

In my mind, the people of Israel would be less likely to lose their lives and limbs if the Arab/Islamic world could have its list of grievances simply heard by Uncle Sam. And I knew hearings would eventually lead to the stalemate over Palestine. It did not happen because the Jewish political establishment in the United States – not necessarily in Israel – was determined to close off serious political discourse with the Arab-Islamic world in the mistaken belief that in so doing it is protecting Israel. It is the worst possible thing to do, practically inviting terrorism, but it grows out of a deeply-held conviction by those Americans – Jew and Gentile – who decide upon such matters that the Arab world is *the enemy* of Israel and that *maximum* force and *minimum* diplomacy is the correct posture.

Remaining Charges

LID: We have a few more questions that are wide-ranging, though not directly connected one to the other. Didn't Saddam Hussein drive all the Jews out after the 1967 Israeli war against Egypt?

JW: No, it was the government of Abdul Rahman Arif that encouraged – though there was no official "expulsion" – the 200,000 some Jews of Iraq to leave, given the hostile reaction to the '67 war among Iraqis. The Ba'ath

Party government that followed did hang some Jews as Israeli spies, but there has never been persecution of Iraqi Jews by the Ba'ath government as such, and there are still two functioning synagogues in Iraq. And seven percent of the population is Catholic.

Yet the position of Saddam and the Ba'ath Party was and is uncompromisingly opposed to Israel. At a press conference on July 19, 1981, Saddam made his position very clear:

> The conflict between the Arabs and the Zionist entity is a historical and cultural conflict that is bound to continue for a long time. But we are confident that in the end the Arab nation will be in a better condition, whereas the Zionist entity will be in an acute historical crisis, because it is an aggressive, expansionist, and racist entity. I have just referred to our view of the Arab people and their land, saying that *wherever* they are exposed to humiliation we stand by them. We consider the occupation of any Arab territory as an occupation of Iraqi territory. Hence it is only natural that we stand by all our Arab brothers in defense of our occupied Arab land whether it is Syrian, Palestinian, or belonging to any other Arab country.

To some in the West that might appear an unacceptably hard line, but it is the authentic voice of the Arab in the street, whatever their governments say to the contrary. Saddam is a hero for many ordinary Arabs because he has stood up, defiantly, to both Israel and the country that has made Israel possible – from the point of view of diplomatic cover, huge financial aid, and military technological transfers – the United States.

LID: What about President Bush's charges during his UN speech in October 2002 that Iraq's government openly praised the attacks of September 11?

JW: This is simply not true. In fact, Iraq expressed sympathy for the families of the victims of the 9/11 attacks. I have no idea how the President was fed that line.

LID: The White House claimed that Iraq trained terrorists who were a threat to the Western democracies. Is this true?

JW: That is likewise false. Iraq did support a network of Palestinian resistance groups prior to 1983, but at that time the U.S. offered to provide support for Baghdad in its war against Iran on condition that it withdraw support from the network. The Hussein government did so for practical reasons.

Of course, some would argue that the various armed factions of the Palestinian movement are terrorists, and thus Saddam represented a state sponsor of terrorism. Perhaps things are not so clear to the Palestinian people who have suffered, and are suffering, a brutality that is so endemic and systematic that it might be called "slow genocide." One does not have to be Palestinian to know that the recent Israeli governments have been very far from what could be termed "democratic" in any Western sense of the word. It reminds me of Edward Peck, our Envoy to Baghdad during the Carter administration, and the Deputy Director of the Task Force on Terrorism in the Reagan administration. The Task Force spent seven months coming up with 51 ideas on how to combat political terrorism, but the then Vice President, George H. W. Bush – who chaired the Task Force – told people not to worry about the *causes* of terrorism, but to concentrate on the *defenses* against it. Peck says that it was generally assumed that political terrorism was the province of the Arab/Islamic world in that period, with its base being the Palestinian problem. But how does one combat an effect if one is ignorant of the cause?

Peck says that he recalls a discussion about how to tell the difference between a terrorist and a freedom fighter. The conclusion was that a *terrorist* is someone financed *by them*, and *freedom fighters* are financed *by us*.[1] Secretary of State, George Schultz, rejected the inference, in the sense that there is no "moral equivalence" between them and us. If we are better than they are, our terrorists cannot be considered criminal, no matter how illegal the activities, no matter how many innocents are killed.

That twisted mentality still dominates American government circles. Thus we find an interesting snippet of news in the *New York Times* for June 9, 2004, by Joel Brinkley, entitled, "Ex-CIA Aides Say Iraq Leader Helped Agency in 90s Attacks." Some people will be disappointed to hear that the "Iraq Leader" in question was not Saddam, but the one chosen by the U.S. government to head the Interim Government, Iyad Allawi. It seems that Allawi was recruited by the CIA in 1992 when he formed the Iraqi National Accord. Some of its activities included sabotaging government buildings, and detonating car bombs. Brinkley continues:

> When Dr. Allawi was picked as interim Prime Minister, he said his first priority would be to improve the security situation by stopping bombings and other insurgent attacks in Iraq – an idea several former officials familiar with his past said they found 'ironic.'"

Irony is one way of putting it, but a better one might be hypocrisy. But the saddest thing in the piece is the statement by an intelligence officer:

---

1. See Dr. Record's discussion of this in his interview on the subject of America's "War on Terror" in the companion to the present volume, *Neo-CONNED! Again*, pp. 309–327.—Ed.

"no one had any problem with sabotage in Baghdad back then." The lesson appears to be that it is all right *for us* to attack Iraqis in *their* country, but it is not alright *for them* to attack *us* in *their* country.

LID: What comment do you have on the fact that Osama bin Laden's al-Qaeda terrorist forces, or at least those who are supposed to be allied to them, were operating inside Iraq while Saddam was still in power?

JW: That is true in one sense, but an important distinction must be made. The al-Qaeda operatives who are said to have been in Iraq were in Kurdistan, which was outside the reach of the Baghdad government, and had been ever since the close of the first Gulf War. The illegal "no-fly" zones made that possible.

LID: A final charge you hear from time to time is that Saddam Hussein ordered the assassination of former President Bush in 1993, while he was visiting Kuwait City, the assassin confessing that he had been given a bomb by the Iraqi secret service.

JW: You hear it, but there's more to the story than meets the eye. At the time, the CIA reported the Iraqi secret service must have been involved since the bomb found by the Kuwaiti police had the wiring "signature" of the Iraqi secret police. In his December 5, 1993, investigative report in *The New Yorker*, "A Case Not Closed," Seymour Hersh discovered that the wiring was of the most common sort. It was more likely that Kuwait was alarmed at the statements of the new President, Bill Clinton, who said he was open to negotiations with Baghdad and the lifting of the sanctions. The "assassination" report appeared in the *New York Times* on January 14, 1993, under the pen of Thomas Friedman, a supporter of what is now called "neoconservatism," and someone who openly advocated the assassination of Saddam Hussein – who, whether we like it or not, was the legitimate head of state in Iraq. Friedman's piece ended all possibility of Clinton following through on his statements, and left him with the "regime change" policy.

My informed guess is that it was a CIA operation, as the CIA Director at the time, James Woolsey – another neoconservative – was almost certainly among those alarmed by President Clinton's conciliatory remarks. It can be no coincidence that at the very first news report of the attempted assassination on Bush Sr. in Kuwait City, Woolsey urged Clinton to go to war against Iraq. It is also worth noting that Hersh pointed out that Woolsey was insinuated into his CIA job by Richard Perle, one of the foremost warmongers in the neoconservative camp. Hersh has always said that the whole thing smelled to high heaven, but CIA ranks closed and they have remained closed ever since.

Furthermore, it would not even make sense for Saddam to attempt such an assassination, especially since at the time of the alleged attempt he was trying to show the new President, Bill Clinton, that he was not such a bad guy after all. In his 1993 article, Hersh makes this very point. I have studied politics going back a long way, and for the life of me I cannot recall a regime in power putting out a contract on a politician who was not only retired, but of an age where he clearly would never come back to power again. Perhaps one of the reasons the Iraqi government spent so little time in the last ten years tackling this allegation was that they could not believe anyone in the United States could fall for this feeble line of argument. That said, John Kerry fell for it when he remarked on *Meet the Press* with Tim Russert that one reason for being glad that Saddam is under lock and key is that he once tried to assassinate former President Bush!

The Big Picture

LID: What should we think about the upcoming trial of Saddam Hussein?

JW: Because no weapons of mass destruction have been found in Iraq and no meaningful links discovered between Saddam and al-Qaeda, it does look like Saddam's prosecutors will have to prove he indeed murdered his own people. Questions about his truthfulness as a witness are irrelevant, as we can assume in advance he will deny all charges. According to CNN, during the interrogation following his capture, he was asked about the killings and mass graves and "dismissed the question" by saying those who were executed were "thieves." He may be referring to the first reports of "mass graves" reported by CNN after the coalition forces took control of Baghdad, which in fact turned out to be cemeteries of marked graves of Iraqi men convicted of a variety of civil crimes. What any court will have to be shown is that his regime was responsible for genocidal political killings.

Proving this, however, will not be as easy it as sounds. On December 7, 2003, the *Associated Press* listed the major suspected mass graves sites as being six in number, with an actual body count by authoritative sources as being less than 4,000. Of this number, 3,115 were unearthed at Mahaweel in southern Iraq, identified as being killed in the Shiite uprising of 1991 against the Baghdad regime, an uprising promoted by the CIA. A war crime? In the north, at Hatra, a mass grave of women and children was discovered, 25 by actual count, but with no report of forensics on just when they died. The site is listed as "major" because "local people" say a complete investigation will turn up 5,000 dead. Since we know that there are such graves all over Iraq dating back to the late 1960s, forensic experts would have to certify the corpses' time of death, and that kind of work is not now being done, as I understand it.

The fact is, however, that all kinds of figures have been, and are being, thrown about with wild abandon when it comes to Saddam's alleged atrocities, as we have discussed. The wildest claims seem to be those of Paul Wolfowitz, who suggested "perhaps a million Iraqi deaths," and the new interim human rights minister for Iraq, Bakhtiar Amin, a Kurd, who recently said simply "millions." It seems that the sky's the limit – but assuming a fair trial such numbers are going to have to be proved by material evidence, and *that*, as I have said, is going to be much harder than most people realize.

But to answer your question, I am pleased with the capture of Saddam Hussein and the upcoming trial because only then will we get to the bottom of this story. While I believe the charges may not stick, or the mass graves would have already been found, I think the exercise may produce an interesting and unwelcome result, especially if Saddam gets *a fair trial*, with judges not hand-picked by the occupying coalition.

One piece of news that I received recently – we'll see whether it's ever confirmed – came from Dr. al-Obaidi in the U.K., who said that the team prosecuting Saddam for crimes against humanity has dropped the genocide charge "due to insufficient evidence." That would certainly be consistent with the facts as I know them, but I wouldn't underestimate the tenacity of those who are hell bent on convicting Saddam on the last remaining point that would justify the American invasion.

LID: What would you say to those who interpret this whole interview as simply a defense of Saddam Hussein and an attack on our own President? Does it not strike you that you are being un-American?

JW: I completely repudiate the idea that I am being un-American because I refuse to be taken in by lies and propaganda. In America, our legal system enshrines the idea – at least theoretically – that a man is innocent until he is proven guilty. I do not see why that should not apply to Saddam Hussein in spite of the media hate campaign that seeks to condemn him beforehand. I believe that anyone who is charged with a "crime" should have the right to a legal defense, and in our system, public defenders are hired by the relevant political jurisdiction and paid by the taxpayers. Over the several decades of my career as a journalist and as a consultant on the political economy, I have never been paid by anyone for playing defense advocate or "devil's advocate" for people in the news.

As far as Saddam Hussein goes, in the last few years I have written myriad commentaries about him on my website, including several explicit memos, "In Defense of Saddam Hussein." The only reason I can write in this vein is because I believe he has been unjustly accused of a specific charge. I cannot defend him or his regime against charges that are beyond my ken and I have never done so. But where I have had access to information and expertise on other serious charges leveled against Saddam, and have concluded he was innocent of those charges, I could in good conscience step forward in his defense.

This is not something I undertook in the last two years, but an enterprise I began in 1990, at the time of Iraq's invasion of Kuwait. In the years since, I have concluded that he could be defended for his decisions in the war with Iran, defended for his decisions in Iraq's conflict with Kuwait, defended against the charge that he committed genocide against the Kurds, defended against the charge that he tried to assassinate former President Bush in 1993. I concluded years ago that he had destroyed whatever leftovers from the 1980s Iraq had of "weapons of mass destruction" and so advised anyone who would listen to me. And all the while I assured the politicians I talked to about my defenses of Saddam that if it could be shown that he was hiding WMDs, or that "mass graves" could be found showing he had slaughtered 200,000 Kurds in 1988, I would instantly confess my error and drop my defense.

One of the things history shows us over and over again is that men and women who were thought to be *evil* incarnate in their own day – and had to be eliminated – are not so bad in hindsight. I have told my family and friends these last several years that I really wish information would be unearthed to show that Saddam Hussein did all the evil things he has been accused of doing, so I could shed my defense of him. Until that happens, I am stuck with him.

LID: Don't you think, though, in spite of everything, that our liberation of the Iraqis from tyranny has been worthwhile?

JW: The simple answer is no.

I do not believe that it has been worthwhile sacrificing the lives of 1800 American soldiers.

I do not believe that it has been worthwhile sacrificing the 25,000 or so American troops who have come back to America either mutilated or mentally unbalanced.

I do not believe that it has been worthwhile sacrificing the more than 100,000 Iraqis who died in the war, and who are dying by the hundreds every day.

I do not believe that it has been worthwhile sacrificing the colossal amount of political capital that has been expended, and which has strained our relations with virtually the entire world, and has made us hated throughout the world – not merely in the Arab and Islamic world, but also in Asia, Latin America and, most sadly of all, in Europe.

I do not believe that it has been worthwhile sacrificing the immense sums of money involved. Even in September 2003, the cost of the war in Iraq was already an incredible $166 billion. According to Yale economist William Nordhaus, this was greater than costs of the Revolutionary War, the War of 1812, the Mexican War, the Civil War, the Spanish-American War, and the Persian Gulf War *combined*, and these figures are inflation-adjusted. More than a year on, God only knows how much more has been wasted – and will yet be wasted – on this war, which could have been spent more productively in sorting out America's many domestic problems.

At the end of the day, I cannot see how any normal person can deny what Paul Craig Roberts, former Assistant Secretary of the Treasury during the Reagan era, said just after this current Iraq war finished. He said that it was "a strategic blunder, the costs of which will mount over the next half century," and he suggested that the only likely good to come from it would be the public's realization "that the neoconservative agenda of conquest of the Muslim Middle East is beyond our available strength."

"The Iraqi people are emerging from decades of tyranny and oppression."

—George W. Bush, June 28, 2005

THE EDITORS' GLOSS: Muhammad al-Baghdadi is a former low-level official of the Iraqi government prior to its overthrow by the United States. His biographical details are not publicly available, for reasons that should be obvious. Through contact we have had with individuals who corresponded directly with him, we have been able to verify beyond reasonable doubt that he is a credible witness to what he writes of in what follows.

Much has been made of Saddam's "oppression" of the Shiite population of Iraq. That "oppression" has furthermore been adduced as a more recent justification for a war that was predicated on something else altogether – something, it should be added, that now has no credibility whatsoever.

Al-Baghdadi's testimony is proof enough – even for those unwilling to accept the totality of what he writes – that plenty of contrary evidence exists in the case of this so-called oppression of the Shiites. While no one will deny that the Iraqi government under Saddam Hussein suppressed, even "brutally," seditious and unrepresentative Shiite insurrections, these actions can in no way be offered as justification for the invasion and occupation of a sovereign state.

Would Americans have tolerated, let alone attempted to justify with labyrinthine "just-war" distinctions, a French and British invasion of their country in 1865 in order to overthrow the recognized government of the United States, which "brutally suppressed" an ongoing insurrection in its southern states? Is it remotely credible to maintain that just-war doctrine affords any nation a right to launch an aggressive war against another sovereign nation based upon allegations of historical events that are themselves both subjects of conflicting testimony, and connected with a government's exercise of its internationally recognized right to suppress sedition and rebellion within its own territory?

Al-Baghdadi's comments illustrate that tales of Shiite "oppression" are *at least* open to doubt, and, as it is never licit to go to war for a questionable cause (as opposed to a just and morally certain one), one cannot therefore maintain that the war in Iraq was justified by Saddam's "oppression" of his Shiite countrymen. And if it was not so justified, *then it was unjust.*

CHAPTER
1
p o s t s c r i p t

The "Oppression of the Shiites"
. . . .
Muhammad al-Baghdadi

W E HAVE HEARD a lot about how the Shiites were supposedly oppressed during the time when the Arab Socialist Ba'ath
Party ruled Iraq. We've heard about how they supposedly were
not treated equally with other Iraqis.

In fact, however, these are nothing but lies fabricated as part of a psychological warfare propaganda campaign aimed at Iraqi citizens – a campaign waged by the U.S. government and its experts in psychological warfare in order to pave the way for its occupation of Iraq.

I don't plan to delve into the details or goals of that campaign here.
Instead I hope to respond briefly to some of the claims they make.

I'll begin with myself. I come from a Shiite background, which is to say
that my father is a scion of a Shiite family. Nevertheless, I worked as a government employee in the Iraqi state, close to the policy makers, and in fact
I participated in the making of policy in the areas of the economy and the
administration of the state. No one ever asked me what sect I belonged to
or what my religion was. Furthermore, I have never heard of anyone asking
such questions, nor have I heard of any discrimination among the people
in whose proximity I worked and who had responsibilities and functions
both above and below me. I might point out that some of my co-workers
took on ministerial-level posts and high-ranking military commands, but
never once did I hear any questions raised about anyone's religious affilia-
tion. When we used to discuss the evaluation of an official as a candidate
for a high-ranking post in the Iraqi government, it didn't occur to anyone
to ask about what religion he belonged to or what sect he was a member of
– as is suggested by the nonsensical ideas being spread in accordance with
the occupation's psychological warfare plans.

Such lies on the part of the invaders and their stooges, whereby they
try to hoodwink people in order to break the unity of Iraq, have prompted

me to set out the facts about the nature of the cadres of the Iraqi state and their backgrounds, in order to refute these mendacious claims. My aim is *not* to deepen sectarian differences or bring them into higher relief in any way, nor am I just trying to defend a political regime, as those who are trying to distort reality might have people believe. My only purpose is to set forth the facts and bring out the truth. To that end I set out the following facts – and they are just a few of many, many more that could be cited.

The first Shiite to be appointed Minister of Defense in Iraq – Staff General Sa'di Tu'mah al-Jabburi – was named to that post during the rule of the Ba'ath Party.

The first Shiite to be appointed Chief-of-Staff of the Iraqi Army – Lieutenant General 'Abd al-Wahid Shannan Al Ribat – was named to that post during the rule of the Ba'ath.

The person who held the post of Foreign Minister the longest was a Shiite, and his term was during the time the Ba'ath ruled the country. Dr. Sa'dun Hammadi had that honor. Thereafter the post was held throughout the 1990s by Muhammad Sa'id as-Sahhaf, and he was also a Shiite.

The person who held the post of Minister of Petroleum in the Ba'ath period was a Shiite – Dr. Sa'dun Hammadi.

The first time in the history of Iraq that Shiite individuals held the post of Minister of Petroleum in succession was during the rule of the Ba'ath. They were: Dr. Sa'dun Hammadi, Qasim Ahmad Taqi, and 'Isam al-Chalabi (the cousin of Ahmad Chalabi). Thus, Shiites occupied the post of Minister of Petroleum more than any other group in the history of Iraq and of the Ba'ath.

The longest period during which Shiites held the post of Governor of the Central Bank of Iraq was in the period of Ba'ath rule, the individual governors being Dr. 'Abd al-Hasan Zalzalah and Tariq at-Takmah Ji. This had never happened in any earlier period in Iraq.

It was under the Ba'ath that for the first time in the history of the Iraq a Shiite held the post of Director of Public Security in Iraq. That individual was Nazim Kazzar. His assistant in that post was 'Ali Rida Bawah, who was a Shiite of Kurdish background.

The top official responsible for investigating crimes by members of the Da'wah Party, which functioned as an agency of Iran and set off bombs inside Iraq during the 1980s and 1990s, and the man who put an end to the sabotage wrecked by that party was himself a Shiite – Security Colonel 'Ali al-Khaqani, a native of the Shiite holy city of an-Najaf. This is something that no one, including Husayn ash-Shahrastani, can deny.

The Presidency of the Revolutionary Court specially formed to deal with cases of conspiracy was held by two Shiites, namely Hadi 'Ali Watut and Muslim al-Jabburi.

It was under the Ba'ath that for the first time in the history of Iraq two Shiites succeeded one another as Prime Minister of Iraq. They were Dr. Sa'dun Hammadi and Muhammad Hamzah az-Zubaydi.

The man who held the post of Speaker of the National Assembly the longest was a Shiite – also Dr. Sa'dun Hammadi.

The National Oil Company, which was responsible for the extraction and export of Iraqi oil, was headed by four Shiite individuals who held the post for the longest time. They were: 'Abd al-Amir al-Anbari, 'Isam al-Chalabi (the cousin of Ahmad Chalabi), Fadil al-Chalabi (another cousin of Ahmad Chalabi), and Ramzi Salman.

More than 60 percent of the General Directors of state companies in the military industries were Shiites. More than 70 percent of the advanced engineering and technical cadres in the military industries were Shiites.

The person to hold the post of Chairman of the Atomic Energy Organization in Iraq for the longest period was a Shiite – Dr. 'Abd ar-Razzaq al-Hashimi. Most of the specialists and scientists in the Atomic Energy Organization were Shiites, among them Diya' Ja'far, Husayn Isma'il al-Bahadili, and Husayn ash-Shahrastani.

The Deputy Chairman of the Military Industrial Board for Technical Affairs, Dr. Nizar al-Qusayr, the most important person on the board because he was in charge of all production development projects, was also a Shiite.

More than 60 percent of both the General Directors in the Iraqi state sector and their technical and scientific cadres who held high official posts and positions in that sector were Shiites.

The person who held the position of General Director in the Iraqi state sector the longest, since the foundation of the state sector and until the U.S. invasion, was a Shiite – namely Midhat al-Hashimi, the General Director of the Public Company for Automobiles.

All the General Directors for the Education Departments in the provinces in Iraq's central and southern area, throughout the entire period of Ba'ath Party rule, were Shiites.

More than 60 percent of Ba'ath Party members were Shiites. The middle-ranking cadres in the Ba'ath Party were more than 70 percent Shiite. They were the foundation of the Party's organizational and formational structure, and they undertook organizational and mass work in the party.

During the time of the Iran-Iraq War, the Commander of Iraqi Artillery was Staff Major General Hamid al-Ward, a Shiite. The Commander of the Armored Forces was Staff Major General Sabih 'Umran at-Tarafah, a Shiite. The General Secretary of the Ministry of Defense – that is, the number two man in the ministry after the Minister of Defense himself – was Staff Major General Sa'd al-Maliki, a Shiite. Then later there was Staff Major General Jiyad al-Imarah, a Shiite. The Commander of the Third Division, Lieutenant General Sa'di Tu'mah al-Jabburi, was a Shiite. The Director of administration of Political Guidance was 'Abd al-Jabbar Muhsin al-Lami, a Shiite. This is to say nothing of the large number of brigade generals, sectional commanders, army officers, and military advisers who were Shiites.

Ten men served as the Permanent Representative of Iraq to the United Nations during the period of Ba'ath Party rule. Of them, four were Shiites, namely: Talib Shabib,'Abd al-Amir al-Anbari – who held the post the longest and occupied the position twice, Muhammad Sadiq al-Mashat, Sa'id al-Musawi.

The post of Permanent Representative of Iraq to the UN was held by one Kurd during the Ba'ath period – 'Ismat Kattani – and by one Shiite of Kurdish origin – 'Abd al-Karim ash-Shaykhli.

The Sunnis who held the post of Permanent Representative in the UN were: 'Adnan al-Bajah Ji, Salah t'Umar al-'Ali, Nizar Hamdun, and Muhammad ad-Duri.

The two Representatives of Iraq to UNESCO were both Shiites: 'Aziz al-Hajj, a Shiite of Kurdish origin, and 'Abd al-Amir al-Anbari, a Shiite.

The last editor-in-chief of the Ba'ath Party's official newspaper, *ath-Thawrah*, was Sami Mahdi, who is a Shiite of Iranian descent.

The Information Adviser to President Saddam Hussein was 'Abd al-Jabbar Muhsin, a Shiite.

The main adviser to President Saddam Hussein for Ba'ath Party affairs was Muhsin Radi Salman, a Shiite.

President Saddam Hussein's aide throughout the 1970s, 1980s, and until the beginning of the 1990s was Sabah Mirzah Mahmud, a Shiite of Kurdish background.

The criteria for nomination of a person to the post of General Director or to a special position (such as the head of an institution or a board, an assistant minister, an ambassadorship, or a minister) in the Iraqi state were competence and specialization in the first place; loyalty to Iraq in the second place; good morals and lifestyle was third; and then came working in accordance with the ideals of the July 17 Revolution – the untarnished ideals of serving Iraq, its progress, and its advancement.

All the singers and songwriters who sang of the Ba'ath Party and of love for the leader in the period of Ba'ath Party rule were Shiites.

All the popular poets who wrote long poems in honor of the Ba'ath Party and the President in the period of Ba'ath Party rule were Shiites.

One of the most tragi-comic features of the present time is the fact that those Ba'ath Party members who turned against the Ba'ath and threw themselves into the arms of the American CIA and collaborated with the Americans in their aggression against Iraq and their occupation of the country were Shiites, and it is *they* who today weep and wail about the "oppression" of the Shiites in the time of the Ba'ath, during which they held positions. But those people are not true children of Iraq, whether they be Shiites or anything else. They are nothing but a gang of hired stooges who promote the plans of the occupation for their petty aims.

Among them, for example, are:

- Iyyad 'Allawi, a Shiite who was a member of a Ba'ath Party Section;
- Tahir al-Baka', a Shiite who was a member of a Ba'ath Party Section;
- Rasim al-'Awwadi, a Shiite who was a member of a Ba'ath Party Branch;
- Hazim ash-Sha'lan, a Shiite who was a member of a Ba'ath Party Base;
- Dawud al-Basri, a Shiite who writes in the newspapers and was a high-ranking official in the Iraqi Embassy in Kuwait;
- Zuhayr Kazim 'Abbud, a Shiite who was a member of a Ba'ath Party Division;
- Mundhir al-Fadl, a Shiite who was a member of a Ba'ath Party Division;
- Brigadier General Sa'd al-'Ubaydi, a Shiite who was a member of a Ba'ath Party Section;
- Falih Hassun ad-Darraji, a Shiite who was a member of a Ba'ath Party Section;
- Hashim al-'Aqqabi, a Shiite who was an active member of the Saddam Branch organizations;
- Hasan al-'Alawi, a Shiite who was a member of a Ba'ath Party Division;
- Amir al-Hilw, a Shiite journalist who was General Director in the Ministry of Information and a member of a Ba'ath Party Division (the al-Muthanna Division, the area of Zayunah in Baghdad); and

- Abd al-Karim al-Muhammadawi, a Staff Sergeant who deserted from the Iraqi military, a Shiite who was a high-ranking aide in the organizations of the ar-Rafidayn military Section in the Ba'ath Party Military Branch in Dhi Qar Province.

Before I conclude this little piece, I feel that I must mention a few things that might perhaps be unknown to some people.

First, Dr. 'Adnan 'Aziz Jabiru was a General Director in the state. He is a Christian who was nominated to ministerial posts on several occasions, but he emphatically rejected them because he preferred to stay in his position where he served the citizens. He was the boldest person I have ever known in my life in his frank confrontations with all officials and members of the leadership. He wasn't a Ba'ath Party member and he was little more than one meter tall.

Second, Dr. Umid Midhat Mubarak, a Kurd and an independent as far as political membership went, was a member of the National Assembly. As a physician he was a member of the social and health committee in the Assembly, whose task it was to evaluate the work and services of the Ministry of Health. In this capacity, in one Assembly session he spoke boldly and criticized the Minister for weaknesses in the Ministry's services. At the time the Minister of Health was Dr. Sadiq Hamid 'Allush, a Member of the Command of the Central Committee of the Ba'ath Party and a veteran Ba'athist. When that Minister was dismissed following the criticisms leveled by Dr. Umid Midhat Mubarak, a decree was issued naming Dr. Umid Midhat Mubarak counselor to the Presidency and then, later, Minister of Health. I don't know what kind of "oppression" anybody can speak of there, unless they are stooges of the occupation and participants in its plans.

Third, for the first time in the history of the Iraqi state, the Governor of the Iraqi Central Bank was one of our Christian brothers, Mr. Subhi Farankul. That was during the period of Ba'ath Party rule. He enjoyed unprecedented respect over all others who held that post for his high professionalism and great expertise. His position as the head of the bank was repeatedly extended, despite the fact that he had passed the legal age of retirement and despite his permanent desire to retire from work. The two deputy Bank Governors during that period were 'Asim Muhammad Salih, a Shiite, and Usamah al-Chalabi, a Shiite (and one of Ahmad Chalabi's cousins).

Fourth, the General Directors and high officials in the Iraqi state were provided with a personal car by the state every two years at the cost of its importation with no customs charges attached – a practice aimed at facilitating their work. This system was instituted after the earlier policy of supplying government departments with their own cars was cancelled. Just like those top officials, the Shiite religious authorities of the al-Haydariyah, al-Husayniyah, al-'Abbasiyah, and al-Kazimiyah religious centers were provided with their own cars on the same terms as those given to those high government officials. The same practice even extended to the major Shiite religious leaders in Karbala', an-Najaf, Baghdad, and al-Basrah, and one of those to receive a car on such terms was 'Ali as-al-Sistani. These Shiite religious figures also received the same financial perquisites given to top government officials in order to allow them to spend more as needed during the difficult times of the embargo. I am a witness to the truth of this before God, and before anyone else, because that was my former official responsibility. I will remain a witness to the fact that orders were issued from the Republican Palace transportation unit to give a Mercedes car to many of them, and one of those who benefited from this was the late Muhammad Sadiq al-Sadr.

Fifth, I must mention one of the Iraqi military commanders, Staff Lieutenant General Yaljin 'Umar 'Adil, a Turkoman. For the first time in history a Turkoman was appointed commander of a division. He was one of the heroes of the war with Iran and commander of the 6th Division in the 1991 war. He then served as an aide to the Chief-of-Staff in the 1990s, despite all the wounds from which his body suffered for the sake of Iraq.

These are just a few bits of evidence to show that Iraq was a real state, and certainly not a regime based on religious sectarianism as the occupation forces and their stooges now claim in order to push their program for splitting up Iraq. I wished to set this down and to relate the story of a cousin, Colonel "A. M.," whose house was seized by the Badr Brigade gang who claim to be Shiites. They expelled him and his family from their home and they attacked his wife after they heard that he might be a member of the Iraqi Resistance. Even though *he is of Shiite background,* he is Iraqi before all else, and this is something that the stooges and the depraved cannot comprehend.

THE EDITORS' GLOSS: In *Neo-CONNED! Again*, Alex Cockburn rightly calls the period between the first and second Gulf Wars the "thirteen years' war," for the attack on Iraq continued unabated, though it was disguised as sanctions and "no-fly-zone" bombing runs.

What follows are articles dealing with that disastrous period. The first is an excerpt from a working paper (UN doc. no. E/CN.4/Sub.2/2000/33) prepared by the impeccably credentialed (see his bio., p. 437) Belgian Judge Marc Bossuyt for the 52nd session of the UN's Economic and Social Council, Sub-Commission on the Promotion and Protection of Human Rights, submitted on June 21, 2000 (modified to reflect the dissolution of UN sanctions following the 2003 U.S. invasion).

Bossuyt's remarks are the considered judgment of a career human-rights-law professional. He says: "the sanctions regime against Iraq was unequivocally illegal under existing international humanitarian law and human rights law." The best the U.S. ambassador to the UN could manage was a sanctimonious dismissal of Bossuyt's report as "incorrect, biased, and inflammatory." Still, the UN sub-commission that received Bossuyt's paper decided, at its 26th meeting, August 26, 2001, to appeal "to the Security Council . . . for the embargo provisions affecting the humanitarian situation of the population of Iraq to be lifted," because it considered "any embargo that condemns an innocent people to hunger, disease, ignorance and even death to be *a flagrant violation of the economic, social and cultural rights and the right to life of the people concerned and of international law*" (emphasis ours).

A review of the same sanctions in light of the moral law and just-war doctrine is just as damning, as Prof. Gordon shows. Both "positive law" and the moral law, then, reveal the sanctions regime to have been legally insufficient and therefore not binding. Any government in a position like that of the Iraqi government at the time would no doubt have sought – and licitly – to evade such a brutal and inhuman embargo.

So much, then, for the excitement surrounding the Iraqi government's alleged attempts to work around the UN sanctions and the "Oil-for-Food" Program they created. Prof. Gordon calls it a "weapon of mass distraction," and Hans Blix tags U.S. criticism of the UN as simply "revenge from American political circles for the defeat [in the UN] over Iraq." The real focus should be on the criminal onslaught waged against the Iraqi people not only in an unjust war in 2003, but in the unjust and illegal quasi-military aggression of the 12 years preceding it.

The Adverse Consequences Economic Sanctions Had on the Enjoyment of Human Rights in Iraq

• • • • • • • • •

Marc Bossuyt, Ph.D., J.D.

1. Implementation of Sanctions

The Security Council imposed multilateral comprehensive economic sanctions in its resolution 661 of August 6, 1990. Under the sanctions all imports and exports to and from Iraq were banned, exemptions being allowed for supplies intended strictly for medical purposes and, in certain circumstances, foodstuffs.[1] The Security Council imposed marine and air blockades in its resolutions 665 (1990) and 670 (1990).

Following the first Gulf War, the Security Council, in its resolution 687 (1991) authorized the continuation of sanctions, with the same humanitarian caveats. The Sanctions Committee was authorized to permit exports of petroleum originating from Iraq, in order to enable Iraq to pay for imports of foodstuffs, medicines and essential civilian supplies. In resolution 687 (1991), the Security Council also imposed a comprehensive arms embargo and established a technical commission of experts (UNSCOM) to monitor and destroy any weapons of mass destruction in Iraq.

In 1991, the Council adopted resolutions 706 (1991) and 712 (1991), authorizing the sale of up to $1.6 billion worth of petroleum and petroleum products by Iraq each six months. The resolutions were never implemented and it was not until 1996 that the "Oil-for-Food" Program came into effect. Resolution 986 (1995) permitted the sale of $2 billion of Iraqi oil over 180 days, the proceeds from which were to be placed in a United Nations-controlled bank account. Of the revenues from the sale, however, only about half ended up going towards the purchase of humanitarian goods, the ma-

---

1. In its resolution 666 (1990), the Security Council established that the Security Council and its Sanctions Committee had the sole power to determine whether humanitarian circumstances mandated the provision of foodstuffs.

jority of the rest going towards reparations and administrative costs. This resolution was implemented with the signing of a memorandum of understanding between the Secretariat and the Government of Iraq on May 20, 1996. The program went into effect December 10, 1996. Although it was conceived of as a temporary measure, the "Oil-for-Food" scheme remained in effect, having been extended several times. The amount Iraq was allowed to sell was increased considerably in resolution 1153 (1998), and the cap was dropped altogether in December 1999 in resolution 1284 (1999). More money was also allowed for the repair of Iraq's greatly damaged oil industry. However, this mitigation of the sanctions in no way solved the crisis; as the United Nations Secretary-General stated in March 2000, "Even if [the "Oil-for-Food" Program] is implemented perfectly, it is possible that our efforts will prove insufficient to satisfy the population's needs."[1]

2. Effects on Civilians

As has been documented by United Nations agencies, NGOs, humanitarian and human rights organizations, researchers, and political leaders, the sanctions upon Iraq produced a humanitarian disaster comparable to the worst catastrophes of the past decades. There is broad controversy and little hard evidence concerning the exact number of deaths directly attributable to the sanctions; estimates range from half a million to a million and a half, with the majority of the dead being children. It should be emphasized that much of the controversy around the number of deaths is only serving to obfuscate the fact that any deaths at all caused by the sanctions regime indicate grave breaches of humanitarian law and *are unacceptable.*

In 1999, after conducting the first surveys since 1991 of child and maternal mortality in Iraq, UNICEF concluded that in the heavily populated southern and central parts of the country, children under five were dying at more than twice the rate they were 10 years before.[2] An expert on the effects of sanctions on civilians stated that "the underlying causes of these excess deaths include contaminated water, lack of high quality foods, inadequate breastfeeding, poor weaning practices, and inadequate supplies in the curative health-care system."[3] The lack of food due to sanctions trans-

1. Press release SG/SM/7338 (March 24, 2000).

2. UNICEF press release CF/DOC/PR/1999/29 (August 12, 1999). UNICEF Executive Director Carol Bellamy said at the press conference that the findings reveal "an ongoing humanitarian emergency."

3. Richard Garfield, "Morbidity and Mortality among Iraqi Children from 1990 to 1998: Assessing the Impact of Economic Sanctions," Occasional Paper no. 16:OP:3, Joan B.

lated into a 32 percent drop in per capita calorie intake compared to before the first Gulf War.[1] According to the Government of Iraq, by 1997, only half of the water treatment capacity of the country was operational.[2]

Owing to the lack of medical supplies, it was estimated that, by 1997, 30 percent of hospital beds were out of use, 75 percent of all hospital equipment did not work and 25 percent of Iraq's 1,305 health centers were closed.[3] A March 1999 Security Council-appointed panel summarized the health and sanitation situation as follows:

In marked contrast to the prevailing situation prior to the events of 1990–1991, the infant mortality rates in Iraq today are among the highest in the world, low infant birth weight affects at least 23 percent of all births, chronic malnutrition affects every fourth child under five years of age, only 41 percent of the population have regular access to clean water, 83 percent of all schools need substantial repairs. The ICRC states that the Iraqi health-care system is today in a decrepit state. UNDP calculates that it would take 7 billion U.S. dollars to rehabilitate the power sector countrywide to its 1990 capacity.[4]

Although some noted a slow improvement in health and nutrition indicators since 1997,[5] the disaster and deaths continued, and still in March 2000 the Secretary-General had expressed particular concern for the plight of Iraqi children.[6]

The health crisis in Iraq intertwined with the general social and economic crises which the sanctions prompted. Even if the deaths had ceased as the result of humanitarian exemptions (as the Secretary-General and others deemed impossible), there would still have been massive, systematic violations of Iraqi citizens' other rights attributable to the sanctions. The economic, social and cultural rights of the Iraqi people were being swept aside, as were their rights to development and to education. For example, the purchasing power of an Iraqi salary by the mid-1990s

---

Kroc Institute for International Peace Studies, University of Notre Dame, July 1999 (http://www.cam.ac.uk/societies/casi).

1. *Ibid.*

2. *Ibid*

3. *Ibid.*

4. Report of the Second Panel Established Pursuant to the Note by the President of the Security Council of 30 January 1999 (S/1999/100) Concerning the Current Humanitarian Situation in Iraq, S/1999/356, annex II (March 30, 1999).

5. Report of the Secretary-General Pursuant to Paragraph 4 of Resolution 1143 (1997) (S/1998/477), June 5, 1998.

6. Press release SG/SM/7338 (March 24, 2000).

was about 5 percent of its value prior to 1990[1] and, as the United Nations Development Programme field office recognized, "the country has experienced a shift from relative affluence to massive poverty."[2] The previous advances in education and literacy were completely reversed from 1990 to 2000. As Denis Halliday, former United Nations Assistant Secretary-General and Humanitarian Coordinator in Iraq, declared after his resignation in September 1998, "sanctions have had a serious impact on the Iraqi extended family system. We're seeing an increase in single-parent families, usually mothers struggling alone. There's an increase in divorce. Many families have had to sell their homes, furniture and other possessions to put food on the table, resulting in homelessness. Many young people are resorting to prostitution."[3] In addition, crime rose and emigration skyrocketed. Researchers have also shown how sanctions have an overwhelmingly greater negative medical and social impact on women, as women bear the brunt of the social and economic displacements and upheaval.[4]

3. The Response to Sanctions

The outcry against the sanctions on Iraq came from all sides. From within the United Nations, the Secretary-General himself has been at the forefront of the criticism, leveling serious charges against the sanctions regime in his report to the Security Council of 10 March 2000 (S/2000/208) and stating two weeks later that "the Council should seek every opportunity to alleviate the suffering of the population, who after all are not the intended targets of sanctions."[5] The sanctions led to the resignation of three United Nations officials, two in 2000 alone. First, Denis Halliday, former United Nations Assistant Secretary-General and Humanitarian Coordinator in Iraq, resigned in September 1998, declaring: "We are in the process of destroying an entire society. It is as simple and terrifying as that. It is illegal and immoral."[6] Hans von Sponeck, Halliday's successor as Humanitarian Coordinator in Iraq, resigned on 13 February 2000,

---

1. UNICEF, *Situation Analysis of Children and Women in Iraq*, Baghdad, April 30, 1998, quoted in Garfield, *loc. cit.*

2. S/1999/356, annex II.

3. Speech delivered by Denis Halliday on Capitol Hill, October 6, 1998 (http://www.cam.ac.uk/societies/casi/halliday/quotes.html).

4. See Nadje Al-Ali, "Sanctions and Women in Iraq," *Sanctions on Iraq: Background, Consequences, Strategies*, Proceedings of the Conference hosted by the Campaign Against Sanctions on Iraq (CASI), November 13–14, 1999 (Cambridge:: CASI, 2000), pp. 73–84.

5. Press release SG/SM/7338 (March 24, 2000).

6. *The Independent* (U.K.), October 15, 1998.

explaining that he could not any longer be associated with a program that prolonged the sufferings of the people and which had no chance of meeting even the basic needs of the civilian population.[1] Two days later, Jutta Burghardt, head of the World Food Programme in Iraq, also resigned, stating "I fully support what Mr. von Sponeck is saying."[2]

Both in the Security Council, the body which has *supposedly* provided legitimization of the sanctions regime, and in other United Nations forums, a number of countries expressed concerns over the impact of the sanctions; they include Brazil, China, Egypt, the Republic of Korea, Kenya, France, Russia and Slovenia.

The sanctions also produced an outcry from civil society. Ending the sanctions became a focus for NGOs, human rights groups, and humanitarian organizations across the world and demonstrations, petitions, lobbying campaigns, and conferences were devoted to the issue. Civil society groups sprang up whose sole purpose was to end the sanctions and which worked to bring together academics, activists, and political leaders who shared that goal. At the Commission on Human Rights, there were a multitude of statements condemning the sanctions.[3] Many groups defied the embargo and brought humanitarian aid to Iraq in acts of international civil disobedience.[4] In legal terms, this popular protest clearly established the "dictates of the public conscience."

4. Iraqi Sanctions and International Law

The sanctions regime against Iraq *was unequivocally illegal under existing international humanitarian law and human rights law.* Some would go

---

1. *Reuters*, "Top UN Official Leaves Iraq, Says Programme Failed," February 17, 2000.

2. *Washington Post*, "Aide Who Quit in Protest Plans Report on Airstrikes on Iraq," February 17, 2000.

3. See the debates in the Sub-Commission on the Promotion and Protection of Human Rights and Commission on Human Rights of the UN's Economic and Social Council (ECOSOC), as well as in reports circulated at the Sub-Commission and Commission by human rights NGOs. See, e.g., Karen Parker and Alexandra Menegakis, *Memorandum: Sanctions in Light of Human Rights and Humanitarian Law* (International Educational Development/Humanitarian Law Project, 1998); oral statements by, among others, the American Association of Jurists, Centre Europe-Tiers Monde, the General Arab Women's Federation, the Women's International League for Peace and Freedom, North-South XXI, the Union of Arab Jurists and International Educational Development; and joint oral statements by as many as 21 NGOs. Written statements include: E/CN.4/Sub.2/1996/NGO/7; E/CN.4/Sub.2/1998/NGO/24; and E/CN.4/1999/NGO/119.

4. Ramsey Clark, although among many, is perhaps one of the most famous individuals to have personally defied the blockade.

as far as making a charge of genocide.[1] Article II of the Convention on the Prevention and Punishment of the Crime of Genocide, which entered into force on 12 January 1951, defines genocide as follows:

Any of the following acts committed with intent to destroy, in whole or in part, a national, ethnical, racial or religious group, as such:

(a) Killing members of the group;
(b) Causing serious bodily harm or mental harm to members of the group;
(c) Deliberately inflicting on the group conditions of life calculated to bring about its physical destruction in whole or in part.

The sanctions regime against Iraq had as its clear purpose the deliberate infliction on the Iraqi people of conditions of life (lack of adequate food, medicines, etc.) calculated to bring about its physical destruction in whole or in part. It does not matter that this deliberate physical destruction had as its ostensible objective the security of the region. Once clear evidence was available that thousands of civilians were dying and that hundreds of thousands would die in the future as the Security Council continued the sanctions, the deaths were no longer an unintended side effect – *the Security Council was responsible for all known consequences of its actions*. The sanctioning bodies cannot be absolved from having had the "intent to destroy" the Iraqi people. The United States Ambassador to the United Nations in fact admitted this; when questioned whether the half million deaths were "worth it," she replied: "we think the price is worth it."[2] The states imposing the sanctions could raise questions under the Genocide Convention.

Any sanctions that are imposed as a result of war or as a part of war are regulated by the laws of armed conflict. Of course, the "six-prong test"[3] is still applicable, but in the Iraqi case it must be interpreted in the light of established armed-conflict law. The sanctions against Iraq were first

---

1. For an in-depth discussion of genocide and other possible violations of international human rights and humanitarian law, see Elias Davidsson, "The Economic Sanctions Against the People of Iraq: Consequences and Legal Findings" (http://www.juscogens. org or http://www.lancs.ac.uk/ug/greenrd/project/elias.htm).

2. "Punishing Saddam," *60 Minutes*, May 12, 1996. The interview went as follows: Lesley Stahl (referring to sanctions against Iraq): "We have heard that a half million children have died. I mean, that's more children than died in Hiroshima. And . . . and you know, is the price worth it?" Madeleine Albright: "I think this is a very hard choice, but the price, we think the price is worth it."

3. The six-prong test is composed of the following questions: (1) are the sanctions imposed for valid reasons; (2) do the sanctions target the proper parties; (3) do the sanctions target the proper goods or objects; (4) are the sanctions reasonably time-limited; (5) are the sanctions effective; and (6) are the sanctions free from protest arising from violations of the "principles of humanity and the dictates of the public conscience"?

imposed in the context of Iraq's military invasion of Kuwait, were maintained during the Gulf War, and then were extended indefinitely after the first phase of military hostilities ended. Also, the continuing air strikes by United States and United Kingdom planes qualified the situation as an armed conflict. Thus, the strict measures stipulated in international humanitarian law for the protection of civilians in armed conflict was applicable to the sanctions regime and its instigators, and violations of those laws can be prosecuted as war crimes.[1] Particularly germane are the provi-

1. Any sanctions regime imposed during a war or as a consequence of a war is governed by humanitarian law. (Cf., for example, The 26th International Conference of the Red Cross and Red Crescent, "Humanitarian Consequences of Economic Sanctions," in *Principles and Response in International Humanitarian Assistance and Protection* (1995): "Any sanctions regime established in the context of armed conflict is governed by international humanitarian law, which requires that the survival and essential needs of the civilian population be ensured." Extreme sanctions could also be considered a weapon of war in themselves.) Under humanitarian law the civilian population must be protected from war and its consequences as much as possible. This requires that the civilian population must always be provided with or allowed to secure the essentials for survival: food, potable water, shelter, medicines, and medical care. As humanitarian law is, like human rights law, considered *jus cogens*, sanctions in contravention of humanitarian law are void.

(1) The Hague Convention and Regulations of 1907 (Convention IV respecting the Laws and Customs of War on Land and its annex: Regulations respecting the Laws and Customs of War on Land) contain a number of provisions that could substantially limit sanctions regimes. For example, the Martens Clause (eighth preambular paragraph, restated in the Geneva Conventions (GCs) of 1949 and Additional Protocol (AP) I thereto (see GCs I, Art. 63; II, Art. 62; III, Art. 142; IV, Art. 158; and AP I, Art. 1, paragraph 2)) mandates that all situations arising from war be governed by principles of law of civilized nations, principles of humanity, and the dictates of the public conscience. Art. 50 of the Regulations provides: "No general penalty, pecuniary or otherwise, shall be inflicted upon the population on account of the acts of individuals for which they cannot be regarded as jointly and severally responsible."

(2) The GCs have many provisions relevant to the imposition of sanctions. For example, they mandate the free passage of medical provisions and objects necessary for religious worship (see, for example, Convention IV, Art. 23).

The Conventions also set out rules relating to medical convoys and evacuation (see, for example, Convention IV, Arts. 21–22), which could be violated by a sanctions regime that limited land or air convoys of humanitarian goods. Because the fundamental purpose of the GCs is to provide for the medical needs of military personnel wounded in battle as a result of armed conflict, any provision of a sanctions regime that limits the ability of a state to provide for its war wounded must be viewed as illegal. GC rights may not be abrogated or waived in any circumstance. (Common Article (CA) I, 7; II, 7; III, 7; IV, 8 of the GCs.)

The two APs to the GCs reinforce some of the provisions. For example, Protocol I, Art. 54, requires the protection of objects indispensable to the survival of the civilian population. A provision of a sanctions regime that authorizes military action against such objects or that denies the repair and recommissioning of those illegally damaged in the course of armed conflict must be viewed as illegal. Protocol I, Art. 70, provides for relief actions for the benefit of the civilian population and would be violated by any provision of a sanctions regime that limits or modifies relief action.

Protocol II contains parallel provisions to many of the provisions set out in Protocol I.

sions of the Geneva Conventions allowing for exemptions for medical supplies and for goods needed for the survival of the civilian population, the prohibition in Protocol I, Article 54, paragraph 1, of "starvation of civilians as a method of warfare," and the provisions relating to the protection of women and children, the two groups most injured by the sanctions regime. Finally, humanitarian law, in accordance with the Martens Clause, clearly establishes that the "dictates of the public conscience" are to be considered binding in cases where the law is not specific. The popular outcry against the sanctions, as mentioned above, constituted these dictates, rendering the sanctions illegal.

For example, AP II, Art. 14, provides for the protection of objects indispensable to the survival of the civilian population.

(3) The General Assembly (GA) has passed many resolutions relating to the protection of persons in times of armed conflict. (See, for example, GA resolutions 2675 (XXV) and 2677 (XXV), adopted in 1970, and 3318 (XXIX), adopted in 1974.) For example, GA Resolution, 3318 (XXIX), of December 14, 1974, on the Declaration on the Protection of Women and Children in Emergency and Armed Conflict provides, in paragraph 6:

"Women and children belonging to the civilian population and finding themselves in circumstances of emergency and armed conflict ... shall not be deprived of shelter, food, medical aid, or other inalienable rights, in accordance with the provisions of the Universal Declaration of Human Rights, the International Covenant on Civil and Political Rights, the International Covenant on Economic, Social and Cultural Rights, the Declaration on the Rights of the Child or other instruments of international law." [The foregoing note is adapted from paragraphs 32–38 of Prof. Bossuyt's June 21, 2000, paper, to which the original footnote reference pointed.—Ed.]

C H A P T E R
1
p o s t s c r i p t

The Real "Oil-for-Food" Scandal
• • • • • • • • • •
Prof. Joy Gordon, Ph.D.

S OME WOULD SAY that the lesson to be learned from September 11 is that we must be even more aggressive in protecting what we see as our security interests. But perhaps that's the wrong lesson altogether. It is worth remembering that the worst destruction done on U.S. soil by foreign enemies was accomplished with little more than hatred, ingenuity, and box cutters. Perhaps what we should learn from our own reactions to September 11 is that the *massive destruction of innocents* is something that is *unlikely to be either forgotten or forgiven.* The destruction accomplished in Iraq – not just in the second Gulf War, but with the sanctions regime imposed for more than a decade prior to it[1] – is unlikely to bring the security we have gone to such lengths to preserve.

I. Cool War

In searching for evidence of the potential danger posed by Iraq, the Bush Administration need have looked no further than the well-kept record of U.S. manipulation of the sanctions program since 1991. If any international act in the last decade was sure to have generated enduring bitterness toward the United States, it was the epidemic suffering needlessly visited on Iraqis via U.S. fiat inside the United Nations Security Council. Within that body, the United States had consistently thwarted Iraq from satisfying its most basic humanitarian needs, using sanctions as nothing less than a deadly weapon, continuing to do so even in spite of the sanctions' eventual reforms. Invoking security concerns – including those not corroborated by

---

1. It is in reference to those sanctions, "book-ended" by two Anglo-American wars, that Alexander Cockburn entitles his lead-off essay on pp. 3–11 of the companion to the present volume, *Neo-CONNED! Again,* "The Thirteen Years War."—Ed.

UN weapons inspectors – U.S. policymakers effectively turned a program of international governance into a legitimized act of mass slaughter.

Since the UN adopted economic sanctions in 1945, in its Charter, as a means of maintaining global order, it has used them fourteen times (twelve times since 1990). But only those sanctions imposed on Iraq have been comprehensive, meaning that virtually every aspect of the country's imports and exports were controlled, which was particularly damaging to a country recovering from war. Since 1991, international agencies documented Iraq's explosion in child mortality rates, water-borne diseases from untreated water supplies, malnutrition in large sectors of the population, and on and on. The most reliable estimate holds that 237,000 Iraqi children under five are dead as a result of sanctions, with other estimates going as high as one million[1] – several times as many as the number of Japanese killed during the U.S. atomic bomb attacks. The deaths from sanctions are also far greater than the number of Iraqis directly killed in the first Gulf War – an estimated 40,000 casualties, both military and civilian.[2] The sanctions are shocking not only because of the extent of the human damage, but also because the suffering has been borne primarily by women, children, the elderly, the sick, and the poor; the state and the wealthy classes seem to be inconvenienced, but are otherwise exempt from extreme hardship.

News of Iraqi fatalities was well documented (by the United Nations, among others), though underreported by the media. What remained invisible, however, was any documentation of how and by whom such a death toll had been justified for so long. How was the danger of goods entering Iraq assessed, and how was it weighed, if at all, against the mounting collateral damage? As an academic who studies the ethics of international relations, I was curious. It was easy to discover that for the last ten years a vast number of lengthy "holds" had been placed on billions of dollars' worth of what seemed unobjectionable – and very much needed – imports to Iraq. But I soon learned that all UN records that could answer my questions were kept from public scrutiny. This is not to say that the UN is lacking in public documents related to the Iraq program. What are unavailable

---

1. Richard Garfield, "Morbidity and Mortality among Iraqi Children from 1990 to 1998: Assessing the Impact of Economic Sanctions," Occasional Paper no. 16:OP:3, Joan B. Kroc Institute for International Peace Studies, University of Notre Dame, p. 1. Note that this figure does not include the adult deaths resulting from the sanctions, for which figures are generally not given because of the difficulty of documenting specific sources of mortality using the methods applicable to infants and young children.

2. See also Garfield's summary of measurements of Gulf War mortality, *ibid.*, p. 17.

are the documents that show how the U.S. policy agenda had determined the outcome of humanitarian and security judgments.

The operation of Iraq sanctions involved numerous agencies within the United Nations. The Security Council's 661 Committee was generally responsible for both enforcing the sanctions and granting humanitarian exemptions. The Office of Iraq Program (OIP), within the UN Secretariat, operated the "Oil-for-Food" Program. Humanitarian agencies such as UNICEF and the World Health Organization worked in Iraq to monitor and improve the population's welfare, periodically reporting their findings to the 661 Committee. These agencies were careful not to discuss publicly their ongoing frustration with the manner in which the program was operated.

Over the last three years, through research and interviews with diplomats, UN staff, scholars, and journalists, I have acquired many of the key confidential UN documents concerning the administration of Iraq sanctions. I obtained these documents on the condition that my sources remain anonymous. What they show is that the United States fought aggressively throughout the last decade to minimize purposefully the humanitarian goods that entered the country. And it did so in the face of enormous human suffering, including massive increases in child mortality and widespread epidemics. It sometimes gave a reason for its refusal to approve humanitarian goods, sometimes gave no reason at all, and sometimes changed its reason three or four times, in each instance causing a delay of months. From August 1991 the United States blocked most purchases of materials necessary for Iraq to generate electricity, as well as equipment for radio, telephone, and other communications. Often restrictions hinged on the withholding of a single essential element, rendering many approved items useless. For example, Iraq was allowed to purchase a sewage-treatment plant but was blocked from buying the generator necessary to run it; this in a country that had been pouring 300,000 tons of raw sewage daily into its rivers.

* * *

Saddam Hussein's government was well known for its human-rights abuses against the Kurds and Shiites, and for its invasion of Kuwait. What is less well known is that this same government had also invested heavily in health, education, and social programs for the two decades prior to the first Gulf War. The social programs and economic development continued, and expanded, even during Iraq's grueling and costly war with Iran from 1980 to 1988, a war that Saddam Hussein might not have survived without substantial U.S. backing. In 1980, the Iraqi government initiated a program to reduce infant and child mortality rates by more than half within ten years. The result was a rapid and steady decline in childhood mortality.[1] Prior to the Gulf War, there was good vaccination coverage; the majority of women received some assistance from trained health professionals during delivery; the majority of the adult population was literate; there was nearly universal access to primary school education; the vast majority of households had access to safe water and electricity; and there was a marked decline in infant mortality rate, and in the under-five mortality rate.[2] According to the World Health Organization (WHO), 90 percent of the population had access to safe water[3] and 93 percent had access to health care. In sum, the country had one of the highest standards of living in the Arab world.

The devastation of the Gulf War and the sanctions that preceded and sustained such devastation changed all that. Often forgotten is the fact that sanctions were imposed before the war – in August of 1990 – in direct response to Iraq's invasion of Kuwait. After the liberation of Kuwait, sanctions were maintained, their focus shifted to disarmament. In 1991, a few months after the end of the war, the UN secretary general's envoy reported that Iraq was facing a crisis in the areas of food, water, sanitation, and health, as well as elsewhere in its entire infrastructure, and predicted an "imminent catastrophe, which could include epidemics and famine, if massive life-supporting needs are not rapidly met." U.S. intelligence assessments took the same view. A Defense Department evaluation noted that "[d]egraded medical conditions in Iraq are primarily attributable to the breakdown of public services (water purification and distribution, preventive medicine, water disposal, health-care services, electricity, and transportation). . . . Hospital care is degraded by lack of running water and electricity."

According to Pentagon officials, that was the intention. In a June 23, 1991, Washington Post article, Pentagon officials stated that Iraq's electrical grid had been targeted by bombing strikes in order to undermine the civilian economy. "People say, 'You didn't recognize that it was going

---

1. UNICEF, *Iraq Immunization, Diarrhoeal Disease, Maternal and Childhood Mortality Survey 10* (1990).

2. Manuelle Hurwitz & Patricia David, *The State of Children's Health in Pre-War Iraq* (London: Centre for Population Studies, London School of Hygiene and Tropical Medicine, 1992), p. 15.

3. World Health Organization, *Health Conditions of the Population in Iraq Since the Gulf Crisis* (1996), p. 2.

to have an effect on water or sewage,'" said one planning officer at the Pentagon. "Well, what were we trying to do with sanctions – help out the Iraqi people? No. What we were doing with the attacks on infrastructure was to accelerate the effect of the sanctions."

Iraq could not legally export or import any goods, including oil, outside the UN sanctions system. The "Oil-for-Food" Program, intended as a limited and temporary emergency measure, was first offered to Iraq in 1991, and was rejected. It was finally put into place in 1996. Under the program, Iraq was permitted to sell a limited amount of oil (until 1999, when the limits were removed), and was allowed to use almost 60 percent of the proceeds to buy humanitarian goods. From the time the program began, Iraq earned approximately $57 billion in oil revenues, of which it spent about $23 billion on goods that actually arrived. This came to about $170 per year per person, which was less than one half the annual per capita income of Haiti, the poorest country in the Western Hemisphere. Iraqi diplomats noted that this was well below what the UN spent on food for dogs used in Iraqi de-mining operations (about $400 per dog per year on imported food, according to the UN).

The severe limits on funds created a permanent humanitarian crisis, but the situation worsened considerably by chronic delays in approval for billions of dollars' worth of goods. In July 2001, for instance, more than $5 billion in goods were on hold.

The Office of Iraq Program did not release information on which countries were blocking contracts, nor did any other body. Access to the minutes of the Security Council's 661 Committee was "restricted." The committee operated by consensus, effectively giving every member veto power. Although support for the sanctions eroded considerably, the sanctions were maintained by "reverse veto" in the Security Council. Because the sanctions did not have an expiration date built in, ending them would have required another resolution by the council. The United States (and Britain) would have been in a position to veto any such resolution even though the sanctions on Iraq had been openly opposed by three permanent members – France, Russia, and China – for many years, and by many of the elected members as well. The sanctions, in effect, could not be without the agreement of the United States.

Nearly everything for Iraq's entire infrastructure – electricity, roads, telephones, water treatment – as well as much of the equipment and supplies related to food and medicine was subject to Security Council review. In practice, this meant that the United States and Britain subjected hundreds of contracts to elaborate scrutiny, without the involvement of any other country on the council; and after that scrutiny, the United States, only occasionally seconded by Britain, consistently blocked or delayed hundreds of humanitarian contracts.

In response to U.S. demands, the UN worked with suppliers to provide the United States with detailed information about the goods and how they would be used, and repeatedly expanded its monitoring system, tracking each item from contracting through delivery and installation, ensuring that the imports were used for legitimate civilian purposes. Despite all these measures, U.S. "holds" actually increased. In September 2001 nearly one third of water and sanitation and one quarter of electricity and educational supply contracts were on hold. Between spring 2000 and spring 2002, for example, holds on humanitarian goods tripled.

Among the goods that the United States blocked during the winter of 2001: dialysis, dental, and fire-fighting equipment, water tankers, milk and yogurt production equipment, and printing equipment for schools. The United States even blocked a contract for agricultural-bagging equipment, insisting that the UN first obtain documentation to "confirm that the 'manual' placement of bags around filling spouts is indeed a person placing the bag on the spout."

Although most contracts for food in the last few years bypassed the Security Council altogether, political interference with related contracts still occurred. In a March 20, 2000, 661 Committee meeting – after considerable debate and numerous U.S. and U.K. objections – a UNICEF official, Anupama Rao Singh, made a presentation on the deplorable humanitarian situation in Iraq. Her report included the following: 25 percent of children in south and central governorates suffered from chronic malnutrition, which was often irreversible, nine percent from acute malnutrition, and child mortality rates had more than doubled since the imposition of sanctions.

A couple of months later, a Syrian company asked the committee to approve a contract to mill flour for Iraq. Whereas Iraq ordinarily purchased food directly, in this case it was growing wheat but did not have adequate facilities to produce flour. The Russian delegate argued that, in light of the report the committee had received from the UNICEF official, and the fact that flour was an essential element of the Iraqi diet, the committee had no choice but to approve the request on humanitarian grounds. The delegate from China agreed, as did those from France and Argentina. But the U.S. representative, Eugene Young, argued that "there should be no hurry" to move on this request: the flour requirement under Security Council Resolution 986 had been met, he said; the number of holds on contracts for milling equipment was "relatively low"; and the committee should wait for the results of a study being conducted by the World Food Program first. Ironically, he also argued against the flour-milling contract on the grounds that "the focus should be on capacity-building within the country" – even though that represented a stark reversal of U.S. policy, which had consistently opposed any form of economic development within Iraq. The British delegate stalled as well, saying that he would need to see "how the request would fit into the Iraqi food program," and that there were still questions about transport and insurance. In the end, despite the extreme malnutrition of which the committee was aware, the U.S. delegate insisted it would be "premature" to grant the request for flour production, and the U.K. representative joined him, blocking the project from going forward.

Many members of the Security Council were sharply critical of these practices. In an April 20, 2000, meeting of the 661 Committee, one member after another challenged the legitimacy of the U.S. decisions to impede the humanitarian contracts. The problem had reached "a critical point," said the Russian delegate; the number of holds was "excessive," said the Canadian representative; the Tunisian delegate expressed concern over the scale of the holds. The British and American delegates justified their position on the grounds that the items on hold were dual-use goods that should be monitored, and that they could not approve them without getting detailed technical information. But the French delegate challenged this explanation: there was an elaborate monitoring mechanism for telecommunications equipment, he pointed out, and the International Telecommunication Union had been involved in assessing projects. Yet, he said, there were holds on almost 90 percent of telecommunications contracts. Similarly, there was already an effective monitoring mechanism for oil equipment that had existed for some time; yet the holds on oil contracts remained high. Nor was it the case, he suggested, that providing prompt, detailed technical information was sufficient to get holds released: a French contract for the supply of ventilators for intensive care units had been on hold for more than five months, despite his government's prompt and detailed response to a request for additional technical information and the obvious humanitarian character of the goods.

Dual-use goods, of course, were the ostensible target of sanctions, since they were capable of contributing to Iraq's military capabilities. But the problem remained that many of the tools necessary for a country simply to function could easily be considered dual use. Truck tires, respirator masks, bulldozers, and pipes had all been blocked or delayed at different times for this reason. Also under suspicion was much of the equipment needed to provide electricity, telephone service, transportation, and clean water.

Yet goods presenting genuine security concerns had been safely imported into Iraq for years and used for legitimate purposes. Chlorine, for example – vital for water purification, and feared as a possible source of the chlorine gas used in chemical weapons – had been aggressively monitored, and deliveries had been regular. Every single canister was tracked from the time of contracting through arrival, installation, and disposal of the empty canister. With many other goods, however, U.S. claims of concern over weapons of mass destruction were a good deal shakier.

In 2001 the United States blocked contracts for water tankers, on the grounds that they might be used to haul chemical weapons instead. Yet the arms experts at UNMOVIC had no objection to them: water tankers with that particular type of lining, they maintained, were not on the "1051 list" – the list of goods that required notice to UN weapons inspectors. Still, the United States insisted on blocking the water tankers – this during a time when the major cause of child deaths was lack of access to clean drinking water, and when the country was in the midst of a drought. Thus, even though the United States justified blocking humanitarian goods out of concern over security and potential military use, it blocked contracts that the UN's own agency charged with weapons inspections did not object to. And the quantities were large. In September 2001, "1051 disagreements" involved nearly 200 humanitarian contracts. In March 2002, there were $25 million worth of holds on contracts for hospital essentials – sterilizers, oxygen plants, spare parts for basic utilities – that, despite release by UNMOVIC, were still blocked by the United States on the claim of "dual-use."

Beyond its consistent blocking of dual-use goods, the United States found many ways to slow approval of contracts. Although it insisted on reviewing every contract carefully, for years it didn't assign enough staff to do this without causing enormous delays. In April 2000 the United States informed the 661 Committee that it had just released $275 million in holds. This did not represent a policy change, the delegate said; rather, the United States had simply allocated more financial resources and personnel to the task of reviewing the contracts. Thus millions in humanitarian contracts had been delayed not because of security concerns but simply because of U.S. disinterest in spending the money necessary to review them. In other cases, after all U.S. objections to a delayed contract were addressed (a process that could take years), the United States simply changed its reason for the hold, and the review process began all over. After a half-million-dollar contract for medical equipment was blocked in February 2000, and the company spent two years responding to U.S. requests for information, the United States changed its reason for the hold, and the contract remained blocked. A tremendous number of other medical equipment contracts suffered the same fate. By September 2001, nearly a billion dollars' worth of medical equipment contracts were on hold, even though all the information sought had been provided.

* * *

Among the many deprivations Iraq had experienced, none was so closely correlated with deaths as its damaged water system. Prior to 1990, 95 percent of urban households in Iraq had access to potable water, as did three quarters of rural households. Soon after the first Gulf War, there were widespread outbreaks of cholera and typhoid – diseases that had been largely eradicated in Iraq – as well as massive increases in child and infant dysentery, and skyrocketing child and infant mortality rates. By 1996 all sewage treatment plants had broken down. As the state's economy collapsed, salaries to state employees stopped, or were paid in Iraqi currency rendered nearly worthless by inflation. Between 1990 and 1996 more than half of the employees involved in water and sanitation left their jobs. By 2001, after five years of the "Oil-for-Food" Program's operating at full capacity, the situation had actually worsened.

In the late 1980s the mortality rate for Iraqi children under five years old had been about 50 per thousand. By 1994 it had nearly doubled, to just under 90. By 1999 it had increased again, this time to nearly 130; that is, 13 percent of all Iraqi children were dead before their fifth birthday. For the most part, they died as a direct or indirect result of contaminated water.[1]

The United States had anticipated the collapse of the Iraqi water system early on. In January 1991, shortly before the first Gulf War began and six months into the sanctions, the Pentagon's Defense Intelligence Agency projected that, under the embargo, Iraq's ability to provide clean drinking

---

1. See UNICEF, *Child Mortality: Iraq, Current Estimates* (1999). Additionally, between 1990 and 1998, the infant mortality rate went from 40/1000 to over 100/1000. UNICEF estimates that if the public health trend from 1960–1990 had continued throughout the 1990s, there would have been a half million fewer deaths of children under five in Iraq from 1991 to 1998 (UNICEF, *Child and Maternal Morality Survey 1999*). There would also have been, as a result of conditions in the 1990s, fatalities among older children and adults, which cannot be measured with precision.

water would collapse within six months. Chemicals for water treatment, the agency noted, "are depleted or nearing depletion," chlorine supplies were "critically low," the main chlorine production plants had been shut down, and industries such as pharmaceuticals and food processing were already becoming incapacitated. "Unless the water is purified with chlorine," the agency concluded, "epidemics of such diseases as cholera, hepatitis, and typhoid could occur."

All of this indeed came to pass.[1] And got worse. Yet U.S. policy on water-supply contracts remained as aggressive as ever. For every such contract unblocked in August 2001, for example, three new ones were put on hold. A 2001 UNICEF report to the Security Council found that access to potable water for the Iraqi population had not improved much under the "Oil-for-Food" Program, and specifically cited the half a billion dollars of water and sanitation-supply contracts then blocked – one third of all submitted. UNICEF reported that up to 40 percent of the purified water run through pipes was contaminated or lost through leakage. Yet the United States had blocked or delayed contracts for water pipes, and for the bulldozers and earth-moving equipment necessary to install them. And despite approving the dangerous dual-use chlorine, the United States had blocked the safety equipment necessary to handle the substance – not only for Iraqis but for UN employees charged with chlorine monitoring there.

* * *

It was no accident that the operation of the 661 Committee was so obscured. Behind closed doors, ensconced in a UN bureaucracy few citizens could parse, American policymakers had been in a good position to avoid criticism of their practices; but they were also, rightly, fearful of public scrutiny, as a fracas over a block on medical supplies in 2001 illustrates.

Early that year the United States had placed holds on $280 million in medical supplies, including vaccines to treat infant hepatitis, tetanus, and diphtheria, as well as incubators and cardiac equipment. The rationale was that the vaccines contained live cultures, albeit highly weakened ones. The Iraqi government, it was argued, could conceivably extract these, and

---

1. Immediately prior to the first Gulf War, the incidence of typhoid was 11.3 per 100,000 people; by 1994 it was more than 142 per 100,000. In 1989, there were zero cases of cholera per 100,000 people; by 1994, there were 1,344 per 100,000 (World Health Organization, *op. cit.*, p. 10). The untreated water and sewage generated a large increase in other gastrointestinal diseases. Of these, dysentery had a particularly high impact on infants and children under five, contributing to the changes in mortality rates noted above.

eventually grow a virulent fatal strain, then develop a missile or other delivery system that could effectively disseminate it. UNICEF and UN health agencies, along with other Security Council members, objected strenuously. European biological weapons experts maintained that such a feat was in fact flatly impossible. At the same time, with massive epidemics ravaging the country, and skyrocketing child mortality, it was quite certain that preventing child vaccines from entering Iraq would result in large numbers of child and infant deaths. Despite pressure behind the scenes from the UN and from members of the Security Council, the United States refused to budge. But in March 2001, when the Washington Post and Reuters reported on the holds – and their impact – the United States abruptly announced it was lifting them.

A few months later, the United States began aggressively and publicly pushing a proposal for "smart sanctions," sometimes known as "targeted sanctions." The idea behind smart sanctions was to "contour" sanctions so that they affected the military and the political leadership instead of the citizenry. Basic civilian necessities, the State Department claimed, would be handled by the UN Secretariat, bypassing the Security Council. Critics pointed out that in fact the proposal would change very little since everything related to infrastructure was routinely classified as dual-use, and so would be subject again to the same kinds of interference. What the "smart sanctions" would accomplish was to mask the U.S. role. Under the new proposal, all the categories of goods the United States ordinarily challenged would instead be placed in a category that was, in effect, automatically placed on hold. But this would now be in the name of the Security Council – even though there was little interest on the part of any of its other members (besides Britain) for maintaining sanctions, and even less interest in blocking humanitarian goods.

After the embarrassing media coverage of the child vaccine debacle, the State Department had been eager to see the new system in place, and to see that none of the other permanent members of the Security Council – Russia, Britain, China, and France – vetoed the proposal. In the face of this new political agenda, U.S. security concerns suddenly disappeared. In early June 2001, when the "smart sanctions" proposal was under negotiation, the United States announced that it would lift holds on $800 million of contracts, of which $200 million involved business with key Security Council members. A few weeks later, the United States lifted holds on $80 million of Chinese contracts with Iraq, including some for radio equipment and other goods that had been blocked because of dual-use concerns.

In the end, China and France agreed to support the U.S. proposal. But Russia did not, and immediately after Russia vetoed it, the United States placed holds on nearly every contract that Iraq had with Russian companies. Then in November 2001, the United States began lobbying again for a smart sanctions proposal, now called the Goods Review List (GRL). The proposal passed the Security Council in May 2002, this time with Russia's support. In what one diplomat, anonymously quoted in the Financial Times of April 3, 2002, called "the boldest move yet by the U.S. to use the holds to buy political agreement,"[1] the Goods Review List had the effect of lifting $740 million of U.S. holds on Russian contracts with Iraq, even though the State Department had earlier insisted that those same holds were necessary to prevent any military imports.

Under the new system, UNMOVIC and the International Atomic Energy Agency made the initial determination about whether an item appeared on the GRL, which included only those materials questionable enough to be passed on to the Security Council. The list was precise and public, but huge. Cobbled together from existing UN and other international lists and precedents, the GRL had been virtually customized to accommodate the imaginative breadth of U.S. policymakers' security concerns. Yet when UN weapons experts began reviewing the $5 billion worth of existing holds in July 2002, they found that very few of them were for goods that had ended up on the GRL or warranted the security concern that the United States had originally claimed. As a result, hundreds of holds were lifted in the ensuing few months.

This mass release of old holds – to have been completed in October 2002 – should have made a difference in Iraq. But U.S. and British maneuvers on the council the year before made genuine relief unlikely. In December 2000, the Security Council had passed a resolution allowing Iraq to spend 600 million euros (about $600 million) from its oil sales on maintenance of its oil production capabilities. Without this, Iraq would still have had to pay for these services, but with no legal avenue to raise the funds. The United States, unable in the end to agree with Iraq on how the funds would be managed, blocked the measure's implementation.[2]

---

1. Ironic, in light of recent accusations that Saddam awarded "Oil-for-Food" contracts to nations or individuals who supported him politically. Perhaps he was not the only head of state to make decisions based upon his conception of "national interest."—Ed.

2. Hans von Sponeck, the former UN assistant secretary general and humanitarian coordinator for Iraq, pointed out in December 2000 how insufficient these maneuvers were that would supposedly have provided Iraq with the opportunity to improve its oil infrastructure and increase production. "The announcement by the Security Council,

II. Sanctions, Just-War Doctrine, and the "Fearful Spectacle of the Civilian Dead"

Economic sanctions are rapidly becoming one of the major tools of international governance of the post-Cold War era. The UN Security Council, empowered under Article 16 of the UN Charter to use economic measures to address "threats of aggression" and "breaches of peace," approved partial or comprehensive sanctions on only two occasions from 1945 to 1990. By contrast, since 1990 the Security Council has imposed sanctions on eleven nations, including the former Yugoslavia, Libya, Somalia, Liberia, Haiti, and several other nations. However, the U.S. has imposed sanctions, unilaterally or with other nations, far more frequently than any other nation in the world, or any multinational body in the world, including the United Nations. More than two-thirds of the sixty-plus sanctions cases between 1945 were initiated and maintained by the United States, and three-quarters of these cases involved unilateral U.S. action without significant participation by other countries.[1] Thus, while the question of ethical legiti-

---

and also reflected in UNSCR 1284, to lift the ceiling on the amount of oil Iraq could pump . . . [i]n theory . . . can only be welcomed; in practice, it has little consequence unless a wide range of measures is adopted concurrently. The likelihood of this happening is slim. Sanctions regulations do not allow oil-field development, nor do they permit comprehensive rehabilitation of existing up- and downstream facilities. In any case, the allocated funds of $600 million per phase are dismally short of what is needed for even basic repairs of the oil industry. To complicate matters further, oil spares often are not off-the-shelf items and therefore need to be tailor-made, and oil spare-part contracts are frequently put on hold by the UN Sanctions Committee. Oil missions appointed by the UN secretary general and led by Sayboldt, a Dutch firm of oil overseers, have regularly visited Iraq and referred to the extremely dangerous state of Iraq's oil fields. Under present conditions [absent rehabilitation of infrastructure], Iraq is not going to increase oil output much beyond the present 2.9 to 3.1 million barrels per day, simply because the oil industry in its present state is not able to do so" ("Iraq: International Sanctions, and What Next," a presentation to the Peterborough Coalition for Social Justice, Ontario, Canada, December 8, 2000 (http://www.web.net/~pcsj/articles/00/iraq-sanction_what-next.html)).

1. George A. Lopez and David Cortright, "Economic Sanctions in Contemporary Global Relations," in George A. Lopez and David Cortright, ed., *Economic Sanctions: Panacea or Peacebuilding in a Post-Cold War World?* (Boulder: Westview, 1995), p. 5. These figures are consistent with the most extensive database regarding sanctions in the twentieth century, see Gary Clyde Hufbauer, Jeffrey J. Schott, and Kimberly Ann Elliott, ed., *Economic Sanctions Reconsidered*, 2nd ed. (Washington, D.C.: Institute for International Economics, 1990). Elliott notes (in 1995, after the second edition was published), that: "Of 104 sanctions episodes from World War II through the UN embargo of Iraq, the United States was a key player in two-thirds. In 80 percent of U.S.-imposed sanctions, the policy was pursued with no more than minor cooperation from its allies or international organizations." Ellliott, "Factors Affecting the Success of Sanctions," *op. cit.*, p. 51.

macy has implications for the UN strategies of international governance, it has far greater implications for the U.S., which uses sanctions more frequently and in many more contexts, from trade regimes and human rights enforcement to its efforts to maintain regional and global hegemony.

Sanctions *seem* to lend themselves well to international governance. They seem more substantial than mere diplomatic protests, yet they are politically less problematic, and less costly, than military incursions. They are often discussed as though they were a mild sort of punishment, not an act of aggression of the kind that has actual human costs. Consequently, sanctions have for the most part avoided the scrutiny that military actions would face, in the domains of both politics and ethics.

Sanctions as applied to Iraq, however, and the massive, long-term human suffering they inflicted – as detailed in the preceding section – have undermined this view. In fact, they make a compelling argument for us to re-examine the moral basis of economic sanctions. Because it is now clear that sanctions can do fully as much human damage as warfare, it seems to me critical that we begin applying a higher level of scrutiny than has been the case since the end of World War I. Furthermore, because sanctions are themselves a form of violence, I would argue that they cannot legitimately be seen merely as a peacekeeping device, or as a tool for enforcing international law. Rather, I will suggest, *they require the same level of justification as other acts of warfare.* Thus, in this essay, I will look at principles of just-war doctrine, applicable in the case of Iraq, but I will also look at just-war doctrine as it applies to sanctions generally, even where the human consequences are less extreme than they were in Iraq.

I will argue that economic sanctions violate just-war principles of both *jus ad bellum* and *jus in bello. Jus ad bellum* requires that a belligerent party have valid grounds for engaging in warfare, whereas *jus in bello* requires that the war be fought in accordance with certain standards of conduct. To engage in warfare at all, the belligerent party must have a just cause. "Just cause" requires "a real and certain danger," such as protecting innocent life, preserving conditions necessary for decent human existence, and securing basic human rights.[1] Secondly, under the requirement of proportionality, the damage inflicted "must not be greater than the damage prevented or the offense being avenged."[2] Finally, there must be a probability of success.

---

1. U.S. Catholic Bishops, "The Challenge of Peace: God's Promise and Our Response," May 1983 pastoral letter, in Malham M. Wakin, ed., *War, Morality, and the Military Profession,* 2nd ed. (Boulder: Westview Press, 1986), pp. 245–46.

2. John Howard Yoder, *When War is Unjust* (Maryknoll, N.Y.: Orbis Books, 1996), p. 156.

The "probability of success" criterion prohibits resort to force when the outcome will be futile.[1]

In the case of Iraq, the initial justification for sanctions was Iraq's incursion into Kuwait. Yet, the invasion of Kuwait clearly had a human cost that was far less than the casualties from sanctions; estimates range as high as 20,000 Kuwaiti casualties (combined military and civilian). Furthermore, the sanctions dragged on for years following Iraq's withdrawal from Kuwait; thus the sanctions could no longer be justified as a means of stopping a *present* act of aggression. The justification for sanctions the became that Iraq possessed the means to produce chemical and biological weapons. However, it is not clear that this justification meets the proportionality test.[2] Although they are called "weapons of mass destruction," biological and chemical weapons, in contrast to nuclear weapons, are not in fact prohibited for the scale of harm done, but for the type of suffering they cause to individuals and its indiscriminate character. In any event, even according to UNSCOM's claims *at the time*,[3] Iraq was not using any such weapons and was not actually accused of possessing the weapons themselves, but only of possessing the means to produce them. It is hard to see how a quarter million civilian deaths is a proportional response, not to a present act of aggression, but something fairly far removed from that – the possession of the means to produce weapons which *might* do indiscriminate harm, *if* they are constructed, and *if* they are then used. Yet, to constitute "just cause," the offense must be "actual, not only possible," according to Yoder.[4]

If we were to hold that possession of such weapons itself justifies retaliation against an entire population, then there is a larger problem. Virtually every country in the world, including many other countries in unstable regions, possess such means, if not the actual weapons themselves. Chemical and biological weapons are notoriously easy to produce; they require little more than a college chemistry lab. Any country which produces pharmaceuticals, or for that matter pesticides, possesses the means to produce

---

1. U.S. Catholic Bishops, *op. cit.*, 248.

2. There are plausible grounds to suggest that economic sanctions are themselves weapons of mass destruction. A 1999 article in *Foreign Affairs* (John Mueller & Karl Mueller, "Sanctions of Mass Destruction," *Foreign Affairs*, May/June 1999, pp. 43ff), written by a military historian and a military strategist, observes that economic sanctions have produced more casualties in the 20th century than every use of every weapon of mass destruction combined.

3. How right they were!—Ed.

4. Yoder, *op. cit.*, p. 150.

chemical and biological weapons. Furthermore, in practice, their use has by no means been consistently treated by the world community as a war crime. There was no such response, for example, to the widespread use of Agent Orange, a biological weapon, by the U.S. throughout the Vietnam War.

The "probability of success" criterion is likewise problematic in the case of Iraq. As the sanctions continued for years, it should have become harder and harder to see how one could plausibly claim that they were likely to succeed in achieving various changes in Iraq state policies, including the removal of Saddam Hussein, given that over time it was obvious that they had been so patently ineffectual.[1] Sanctions are notorious for their low rate of success in achieving political goals. The most extensive study of sanctions episodes in this century estimates that sanctions are "a factor" in achieving the target state's compliance about one-third of the time.[2] But even this figure has been challenged as far too optimistic.[3] The typical response of a people in the face of sanctions is in fact to "rally 'round the flag," and support the leadership in the face of foreign coercion.[4] That response has characterized sanctions situations from Italian support for Mussolini in the face of the League of Nations' boycott and Serbian support of Slobodan Milosevic, to the U.S. response to the Arab oil boycott of the 1970s. The situations where outside sanctions actually help erode the internal legitimacy of the state, such as in South Africa, are infrequent.

In South Africa, for example, the external sanctions imposed on the country were accompanied by extensive political activity toward democracy inside South Africa. The sanctions were also explicitly supported by several sectors of the black population, the population hardest hit by the

---

1. I will not address here the question of the legitimacy of particular political goals, such as the removal of a country's leader from office.

2. Hufbauer, Schott, and Elliott, *op. cit., passim.*

3. Robert Pape argues that in most of these cases, there were other factors as well as sanctions, such as military actions, such that it is impossible to say with any certainty what role was played by the sanctions themselves. In only about 5 percent of the situations was there some political change that could clearly be attributed directly to sanctions. "Why Economic Sanctions Do Not Work," *International Security,* Vol. 22, no. 2 , Fall, 1997, pp. 90–136.

4. Johann Galtung's work in the 1960s has been widely cited in this regard. See, for example, Ivan Eland's comment that "Galtung used the term rally-around-the-flag effect to argue that leaders in target nations could use the economic pain caused by foreign nations to rally their populations around their cause. Rather than creating disintegration in the target state, sanctions would invoke nationalism and political integration." Ivan Eland, "Economic Sanctions as Tools of Foreign Policy," in Lopez and Cortright, *op. cit.,* p. 32.

THE REAL "OIL-FOR-FOOD" SCANDAL

sanctions. The first factor contributed directly to the end of apartheid, and it is not clear whether the changes which finally took place were attributable to the sanctions themselves, or to the political movements within and outside the country. The second factor changes the ethical context, since there was explicit, informed consent by those harmed. It seems to me that the example of South Africa does not offer a justification of sanctions that extends beyond the particulars of that situation, any more than a boxer who consents to risk being harmed in a fight provides a general justification for other kinds of assault, including assault against non-consenting individuals.

Thus, sanctions do not appear to be morally defensible in the ways they were used against Iraq, under the principle of *jus ad bellum*. But of course the issues of proportionality and just cause will vary from situation to situation. It is conceivable within this framework that if the cause were different, if the sanctions were less extreme, and if they were more efficacious, there could well be a situation where it would be permissible to engage in warring acts, including sanctions. However, I would suggest in this case, sanctions are inherently indefensible as a *means* of conducting warfare.

The *jus in bello* principle of discrimination holds that the means used for warfare must not be indiscriminate. The means used "must respect the immunity of the innocent," where "innocent" refers to "those who are no threat." This encompasses (1) women, children, the aged, infirm; (2) clergy, religious, foreigners; (3) unarmed persons going about their ordinary vocations; and (4) soldiers on leave or who have become prisoners. "*Innocent* does not mean that persons are not patriotic, do not morally support the war effort, or do not participate in the wartime economy, but only that they are no threat, are not combatant."[1]

The principle of discrimination in just-war doctrine requires the attacker to distinguish between combatants and non-combatants; between combatants who are injured and those who are uninjured; between combatants who are armed and those who have surrendered and are defenseless; etc.[2] Under just-war doctrine, there is no strict prohibition against killing

---

1. Yoder, *op. cit.*, p. 157. Yoder notes that the clarity of this definition "has recently been compromised, though not logically set aside, by the notion of a quasi-combatant work force." But this is exactly the heart of the issue: if the economy as a whole supports the military or the political leadership – even if it is just by having roads which the military uses, along with everyone else; or even if it is just by feeding the civilian populace, which frees up food for the soldiers – then, the argument goes, the economy itself is fair game.

2. See generally Ian Clark, *Waging War: A Philosophical Introduction* (Oxford: Oxford University Press, 1988), pp. 87–97; James Turner Johnson, *Just War Tradition and the*

civilians, or killing injured or unarmed combatants, when it is required by "military necessity" or as an unavoidable consequence of an attack on a legitimate military target. A common example is that an ammunition factory is a legitimate military target in wartime; if in bombing the factory, civilians who live nearby are also killed, no war crime has been committed. What is prohibited is to target civilians directly, or injured or defenseless combatants; or to bomb indiscriminately, where the deaths of civilians are foreseeable.

As Walzer notes, siege is the oldest form of war waged against both soldiers and civilians. In siege, non-combatants are not only exposed, but in fact are more likely to be killed than combatants, given that the goal of siege "is surrender, not by defeat of the enemy army, but by the fearful spectacle of the civilian dead."[1] Thus, siege warfare has the quality of actually inverting the principle of discrimination. Siege operates by restricting the economy of the entire community, creating shortages of food, water, and fuel. Those who are least able to survive the ensuing hunger, illness, and cold are the very young, the elderly, and those who are sick or injured. Thus the direct consequence of siege is that harm is done to those who are least able to defend themselves, who present the least military threat, who have the least input into policy or military decisions, and who are most vulnerable to hunger, cold, and illness. The harm done by the enemy's deprivation is exacerbated by domestic policy, which typically shifts whatever resources there are to the military and to the political leadership. This is sometimes done for security reasons, in the belief that defending against military attack is the highest priority, and is more immediately urgent than the slower damage of hunger and illness to which the civilian population is subjected. It may also happen because the leadership is corrupt, or because the desperation creates conditions for black marketeering. Both of these consequences – the suffering of the innocent and helpless, and the shifting of resources to the military and to the privileged – are as old as siege itself. In a siege,

> civilians and soldiers are exposed to the same risks. Scarcity and proximity make them equally vulnerable. Or perhaps not equally so: in this kind of war, once combat begins, non-combatants are more likely to be killed. The soldiers fight from protected positions, and the civilians, who don't fight at all, are

---

Restraint of War (Princeton: Princeton University Press, 1981); and Telford Taylor, "War Crimes," in *Nuremberg and Vietnam: An American Tragedy* (New York: Times Books, 1970).

1. Michael Walzer, *Just and Unjust Wars*, 2nd ed. (Glenview, Ill.: Basic Books, 1977).

quickly made over . . . into "useless mouths." Fed last, and only with the army's surplus, they die first.[1]

In addition, although the harm to the civilian population is slower than that done by warfare, it is not necessarily any less severe. Walzer quotes a passage from an account of the Roman siege of Jerusalem:

> The restraint of liberty to pass in and out of the city took from the Jews all hope of safety, and the famine now increasing consumed whole households and families; and the houses were full of dead women and infants; and the streets filed with the dead bodies of old men. And the young men, swollen like dead men's shadows, walked in the market place and fell down dead where it happened. And now the multitude of dead bodies was so great that they that were alive could not bury them, nor cared they for burying them . . . And those who were yet living, without tears beheld those who being dead were now at rest before them. There was no noise heard from within the city.[2]

Thus, the argument can be made that siege has the character of being a form of warfare which itself constitutes a war crime. By its very nature, it is easily foreseeable or calculated to cause *direct* harm to those who are, in just-war doctrine, supposed to be exempt from warfare – the apolitical and the unarmed – in order to influence *indirectly* those who are armed and those who are responsible for military and political decisions. Let us place siege in the context of war crimes and just-war doctrine: in just-war doctrine, we could demand a justification for a military strategy in terms of the obligation to minimize harm to civilians – the ammunition factory was a legitimate target, and there was no way to bomb it without collateral damage to nearby residential areas. But siege is peculiar in that it resists such an analysis – the immediate goal is *precisely* to cause suffering to civilians. In the case of the ammunitions factory, we can answer the question: how is this act consistent with the moral requirement to discriminate? In the case of siege, we cannot.

It may be argued that military necessity sometimes justifies the use of siege warfare, and that in this case, military necessity overrides the principle of discrimination. "Military necessity" is sometimes defined as consisting of acts "which are indispensable for securing the complete submission of the enemy as soon as possible," according to a version of the U.S. Army Field Manual. Alternatively, military necessity is sometimes understood to include, by definition, whatever limitations are required by international

---

1. *Ibid.*, p. 160.

2. *Ibid.*, p. 161, citing *The Works of Josephus*, Tho. Lodge, trans. (London, 1620), *The Wars of the Jews*, Bk. VI, ch. XIV, 721.

law, including humanitarian principles and the principle of discrimination.[1] If military necessity legitimizes *any act of war*, then the principle of discrimination becomes a luxury rather than a limitation of military conduct; it would hold only that one may not target civilians gratuitously. On the other hand, if military necessity is constrained by the principle of discrimination, then one may not target civilians, even where it would be of great value to the war effort. The "unanswered question," however, "is whether the function of laws of war is to protect all militarily necessary acts or to serve as a judge of those militarily necessary acts that should be forbidden," given that "there is a widespread suspicion that there really are no laws of war. After all, the Hague Conventions were prefaced by the formula, 'if military circumstances permit,' and the Conventions of Geneva provided that nations could renounce them."[2]

It is sometimes said that military necessity is the exception that swallows just-war doctrine altogether, since virtually anything can be justified – by the party doing it – as having a military purpose. An argument can be made, at least by the acting party, that there are circumstances in which it would be militarily necessary to demoralize the civilian population by conducting carpet bombing as a method of psychological warfare, or as a means of undermining the entire industrial base and labor force upon which military production depends. If military necessity can legitimate harm directly and intentionally done to civilians, then it is true that siege can invoke this justification; but if so, then the principle of discrimination has been lost altogether. If the principle of discrimination is to have any meaning at all, then directly harming children, the sick, and the elderly, in order to influence indirectly military and political leaders, must be ethically precluded, and this preclusion must not be overridden by a claim of military necessity. The alternative – to hold that military necessity can legitimize direct and intentional harm to civilians – is effectively to take a realist or nihilist position that ethical restraint has no place in war. But while that position would be available to those engaged in warfare, it would seem to be unavailable to those seeking to impose or justify sanctions on such grounds as international law or human rights, since these claims themselves invoke a legal and ethical framework.

---

1. Robert L. Holmes, *On War and Morality* (Princeton: Princeton University Press, 1989), pp. 101–6; William O'Brien, *The Conduct of Just and Limited War* (New York: Praeger, 1981), pp. 64–67; Johnson, *op. cit.*, pp. 86–94.

2. Donald A. Wells, ed., *An Encyclopedia of War and Ethics* (Westport, Conn.: Greenwood, 1996), s.v. "Military Necessity," p. 306.

In certain respects, sanctions are obviously the modern version of siege ⭐ warfare – each involves the systematic deprivation of a whole city or nation of economic resources. Although in siege warfare this is accomplished by surrounding the city with an army, the same effect can be achieved by using international institutions and international pressure to prevent the sale or purchase of goods, and to prevent migration. It is sometimes argued that an embargoed nation can still engage in some marginal trade, despite sanctions; but similarly in a siege there may be marginal ways of getting goods through gaps in the blockade. In both cases, however, the unit under embargo or siege is a mixed population rather than a military installation, or is entirely civilian. In both cases, the net effect is the same, which is the disruption or strangulation of the economy as a whole.[1]

Christiansen and Powers argue that the just-war doctrine, which holds that civilians and non-combatants should be immune from direct attack, does not apply to peacetime sanctions in the same way that this doctrine applies to sieges and blockades imposed as part of a war effort.[2] Scholars in the just-war tradition, they note, "often treat economic sanctions as analogous with acts of war . . . along with blockades and sieges."[3] However, Christiansen and Powers argue that sanctions without war have a different moral status, for three reasons: first, unlike wartime blockades, economic sanctions are not imposed as a form of war, but as an alternative to warfare; second, some kinds of harms may in fact be justified, either because the population has consented to the state's policies or because it shares responsibility for them in some fashion; and third, with appropriate humanitarian measures built in, the harm inflicted by sanctions is not as extreme as the harm done by war.[4] The fundamental difference, they hold,

---

1. This article does not address the implications of "smart sanctions," which are those that affect only the military and political leadership, such as the seizure of foreign bank accounts of individual leaders. Obviously such sanctions do not raise any of the same ethical issues. However, the fact that it may be possible to target sanctions in this way does not in any way resolve the ethical problems raised by sanctions which are not "smart," and do affect an economy as a whole.

2. Drew Christiansen, S.J., and Gerard F. Powers, "Economic Sanctions and Just-War Doctrine," in Lopez and Cortright, *op. cit.*, p. 102.

3. *Ibid.*, p. 101.

4. *Ibid.*, p. 103. Interestingly, John C. Scharfen, a military theorist, takes the opposite view in *The Dismal Battlefield: Mobilizing for Economic Conflict* (Annapolis: Naval Institute Press, 1995): "Economic force produces casualties," he says bluntly. "The collateral damage is almost always indiscriminate" (p. 4). There may be political reasons to use different terms, but, he suggests, that is just a matter of rhetoric. "*Economic war* implies aggression on the part of those who employ the economic weapon. It is a term favored by the target of that force and those moralists who would class the use of the

is that the use of economic sanctions is rooted in the intention to avoid the use of armed force, as opposed to the intent to multiply the effects of war; and that as a lower-level exercise of coercion, it raises the threshold for the use of actual force, thereby lowering the likelihood of actual warfare.[1]

To some extent, their reasons reiterate the same arguments made by others – that sanctions are less harsh than warfare; that the population consented to, or for other reasons can properly be held responsible for, the acts of the leadership; that structuring in humanitarian exceptions will prevent sanctions from causing death or great suffering. I have addressed these issues elsewhere.[2] Here I want to look at Christiansen and Powers to draw a distinction between sanctions-as-war and sanctions-without-war. The distinction does not resolve the underlying question: are sanctions a device that keeps the peace and enforces international law, or are they intrinsically a form of violence, which in fact violates the laws of warfare? Woodrow Wilson, in urging the adoption of sanctions as a method by which the League of Nations would keep the world free of war, described them as a "peaceful, silent, deadly remedy." And indeed, before the Iraq situation showed us how extensive and extreme the human damage from sanctions can be, economic sanctions were most commonly portrayed in the U.S. as a kind of stern but peaceful act – a punishment which inconveniences or embarrasses, but does no damage of the sort that raises moral issues. In fact, it was the peace activists who, in 1990, were in the forefront arguing that sanctions be used in the case of Iraq rather than military undertakings.

Like many other commentators, Christiansen and Powers are partly basing their claim on two sets of empirical assumptions regarding the speed and degree of damage done by sanctions: "Whereas war's impact is speedy and frequently lethal, the impact of sanctions grows over time and allows more easily for mitigation of these harmful effects and for a negotiated solution than acts of war."[3] Christiansen and Powers suggest that the way to conceptualize sanctions is that warfare is akin to the death penalty, whereas sanctions are more like attaching someone's assets in a civil proceeding.[4] In this analogy, the economic domain is seen as fully separate,

---

economic instrument as unscrupulous. *Economic sanctions* is a milder term and one favored by those employing the instrument" (p. 8).

1. Christiansen and Powers, *op. cit.*, p. 103.

2. "Peaceful, Silent, Deadly Remedy: The Ethics of Economic Sanctions," *Ethics and International Affairs*, Vol. 13, 1999.

3. Christiansen and Powers, *op. cit.*, p. 107.

4. *Ibid.*

and of a different nature altogether, than the domain of power and of violence. But economic harm, while it is not directly physical, can also be a form of violence. The sanctions-as-mere-seizure-of-assets theory, whether on the level of the individual or an entire economy, implicitly assumes a starting point of relative abundance. Whether the seizure of someone's assets is inconvenient or devastating depends entirely on what their assets are, and how much is left after the seizure. For an upper-middle-class person with, say, $50,000 in stocks and an annual income of $80,000, seizing $1000 from a checking account would at most cause inconvenience, annoyance, perhaps some slight reduction in luxuries or indulgences. For someone living at poverty level, seizing $1000 may mean that a family has lost irreplaceably the ability to pay for fuel oil for a winter's heating season, or lost their car in a rural area with no other transportation, or lost the security deposit and first month's rent on an apartment that would have given them a way out of a homeless shelter. Living in a home with a temperature of 40 degrees in the winter does not kill quickly, in the way that a bullet does, and may not kill at all. It may only make someone sick, or over some time, worsen an illness until death occurs. Living in a shelter or on the street for a night or for a week or for a month doesn't kill in the way that a bullet does, but it exposes someone to a risk of considerable random violence, including killings. To conceptualize economic deprivation in terms of mild punishment whose effects are reversible with no permanent damage – inconvenience, embarrassment, living on a budget – is to misunderstand the nature of the economic. "Economic deprivation" is not a uniform phenomenon; the loss of conveniences constitutes a different experience than the loss of the means to meet basic needs. There is a reason that infant mortality rates and life expectancy rates are used as measures of economic development: poverty manifests itself in malnutrition, sickness, exposure to the elements, exhaustion, dirty drinking water, the lack of means to leave a violent country or neighborhood – the shortening of one's life. It is for this reason that liberation theologians and others have argued that poverty is indeed a form of violence, although it doesn't kill in the way that a bullet does.

Christiansen and Powers argue that sanctions differ from siege partly on the grounds that the intent of sanctions is to prevent violence rather than exacerbate it. Under the doctrine of double effect, however, this does not seem to hold. The doctrine of double effect provides that

> the foreseen evil effect of a man's action is not morally imputable to him, provided that (1) the action in itself is directed immediately to some other result,

(2) the evil effect is not willed either in itself or as a means to the other result, (3) the permitting of the evil effect is justified by reasons of proportionate weight.[1]

Although the doctrine of double effect would seem to justify "collateral damage," it does not offer a justification of sanctions. "Collateral damage" entails the unintended secondary harm to civilians. If a bombing raid is conducted against a military base, the collateral damage would be that the schoolhouse half a mile away was destroyed by a bomb that missed its intended target, which was the military base. In that case, the bombing raid would be equally successful if the base were hit, and the schoolhouse were undamaged. But the damage done by indirect sanctions is not in fact "collateral," in that the damage to the civilian population is necessary and instrumental. The *direct* damage to the economy is intended to influence the leadership *indirectly*, by triggering political pressure or uprisings of the civilians, or by generating moral guilt from the "fearful spectacle of the civilian dead." Sanctions directed against an economy would in fact be considered unsuccessful if no disruption of the economy took place. We often hear commentators objecting that "sanctions didn't work" in one situation or another because they weren't "tight" enough – they did not succeed in disrupting the economy. Thus, sanctions are not defensible under the doctrine of double effect. Although the end may indeed be legitimate, the intended intermediate means consists of the generalized damage to the economy, which violates both the first and second requirements of the doctrine. But there is a second reason why good intent can not avail as a justification for sanctions: the intent cannot in good faith be reconciled with the history and the logic of sanctions, and with the likely outcome. We know from the history of siege warfare that, legitimately or not, in the face of economic strangulation, the military and political leadership will insulate themselves from its consequences, and place a disproportionate burden on the civilian population. We also know from history that economic strangulation will consolidate the state's power rather than undermine it; we know that sanctions are, for the most part, unlikely to prevent military aggression, or stop human rights violations, or achieve compliance with *any* political or military demand, even when sanctions drag on for decades. It is hard to reconcile the claimed "good intent" of sanctions with a history that makes it easy to foresee that those intentions are not likely to be realized. Thus,

---

1. John C. Ford, S.J., "The Morality of Obliteration Bombing," in Richard A. Wasserstrom, ed., *War and Morality* (Belmont, Calif.: Wadsworth, 1970), p. 26.

I would suggest that while sanctions may have very different goals from siege warfare – including goals such as international governance – they are nevertheless subject to many of the same moral objections: that they intentionally, or at least predictably, harm the most vulnerable and the least political; and that this is something which the party imposing sanctions either knows, or should know. To the extent that economic sanctions seek to undermine the economy of a society, and thereby prevent the production or importation of necessities, they are functioning as the modern equivalent of siege. To the extent that sanctions deprive the most vulnerable and least political sectors of society of the food, potable water, medical care, and fuel necessary for survival and basic human needs, sanctions should be subject to the same moral objections as siege warfare.

I do not deny that the contexts in which sanctions and sieges occur may be different, the intent of each may differ, the nature of the demands may be different, and the options of the besieged or sanctioned states may be different. But the moral objection to sanctions does not rest on the analogy; sanctions do not have to be identical to siege warfare in order to be subject to condemnation under just-war principles. Indeed, if the intent of sanctions is peaceful rather than belligerent, then the usual justifications in warfare are unavailable. I am morally permitted to kill where my survival is at stake; and in war, I am morally permitted to kill even innocents, in some circumstances. But if one's goal is to see that international law is enforced or that human rights are respected, then the stakes and the justificatory context are quite different. It is hard to make sense of the claim that "collateral damage" can be justified in the name of protecting human rights; or that international law might be enforced by means that stand in violation of international laws, including the just-war principle of discrimination. Thus, if sanctions are analogous to siege warfare, then they are problematic for the same reasons – both effectively violate the principle of discrimination. But if sanctions are not analogous to siege, then sanctions are even more problematic. *If the goals of sanctions are the enforcement of humanitarian standards or compliance with legal and ethical norms, then extensive and predictable harm to civilians cannot even be justified by reference to survival or military advantage.* Insofar as this is the case, sanctions are simply a device of cruelty garbed in self-righteousness.

To the extent that we see sanctions as a means of peacekeeping and international governance, sanctions effectively escape ethical analysis – we do not judge them by the same standards we judge other kinds of harm done to innocents. Yet, concretely, the hunger, sickness, and poverty, which are ostensibly inflicted for benign purposes, affect individuals no differently than hunger, sickness, and poverty inflicted out of malevolence. To describe sanctions as a means of "peacekeeping" or "enforcing human rights" is an ideological move, which, from the perspective of concrete personal experiences, is simply counterfactual. Sanctions are, at bottom, a bureaucratized, internationally organized form of siege warfare, and should be seen, and judged, as such.

III. A Weapon of Mass Distraction

Congressman Ralph Hall opened a set of Congressional hearings on July 8, 2004, with a dramatic flourish, denouncing "the deaths of thousands of Iraqis through malnutrition and lack of appropriate medical supplies." The Texas Republican told a subcommittee of the House Energy and Commerce Committee: "We have a name for that in the United States. It's called murder."

But the target of Hall's accusation were not the sanctions that had helped to double the rate of mortality among children under five in central and southern Iraq over the preceding decade. Rather, the Congressman was introducing yet more hearings simply to air allegations of incompetence, manipulation, and personal corruption in the so-called "Oil-for-Food" Program established by the UN Security Council in 1995 to ameliorate the humanitarian emergency in Iraq. According to these allegations, UN mismanagement allowed Saddam Hussein to pocket billions of dollars in oil sales at the expense of the Iraqi people.

The present criticism is based mainly on an April 2004 report by the General Accounting Office (GAO) – now the Government Accountability Office – as well as upon a list published in January 2004 by the Iraqi newspaper *Al-Mada*, which claims to identify those who received vouchers to buy oil from Iraq. The heart of the GAO's accusation is that "from 1997 through 2002 . . . the former Iraqi regime acquired $10.1 billion in illegal revenues related to the 'Oil-for-Food' Program." The CIA's October 2004 Duelfer Report provided a more detailed version of the accusations.

Given the elaborate safeguards built into the "Oil-for-Food" Program, UN critics argue, how could such theft have occurred without complicity? The alleged "loss" of billions of dollars and countless Iraqi lives is laid at the feet of the United Nations, when it is not blamed on Saddam Hussein himself. For example, Benon Sevan, former head of the Office of Iraq Program, which housed the now dissolved "Oil-for-Food" Program, has been named as one UN official who purportedly took what amount to bribes to look the other way.

No fewer than nine different investigations into these claims have been launched: three in the House of Representatives, one in the Senate, one each at the Treasury Department and U.S. Customs Service, one in New York courts and one by the U.S.-appointed Iraqi Board of Supreme Audit, as well as an internal UN investigation headed by Paul Volcker, former head of the Federal Reserve Bank. One House inquiry has issued a subpoena for relevant records from the Paris-based bank, BNP Paribas, where the UN kept the "Oil-for-Food" funds on deposit; Exxon-Mobil has also received a subpoena from a U.S. attorney's office in New York.

This raft of investigations has been accompanied by a loud campaign of Bush-administration supporters eager to take note of a dramatic new "scandal" involving Iraq. William Safire called the "scandal" the "richest rip-off in world history," though the well-known Enron scandal involving Kenneth Lay, a long-time friend of President Bush, resulted in similar losses, including billions of dollars of employee pension funds. Claudia Rosett, one of the most vitriolic critics, wrote in the April 28, 2004, *Wall Street Journal,* "It's looking more and more as if one of the best reasons to get rid of Saddam Hussein was that it was probably the only way to get rid of 'Oil-for-Food.'" While mostly neoconservative columnists have worked to discredit the "Oil-for-Food" Program in the public mind, even the *New York Times* got into the act, with "How Hussein Stole Billions Under the Eye of the United Nations' 'Oil-For-Food' Program" as a recent headline.

At the July 2004 Congressional hearings chaired by Congressman Hall, Jed Babbin, a former Defense Department official and author of a UN-bashing tract, *Inside the Asylum,* ludicrously described the UN as "the handmaiden of terrorism, the errand boy of despots and dictators, and a quagmire that is the antithesis of our policy to pre-empt terrorist attacks." The congressman spoke of "the trail of corruption unfolding on the world stage."

Perhaps not coincidentally, the unfolding investigations into "Oil-for-Food" came at a time when the terms of the UN's future involvement in Iraq were unclear. Security Council Resolution 1483, passed in May 2003 under enormous pressure from the U.S., removed all UN monitors from Iraq, eliminated the 661 Committee, suspended the role of UNMOVIC, the UN disarmament agency, and eliminated any UN oversight of oil sales or disposition of oil proceeds. The resolution also endorsed the "Occupying Authority" of the U.S. and Britain in Iraq. One year later, the Bush administration again induced the Security Council to approve a mandate for a U.S.-dominated "multinational force" and left the UN role in Iraq's troubled political transition undefined. Despite its substantial experience in reconstruction, development and the supervision of free elections, the UN's ability to negotiate a larger role was arguably compromised by the sensational accusations involving the "Oil-for-Food" Program. How seriously should they be taken?

Humanitarian Emergency

"Oil-for-Food," though never more than a stopgap measure, saved Iraqi civilians from privations even worse than those they actually suffered. The economic sanctions imposed by the Security Council following the first Gulf War in 1990, combined with the massive destruction of infrastructure during that war and the consequent refugee flight afterwards, had resulted in a huge humanitarian crisis by the summer of 1991. A UN team found a threefold increase in under-five mortality over the first eight months of that year. Iraq rejected the terms of the Security Council's initial proposal to permit very limited oil sales, and, over the next four years, the nearly comprehensive sanctions helped to cause increases in malnutrition and waterborne diseases. In 1995, the Security Council authorized a new proposal allowing Iraq to sell larger amounts of oil and then use the proceeds to buy food, medicine and other humanitarian goods.

Several different UN agencies provided expertise, service delivery and monitoring once the "Oil-for-Food" was finally implemented in March 1997. These included UNICEF, the World Health Organization, the World Food Program, the Food and Agriculture Organization and the UN Development Program. When the program was formally terminated in November 2003, $31 billion of humanitarian aid had been delivered – primarily food and medicine – but also some items for water and sewage treatment, electricity production, transportation and agriculture. Within the repressive strictures of the sanctions regime, the "Oil-for-Food" Program accomplished a great deal, according to statistics kept by these agencies and independent observers. Between 1997 and 2002, the nutritional value of the food basket distributed monthly by the program almost doubled, from 1,200 calories per person per day to about 2,200. The incidence of communicable diseases, including cholera and malaria, was cut down substantially. Electricity became more reliable, as did the availability of potable water. Despite these improvement, however, sanctions continued to take a terrible toll.[1]

---

1. Von Sponeck pointed out, in his presentation referenced previously, how ultimately

In the late 1990s and the early days of the current Bush administration, most of the debate over "Oil-for-Food" focused on its limitations as a remedy for Iraq's humanitarian crisis. Today's spotlight on alleged corruption in the program, in addition to being tinged with reflexive neoconservative hostility to the UN, reveals the collective amnesia about the effects of the economic sanctions that made "Oil-for-Food" necessary in the first place. During the congressional hearings, Hall noted the "fraud and deception that probably resulted in the deaths of thousands of Iraqis through malnutrition." But regardless of whether or not "Oil-for-Food" funds may have improperly ended up in the hands of Saddam Hussein's government, the fundamental responsibility for the humanitarian crisis was the sanctions regime imposed on Iraq by the Security Council, and then enforced in an extraordinarily harsh way at the insistence of the U.S. and Britain.[1]

Smuggling

It is important to separate out accusations implicating the UN agencies, as distinct from individuals working at the UN, or the policies of member nations. The GAO report estimated that Iraq received $5.7 billion in proceeds from oil smuggling between 1997 and 2002. Critics like Safire and Rosett charge the UN with incompetence, if not complicity, in this "illicit" trade that bypassed the "Oil-for-Food" mechanism.

---

inadequate "Oil-for-Food" was as a long-term solution. "In phases one to three [of the program], the net amount available for survival was $1.3 billion; for phases four to six this increased to $2.9 billion; and in phases seven to nine to $4.2 billion. What is consistently overlooked is that these amounts translate into $113, $252 and $408 respectively per person per annum. No one can defend such funding as adequate, given the knowledge of the human conditions in Iraq . . . " (Von Sponeck, *loc. cit.*).

1. An example of the accusations leveled against the government of Iraq is the assertion that it failed to distribute humanitarian supplies obtained under "Oil-for-Food." Former U.K. Defense Secretary George Robertson, for instance, said in January 1999 that Saddam Hussein "has in warehouses $275 million-worth of medicines and medical supplies which he refuses to distribute," and he asked rhetorically, "'what kind of leader watches his children die and his hospitals operate without drugs, but keeps $275 million-worth of medicines and medical supplies locked up in a warehouse?" Von Sponeck (*ibid*) provides a counter to this assertion: " . . . it was shown in a stock analysis published by the United Nations in February 2000 that 91.7 percent of all humanitarian supplies had been distributed to end users since the inception of the program. This is a figure the U.S. government simply ignores. Instead there is the continued accusation of hoarding by the Iraqi regime, a completely incorrect assertion. . . . [while] it would be wrong to defend at all costs the total accuracy of data collected by the United Nations. . . . [w]hat can be said with confidence . . . is that the trends identified with UN statistics are correct and allow the conclusion that the distribution picture, including for medicines, is satisfactory. Contrary to U.S./U.K. statements, the United Nations has no evidence of willful withholding of any humanitarian supplies."

Yet it is somewhat misleading to portray smuggling as a failure on the part of the UN. In 1990, Security Council Resolution 665 invited member states to interdict suspected smuggling with their own military forces, leading to the establishment of the Multinational Interception Force patrolling the Persian Gulf. The U.S. Navy provided most of the ships for the force, which had operated under the command of a series of American rear and vice admirals from the Fifth Fleet based in Bahrain. Yet in May 1991, under the first Bush Administration, as Iraq's neighbors began to complain about the effects of the sanctions on their countries, the United States quietly decided to grant an informal "exemption" to Jordan, permitting it to import Iraqi oil in clear violation of the sanctions. This arrangement continued for the next decade, with the blessing of three U.S. administrations. According to the Duelfer report, Iraq's income from these arrangements with Jordan totaled some $4.4 billion. Turkey, like Jordan, also complained that the sanctions were harming its economy. And Turkey, like Jordan, was a crucial ally the United States needed to appease. The result was a decision by the United States "to close our eyes to leakage via Turkey," according to former Assistant Secretary of State Robert Pelletreau. By 1997 the volume of oil being smuggled from Iraq to Turkey had grown to 1,000 trucks per day, transporting millions of tons of oil per year, all while U.S. planes enforcing no-fly zones flew overhead. Iraq's illicit income from Turkey, according to the Duelfer report, came to $710 million.

Kickbacks

The GAO report estimated that Iraq received $4.4 billion in "illicit" income from kickbacks on import contracts and on oil surcharges. According to interviews with Iraqi ministry officials cited in the report, it was the practice of the Iraqi government to inflate by 5 to 10 percent the price it would pay for humanitarian imports channeled through "Oil-for-Food." The vendor would then, it was claimed, return the surplus to the Iraqis under the table.

It would have been difficult for UN officials to detect and stop these kickbacks. As the Deputy Director of the Defense Contract Audit Agency testified before Congress on April 21, his agency had found that of several hundred contracts reviewed, 48 percent were "potentially overpriced" by at least 5 percent, based on market prices. "Oil-for-Food" contracts were not signed under normal market conditions, and a 5 percent price difference is not outside even the normal variations of commerce. Many con-

tracts were for specially designed items, such as parts for sewage treatment plants, for which there was no "market price." In addition, there were
extraordinary transaction costs: to be able to sell Iraq goods under the
"Oil-for-Food" Program, a vendor had to go through an elaborate application procedure, provide detailed documentation and often answer additional questions about component parts and chemical makeup. The process sometimes dragged on for years. It would be surprising if, under these
circumstances, vendors always sold their goods at the "normal" rates given
the extra amount of time and expense that they were put to in simply selling their wares.

On more than 70 occasions when there were obvious price discrepancies, the Office of the Iraq Program did bring them to the attention of the
so-called 661 Committee – composed of all 15 Security Council members – which reviewed all proposed "Oil-for-Food" contracts. In testimony
submitted to Congress on April 28, John Ruggie, the assistant secretary
general charged with relations with the U.S. mission, recalled that the
committee "approved roughly 36,000 contracts over the life span of the
program. Every member had the right to hold up contracts if they detect-
ed irregularities, and the U.S. and Britain were by far the most vigilant
among them. Yet, as best as I can determine, of those 36,000 contracts not
one – not a single solitary one – was ever held up by any member on the
grounds of pricing."

The U.S. delegation alone had 60 people examining contracts, and, over
the course of the program, this delegation blocked thousands of contracts
worth billions of dollars. Yet, in placing contracts on hold, the U.S. and
Britain were almost exclusively concerned with preventing potential "dual-
use" goods – items that theoretically could have military uses – from entering Iraq. From time to time, according to sources who served on the
661 Committee staff, Americans on the staff did claim to have espied kickbacks, but simply offered no *evidence* of such.

Surcharges

In late 2000, Iraq began a practice of selling oil at low prices, often to
middlemen, who would then resell the oil at higher prices and pay Iraq a
surcharge under the table. The "oil overseers" – oil industry consultants
working for the "Oil-for-Food" Program – brought this practice to the attention of the Security Council. The U.S. and Britain responded in 2001 by
implementing a "retroactive oil pricing policy." Normal commercial practice

is to set the sale price for some period of time, such as a month. Under "Oil-for-Food," the oil overseers submitted a proposed price, the 661 Committee then approved it and oil was then sold for the following month at that price. As the 661 Committee operated by consensus, every member could effectively exercise a veto over any measure. Making "creative use of the consensus rule," in the words of Ambassador Patrick Kennedy, a U.S. official familiar with the 661 Committee, the U.S. and Britain simply withheld their approval of contracts until the sales period had passed. The 661 Committee then decided what the market value would have been the *previous* month – a determination that can be somewhat arbitrary – and required the buyer to pay that amount. Thereafter, buyers had to sign a contract to purchase oil literally without knowing the price until well afterwards.

Few buyers would commit to purchases under these conditions, and the oil overseers warned the committee that Iraqi oil sales were likely to collapse. In fact, Iraqi petroleum exports dropped from an average of 1.7 million barrels per day in 2001 to less than one quarter of that amount in September 2002. Meanwhile, Iraq had ended its surcharges – oil prices were raised and the profit margin was simply too low for surcharges to be possible. Still, the U.S. and Britain would *not* suspend the retroactive pricing gambit, with which they continued until the U.S.-led coalition invaded Iraq in March 2003.

The result was that the "Oil-for-Food" Program was, in substantial measure, bankrupted. Speaking before Congress on April 21, 2004, Kennedy bragged that, through retroactive pricing, "we were able to save the people of Iraq significant sums of money in illegal oil charges," yet the policy also, more importantly, prevented the program from raising billions of dollars in revenue for critical humanitarian goods. In February 2002, Benon Sevan announced that revenues had dropped so drastically that $1.6 billion of approved contracts could not be funded. If the contracts then on hold – largely at the behest of the Bush and Blair governments – had been approved, the shortfall would have totaled $6.9 billion. While the former Iraqi regime may well have reaped ill-gotten gains from the surcharges, that practice had far less impact on the Iraqi population than the punishing response of the U.S. and Britain, which substantially undermined the entire humanitarian program. The "Oil-for-Food" Program, the lifeline for the entire Iraqi population, was badly compromised – not because Saddam Hussein had skimmed 5 percent or 10 percent but because the United States and Britain had adopted a punitive measure so extreme that it nearly bankrupted the entire program.

Profiteering

In January 2004, the Iraqi newspaper *al-Mada* published a list of individuals and companies from around the world that supposedly received certificates from the government of Iraq that entitled them to buy a certain amount of oil from Iraq. It is rumored that the list was provided to *al-Mada* by Ahmed Chalabi, the former member of the Iraqi Governing Council in disrepute for providing the U.S. with false information about weapons of mass destruction in pre-war Iraq. Thus far no documentation of the list's authenticity is in evidence.

While Saddam Hussein's regime may have found ways to capture funds that were meant to serve the Iraqi population, abuse of oil monies seems to be occurring on a similar – and perhaps even greater – scale in U.S.-occupied Iraq. For example, Halliburton, under its contract with the U.S. Army Corps of Engineers, provided fuel to the military at $1.59 per gallon, while the Iraqi national oil company could buy the fuel at 98 cents per gallon. The difference came to $300 million, and the profits were funneled into the coffers of an American corporation, rather than pumped into the Iraqi economy. In October 2003, a leading British aid agency, Christian Aid, released a study showing that of the $5 billion in Iraqi oil money transferred to the Coalition Provisional Authority, the CPA could only account for $1 billion. The accounts were still incomplete upon the CPA's dissolution, according to Christian Aid. On July 15, 2004, the International Accounting and Monitoring Board, created by the Security Council to watch over the CPA's stewardship of Iraqi oil funds, found that controls over the funds from November 2002 to May 2003 had been inadequate. The CPA, for instance, was unable to certify that crude had not been smuggled out of Iraq. Another independent NGO, the Iraq Revenue Watch project of the Open Society Institute, reported that in the weeks before the June 28, 2004, handover of "sovereignty," the CPA rushed to commit nearly $2 billion in Iraqi funds with no planning and questionable justification. In many cases, billions of dollars of U.S. funds had already been committed in the same areas. Perhaps not surprisingly a January 2005 report from a special Iraq reconstruction inspector general revealed the general inability of the U.S. to keep track of almost $9 billion in reconstruction funds transferred to Iraqi ministries, citing the lack of any way to verify that the money allocated was used for its intended purposes.[1]

---

1. In terms of corruption, the post-CPA Iraqi economy under continued U.S. occupation is no model either. An April 2005 article appearing in the *Chicago Tribune* cited "bur-

Putting Things in Perspective

Critics are at great pains to portray the trade Iraq conducted with these nations as "illicit." However, the entire sanctions regime, given its devastating humanitarian effect, has been persuasively criticized as contrary to international law (see jurist Marc Bossuyt's comprehensive, June 2000 report, commissioned by the Sub-Commission on the Promotion and Protection of Human Rights of the UN's Economic and Social Council, which calls the sanctions "unequivocally illegal under existing international humanitarian law and human rights law"). The very purpose of the sanctions is also subject to legal criticism, insofar they were intended not to enforce compliance with certain resolutions but rather to change the recognized government of Iraq.[1] Certainly the Iraqi government under Hussein could have understood the sanctions in this way, and it would have been justified in doing so. On many times American officials expressed a reluctance to ever remove sanctions; the March 26, 1997, statement of then-Secretary of State Madeleine Albright is simply one example: "We do not agree with those nations who argue that if Iraq complies with its obligations concerning weapons of mass destruction, sanctions should be lifted."[2] Indeed, as

geoning corruption" as one of the biggest problems. "Corruption is siphoning as much as 95 cents from every contract dollar, according to people already working there," it said. Corruption allegations abound, according to the report: "Officials in the Trade Ministry, which is responsible for distributing food in Iraq, are accused of getting involved with highway bandits who pilfer food shipments. There are fresh allegations that some officials in the outgoing Interim Government are feathering luxury nests abroad in preparation for forced early retirement.... In just the past two months, Iraqi press reports have claimed that corruption taints the judiciary, the Baghdad government, the police, several regional governments and the Federal Ministries of Oil, Health, Construction and Housing, Defense and Electricity."

A London-born Iraqi businessman alleged that "graft accounts for anywhere from 80 percent to 95 percent of Iraqi-controlled contracts." His figures were confirmed by several other Iraqi businessmen (Cam Simpson, "Graft, Fear Bind Iraqis Trying to Do Business," *Chicago Tribune*, April 10, 2005, online).—Ed.

1. A politics professor from the University of Bristol in the U.K. pointed out that " ... U.S. policy can be construed as being in violation of the very UN resolutions with which Iraq is being expected to comply because SCR 687 affirms explicitly the 'sovereignty, territorial integrity and political independence' of Iraq." (Eric Herring, "Between Iraq and a Hard Place," *Review of International Studies*, vol. 28, no. 1 (January 2002), pp.39ff). He also notes that "Iraqi suspicions about British intentions must [have been] fuelled even further by the firing of over 1,000 British and U.S. missiles at Iraqi targets since their Operation Desert Fox attacks on Iraq in December 1998.... the no-fly-zones [had] not received UN authorization, and many believe[d] that Britain and the United States [provoked] the incidents in order to chip away at Iraq's conventional forces."

2. Other statements compiled by the Institute for Public Accuracy include:

May 20, 1991. James Baker, Secretary of State: "We are not interested in seeing a relax-

Hans von Sponeck put it, "the refusal by the Security Council to recognize progressive compliance and reward such compliance with concurrent incremental easing of sanctions" was "a fundamental mistake of historic proportions."[1]

* * *

It may prove to be the case that particular individuals in the UN did receive payoffs from Iraq in the form of oil vouchers, but fraudulent acts by individuals – in direct violation of their employer's policies – are not the same thing as institutional failure; the UN barred employees from engaging in financial transactions with Iraq. And Saddam Hussein *may* have ended up with more money in his pockets than he should have had. But little of the blame can credibly be laid at the feet of "the UN bureaucracy."

Far more of the fault lies with policies and decisions of the Security Council in which the United States played a central role. It is particularly ironic to hear the United States speak of the UN as a global center of corruption and incompetence. We might want to remember one occasion in particular when the UN exercised its responsibility for careful oversight. It was January of 2003, when Colin Powell insisted that Iraq was rife with

---

ation of sanctions as long as Saddam Hussein is in power."

January 14, 1993. President Clinton: "There is no difference between my policy and the policy of the present Administration. . . . I have no intention of normalizing relations with him."

March 26, 1997. Secretary of State Madeline Albright: "We do not agree with the nations who argue that if Iraq complies with its obligations concerning weapons of mass destruction, sanctions should be lifted. Our view, which is unshakable, is that Iraq must prove its peaceful intentions. . . . And the evidence is overwhelming that Saddam Hussein's intentions will never be peaceful."

November 14, 1997. Clinton: [When Iraq broke the inspections regime] "What he has just done is to ensure that the sanctions will be there until the end of time or as long as he lasts."

November 14, 1997. National Security Adviser Sandy Berger: "[Saddam Hussein] can't be in compliance if he's thrown the UNSCOM people out. So it's a necessary condition. It may not be a sufficient condition."

December 16, 1997. Clinton: "I think that he felt probably that the United States would never vote to lift the sanctions on him no matter what he did."

August 20, 1997. Ambassador Bill Richardson: "Sanctions may stay on in perpetuity."

September 15, 1998. Assistant Secretary of State Martin Indyk: " . . . the Security Council resolutions provide in very specific terms for the lifting of sanctions when Iraq has fully complied with all the Security Council resolutions. And that is the crux of the matter; it's not a question that they'll never be lifted, but the conditions on which they'll be lifted will never appear to be fulfilled."

See *The Institute for Public Accuracy,* "Autopsy of a Disaster: The U.S. Sanctions Policy on Iraq," December 13, 1998, online (http://www.accuracy.org/article.php?articleId=1028).

1. Von Sponeck, *loc. cit.*

weapons of mass destruction ready to be unleashed against Iraq's neighbors, and against the United States. The Security Council would not authorize an invasion of Iraq. The members of the Council wanted *evidence*, not speculation; and there wasn't any, because there weren't any weapons of mass destruction. Perhaps it is unsurprising that today the only role it seems the United States expects the UN to play in the continuing drama of Iraq is that of scapegoat.

More to the point, the "Oil-for-Food" flap fits into the decade-old pattern whereby Washington and London place exclusive blame for the humanitarian crisis in Iraq before the invasion – and now for the country's hobbled economy as well – upon the "neglect" of the former regime. Under the sanctions, Iraq's annual gross domestic product dropped from about $60 billion to about $13 billion, according to a joint Food and Agriculture Organization and World Food Program estimate released in 1997. Let's assume that *all* the accusations of corruption are true, and the government of Saddam Hussein did indeed salt away $11 billion over the six years in which the "Oil-for-Food" Program was in operation. Even if those funds had purchased humanitarian goods, the Iraqi GDP would have risen to only $15 billion annually – not an amount that could have compensated for the loss of 75 percent of the economy or rebuilt the dilapidated infrastructure.

It is for this reason that British MP, George Galloway, in his May 17, 2005, appearance before the Senate Investigations Subcommittee (of the Homeland Security and Governmental Affairs Committee), told Senator Norm Coleman that he opposed the "Oil-for-Food" Program with "all his heart."

> Not for the reasons that you are troubled by, but because it was a program which saw the death – I'm talking about the death now; I'm talking about a mass grave – of a million people, most of them children, in Iraq. The "Oil-for-Food" Program gave 30 cents per day per Iraqi for the period of the "Oil-for-Food" Program – 30 cents for all food, all medicine, all clothes, all schools, all hospitals, all public services. I believe that the United Nations had no right to starve Iraq's people because it had fallen out with Iraq's dictator.
>
> David Bonior, your former colleague, Senator, whom I admired very much – a former chief whip here on the Hill – described the sanctions policy as "infanticide masquerading as politics." Senator Coleman thinks that's funny, but I think it's the most profound description of that era that I have ever read – infanticide masquerading as politics.
>
> So I opposed this program with all my heart. Not because Saddam was getting kickbacks from it – and I don't know when it's alleged these kickbacks

started. Not because some individuals were getting rich doing business with Iraq under it. But because it was a murderous policy of killing huge numbers of Iraqis. That's what troubles me.

History may yet record the sanctions regime iteslf, imposed by the Security Council and shaped at every juncture by the U.S. and Britain, as the *real* "Oil-for-Food" scandal.

THE EDITORS' GLOSS: Adding further reason for sincere and open-minded Catholics to question the legitimacy of the war in Iraq is the clear and public evidence impugning the *motives* (or "right intention," in just-war language) of the architects of the war. It was no secret that those making the most noise in favor of war possessed an ideological and fanatical obsession with "transforming" the Middle East by reforming (read: overthrowing, via unprovoked military aggression) Iraq's government and social order. Pat Buchanan's article, slightly adapted from its original form as published in *The American Conservative* on March 24, 2003, illustrates that obsession, and impugns the rectitude of the intention of those pushing for war in Iraq in the period leading up to the invasion of March 2003.

Maybe the neoconservatives who Buchanan critiques really believed in the "justice" of their cause. But no document of international law, moral theology, or Catholic dogma supports the idea that a nation can go to war in order to transform a nation's or a region's politics. The inadequacy of the neocons' cause is reminiscent of the vagueness that well-known Catholic philosopher Elizabeth Anscombe condemned in the cause of the British government as it considered making war on Germany during World War II: " . . . it is a condition of a just war that it should be fought with a just intention; not that it should not be fought with an unjust intention. If the government's intentions cannot be known to be unjust because they are vague, that vagueness itself vitiates them." Contributing even more to the sense that she just as easily could have been writing of the neocons' "war on terror," she said, furthermore: " . . . the truth is that the government's professed intentions are not merely vague, but unlimited. They have not said: 'When justice is done on points A, B and C, then we will stop fighting.' They have talked about 'sweeping away everything that Hitlerism [read: Ba'athism] stands for' and about 'building a new order in Europe' [read: spreading "freedom"]. What does this mean but that our intentions are so unlimited that there is no point at which we . . . could say to our government: 'Stop fighting; for your conditions are satisfied.'"

What is important, then, for Catholics and all men and women of good will to realize, from Anscombe's critique, by analogy, and from Buchanan's article, is that the cause espoused by the Bush administration and its supporting cast of ideologues is not a cause that did – nor could it ever, under any circumstances – justify war.

CHAPTER
2

Whose War?

• • • • • • • • •

Patrick J. Buchanan

THE WAR PARTY may have gotten its war. But it has also gotten something it did not bargain for. Its membership lists and associations have been exposed and its motives challenged. In a rare moment in U.S. journalism, Tim Russert put this question directly to Richard Perle: "Can you assure American viewers ... that we're in this situation against Saddam Hussein and his removal for American security interests? And what would be the link in terms of Israel?"

Suddenly, the Israeli connection is on the table, and the War Party is not amused. Finding themselves in an unanticipated firefight, our neoconservative friends are doing what comes naturally, seeking student deferments from political combat by claiming the status of a persecuted minority group. People who claim to be writing the foreign policy of the world superpower, one would think, would be a little more manly in the schoolyard of politics. Not so.

Former *Wall Street Journal* editor Max Boot kicked off the campaign. When these "Buchananites toss around 'neoconservative' – and cite names like Wolfowitz and Cohen – it sometimes sounds as if what they really mean is 'Jewish conservative.'" Yet Boot readily concedes that a passionate attachment to Israel is a "key tenet of neoconservatism." He also claims that the *National Security Strategy* of President Bush "sounds as if it could have come straight out from the pages of *Commentary* magazine, the neocon bible." (For the uninitiated, *Commentary*, the bible in which Boot seeks divine guidance, is the monthly of the American Jewish Committee.)

David Brooks of the *Weekly Standard* wails that attacks based on the Israel tie have put him through personal hell: "Now I get a steady stream of anti-Semitic screeds in my email, my voicemail and in my mailbox. . . . Anti-Semitism is alive and thriving. It's just that its epicenter is no longer on the Buchananite right, but on the peace-movement left."

Washington Post columnist Robert Kagan endures his own purgatory abroad: "In London ... one finds Britain's finest minds propounding, in sophisticated language and melodious Oxbridge accents, the conspiracy theories of Pat Buchanan concerning the 'neoconservative' (read: Jewish) hijacking of American foreign policy."

Lawrence Kaplan of the *New Republic* charges that our little magazine, *The American Conservative*, "has been transformed into a forum for those who contend that President Bush has become a client of ... Ariel Sharon and the 'neoconservative war party.'"

Referencing Charles Lindbergh, he accuses Paul Schroeder, Chris Matthews, Robert Novak, Georgie Anne Geyer, Jason Vest of the *Nation*, and Gary Hart of implying that "members of the Bush team have been doing Israel's bidding and, by extension, exhibiting 'dual loyalties.'" Kaplan thunders:

> The real problem with such claims is not just that they are untrue. The problem is that they are toxic. Invoking the specter of dual loyalty to mute criticism and debate amounts to more than the everyday pollution of public discourse. It is the nullification of public discourse, for how can one refute accusations grounded in ethnicity? The charges are, *ipso facto*, impossible to disprove. And so they are meant to be.

What is going on here? *Slate*'s Mickey Kaus nails it in the headline of his retort: "Lawrence Kaplan Plays the Anti-Semitic Card."

What Kaplan, Brooks, Boot, and Kagan are doing is the same thing that the Democratic race-relations hucksters do when caught with some mammoth contribution from a Fortune 500 company they had previously accused of discrimination. They play the race card. So, too, the neoconservatives are trying to fend off critics by assassinating their character and impugning their motives.

Indeed, it is the charge of "anti-Semitism" itself that is toxic. For this venerable slander is designed to nullify public discourse by smearing and intimidating foes and censoring and blacklisting them and any who would publish them. Neocons say we attack them because they are Jewish. We do not. We attack them because their warmongering threatens our country, even as it finds a reliable echo in Ariel Sharon.

And this time the boys have cried "wolf" once too often. It is not working. As Kaus notes, Kaplan's own *New Republic* carries Harvard professor Stanley Hoffman. In writing of the four power centers in this capital that are clamoring for war, Hoffman himself describes the fourth thus:

> And, finally, there is a loose collection of friends of Israel, who believe in the identity of interests between the Jewish state and the United States. . . . These analysts look on foreign policy through the lens of one dominant concern: is it good or bad for Israel? Since that nation's founding in 1948, these thinkers have never been in very good odor at the State Department, but now they are well ensconced in the Pentagon, around such strategists as Paul Wolfowitz, Richard Perle and Douglas Feith.

"If Stanley Hoffman can say this," asks Kaus, "why can't Chris Matthews?" Kaus also notes that Kaplan somehow failed to mention the most devastating piece tying the neoconservatives to Sharon and his Likud Party.

In a Feb. 9, 2003, front-page article in the *Washington Post*, Robert Kaiser quotes a senior U.S. official as saying, "The Likudniks are really in charge now." Kaiser names Perle, Wolfowitz, and Feith as members of a pro-Israel network inside the administration and adds David Wurmser of the Defense Department and Elliott Abrams of the National Security Council. (Abrams is the son-in-law of Norman Podhoretz, editor emeritus of *Commentary*, whose magazine has for decades branded critics of Israel as anti-Semites.)

Noting that Sharon repeatedly claims a "special closeness" to the Bushites, Kaiser writes, "For the first time a U.S. administration and a Likud government are pursuing nearly identical policies." And a valid question is: how did this come to be, and while it is surely in Sharon's interest, is it in America's interest?

This is a time for truth. For America has made a momentous decision, potentially launching a series of wars in the Middle East that we believe would be a tragedy and a disaster for this Republic.

We charge that a cabal of polemicists and public officials has sought to ensnare our country in a series of wars that are not in America's interests. We charge them with colluding with Israel to ignite those wars and destroy the Oslo Accords. We charge them with deliberately damaging U.S. relations with every state in the Arab world that defies Israel or supports the Palestinian people's right to a homeland of their own. We charge that they have alienated friends and allies all over the Islamic and Western world through their arrogance, hubris, and bellicosity. Not in our lifetimes has America been so isolated from old friends.

They charge us with anti-Semitism -i.e., a hatred of Jews for their faith, heritage, or ancestry. False. The truth is, those hurling these charges harbor a "passionate attachment" to a nation not our own that causes them to subordinate the interests of their own country and to act on an assumption that, somehow, what's good for Israel is good for America.

The Neoconservatives

Who are the neoconservatives? The first generation were ex-liberals, socialists, and Trotskyites, boat-people from the McGovern revolution who rafted over to the GOP at the end of conservatism's long march to power with Ronald Reagan in 1980.

A neoconservative, wrote Kevin Phillips back then, is more likely to be a magazine editor than a bricklayer. Today, he or she is more likely to be a resident scholar at a public policy institute such as the American Enterprise Institute (AEI) or one of its clones like the Center for Security Policy (CSP) or the Jewish Institute for National Security Affairs (JINSA). As one wag writes, a neocon is more familiar with the inside of a think tank than an Abrams tank.

Almost none came out of the business world or military, and few if any came out of the Goldwater campaign. The heroes they invoke are Woodrow Wilson, FDR, Harry Truman, Martin Luther King, and Democratic Senators Henry "Scoop" Jackson (Wash.) and Pat Moynihan (N.Y.).

All are interventionists who regard Stakhanovite support of Israel as a defining characteristic of their breed. Among their luminaries are Jeane Kirkpatrick, Bill Bennett, Michael Novak, and James Q. Wilson.

Their publications include the *Weekly Standard, Commentary,* the *New Republic, National Review,* and the editorial page of the *Wall Street Journal.* Though few in number, they wield disproportionate power through control of the conservative foundations and magazines, through their syndicated columns, and by attaching themselves to men of power.

Beating the War Drums

When the cold war ended, these neoconservatives began casting about for a new crusade to give meaning to their lives. On Sept. 11, their time came. They seized on that horrific atrocity to steer America's rage into all-out war to destroy their despised enemies, the Arab and Islamic "rogue states" that have resisted U.S. hegemony and loathe Israel.

The War Party's plan, however, had been in preparation far in advance of 9/11. And when President Bush, after defeating the Taliban, was looking for a new front in the war on terror, they put their pre-cooked meal in front of him. Bush dug into it.

Before introducing the script-writers of America's future wars, consider the rapid and synchronized reaction of the neocons to what happened after that fateful day.

On Sept. 12, 2001, Americans were still in shock when Bill Bennett told CNN that we were in "a struggle between good and evil," that the Congress must declare war on "militant Islam," and that "overwhelming force" must be used. Bennett cited Lebanon, Libya, Syria, Iraq, Iran, and China as targets for attack. Not, however, Afghanistan, the sanctuary of Osama's terrorists. How did Bennett know which nations must be smashed before he had any idea who attacked us?

The Wall Street Journal immediately offered up a specific target list, calling for U.S. air strikes on "terrorist camps in Syria, Sudan, Libya, and Algeria, and perhaps even in parts of Egypt." Yet, not one of Bennett's six countries, nor one of these five, had anything to do with 9/11.

On Sept. 15, according to Bob Woodward's *Bush at War,* "Paul Wolfowitz put forth military arguments to justify a U.S. attack on Iraq rather than Afghanistan." Why Iraq? Because, Wolfowitz argued in the War Cabinet, while "attacking Afghanistan would be uncertain . . . Iraq was a brittle oppressive regime that might break easily. It was doable."

On Sept. 20, forty neoconservatives sent an open letter to the White House instructing President Bush on how the war on terror must be conducted. Signed by Bennett, Podhoretz, Kirkpatrick, Perle, Kristol, and *Washington Post* columnist Charles Krauthammer, the letter was an ultimatum. To retain the signers' support, the President was told, he must target Hezbollah for destruction, retaliate against Syria and Iran if they refuse to sever ties to Hezbollah, and overthrow Saddam. Any failure to attack Iraq, the signers warned Bush, "will constitute an early and perhaps decisive surrender in the war on international terrorism."

Here was a cabal of intellectuals telling the Commander-in-Chief, nine days after an attack on America, that if he did not follow their war plans, he would be charged with surrendering to terror. Yet, Hezbollah had nothing to do with 9/11. What had Hezbollah done? Hezbollah had humiliated Israel by driving its army out of Lebanon.

President Bush had been warned. He was to exploit the attack of 9/11 to launch a series of wars on Arab regimes, none of which had attacked us. All, however, were enemies of Israel. "Bibi" Netanyahu, the former Prime Minister of Israel, like some latter-day Citizen Genet, was ubiquitous on American television, calling for us to crush the "Empire of Terror." The "Empire," it turns out, consisted of Hamas, Hezbollah, Iran, Iraq, and "the Palestinian enclave."

Nasty as some of these regimes and groups might be, what had they done to the United States?

The War Party seemed desperate to get a Middle East war going before America had second thoughts. Tom Donnelly of the Project for the New American Century (PNAC) called for an immediate invasion of Iraq. "Nor need the attack await the deployment of half a million troops. . . . [T]he larger challenge will be occupying Iraq after the fighting is over," he wrote.

Donnelly was echoed by Jonah Goldberg of *National Review*: "The United States needs to go to war with Iraq because it needs to go to war with someone in the region and Iraq makes the most sense."

Goldberg endorsed "the Ledeen Doctrine" of ex-Pentagon official Michael Ledeen, which Goldberg described thus: "Every ten years or so, the United States needs to pick up some small crappy little country and throw it against the wall, just to show we mean business." (When the French ambassador in London, at a dinner party, asked why we should risk World War III over some "shitty little country" – meaning Israel – Goldberg's magazine was not amused.)

Ledeen, however, is less frivolous. In *The War Against the Terror Masters*, he identifies the exact regimes America must destroy:

> First and foremost, we must bring down the terror regimes, beginning with the Big Three: Iran, Iraq, and Syria. And then we have to come to grips with Saudi Arabia. . . . Once the tyrants in Iran, Iraq, Syria, and Saudi Arabia have been brought down, we will remain engaged. . . . We have to ensure the fulfillment of the democratic revolution. . . . Stability is an unworthy American mission, and a misleading concept to boot. We do not want stability in Iran, Iraq, Syria, Lebanon, and even Saudi Arabia; we want things to change. The real issue is not whether, but how to destabilize.

Rejecting stability as "an unworthy American mission," Ledeen goes on to define America's authentic "historic mission":

> Creative destruction is our middle name, both within our society and abroad. We tear down the old order every day, from business to science, literature, art, architecture, and cinema to politics and the law. Our enemies have always hated this whirlwind of energy and creativity which menaces their traditions (whatever they may be) and shames them for their inability to keep pace. . . . [W]e must destroy them to advance our historic mission.

Passages like this owe more to Leon Trotsky than to Robert Taft and betray a Jacobin streak in neoconservatism that cannot be reconciled with any concept of true conservatism.

To the *Weekly Standard*, Ledeen's enemies list was too restrictive. We must not only declare war on terror networks and states that harbor terrorists, said the *Standard*, we should launch wars on "any group or government inclined to support or sustain others like them in the future."

Robert Kagan and William Kristol were giddy with excitement at the prospect of Armageddon. The coming war "is going to spread and engulf a number of countries. . . . It is going to resemble the clash of civilizations that everyone has hoped to avoid. . . . [I]t is possible that the demise of some 'moderate' Arab regimes may be just round the corner."

Norman Podhoretz in *Commentary* even outdid Kristol's *Standard*, rhapsodizing that we should embrace a war of civilizations, as it is George W. Bush's mission "to fight World War IV – the war against militant Islam." By his count, the regimes that richly deserve to be overthrown are not confined to the three singled-out members of the axis of evil (Iraq, Iran, North Korea). At a minimum, the axis should extend to Syria and Lebanon and Libya, as well as "'friends" of America like the Saudi royal family and Egypt's Hosni Mubarak, along with the Palestinian Authority. Bush must reject the "timorous counsels" of the "incorrigibly cautious Colin Powell," wrote Podhoretz, and "find the stomach to impose a new political culture on the defeated" Islamic world. As the war against al-Qaeda required that we destroy the Taliban, Podhoretz wrote,

> We may willy-nilly find ourselves forced . . . to topple five or six or seven more tyrannies in the Islamic world (including that other sponsor of terrorism, Yasser Arafat's Palestinian Authority). I can even [imagine] the turmoil of this war leading to some new species of an imperial mission for America, whose purpose would be to oversee the emergence of successor governments in the region more amenable to reform and modernization than the despotisms now in place. . . . I can also envisage the establishment of some kind of American protectorate over the oil fields of Saudi Arabia, as we more and more come to wonder why 7,000 princes should go on being permitted to exert so much leverage over us and everyone else.

Podhoretz credits Eliot Cohen with the phrase "World War IV." Bush was shortly thereafter seen carrying about a gift copy of Cohen's book that celebrates civilian mastery of the military in times of war, as exhibited by such leaders as Winston Churchill and David Ben Gurion.

A list of the Middle East regimes that Podhoretz, Bennett, Ledeen, Netanyahu, and the *Wall Street Journal* regard as targets for destruction thus includes Algeria, Libya, Egypt, Sudan, Lebanon, Syria, Iraq, Saudi Arabia, Iran, Hezbollah, Hamas, the Palestinian Authority, and "militant Islam."

Cui Bono? For whose benefit these endless wars in a region that holds nothing vital to America save oil, which the Arabs must sell us to survive? Who would benefit from a war between America and Islam?

Answer: one nation, one leader, one party. Israel, Sharon, Likud.

Indeed, Sharon has been everywhere the echo of his acolytes in America. In February 2003, Sharon told a delegation of Congressmen that, after Saddam's regime is destroyed, it is of "vital importance" that the United States disarm Iran, Syria, and Libya.

"We have a great interest in shaping the Middle East the day after" the war on Iraq, Defense Minister Shaul Mofaz told the Conference of Major American Jewish Organizations. After U.S. troops enter Baghdad, the United States must generate "political, economic, diplomatic pressure" on Tehran, Mofaz admonished the American Jews.

Are the neoconservatives concerned about a war on Iraq bringing down friendly Arab governments? Not at all. They would welcome it.

"Mubarak is no great shakes," says Richard Perle of the President of Egypt. "Surely we can do better than Mubarak." Asked about the possibility that a war on Iraq – which he predicted would be a "cakewalk" – might upend governments in Egypt and Saudi Arabia, former UN ambassador Ken Adelman told Joshua Micah Marshall of *Washington Monthly*, "All the better if you ask me."

On July 10, 2002, Perle invited a former aide to Lyndon LaRouche named Laurent Murawiec to address the Defense Policy Board. In a briefing that startled Henry Kissinger, Murawiec named Saudi Arabia as "the kernel of evil, the prime mover, the most dangerous opponent" of the United States.

Washington should give Riyadh an ultimatum, he said. Either you Saudis "prosecute or isolate those involved in the terror chain, including the Saudi intelligence services," and end all propaganda against Israel, or we invade your country, seize your oil fields, and occupy Mecca.

In closing his PowerPoint presentation, Murawiec offered a "Grand Strategy for the Middle East." "Iraq is the tactical pivot, Saudi Arabia the strategic pivot, Egypt the prize." Leaked reports of Murawiec's briefing did not indicate if anyone raised the question of how the Islamic world might respond to U.S. troops tramping around the grounds of the Great Mosque.

What these neoconservatives seek is to conscript American blood to make the world safe for Israel. They want the peace of the sword imposed on Islam and American soldiers to die if necessary to impose it.

Washington Times editor at large Arnaud de Borchgrave calls this the "Bush-Sharon Doctrine." "Washington's 'Likudniks,'" he writes, "have been

[142]

in charge of U.S. policy in the Middle East since Bush was sworn into office."

The neocons seek American empire, and Sharonites seek hegemony over the Middle East. The two agendas coincide precisely. And though neocons insist that it was Sept. 11 that made the case for war on Iraq and militant Islam, the origins of their war plans go back far before.

"Securing the Realm"

The principal draftsman is Richard Perle, an aide to Senator Scoop Jackson, who, in 1970, was overheard on a federal wiretap discussing classified information from the National Security Council with the Israeli Embassy. In *Jews and American Politics,* published in 1974, Stephen D. Isaacs wrote, "Richard Perle and Morris Amitay command a tiny army of Semitophiles on Capitol Hill and direct Jewish power in behalf of Jewish interests." In 1983, the *New York Times* reported that Perle had taken substantial payments from an Israeli weapons manufacturer.

In 1996, with Douglas Feith and David Wurmser, Perle wrote "A Clean Break: A New Strategy for Securing the Realm," for Prime Minister Netanyahu. In it, Perle, Feith, and Wurmser urged Bibi to ditch the Oslo Accords of the assassinated Yitzak Rabin and adopt a new aggressive strategy:

> Israel can shape its strategic environment, in co-operation with Turkey and Jordan, by weakening, containing, and even rolling back Syria. This effort can focus on removing Saddam Hussein from power in Iraq – an important Israeli strategic objective in its own right – as a means of foiling Syria's regional ambitions. Jordan has challenged Syria's regional ambitions recently by suggesting the restoration of the Hashemites in Iraq.

In the Perle-Feith-Wurmser strategy, Israel's enemy remains Syria, but the road to Damascus runs through Baghdad. Their plan, which urged Israel to re-establish "the principle of preemption," has now been imposed by Perle, Feith, Wurmser & Co. on the United States.

In his own 1997 paper, "A Strategy for Israel," Feith pressed Israel to re-occupy "the areas under Palestinian Authority control," though "the price in blood would be high."

Wurmser, as a resident scholar at AEI, drafted joint war plans for Israel and the United States "to fatally strike the centers of radicalism in the Middle East. Israel and the United States should . . . broaden the conflict to strike fatally, not merely disarm, the centers of radicalism in the region – the regimes of Damascus, Baghdad, Tripoli, Tehran, and Gaza. That would establish the recognition that fighting either the United States or Israel is suicidal."

He urged both nations to be on the lookout for a crisis, for as he wrote, "Crises can be opportunities." Wurmser published his U.S.-Israeli war plan on Jan. 1, 2001, *nine months before 9/11*.

About the Perle-Feith-Wurmser cabal, author Michael Lind writes:

> The radical Zionist right to which Perle and Feith belong is small in number but it has become a significant force in Republican policy-making circles. It is a recent phenomenon, dating back to the late 1970s and 1980s, when many formerly Democratic Jewish intellectuals joined the broad Reagan coalition. While many of these hawks speak in public about global crusades for democracy, the chief concern of many such "neoconservatives" is the power and reputation of Israel.

Right down the smokestack.

Perle, until recently, chaired the Defense Policy Board, Feith is an outgoing Under Secretary of Defense, and Wurmser – now Middle East Adviser in the Office of the Vice President – was special assistant to John Bolton, who, as Under Secretary of State for Arms Control, dutifully echoed the Perle-Sharon line. According to the Israeli daily newspaper *Ha'aretz*, in late February 2003,

> U.S. Under Secretary of State John Bolton said in meetings with Israeli officials . . . that he has no doubt America will attack Iraq and that it will be necessary to deal with threats from Syria, Iran and North Korea afterwards.

On Jan. 26, 1998, President Clinton received a letter imploring him to use his State of the Union address to make removal of Saddam Hussein's regime the "aim of American foreign policy" and to use military action because "diplomacy is failing." Were Clinton to do that, the signers pledged, they would "offer [their] full support in this difficult but necessary endeavor." Signing the pledge were Elliott Abrams, Bill Bennett, John Bolton, Robert Kagan, William Kristol, Richard Perle, and Paul Wolfowitz. Four years before 9/11, the neocons had Baghdad on their minds.

The Wolfowitz Doctrine

In 1992, a startling document was leaked from the office of Paul Wolfowitz at the Pentagon. Barton Gellman of the *Washington Post* called it a "classified blueprint intended to help 'set the nation's direction for the next century.'" The Wolfowitz Memo called for a permanent U.S. military presence on six continents to deter all "potential competitors from even aspiring to a larger regional or global role." Containment, the victorious strategy of the cold war, was to give way to an ambitious new strategy designed to "establish and protect a new order."

Though the Wolfowitz Memo was denounced and dismissed in 1992, it became American policy in the 33-page *National Security Strategy* (*NSS*) issued by President Bush on Sept. 21, 2002. *Washington Post* reporter Tim Reich describes it as a "watershed in U.S. foreign policy" that "reverses the fundamental principles that have guided successive Presidents for more than 50 years: containment and deterrence."

Andrew Bacevich, a professor at Boston University, writes of the *NSS* that he marvels at "its fusion of breathtaking utopianism with barely disguised *machtpolitik*. It reads as if it were the product not of sober, ostensibly conservative Republicans but of an unlikely collaboration between Woodrow Wilson and the elder Field Marshal von Moltke."

In confronting America's adversaries, the paper declares, "We will not hesitate to act alone, if necessary, to exercise our right of self-defense by acting preemptively." It warns any nation that seeks to acquire power to rival the United States that it will be courting war:

> [T]he President has no intention of allowing any nation to catch up with the huge lead the United States has opened since the fall of the Soviet Union more than a decade ago. . . . Our forces will be strong enough to dissuade potential adversaries from pursuing a military buildup in hopes of surpassing or equaling the power of the United States.

America must reconcile herself to an era of "nation-building on a grand scale, and with no exit strategy," Robert Kagan instructs. But this *Pax Americana* the neocons envision bids fair to usher us into a time of what Harry Elmer Barnes called "permanent war for permanent peace."

The Munich Card

As President Bush was warned on Sept. 20, 2001, that he will be indicted for "a decisive surrender" in the war on terror should he fail to attack Iraq, he is also on notice that pressure on Israel is forbidden. For as the neoconservatives have played the anti-Semitic card, they will not hesitate to play the Munich card as well. In early 2002, when Bush called on Sharon to pull out of the West Bank, Sharon fired back that he would not let anyone do to Israel what Neville Chamberlain had done to the Czechs. Frank Gaffney of the Center for Security Policy immediately backed up Ariel Sharon:

With each passing day, Washington appears to view its principal Middle Eastern ally's conduct as inconvenient – in much the same way London and Paris came to see Czechoslovakia's resistance to Hitler's offers of peace in exchange for Czech lands.

When former U.S. NATO commander Gen. George Jouwlan said the United States may have to impose a peace on Israel and the Palestinians, he, too, faced the charge of appeasement. Wrote Gaffney,

They would, presumably, go beyond Britain and France's sell-out of an ally at Munich in 1938. The "impose a peace" school is apparently prepared to have us play the role of Hitler's Wehrmacht as well, seizing and turning over to Yasser Arafat the contemporary Sudetenland: the West Bank and Gaza Strip and perhaps part of Jerusalem as well.

Podhoretz agreed Sharon was right in the substance of what he said but called it politically unwise to use the Munich analogy.

President Bush is on notice: should he pressure Israel to trade land for peace, the Oslo formula in which his father and Yitzak Rabin believed, he will, as was his father, be denounced as an anti-Semite and a Munich-style appeaser by both Israelis and their neoconservative allies inside his own Big Tent.

Yet, if Bush cannot deliver Sharon, there can be no peace. And if there is no peace in the Mideast there is no security for us, ever – for there will be no end to terror. As most every diplomat and journalist who travels to the region will relate, America's failure to be even-handed, our failure to rein in Sharon, our failure to condemn Israel's excesses, and our moral complicity in Israel's looting of Palestinian lands and denial of their right to self-determination sustains the anti-Americanism in the Islamic world in which terrorists and terrorism breed.

Let us conclude. The Israeli people certainly have a right to peace and security. But U.S. and Israeli interests are not identical. They often collide, and when they do, U.S. interests must prevail. Moreover, we do not view the Sharon regime as "America's best friend."

Since the time of Ben Gurion, the behavior of the Israeli regime has been Jekyll and Hyde. In the 1950s, its intelligence service, the Mossad, had agents in Egypt blow up U.S. installations to make it appear the work of Cairo, to destroy U.S. relations with the new Nasser government. During the Six Day War, Israel ordered repeated attacks on the undefended USS Liberty that killed 34 American sailors and wounded 171 and included the machine-gunning of life rafts. This massacre was neither investigated nor punished by the U.S. government in an act of national cravenness.

Though we have given Israel $20,000 for every Jewish citizen, Israel refuses to stop building the settlements that are the cause of the Palestinian *intifada*. Likud has dragged our good name through the mud and blood of Ramallah, ignored Bush's requests to restrain itself, and sold U.S. weapons technology to China, including the Patriot, the Phoenix air-to-air missile, and the Lavi fighter, which is based on F-16 technology. Only direct U.S. intervention blocked Israel's sale of our AWACS system.

Israel suborned Jonathan Pollard to loot our secrets and refuses to return the documents, which would establish whether or not they were sold to Moscow. When Clinton tried to broker an agreement at Wye Plantation between Israel and Arafat, Bibi Netanyahu attempted to extort, as his price for signing, release of Pollard, so he could take this treasonous snake back to Israel as a national hero.

Do our allies behave like this?

Though we have said repeatedly that we admire much of what this President has done, he must at some point jettison the neoconservatives' agenda of endless wars on the Islamic world that serve only the interests of a country other than the one he was elected (twice) to preserve and protect.

. . . one might begin the argument by considering the present historical situation of humanity as dominated by the fact of Communism. The essential fact here is that Communism, as an ideology and as a power-system, constitutes the gravest possible menace to the moral and civilizational values that form the basis of "the West," understanding the term to designate not a geographical entity but an order of temporal life that has been the product of valid human dynamisms tempered by the spirit of the Gospel. Arguing from this standpoint alone one could well posit, in all logic, the present validity of the concept of the "holy war." Or one might come to some advocacy of "preventive" war or "pre-emptive" war. Or one might be led to assert that, since the adversary is completely unprincipled, and since our duty in face of him is success in the service of civilization itself, we must jettison the tradition of civilized warfare and be prepared to use any means that promise success.

NONE OF THESE CONCLUSIONS IS MORALLY ACCEPTABLE.

—Fr. John Courtney Murray, S.J.
"The Uses of a Doctrine on the Uses of Force,"
We Hold These Truths, 1960

Conservative and Anti-War: Patriotism, Prudence, and the Moral Law

THE EDITORS' GLOSS: As many will be aware who followed (and continue to follow) the controversy surrounding the Iraq war, numerous respectable and even "mainstream" opponents of the war were tarred by the more ideologically aggressive neocons as "unpatriotic."

It is this charge to which the late Samuel Francs responds, in one of the last essays he was to write before his untimely and early death.

In general terms, it is insane to imagine that attempting to steer one's country away from an unnecessary, costly (in blood and treasure), and unjust – and therefore immoral – war, through reasoned, non-violent discourse, should be thought of as anything *other* than patriotic. Ideologues of the stripe of David Frum have never shied away from arguing for insane theses, however, when they prove necessary to – or follow from – a preconceived line of argument. As Frum imagined "regime change" in Iraq to be in the American interest as he conceived it, anyone disagreeing was therefore smeared as a traitor.

What Francis offers is a welcome antidote to the insanity of a parochial and narrow-minded conception of patriotism, which mistakes towing a party line, submitting to partisan diktat, and blind adherence to government decree for a selfless attachment to the true interests of one's nation. Interestingly, Francis's perspective is no less a product of the moral law as defended by the Catholic Church than is the just-war doctrine itself. As Fr. Edward Cahill, noteworthy moral theologian and political thinker, wrote way back in 1932, "love of country means . . . a love or benevolence for one's countrymen as such, implying *an efficacious desire to promote their interests*" (emphasis ours). So if Frum and his cohorts succeeded in orchestrating a war that was indeed injurious to America's interests, by compromising both her security and tarnishing her public moral character and reputation, who was it, then, who was being "unpatriotic"?

Refuge of Scoundrels: Patriotism, True and False, in the Iraq War Controversy

• • • • • • • • • •

Samuel Francis, Ph.D.

THE BEST-KNOWN and most controversial claims that the Bush administration asserted to justify the war against Iraq in 2002 and 2003 involved allegations about Iraq's possession of "Weapons of Mass Destruction" and its supposed links with al-Qaeda and other terrorist groups. These claims have been largely refuted or at least not substantiated by post-war investigations, but they were by no means the only arguments the administration and other supporters of the war invoked as justifications. Underlying the case of war, regardless of factual claims and their reliability, was the unexamined assumption that patriotism invariably demands support for war – that unless one supports the war against Saddam Hussein (and, by extension, any other war that the government – more specifically the executive branch – has decided to fight), one's patriotism is in question.

Since the attacks of September 11, 2001, invocations of patriotism have become commonplace – and often tendentious, if not actually insulting and occasionally dangerous. What is called by the label "USA PATRIOT" Act of 2001, a clever and catchy acronym for an enormous piece of awkwardly titled legislation known officially as "an Act for Uniting and Strengthening America by Providing Appropriate Tools Required to Intercept and Obstruct Terrorism," is one of the obvious instances. Enacted by Congress in the aftermath of the 2001 attacks after only the most cursory deliberations by lawmakers, the law conscripts for partisan political purposes a word and concept that should denote a virtue praiseworthy in itself and vital to national and social cohesion. The proliferation of American flags on lapel pins, car bumpers, articles of clothing, highway overpasses, advertisements, car dealers' lots, cocktail glasses, tissue paper, match books, and other inappropriate and often degrading locations is yet another instance of the mass cheapening of perfectly legitimate and important patriotic sentiment. It is hardly surprising that such sentiments became commonplace after 9/11, nor is it surprising that partisans and what can only be called warmongers should seek to exploit them for their own purposes.

The neoconservatives who promoted the war with Iraq almost from the very moment of the 9/11 attacks have been the first to reach for patriotic emotions in mobilizing support for what is essentially a war fought on behalf of the interests of a foreign country. For the neocons themselves, this appeal to patriotism was critical in establishing their own credentials as "real" conservatives. Prior to the war with Iraq, they were regarded, in so far as they possessed any profile outside the ranks of an increasingly marginalized and withering "conservative movement," as simply a rather narrowly focused band of policy-wonks lodged in the think tanks, highbrow journals, and occasional academic or administrative labyrinths of Washington, New York and other metropolises. Unable to acquire either a mass following of the kind that earlier conservative figures such as Joseph McCarthy, Barry Goldwater, Jesse Helms, Ronald Reagan, or Pat Buchanan had attracted, the neocons were obliged to curry political favor with whatever political figures would pay attention to them. They were generally unsuccessful in such efforts until the advent of the Bush administration. The war with Iraq and the 9/11 attacks, if they accomplished nothing else for neoconservatives, afforded them the opportunity to enlist themselves on the side of the vast majority of Americans who experienced profound anger and fear as the result of the 9/11 attacks and who demanded a swift, just, and retributive response. By successfully – at least for a time – linking such emotions to Iraq rather than to the actual perpetrators of 9/11, the neocons came close to establishing in the minds of many conservatives and Republicans what they had always heretofore lacked – legitimacy as conservative patriots – as well as a mass following that echoed its patriotic appeals.

That the neoconservatives were entirely willing not only to exploit mass patriotic sentiment but also to deny the patriotic loyalties of their critics soon became obvious. Indeed, this was a tactic employed by Republican partisans as well in the 2004 election campaign, when opponents of John Kerry were quick to point to photographs of the Democratic nominee with Jane Fonda during the Vietnam era and later to raise questions about Kerry's credentials as a war hero. But even before Kerry became the target of partisan innuendo, the neoconservatives were lodging similar accusations against their principal ideological rivals within the ranks of organized conservatism, the paleo-conservatives. The chief expression of this tactic was the long cover article in *National Review* of April 7, 2003, by former Bush speechwriter David Frum on the "Unpatriotic Conservatives" who dissented from the Iraq war.

Frum was explicit about who these unpatriotic "antiwar conservatives" are – "Some are famous: Patrick Buchanan and Robert Novak. Others are not: Llewellyn Rockwell, Samuel Francis, Thomas Fleming, Scott McConnell, Justin Raimondo, Joe Sobran, Charley Reese, Jude Wanniski, Eric Margolis, and Taki Theodoracopulos" – and he was equally clear as to why they are "unpatriotic."

Not only, Frum wrote, do they "aspire to reinvent conservative ideology: to junk the 50-year-old conservative commitment to defend American interests and values throughout the world – the commitment that inspired the founding of this magazine – in favor of a fearful policy of ignoring threats and appeasing enemies," but also they

> have gone far, far beyond the advocacy of alternative strategies. They have made common cause with the left-wing and Islamist antiwar movements in this country and in Europe. They deny and excuse terror. They espouse a potentially self-fulfilling defeatism. They publicize wild conspiracy theories. And some of them explicitly yearn for the victory of their nation's enemies.

Frum's editorializing suggested that he was at least hypothetically willing to grant that dissent on the war might be legitimate if it offered or endorsed "alternative strategies" – presumably, alternatives to war for destroying the Iraqi regime – but only if dissent shared that goal. The presumption, in other words, was that while dissent on the means of destroying the Iraqi government might be legitimate and consistent with his concept of "patriotism," there could be no disagreement on the goal of destroying the regime. Anyone who did not wish to destroy the regime was therefore "unpatriotic."

In fact, nowhere in his article or anywhere else did Frum substantiate any of the extreme accusations he alleged. His specifics against the anti-war right included a number of charges (most of which he claimed to document with only a single quotation from the individuals he named), such as making "common cause" (with the anti-American left). The only substance in this particular charge is that some anti-war critics on the right, more especially libertarians, have websites that "approvingly cite and link to" the writings of "anti-Americans of the far Left" like Noam Chomsky, Gore Vidal, and Alexander Cockburn. But web linkages are virtually meaningless as to establishing "common cause" with much of anything. People who are interested in the war and the case for and against it have an obvious interest in connecting to such websites. The anti-war libertarian website LewRockwell.com, for example, links not only to Noam Chomsky's website, but also to those of *National Review* itself, the *Weekly Standard*, the *American Spectator*, and the *New York Times*, among many others. Do those links show that the Rockwell site has made "common cause" with those who manage those sites? Frum offers no evidence other than website linkages to substantiate his claim that the antiwar right has made "common cause" with the "anti-American Left." (Nor does he even try to substantiate his assertion that such left-wing anti-war critics are "anti-American.")

In addition, Frum also cited what he called "terror denial," "espousing defeatism," "excuse-making," "conspiracy theorizing," and "yearning for defeat" as characteristics of the anti-war right. Not one of these characteristics, even if true, would establish that the anti-war right is "unpatriotic" in the real sense of being opposed or indifferent to loyalty and love for their country, but each of Frum's substantiations for these charges is weak or invalid. Only in the last charge of "yearning for defeat" did he mention an attitude that might constitute absence of patriotism. The only example he offered was a passage from Canadian journalist Eric Margolis that Frum described as appealing to Arab leaders "to unite in battle against the U.S." Yet the passage he quoted from Margolis said nothing of the kind. It suggested peaceful means by which Arab leaders could dissuade or halt the United States from waging war on Iraq. "What could Arabs do to prevent a war of aggression against Iraq that increasingly resembles a medieval crusade?" Margolis asked. He proposed that they

> form a united diplomatic front that demands UN inspections continue. Stage an oil boycott of the U.S. if Iraq is attacked. Send 250,000 civilians from across the Arab World to form human shields around Baghdad and other Iraqi cities. Boycott Britain, Turkey, Kuwait, and the Gulf states that join or abet the U.S. invasion of Iraq. Withdraw all funds on deposit in U.S. and British banks. Accept payment for oil only in Euros, not dollars. Send Arab League troops to Iraq, so that an attack on Iraq is an attack on the entire League. Cancel billions worth of arms contracts with the U.S. and Britain. At least make a token show of male hormones and national pride.

Frum also quoted a column by anti-war libertarian Justin Raimondo in which Raimondo wrote that the possible consequences of a victorious war with Iraq would be "a high price to pay for 'victory' – so high that patriots might almost be forgiven if they pine for defeat." Of course, the operative words here are "might almost," a formulation that stops well short of actually "pining for defeat" of one's own country. Raimondo's argument in any case is clearly rhetorical and ironic – the results of a victory over Iraq would be so bad that defeat might be better.

The remainder of Frum's 6,500 word article is largely taken up with a vituperative account of "paleo-conservatism" – "the writers I quote call themselves 'paleoconservatives,' implying that they are somehow the inheritors of an older, purer, conservatism than that upheld by their impostor rivals." Actually those who call themselves "paleo-conservatives" do say that and accurately so[1], but by no means all those on the anti-war right embrace the "paleo" label, and even those who do embrace it do so with reservations and qualifications. Some (like Rockwell and Raimondo) are libertarians; others like Scott McConnell of *The American Conservative* are ex-neoconservatives who explictly reject the label "paleo-conservative," and others still (like myself) accept it only as a label of convenience. Robert Novak, for example, does not consider himself to be a paleo-conservative at all and would not be considered one by real paleo-conservatives. (It's interesting that *National Review* in the issue – April 21 – following the one in which Frum's article appeared felt the need to qualify considerably his allegations about the individuals he had specified – "the piece did not attribute to every figure mentioned in it, charges made against others," a statement that (a) is not true; Frum never made any such qualification and spoke of all the individuals he mentioned as a unit, and (b) effectively renders the allegations he did make worthless – to which specific individuals should his charges be attributed and to which should they not be attributed? While the editorial note specifically withdrew Frum's charges against Novak, it did make clear that Novak "is not to be confused with Sam Francis," a confusion that presumably few would be disposed to make in any case. The magazine's withdrawal of Frum's accusations against Novak also considerably weakened Frum's case since Frum had showcased Novak as a major paleo and quoted him as an "unpatriotic conservative" at least three times in the article.)

Frum's account of the background of "paleo-conservatism" is thus deeply flawed with inaccuracies and displays several clearly personal grudges and *ad hominem* invective against certain paleos – historian Paul Gottfried, Frum writes, is "perhaps the most relentlessly solipsistic of the disgruntled paleos,"

---

1. For an extended critique of Frum's conception of what the "older, purer conservatism" is, see my column "Infamies" in *Chronicles*, June, 2003, pp. 33–34.

while *Chronicles* editor Thomas Fleming is "a jumpy, wrathful man so prone to abrupt intellectual reversals that even some of his friends and supporters question his equilibrium." I myself am denounced as advocating "a politics of uninhibited racial nationalism" and misquoted as writing in 1991 that "A 'nationalist ethic' may often require government action." I have no recollection of writing such a sentence and am unable to locate any such passage in my work, although I fail to see what precisely is wrong with the sentiment expressed in it or why a neoconservative in particular would object to it. Unable to substantiate his charges that the paleos have essentially committed treason or harbor treasonous sentiments (there is no other word to describe people who "explicitly yearn for the victory of their nation's enemies"), Frum falls back on smears of "racism," "anti-Semitism," "protectionism," and "isolationism." Any or all such charges may or may not be true of one or another of the anti-war right, but none of them has anything to do with what Frum started out claiming – that they are "unpatriotic" or disaffected from the country or "explicitly yearn for the victory of their nation's enemies."

The paleos in general are disaffected not from the country itself but from the determination of the U.S. government to wage unnecessary wars that either border on the unjust or actually go well over the line of injustice, wars that are manifestly unprovoked and are not clearly in the interests of the nation, whether just or unjust, and wars that, even if victorious, may lead to so many entanglements, complications, injustices, and costs (human, economic, diplomatic, technological) that they are better avoided, regardless of their moral character. What most paleos have written about the Iraq war before and after has been along these lines – lines that are perfectly consistent with and indeed reflect a serious patriotism, as opposed to the kind of sophomoric chauvinism that demands blind obedience to whatever wars the government launches.

The unspoken assumption that underlies the neoconservative accusations against the anti-war right (and indeed the anti-war left) seems to be that dissent from or opposition to the state in war is evidence of a lack of "patriotism" and actual sympathy for the enemy. This assumption in turn betrays an unquestioning faith in the infallibility of the state. Indeed the blind faith in the state that the neoconservative attitude toward war discloses seems to be representative of them and their ideology, which emerged from the conventional liberalism and democratic socialism that prevailed among mainstream intellectuals from the New Deal through the Great Society eras and of which an unguarded faith in "big government" and the state was characteristic.

The older generation of neoconservatives was explicit in its disagreement with Old Right conservatism in its view of the proper scale of the state. While Old Right conservatism rejects anarchism and the minimal state doctrines of libertarian ideology, it adheres to a constitutionalist view of the limits of the American federal government in particular and to a commitment to a severely restricted and reduced scale and size of the state in general. Neoconservative theorists have long made it plain that they do not share the Old Right conservative view of the state.

Thus Irving Kristol, one of the principal founders of neoconservatism, has written in the *Weekly Standard* (Aug. 25, 2003) that, in distinction to older conservatives, "Neocons do not feel that kind of alarm or anxiety about the growth of the state in the past century, seeing it as natural, indeed inevitable" and (as long ago as 1979), "A conservative welfare state – what once was called a 'social insurance' state – is perfectly consistent with the neoconservative perspective." Kristol is by no means alone in this view of the state. Norman Podhoretz, also one of the main founders of neoconservatism, has written (in 1995) that, in contrast to the old conservatives, "the neoconservatives dissociated themselves from the wholesale opposition to the welfare state which had marked American conservatism since the days of the New Deal" and that while neoconservatives supported "setting certain limits" to the welfare state, those limits did not involve "issues of principle, such as the legitimate size and role of the central government in the American constitutional order" but were to be "determined by practical considerations."

Indeed this view of the state is just as characteristic of the younger neoconservatives. Thus neoconservative Bill Kristol, son of Irving and editor of the *Weekly Standard*, today the principal neoconservative news and opinion magazine, reflects this readiness to embrace the state faithfully.

In an opinion column in the *Wall Street Journal* of September 15, 1997, Kristol and fellow neoconservative David Brooks assert that the "national greatness conservatism" they were espousing "isn't unfriendly to government, properly understood" and demand to know "How can Americans love their nation if they hate its government?" Interviewed by liberal journalist E.J. Dionne two days later in the *Washington Post*, Kristol acknowledged that "there is absolutely no mass base for his brand of conservatism," but commented that New York Mayor Rudolph Giuliani "fits his mold." As Dionne noted, "Using government on behalf of 'national greatness' could get you right back to the New Deal" but

> New Dealism doesn't bother Kristol. "Franklin Roosevelt and John Kennedy and, for that matter, Lyndon Johnson are big facts in American history. . . . Are

we willing to say that the country is worse off because of FDR or JFK or LBJ? I'm not willing to say that."

As Dionne concluded, not unhappily, with the triumph of neoconservatism over Old Right conservatism, "The era of bashing big government is ending."

Authentic conservatism (of which so-called "paleo-conservatism" is one variety) is in no sense anti-patriotic, but it does draw a firm and clear distinction between love of or attachment to country, on the one hand, and deference to the state or the incumbent masters of the state, on the other. Especially in the contemporary world, conservatives distinguish between the people, traditions, norms, and institutions that have defined and characterized the country – the nation – throughout its history, on the one hand, and the structures, ideas, and groups that embody forces that are inimical to the country but are at present dominant, on the other. Most serious conservatives today perceive the dominant forces – in the state as well as the culture and economy – as fundamentally antagonistic to the traditional identity of the nation.

Conservatism in this sense thus ceases to be an ideology offering justifications for the current distribution of power in American society and becomes a far more radical persuasion that seeks fundamental change that would dislodge the dominant and antagonistic powers and restore or make possible a restoration of the historic national identity. It is loyalty and commitment to that identity that constitutes patriotism – not attachment or obedience to the government or the state *per se,* regardless of who or what is currently in control of it – and attachment to the state is incumbent on real patriots only in so far as the state reflects the national identity and protects its existence and welfare through just means. With the emergence and triumph since the 1980s of neoconservatism as the dominant expression of the "right" in the United States, the conservatism of national identity has begun to dwindle, and the neoconservative success in manipulating legitimate patriotic sentiments is a major reason for its decline. Nevertheless, as the war that the neocons instigated lurches from embarrassment to disaster and perhaps tragically to yet another massive atrocity on the scale of the original 9/11, Americans who have supported the war with Iraq because of their embrace of an authentic patriotism may come to see that their sentiments have been misplaced and that they have been grievously deceived by a faction that only purported to have the real interests of the nation at heart.

www.informationclearinghouse.info

Iraq, April 2003. "Where they make desolation, they call it peace." —Tacitus

THE EDITORS' GLOSS: Joe Sobran's pithy contribution to this anthology illustrates what many of his fans have known for years: he's got the courage to say what many others fear to.

"An unjustified war is mass murder," he says. That's a pretty strong statement, but it's no less true for being so. It's all very well to "support the troops" if that means not blaming them for being put in harm's way, and hoping and praying that they come home before their leaders send them on another undefined and unnecessary mission that has nothing to do with "defending the Constitution." But what about those leaders, who went to war supposedly to "enforce UN resolutions" or "protect the national security of the United States"? It is now manifest that the war was unnecessary on both counts, illegal as regards the former (as detailed by Dr. John Burroughs in *Neo-CONNED! Again*), and counter-productive as regards the latter. There's at least one man who *should be held responsible* for thousands of deaths and a gross violation of the natural and international law, and he sits in the White House..

Elsewhere Sobran takes issue with the idea that "attacking invading sol-diers in your own country is 'terrorism.'" (Readers who find this theme interesting should see the section of *Neo-CONNED! Again* called "One Good Scandal Deserves Another," on the hypocrisy plaguing American foreign policy, and its supporting rhetoric regarding "terror" and "extremism.") Most revealing about what Sobran writes is the stark fact that it throws into relief: if it is true that the U.S. invasion of Iraq was both immoral and illegal – as no one can now seriously dispute – it's hard to avoid the conclusion that it is the Iraqis who have a right to self-defense, and the Americans who continue an act of aggression, no less illegal now than at the outset. That's the burden of just-war theory: both sides cannot be right, and the one in the wrong has no objective right to commit belligerent acts, even in self-defense. As Michael Mandel, a professor at Osgoode Hall, York University's law school, points out, there's no such thing as self-defense when you are an aggressor: "When General Brooks said the soldiers at the Karbala checkpoint were exer-cising their 'inherent right to self-defense,' he was talking nonsense: an aggressor has no right to self-defense. If you break into someone's house and hold them at gunpoint, and they try to kill you but you kill them first, they're guilty of nothing and you're guilty of murder."

That's a pretty rotten position for American citizens and soldiers to be put in. And those who put them there ought to be in the dock for it.

CHAPTER
4

On Morals, Motives, and Men
• • • • • • • • •
Joseph Sobran

> "A truth that's told with bad intent
> Beats all the lies you can invent."

S O SAID THE poet William Blake. His words came to mind when I read the hawkish British weekly, *The Economist*, on whether President Bush and Prime Minister Tony Blair had lied about the Iraqi "threat" that turned out to be non-existent after the war had already been fought. Both rulers have been cleared of outright mendacity by official investigations; the magazine called them "sincere deceivers" who "believed what they said, but . . . said more than they really knew."

Many people argue that we should believe our rulers because "they know so much more than we do." Yes, they have access to far more information than we do; and furthermore, they have the power to *withhold* it from us. A curious reason for trusting them. Jefferson said that freedom depends on "jealousy" – suspicion of government – and not "confidence" in it.

We have more to fear than rulers' factual lies; we also have to worry about their bad judgment and exaggerations. The Senate Intelligence Committee concluded that Bush had "overstated" the supposed Iraqi threat. Are we expected to write this off as an honest mistake, when the "overstatement" meant the difference between war and peace, life and death?

While Bush was "overstating" the danger, he allowed his underlings to go further. Vice President Dick Cheney, the administration's answer to Whoopi Goldberg, said there was "no doubt" that Saddam Hussein had an active nuclear program; National Security Adviser Condoleezza Rice warned that we faced nuclear attack; even Secretary of State Colin Powell, the only member of the Bush team known for measuring his words, joined in the hyperbole contest, asserting positively things unwarranted by the facts.

Yes, in a sense they all knew more than we did. That's what makes their feigned certitude not only false, but criminal. They misled the American public into thinking a "preemptive" war was necessary for American survival, when it was not.

Even so, many Americans didn't believe them. Politicians lie a lot; that's a fact of life, sadly. But in this case, it also defied common sense to think Saddam Hussein would dare to launch an attack on the United States, the latter having weapons of mass killing so far superior to anything he could possibly have possessed. He had already been decisively deterred from invading tiny Kuwait next door, which he had once attacked only because he thought it was safe to do so, in the light of his discussion with American Ambassador to Iraq, April Glaspie. Why would he launch a suicidal war on the West?

Moreover, neoconservatives in the press, who hungered for war on Iraq, went beyond exaggeration to sheer fantasy, warning that the United States was in danger of total destruction – "holocaust," in the word of Richard Perle and David Frum, in their hysterical book *An End to Evil*. Bush did nothing to temper these diatribes, which were useful to him; just as he didn't bother correcting the many Americans who didn't even know the difference between Saddam Hussein and Osama bin Laden. Such absurd confusion was also useful, and was put to good use.

So outright lying was hardly necessary. Just encouraging hysteria and letting it run its natural course did the job. Time and again the Bush spokesmen said there was "no doubt" of the Iraqi threat; and those who did have doubts should trust their rulers. "The risks of inaction," Secretary of Defense Donald Rumsfeld said, "are greater than the risks of action." War was the *prudent* course.

The country is now having severe second thoughts about the war, but one risk was hardly taken into account: the risk of killing innocent people, including Iraqi soldiers whose only crime was trying vainly to defend their country from an unprovoked invasion. We still hear a great deal about American casualties, but almost nothing about American guilt.

An unjustified war is mass murder. That obvious truth has carried very little weight in the whole debate over this war. Our government has slaughtered countless people. Those who still resist are called rebels and even terrorists, no different from the fanatics of 9/11.

The hawks, within the administration and in its volunteer propaganda corps in the media, have never evinced much (if any) regret at the cost to the other side. How can anyone call these deceivers "sincere" if they never even paused to face the simple moral question "But what if we are wrong?" If they had been sincere then, they would be facing this question today, tens of thousands of deaths later, when there is little doubt how wrong they were.

As it happens, we heard from the other side: "I call upon the American people to stand beside their brothers, the Iraqi people, who are suffering an injustice by your rulers and the occupying army, to help them in the transfer of power to honest Iraqis. Otherwise, Iraq will be another Vietnam for America and the occupiers."

This plea, from the popular Shiite leader' Sheik Muqtada al-Sadr, was notable on several counts. First, he appealed to our conscience – our sense of justice as well as our prudence. Second, he addressed us as "brothers," not "infidels." (Dale Carnegie would admire his Islamic tact.) Third, he didn't threaten us with retaliation in our homeland; he merely asked us to get *our* government out of *his* homeland. Otherwise, he warned, Iraq will become another big problem for us – like Vietnam.

Muqtada was then ordered arrested by the occupiers, alias "us," the Americans. But he could hardly be called a "Saddam loyalist"; Saddam Hussein executed his father and brother.

Is he a terrorist? He "issued [a] call for terrorism against allied troops," as the hawkish *Washington Times* puts it. That phrase shows how badly Americans now abuse the English language: attacking invading soldiers in your own country is "terrorism"!

What Muqtada warned of was worlds away from murdering innocent people in New York. He was talking about fighting in his own country. From his point of view, Iraq has a massive problem with illegal aliens.

It used to be called "guerrilla warfare." It's often the only military option available against a powerful invader. The French Resistance is still praised for using guerrilla tactics against the German occupation during World War II.

Guerrilla warfare can be pretty ugly, as the Fallujah killings and corpse mutilations in the spring of 2004 reminded us. But "conventional" warfare, especially with modern high-tech weapons, isn't pretty either. American television was criticized for declining to show what was done to four American bodies; but neither has it shown, to this day, the Iraqi carnage caused by American weapons. We've been spared thousands of gruesome pictures showing the victims of "liberation." That includes civilians as well as brave Iraqi soldiers fighting the invaders against hopeless odds.

In the American media, only American soldiers in Iraq count as *fully human*, even as "heroes"; their deaths and injuries are tragic. Iraqis who don't welcome their "presence" are all lumped together as "terrorists."

Their deaths are like those of insects and only make us safer. We stand for freedom. Those who resist us hate freedom.

The Bush administration prepared us for war with lies that have been exposed. It said things it knew were false and things it had "no doubt" were true when they were only wild guesses. Saddam has been overthrown, but the people he oppressed and persecuted – the people we were supposedly saving from him – are now treated as enemies too. Do they also have "weapons of mass destruction" that threaten us?

The U.S. Government keeps justifying its huge and expanding power with dizzyingly rotating rationales. Consistency, as they say, is "not a problem." With all this propaganda, just keeping your head is a full-time job.

Muqtada's simple plea was ignored. Bush's opponent John Kerry could have exploited it if he had wanted to, having, after all, made his first fame speaking out against the Vietnam war. But he chose not to.

The closer you get to power, it seems, the less you are inclined to pipe up against it. Politicians who inveigh against abuses of power never mean they want to abolish the power itself; *they merely mean that they want it for themselves.*

As President, Kerry would have continued the war on "terrorism," a useful excuse for U.S. power, even if he had somewhat changed its guise with a multilateral approach. He might be compared to a politician who – this may sound far-fetched – marries an immensely rich woman and makes crude, demagogic attacks on "the rich" while living off her money.

What would Bush have done if he had reviewed the situation and realized that the Iraq war was wrong? Would he have repented, apologized, and withdrawn the troops, even at risk of losing the election? Or would he have admitted nothing and persisted in his course for the sake of keeping power?

We may never know. Yet it's even possible that it has already happened: that he realizes even now that he has created another Vietnam but chooses to keep it going, at whatever cost to others, rather than pay any price himself. After all, when a politician wrestles with his conscience, he usually wins.

In March 2004, a caravan including families from Military Families Speak Out (MFSO), who had lost their soldier-children in Iraq or whose children were serving in Iraq, families who had lost loved ones in N.Y. on 9/11, and Vets for Peace gathered at Dover Air Force Base, where the bodies of soldiers killed in Iraq are returned. On day two, the group gathered at Walter Reed Army Medical Center to highlight the treatment of more than 10,000 service men and women served in crowded, understaffed facilities. These families are angered by the deceptions for going to war and the attempt to hide the human cost.

THE EDITORS' GLOSS: Charley Reese brings to our attention the comments of Elizabeth Wilmshurst, a straight-talking London international lawyer who served as deputy legal advisor in the British Foreign and Commonwealth Office, where she worked for 29 years until her resignation of March 18, 2003. She resigned because, she said, "[she] did not agree that the use of force against Iraq was lawful, and in all the circumstances [she] did not want to continue as a legal adviser." Her resignation letter said of the Anglo-American war that "an unlawful use of force on such a scale amounts to the crime of aggression." She also referred to her conscience! It's nice to see some integrity in the land of St. Thomas More – if only occasionally.

Ms. Wilmshurst has spoken candidly on a number of issues. As Reese notes, she has questioned the "war on terror," and she's also indicated, with a lawyerly precision that one might wish for in the U.S. attorney general's or White House counsel's office, that going to war should be based on "facts" and not on an "assertion." Too bad no one in the U.S. or U.K. governments asked for her opinion in advance.

What is also unfortunate is that she knows so much more about just-war doctrine – though she is presumably neither a Catholic nor a moralist – than the self-professed, neocon "doctors of the Church." Michael Novak, for instance, tried to tell the Vatican in February 2003 that the U.S. was justified in attacking Iraq because of what "a spark of contact" between Saddam and terrorists "could" have accomplished, implying that America's right to make war arose from the *possibility* that Saddam *could* have done something to the U.S. His "just-war doctrine" includes the idea that America must ensure that no nation possesses the capacity to inflict harm on it, and make preemptive war in any direction it thinks will best "protect the lives and rights" of its people.

Happily, Novak's fantasy isn't part of any just-war doctrine permitted to Catholics, for a true title to make war comes only from an ongoing or imminent, grave and actual *violation* of a nation's rights – not from a merely *potential* one, regardless of whether the potential might be a clandestine, unannounced (terrorist-style) attack. Nor does it particularly matter, from a moral point of view, that submitting to the moral law in foreign affairs carries perhaps more risk than ignoring it and obliterating anyone who possesses the capacity to do us harm.

To their credit, the Novak line isn't part of any just-war doctrine that Charley Reese or Elizabeth Wilmshurst are familiar with either.

Legal Nonsense
• • • • • • • • •

Charley Reese

I LOVE THE SHARP tongue of the British. A former legal adviser to the British Foreign Office has said George Bush's war on terrorism is "legal nonsense" and confers no more power on the United States to detain people than the war against obesity.

That's true. The British lady, Elizabeth Wilmshurst, is quite correct, too, that the war against Iraq was illegal and thus the occupation of Iraq was/is illegal. I say "was/is" because that depends on whether you believe the fairy tale of Iraqi sovereignty.

So it turns out old Saddam Hussein was correct. He is still the legal President of Iraq; the new Iraqi government is illegal and has no right to try him. That, of course, will not prevent him from being tried and eventually hanged. One of the things I hope Americans are learning, besides the fact that the war wasn't worth it, is that the rule of law is a farce. Like language, the law is twisted to justify what the Bush administration wants to do. This administration is bound by neither law nor truth. ✗

I'm no lawyer, but I pointed out some time ago that you can't declare war on a tactic, and that's all terrorism is – a tactic. Real terrorists, as opposed to people resisting occupation of their country or guerrillas fighting to overthrow a government, are criminals, and as criminals deserve to be hunted down. That, however, is not a war. *Its county hunting.*

For all time, when bad governments wanted to increase their power, they spread fear and claimed the new power would allow them to "protect" the people. If there were no real enemies at the gate, they would invent them. The threat of terrorism has been enormously exaggerated by this administration to justify a very un-American lust for power. It has spread fear like a glutton spreads butter on hot pancakes.

Some local law-enforcement officers also fearmonger to get bigger budgets. Some in burgs no international terrorist could find with a satellite are warning the local folks to suspect everybody they see.

Another word that is vastly abused in this crazy time is "intelligence." Do you know what intelligence is? It's just knowledge, and knowledge must be factual. Assertions are not knowledge. Beliefs are not knowledge. Fears are not knowledge. Regardless of what so-called "intelligence" said, the facts are that Iraq had no stockpiles of weapons of mass destruction, had no programs to produce them and had no cooperative arrangements with al-Qaeda.

Vice President Dick Cheney, who probably should see a psychologist as well as a cardiologist, continues to claim a connection, but what he calls a connection is one or two meetings in a period of years from which nothing ever came. If a mere meeting is a "connection," then all of us have connections with every human being we've ever met, however briefly. This is another example of language abuse.

Another architect of the illegal war, former Deputy Secretary of Defense Paul Wolfowitz, coyly claimed for the longest time that just because we didn't find the weapons doesn't mean they don't exist. That's true. We haven't found any Martians, either, but perhaps they do exist, perhaps even in the offices of the Pentagon. It's always been hard to prove a negative.

This is an administration of sick puppies whose minds are haunted by lust for power, ideological phantoms and a profound contempt for the American people. A willingness to deceive is always proof of contempt.

I had hoped, in November of last year, that a majority of Americans would decide that this administration, like its illegal war, wasn't worth re-electing. But there is justice in the universe. At least now President Bush will have to clean up his own mess.

Chelle Pokorney touches her husband's casket as daughter Taylor, 2, holds the flag during Lieutenant Frederick Pokorney Jr.'s funeral, April 14, 2003, at Arlington National Cemetery.

THE EDITORS' GLOSS: The "insurgency" in Iraq is often thought of as a rear-guard action motivated by "dead-enders" and outright "terrorists" who ungratefully refuse the "blessings of democracy" foisted on them by the bombs and bullets of American diplomacy.

It is just possible, however, that people who fight foreign invasion do so because they don't like foreign invasion, and don't feel inclined to submit to it – even at the risk of death. As the Irish Jesuit Fr. Edward Cahill wrote in 1932, "the political unity and the independence of the nation have the first place. They are the primary rights of a nation, and the violent invasion of them by a foreign power has always been recognized by the common consent of mankind as the greatest national evil that a people can suffer. For, as with the individual, so also with the nation, slavery is justly regarded as an evil and a degradation, which no earthly advantage can outweigh. To be deprived of its independence has always been looked upon as a greater disaster for a nation than any loss of material resources, no matter how severe, greater even than the destruction of the flower of the nation's manhood in the horrors of war."

History would seem to indicate that no one in the region that is modern Iraq is prepared to live under foreign domination, though they *are* quite prepared to exercise their right to resist it. Attempts to portray that resistance as "terrorism" – as even many conservative Catholic self-appointed experts do – ignore this truth in an effort to spin the conflict as yet another battle in the great American crusade against "terror." Yet this is a jingoistic and chauvinistic interpretation supported by neither the moral truth, which recognizes a people's right to defend itself, nor the facts ... facts like recent studies, reported in a July 18, 2005, *Christian Science Monitor* piece by Tom Regan, indicating that even the "foreign" fighters in Iraq are "not extremists who wanted to attack the U.S. in an al-Qaeda-like manner" but are simply "heeding the calls from clerics and activists to drive infidels out of Arab land."

A serious and realistic approach to statesmanship – rather than an ideological and fideistic one – would bear in mind not only these recent facts but also an understanding of Iraq's history, such as that hinted at by Dr. Fleming in what follows. Such an understanding would reveal to our governing class just how unlikely it is that people in the region would submit to even temporary foreign domination, thus calling into question the prospects of success for a war such as ours, and impugning thereby the war's alleged justice.

Riding the Red Horse:
War and the Prospects of Success
. . . .
Thomas Fleming, Ph.D.

> "And there went out another horse that was red: and power was given to him that sat thereon to take peace from the earth, and that they should kill one another: and there was given unto him a great sword."
>
> —Apocalypse vi:4

IN THE APOSTLE'S revelation, the rider of the red horse has the power to take peace from the earth so that men will kill each other. It is a frightening power, and the great novel by Eugenio Corti that takes its name from this passage, *Il cavallo rosso*, documents the author's first-hand experience as an artillery officer on both sides of the Second World War, first as an Italian soldier fighting on the Russian front as a German ally and then as one of *The Last Soldiers of the King* (the title of another of his books) defending Italy from its former ally. Why does he fight the Germans? He is Italian, and they, who are occupying Italy, must be expelled. Faced with the desertions, incompetence, and, indeed the cowardice of many Italian soldiers, Corti feels unequal to the task, but he imagines the faces of friends and feels "ashamed for having begun to give up; we simply had to continue behaving like men, that was all." He fought, in other words, because not to fight would be an act of betrayal.

Corti was a brave and dutiful soldier, but he also understood the horror of war too well to think of it as the first or even the second recourse of foreign policy. "Poveri cristi," he repeatedly calls the Italian soldiers on the Russian front (in his war diary *Few Returned*), "Poor Christs," an evocative Italian expression for innocent suffering.

Refusal to fight may be cowardice and treason that darkens the soul of a single man, but the opposite mistake – an impetuous and reckless decision to make unnecessary war – may cost the lives of millions. And, most moral people will condemn any declaration of war to the extent that it is made out of pride or cupidity or even self-interest – as opposed to Corti's simple desire to defend his country.

How, then, are such decisions to be made? Catholics, both liberal and conservative, trot out the principles of just-war theory as self-evident truths. Unfortunately, they are not self-evident to most non-Christians, and unless these principles can be put in the abstract form of the liberal philosophical tradition, we can scarcely hope to see them taken seriously by political commentators, much less applied by men who have hardened their hearts to wage undeclared wars by pushing buttons.

The criteria for a just war are sometimes presented as a list of arbitrary commandments with no obvious relation to each other. However, the theoretical criteria can be resolved into three questions that, perhaps, even liberals should be able to grasp. In contemplating any proposed war, we must consider the *justice* of the causes of the war, the *methods* to be employed, and the *consequences* that can be expected. While I propose to concentrate only on the last question and to treat it only from an historical point of view, it is worth considering the basic case for the U.S. invasion and occupation of Iraq.

Peace, as St. Thomas explained, is the object of a just war, and administration spokesmen have duly justified the invasion of Iraq because the ultimate purpose was to bring peace. Saddam Hussein had, it was alleged, actively collaborated with the al-Qaeda terrorists who attacked the World Trade Center; he was stockpiling "weapons of mass destruction" and was on the point of being able to strike the United States and its allies with nuclear weapons; Saddam was a tyrant and American forces would be greeted as liberators; his removal, at the cost of minimum civilian damage, would bring democracy, peace, and prosperity to the Middle East. In the event, none of the acts in this scenario were played out according to the administration's plan, but even if weapons of mass destruction had been found and the occupation were peaceful, a broader historical context suggests that even by the administration's own standards, war would not have been justified, not, certainly, on the grounds that it would bring peace.

Americans are not fond of studying history, even recent history. They would like to confine their knowledge of Iraq to the period beginning roughly in 1990. Conveniently forgotten is the part played by the United States and its allies in supplying weapons – including chemical and biological weapons – to Saddam, when he was seen as an ally against Iran.

Forgotten, too, is American policy in Afghanistan (since the Carter years), where Islamic guerrillas were armed and trained by the United States, which also furnished fundamentalist imams to promote jihad against the Russians. In the 911 Commission hearing, there was no mention of this policy nor of our support for Islamic terrorists in Kosovo and Bosnia, where Osama bin Laden – then the ally and protégé of the CIA – was given citizenship and permitted to establish a base of operations in Europe. There is nothing to prevent an Iraqi fighter from citing the old proverb, what is sauce for the goose is sauce for the gander. If manufacturing chemical and biological weapons and distributing them to terrorists is a crime for Iraq, it is also a crime for the United States; if the charge of aiding and abetting Islamic terrorists justifies the invasion of Iraq and the massive destruction of civilian life, then why should the United States, which has consistently aided and abetted Islamic terrorists, express outrage against attacks on its citizens?

We also need to look at this war in a broader historical context, if we are to assess the probable consequences. In the first Gulf War, there was considerable loss of civilian life and damage to the Iraqi infrastructure. Because of the destruction and the embargo, hundreds of thousands – some estimates exceed 750,000 – Iraqis died in the years following the war. There is no conceivable justification for so massive a loss of life, for which the United States bears overwhelming responsibility. While the results of the second Gulf War may or may not reach the catastrophic proportions of the first, the inevitable loss of life, the destruction of the economy and infrastructure, and the demolition and vandalizing of precious historic monuments should be matters of grave concern.

There is, however, another criterion by which the consequences of a war can be judged: the probability of success. To make such a judgment requires an exercise of prudence, the virtuous faculty that enables us to judge the probable outcomes of our actions by applying universal rules to specific acts. As St. Thomas states (*Summa Theologica*, II, ii, Q. 47), "since it belongs to prudence rightly to counsel, judge, and command concerning the means of obtaining a due end, it is evident that prudence regards not only the private good of the individual, but also the common good of the multitude."

To be prudent, a ruler in deciding to go to war must examine the historical evidence at his disposal. Before launching an invasion of Iraq, an American President would have to consider how likely is it that Iraq, of all the Arabic-speaking provinces of the former Ottoman Empire, should develop the institutions of a peaceful democracy? The history of the Middle East gives little encouragement to those who imagine that an oil-rich Switzerland can be established among the ruins of Nineveh and Babylon.

The Persians

The United States is by no means the first powerful nation that imagined it could impose peace and justice upon the Middle East. We are walking in the footsteps of the Ottomans, the Byzantines, the Romans, the Macedonians, and the Medes and Persians, who overthrew the Assyrian Empire, conquered Babylon, and sent some of the Babylonian Jews back to Jerusalem to restore the temple.

> In the first year of Cyrus the king, the same Cyrus the king made a decree concerning the house of God at Jerusalem, Let the house be builded, the place they offered sacrifices, and let the foundations thereof be strongly laid. . . . And also let the golden and silver vessels of the house of God, which Nebuchadnezzar took forth out of the temple which is at Jerusalem, and brought unto Babylon, be restored.

The Persians were a great people, whose simple code of honor – ride a horse, shoot straight, and tell the truth – was admired by their Greek enemies. The conquest of Babylon in 537, the occasion of Cyrus's edict, although it sealed Persia's fate as an imperial nation doomed to degenerate and fail, shows the Persians flushed with success but determined to deal justly with their subjects. Although it has been conjectured that the Persians were rewarding the Babylonian Jews for covert assistance in the defeat of Nabonidus, the last Babylonian king, there is no need to posit any special relationship between a tiny and impotent people and the greatest ruler of the day. It was Cyrus's general policy to reverse the oppression inflicted on subject nations by Babylonian and Assyrian rulers, who had driven defeated enemies into exile and resettled foreigners in the vacated lands. This *divide et impera* strategy would be emulated by later tyrants.

The Assyrians had permanently destroyed the northern kingdom of Israel, and the Babylonians, after conquering the people of Judah, although they did allow most Jews to remain in their country, drove many skilled workers and much of the elite class into exile, and they destroyed the temple whose ruins were a potent symbol of cultural genocide.

The Assyrians were a thoroughly nasty lot, who excelled in the refinements of mayhem and torture – skinning alive was a favorite technique. An educated Iraqi, whom I met at the Oriental Institute in Chicago, tried to claim that the Assyrians had been given a bad press by their enemies. Alas, the bad press comes from the Assyrians themselves, whose chronicles and sculptured reliefs offer gloating accounts of mass murder. And, if we were inclined to think the Assyrian chroniclers had exaggerated the violence, the ruins of Ashdod, a Philistine city, which tried to reassert its independence from Sargon II, reveal the grisly reality. Israeli archaeologists, Moshe and Trude Dothan, found dozens of dismembered bodies thrown into a pit, a stack of ten skulls, as well as the remains of hundreds of children, adolescents, and adults – all in one small area. Egypt, which might once have come to the rescue of its Philistine satellite, had been reduced to a cipher, and the rulers of Ashdod had made the mistake of thinking they could stand up to their world's only remaining superpower.

The Assyrians were hardly any kinder to their own citizens. While Sumerian and Babylonian laws had been temperate and proportional, Assyrian punishments even for fairly trivial offenses were extreme. As C. J. Gadd (in the *Cambridge Ancient History*) describes them: "These laws abound, in almost every section, with heavy fines and convict-labour, superadded to savage beatings and ghastly physical mutilations, inflicted upon men and women alike, to which the death-penalty, also freely awarded, can seem only an alleviation." Gadd connects the savagery of their laws with the unwholesome life in the Assyrian palace, which served as a prison for the king's family and household.

The Assyrians and their Babylonian successors wrote the book on tyranny and empire, setting an example to be imitated by future conquerors, no matter how noble their motives. The Persian Cyrus, for example, understood (as the Assyrians had not) that leaving people alone to enjoy their own customs and worship their own gods, is a better means of securing the loyalty of subjects than the orgy of destruction and bloodshed over which the Assyrian documents so lovingly gloat. But the comparative decency and humanity of the Persians, glorified not only by Ezra but also by Isaiah (who calls him *messiah*), must have come as a relief, a gentle morning after the long nightmare of Assyrian and Babylonian misrule.

The last Babylonian king, Nabonidus, was not so much a tyrant as he was an eccentric. His elderly mother came from Haran (one of Abraham's cities), where she was priestess of the moon-god Sin, and as king, Nabonidus devoted much of his time to elevating his mother's deity over the gods of the Babylonian pantheon. Many Babylonians thought the old man was insane – claiming victory in battles that had never taken place. And yet this "archaeologist king" had apparently been a successful military commander in his youth and as king he not only rebuilt the temple of Sin, but also restored ancient temples and revived the religious and cultural traditions of the Sumerian and Akkadian peoples.

Those traditions can be traced in written documents back to the early Third Millenium, when the peoples of Sumerian city-states were laying the groundwork for the civilization that was later enriched and reinvented by Greeks and Romans, before being passed down to us. Outside of Mesopotamia and Egypt, other early peoples are only so much bones and rubbish, and their "histories" are told as catalogues of pottery styles and methods of interment. But Sumerians and Akkadians, and the peoples of Mari and Nineveh who followed them, we know as distinctive human beings, who lived and died, killed and loved and worshipped their gods whose deeds comprised the central subject of their literatures. And if the Sumerians created civilization, their Akkadian successors gave birth to the first empire.

The founder of the Akkadian empire was Sargon, the first "Great Man" of history. We know few facts about his early career – not even his name. He must have adopted Sargon, which means "the true king," after he came to power. But the story of his life impressed itself upon the imagination of later generations. According to the legend, he was the illegitimate child of a priestess in Kish and as an infant he was exposed, like Moses and Romulus, in a basket set into the river and was raised by a humble water-carrier. Eventually, he found favor with Ishtar (the Semitic Venus) and he was made cup-bearer (something like chancellor) to Ur-Zababa, the Sumerian king of Kish. Sargon's chief rival for power, Lugalzagessi, the Sumerian king of Umma, had apparently dethroned and probably killed king Ur-Zabba, when he conquered Kish, but Sargon raised an army, and took Lagash by surprise and went on to smite Lagash. Afterwards he made a ceremonial ritual of washing his weapons in the Persian Gulf.

This little detail is a hint that Sargon self-consciously regarded himself as a man of destiny. And it was not just his impressive conquests that made him different. His decision to impose a uniform system of weights and measures is typical. Earlier rulers had ruled over all of Sumer, but they had been content to leave the city-states independent and, therefore, capable of rebellion. Sargon thoroughly dominated the cities and subjected them to a centralized administration – creating the first conscription for a world empire.

Sargon's successors were faced with revolts and invasions, but they managed to hold his empire together. Sargon's grandson Naram-Sin ruled over a territory stretching from the Mediterranean Sea to the Taurus Mountains in southern Turkey. He declared himself "king of the four quarters of the world" – usually interpreted as something like ruler of the universe. He also took to wearing a horned helmet that had previously been reserved to the gods and had himself proclaimed a god – another first step for the Akkadian dynasty that was imitated by later rulers. Although his empire was invaded and overthrown by wild Gutians from the East, the Assyrians remained loyal to Sargon's imperial vision.

To visualize the empire of Sargon the Great and the lands ruled by his successors, it is helpful to imagine a map. Babylon was on the Euphrates River, southwest of modern Baghdad (on the Tigris). Upstream from Babylon lay Mari, whose records give us so lively a picture of early Semitic life, as well as Assur and Nineveh, the Assyrian capitals. Downstream on the Euphrates lay Ur, the "imperial city" of the Sumerians. Ancient Babylon was not far from Agade, the city that commemorates the name of the Akkadians, the Semitic people that intermingled with the Sumerians and eventually, without ever forgetting their debt, took over political and cultural hegemony.

In terms of modern cities, this land between the two rivers, or Mesopotamia, stretches from Mosul in the north and southeastward down the Euphrates to Basra, which lies east of Ur and Eridu. This "cradle of civilization," which gave birth to the idea of global empire – and was so often the graveyard of empires – lies within the confines of modern Iraq.

The Persians came into Assyria and Babylonia as high-minded liberators, but within a generation or two they had gone native, imitating the quaint customs of the locals. By the time they attempted the conquest of Greece in the early 5th century, Herodotus, who appreciated their good qualities, was able to see the Persian Wars as part of the ongoing struggle between Hellenic Europe and barbaric Asia. The Macedonians and Greeks who overthrew the Persians and took over Mesopotamia also began on a high note, but they too fell in with local traditions, and the record of the later Seleucid rulers is stained in the blood of patriots and tyrants.

The Romans, who were invited by the Jews to intervene on their behalf, succeeded to the Macedonians, but, although Rome's eastern provinces brought great wealth, the project was a costly adventure that entailed generations of warfare against the Parthians and later the revived kingdom of the Persians. Some of the greatest defeats suffered by the Roman army were in these wars. The struggle for control of Mesopotamia dragged on for centuries. Marching against the Persians, the Emperor Julian met defeat and death in 363. The Byzantine Emperor, Heraclius, finally conquered the Persians, but the victory proved very costly. Not only had the empire exhausted its resources in the struggle, but, with Persia out of the way, they had to face the gathering storm of Islamic expansionism, alone.

The impression is sometimes given that Roman emperors simply invaded territories without any pretext of a just cause. Such is not the case. Whatever the facts might have been, Roman generals and their masters typically claimed they were acting justly in responding to aggression against Rome or a Roman ally or in punishing the violators of a treaty. Like every other great nation in the history of the world, Romans waged wars for loot and plunder, but they were generally able to pretend to a just cause. The same can be said of the Persians, Egyptians, and Hittites. A war of pure aggression was viewed as a risky business, partly because it might bring on divine wrath, and partly because it might drive enemies into a defensive alliance. Even Assyrian rulers tried to justify their wars of conquest as acts of divinely ordained justice. In 741 B.C. Sargon II attacked Urartu more or less for the hell of it: "because I had never yet come near Ursa . . . nor poured out the blood of his warriors on the field." Nonetheless, Sargon prayed to Ashur for permission to attack his enemy" – to make him bear his sin" – on the grounds of impiety. The Assyrian attack on Israel had still firmer grounds. Although king Hoshea had wisely submitted himself and what was left of his kingdom to Tiglath-Pileser III, he was caught intriguing with Egypt against Tiglath-Pileser's successor. When the crunch came, Egypt failed to come to Israel's rescue, and that tiny kingdom learned too late not to get involved in the conflicts of great nations.

The Assyrians were replaced by the Persians who were themselves conquered by the Macedonians, who were forced to give way to the power of Rome. The Romans and Byzantines were not the last western people to attempt to dominate Mesopotamia. They were followed, 400 years later, by the Crusaders, who came to rescue the Holy Land and remained to become, in a surprisingly short time, as ruthless – and degenerate – as the Assyrians themselves. Britain arrived in force after WWI, to ensure a stable and pro-British government and, as time went on, control of the oilfields. Their mischievous creativity in making "nations" – such as Kuwait – by drawing lines on maps has only contributed to the instability of the Middle East. They also bear principal responsibility for the *unwise* establishment of Israel and the destruction of the Palestinians. If any of these Western powers thought they could rid the Middle East of violence and tyranny, they should have been quickly disabused.

Now enter the not-so-quiet Americans. There should have been no doubt about the Americans' capacity to conquer the "Cradle of Civilization," but at what cost and to what purpose? There are less violent ways to secure the oil that fuels the U.S. economy, and no one should have any illusions – after 5000 years – about bringing peace and democracy to Babylonia and Assyria.

Our grandchildren will not live to see that day, but, should our grandchildren wish to prowl among the ruins of a civilization that died in their grandparents time, will they still be able to visit Ur and Nineveh? Many important monuments were damaged in the first Gulf War, and during the period of embargo and illegal "no-fly zones," the Iraqi government was unable to protect such important sites as Nineveh. But these vandalisms were only the prelude to the massive looting and destruction of Mesopotamian antiquities that has taken place under the American occupation. Even if many of the larger works of art can be recovered, precious collections of documents and artifacts, so painfully assembled by scholars and archaeologists, can never be put back together. Imagine our reaction if Israel were to carry out the threat made by a leading defense advisor, Martin van Creveld, to strike Rome with nuclear weapons.

Empire – or rather, the concept of benevolent global hegemony – is one of the gifts of Mesopotamia, but it is a poisoned chalice. The story of the Tower of Babel is the Bible's commentary on the Babylonians' attempt to build a multi-ethnic state, and the ruins of Nineveh and Babylon and Persepolis should warn the most rugged imperialist against the danger of walking in the footsteps of Sargon and Sennacherib.

Cicero's admonition on the lessons of history is by now a cliché but true, nonetheless: he who does not know what took place before he was born remains forever a child. Unfortunately, the ruling class of the United States, children all in their historical ignorance, control a military machine that would have inspired awe in Sargon and Sennacherib. But if they cannot take prudential lessons from history, perhaps they can learn humility by contemplating the consequences, becoming more evident every day, of their folly.

The consequences of this invasion, whether measured in terms of the thousands of dead Iraqi civilians, the destruction of precious monuments and documents, or even the loss of money generated by the Iraqi oil industry, are already terrible and should convince any war hawk that this war was a mistake. But for Americans, the gravest consequences may well lie in the not so distant future. The United States' policy in the Middle East has succeeded in doing what no one else has done in several centuries. It has united Muslims around the world in a common cause: the desire to inflict pain on the American people. In the looming struggle with Islam, we have lost most of our principal allies, and our rivals for world domination, China and Russia, can afford to sit back and enjoy the spectacle of one more ruler of the four quarters meeting its end in the deserts of Babylonia.

Rudyard Kipling, contemplating the fate of the British Empire, issued a warning in his great hymn "Recessional."

> Far-called, our navies melt away;
> On dune and headland sinks the fire:
> Lo, all our pomp of yesterday
> Is one with Nineveh and Tyre!
> Judge of the Nations, spare us yet,
> Lest we forget – lest we forget!

For Iraqi mothers, Bush's Operation IRAQI FREEDOM has brought the Wild West to the Middle East.

THE EDITORS' GLOSS: The U.S.-created "new Iraq" is a mess, and the logic, facts, and argument marshaled in support of that thesis by Eric Margolis give the lie to one of the most absurd justifications for the war in Iraq: it's OK because it's better now than when Saddam was in power.

But what if Iraq indeed *were* better off? Saddam was a "rough" character, and his forcible removal from power may even have heralded the end of things that some Iraqis would rather not have lived with over the last several decades (though many of Saddam's critics tend to be notoriously short on reliable details, and many of them turn out to be outright liars). But nowhere in just-war theory is there granted a right to make war on a sovereign state simply to make life "better" for its people.

Yet this is what we now hear, given especially the missing WMD and the non-existent ties between Baghdad and al-Qaeda: the 2003 war in Iraq was for "democracy." The President told peoples around the world during his second inauguration, "when you stand for liberty, we will stand with you." Charles Krauthammer wanted the war in order to "revolutionize the region," and Thomas Friedman defended it as a way "to build a progressive Arab regime."

None of these pie-in-the sky aims justifies war. The allegedly "undemocratic" nature of pre-war Iraqi society in no way constituted a *violation* of America's *rights*, required by just-war doctrine before the U.S. could claim a corresponding right to make war. Indeed, as a saintly Pontiff put it back in 1910, forms of government are essentially irrelevant. Far from justifying death and destruction in its pursuit, "the advent of universal Democracy is of no concern to the action of the Church in the world," he said. "Giving themselves the form of government which they think most suited to their needs" is a task that "the Church has always left to the nations."

She certainly did not leave it to the United States and its military machine.

CHAPTER
7

A Mirage Too Far
• • • • • • • • • •
Eric S. Margolis

THE GRAVEST ISSUE continuing to confront President George W. Bush during this second term of his is the painful fact that the war he unleashed against Iraq is lost, both on the strategic as well as the tactical level.

No matter how much the Iraq war is justified by its neocon engineers as a self-defensive conflict, each bloody new day in Iraq makes clear that the Bush administration plunged into a war based on disastrously bad intelligence, falsified data, and deeply flawed political and military planning.

Neither Iraq's U.S.-"guided" January elections, nor intensifying military operations against the Iraqi resistance, will change the reality that President George Bush's crusade in Mesopotamia looks more each day like a 20th century colonial war of increasingly violent repression. Watching American tanks firing into buildings in Fallujah conjures up ugly memories of Soviet armor in 1956 Budapest rather than images of a war of self-defense or democratic liberation. In fact, President Bush's varying reasons for invading Iraq often sound remarkably like the ones Moscow used to justify crushing free Hungary.

By failing to win quickly a clear victory in Iraq in either a political, military, or economic sense, America has already lost the war. Victory, in the case of Iraq, remains indefinable. Defeat, however, can easily be delineated. We are looking at it each day.

In 2003, this writer joined his voice to those of other Mid-east veterans in warning that an invasion of Iraq promised to immerse the U.S. in a boiling cauldron of Mesopotamian conflict that would defy political resolution and inflict disaster on all concerned.

Unfortunately, none of the administration's war hawks appears to have read the finest military thinker of the 20th century, Britain's Major General J.F.C Fuller. He coined a basic maxim of grand strategy: the objective of war is not victory, as many mistakenly imagine, but the peace that ensues. In fact, the Iraq fiasco perfectly illustrates the general's point that military victory is empty unless it achieves desired political objectives.

In Iraq, as well as Afghanistan, the Bush administration replaced the regimes it overthrew by political puppets that lacked any national or even regional following, had no claim to legitimacy, and, most important in the Muslim World, were totally bereft of any popular respect. The survival of these rent-a-regimes was entirely dependent on American and British bayonets.

The man Washington put in charge of Iraq, Iyad Allawi, a longtime CIA and MI6 "asset," was viewed by most Iraqis as a foreign hireling, and a Saddam wannabe. Saddam Hussein could at least walk in downtown Baghdad; Allawi, like CIA "asset" Hamid Karzai (Afghanistan's figurehead leader), needed to be constantly surrounded by a ring of American mercenary bodyguards and U.S. troops.

Iraq's January elections were trumpeted by the White House as that nation's democratic coming of age. But they excluded all significant opposition parties and are regarded by all in the cynical Mid-east as rigged in spite of Washington's claims true democracy has been established in Iraq.

In Afghanistan, the shura, or national council, that "elected" Hamid Karzai as interim president was also ringed by U.S. troops, and its members were bought with tens of millions in bribes. The whole process was rightly dismissed across Afghanistan as a rigged, political farce identical to a similar shura that was held by the Soviets in 1986, and which produced Afghanistan's new, "democratic president," Moscow's man in Kabul, Najibullah.

The only way Iraqi elections could have been considered honest is if parties opposed to U.S. rule of Iraq – including Islamist parties – were allowed to run *and actually win.* In recent Afghan "democratic" elections ballyhooed by the Bush administration, parties and figures opposed to U.S. occupation were excluded – as they were in Iraq. While the U.S. rightly called for honest elections in Ukraine, votes in its Mid-east satrapies, like Iraq, Egypt, Tunisia, and Morocco, are as rigged as any in the old Soviet Union.

When a regime emerges in Baghdad that demands all foreign forces get out, promises to re-arm Iraq, and calls for renewed confrontation with Israel, then we will know that true democracy has bloomed in Iraq.

By contrast, the Bush administration's version of democracy in Iraq means a compliant regime that hosts U.S. bases, pumps cheap oil, allows U.S. firms to harvest Iraq's wealth, keeps Islamists in check, and makes nice to Israel.

This is a mirage. It will not happen. Iraq can never be reformed into a politically stable nation until the nationalists and other Islamist parties are allowed into the political process and given power commensurate with their numbers.

Washington cannot rule Iraq indefinitely through a Vichy-style regime.

Nor has it been so far able to achieve any national accord between Shiites, Sunnis, and Kurds, only the latter of whom support the U.S. presence. In other words, Iraq remains a politically shattered nation where fierce tribalism has re-emerged in the void created by the fall of the brutal but efficient regime of Saddam Hussein. The same process has occurred in Afghanistan, where the feeble Karzai regime rules only Kabul.

These painful verities were perfectly clear before the invasions of either nation. Veteran observers warned that no stability was possible in either Iraq or Afghanistan without the political inclusion of all parties and ethnic groups. But the Bush administration's born-again cold warriors did precisely the opposite, imposing puppet minority regimes that would never be accepted by the majority.

Political failure in Iraq means the growing national resistance to U.S.-led foreign occupation will continue and intensify. Hard on the heels of political failure comes increasingly grim operational and tactical reverses that may portend an actual military defeat, or at least bloody stalemate, for America's mighty armed forces.

One of the most important concepts in the military arts is that of initiative. An attacker holds the initiative, and derives potent advantage from it, by keeping the defender off balance and unable to develop his own strategies and tactics. Think of one boxer pummeling another into a corner.

In a grave development, U.S. forces in Iraq have lost strategic and, frequently, tactical initiative. The 150,000 U.S. troops garrisoning Iraq are stretched perilously thin, unable to control large swathes of territory, and tied down protecting bases and economic targets.

U.S. forces are unable for moral, humane, and public relations reasons to raze entire rebellious Iraqi cities and slaughter thousands at a time, as the Russians have done in Chechnya, though they came close to Moscow's Mongol tactics by destroying the rebellious city of Fallujah as a warning to other resisters. As soon as Fallujah was "liberated," resistance forces slipped back in, forcing the U.S. to garrison yet another city.

In Iraq, U.S. troops are becoming painfully aware the war has no apparent end and is growing more, not less intense. Like young Soviet soldiers in Afghanistan who were told they were "liberating" that nation from foreign imperialist occupation, even the most naïve U.S. troops must by now understand that they are not liberators, but unwanted occupiers stuck in what appears a pointless, incomprehensible war. The much-publicized mutiny of a transport unit is gripping evidence of the erosion of morale in Iraq.

Almost all previous colonial wars of the 20th century showed that garrison duty and anti-insurgency operations relentlessly sapped military morale, engendered torture and brutality, and corrupted even the best-trained troops. The examples of Algeria, Angola, Indochina, and Afghanistan in the 1980s come immediately to mind.

On the tactical level, lines of communications have proven the Achilles heel of the U.S. expeditionary force in Iraq ever since the first days of the invasion. Iraqi irregulars and resistance forces quickly attacked vulnerable U.S. supply convoys without whose constant provisions logistically voracious American forces could not effectively operate. Such attacks actually slowed or even halted U.S. armored spearheads as they raced north to Baghdad.

During the course of the last year, attacks against the long U.S. supply lines that stretch from Kuwait north into Iraq have risen steadily. In a horrifying new element in what the Pentagon calls asymmetric warfare, Iraqi guerillas found that chopping off the heads of foreign truck drivers was a highly effective way of undermining the U.S. supply system. Many of the 20,000 or so foreign mercenaries hired to fight and perform services in Iraq for U.S. and British forces simply decamp in the face of growing atrocities and kidnappings.

The U.S. cannot adequately guard its supply lines, nor the oil pipelines that are regularly targeted by Iraq's resistance. More troops are needed, but they are not available. The so-called "coalition of the willing" continues to shrink. The Bush administration has been unsuccessful in cajoling or bribing any new nations to send troops into combat in Iraq.

Efforts by the U.S. to achieve a classic goal of all occupying powers – forming native armed forces to perform dirty, dangerous jobs and routine security, are proving unsuccessful. The 170,000 Iraqis who have been put into police and army uniforms by the Pentagon enlisted solely because no other means of income was available.

In another classic truism of colonial warfare, these native troops do the bare minimum to earn their paychecks, routinely inform the resistance on U.S. plans, sometimes fight against their paymasters, and are almost entirely unreliable. Suicide car bombings of police stations and enlistment offices do not encourage morale among Washington's Iraqi sepoys. Hopes inspired by Iyad Allawi that Iraqi government troops will go do the heavy fighting are another Pentagon necon fantasy that will cost more billions of wasted dollars.

The bitter lessons learned in Vietnam have been entirely forgotten.

Resistance attacks by 20 odd groups ranging from Islamists, Nasserites, Ba'athists, to al-Qaeda and foreign mujahedin, have increased dramatically since the insurgency's beginning over two years ago. U.S. estimates say resistance forces have grown at least fourfold, from 5,000 to 20,000, a figure this writer believes is a woeful underestimate.

U.S. forces have killed some 12,000–20,000 (one reputable study by Johns Hopkins claims 100,000) Iraqi civilians since invading Iraq, and continue to slay large numbers in urban battles against guerillas and by punitive bombings against rebellious cities, most notably, Fallujah, which has become a symbol of national resistance to occupation. Every new civilian killed earns the U.S. five new enemies in Iraq.

As the resistance grows, U.S. forces are spending more time protecting their bases and supply convoys than fighting the enemy, another classic waypoint in guerilla conflicts marking a major loss of tactical initiative.

While U.S. troop morale declines, the war is also causing serious strain to the military's assets. The U.S. lacks sufficient troops to "pacify" Iraq. So thinly stretched are U.S. forces that 60-year old reservists are being recalled to arms. Over half of all U.S. combat units are stuck in Iraq.

Tanks and Bradley fighting vehicles are not designed for fighting insurgents: their delicate tracks are being worn out and their engines degraded by sand and dust, The same applies to the U.S. helicopter fleet in Iraq, which has proven to be remarkably vulnerable to small arms fire.

U.S. war stocks and spare parts are being used up at rates that will take years, if not decades, to replenish. Aircraft and ships are being pressed into service way beyond their normal operational cycles. Maintenance, readiness and replacements are being gravely compromised by the wars in Iraq and Afghanistan. Pentagon funds allocated for replacement and modernization of equipment are being consumed by combat operations.

While non-Kurdish regions of Iraq remain in semi-chaos, the U.S. will continue to pour $6 billion monthly into Iraq's desert sands just to keep the

Frankenstein state it has acquired from collapsing. Meanwhile, Iraq acts both as a magnet and incubator for every sort of fanatical anti-American group and, like Afghanistan in the 1980s, a rallying point for the Muslim world.

President Bush and his neocon praetorians may call this a victory, but to one who has covered a dozen insurgencies, Iraq looks like a disaster well into the making. America has stuck its head into a hornet's nest. It cannot pull out without enormous loss of face that will undermine its existing Mid-east oil imperium and embolden anti-U.S. groups everywhere. Bush, who staked his presidency on fighting Muslims, cannot be seen to be beaten by a despised nation of Arabs.

But if the U.S. stays in Iraq – and Afghanistan – the result will be more soldiers killed, more treasure wasted, more enemies created, and all without anything to show for it. Except, of course, for a delighted Osama bin Laden who has repeatedly told his followers that the only way to defeat the mighty U.S.A is to get it stuck into small wars and slowly bleed it dry. President Bush has kindly obliged.

Faced by a monstrously expensive, stalemated war of attrition, a good general would cut his losses and retreat. After all, who today really cares about the humiliating retreat from Vietnam? Prestige is for politicians, not the soldiers who are facing death on Iraq's lethal streets.

But Bush and his necon desk warriors are the very worst of military leaders. They went to war without a plan for the peace, made hope and wishful thinking into a strategy, and listened to fraudsters, mountebanks, and agents of influence of a foreign nation, rather than the Pentagon's battle-tested veterans. On their heads rests the deaths of so many Americans and Iraqis.

There is nothing more tragic nor more wasteful than a lost war. And there is not a scintilla of right, justice, or vindication in a war of pure colonial aggression. The 20th century taught us those hard lessons, even if Bush and Co. obstinately refuse to heed them.

A flag is folded at the grave site for Army Sergeant First Class John W. Marshall, who was killed in Baghdad. His children, although they live far from the Washington area, chose a burial at Arlington National Cemetery for their father.

THE EDITORS' GLOSS: One clear sign of the corruption of American politics is the way in which the affixing of labels has come to replace the serious exchange of ideas. Those who defend the idea of a just war are often called "war mongers," while those who wish to prevent war however possible are dismissed as "peaceniks" and "pacifists."

All this name-calling has disguised the true position of the Catholic Church on matters of war and peace (straightforwardly presented in the Appendices). The work of Catholic neocon (and American Enterprise Institute hack) Michael Novak has the same negative effect. For him, just-war doctrine "sets forth the rules under which public authorities are obliged to move to defend their own peoples." But the truth is the opposite: it *limits* when armed force *can* legitimately be used, and says almost nothing about when it *should* be.

Nor is war a "virtue," as Islamophobes Webster and Cole maintain in their interesting but fundamentally wrong treatise *The Virtue of War.* Nor is it "beautiful," as Atila Guimarães maintains in the last chapter of his disastrous and even childish book *War, Just War,* laced as it is with platitudes and assertions – such as "life is a just war" – that serve only to short-circuit logic and stifle discourse.

War is in reality a plague from which the Church prays to be delivered, like famine and pestilence. St. Thomas treats of it in the *Summa* as a vice under the heading of "charity," and the Catechism of the Council of Trent deals with it as an exception to the prohibition against murder in its discussion of the 5th Commandment. "A just war is always a sad thing," says Catholic philosopher Romano Amerio in his *Iota Unum,* "because it is a form of fratricide and, if fought among Christians, also a sort of sacrilege, given the sacred character of a baptized man." Mgr. Beguin, Bishop of Belley, France, wrote in 1931 that "considered in itself, in abstraction from the motives which can sometimes justify it, war is murder, an accumulation of murders. It is, says Pius XI, a monstrous homicide, a fratricidal combat, the accursed fruit of discord. All those who have seen the atrocities of war at close quarters will endorse this condemnation without reserve." And the Malines Social Union's *Code of International Ethics* refers to war, and material force in general, though "required by natural law as the servant of justice," as not something to celebrate but rather "a regrettable necessity."

Let Catholics and other "red-blooded" types who might be inclined to dismiss what follows consider these truths before they do so.

CHAPTER
8

The Failure of War
• • • • • • • • •
Wendell Berry

> "All modern war is to be forbidden."
> —Alfredo Cardinal Ottaviani

IF YOU KNOW even as little history as I do, it is hard not to doubt the efficacy of modern war as a solution to any problem except that of retribution – the "justice" of exchanging one damage for another.

Apologists for war will insist that war answers the problem of national self-defense. But the doubter, in reply, will ask to what extent the cost even of a successful war of national defense – in life, money, material, foods, health, and (inevitably) freedom – may amount to a national defeat. National defense through war always involves some degree of national defeat. This paradox has been with us from the very beginning of our republic. Militarization in defense of freedom reduces the freedom of the defenders.

In a modern war, fought with modern weapons and on the modern scale, neither side can limit to "the enemy" the damage that it does. These wars damage the world. We know enough by now to know that you cannot damage a part of the world without damaging all of it. Modern war has not only made it impossible to kill "combatants" without killing "non-combatants," it has made it impossible to damage your enemy without damaging yourself.

That many have considered the increasing unacceptability of modern warfare is shown by the language of the propaganda surrounding it. Modern wars have characteristically been fought to end war; they have been fought in the name of peace. Our most terrible weapons have been made, ostensibly, to preserve and assure the peace of the world. "All we want is peace," we say, as we increase relentlessly our capacity to make war.

Yet at the end of a century in which we have fought two wars to end war and several more to prevent war and preserve peace, and in which scientific and technological progress has made war ever more terrible and less controllable, we still, by policy, give no consideration to nonviolent means of national defense. We do indeed make much of diplomacy and diplomatic relations, but by diplomacy we mean invariably ultimatums for peace backed by the threat of war. It is always understood that we stand ready to kill those with whom we are "peacefully negotiating."

Our century of war, militarism, and political terror has produced great – and successful -advocates of true peace, among whom Mohandas Gandhi is a paramount example. The considerable success that they achieved testifies to the presence, in the midst of violence, of an authentic and powerful desire for peace and, more important, of the proven will to make the necessary sacrifices. But so far as our government is concerned, these men and their great and authenticating accomplishments might as well never have existed. To achieve peace by peaceable means is not yet our goal. We cling to the hopeless paradox of making peace by making war.

Which is to say that we cling in our public life to a brutal hypocrisy. In our century of almost universal violence of humans against fellow humans, and against our natural and cultural commonwealth, hypocrisy has been inescapable because our opposition to violence has been selective or merely fashionable. Some of us who approve of our monstrous military budget and our peacekeeping wars nonetheless deplore "domestic violence" and think that our society can be pacified by "gun control." And some of us are against capital punishment but for abortion.

If we give to these small absurdities the magnitude of international relations, we produce, unsurprisingly, some much larger absurdities. What could be more absurd, to begin with, than our attitude of high moral outrage against other nations for manufacturing the selfsame weapons that we manufacture? The difference, as our leaders say, is that we will use these weapons virtuously, whereas our enemies will use them maliciously – a proposition that too readily conforms to a proposition of much less dignity: we will use them in our interest, whereas our enemies will use them in theirs.

Or we must say, at least, that the issue of virtue in war is as obscure, ambiguous, and troubling as Abraham Lincoln found to be the issue of prayer in war: "Both [the North and the South] read the same bible, and pray to the same God, and each invokes his aid against the other . . . The prayers of both could not be answered – that of neither could be answered fully."

Recent American wars, having been both "foreign" and "limited," have been fought under the assumption that little or no personal sacrifice is required. In "foreign" wars, we do not directly experience the damage that we inflict upon the enemy. We hear and see this damage reported in the news, but we are not affected. These limited, "foreign" wars require that some of our young people should be killed or crippled, and that some families should grieve, but these "casualties" are so widely distributed among our population as hardly to be noticed.

Otherwise, we do not feel ourselves to be involved. We pay taxes to support the war, but that is nothing new, for we pay war taxes also in time of "peace." We experience no shortages, we suffer no rationing, we endure no limitations. We earn, borrow, spend, and consume in wartime as in peacetime.

And of course no sacrifice is required of those large economic interests that now principally constitute our economy. No corporation will be required to submit to any limitation or to sacrifice a dollar. On the contrary, war is the great cure-all and opportunity of our corporate economy, which subsists and thrives upon war. War ended the Great Depression of the 1930s, and we have maintained a war economy – an economy, one might justly say, of general violence – ever since, sacrificing to it an enormous economic and ecological wealth, including, as designated victims, the farmers and the industrial working class.

And so great costs are involved in our fixation on war, but the costs are "externalized" as "acceptable losses." And here we see how progress in war, progress in technology, and progress in the industrial economy are parallel to one another – or, very often, are merely identical.

Romantic nationalists, which is to say most apologists for war, always imply in their public speeches a mathematics or an accounting of war. Thus by its suffering in the Civil War, the North is said to have "paid for" the emancipation of the slaves and the preservation of the Union. Thus we may speak of our liberty as having been "bought" by the bloodshed of patriots. I am fully aware of the truth in such statements. I know that I am one of many who have benefited from painful sacrifices made by other people, and I would not like to be ungrateful. Moreover, I am a patriot myself and I know that the time may come for any of us when we must make extreme sacrifices for the sake of liberty.

But still I am suspicious of this kind of accounting. For one reason, it is necessarily done by the living on behalf of the dead. And I think we must be careful about too easily accepting, or being too easily grateful for, sacrifices made by others, especially if we have made none ourselves. For another reason, though our leaders in war always assume that there is an acceptable price, there is never a previously stated level of acceptability. The acceptable price, finally, is whatever is paid.

It is easy to see the similarity between this accounting of the price of war and our usual accounting of "the price of progress." We seem to have agreed that whatever has been (or will be) paid for so-called progress is an acceptable price. If that price includes the diminishment of privacy and the increase of government secrecy, so be it. If it means a radical reduction in the number of small businesses and the virtual destruction of the farm population, so be it. If it means the devastation of whole regions by extractive industries, so be it. If it means that a mere handful of people should own more billions of wealth than is owned by all of the world's poor, so be it.

But let us have the candor to acknowledge that what we call "the economy" or "the free market" is less and less distinguishable from warfare. For about half of the last century, we worried about world conquest by international communism. Now with less worry (so far) we are witnessing world conquest by international capitalism.

Though its political means are milder (so far) than those of communism, this newly internationalized capitalism may prove even more destructive of human cultures and communities, of freedom, and of nature. Its tendency is just as much toward total dominance and control. Confronting this conquest, ratified and licensed by the new international trade agreements, no place and no community in the world may consider itself safe from some form of plunder. More and more people all over the world are recognizing that this is so, and they are saying that world conquest of any kind is wrong, period.

They are doing more than that. They are saying that local conquest also is wrong, and wherever it is taking place local people are joining together to oppose it. All over my own state of Kentucky this opposition is growing – from the west, where the exiled people of the Land Between the Lakes are struggling to save their homeland from bureaucratic depredation, to the east, where the native people of the mountains are still struggling to preserve their land from destruction by absentee corporations.

To have an economy that is warlike, that aims at conquest and that destroys virtually everything that it is dependent on, placing no value on the health of nature or of human communities, is absurd enough. It is even more absurd that this economy, that in some respects is so much at one with our military industries and programs, is in other respects directly in conflict with our professed aim of national defense.

It seems only reasonable, only sane, to suppose that a gigantic program of preparedness for national defense should be founded first of all upon a principle of national and even regional economic independence. A nation determined to defend itself and its freedoms should be prepared, and always preparing, to live from its own resources and from the work and the skills of its own people. But that is not what we are doing in the United States today. What we are doing is squandering in the most prodigal manner the natural and human resources of the nation.

At present, in the face of declining finite sources of fossil fuel energies, we have virtually no energy policy, either for conservation or for the development of safe and clean alternative sources. At present, our energy policy simply is to use all that we have. Moreover, in the face of a growing population needing to be fed, we have virtually no policy for land conservation and no policy of just compensation to the primary producers of food. Our agricultural policy is to use up everything that we have, while depending increasingly on imported food, energy, technology, and labor.

Those are just two examples of our general indifference to our own needs. We thus are elaborating a surely dangerous contradiction between our militant nationalism and our espousal of the international "free market" ideology. How do we escape from this absurdity?

I don't think there is an easy answer. Obviously, we would be less absurd if we took better care of things. We would be less absurd if we founded our public policies upon an honest description of our needs and our predicament, rather than upon fantastical descriptions of our wishes. We would be less absurd if our leaders would consider in good faith the proven alternatives to violence.

Such things are easy to say, but we are disposed, somewhat by culture and somewhat by nature, to solve our problems by violence, and even to enjoy doing so. And yet by now all of us must at least have suspected that our right to live, to be free, and to be at peace is not guaranteed by any act of violence. It can be guaranteed only by our willingness that all other persons should live, be free, and be at peace – and by our willingness to use or give our own lives to make that possible. To be incapable of such willingness is merely to resign ourselves to the absurdity we are in; and yet, if you are like me, you are unsure to what extent you are capable of it.

Here is the other question that I have been leading toward, one that the predicament of modern warfare forces upon us: how many deaths of other people's children by bombing or starvation are we willing to accept in order that we may be free, affluent, and (supposedly) at peace? To that question I answer: none. Please, no children. Don't kill any children for my benefit.

If that is your answer too, then you must know that we have not come to rest, far from it. For surely we must feel ourselves swarmed about with more questions that are urgent, personal, and intimidating. But perhaps also we feel ourselves beginning to be free, facing at last in our own selves the greatest challenge ever laid before us, the most comprehensive vision of human progress, the best advice, and the least obeyed:

> But I say to you, Love your enemies: do good to them that hate you: and pray for them that persecute and calumniate you: That you may be the children of your Father who is in heaven, who maketh his sun to rise upon the good, and bad, and raineth upon the just and the unjust (St. Matt. v: 44–45).

www.robert-fisk.com

Innocent Iraqi children – known only to God and to their grieving families.

THE EDITORS' GLOSS: As noted in an earlier gloss, today's political landscape is littered with epithets, labels, and pigeon-holes, all of which substitute for a serious consideration of ideas. Those who seek to avoid war are denounced by the "right" as "pacifists," even though the pejorative sense of the term cannot accurately be applied to those who, like the late Cardinal Ottaviani of the Vatican's Holy Office, object to modern war on the grounds that it cannot be conducted justly, or those like the current Pope who point out that "preventive" war is not countenanced by Catholic just-war doctrine. A biographer of the previous Pope Benedict called him a "pacifist," and Dorothy Day, Eric Gill, and others thought of themselves that way. Yet none of them denied a person's (or a nation's) right to defend itself with armed force from actual, ongoing attack (see, e.g., the Eric Gill interview on pp. 379–383). The pacifism condemned by the Church is the absolute rejection of the use of force, including when it would be the only way for a man to defend his wife and children or defend his nation. Few, if any, would go to this extreme, as Marine General Smedley Butler pointed out when he said, based on his own experience, that even his Quaker forebears would have leapt to their feet if it were a matter of defending their families.

But it's much easier simply to condemn people with vague and sophistical labels than it is to examine what they mean when they use them.

Likewise, it is easier for George Will to cry "slander" – because a Democrat is saying it – when Congressman Jim McDermott (D-Wash.) suggested that the Bush administration might have used "deceit" to launch a war with Iraq. And as easy for Jack Shafer of *Slate* to dismiss as "liberal" a critique of Bush's conflation of Iraq with the "war on terror." Yet what do liberalism, conservatism, Republicans, and Democrats have to do with issues such as truth, lies, justice, and honesty? Should it matter that "conservatives" support a war and "liberals" oppose it? Do people who use these terms really even know what they mean?

It is this silliness that Prof. Gottfried cuts through in what follows, offering a healthy reminder that issues of war and peace are too important to be a matter of mere semantics and party loyalty. And if we must take sides, let us not operate within the broken and increasingly useless categories of left and right, but rather good and bad, true and false, right and wrong. Smedly Butler said "to hell with war." He might have added "to hell with parties" too.

C H A P T E R
9

A Conservative War?
• • • • • • • • •
Prof. Paul Gottfried, Ph.D.

FROM THE OUTSET of the war launched by the American government against the Iraq of Saddam Hussein, it has been taken for granted by the mass media on both sides of the spectrum, with few exceptions, that the war was a "conservative" one. For liberals in the mold of Michael Moore, the war was a positive unleashing of extreme violence from "the far right." For pro-war Republicans, opposition to the war is typically "left-wing" and "liberal."

Gore Vidal, in roundly criticizing the war and the political climate that paved the way for it, warns of the "right wing" who, he says, are "the bad guys."[1] The evidence cited by *Frontpagemag.com* about the academic perceptions of the war as "conservative" is also entirely accurate. Over the last year, I participated in several gatherings of professors called to discuss recent international events, and I was more than ever amazed by just how pervasive this characterization of the war is. Intellectuals and educators consider this conflict in the way Michael Moore does in his movie, *Farenheit 9/11*, as violence being unleashed by "the far right."

On the Republican side most commentators buy into and foster this perception. Jack Shafer, in an illustrative posting on *Slate.com*, labels reasoned and substantive criticism of the Iraq war as "liberal critique."[2] When *Boston Globe* journalist Jeff Jacoby came to my own Elizabethtown College on February 23 of this year, he responded to a question from my colleague, "Why isn't it conservative to *reject* messianic global democracy?" with, "You sound like Teddy Kennedy." David Frum, in his notorious *National Review* piece excommunicating "conservatives" from the movement who failed to tow the truly "conservative" line on the war, situates the attack on

1. *Dreaming War* (New York: Thunder's Mouth Press/Nation Books, 2002), p. 197.
2. "Case Open," November 18, 2003.

Iraq in the context of "the 50-year-old *conservative* commitment to defend American interests and values throughout the world"(emphasis mine).[1]

For whatever reason, "mainstream" voices from all sides of the spectrum have long ago arrived at a consensus that this is a "conservative" or "right-wing" war, and that the war's supporters or opponents therefore fall into "conservative" or "liberal" camps depending upon whether they are "pro-" or "anti-" war.

Now it seems to this writer that there is no real basis in fact for believing that the Bush administration's war against Iraq is a conservative one at all. Nevertheless, the notion has been foisted on the American people with tremendous ease. Perhaps this is because in popular parlance, terms such as "conservative" and "right-wing" are vague and undefined, allowing people both sincere and insincere to make them mean *anything they like*. It is nonetheless surprising that no one seems to have challenged this most basic of assumptions.

The Bush administration, of course, claims that the war was initiated for security purposes, to take possession of Saddam Hussein's alleged weapons of mass destruction and to cut off al-Qaeda's links to the U.S.-designated "rogue" government of Iraq. When these justifications fell flat, another reason thrown out by way of justification has been that the war's aim is to spread the blessings of democracy, including women's rights (from the "right" to wear cosmetics to the right to kill the unborn child in the womb), to a benighted part of the world.

The administration has also gone out of its way to stress the religiously pluralistic character of America's human rights and anti-terrorist missions. Three months after the bombing of the World Trade Center, Bush with great fanfare invited Muslim clergy to the White House to call benign public attention to the Feast of Ramadan. Since then the President has denied repeatedly that an anti-Islamic animus fuels the Asian wars in which the U.S. has become embroiled. In 2003 an evangelical officer, who did try to present the war against Islamic "terrorists" as a resumption of the Crusades, immediately found himself relieved of his command, with neoconservative columnists, Jonah Goldberg and John Podhoretz, hailing this decision as necessary for the prosecution of a non-sectarian war to establish something they call "pluralism" in the Middle East.

One might reasonably ask what these justifications have to do with traditionally "conservative" motivations for war. It can be admitted that what

---

1. "Unpatriotic Conservatives," *National Review*, April 7, 2003, online.

is meant here by a "conservatively" motivated decision to go to war does encompass *the totality of* the traditional Christian teachings about just war. Arguably a war might claim a conservative foundation even where the civilian population is not consistently spared, laws of proportionality are not properly observed, and even where just cause is not entirely evident. What makes the launching of a war "conservative," from a strictly historical perspective, is the declared intention of those who embark on the struggle to achieve recognizably conservative ends. Attempts to preserve a customary way of life against outside threats, and to resist violence directed against persons and property fit the definition of a conservative war. By this standard the Nationalist uprising in Spain in July 1936 against a violent, anti-clericalist regime that could not or would not maintain civil order, was a conservatively motivated act. This judgment can be applied without necessarily giving moral approval to everything the Nationalists did to achieve victory and to eradicate their enemies. One might also admit, from this standpoint, that the definition of a "conservative war" includes any struggle intended to protect one's historical homeland from a foreign invader. Such a definition might apply to a wide range of homeland defenders, from Robert E. Lee commanding the Army of Northern Virginia, to the German *Heimwehr* fending off Russian soldiers attacking German women and family homes, to Soviet tanks repelling German invaders at Stalingrad. It is a definition that the Left might also accept, while imposing its own value grid on the sides involved in the conflict.

What is *not* a conservative war is one that is advocated as part of a "permanent revolution," to destabilize traditional societies and to impose American modernity. It is precisely in these terms that Charles Krauthammer, Stephen Schwarz, Michael Ledeen, Peter Brookes, and William Kristol, among other likeminded apologists for Bush's war policy, understand America's role in the Middle East and throughout the rest of the world. Aside from the now-discredited "national security" justifications put forward by the Bush administration, it is also in these terms that Bush and Co. justified the Iraq war. Claes G. Ryn's *America the Virtuous* piles up a mountain of quotations to document the obvious, that the pro-war rhetoric of the neoconservatives, which the media holds up to the world as "the American Right," indicates a family resemblance to the speeches of French Jacobins about to fight their counter-revolutionary neighbors. Ryn and other critics have likened the war's defenders to the Marxist-Leninists who argued that their revolution could not be safe unless it was *exported.*

One wonders *why* the critics of the "right wing war unleashed by Bush" do not notice the *radically leftist* propaganda being pulled out to defend it.

Part of this propaganda involves the attempt to spin the influence of German-Jewish political philosopher, Leo Strauss, on those who agitated for war as a "conservative" phenomenon. In 2003 the *Boston Globe, Los Angeles Times, New York Times, Washington Post, Le Monde, The Guardian,* and most of the German press featured stories on Strauss and his so-called "right wing" students. Supposedly Strauss – particularly as presented by Canadian leftist critic Shadia Drury – was the unacknowledged mental slave of the German anti-democratic thinkers Friedrich Nietzsche and Carl Schmitt. He taught his disciples at the University of Chicago to pretend to be "democrats," until they could take power and become "philosopher kings." Once in power, Strauss's students, who only pretend to celebrate Roosevelt and Martin Luther King as American heroes, would rule in accordance with their will to power. These students had allegedly begun to assume this ominous role under Bush, when they convinced him to launch a war that would increase their hold on the government. Bush's security advisors, most prominently Paul Wolfowitz and Richard Perle, were the visible tips of an iceberg leading down to Leo Strauss. So far so good, but from there the story leads to a German "fascist," "anti-democratic," and therefore "conservative" connection.

There is *nothing* "right-wing" or "Teutonophile" about these so-called Straussian "fascists" whom journalists claim to be outing. Most of them, as Straussian Mark Blitz accurately explains,[1] preach global democracy, human rights, secularism, and equality – not exactly the stock-in-trade of "the right" or "fascists" however you define them! As that best-selling tract by Straussian Professor Allan Bloom, *The Closing of the American Mind,* made clear to millions, what Straussians like best about the U.S. is its willingness to pursue bloody "educational experiments" in the name of democracy and equality against those who think differently. Having authored works on the German Catholic conservative jurist, Carl Schmitt, and on Strauss and the Straussians, I have yet to establish that tight connection between my subjects that national newspapers very confidently claim to have found. The assumed ties between Schmitt and the invasion of Iraq are doubtful, in addition, because of Schmitt's known aversion to American empire-building, as well as his unambiguous statements in the 1950s and 60s about the danger to European civilization posed by the American pres-

---

1. "Leo Strauss, the Straussians, and American Foreign Policy," *Open Democracy,* November 13, 2003, online.

ence. The fabrication of this imaginary link between the "anti-democratic" Schmitt and the "democratic imperialist" Straussians shows the lengths to which some will go to affix a "rightist" label to Bush's foreign policy.

Other critics of the war see it as scripted by the "Religious Right," and portray the war as part and parcel of "conservative" politics. Whether Bush takes a stand against third-term abortions, expresses reservations about gay marriages, or sends an army into a Muslim country, it is supposedly Pat Robertson, Congressman Tom DeLay, or some other known fundamentalist or evangelical who is pulling the strings. A book by Sara Diamond, *Roads to Dominion: Right-Wing Movements and Political Parties in the U.S.* (New York, 1996), purports to uncover the snowball of intrigue extending from the early *National Review* to the religious right. Bush, we are told, takes positions with an eye toward the Evangelical vote, which would vanish, or so he fears, unless he accommodates the "Christians." Then, too, there are the "big business" contacts (read "conservative") of his family and of Vice President Cheney, which provide further incentive to fight a war that will have the effect of securing America's control of Middle Eastern oil. From the European Right to the European Left, the belief prevails that oil, and the opportunity for profiteering that it offers, led to the attack on Iraq (though the Right has a more nuanced view of this matter, seeing oil as being just one element in a mosaic of reasons).

Such interpretations contain *some* elements of truth, but they are hardly "conservative" ones. The Zionist sympathies of the Religious Right and Republican attempts to "reach out" to normally Democratic Jewish voters would have made the overthrow of the fervently anti-Israeli Saddam Hussein seem electorally useful, providing that the war went well. The lack of an exit strategy did create problems, but it is altogether possible that such an exit was taken for granted assuming that Saddam could be ousted. The war in fact may have been a sop to the Religious Right, particularly since Bush, under the prodding of his advisor Karl Rove, has persistently tried to make up to soccer moms and Democratic voters. In March and April of last year, the President campaigned vigorously for the very liberal Jewish Republican Senator Arlen Specter, who was facing a tough primary challenge in Pennsylvania from Congressman Pat Toomey. The challenger, an anti-abortion Catholic with strong Evangelical support, went down to a close defeat (of less than two points) after Bush and "Catholic" Republican Senator Rick Santorum went to bat for the enthusiastically pro-choice Specter. The result is that some conservative Protestants have refused to back Bush as well as Specter. It is not unlikely that Bush saw the war as being a conciliatory gesture in the direction of Dispensationalist Christians, which would play equally well among Zionists. It is possible that the administration regarded their projected attack as a way of ensuring the continued flow of Iraqi oil to Europe and Japan. However, since Saddam never ever talked about cutting the flow of oil, it seems to me that such a material end could have been served by less drastic means than what was undertaken, namely, the occupation and "democratic re-education" of Iraq's diverse populations.

In any case, none of these concerns demonstrates that Bush is waging a "conservative" crusade. Opportunistic political gestures to the "religious right" and sympathy for its Christian Zionist sentiments hardly make the war in Iraq a "conservative" undertaking. As for the oil interests, economic motives are always there to be ascribed to any conflict, and the Left is notoriously inconsistent in attaching unworthy material ambitions to those it dislikes, while treating progressive third world or leftist governments less suspiciously when they attack other countries. Sometimes the "isolationist Right" has played the same game. Thus it has tried to explain America's entry into World War One with reference to the generous loans that J.P. Morgan bestowed on England. One might show with equal ease, however, that pro-German bankers, led by Jacob Schiff, were simultaneously feeding loans to the other side. Such loans in either case were driven less by profit motives than by sentimental and cultural affinities, though one might speculate upon other possible reasons.

There are several probable reasons for this ideological misrepresentation of the war in Iraq as a "conservative" undertaking. One, electoral politics in the U.S., and the relative positioning of the two national parties, requires that a war begun by Republicans be made to *appear* right wing for the benefit of those Democrats who oppose both the war as well as "all things conservative." One suspects that if the Republicans, and not Clinton, had been in the driver's seat when the illegal decision was made four years ago to bomb Serbia, that action too would have been condemned as a "right-wing" enterprise. Anti-war filmmaker, Michael Moore, a known backer of Clinton, and the 2004 presidential contender, General Wesley Clark, both major actors in the war against Serbia, never bothered to protest the Democratic Party's act of military aggression. Partisanship dictates whether wars are "right wing" or "humanitarian," depending on which party is in power. It is also irrelevant in assigning these labels whether the party out of power supported a particular military action. Thus the senatorial votes in favor of the war cast by Democratic presidential candidate, John Kerry, are not seen to implicate him in the current "right wing" struggle; similarly the heavy approval given by Republicans to Clinton's bombing of Serbia does not change the presentation of this offensive war as Democratic and therefore "progressive." Immediately after Kerry had won the Democratic nomination in the spring of 2004, David Broder, Haynes Johnson, and Robert Dallek all expressed a predictable opinion that this would be the "most ideologically divisive" presidential race "since FDR ran against Hoover in 1932." The superlatives applied to this drab presidential race might seem ludicrous, unless one recalls that the two parties appeal to different ideological electorates. Some of their backers – for example, the aforementioned writers and the maker of *Fahrenheit 911* – may see party differences as being greater than the actual facts warrant. Clearly the same is true for those on Fox News and for Republican commentators who try to keep self-identified conservatives in their party, by exaggerating its differences from that of the Democrats.

Another important factor contributing to the "right wing" image of the war (favored by its critics on the left) was the refusal of the Bush administration in the stages leading up to the war to cooperate fully with the UN and its European "allies." The multilateralism demanded by the Left is consistent with its post-national and globalist perspective and this reason for treating the war as "conservative," in its avoidance of internationalist solutions, has some merit. What must however be factored in is that the war party has disputed the UN's claim to global leadership by *underscoring* its commitment to human rights. Unlike the UN and the European opponents of the war, American hawks claim that American armies are truly fighting for women's rights and universal democracy. They are not occupying Iraq to pursue other ideals except the democratic universalist (and hardly "conservative") ones that Saddam Hussein had allegedly stifled. It might also be asked whether the same invectives would be hurled at the American administration were it a Democratic one taking action against a politically incorrect European Christian state? Could one imagine the same hullabaloo from engaged leftists and committed Democrats if Kerry, had he been elected, moved to overthrow a genuinely conservative nationalist government in the Balkans – or decided to quarantine a European country that had fallen into "right wing" populist hands? The second case is not improbable, given the threatening communications that in 1999 went from Clinton's National Security Advisor and Secretary of State to the Austrian government. At that time the dominant Austrian Volkspartei was considering the inclusion of the anti-immigration populist Jorg Haider in its cabinet.

Although there are well meaning but misguided patriots who cheer any war into which the U.S. has slipped, it might be noted that such a cheering gallery is not an *inherently* conservative force. *Patriotism is usually a conservative sentiment, but those who express it may not be serving conservative ends.* Is there any reason to doubt that those who are now decorating their porches with expressions of support for American troops would being doing the same for *any* struggle in which the American government chose to get involved? Why would they be any less demonstrative in their patriotism if a hypothetical President Kerry decided to educate by invading a country that reputedly oppressed women? The self-justifications I typically hear from my flag-waving, bellicose neighbors are that "you have to support the President" and that "we're behind our soldiers." Such statements could be pulled out to defend any American military action, although given the party orientation of Lancaster County, one might be hearing Republican partisanship as well as garden-variety jingoism.

Of all the reasons for the mislabeling of the present war, the one that seems the most compelling is the transformation of the "American Right" that is now going on. In a syndicated column on May 12, 2004, George Will called for the restoration in foreign policy of a conservative, as opposed to neoconservative, perspective, which avoids abstract democratic ideals. Will had weighed in for two decades behind the creed he now laments. During the first Gulf War, he advocated an American-controlled experiment in democracy for the Kuwaitis, and in the 1980s and 90s he talked up the contributions of the Kristol family in helping to make American "conservatism" more intelligent and more moderate. Will, among other establishment conservatives, is registering second thoughts about his erstwhile companions, but by now he may be looking at a juggernaut. In view of their control of movement conservative foundations, philanthropies, newspapers, magazines, and a TV Channel, and their access to establishment liberal news forums, the neoconservatives' hegemony will not likely yield in the near term to competing forces. This highly visible group is the one on the "conventional right" that rattles liberals *the least*. They are the *only* "conservatives" whom liberals do *not* attack as racists, homophobes, and anti-Semites. The discrepancy in wealth and media resources between this relabeled camp of welfare state New Deal Democrats and irritable Zionists, and the "Old Right" remains a factor to be dealt with.

But more relevant here than the extent of this neoconservative occupation is its *effect* on views about the war. Because both the neoconservative press and Bush's neoconservative advisors pushed for this conflict, it is therefore said to be *a conservative action.* What makes it "conservative" is where its advocates are positioned. The neoconservatives are those whom the liberal media choose to call the "respectable right." Moreover, this designated "right" sets up litmus tests for its team players. Although these tests have nothing more to do with non-leftist credentials than rooting for the LA Dodgers or preferring vanilla to chocolate ice cream, they have become the marks of conservative identity *as defined by the neoconservative media.* And the liberal left, which has no problem with the new labeling system, also accepts these arbitrary litmus tests of acceptable "conservative" orthodoxy, e.g., supporting the Sharon government in Israel unconditionally, lecturing about global democracy, and instigating Middle Eastern wars. After all, the neoconservatives are mostly open to those liberal social reforms being pushed by the media, unlike those who might be termed "traditional conservatives." Young neoconservatives John Podhoretz, David Brooks, and Jonah Goldberg happily endorsed gay marriage and the amnestying of illegals, when these became liberal issues.

Note, too, how readily Bill Kristol, in an interview in the *New York Times,* admitted to how much closer he and his colleagues stood to Kerry than to "right-wingers" who do *not* share their enthusiasm for global democracy. The neoconservative media have declared the acceptance of the war in Iraq, as a democratic educational experiment, as *essential* for "conservative" membership. Those who fail this litmus test may end up as *bona fide* members of the "unpatriotic Right," as neocon scribblers such as Frum term them. Such bullying is effective in some situations. Foundations and publications that receive subsidies from neoconservative sources or are involved with the Republican Party only employ self-identified conservatives. Such employees can hurt themselves by disagreeing with neoconservative censors; and since the war has become a *test* of conservative and Republican loyalties, those who *depend* on the party or the movement may try not to seem out of step. But there is no reason to mistake this acquiescence for a particularly "conservative" affirmation.

Many people of conviction on both sides of the political spectrum have come to a principled opposition to the Bush administration's war. That this war has been popularly and incorrectly labeled "conservative" should not lead sincere liberals on the "left" to oppose it simply for its so-called "conservatism," any more than it should lead true conservatives on the "right" to support it for the same reason. The most tragic success of the popular campaign to portray the war as "conservative" may be the way in which such a label has prevented sincere, if qualified, collaboration between those on the "left" and "right" in opposition to the war. Attacking each other for support of or opposition to a "conservative" cause (with more focus on the "conservative" than on the cause), the sincere, anti-war left alienates the traditionally conservative right, while the right for its part is pushed into supporting the "party line" while denouncing the liberal, anti-war left. The common enemy – in this case the war, and those who support it – thus gets lost in the fray of frequently meaningless, partisan name-calling. Recognizing the complete misapplication of the name would make "conservatism" a mere side issue in the face of a larger struggle. It would allow both sides to realize – to the profit of the nation – that the enemy of my enemy may indeed sometimes be my friend.

THE VENERABLE TRADITION: PUTTING THE BRAKES ON AGGRESSION AND SECURING JUSTICE FOR IRAQ

THE EDITORS' GLOSS: In February of 2003, the "usual suspects" – and some others – posted to a Catholic just-war website an open letter to the President in defense of the then-upcoming war with Iraq. These included well-known "conservative" Catholics such as Fr. Joseph Fessio, S.J., Deal Hudson, Bill Bennet, Princeton's Robert George, Elizabeth Fox-Genovese, Robert Royal, Patrick Madrid, William Donahue, Robert Reilly, George Sim Johnston, Mary Kay Clark, and Charles M. Wilson. In their letter they maintained that "the proposition sometimes asserted . . . that preventive or preemptive military action can never be defensive within the meaning of just war doctrine is simply erroneous."

The article that follows is a refutation of that contention, insofar as refutation of such a vague and confused assertion is possible. For what most characterizes their statement – and many of the others in their letter – is a vague mixing of categories and principles such that their assertions contain some truth and some error (like heresy!), "all the better to mislead you with, my dear." For preventive war and preemptive war are two different things, and they cannot be said together and without distinction to enjoy the sanction of law and morality. "Operation IRAQI FREEDOM was a preventive war, which traditionally has been indistinguishable from aggression," Prof. Jeffrey Record of the U.S. Air Force's Montgomery, Alabama, Air War College has written, referring in fact to "the Defense Department's official definition of the term." Preemption, he notes, is "an attack initiated on the basis of incontrovertible evidence that an enemy attack is imminent," while preventive war is "a war initiated in the belief that military conflict, while not imminent, is inevitable, and that to delay would involve greater risk."

One is at times justifiable; the other – as Fr. Iscara's essay makes perfectly clear – is not.

10

Might Is Not Right:
Why "Preventive War" Is Immoral

• • • • • • • • •

Fr. Juan Carlos Iscara

TO STATE THE conditions in which a just war is morally licit is an ethical judgment, whereas to decide whether, here and now, a war should be fought is a judgment of political prudence. In other words, to know the conditions in which a just war may be fought is one thing; to establish whether those conditions are or are not realized in a particular case is a different and far more difficult matter. We must be guided to concrete decisions by a body of principles of justice, previous to any conflict, grounded in the Eternal Reason of God; but our prudential judgment depends on the knowledge of all the relevant facts in the concrete case.

To justify the Iraqi war, many have spoken of "preemptive strikes" and of "preventive war" as particular applications of the moral notion of self-defense. Upon reflection, it would seem that even Catholic analysts advance such arguments not because they offer a true moral justification of the war, but because they are the most likely to sway public opinion. We must be acutely aware of the danger of error and of moral failing through the manipulation of propaganda and the easy slogans of a sentimental patriotism.

In the end, "people of good will may differ on how to apply the just-war norms in particular cases. Nevertheless, there is always a serious obligation for all to justify their own conclusions as measured against the moral norms of Catholic teaching."[1]

I. Self-Defense

Catholic Tradition has always held that, under certain given conditions, it is licit to take up arms, that there are some circumstances in which war

---

1. Office for Social Justice (Archdiocese of St. Paul and Minneapolis), *War With Iraq: Is It Just?* (St. Paul: Office for Social Justice, 2003), p. 1.

is not merely licit but even necessary, which would mean it is not only a right, but also a duty.[1] Even Pius XII, who passed an otherwise severe judgment on the evils of modern warfare, conceded this fundamental right of nations, a right without which their national independence would be more truly an international joke, depending solely on the whim of the surrounding nations. It stands to reason, for if the governing authority in a sovereign state were to lack the means necessary for preserving that state and its common good, then such an authority would be fundamentally flawed.

Just Cause for War

St. Thomas Aquinas approached the question from the moral aspect and briefly considered it in his treatise on Charity, as war is obviously opposed to one of charity's effects, *peace*. The direct destruction of peace and the indirect attack on charity show the malice of war. This malice is only avoided if the war is ultimately oriented towards peace. However, waging war to make peace appears as a rather paradoxical principle. Therefore, in determining whether war is sinful or not, St. Thomas treated the issue in terms of Justice. War is licit – that is, it can be waged without sin – if it is just, and then only if it is just.[2] If the conditions of justice are met, then the recourse to armed force is truly an instrument for peace.

Thus, the Catholic "just-war theory" is the acknowledgment of the right of nations to self-defense against an unjust aggression.[3] This is simply an application of the natural law – legitimate defense is a natural right. Just as it is obvious that every man has the right to preserve his own existence, so too does the state have the natural right to defend itself against a real, immediate and grave threat to its very existence and essential good.[4]

Defense

The term "defense" has been understood by Catholic theologians in a wide sense. Hence, it is taught that military force may be rightfully employed either as *self-defense* against an unjust attack; or for the *restoration* or recuperation of what was unjustly taken; or for the *punishment* of unjust aggressors.[5]

---

1. See the excellent explanation of the principles of the just-war doctrine in the appendix of Fr. Francis Stratmann, pp. 387–417.

2. *Summa Theologica* (henceforth *ST*), II, ii, Q. 40, A. 1.

3. *ST*, II, ii, Q. 40, A. 2, obj. 1.

4. Leo XIII, "Allocution to Cardinals," February 11, 1889.

5. For a longer treatment of this question, see my article, "Just War: Catholic Doctrine

Contemporary international law has narrowed the Thomistic notion of "just cause" to defense. This defense may be understood in the traditional sense of one nation or group of nations repelling military attacks made by another nation, or in the wider sense of an internationally sanctioned defense against breaches of international peace.[1] Nevertheless, this one concept of "defense" is broad enough to include the other two concepts of recuperation and punishment. Thomistic principles continue to underlie the present international laws on war even though the legal vocabulary has changed, still reflecting the traditional view that the first use of force in a conflict is morally suspect, while the second use is not and it is simply considered "defense."

In Catholic doctrine, the time for the self-defense of the private individual is limited to the time of the unjust aggression. However, for the public authority, not only defense against an actual attack, but also retaliation against a past aggression may be still legitimately called a matter of defense because the injury continues being inflicted (and so violence is still being exercised) throughout the entire time that the aggressor refuses to return what he has taken or to amend the violation he has made. The use of force to recover what was lost thereby becomes legitimate, if force is the only means to do so.

The public authority also has the right, and sometimes even the duty, to punish evildoers – to take "vengeance." As the goal of war is the restoration of peace – that is, of the just order – justice demands more than simply rendering the aggressor incapable of doing further damage and despoiling him of what he had unjustly taken. Justice requires that the criminal also make satisfaction for his evildoing, and this is the object of vengeance. As long as such satisfaction has not been made, it can be said that the order of justice continues to be violated, that an injury continues to be inflicted – against which a nation can defend itself.

This is not "getting even," but an act of vindictive justice from which will result manifold benefits. The culpable party makes amends for his crime, or he is at least kept from doing further damage. The authority maintains public order by repressing evils as they appear. It is a safeguard for future justice since others will be deterred from similar crimes by fear of similar retribution. And it upholds the honor of God, the Just Judge, whom men are called to imitate.

and Some Modern Problems," in *The Angelus*, July, 2002, pp. 2–16.

1. James Turner Johnson, *Morality and Contemporary Warfare* (New Haven: Yale University Press, 1999), p. 29.

Nonetheless, this right of defense has limits. Not every injustice may be countered by war. The injustice must be, at the same time, evident, extremely grave and otherwise inevitable.[1] When the damages that a war will certainly provoke are out of all proportion with the injustice inflicted, there may even exist a duty to endure such injustice.[2]

II. "Pre-Emptive Strike"

As we have said, the first use of force in any given conflict is always morally suspect, as it appears to be aggression. The second use, as it is reaction to the attack, is not so suspect, in principle, and is considered purely defensive. But in certain complex circumstances the first use of force may be in reality defensive, although it cannot be easily perceived as such. It is in these cases that the terms "preemptive strike" and "preventive war" are likely to be used. They must be clearly defined, if we are to understand their moral status.

Definition

The "use of preemptive force" – or a "preemptive strike" – means that *we attack our adversary, although he has not yet actually attacked us.* The adversary has already started preparing for it, but the attack has not yet physically happened.

Moral Argument

Such a course of action may be allowed only when it constitutes *self-defense* in the wider sense stated above. That is, it is morally permissible only when there is, on the part of the adversary, a *"manifest intent to injure,* a *degree of active preparation* that makes that intent a positive danger, and a general situation in which waiting or doing anything other than fighting greatly magnifies the risk."[3]

If the "preemptive" force is to be used either as a means of obtaining satisfaction for damage previously inflicted or to punish evildoers, it has to be proven beyond any reasonable doubt (because of the evils that war will

---

1. Pius XII, Allocution to the World Congress of Medicine, September 30, 1954.

2. Pius XII, Allocution to Military Doctors, October 19. 1953.

3. Michael Walzer, quoted in Maryann Cusimano Love, "Real Prevention: Alternatives to Force," *America*, Vol. 188, No. 2, January 20-27, 2003, p. 13.

unleash) that it is defensive – that is, that the adversary is the cause of such damage, or that he has efficaciously cooperated in inflicting it.

Burden of Proof

It is an acknowledged legal principle that the burden of proof rests on him who affirms or accuses. In our case, it is the responsibility of the government that decides to launch a preemptive strike to prove the existence of one of the following three criteria: (1) that there is such "manifest intent," or (2) that the threat of the adversary's attack is impending, *"overwhelming, and leaving no choice of means and no moment for deliberation,"*[1] or (3) that the adversary is the cause of the damage inflicted.

It may be argued that, given the complexities of the contemporary international situation, the dangers of "asymmetrical warfare" and the existence of clandestine networks of terrorism, only the public authorities are *"close to the facts of the case and . . . privy to highly restricted intelligence,"*[2] and, therefore, they are not obliged to disclose their evidence when doing so may endanger their sources or jeopardize the outcome of the war. Catholic moral doctrine has always made allowances for such a case, stating that the common citizen must, *a priori*, trust his government and presume the justice of the war.[3]

---

1. *Ibid.,* p. 13.

2. Michael Novak, "An Argument That War Against Iraq is Just," *Origins,* Vol. 32, No. 36, February 20, 2003, p. 595.

3. "Since the processes of diplomacy are so complicated and obscure in our times, soldiers and inferior officials are scarcely able to judge competently concerning this certainty of the rectitude, generally, as of the rest of the conditions of a just war." Zalba, Marcelino, S.J., *Theologiae Moralis Summa,* (Madrid: Biblioteca de Autores Cristianos, 1957), II, 104 (n. 244); Prümmer, Dominic M., O.P., *Manuale Theologiae Moralis* (Barcelona: Herder, 1961), II, 123. [While it is true that the government deserves the *benefit* of any *reasonable doubt,* it should not be forgotten that any assessment of the justice or injustice of a war proposed by the government – an assessment presumed necessary even by moralists who teach that the government enjoys a high degree of presumption of rectitude – assumes the right and duty of the individual conscience to make proper investigations into the claims of justice made by the government, in all but the most evident and pressing cases of actual national self defense. Theologians such as Suárez, de Vitoria, Bellarmine, Sylvester Mazzolini, and Pope Adrian VI have made allowances for this. More recently, the English Carmelite Fr. Brocard Sewell in his memoirs, *My Dear Time's Waste* (Aylesford: St. Albert's Press, 1966), has suggested that the "old" attitude which saw the laity as "not possibly well informed enough to question the justice of a war embarked on by the lawful authority of the State" was "reasonable enough" when the laity were mostly uneducated. His gloss on this, referring even to a period as early as the 1930s, is: "but times had changed." This conclusion is consistent with the position taken in the 1941 study by the Ethics Committee of the Catholic Association for International Peace (CAIP), chaired by Mgr. John A Ryan, entitled *The Morality of*

But that presumption, while justifiable for the individual citizen, is not appropriate for the international community. Because of today's increased solidarity and mutual interaction of nations, military conflicts have the capacity to expand and to compromise severely the international order. In consequence, today's threshold of what constitutes the "common good" must be raised to include, in certain extraordinary cases, the higher common good of that international order.

It is only just, therefore, for the international community – before committing itself or giving its sanction to a proposed military action – to demand not only assurances but also proofs of a clear case for a war that has the potential to endanger both the common good of each member (for which each is responsible before God and its own citizens), and the international common good in whose pursuit all must collaborate.

During the Cuban missile crisis of 1962, the U.S. Ambassador to the United Nations, Adlai Stevenson, justified the American readiness to use military force to confront the specific threats from Russia by presenting photographs that unquestionably showed the Russian missile array in Cuba. For the war against Iraq, the present U.S. administration did not offer such convincing proof to the international community. Consequently, the UN Security Council remained unconvinced, and unwilling to endorse the American military action against Iraq.

It may be argued that the nation-members of the Security Council have their own political agendas and that perhaps they would have denied such endorsement even with undeniable proof of Iraq's threat. Perhaps – but the fact remains that a reasonable demand of justice has not been satisfied.

III. "Preventive War"

The notion of "preventive war," in its concrete application to the Iraqi war, was presented to the Catholic world by Michael Novak[1] in a lecture

---

Conscientious Objection to War (Washington, D.C.: CAIP, 1941). See also the discussion of conscientious objection by Dr. Peter Chojnowski on pp. 361–373 of the present volume, along with the detailed discussions of the notion of moral certainty in the decision to make war in the essay by Dr. Thomas Ryba and the appendix of Fr. Francis Stratmann, respectively on pp. 223–244 and pp. 387–417 of the present volume.—Ed.]

1. Nearly ordained a priest in the Congregation of the Holy Cross after completing his seminary training, Novak, after being a liberal critic of the Church and of Republican administrations, has now "reinvented" himself as a "neoconservative" Catholic intellectual.

given in Rome at the invitation of the U.S. Ambassador to the Holy See, James Nicholson.

Definition

The notion of "preventive war" was presented, not as a new theory, but as an application of the Catholic just-war doctrine. As Michael Novak, in his vagueness,[1] did not offer a definition of it, we are entitled to extrapolate from his text a definition of "preventive war" as the *unilateral attack that neutralizes what is, at present, only the mere possibility of a future attack by a potential adversary.* In other words, military force is brought to bear upon a country to prevent a threat that such a country may or may not pose in the future, but which we fear it may. Thus, *the rationale for war is not the adversary's actual threat, but our own assessment of his possible future intentions* – that is, the debatable conclusion of our own guesswork *becomes* the motive for war.

Thesis

As we have said, a case may be made in support of the moral permissibility of the use of "preemptive force," but the "preventive war," as defined above, *is indefensible on moral grounds.*

Terminology

Many speak, indistinctly, of "preemptive strikes" and of "preventive war." On a moral basis, attention must be called to the fact that – precisely because the notion of preemptive strike may have some moral permissibility in certain circumstances, while the preventive war has no justification at all – the moral discourse that ties both notions together and uses them as equivalent is, to say the least, confusing.

Moral Argument

Why? Because *war is morally permissible only as a means of self-defense.* Even the "anticipatory self-defense" – or "preemptive strike" – is a morally

---

1. Novak affirmed that the "preventive war" against Iraq was simply a follow-up of previous UN sanctions, bringing to a close the 1991 Gulf War; in that case, one does not see the need to talk of it as "preventive." A few sentences later, though, the war is nonetheless "preventive" because it removes the possibility that, one day, terrorists and Saddam Hussein may collaborate to attack America.

permissible action because it is, after all, defense of self against an unjust aggression already underway. In such a case, and at least morally speaking, the attack upon us has started.

(a) It is not defense

In a "preventive war," on the other hand, as we have defined it, there is no "defense" in the sense that there is *no actual attack underway to defend oneself against.* Or, rather, the term "underway" has been so expanded to include also our own assessment of the *mere possibility of, or potentiality for, a future attack* – that is, it is "underway" when we guess so.

In a "preventive war" so defined, the *dubious conclusions* of our conjectures about the adversary's possible but unproven intentions are taken as *certainty* of his intent to injure us. Once such spurious "certainty" has taken the place of real proof, it is argued (wrongfully and unlawfully) that the attack is "underway," and one slithers easily (but still wrongfully and unlawfully) into the moral argument of "self-defense."

(b) Certainty is required

To act morally, one must have moral certainty of the justice of the war. "Moral" certainty is that which, although it refers to contingent facts and thus it cannot exclude all possibility of error, nonetheless leaves no reasonable and prudent doubt about the rectitude of the decision to be taken.

Now, certainty is the effect of evidence. As the damage to be inflicted by a war upon the adversary is real, absolutely certain and much of it irreparable, the decision to wage war must be based upon proportional, morally certain reasons. Presumption in the absence of evidence is not sufficient to justify morally an action with such dreadful consequences.

(c) Modern risks do not justify it

It is undeniable, as Michael Novak and George Weigel have pointed out, that the development of new technologies and the increased threat of global terrorism have changed the face of war in the modern world. Since the end of the cold war, as there remains no possible enemy of the United States with the means to resist the full engagement of American military power, military and political analysts consider that only "asymmetrical" attacks would seem to be viable for an adversary in the foreseeable future – terrorism against civilian targets, "cyberwar" against computer systems, etc.

Thus, the normal criteria to be examined in the assessment of a just-war situation may not be present – no conventional military movements (as

Weigel puts it, no more question "of waiting for the redcoats to crest the hill at dawn"), no visible signs of imminent attack, no authority of a hostile state who assumes responsibility for the attack.[1]

Even so, the mere ability of a country, even an unfriendly one, to launch a war is not sufficient cause for a just war.[2] The just war is a defensive one. The notion of "defense" may be construed so as to cover a wide array of concrete situations, but it is always reaction to an actual attack or to the adversary's "manifest intent" to injure.

Thus, however reasonable may be the fears for the safety of one's country, however much the risks may have increased in modern times, however tactically expedient and, in the long run, safer, it may be to neutralize such odds, the moral principle remains unchangeable: *non faciamus mala ut veniant bona* – it is not permissible to do what is morally evil, not even to obtain a good result. A government certainly has the right and the duty to protect its citizens, but it also has the higher obligation of submitting to the moral law (which is, in the end, nothing else than the Law of God).

(d) It is aggression

Whatever terms we choose to designate such action, "the 'preventive war' is a war of aggression, unjustifiable on moral grounds and according to international law. To intervene, it is required to have proofs."[3]

In practice, some analysts and commentators have expanded the traditional notion of "anticipatory self-defense" to the point where it includes the first use of force, on the basis of the presumption of the hostile intentions of the adversary. Thus expanded, such action ceases to be self-defense and fits the definition of aggression. Thus, it is unjust.

IV. Closing Reflection

Two final reflections, one theological, and the other political.

Our Lord blessed those *"who hunger and thirst after justice"* and those who are persecuted *"for justice's sake."* Of such is the kingdom of Heaven,

---

1. Novak, "An Argument That War Against Iraq is Just," pp. 595–596; George Weigel, "The Just War Case for the War," *America*, Vol. 188, No. 11, March 31, 2003, p. 8.

2. See Philip F. Lawler, "A Lost Chance for Moral Leadership," *The Catholic World Report*, March, 2003, p. 1.

3. Archbishop Renato Raffaele Martino, President of the Pontifical Council for Justice and Peace, quoted in Gianni Cardinali, "Una vera azione preventiva? Evitare la guerra," Interview with Archbishop Martino, *30 Giorni*, February, 2003, online.

not of those who desire freedom above all, a liberty so elevated and absolute that it will necessarily attempt to free itself from dependence on God. In war, a nation that fights for freedom, without reference to justice, divorced as it were from the strict observance of the moral law, has no right to war, because it does not know why it wants to be free, or why it wants anyone else to be free. Catholics, in opposition to the spirit of the world, should think first and primarily in terms of justice. Whenever there is justice, there is true freedom. *"Seek ye first the kingdom of God and His justice, and all these things shall be added unto you."*

On the political side, analysts speak of a new American strategy, which seems to be focused on the preservation of the unipolarity of American hegemony achieved with the end of the cold war. In practice, it would mean that America is ready to intervene anywhere, any time, to neutralize any serious threat to its global dominance. If this is true, non-aligned states, by the mere fact of their non-alignment, will be deemed to pose a threat, and the mere possession of weapons of mass destruction by an unfriendly government, even without the violation of any existing international law, will be considered as a threat that has to be counteracted, and that on an anticipatory basis.[1] Many see in the present war against Iraq the *"first and paradigmatic application"* of this new and fateful strategy.[2]

The author of this article is no political analyst, but a priest, and thus his final words must be fittingly a prayer: may the Lord God of Armies, *Dominus Deus Sabaoth*, grant – to us and to those in authority over us – light for our intelligences and strong and serene hearts to walk in righteousness in His sight.

---

1. G. John Ikenberry, "America's Imperial Ambition," *Foreign Affairs*, September-October, 2002, pp. 52–53.

2. Drew Christiansen, S.J., "Whither the 'Just War'?" *America*, Vol. 188, No. 10, March 24, 2003, p. 7.

Sandro Botticelli, c1481, Abegg-Stiftung
Museum, Riggisberg, Switzerland

ST. THOMAS AQUINAS, O. P. (c1225–1274)

MARCUS TULLIUS CICERO (106–43 B.C.)

FRANCISCO SUÁREZ, S. J. (1548–1617)

THE EDITORS' GLOSS: The insanity of the arguments adduced in support of an attack on Iraq – both before and after the fact – is not limited to the "open letter" which we noted in our earlier gloss on Fr. Iscara's essay. A relatively unknown but telling admission relating to the argument in favor of war was made by Doug Feith, outgoing no. 3 man at the Pentagon and one of the chief architects of the war. Speaking to the American Enterprise Institute on May 4, 2004, he dealt with the criticism that swirled around the administration regarding its notorious failure to find Saddam's much-discussed WMD.

"The principal strategic danger to the United States in the war on terrorism," he said (emphasis ours in the following), "is the *possibility* that terrorists *could* get their hands on chemical, biological or nuclear weapons." He continued: "Given Iraq's record of hostility, aggression, WMD use, and ties to terrorists . . . President Bush concluded in light of the 9/11 attacks [which have what to do with the subject at hand?] that it was necessary to remove the Saddam Hussein regime by force." And here's the kicker: "The danger was too great that Saddam *might* give the fruits of his WMD programs to terrorists for use against the United States. This danger *did not hinge on whether Saddam was actually stockpiling chemical or biological weapons.*"

What this outrageous (but not entirely unexpected) admission shows is that the Bush administration couldn't have cared less whether or not Saddam actually possessed "forbidden" weapons, notwithstanding its expressions of affected outrage at his refusal to provide the UN with a list of everything he didn't have. President Bush and his neocon cohorts launched an aggressive war of political conquest: the aim, says Feith, was "to remove the Saddam Hussein regime by force," notwithstanding his lack of even the means to do us harm.

The admission also effectively makes Dr. Ryba's case: that whatever approach to pre-war decision-making the President was taking, it wasn't one saddled with worry about the need to fight a truly just war.

C H A P T E R

11

Epistemic Inadequacy, Catholic Just-War Criteria, and the War in Iraq
• • • • • • • • •
Prof. Thomas Ryba, Ph.D.

A S JUST WAR theory has historically developed, just-war theoreticians have expanded the set of concomitant criteria necessary to judge a war just. Although there is widespread agreement about what these concomitant criteria are, the difficulty is that different theoreticians of the model require different levels of certainty that these criteria have been met. In the doctrines of Augustine, Thomas, Bañez, Vasquez and Liguori the aggrieved state must have moral *certainty* about its cause, while in the thought of Suárez (and those who follow him), what is required is that justice simply be more probably on the side of the aggrieved state.

The Argument

What I would like to do in this essay is to show that formulations of just-war theory that concentrate on the criterion of probable just cause – and particularly the Bush administration's theory of the justification of the recent war in Iraq (insofar as it may be called a theory in any important sense) – attempt to dodge the issue of moral certainty in favor of the certainty of the preponderance of justice (a probabilistic and material criterion). What I will attempt to show is that, certainty about the *probability* of justice liberalizes the grounds for war, and that such a liberalization is problematic.

A Comprehensive List of Just-War Criteria

The notion of a just war within the Roman Catholic tradition has been an ethical "work in progress." To the presumptively original criteria provided by Augustine (relying as he did on Cicero), a series of thinkers – Aquinas,

Bañez, Vasquez, Vitoria, Suárez and Liguori – have contributed or provided justifications for additional criteria, so that the notion inherited by contemporary Catholics is one much richer and more stringent than those promulgated in earlier centuries.[1] Although many 21st century moral theologians provide slightly shorter lists, a comprehensive list of the *ad bellum* ("going to war") just-war criteria includes the following:

1. The war must have a just cause, such as defense, intentional threats to innocent life, intentional violations of human rights, vindication of justice, avenging intentional wrongdoing.

2. The war must be prosecuted by a competent, politically legitimate, authority in charge of the public order.

3. There must be right intention behind the war that excludes revenge and bloodlust, and is confined to the accomplishment of the goals connected with just causes.

4. The war must be initiated only as a last resort after all other reasonable avenues of peaceful resolution have been exhausted.

5. Justice must be relatively greater on the side of the offended nation, but cannot be absolute.[2]

6. The benefits of the war – the wrongs righted and good established – must proportionally outweigh the costs of the war – measured in suffering and destruction.

7. There must be a reasonable hope of success.

In addition, there are two *in bello* ("in war") criteria:

---

1. The major stages in this development are the formulations of Cicero, Augustine, Thomas Aquinas, Francisco de Vitoria, and Francisco Suárez, and then the Papal additions of the 20th century.

2. This means that "no state should act on the basis that it has 'absolute justice' on its side. Every party to a conflict should acknowledge the limits to its 'just cause' and the consequent requirements to use *only* limited means in pursuit of its objectives." The Catholic Bishops in *The Challenge of Peace*, §93, cited by Richard B. Miller, *Interpretations of Conflict: Ethics, Pacifism and the Just War Tradition*, (Chicago: University of Chicago Press, 1991), p. 66. [This notion, introduced by the American Bishops, is problematic in light of traditional just-war doctrine. See the appendix of Fr. Francis Stratmann, on pp. 387–417 of the present volume, which rules out the initiation of war without moral certainty of the justice of the cause on the side of the party initiating war. See also the enlightening remarks made upon this notion of "relative justice" by Dr. David Lutz on pp. 127–169 of the companion to the present volume, *Neo-CONNED! Again*.

1. Civilians (those not intentionally cooperating with combatants) must be discriminated from combatants and no intentional force is to be directed against them.

2. The tactics employed – measured in suffering and destruction – must not be proportionately greater than the wrongs righted and good established.[1]

An important feature of both the list of seven *ad bellum* criteria and the list of the two *in bello* criteria is that both are lists of *concomitant* criteria. They represent concomitant necessary conditions for a just war. However, in conception, these criteria have not been fixed but have grown *in* precision as well as *by* accretion, both kinds of growth having effected a narrowing of the circumstances under which just war is possible. This means that because it is in the process of development, new criteria can be added, and for this reason the criteria provided are necessary but not ultimately sufficient.

In fact, in the late 20th century further qualifications have been added to these criteria including: the unconditional condemnation of total war, the unconditional denial of any war of aggression (and the questioning of any justification of preemption), the unconditional denial of wars of subjugation, the exclusion of preemptive attack, the necessity of establishing an international authority to adjudicate international disputes and the affirmation of the primacy of negotiated settlements with just war reserved as a last resort. The Popes and Bishops have also backed away from affirming the *unequivocal right* to wage just war as well as the notion of a *moral obligation* to wage just war when the criteria of just cause have been fulfilled.[2]

Two Interpretive Frames for Just-War Criteria

Historically, the above criteria have been construed according to two different interpretive approaches as to what constitutes the admissible triggering condition of just war. The first, which is most closely connected

---

1. In listing this comprehensive set of criteria, I follow Richard Miller, *op. cit.*, pp. 13–15, and the U.S. Conference of Catholic Bishops.

2. These additional qualifications are found in the writings of the great 20th century Popes, including Pius XII, *Summi Pontificatus* (1939) and "Christmas Message" (1944), John XXIII, *Pacem in Terris* (1963), Paul VI, *Populorum Progressio* (1967), John Paul II, "Disarmament," Message to the UN General Assembly (1988) and *Evangelium Vitae* (1995), and, from the Documents of the Second Vatican Council, *Gaudium et Spes* (1965).

to the stringent interpretation of just war within the Roman Catholic tradition, makes the argument that a state of certainty must be met for each condition. Thus, one must be certain that there is a just cause, certain that the authority is competent, certain that there is a right intention, certain that it is a last resort, certain that there is relative justice, certain that there are proportional benefits and certain that there is a reasonable hope of success. This is the tradition connected with Augustine of Hippo, Thomas Aquinas and the Thomists down to the 17th century.[1] Gabriel Vasquez, S.J., and Dominicus Bañez, O.P., both assert this principle unequivocally. In Bañez's words, "[T]he state that wishes to declare war must not entertain a single doubt, the justifying reasons must be clearer than day. A declaration of war is equivalent to a sentence of death; to pronounce the latter with a doubtful conscience is murder."[2] St. Alphonsus de Liguori confirms the point: "There is no doubt that since war generally brings in its train so many evils and so much harm to religion, to innocent people, to the honor of women, etc., in practice it is hardly ever just if declared on probable reasons of justice alone and not certain reasons."[3]

Francisco de Vitoria, O.P., argues that the subjective belief of even a prince is not enough to determine whether war has been declared just, because the prince's judgment may be *vincibly* erroneous because under the influence of the passions.[4] The justice and causes must be examined with great care with every opportunity for the opponents to make their case.[5] All of this must be judged in such a way that the belief resulting must be the belief "formed according to [the Aristotelian notion of] the judgment of the wise man."[6] What is required is a prudential judgment of the highest order reckoning an intrinsic injustice.

---

1. Cyprian Emanuel, O.F.M., Ph.D., and the Committee on Ethics, *The Ethics of War: A Report of the Ethics Committee* (Washington, D.C.: The Catholic Association for International Peace (CAIP), 1932), p. 24.

2. Dominicus Bañez, quoted *ibid.*

3. *De Quinto Praecepto Decalogi*, Art. II, Par. 404, quoted in John Eppstein, *The Catholic Tradition of the Law of Nations* (Washington, D.C.: CAIP, 1935), p. 112.

4. Francisco de Vitoria, O.P., *De Iure Belli*, in Ernest Nys and John Pawley Bate, trans., *De Indis et de Iure Belli Relectiones* (Washington, D.C.: Carnegie Institution, 1917; reprinted, Buffalo: William S. Hein & Co., Inc., 1995), parts V and VI of *Relectiones Theologicae XII* (published previously, Johan Georg Simon, J.U.D., ed., Cologne and Frankfort: August Boetius, 1696), 20 and 21, p. 173.

5. *Ibid.*, 21.

6. *Ibid.*, 20. De Vitoria's citation of Book 2 of Aristotle's *Nicomachean Ethics* at this point is apparently to highlight the fact that the object of the unjust action must be intrinsically evil and must be judged to be such. It may also be to suggest the virtues that the wise ruler must possess.

The second interpretive frame for the conditions for just war focuses not on the certainty of the judgment but according to a virtually *equiprobabilist* understanding of the relative justice connected with the material conditions for war.[1] One approach within this frame requires merely a general judgment of the probability that more justice is on the side of the offended to justify him in initiating the war. This is the position of Francisco Suárez.[2]

Suárez distinguishes the practical certitude expressed in statements such as, "It is lawful *for x* to make war," from the theoretical certitude expressed in statements such as, "This cause of war is just *in itself*" or, "This thing *t* sought through war *is rightfully x's*."[3] Although holding that "war is a matter of the gravest character" and that the deliberation concerning it must be applied according to the principle of reason as "commensurate [or in due proportion] with its importance," Suárez notes that when a king's claim to territory is "carefully examined" and "the truth of that claim clearly established" then the going to war to reclaim it is just.[4] However, when each side claims that territory with some probability, then the most probable claim makes the war just.[5] This, he believes, follows from a creative interpretation of the principle of distributive justice that entails "the more worthy party is to receive the preference."[6] His interpretation makes the more worthy party him "who enjoys the more probable right."[7] Probabilities being equipollent, possession establishes right, and if neither party is in possession, then the desired thing should be divided equally between claimants.[8] When the issue is not the possession of a thing (or a commodity) but a question of a violation of justice or charity, then again the more worthy party is he who is more *probably* worthy. Suárez's virtual

---

1. "Equiprobabilism" is the casuist system which proposes to resolve questions of the goodness or evil of an action on the basis of whether the greater probability is on the side of law or freedom. If on the side of the law, then one is bound by it. If on the side of freedom, then one is free to act.

2. Emanuel, *op. cit.*, p. 24.

3. Francisco Suárez, S.J., *De Caritate*, from *On the Three Theological Virtues: Faith, Hope, and Charity* (originally published, Coimbra: Nicolas Carvalho, 1621) in Gwladys L. Williams, *et al.*, trans., *Selections from Three Works* (London: Humphrey Milford, 1944; reprinted, Buffalo: William S. Hein & Co., Inc., 1995), Disputation XIII (*De Bello*), Sect. VI, p. 828.

4. *Ibid.*, Sect. VI, 2, p. 828.

5. *Ibid.*

6. *Ibid.*

7. *Ibid.*

8. *Ibid.*, Sect. VI, 4, pp. 829–830.

equiprobabilism extends only to the causes of war, but without a just cause the war's legitimacy is invalidated anyway.

Notice, here, that a shift has been made from the original Thomist position, which stipulates that certainty about the going-to-war criteria must be met, to the probabilist's (or equiprobabilists') position that clears the way for bellicose action under circumstances with no *certain* moral status. Suárez's interpretation begins with a presupposition of moral uncertainty and, with that uncertainty given, interprets the *freedom* to wage war as a function of the barest probability that justice is on the side of the state that declares war.

Luis Molina, S.J., further broadens the grounds for just war by removing the stipulation that the injustice of the offender be intentional (or formally unjust) in favor of *material* (or unintentional) grounds. Even if *no intent* to do harm or to commit injustices is provable on the part of one's opponent, Molina argues the aggrieved state has the right to go to war against its offender.[1] Here, the intention of one's opponent becomes nearly irrelevant. This approach had the effect of shifting consideration from certainty to the material circumstances which precipitate war, but in such a way that specific criteria were blurred in favor of a simple general judgment that more justice be probably on the side of the initiator. It also tends to remove the issue of intentional agency of one's opponent as a cause. According to Molina, what is required to go to war is that one must be certain that the probabilities are greater than equal that a material injustice has been committed. Note how different this is from the clear criteria identified by Francis Stratmann that "gross *formal* moral guilt [must be evident] on one side – material wrong is not sufficient."[2]

In the framing of the *ad bellum* criteria, it would seem that there are two different kinds of warrant at issue. One conception of warrant is that expressed in the following sentence: "I have good grounds to go to war because I am certain that an injustice was done." The other is that expressed in the quite different statement: "I have good grounds to go to war because it is probable that an injustice was done to me." Or even more startling: "I have good grounds to go to war because the probability that an injustice was done to me is greater than or equal to the probability that an injustice was not done to me." The first formulation looks to a set of judgments to

---

1. Emanuel, *op. cit.*, p. 26.

2. From Fr. Francis Stratmann's *The Church and War* (New York: P. J. Kennedy and Sons, 1928), Chapter III, reproduced in the present volume as Appendix I, pp. 387–417.

establish the certainty of a just cause for war; the latter accepts probable uncertainties as a just cause.

Clearly the latter is an attempt to remove the stringent requirement of grounding the practical judgment in realities and to ground it in mere probabilities. Even though this equiprobabilism is weighted toward giving the moral actor freedom (especially when the Magisterium has not pronounced with certainty on a specific moral case[1]), its employment to establish grounds for war can only issue in reckless freedom, equivalent to an unconscionable disregard for life. Here, the stakes are much higher than in a casuistic case involving an individual's freedom. They are not the individual's possible commission of a single sin or the preservation of the individual's freedom from scrupulosity; they are the potential loss of millions of lives and unlimited material destruction – circumstances precisely under which a little scrupulosity goes a long way to preserve life. It is not surprising, therefore, that later moral theologians were wont to dismiss the equiprobabilist position quite definitively; the judgment of Edward Génicot (1856–1900) is illustrative: "The principal reason (why moral certitude of the justice of the cause is required before war may lawfully be declared) is this: that war brings in its train so many evils that it cannot be permitted except for vindicating really certain rights. Hence the opinion of many authors, who think it is sufficient that the right of the party declaring war should be merely 'probable' or 'more probable,' is altogether to be rejected and condemned as intrinsically dangerous."[2]

It is my contention that the present war in Iraq has been prosecuted on the basis of reasoning which more closely resembles the Suárezian and Molinian approaches to the conditions for war than the model which requires certainty and which is in the mainstream of the tradition of the Church. Though it is not very likely that the governmental officials responsible for declaring war on Iraq have heard of, or would be interested in, the theories elaborated by Suárez and Molina, that does not excuse them from culpability for applying arguments very much like them, especially when there has been opportunity to become familiar with sounder formulations. In their avoidance of such familiarization, they lapse into a variety of thinking which tailors the excuse for going to war to the ends they hope to achieve. At any rate, to make this case as forcefully as possible, I will need to engage in a few more preliminary discussions as background to building a case for their culpability.

1. See the article by Dr. William Cavanaugh in the present volume, pp. 269–289.—Ed.
2. *Institutiones Theologicae Morales*, quoted by Eppstein, *op. cit.*, p. 168.

Implicit Structures in the Just-War Criteria

In the difference between the two interpretations for the certification of a just war, more is at stake than what meets the eye. An example, I think, will make this clear. In his classic article, "The Ethics of War," Cyprian Emanuel, O.F.M., summarizes the conditions for determining whether a war is just as follows: "Wars are just or unjust according as the conditions for justification are present or not."[1]

Although Emanuel obviously does not intend it, in his description there is a telling ambiguity that is the crux of the judicative task.[2] In the above statement, it is the interpretive moment that is veiled. This is common in many treatments of these criteria. Now in actual circumstances, the conditions for a just war are not always *unequivocally* given. Circumstances are not always black and white, and the way the various criteria are interrelated muddies the judgment about the nature of the conditions. It is possible, therefore, to describe two aspects of the overall assessment of a war's justice – or prior to the commencement of hostilities, the assessment of whether a contemplated war would be just – which require interpretation. First are what we might call ontological conditions for justification – the states of affairs in the external world that determine whether a war is indeed just. These are the conditions *that exist in actual fact* and independently of anyone judging them to be such. Second, there are the elements that constitute the level of "certainty" that the actors involved possess – i.e., the actors' own assessment of the relation between the aforementioned realities and the belief states of the actors (which is to say, are the actors confident that, in reflecting upon their level of "certainty," their *judgments* about the degree to which the conditions for a just war are met correspond to the *reality* of whether those conditions are truly met).

The ontological (or *de re*) features of the "going-to-war" situation are about whether certain features *obtain*. Certainty is *about* these features. Judgments are about the relations of ontological features to the one judging, that is about *how one is certain* that they obtain. Certainty constitutes a reflexive moment; it is a judgment about how accurately one has *assessed* the realities not about the realities *per se*. It is a judgment about

---

1. Emanuel, *op. cit.*, p. 6

2. Here, I am using the ambiguity of one of his descriptions to make the point that it is easy to lapse into descriptions of just war that deemphasize the complexity of judgment, not to claim that Emanuel actually is guilty of ignoring that complexity. My point is that the interpretation of the circumstances surrounding war sometimes lead to a conscionable certainty that does not reflect the real grounds for justification.

whether one has correctly interpreted the realities or that one has been deceived. Thus, judgment is about dubitability of the evidence presented to consciousness. Probabilistic judgments about going to war signal the insufficiency of our data, our interpretations, our understanding, or our judgments to bring us to certainty. Thus, it is quite different to say that "I am certain that the criteria for capital punishment have been met in the case of Scott Peterson" and to say that "I think that the probability that Scott Peterson is guilty is 51% *and* that probability is sufficient to warrant his execution." The latter would seem to lead to an unconscionable act in a way that the former would not. Even so, it is possible to be conscionably certain and wrong.

The distinction above has relevance to the classical Roman Catholic formulation of the ethical situation which recognizes a distinction be-tween the object of the moral act, the intention of the moral act and the knowledge of the moral act. Accordingly, we may distinguish the following situations:

1. The situation in which circumstances make war just, we have certainty about them, and our intentions are just.

2. The situation in which circumstances make the war just, but we do not have certainty about those circumstances, and our intentions are just.

3. The situation in which circumstances do not make war just, but we are certain that they make war just (but are mistaken), and our intentions are just.

4. The situation in which circumstances do not make war just, and we are certain about them (that they do not make war just), and our intentions are just.

5. The situation in which we are not certain about whether or not the circumstances make war just, but we pretend that they are just.

In situation (1) we have a case in which the just going-to-war criteria are met, so that if action is taken it is just. In situation (2), because we do not have the requisite certainty, war could not be justly undertaken. Situation (3) represents the situation of fallible judgment, which does not make the going to war just but to which no immediate culpability may be assigned unless the discovery phase was bungled. Bungling would change the situation and make it immoral, owing to culpable ignorance. Situation (4), because it stipulates that our intentions are just, cannot lead to a choice to engage in war, knowing – as we do – that the conditions are not met. Situation (5) is an example of immoral and dishonest belligerency.

The Possible Insufficiency of the Just-War Criteria

Up to this point, we have not addressed the significance of the fact that the seven *ad bellum* criteria are only *necessary* concomitant criteria and that they are not also *sufficient* concomitant criteria. As I suggested earlier, the very fact that they have grown in number through time suggests that they are susceptible to further expansion and are, therefore, merely necessary at best. One can plausibly argue that the improvement of law and morality will make just-war theory ultimately converge with pacifism because, as just-war theory piles stipulation upon stipulation, converging toward sufficiency, just war becomes less morally possible.

If we characterize the sufficiency of just-war theory in this fashion, it is possible to argue that the relationship between the various conditions would seem to be a special instance of the Gettier problem. The Gettier problem was first posed in *Analysis* in 1963 by Edmund L. Gettier establishing the insufficiency of certain standard accounts of what it means to know something.[1] Gettier was able to show that even when something was true, an individual believed it to be true, and that individual was justified in believing it to be true, these conditions, though concomitantly necessary for that belief (or knowing), were not sufficient to ground that belief. For intermittent historical stretches, the *ad bellum* criteria have been treated as necessary *and* sufficient. But this is clearly not defensible, since criteria have been added over the course of history showing the insufficiency of preceding criteria. In the case of just-war theoreticians, this insufficiency is non-culpable only in those circumstances when the perfecting criteria could not be discovered. But Gettier's analysis suggests a deeper insufficiency in the justification of just war, as well. Let's take the example, then, which makes this clear with respect to the war in Iraq.

President Bush can be said to *know* that the grounds for the war with Iraq are just in the following way: (i) "The grounds for war with Iraq are just" *is true*; (ii) President Bush *believes* that "the grounds for war with Iraq

---

1. Gettier, Edmund L., "Is Justified True Belief Knowledge?" in A. Phillips Griffiths, ed., *Knowledge and Belief* (Oxford: Oxford University Press, 1967), pp. 144–146.

are just" is true; and (iii) President Bush *is justified in believing* that "the grounds for war with Iraq are just" is true.

According to the classical accounts, were any of these concomitant conditions false, then clearly President Bush could not claim that he *knows* the war with Iraq is just. One of the necessary conditions would be violated. But what Gettier has shown is that even if all three conditions are met, there may still not be sufficient grounds to go to war. One way in which the insufficiency might be demonstrated is if there were an additional set of reasonable criteria that more precisely defined Bush's justification. If there were, then he would be morally obligated to follow them, as long as they improved sufficiency and could not be improved themselves.

Clearly it is never just to go to war if any of the following conditions are met: (a) the grounds for the war are not just; (b) the President believes the grounds for the war are not just; and/or (c) the criteria for the justification of the war are faulty. Clearly, if the grounds for the war themselves are, in reality, unjust, President Bush may falsely believe they are just because the criteria he applies are faulty. Or, they may be just, in reality, and he may believe them to be just but for the wrong reasons. Or he may pig-headedly (or *demonically*) believe them to be just against their real injustice and a set of criteria that tell him they are unjust. Even when all three conditions obtain, Gettier would argue – and the historical evolution of just-war theory would confirm – that the criteria for just war stipulate necessary criteria but not a set complete in their sufficiency.

Here, the broadly Thomist principle of certainty – bearing most specifically on condition (c) above – namely the certainty of our judgment – is important. Examining more closely the constituent elements of our knowledge, and its "certainty," about the justice of a proposed war, we can see that epistemic adequacy would not obtain (i.e., we could not properly be said to have true "knowledge") most obviously if (i) is not true but both (ii) and (iii) are true – the situation occurring if (iii) is construed in terms of a set of criteria other than those specified within the Roman Catholic tradition. Epistemic adequacy would also not obtain if (i) is not true, (ii) is true and (iii) is not true; or it would not obtain if – according to the most cynical view of President Bush's actions – none of the conditions are met. But even if all of the criteria for just war are met, there is still the possibility, *à la* Gettier, that Bush does not have sufficient knowledge that the war is a just war.

With respect to the war in Iraq, a Gettier case would obtain if the criteria for just war were met, Bush judges the war to be just, Bush certifies the certainty of the justification and Bush's intention is just. These might all be maintained as concomitant necessities without their being sufficient. That the criteria for just war might fall short of sufficiency raises some interesting ethical questions. It suggests that no war is sufficiently just to be considered unequivocally moral, but – by the same token – if the knowledge of what would make the criteria sufficient is beyond our epistemic reach, then we are non-culpably ignorant. However, the very fact that we know them to be insufficient, means that it is impossible to bask in the self-assurance that any war is perfectly just. Precisely because of this, awareness of this insufficiency implies that just wars must be undertaken with trepidation and with the intention to search for more adequate criteria. In President Bush's case, even if operating with a set of necessary criteria, so long as a more adequate model is discoverable, its greater sufficiency makes it morally culpable for him not to adopt it. It is in this sense, that the fifth *ad bellum* criterion has relevance. If we can argue that all definitions of just war are essentially insufficient as shown by (1) its historical evolution and (2) its being a species of the Gettier problem, then we can argue that we might never adequately know what makes a just war *sufficiently* a just war. Without knowledge of sufficient justice, at best we can only claim justice proportionately and, at worst, achieve it accidentally. For this reason, nothing more than a relative justice can be on the side of a nation initiating a just war. This adds a new layer of meaning to the notion of just war. One that recognizes the prosecution of a just war is always relative to the best model available at the time.

This might seem to lead us to the Suárezian position, but in fact it points toward a position which is more rigorous. With respect to all criteria of going to war, we must have certainty relative to the model we employ and a willingness to make the criteria more stringent, if reason beckons us to do so. Inasmuch as Suárez attempted to introduce probable (equiprobable) causes for war into the first criterion, we must reject that liberalization because that liberalization leads to a bellicose adventurism of the worst kind. It weighs human life as insignificant in the face of a merely probable injustice. However, by the relative insufficiency of all just-war models, we must admit – in accord with the fifth criterion – that we cannot claim that justice is absolutely on our side in any circumstances.

To the questionable morality of equiprobabilist interpretations of relative justice, it is possible to add the insufficiency of the just-war criteria, even in their most robust form. Together, these defects bring home the precarious nature of any cavalier rush to war, like the rush to war that characterized the beginning of the war with Iraq.

The logical and unavoidable conclusion of all this is that the inherent insufficiency of just-war criteria may indicate: (1) that the insufficiency of criteria for just war signals that *no criteria* are sufficient to make war just and therefore war *cannot be* just; or (2) that though there may be criteria that are sufficient to make a war just, that sufficiency is unachievable or (3) that though there are sufficient criteria to make a war just, we have not yet achieved an understanding of what they are. The first of these possibilities is the Pacifist position. If one believes it to be the case then there are no conscionable grounds for war. The second and third possibilities make the undertaking of war a matter of relative justice, something to be undertaken only under the most dire circumstances.

The War in Iraq as an Example of Unjust War: An Application of the Preceding

Since 9/11, most of the scholars taking up the question of whether the war in Iraq is a just war – scholars such as Elshtain, Walzer, Temes, Lucas, Hayden, Weigel, Royal, Powers, *et al.* – make use of lists or principles that vary according to the political stance they have.[1] I would even go so far as to argue that, in some cases, they intentionally tailor their criteria to their purposes. This having been said, a typological distinction can be made between them. In the present debate about the Iraq war, the criteria for just war are established either from within the war-realist perspective (and the accompanying positivist view of law) or from the natural law tradition.

---

1. Cf., for example, Jean Bethke Elshtain, *Just War Against Terror: The Burden of American Power in a Violent World* (New York: Basic Books, 2003); Patrick Hayden, "The War on Terrorism and the Just Use of Military Force," in Patrick Hayden, Tom Lansford, and Robert P. Watson, ed., *America's War on Terror* (Burlington: Ashgate, 2003), pp. 105–121; George R. Lucas, "From *Jus Ad Bellum* to *Jus Ad Pacem*: Re-Thinking Just-War Criteria for the Use of Military Force for Humanitarian Ends," in Deen K. Chatterjee and Don E. Scheid, ed., *Ethics and Foreign Intervention* (Cambridge: Cambridge University Press, 2003), pp. 72–96; Peter S. Temes, *The Just War: An American Reflection on the Morality of War in Our Time* (Chicago: Ivan R. Dee, 2003); and Michael Walzer, *Arguing About War* (New Haven, 2004). Of the group, Jean Bethke Elshtain argues that the war in Iraq is just on the basis of the Augustinian criteria. This seems to me to be a clear example of intentionally choosing a regressive model of just war – Augustine's – in order to make an argument that will be consonant with one's political decision. It is the moral equivalent of putting the cart before the horse. That we are said to be once again struggling against "barbarians" does not in any way mean that we must relax the conditions for going to war. Cf. Elshtain, *op. cit.*, pp. 59–70.

In the remainder of this piece, my argument will follow from within the more stringent set of criteria specified in the tradition of Roman Catholicism, so that the war-realist and comparatively truncated (or Suárezian) versions of these criteria will not be engaged. My explanation for the absence of any engagement is that my purpose, here, is not to vindicate the strong version of the Roman Catholic interpretation against the interpretations which would weaken it, even though I think such a vindication is possible. My task is simpler. It is, instead, to use these criteria to evaluate the war in Iraq.

In classical Roman Catholic moral theory, the notion of moral certainty is relatively easy to establish. It is based upon natural law and/or the Church's *Magisterium* or accepted definitions sanctioned by this authority. One achieves moral certainty when a type of action – sometimes called the object of an act – is judged intrinsically licit or illicit, or when other conditions – intention, for example – are also unequivocally grasped. When the moral certainty of some action is questionable, one has recourse to one of the systems of casuistry to decide whether an act is conscionable or not. Here, it should be noted that the conscionable nature of a morally uncertain act at a particular moment does not guarantee its rectitude indefinitely. Although one might want to say that though a President responsible for launching a conscionable war at a given time cannot be held morally culpable for a mistaken decision if that decision was in good faith, that does not mean that he is free from responsibility when it is discovered or made known to him that he was in error. Another way of putting this is that under any circumstance when bellicose action is undertaken presuming moral certainty, that decision possesses a temporal dimension that might cause it to be viewed as mistaken – and therefore culpable – at some future point. Restorative justice might even demand that reparations be paid. And there is also the question of his prior responsibility. A moral actor has the prior responsibility to examine the model of the just war he employs in reaching the conclusion that war is just. Imprudence in the choice of models, in such grave questions, is itself a culpable offense.

In fall 2002, just before the war with Iraq began, I wrote a piece for *Chronicles* in which I argued that according to the criteria of Roman Catholic just-war theory, Bush's war with Iraq was unjust.[1] My argument hinged on three criteria in particular: the criterion of just cause, the crite-

---

1. Thomas Ryba, "Just War or Just Another War?" *Chronicles*, February, 2003, pp. 20–22.

rion of right intention and the criterion of last resort. It seemed to me, then, that the Bush administration's assertion that certain facts (especially bearing on these three criteria) were known with high probability *had not been proven*, and thus a plausible case for just cause, right intention, and last resort could not honestly be made. Though I can hardly claim prescience – the media, early on, were full of the suspicion that the evidence for weapons of mass destruction was very slim – I remain nevertheless surprised by the degree to which the claims made about the presence of WMDs in Iraq have diverged from the evidence (or lack of evidence) for them. This is all the more striking given that the occupation has made the possibility of WMDs' discovery so much better.

Here, I would like to take the opportunity to expand on the analysis I made in *Chronicles*, with the issues addressed above as background.

Bush's Legitimization of the War in Iraq

In every case that the Bush administration has attempted to identify just causes for the war in Iraq, that identification has been based on probabilities that injustices exist which would be causes for war. Since the beginning of the war, the strategy of the Bush administration and its epigones – in the absence of *certainty* – has been five-fold:

(a) to continue to assert that WMDs exist in Iraq, but to extend the temporal horizon for their expected discovery, and thus defer the judgment on the rectitude of this war to the indefinite future;

(b) to claim the essential rectitude of the cause in light of the alleged human rights record of Saddam Hussein and the alleged discovery of the mass graves of his victims – this often according to the claim that Saddam Hussein allegedly *was* the weapon of mass destruction;

(c) to argue that Saddam's regime was already a supporter of al-Qaeda, not merely of "home-grown terrorists" like many other regimes deemed unworthy of intervention;

(d) to argue that Iraq would have become a client State for world-wide terrorism after 9/11, even if not directly involved with al-Qaeda before 9/11; or

(e) to argue that the resistance met at the hands of non-Iraqi Islamist terrorists was a part of the grand strategy of the "roach motel" theory of intervention ("terrorists check in but they don't check out"), in other words, that from the beginning the plan was to attract terrorists to the area instead of spreading military resources around the world.

Except for (b) which *was* a claim made prior to the war (though it hardly constituted the reason action was taken), (c) – for which there is scanty evidence – and (e), these strategies proceed according to retroactive justifications. Now retroactive justifications are often called into service when a probable cause for action has been practically discredited. A species of the *post hoc ergo propter hoc*[1] fallacy, they are an attempt to recover legitimacy when the original reason for action is challenged or is no longer defensible. Retroactive justifications function in one of two ways: either they are the direct result of *post hoc* discovery – this is the justification we would have used, had we been aware of the facts we now have – or they are a matter of realistic motivations which, for political or security reasons, could not be disclosed at the time the war was mounted. Thus, though a reason for war might have been expressed and intended secretly, it was not publicly expressed either because, though a good reason, it was not a *convincing* reason, or because, though a good reason, it was not *safe* to express it.

The latter variety of retroactive justification – that based upon a secret reason later disclosed – is not purely retroactive. It is *post hoc* or retroactive only from the public's point of view, while the war strategists may have known it as the real cause from the start. Now there might be conditions which would warrant the keeping of reasons for war secret, but there are honest and dishonest ways of doing this. If the government asks the public to trust that it has just grounds which may not be disclosed, there is nothing immoral in prosecuting a war in this fashion as long as those grounds are indeed moral. Moreover, even when the government makes use of real just causes that may not be those that are most compelling as an argument for going to war, as long as those causes are a subset of the set of real conscionable reasons – some that may be disclosed and others that cannot – and as long as it does not positively assert those causes to be the only causes, nothing morally objectionable has occurred. Nevertheless, if these strategists disingenuously substitute (in their public discourse) a false though theoretically just reason for the real but just reason, they have lied. Once the real reason for war is known by the public and the lie is retroactively justified to them, they may even countenance it, because it was done for the good of the commonwealth. But this is no way for elected officials to discharge their responsibility to the electorate, unless one believes that they ought to be elected for the express purpose to tell us lies that will move us to action.

The morality of mounting a war on the basis of a positive lie – even with good reasons to back it up – is not defensible. St. Thomas, although

---

1. After which therefore because of which. —Ed.

allowing stratagems such as concealment, does not allow positive lying as one of war's instrumentalities.[1] So, there is a clear moral problem with any call for war that substitutes a convincing but false reason for war in place of the real reason for war, even if the true reason is revealed later. Unless it is a lesser but nevertheless *real* reason, it is at best a lie and at worst a lie coupled to an immoral reason for war.

The Bush administration would not have had to resort to retroactive justifications had it possessed the requisite certainty specified by the Thomist model. In going to war, therefore, it (unconsciously) relied on a Suárezian probabilistic calculus of just cause, but it coupled it to the claim that the superior – if not absolutely superior – justice of the American way of life made less than necessary justifications necessary and sufficient because of this superior moral stance. Remember, in each case of justification the probability that the cause was just fell short – in some cases *far* short – of certainty. Anything less than certainty does not warrant war. According to the Roman Catholic model, the U.S. possesses no inherent right to wage war in *any* circumstance but especially not in those circumstances when it establishes the grounds for war probabilistically and then when it justifies these mistaken grounds on the basis of the moral superiority of its way of life.

But as if that weren't enough, each of the justifications for the war with Iraq possesses further structural problems. Justifications (a), (d) and (e) fiddle with the connection between certainty and temporality in different ways.

Justification (a) contains an implicit argument from analogy. The logic of this argument goes something like this: knowing what we know about the wiliness of Saddam, it is not the case that evidence was lacking nor is it the case that the evidence was misinterpreted. Rather, the evidence was evidence in real time and correctly interpreted. Therefore, if no weapons were discovered, it must be that Saddam has played a shell game with us. This justification – which possesses the weak compulsion of a bare likelihood at best – requires the brilliance of Saddam as a prior high probability, a premise which is highly questionable, given his ignominious circumstances at the time of his capture. It, furthermore, demands from its believers a twisted logic tantamount to fervent hope, each passing frustration at not finding WMDs being counted as evidence that Saddam was even cleverer than we expected. Most importantly, it requires the uncompromising belief in the veracity of the assertion that Iraq possessed weapons of mass destruction in the first place. Instead of using non-discovery as a

---

1. St. Thomas Aquinas, *Summa Theologica* (henceforth *ST*), II, ii, Q. 40, A. 3.

probable argument that WMDs were not possessed by Saddam, it uses non-discovery as a probable proof of Saddam's wiliness. Because the proof of the non-existence of something is virtually impossible, this kind of argument is temporally open-ended. Now it is always possible that Iraqi WMDs will be discovered (somewhere) and the wiliness of Saddam finally proven, but given the accumulated evidence up to the present as well as the vigorous back-peddling this administration has done to name other justifications for war retroactively, this justification, if not promulgated disingenuously, is at least totally irrational. (As I write these words, the U.S. government has officially abandoned its search for Iraqi WMDs inside Iraq!)

One can imagine circumstances where WMDs were involved and in which preemptive war might be just. If, for example, one intercepts launch-orders that are time sensitive, so that one knows that an attack will be mounted with an almost one-hundred percent probability, then this would seem to be an example of when a preemptive attack might be made on the principle that the circumstances set in motion already count as the first act of war. The parallel would be forcibly stopping a thrown sucker punch. However, as the temporal distance between command and execution grows – the *certainty* of the command's execution generally diminishes. In the absence of evidence that a "command" has been given, the existence of WMDs, in themselves, do not constitute a threat without clear intent to use them. And knowing that there is intent to use them but without the capability to use them means that that intent must wait for future realization. Knowing that the intention will likely be carried out at some distant future date, then other measures – beside war – could be taken to prevent the command's being carried out. And these alternative measures must be attempted, for to have other means at one's disposal to prevent an attack, short of war, are almost always preferable. In this way, temporal distance between intention and action weakens the grounds for the justification of a war. Evidence of weapons of mass destruction that is ten years old does not have the same actionable significance as that of satellite telemetry in real time. It weakens the moral certainty of the case for war.

Justification (d) is based upon a supposition which, given everything we know about the intelligence used to justify this war, is not compelling.[1] Other client states were also available. The ideological and religious

---

1. Both *The 9/11 Commission Report* (New York: W. W. Norton & Co., 2004) and Bob Woodward's *Bush at War* (New York: Simon and Schuster, 2002) make the point that (1) there was very little intelligence to link al-Qaeda with Saddam Hussein, and (2) Iraq was already a target for possible intervention before the al-Qaeda attack on the twin towers. One of the effects of 9/11 on war planning was to provide the pretence for including

differences between Osama bin Laden and Saddam Hussein are sufficient to make this justification highly questionable. But because the very act of prosecuting the war erased the conditions leading to its empirical verification, the Bush administration may disingenuously maintain either (i) that it, in fact, succeeded in removing the threat or (ii) that though the threat was far from certain, it was better to be safe than sorry. The second justification is Suárezian in character and, because so uncertain, is ethically problematic as a justification, whereas the first justification if there were no threat in the first place is tantamount to a dishonest ground. Even if there had been a pre-existing political relationship between Saddam and Osama, this does not amount to an imminent threat. The establishment of such a relationship calls for an evaluation of its nature before action is taken. And, again, that action need not be war. Other diplomatic and covert options are available. Preventative war undertaken on the probability that an alliance *might* issue in hostilities is indefensible according to the Roman Catholic theory of just war.

If justification (e) is not an outright lie, a cynical ploy to create a strategy where originally there was none, then it is equivalent to precipitous experimentation. The theoretical underpinnings of such an idea are questionable to say the least, not to mention the relative cost in terms of human carnage to put the theory to an experimental test. Again, how could the administration know that the result of the invasion of Iraq would be to draw Islamist terrorists into armed combat, instead of causing them to fan out into the world as a diffused threat? The effect of the Iraq war *may* be that practically this result was achieved, but before the war attained this character, how could this expected outcome be gauged with any certainty? Even if the Bush administration were in possession of some calculus by which this might be reckoned with high probability, even then the *ad bellum* criteria could not be fulfilled.

There are issues of Iraq's sovereignty connected with this strategy. It is adventurism of the worst kind, and a grave and unjust violation of a state's rights, to attack a state with the intent that one's enemies from outside that state would be drawn into the conflict. Here, one has initiated a conflict

---

Iraq as an aggressor. Rumsfeld, Wolfowitz, and Cheney seem to have been the chief advocates for folding Iraq into the war on al-Qaeda. WMDs, collaboration with al-Qaeda, and Iraq's status as a harbor state for terrorists were some of the reasons given for this inclusion. What is especially surprising about *The 9/11 Commission Report* is its almost complete silence on the planning for the war with Iraq, and this is apparently a function of the almost complete disconnect between the causes of 9/11 and Iraq. See *The 9/11 Commission Report*, pp. 334–338.

that has the potential to make innocents in the attacked state the victims of *my* enemies' hostilities. Whether driven by the "roach motel" theory of intervention, or not, the practical effect of the war in Iraq has been to make innocent Iraqis the enemy of the U.S.'s enemies. Unconscionable as an anticipated outcome of our intervention, our inability to control the violence against innocents at the hands of our provoked enemies raises serious questions about the second *in bello* criterion, not to mention the first.

The additional problem is that this justification amounts ultimately to a strategy of creating an environment whose bellicosity is more internecine than that experienced in the earlier conventional stage. Thus, it is utilitarian in an inadmissible way. It is the preemptive, instrumental use of a limited war to bring about a specific kind of total war – war with an indefinite temporal limit confined within a limited space.

Obviously, none of the justifications possess the requisite certainty to qualify as *ad bellum* reasons to go to war, and all possess other features which are sufficient to disqualify them on other ethical grounds.

In the cases of justification (b) and justification (c), we have two justifications that also fall within the scope of the Suárezian modification of the just-war model. The attempts, here, as with the Suárezian model itself, are not only to establish the probable just cause of the conflict itself, but also to argue that the absolute justice of the American cause constitutes suf-

ficient reason to go to war.

The former strategy of legitimization, (b), would seem to be a species of the Suárezian move to demonstrate that the relative justice of the cause can be construed simply in terms of the greater justice being on the side of the initiator of the war. Here, a number of problems immediately come to mind. First, in examining the criteria of just cause, one wonders who precisely the aggrieved party is. If the aggrieved party is the collective of innocents allegedly persecuted in Saddam's regime, then why has this same justification not been used for intervention in other problem areas around the world? And what are the temporal limits on such a claim? If these human rights violations occurred 12 or more years ago, then does the justification have the same strength? Short of a policy which universalizes the Augustinian notion of the defense of innocents, this argument makes no sense, but if the defense of innocents is the major concern, then why has the same criterion not been used to launch interventions in other countries where genocide has occurred? The application of this criterion as a justification for war in Iraq, but not to other countries, suggests that either it is a cover for ulterior motivations or that it is backed by an arrogant confidence in the absolute moral authority of the U.S. to designate its opponents without culpability.

· In Iraq, the situation is made even more morally complex by the CIA's role in prompting Saddam's suppression of uprisings against his government in Kurdistan during and after Gulf War I and the Shiites in Basra after Gulf War I. If we are responsible for aiding and abetting revolutionary activities, knowing that they will be brutally suppressed, and then claiming that civil rights' violations in the suppression of those activities are grounds for war, are we not guilty of the instrumental use of humans to precipitate human rights abuses in order to use these abuses as a justification for intervention? Is this not an interventionist policy of the most cynical and arrogant variety? Is it not the subordination of human lives to an absolute moral ideal of human rights in a way that is equivalent to the principle that the end justifies the means?

The latter strategy of legitimization, (c) – especially in light of the Report on 9/11 – also seems groundless. As argued above, there is no evidence to support the theory that Saddam Hussein had given succor, to any substantial extent, to al-Qaeda. Thus, to consider Iraq as an ally state of al-Qaeda is baseless. Though we arguably have a case for just war against al-Qaeda, the requisite connection employed by this justification has no substantiality.

Summary of Conclusions

On the basis of the foregoing, it is possible to summarize the reasons why Bush's war with Iraq – according to its *ad bellum* criteria – is unjust.

With respect to the *criteria* for just war, it cannot be established (with certainty) that the regime of Saddam Hussein was responsible for an injustice that was a direct affront to the U.S.A. sufficient to warrant war. Unquestionably, Saddam's alleged violation of the rights and dignity of his people would be a ground for just war according to the Augustinian criteria, but such allegations have not been identified as a principle ground in *this* conflict, or as a principle of our foreign policy. With respect to virtually all other plausible grounds, WMDs, cooperation between al-Qaeda and Saddam Hussein, etc., the unfolding evolution of the conflict has proven them to be baseless. The baselessness of these grounds means that the judgments which reckon the war just are incorrect either because the President and his advisors are deceived or because they are being intentionally deceptive. Even given the possibility that President Bush and his advisors are honestly mistaken in their characterization of the war, the certainty they associate with these judgments is clearly an exaggeration that vitiates the asserted justice of their cause. As the real uncertainties connected with discovery and the war's prosecution come to light, it becomes more and more evident that the war was undertaken overconfidently and without sufficient discernment and wisdom. Finally, with respect to the intention to go to war, there have been suggestions that the expressed intentions for our involvement in Iraq are not the real reasons. Strategic advantage, oil, preventative measures against terrorism, etc., all constitute morally culpable grounds sufficient to negate any just intention.

It is not impossible that President Bush with great (subjective) confidence judges the war with Iraq to be just and that his intentions in prosecuting it are pure. And it is also not impossible that he is operating on the basis of an (undisclosed) model which provides unquestionable grounds for the present conflict, relative to that model. Even if this is so, it does not absolve him from the moral responsibility to come to knowledge of more adequate theories of just war and to bring his policy into conformity with them. President Bush's prosecution of the war in Iraq provides little solace for Roman Catholics, who must find the reasons for this war unconscionable because their own model is so much more demanding.[1] And, from the Roman Catholic point of view, President Bush's subjective certitude is no proof of his rectitude or excuse for exculpable ignorance. Subjective certitude exercised in so reckless a fashion is an example of culpable ignorance, an ignorance whose only remedy is familiarity *with* and education *by* the morally superior Roman Catholic model.[2]

---

1. Cyprian Emanuel, O.F.M., Ph.D., (writing with the Committee on Ethics) summarizes the moral conditions for conscientious objection in *The Morality of Conscientious Objection to War* (Washington, D.C.: CAIP, 1941). Though written in 1941, the arguments make the translation to the Iraq war quite well. [Note also Dr. Peter Chojnowski's article on the Committee's report, in the present volume at pp. 361–373.—Ed.]

2. St. Thomas's most thorough discussion of conscience, culpability, and exculpability is in his *Disputed Question on Truth*, 17: On Conscience (in Ralph McInerny, *Thomas Aquinas: Selected Writings* (New York: Penguin Books, 1998), pp. 217–238). Because President Bush has, at his disposal, the means to come to a more sufficient understanding of just war, he is obliged to do so. He is, therefore, morally culpable in not doing so, providing there is not some incapacity that would make him invincibly ignorant and remove culpability.

Polyptych of Ss. Michael the Archangel and Augustine,
Piero della Francesca, 1454,
Museo de Arte Antiga, Lisbon

Statue in front of the Dominican Convent of St. Stephen,
Salamanca, Spain

St. Augustine (354–c371)

Francisco de Vitoria, O. P. (c1480–1546)

THE EDITORS' GLOSS: Dr. Gordon's title is an ambitious one, for more fallacies have been adduced in support of the war in Iraq than there are pages in which to expose them. Dr. Gordon hits some essential ones; let us simply support his thesis with a couple of additional examples.

Fr. Neuhaus ran a piece in his February 2002 *First Things* which was ironically entitled "Just War Truths and Fallacies." (Maybe "fallacies" was the part of the headline referring to the text that followed it.) The piece included a discussion by David S. Yeago, a Lutheran Professor of Systematic Theology in Columbia, South Carolina, which purported to refute those "opponents of military action [who] seem to deny that the United States has suffered an injury sufficient to provide just cause." (Count us among that number; indeed there is no indication whatsoever that the U.S. *suffered* at the hands of Iraq in a way that would justify a military response; Doug Feith admitted as much to AEI in May 2004). This was a good start, and it got worse from there, because Yeago did not respond to the assertion he began with, but pulled an overt bait-and-switch by raising another and wholly separate assertion: "The United States, it is said, has itself injured and outraged other nations and peoples, and so lacks the moral authority to exact retribution when it is itself injured and outraged in turn." He then attempted to dispense with the first assertion by commenting – as regards the second – "this argument seems to me to be entirely fallacious." The old story about the pot and kettle comes to mind here.

In refuting (and that credibly) the second principle, Yeago did nothing to address the real issue: that the U.S. had not suffered an injury (or in Catholic language, an infringement of a strict right) that would justify going to war. Perhaps he did not address that point because there is no way persuasively to do so

The sad thing is that this kind of illogic characterized (and still does) every argument in favor of making war on Iraq. Were it not for *FOX News* the American people might even have spotted the shady logic. Happily, it's not too late for people to get their heads on straight about the war, even if it's too late to bring back from the dead the British, Iraqis, Americans and others who have been tragically and criminally lost during its prosecution.

C H A P T E R
12

A Review of the Literature: Exposing the Fallacies in Defense of the Invasion of Iraq
• • • • • • • • • •
David Gordon, Ph.D.

W AS THE INVASION of Iraq morally justified? The answer to this question depends crucially on the view of morality one adopts. The evaluation of the war by a utilitarian, for example, may well differ from that of a proponent of traditional just-war theory. I shall adopt the latter perspective here, without essaying the task of showing that this theory ought to be chosen. Our initial question has now been limited: was the invasion of Iraq justified according to the requirements of the traditional view? I shall be concerned with the rules of *jus ad bellum*, which govern when a war may be undertaken. (Disturbing developments indicate that the rules of *jus in bello*, which govern the conduct of war, have not been followed; as an example, American troops have not shrunk from using torture. But these will not be canvassed here, since supporters of the war might claim that they show only that an otherwise just war should be fought in a different manner.)

Once the initial question has been limited in this way, it becomes easy to answer. The invasion of Iraq fails to meet these traditional requirements. The issue is not even close: there is an open and shut case against the war. This is not surprising. As Cardinal Journet has noted, the criteria for a just war are very difficult to meet:

> Following St. Augustine, St. Thomas recalls the conditions for a just war: (1) it must aim at peace; so that a war, however just on other counts, would become absolutely illicit if waged only out of hate or ambition; (2) it must be undertaken for a just cause, for example to constrain a nation to repress great disorders or repair grave injustices; (3) it must be declared by the legitimate authority . . . . After reading this specification for a just war we might well ask

how many wars have been wholly just. Probably they could be counted on the fingers of one hand.[1]

If this is correct, though, we must confront a paradox: several eminent authorities claim that the war in Iraq does meet the traditional just-war requirements. How can this be? Disagreement in moral matters is hardly unusual, but how can there be a dispute about whether a set of clear criteria applies? Jean Bethke Elshtain, in an Epilogue to the 2004 edition of her *Just War Against Terror,* and Alexander F. C. Webster and Darrell Cole, in *The Virtue of War,* maintain that the war in Iraq is just. Am I wrong in thinking it obvious that the war is unjust? I have so far merely asserted my view; what is its basis? I propose to answer this by an examination of the arguments presented in the two books just mentioned. As will soon become evident, to show why these arguments fail is at the same time to show that the war is unjust.

For Elshtain, the justice of the war is simple and straightforward. The war was justified on two grounds, which we shall examine in order. First, was not the United States faced with a buildup of weapons of mass destruction (WMDs) by a hostile power?

> The core around which a justification for war was based is uncontroverted, namely the materials and weapons that were catalogued and that Iraq admitted it possessed as of 1998. If we add to what they admitted having produced what intelligence suggested they were in the process of producing, you have a threat of serious proportions.[2]

At first, I imagined that Elshtain had composed her Epilogue before the failure of all attempts to find these nefarious objects had become manifest.

Quite the contrary, she is well aware that the WMDs are nowhere to be found; nevertheless, she contends that we have good reason to think that they were at one time present. And even if they were not, did not Saddam Hussein at least wish to acquire them? What more can any reasonable person want? The Iraqi regime evaded efforts by UN inspectors to discover their stocks of weapons; surely there can be no reasonable doubt that Saddam had such weapons.

---

1. Charles Journet, *The Church of the Word Incarnate* (London and New York: Sheed and Ward), Volume I, pp.306–307. Carl Schmitt mocks Journet, but fails to refute his analysis. See Schmitt, *The Nomos of the Earth* (New York, Telos Press, 2003), p.58n.

2. Jean Bethke Elshtain, *Just War Against Terror* (New York: Basic Books, 2004), paperback edition, p.187. All subsequent references to this book will be by the page numbers in parentheses in the text.

> The "I told you so's" are, at this point, either ignoring the evidence or rushing to judgment because massive caches of WMDs have not been uncovered. But the interesting, and reasonable, question at this point is: what happened to the weapons and what did Secretary of State Madeleine Albright mean when she said ... that Iraq's weapons program could "destroy all humanity"? Was she "lying" too? If ... the Bush administration made it all up because they wanted a war, it means the UN and the Clinton administration made it all up too (p. 189).

Elshtain suggests that the weapons have been dispersed to Syria or elsewhere.

Her reasoning here is curious. She says that the Bush administration cannot have been lying, because then the Clinton administration would also have been lying. But it does not seem to have occurred to her that the situation between the close of the Clinton years and the invasion might have changed. Did not the UN inspectors destroy large caches of weapons? Even if Iraq at one time had a program to develop such weapons, might not Saddam have changed his mind? It hardly follows that if Albright was right, then Bush must also have been accurate. Further, doubters of either administration need not claim that lying is involved: perhaps overestimates about WMDs were based on reckless misjudgment or simple error. Aside from this, I must confess that it does not seem quite so ridiculous to me as it does to Elshtain that one or both administrations lied.

Let us put all this to one side. Suppose that Saddam did possess WMDs: would this suffice to justify war against him? Certainly, self-defense counts as a legitimate cause of action in just-war theory; but the mere possession of such weapons by an unfriendly power hardly counts as an imminent threat of invasion. Nations have conflicting interests and generally choose to rely in part on armaments to defend these interests. Even powers hostile to the United States are within their rights in acting to secure dangerous armaments. The fact that the position of the United States has been worsened through such an arms buildup by an unfriendly power does not justify war under the traditional criteria. To doubt this at once generates absurd results. Two nations hostile to each other could each be justified in going to war to counter the arms buildup of the other. Was Iraq justified in attacking the United States when the U.S. increased its military presence in the Persian Gulf? If not, why does Elshtain think that we are justified in going to war because of Iraqi armaments? It won't do to answer that the Saddam Hussein regime was in various and sundry respects evil in a way that the Bush administration is not. This point is relevant to her second justification for war, not the one that presently concerns us. (The argument that, since Iraq was obligated by agreement after the Gulf War to end WMD programs, the U.S. could intervene, is a better one and will be considered below. Here I am concerned only to stress that there is no general obligation on nations, the violation of which justifies war, to refrain from buildups of WMDs or other deadly weapons.)

Besides this general point, a specific feature of the situation in Iraq rendered nugatory the threat of WMDs. Even if Saddam had managed to acquire these weapons, how could he use them against the United States? Iraq had no delivery system capable of reaching the United States with them. The distinguished diplomatic historian Paul W. Schroeder has well stated the essential point at issue: "The more one thinks about it, the more implausible it becomes to claim that the United States, a superpower with an historically unprecedented position of unchallenged military superiority, is threatened by an impoverished, ruined, insecure state halfway 'round the world."[1]

Elshtain is aware of this, but she brings to bear a counter-argument.

> [W]hile Saddam certainly did not possess the ability to use conventional weapons against us . . . the threat nevertheless did exist in light of the minute amounts of biological and nerve gas material needed to kill large numbers of noncombatants. Putting together the admitted [by whom?] existence of chemical and biological weapons with the clear and present danger that such weapons could be transferred to international terrorist groups, the prudent statesperson could find reasons to act in order to reduce the threat (p. 188).

Elshtain's argument is, I think, this: because the damage WMDs would inflict is very serious, one does not need conclusive evidence that Saddam planned to use them against us. So long as there is a reasonable chance the weapons may be used against us, may we not act? To argue in this way is to make a fundamental mistake about just-war theory. It is indeed part of prudence to take account of grave dangers that are less than certain. It is not a good argument against giving up smoking that tobacco use only *increases the probability* of lung cancer, rather than rendering *certain* the onset of that disease.

It was then entirely reasonable for the United States to bear in mind the possibility that Saddam had WMDs and planned to use them against us, even in the absence of convincing evidence that he had these weapons. So far Elshtain is right; but she errs in thinking that the bare possibility

---

1. Paul W. Schroeder, "The Case Against Preemptive War," *The American Conservative*, Vol. 1, No. 2, October 21, 2002, p. 12.

suffices to justify war. Just-war theory cannot be reduced *in toto* to the calculations of prudence. Even if, which I do not concede, national self-interest would have justified an assault, it does not follow that just-war theory does so. Morality, after all, sometimes imposes restraints on the dictates of self-interested prudence. In the traditional view, there must be an imminent danger of attack to justify war. To "take out" in advance a dangerous potential enemy is not self-defense.[1]

But, one might object, am I not saying that just-war theory is a suicide pact? Is a nation to ignore grave danger because the precepts of a theory say so? Does not this view convert just-war theory into a recipe for disaster?

Not at all. A nation is free to counter possible threats to its security by, for example, arming itself against the threatening power, forming an alliance against it, endeavoring to persuade it to adopt a friendlier policy, etc. All that just-war theory here rules out is war based on the bare *possibility* of a grave danger.

This is not the place to spell out the alternatives to war against a hostile power. But the failure to realize one point often throws discussions of war on the wrong track. It should not be taken as given that a particular nation is "hostile" when one is considering the justice of going to war. One needs to ask, why is the nation hostile to us? Elshtain falls into this mistake. She says that it is possible Saddam Hussein intended to use WMDs against us: therefore we may interdict such use by initiating war. She fails to ask why he might entertain such hostile designs, if he in fact did so. Might it have something to do with our endeavoring to overthrow him from power? If one country threatens another, it is not a proper use of just-war theory for the threatening power to claim that it is acting in self-defense by going to war when the threatened power responds with aggressive actions of its own. Of course, Elshtain can respond that the hostile actions of the United States were justified responses to previous Iraqi offenses; but this merely pushes back the argument one step. To apply just-war theory correctly, one cannot simply begin *in medias res*, as Elshtain does.[2]

---

1. The "Chicago School" approach of Gary Becker, Richard Posner, Eric Posner, *et hoc genus omne*, supports preemptive action against potentially threatening dangers by appeal to the precepts of decision theory. But these authors do not profess to be following the traditional view. See Eric Posner and Alan O. Sykes, "Optimal War and *Jus Ad Bellum*," University of Chicago Law and Economics, Olin Working Paper Number 211, April, 2004.

2. I am not saying that only a completely "innocent" nation is justified in going to war in response to an invasion. Rather, the point concerns the morality of preemptive actions to deal with possible actions by a hostile power, when one's own actions have helped to bring about that hostility.

I have so far contended that Iraq was within its rights to endeavor to acquire WMDs. (Again, I have put aside the argument that Iraq was bound by the peace terms of the Gulf War not to do so.) But suppose that this contention is mistaken: assume that possession of such weapons by Iraq was illegitimate and, very much contrary to fact, evidence indicated that Iraq at the time of the American invasion held such weapons. Would the United States then have been justified in going to war?

Once more the answer is obvious: it would not have been. As Elshtain herself recognizes, one of the requirements of the traditional view is that a "war should be a last resort after other options have been considered seriously. Other measures need not have been tried, in turn, but they must at least have been considered" (p. 184). Would it not have been possible to take action against WMDs without a full-scale invasion? Elshtain notes that sanctions have not been effective, but this is hardly the only measure short of war that might have been adopted. One could have insisted, under threat of force, that massive inspections be allowed. (I hasten to add that I do not support this in the actual situation. I am considering only the hypothetical situation mentioned in the preceding paragraph.) Elshtain thinks a preemptive invasion was a "judgment call" but fails to show that what President Bush termed "regime change" was needed to deal with the supposed WMDs. Here also is our long-delayed response to the point that the United States had the right, by the truce terms of the 1991 Gulf War, to forbid Iraq from producing WMDs. The fact that a country is in violation of a treaty does not constitute grounds for war, if less drastic measures are available to secure compliance.

In a treatment of just war, it would be entirely inappropriate to engage in unjust tactics of controversy. Were I to end my comments on her discussion here, I would be guilty of exactly this failing. She rests her case for armed intervention not only on the danger of WMDs, but also on the violations of human rights committed by Saddam Hussein's government. May the United States not justifiably act, in Cardinal Journet's phrase, "to repair grave injustices"? Elshtain points out that the Bush "administration cited other reasons [than WMDs] that were more akin to the classic just-war insistence that crimes against the innocent should be punished. These other reasons concerned primarily Saddam's well-documented attempted genocide against the Kurds; his destruction of the entire way of life of the Marsh Arabs; and the mass murders against the Shiite Muslims in the aftermath of the 1991 Persian Gulf War" (p. 186).

Is not Elshtain here relying on a dubious premise? She speaks of the need to "punish" crimes against the innocent. But punishment is a response to past actions: it is not an attempt to prevent or deter present wrongs. Does a nation have the right to assume judicial authority over the affairs of another nation, as Elshtain suggests? Michael Walzer has put well the case that it does not:

> [H]umanitarian interventions to stop massacre and ethnic cleansing can also legitimately result in the installation of a new regime. But now [September 2002] that a zone of (relative) safety has been carved out for the Kurds in the North, there is no compelling case to be made for humanitarian intervention in Iraq. The Baghdad regime is brutally repressive and morally repugnant, certainly, but it is not engaged in mass murder or ethnic cleansing; there are governments as bad (well, almost as bad) all over the world.[1]

Elshtain's doctrine, in which the United States is viewed as a universal enforcer of morality, is an example of what Carl Schmitt aptly termed "the tyranny of values." When a country views its antagonists as criminals, it ignites unprecedented ferocity.

> The discriminatory concept of the enemy as a criminal and the attendant implication of *justa causa* run parallel to the intensification of the means of destruction and the disorientation of theatres of war. Intensification of the technical means of destruction opens the abyss of an equally destructive legal and moral discrimination.... Given the fact that war has been transformed into a police action against troublemakers, criminals, and pests, justification of the methods of this "police bombing" must be intensified. Thus, one is compelled to push the discrimination of the opponent into the abyss.[2]

Elshtain has failed to arrive at a convincing argument that the United States had a just cause for invading Iraq. Alexander F.C. Webster and David Cole, like Elshtain, consider the war against Iraq just, or, in the terminology they prefer, a "justifiable" war; and they use some of the same arguments as she does. But they emphasize to a greater degree the need to counter terrorism. Saddam Hussein supported "terrorist organizations who pose an imminent threat to U.S. citizens."[3]

These authors have painted with an overly broad brush. They warn of a worldwide war of militant Islam against the West, with terrorism the principal weapon of the advocates of *jihad*. Are we not justified, these authors ask, in taking action against this threat? "We need not have any moral qualms

---

1. Michael Walzer, *Arguing About War* (New Haven and London: Yale University Press, 2004), p.149.

2. Carl Schmitt, *op. cit.*, p.321.

3. Alexander F. C. Webster and David Cole, *The Virtue of War* (Salisbury, Mass: Regina Orthodox Press, 2004), p.211.

about the war against international Islamic terrorism."[1] But they fail to tie Saddam's regime to the supposed war of Islam. Attempts to link Saddam to Osama bin Laden have failed. Saddam's support for terrorist organizations consists, one gathers, of subventions to the PLO and other anti-Israel groups. Support for these groups certainly goes counter to American policy; but this hardly constitutes an assault on the very being of the United States.

Against this it may be argued that terrorists are somehow linked in a universal fraternity. Do not Islamic terrorists aim to destroy all enemies of their religion?[2] Let us grant the premise: the question then becomes, whom do these groups consider an enemy? Is it anyone who does not adhere to exactly the brand of Islam that they favor? Quite the contrary, terrorist groups often have local agendas in mind. As Michael Mann has noted,

> In designing his war against terrorism, Bush the Younger ... [makes] no distinction between national and international terrorism. The U.S. State Department's annual list of proscribed terrorist organizations gives details of them all, but it does not tell us whether they have recently attacked Americans. The Bush administration has been attacking both indiscriminately, driving them together in self-defense against the U.S.[3]

If my argument has been so far correct, no just cause for war against Iraq existed at the time of America's invasion. WMDs, whether real or alleged; alleged past atrocities of Saddam's regime; and Saddam's support for "terrorism" fail to meet the requirements for just cause of the traditional view. Nor will it do, I think to argue that the combination of these claims add up to a just cause of action. But suppose that I am wrong. Let us assume that there was adequate grounds for American action. Granted this premise, was America's war a just one?

I do not think so. A crucial part of the traditional view is that the war must be launched with the right intention. It is not enough that a just cause of action be present: the invading power must intend its resort to war to respond to the correct cause, and only to that. Suppose, for example, that the just cause of action was a reasonable belief that Iraq possessed WMDs and intended to use them in a direct attack on the United States. A war begun for this motive must then be intended only to end this threat. If the invasion aimed at other things as well, such as securing oil supplies for

---

1. *Ibid.*, p.19.

2. Besides Webster and Cole's volume, see David Frum and Richard Perle, *An End to Evil: How to Win the War on Terror* (New York: Random House, 2004), which also supports this argument.

3. Michael Mann, *Incoherent Empire* (London and New York: Verso, 2003), p.160.

the United States or gaining a base of operations to strengthen American power in the Middle East, it would not qualify as just.

Elizabeth Anscombe, in an essay written with Norman Daniel at the beginning of World War II, has, with her characteristic incisiveness, arrived at the essence:

> If war is to be just, the warring state must intend only what is just, and the aim of the war must be to set right certain specific injustices. That is, the righting of wrong done must be a sufficient condition on which peace will be made . . . it is a condition of a just war that it *should* be fought with a *just* intention; not that it should *not* be fought with an *unjust* intention. If the government's intentions cannot be known because they are vague, that vagueness itself vitiates them.[1]

It is evident that American policy fails this standard. Far from seeking only a limited end, Bush demanded a "regime change." Neoconsevatives such as Paul Wolfowitz and Richard Perle, who rank high in the counsels of the administration, go further and demand that other countries in the Arab world, including Iran and Syria, be "democratized" so that they will favor American values and interests.[2] In a recent volume by two influential neoconservatives, we read: "There is today not a single Arab state that qualifies as a democracy. . . . But promoting democracy in the Middle East is not a matter of national egotism. It has become a matter of national well-being, even survival."[3] America's invasion will turn Iraq into a democracy; this happy outcome will bring pressure to bear on the governments of Saudi Arabia and Iran. (The thought that people might freely choose to oppose American policy seems not to have occurred to them.)

The war in Iraq, then, fails the tests of just war on numerous grounds. Iraq posed no threat to the United States, nor were there sufficient "humanitarian" grounds to justify America's violent course of action. Even if there had been a valid reason to invade, America's aims in the war went far beyond what the rules of *jus ad bellum* sanction. The war for the idol of "democracy" in Iraq confirms the wise words of Gustav Thibon: a war "waged for idols . . . will itself be an idol. An evil so atrocious and so univer- sal, a course so straight to the abyss of nothingness, cannot be borne with unless it be erected into an absolute in hearts poisoned with hatred."[4]

---

1. "The Justice of the Present War Examined," in G.E.M. Anscombe, *Ethics, Religion, and Politics* (Minneapolis: University of Minnesota Press, 1981), pp.74–75, emphasis in original.

2. The Frum and Perle book earlier cited should be consulted as an example of neoconservative aims in Iraq.

3. Lawrence F. Kaplan and William Kristol, *The War Over Iraq: Saddam's Tyranny and America's Mission* (San Francisco: Encounter Books, 2003), p.110.

4. Thibon's remarks are quoted in Journet, *op. cit.*, p.307.

THE EDITORS' GLOSS: The idea of a juridically established body representing the entire family of nations, exercising authority over its individual members in matters of war and peace, is yet another notion much maligned among "conservative" commentators, and much abused and distorted by their "liberal" counterparts. On this subject, as with so many others, the truth is found in the middle, not just between but above and beyond the opposites that argue either for a tyrannical world government or an absolutist conception of national sovereignty.

The very real abuses of the UN and its questionable founding unfortunately discredit the idea of an authoritative, international tribunal empowered to assist with the resolution of disputes between nations. Cardinal Ottaviani of the Vatican's Holy Office captured the spirit that such an institution might embody when he remarked, at a discussion of war and peace during the Second Vatican Council: " . . . just as we have the United States of America and the United States of Brazil, why cannot man reach the point where there will be . . . a common fatherland for all men, a Christian republic where the peace of Christ would reign in the kingdom of Christ?" The same sentiment animated Pope Pius XII when he declared, in 1945, that "mankind, as it emerges from the dark night in which it has been so long submerged, will be able to hail the dawn of a new and better era of its history" when, to the recognition of the immorality of aggressive war, can be added "the threat of a judicial intervention by the nations and of chastisement inflicted on the aggressor by the society of states, so that war will always be subject to the stigma of proscription, always under surveillance and liable to preventive measures."

We should be careful of arguments that defend the American war in Iraq under cover of UN resolutions, however. As the old *Catholic Encyclopedia* says, " . . . a war, to be just, must be waged by a sovereign power for the security of a perfect right of its own," and not for the security of a right of the "international community." In the case of the war in Iraq, the UN's "failure to act" at U.S. behest was a welcome, if tardy and insufficient, act of justice. It is only when America learns to subordinate its "national claims to the moral ideal of a Christian commonwealth of nations," as Dr. Charles G. Fenwick, President of the Catholic Association for International Peace put it in 1937, that Americans will see in the actions of international bodies anything more than "success" or "failure" as judged by their willingness or refusal to conform to the American will.

C H A P T E R
13

Iraq: Sovereignty and Conscience
• • • • • • • • • •
Prof. James Hanink, Ph.D.

J UST PRIOR TO Gulf War II, President George W. Bush told us, "We
don't need anyone's permission." The United States, a sovereign power,
needed no one's permission to invade Iraq. What are we to make of
such a claim?

I. Introduction

My answer to this question is straightforward. It's a Catholic answer
as well. The sovereignty of the State is *limited* – as is the autonomy of the
citizen. Given, too, the primacy of the common good, developing an international political society, with the right measure of authority – where each
nation's legitimate reciprocal duties and rights are exercised and protected
– is a moral imperative. We must, to be sure, be sober in the development
and pursuit of this political structure.[1]

To give a context for my answer, I note three unpleasant reminders and
pause for an historical interlude. Together, the reminders and interlude sug-

---

1. Alfredo Cardinal Ottaviani reminds us of the moral urgency of this pursuit. Of conflicts between states he writes: "But what of mediation, arbitration, or investigation by an
international tribunal? Are not these also possible means? To me, indeed, they seem of so
obligatory a nature that they alone are the only justifiable and lawful means of vindicating rights in present times; war is out of the question." See Alfredo Cardinal Ottaviani,
Institutiones Juris Publici Ecclesiastici, Vol. I (*Jus Publicum Internum*) Pars I, Titulus
iii, art. 3 (*Relationes societatum perfectarum in statu conflictus*), Principium 2 (Rome:
Vatican Polyglot, 1948, 3rd Edition), pp. 149–55 [included as an appendix in the present
volume, pp. 419–424—Ed]. The translation is from *Blackfriars*, No. 354, September 1949.
Elsewhere in the same piece he writes that war can only be justified precisely when there
is no hope of recourse to a higher authority: " . . . the sole justification of recourse to
warfare was on an occasion when there was little hope of appealing to, or – if a disputed
right were in question – of getting a decision from an authority higher than the state." On
the need for sobriety in our pursuit, we might reflect on Vatican II's recognition of the
established international disorder. "Until a competent international authority equipped
with forces adequate to restrain transgressors has been constituted, governments cannot
be denied the right of legitimate defense" (*Gaudium et Spes* (1965), §79).

gest points of discernment for identifying a just war. These points, in turn, set the stage for "the parent's test," a practical way to locate where "the burden of argument" lies in deciding whether waging a particular war is just.

II. Some Particulars and an Interlude

Suppose we assume, plausibly, that a sovereign State needs no permission to apprehend and disarm a gang of murderous thieves actively engaged in their crimes. If so, Mr. Bush's proclamation has its initial appeal. Yet many dispute the course of the policy he chose to follow. Decent people have argued that it proved to be a policy of naked aggression.

To adjudicate this immediate disagreement, let's consider three particulars; each is a salubrious reminder.

1. It often happens that a gang of murderous thieves comes to control a State.

2. Second, such gangs sometimes prevent a State from falling into anarchy.

3. Third, it is by no means clear who is to discern whether the rule of murdering thieves is better or worse than mere anarchy.

These particulars, in turn, provoke many thoughtful people to appeal to the United Nations. The United Nations, they say, must resolve so patently dismal yet distressingly familiar a dilemma.

Still others, of course, insist that the United Nations, as matters stand, cannot assume such a function, and this for two reasons. The first is that it lacks the military forces to intervene effectively. The second is that the United Nations, despite the authority which some would have it claim, is morally compromised by its past failures to defend the innocent and prosecute the guilty.

Yet, if we are to look to history, who is without moral compromise? Not the State; not even our own United States. Still, since we ignore the past at our peril, we had best allow for a (necessarily selective) historical interlude.

For a start, Catholic thinkers have understood war and military service as shifting social realities. Does military service require worship of the Emperor? Such service must be rejected, and in the early centuries many did. Does war stave off the slaughter of the innocent? Then we must go to war, and in the middle centuries many preached this message. Does war mete out retributive justice? Then it can be offensive. Does war now fail to mete out retributive justice? Then war can only be defensive. In recent times, a consensus emerges: a necessary condition for waging war justly is that we do so to safeguard the innocent. And yet, an imminent threat against the innocent, at home or abroad, can justify a defensive war, whether we act inside or outside our national boundaries.

A second historical observation: Catholic thinking about the common good has long recognized that it extends beyond the boundaries of the State. In the past, the transnational character of the common good has been less apparent, because in so many ways peoples and states were socially and economically independent of one another. In the present, a rapidly increasing interdependence is obvious. Sometimes, to be sure, the strong wrongly impose this interdependence on the weak. Often, however, interdependence is the fruit of a respect for the inherent dignity of man, one that transcends national boundaries, joined with technical advances in communication.

A third point, surely, is the consistent and continuing practice of the Holy See. From the inception of the United Nations to the present time, the Holy See has encouraged its mission. For its part, the United Nations has given the Holy See a respected role in its public deliberations. The images of Paul VI and John Paul II addressing the General Assembly remain vivid. But more than media images are at work. For a decidedly topical example, the convergence between Catholic just-war theory and the treatment of war in the United Nations Charter is striking. The United States, lest we forget, has committed itself, in law, to honoring this Charter.

Yet, despite points of convergence, there are also points of sharp divergence. Most worrisome, perhaps, is the hostility of many in the United Nations to the policies of the Holy See on the family, especially with respect to contraception and abortion. Nonetheless, John Paul II publicly and insistently appealed to President Bush and Coalition Forces to give the United Nations more time to find nonviolent solutions to the crisis in Iraq. As James Francis Cardinal Stafford, the former archbishop of Denver, recently observed "The Pope [has] emphasized the importance not simply of relying upon the UN as it exists now, but of a further enhancement of its peacemaking capacities," while adding that we find ourselves "in a very ambiguous moral situation in which both the wheat and the tares are growing together."[1] The final reckoning, we know, is in God's hands. In human affairs, however, there can come a time to separate life-giving grains from death-dealing weeds. But when, and how, are we to do so?

---

1. Delia Gallagher, "Cardinal Stafford on War and the Church's Thinking," *Zenit*, May 24, 2004, online.

III. Points for Discernment

We can, in part, answer the questions of when and how to separate the wheat and the tares, with respect to critical moral ambiguities of the day, if we think carefully about sovereignty, truth, and the counterfeiting of both patriotism and peacemaking. Doing so will provide us with important points for discernment.

Let's reflect, first, on sovereignty. Here we can do so critically, albeit not exhaustively. The anchor of our analysis is that neither polities nor persons can be sovereign apart from the common good. And what is the common good? In the words of Pope John XXIII, it "embraces the sum total of those conditions of social living whereby men are enabled to achieve their own integral perfection more fully and more easily." (*Pacem in Terris*, §58) This "perfection," of course, does not imply a Promethean, materialist utopia. Rather it evokes a personal and social harmony achieved through obedience to the will of God.

The specifying principles of subsidiarity and solidarity help us identify the common good. Subsidiarity teaches that we best realize our potential in ordered freedom, an order that shows a primary regard for the local and immediate. Solidarity teaches that the first measure of justice for any society is how it treats the most vulnerable. Sovereignty, thus, must promote the common good and honor subsidiarity and solidarity. This common good, in every social dimension, draws each person into it realization. Subsidiarity and solidarity, for their part, dynamically specify how we participate therein.

Given the sources of authentic sovereignty, what grades should we assign to the United States? Or to the United Nations? In each case, respect for the common good, and its specifying principles, is cruelly mixed. (Never forget, since so many deny it, the silent holocaust of abortion.) Yet, apart from a respect for the moral order, no polity – national or international – can rightly claim sovereignty. Note, then, what follows: insofar as sovereignty is taken to be *absolute* and *self-grounding*, it is for this very reason invalidated. On this point Jacques Maritain, for many Catholics (though by no means all) among the foremost Thomist thinkers of the twentieth century, a man who (simultaneously) loved France and the United States and the United Nations, saw only darkness at the end of modern disputations, military or verbal, about sovereignty: "[T]o think in a consistent manner in political philosophy," he insisted, "we have to discard the concept of Sovereignty, which is but one with the concept of Absolutism."[1]

---

1. Jacques Maritain, *Man and the State* (Washington, D.C.: Catholic University of

Let's turn, next, to the fortunes of truth as we find them in the context of war and sovereignty. They are at best precarious, whether we consider either empirical truth (i.e., of facts and figures) or moral truth (i.e., of acting in accord with reason). Indeed, in either case, "truth is the first casualty of war."

Empirical truth, we know, is an almost immediate and often designated casualty. The effective waging of war predictably depends on both deception and distortion. Belligerents publicize and exaggerate the wrongs of their foes, while they ignore or deny the wrongs of their friends. A grim measure of their success in doing both is that, more and more often, reliable statistics on the casualties suffered by innocent noncombatants are "not available." Yet few deny what Alfredo Cardinal Ottaviani, writing just after World War II, feared: that war "will claim its victims more from the civilian population than from the combatant troops."[1] (No one familiar with the history of Vatican Council II would take Ottaviani to be a "liberal.")

Moral truth, too, finds a hostile reception. Not only does deceit become a virtue, but the narrowest consequentialism has also become the presiding judge. The ethics of war collapses into the rule of necessity: "We must choose the lesser of two evils." Yet, this dictum contradicts the Catholic belief in the inviolability of innocent human life. The calculus it proposes is as heartless as the secularity that requires it. Writing during the cold war, the eminent philosopher Elizabeth Anscombe insisted on the moral truth, no matter its demands.

> [W]e have to fear God and keep his commandments, and calculate what is for the best only within the limits of that obedience. . . . Those, therefore, who think they must be prepared to wage a war with Russia involving the deliberate massacre of cities, must be prepared to say to God: "We had to break your law, lest your Church fail."[2]

The more we obfuscate the moral truth, the more difficult it becomes to accept it. This *psychological* truth, however, cannot excuse those of us who, whether we are teachers or students, know that evil must not be done so that good may come.

America Press, 1998), p. 49. Maritain's point is to reject any supposed absolute sovereignty. He does not disallow the relative autonomy of states, one with respect to the other. Nor, of course, does he propose an absolutist internationalism or imperialism.

1. For this grim prediction and an unblinking account of modern war, see Alfredo Cardinal Ottaviani, *loc. cit.*

2. "War and Murder," *Ethics, Religion and Politics: Collected Philosophical Papers* (Minneapolis: The University of Minnesota Press, 1981), Volume III, p. 61.

Blessed are the peacemakers for they shall be called the children of God.

We can now move, briefly, to the third of our points for discernment. It is that both patriotism and peacemaking are often falsified. While this is no surprise, the times are such that, even when counterfeit, many rush to affirm one or other of the counterfeits. In doing so, true patriots and peacemakers find themselves in the company of those who undermine the core values to which true patriots and peacemakers seek to witness.

The true patriot affirms the goodness and worth of his or her country; the pseudo-patriot, however, touts his or her country "whether right or wrong." Yet, insofar as one's country acts wrongly, it compromises its own goodness and worth. The true peacemaker affirms the importance of seeking nonviolent ways of resolving conflict, even at great personal cost; the pseudo-peacemaker seeks not the peace that is the work of justice but rather the comfort of indolence and indifference. But spiritual sloth and moral skepticism are inimical to the work of justice. The double irony in this dialectic of distortion is that a true patriot seeks to resolve conflicts justly and a true peacemaker affirms the goodness of country. In both cases, however, there is a question of limit: neither the patriot nor the peacemaker may sin against innocent life, whether by the commission of its destruction nor the omission of its defense.

Here, of course, we must be candid. Considering these "points for discernment," however critical, might itself lead to heightened perplexity. Yes, we are better able to discern the tares among the wheat. But the question remains: at what point can we say that the weeds, as they multiply, will choke off the wheat? How sure must we be, before we act, that they will do so? In the judging of sovereignty and the waging of war, does prudence always urge us to wait a bit longer before we act? Or does prudence, classically understood as right reason in acting, sometimes tell us to reach a verdict, whether on sovereignty or war, and place the burden of argument – of achieving the requisite sureness – somewhere else? Suppose, for example, that we have *for a very long time* been watching our enemies (often drawn from our own number) sowing weeds among the wheat. Are we now to move from timeless parable to "time present," which is before us now as history's progeny?

IV. On the Burden of Proof

How are we to act in our own time of moral ambiguity? Specifically, how are we to decide whether to support or engage in war when sovereignty is suspect, truth is trampled, and moral reasoning is reduced to technical calculation?

Some have thought that, come what may, we must follow the lead of those in authority. How could any individual access to the wide range of facts that are relevant to a decision to engage in war? Only those in authority can appreciate the positive and negative ramifications of competing diplomatic initiatives and military strategies. The State must pursue what seems to be its best policy in a coherent and unified fashion. To do so would be impossible were individuals to exercise a veto over the State's executive function. It follows, too, that the State alone has the authority to determine the ethics of war with regard to both *jus ad bellum* and *jus in bello*. Hence, only if one is *certain* that the State is acting unjustly may one, in conscience, reject its authority. The individual must carry the burden of argument.

Such an "individual burden argument," in some historical periods, might be plausible. Yet, we cannot ignore its limits. It presupposes, from the start, that the State *is* sovereign. But any State that claims an *absolute* sovereignty claims too much, and any State that systematically undermines the common good squanders its legitimacy. The "individual burden argument," moreover, overlooks the fact that in some instances individuals might well have moral insights that disqualify the State's military policy, regardless of the State's privileged access to information. This is especially true in a state in which the decision making process of government is not informed by a coherent recognition of the natural moral law. For example, a reflective individual might come to recognize that a military policy depends on the State's resolve, in the last analysis, to threaten to use nuclear weapons against entire cities. Such a policy, whatever its goal and whatever other factors might color it, is illegitimate.

Let me, then, propose a markedly different standard for deciding who it is that has the burden of argument. As an initial "reality check," we had best acknowledge that if anything is constant in warfare, it is that the young fight the wars that their elders deem necessary. A chief upshot of this phenomenon is that parents often find themselves trying to explain the moral dimension of military action to their sons (and, sadly, daughters). Such an accounting, I submit, establishes a key moral fulcrum: parents should be free from reasonable doubt that it is right for their sons and daughters to engage in military action under this State, at this time, and in this war. Absent freedom from reasonable doubt, parents should urge their adult children not to support, or take part in, the State's military policy. When parents cannot reach this freedom from reasonable doubt, they should ask their sons and daughters on what grounds they, who will fight the war, think military action is justifiable. This exchange between the generations of the family should be, in the language of public affairs, "frank and candid." Out of this critical dialogue, a family might hope that a prudent course will emerge. In such a dialogue, parents can be honest with their children about the world that they are passing on to them. Adult children, for their part, can come to recognize something of the cost involved in making that world a friend to justice.

V. Iraq: The Burden of Argument

Suppose, then, I follow the proposal at hand. I begin with the question of whether I am free from reasonable doubt that my adult children could justifiably serve in Iraq. On the basis of at least the following reasons, I do not think that I could be free from reasonable doubt.

1. Military training tends to undermine critical thinking and personal responsibility.

2. Military service tends to put a great strain on marriage and family life.

3. Military action often puts young people in situations in which they face great pressure to kill the innocent.

4. It is by no means clear that military action in Iraq is necessary for national self-defense.

5. It is by no means clear that military action in Iraq serves the defense of the innocent.

When I have, in fact, presented these points for reflection, my adult children have seemed largely to recognize their cogency.

In working through such reflections with them, I have readily acknowledged how some might come to think differently about the validity of military training and military action. After all, some criticisms of military training and service are criticisms of modernity itself. Prolonged engagement in bureaucratic structures tends to undermine critical thinking and moral personal responsibility. A too eager immersion in the corporate world, for that matter, often damages marriage and family life.

Indeed, quite apart from these broad comparisons, decent people have made a case for President Bush's policy. Decent or not, we ought to test any such a case. Here sallies from a possible "micro-exchange" come to mind.

> *Question:* Oughtn't we to have trusted UN weapons inspectors?

> *Answer:* Perhaps. But not simply because they are UN inspectors. More than once, the UN has helped to legitimate states that show contempt for their own citizens. Consider China's – duly inspected – coercive population policy.

> *Question:* UN inspectors aside, don't many countries now have the sort of weapons that "hawks" feared Iraq to have?
>
> *Answer:* Surely. But it's a mistake to excuse criminals that one might be able to disarm simply because there are other criminals that one can't disarm.

And so the debate persists and will continue to do so. Nor will history put it to rest, because revisionist history will soon follow.

But from such debate, what does *not* follow, if logic is our standard, is that I must put aside *my own* doubts about the legitimacy of the President's policy. The Coalition's intelligence rightly has been judged flawed and, at some levels, manipulated. Furthermore, John Paul II, no stranger to *realpolitik*, was always a sharp critic of the Bush policy. The cogency of that criticism is increasingly apparent. My conclusion: though on the surface understandable, the Bush policy is not trustworthy *beyond a reasonable doubt*. As a parent, I cannot counsel my adult children to take on military training for, nor to engage in military action in support of, that policy.

To be sure, there will always be wars and rumors of wars. So it is, of course, incumbent on me to explore these and related points with my sons and daughter in the months and years to come. Suppose, for example, we were to discuss their participation in a true humanitarian intervention. If here the whole emphasis of military action would be the *genuine* defense of the innocent, I would anticipate little if any doubt about its necessity. Far more pressing, one suspects, would be the question of its lethal postponement and, too, the provenance of the rationale for such a delay.

VI. Christ the King

Finally, we might return to Mr. Bush's press conference proclamation: "We don't need any one's permission." A provocative remark, it should provoke us beyond "politics as usual" and the secular forces that orchestrate them.

Rulers, to be sure, have a place in the Divine Economy. More than this, they have a place of honor. St. Paul admonishes the Christians of Rome, many of them slaves, "Let every person be subject to the governing authorities; for there is no authority except from God, and those authorities that exist have been instituted by God." To this he adds: "[A]uthority does not bear the sword in vain! It is the servant of God to execute wrath on the wrongdoer" (*Romans* xiii:1, 4).

In virtue of their place of honor, leaders of state face a stern examination of conscience. Are they alert to the lust for domination? (It attends us all but most especially the powerful.) And with what intention do they engage in war? Are they certain that they will protect the innocent? Can heads of state see themselves as servants of God's justice?

If leaders of state are doubtful in answering these questions, how can they justify waging war? How can they expect individual citizens to be confident of acting justly in training for, or waging, war? Yet, unless the leaders of state honor conscience, as formed in light of the moral law, they cannot respect the common good. Insofar as they fail to respect the common good, they forfeit their authority. When statecraft intentionally divorces itself from soul craft, citizens dare not extend the benefit of doubt to those who hold the reins of power.[1]

The Psalmist has it right: "Unless the Lord builds, they labor in vain who build" (Psalm cxxvii). They are vain who insist either that a State, national *or* international, can be sovereign in any absolute sense. No matter how many engage in political idolatry, the historian Daniel Philpott bluntly records the constant verdict of the Roman Catholic Church. "To the sovereign state, it offers this abiding reproach: supreme political authority, within borders, anywhere, of a mortal person, of any sort of human institution is something to which nobody ought to make claim."[2] To suppose otherwise, after all, would be to confuse creature with Creator. In the end, it is always and only persons, in their acts and omissions, who set the policy of a State. Yet, none of us can arrogate a radical autonomy.

Have we not learned that it is in the City that the Lord builds, and there alone, that we find sovereignty? In that City, Christ is King. Hesitating to come before Him as suppliants, we are tempted to seek the permission of idols, tempted even to present ourselves as such to those whom we would teach democracy and its lessons of citizenship.

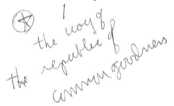

---

1. This is the conclusion reached by the Ethics Committee of the Catholic Association for International Peace, as detailed in their 1941 study, *The Morality of Conscientious Objection to War* (Washington, D.C.: CAIP). See pp. 361–373of the present volume for a detailed discussion of the Committee's findings.—Ed.

2. Daniel Philpott, *Revolutions in Sovereignty: How Ideas Shaped Modern International Relations* (Princeton: Princeton University Press, 2001), p. 262.

Judgment and Inspiration: The Church *Still* Speaks With Authority

THE EDITORS' GLOSS: Much is made by the likes of Michael Novak that the new Catholic Catechism "assigns primary responsibility [for deciding to go to war], not to distant commentators, but to public authorities themselves." What this means is straightforward enough: the legitimate government authority decides *when* to go to war. What it implies is problematic: the President need listen to no outside source of guidance when it comes to making war.

That couldn't be farther from the truth, according to Dr. William Cavanaugh, who explains – in the following essay, expanded significantly since it appeared in the May 23, 2003, *Commonweal* – the nature of the Church's authority over states and souls in matters of war and peace no less than in other temporal affairs that have spiritual components. Mindlessly repeating that "the President makes the decision when to go to war" does nothing to change the fact.

American Churchmen offered meager resistance to the Bush administration's war of aggression in the Gulf. Would that they had earnestly considered – and taken to heart – the writing of their predecessors on the subject, which seems all the more profound in view of the pathetic "we-don't-think-the-war-is-just-but-men-may-disagree" approach they took to the recent conflict. "Since God is the Ruler of nations no less than of individuals," the American Hierarchy wrote (emphasis ours) in 1919 under the leadership of Cardinal Gibbons, "His law is supreme over the external relations of states as well as in the internal affairs of each. The sovereignty that makes a nation independent of other nations, does not exempt it from its obligations toward God; nor can any covenant, however shrewdly arranged, guarantee peace and security, if it disregard the divine commands. These require that in their dealings with one another, nations shall observe both justice and charity. By the former, each nation is bound to respect the existence, integrity and rights of all other nations; by the latter, it is obliged to assist other nations with those acts of beneficence and good will which can be performed without undue inconvenience to itself. *From these obligations a nation is not dispensed by reason of its superior civilization, its industrial activity or its commercial enterprise;* LEAST OF ALL, BY ITS MILITARY POWER."

Neocons may balk at these words, but when Catholics approach their Maker they will be judged on whether they followed their consciences and the teachings of the Church, and not whether they aspired to Irving Kristol's "neoconservative persuasion" and its drive for empire.

14

To Whom Should We Go?
Legitimate Authority and Just Wars

• • • • • • • • • •

Prof. William T. Cavanaugh, Ph.D.

> "War is not a political problem, but moral and religious."
> —Bishop Fulton J. Sheen

A T A RECENT campus discussion about the bishops' authority to speak on matters of war, much airtime was given to whether the bishops had overstepped their competence in judging such matters. Near the end of the session, a genuinely perplexed student stood and echoed the disciples' question to Jesus: "To whom should we go? If we can't rely on the Church's judgment in these matters, where should we form our opinions?"

It is one thing to argue, on just-war grounds, against the overwhelming judgment of the Pope and worldwide bishops, that the recent campaign in Iraq was morally justifiable. It is another thing to argue that the Pope and bishops are not qualified to make such judgments. Neoconservative Catholic commentators and others have been trying to mitigate their embarrassment over being at odds with the Pope on this issue by claiming that it is not really the Church's call to make. Decisions about if and when we Catholics should kill should be left to the President. This line of thinking is dangerously wrong. For while acknowledging the state's power to determine when to go to war, it 1) dismisses the authority of the Church to evaluate actions of the state and 2) falsely relieves the individual Catholic of his or her responsibility to investigate and act according to a well-formed conscience.

An example of this type of thinking can be found in the March 25, 2003, letter to Catholic military chaplains from the U.S. Military Services Archbishop, Edwin O'Brien. In referring to the ongoing debate over the moral justification of the war, O'Brien tells his chaplains, "Given the complexity of factors involved, many of which understandably remain confidential, it is altogether appropriate for members of our armed forces to presume the integrity of our leadership and its judgments, and therefore to carry out their military duties in good conscience." The archbishop assumes that "our leadership" will be understood as referring to the President of the United States, not to the Pope and the bishops of the universal Church to which the chaplains belong. The archbishop continues, "It is to be hoped that all factors which have led to our intervention will eventually be made public, and that the full picture of the Iraqi regime's weaponry and brutality will shed helpful light upon our President's decision." In other words, we may hope that, after the killing is done, it will be found to have been justified. There is always a chance some weapons of mass destruction will turn up after all. In the meantime, Catholic soldiers may safely leave responsibility for moral decision making on the war to the President. The judgment of the Church does not merit a mention in the archbishop's letter.

Michael Novak and George Weigel have applied this argument not merely to soldiers and chaplains but to all Catholics. In an opinion piece in *The Times* (London, February 12, 2003), Novak says that it belongs to public authorities, and not the Church, to judge on matters of war for two reasons: the former have the "primary vocational role and constitutional duty to protect the lives and rights of their people" and they are "privy to highly restricted intelligence." Others have a right to voice their opinions, but "final judgment" belongs to the state. Here Novak cites the Catechism (2309): "The evaluation of these conditions for moral legitimacy [of war] belongs to the prudential judgment of those who have responsibility for the common good." Weigel (*America*, March 31, 2003) cites the same passage from the Catechism and declares that, although "religious leaders and religious intellectuals" should help inform the public debate, "the call is made by others," namely, "responsible public authorities."

It is true but trivial to point out that the nation-state and not the Church makes war. Clearly Novak and Weigel have something more in mind. The "call" being made is about the moral status of the war. According to Novak and Weigel, the final judgment on that status belongs to the state – but what does "final judgment" mean? Does it mean that the Pope's judgment, expressed through his nuncio, that the current war is "unjust and immoral," is simply overridden by the President's judgment, and that the Pope's judgment should be regarded by Catholics as null and void? The implication seems to be that, although the Pope and bishops should be thanked for their input, Catholics should accept the President's judgment and support the war. But there are two issues at stake here. Paramount is the objective question of the "just-ness" of the war. The state might truly and effectively have the final say over whether or not *to go to* war, but that says nothing of the *objective morality* of its decision. With that in mind, the second issue concerns the individual's right and responsibility to evaluate the state's decision, in light not simply of the fact that the decision was made by the state, but of that decision's validity as measured by the Catholic faith and by any particular, official pronouncement upon it made by the Church.

I. The Issue at Stake

One of the most serious of questions before us is: has the Church really handed over its moral decision making on war to the leaders of the secular nation-state? Weigel recognizes that the passage cited from the Catechism is the traditional just-war criterion of competent, or legitimate, authority. He correctly states that in its medieval context this criterion was originally pro-mulgated to separate war from mere murder or brigandage. In other words, only civil authorities, and not private individuals, can declare war. Given that the civil authorities in Christendom were, as John Neville Figgis has noted, "the police department of the Church," however, there was no sense that the application of the just-war theory was somehow taking place outside the Church. Weigel does not acknowledge this, but merely asserts: "For the past several hundred years, 'competent authority' has resided in the nation-state."

Doubtless, much has changed, for better and for worse, in the transition from the medieval to the modern world, but where along the line did the Church hand over to the secular nation-state its responsibility to make judgments on the grave moral issue of war? The main message of the passage from the Catechism is not its recognition that the state must decide when to go to war. Rather, the point is that it lays an *obligation* on civil authorities to consider moral truth, and not merely reasons of state, in deciding issues of lethal force. Further, it nowhere limits the Church's own competence in these matters. The 1983 Code of Canon Law (747, §2) makes this plain: "The Church has the right always and everywhere to proclaim moral principles, even in respect of the social order, and to make judgments about any human matter in so far as this is required by fundamental human rights or the salvation of souls."

Weigel and others regard the just-war theory as a tool of statecraft. The Catholic tradition, in contrast, has understood the just-war theory as an aid to moral judgment in the most serious of moral matters: the taking of human life. Thus, the claim made by Archbishop O'Brien and Michael Novak that the President is privy to *better* information, even if true, would be of secondary importance at best, provided that information is not presented in defense of an argument qualitatively different from what has already been asserted. Moral judgment in the Christian tradition is a matter not just of information, but of being formed in the virtues proper to a disciple of Christ. There is no reason to assume that the leaders of a secular nation-state are so formed, nor that the principles guiding the Christian moral life are at the heart of American foreign policy. War planners are always going to think their wars are justified. There is also no guarantee, to put it mildly, that moral considerations will trump those of narrowly defined national interest and corporate profit when the foreign-policy establishment creates its agenda.

In this case, there is reason to believe that the President was not privy to better information than the rest of us. George W. Bush made public every possible scrap of information supporting the attack on Iraq. The information kept from our view was generally that *calling into question* the necessity for war. Indeed, the passage of time suggests that the evidence supporting arguments favorable to the "preventive" war (e.g., Iraq-al-Qaeda links, WMD) was dubious at best. Still, the main point is that simply having more information does not alter the quality of the decision to go to war as fundamentally one of moral judgment. For the Church to defer to the nation-state in making that moral judgment would be to fail in her divinely ordained mission to teach right from wrong, and it would mark an abdication of her responsibility and power to judge the actions of the state.

II. The Church's Moral Authority over Temporal Matters

What is this power, and to what extent does it bind individual Catholics and the state? To answer these questions one must delve into the roles and relation of Church and state, a volatile issue especially in a post-Christian era that has witnessed the advent of powerful nation-states and the consequent diminishment of the Church's public role.

At the peak of the prestige and power of the papacy in the medieval period, the Popes claimed the absolute supremacy of the Church over the temporal order; they attempted in certain circumstances to act upon that claim. Boniface VIII's bull *Unam Sanctam* stated it most stridently:

> We are informed by the texts of the gospels that in this Church and in its power are two swords; namely, the spiritual and the temporal. For when the

Apostles say: "Behold, here are two swords" [St. Luke xxii:38] that is to say, in the Church, since the Apostles were speaking, the Lord did not reply that there were too many, but sufficient. . . . Both, therefore, are in the power of the Church, that is to say, the spiritual and the material sword, but the former is to be administered for the Church but the latter by the Church; the former in the hands of the priest; the latter by the hands of kings and soldiers, but at the will and sufferance of the priest.[1]

There has been considerable debate over whether the spiritual power claimed here is an actual direct and effective jurisdiction over the civil power or merely an "indirect" spiritual power (as it has been called), in particular circumstances, over temporal affairs. What is clear is that popes claimed the power to excommunicate and depose secular princes when their social as well as personal actions endangered Catholic souls; they excused subjects from their duties to obey these princes; and they judged of the morality of wars. Bishops and regional synods of the Church proclaimed the Peace of God and Truce of God according to which certain holy places and time periods were declared off-limits to war and violators were punished by excommunication and interdict. The Church required penance for killing even in just wars, and the Church demanded (though unsuccessfully) arms limitations in the twelfth century, banning the cross-bow and poisoned arrows, all under pain of excommunication. The theory behind the reality took different forms, but there was ultimate agreement that the temporal did not stand outside the spiritual. The temporal was not a separate space, but rather indicated that coercion by civil authorities was for a time necessary while awaiting the return of Christ. The Church oversaw the temporal authorities and the temporal authorities protected and defended the Church. Despite its limitations, it was a system that took seriously the notion that all things were to be ordered to God.

The neocons of today will surely follow the liberals of yesterday by argu-ing from context – that was then, this is now, and these claims no longer apply. In practice, they have a point. Christendom is effectively no more. The secular nation-state has supplanted medieval Christendom. In con-temporary interpretations of liberalism, a wall separates Church and state. In America today, for the Church to act upon a presumed moral superior-ity that impacts on practical politics (such as, for example, barring from communion pro-abortion-rights politicians) leads to denunciation among Catholics as well as non-Catholics. It is an intrusion of faith into politics where, it is claimed, *it does not belong.*

---

1. *Unam Sanctam* (1302).

Without question the actual relations of Church and state have changed over time. No sane observer of history could see otherwise. The Catholic Church's power in temporal affairs has deteriorated not only in Protestant countries, but in Catholic countries as well. Led by the Church's eldest daughter, France, the rulers of these countries gazed upon the Church as either a tool for or an obstacle to the aggrandizement of their power. The Gallican Articles of 1682 codified within France not only the complete exclusion of the Pope from temporal affairs, but also his subordination in even ecclesiastical and spiritual matters. Meanwhile, Josephinism in the Hapsburg lands witnessed the secular princes arrogating to themselves even the power to determine rubrics for Catholic Masses. By the nineteenth century, many exasperated Catholics helped fuel the liberal revolution that demanded (among other things) the complete divorce of Church and state, as a means of protecting the integrity of the Church. It is that liberalism that reigns today, and the Church, though safe to live in her assigned corner, has lost much of her social and political relevance. With the privatization of the Christian faith, loyalty to state has largely supplanted fidelity to Church and Christ as our highest *public* allegiance.

Notwithstanding this tendency towards secularism of the modern state, the Church has never relinquished her authority to judge regarding temporal matters – as Canon 747, §2, cited above, makes plain – nor has she ever surrendered her prerogative to make pronouncements upon the justice of particular wars, as Weigel and Novak seem to think. A brief survey of 19th and 20th century Catholic thought and practice on this issue should make this clear.

Orestes Brownson, in discussing the doctrinal defeat of Gallicanism at Vatican I, put the Church's position on her ability to judge the moral aspect of temporal matters this way:

> Politics are only a branch of ethics; ethics depend on the moral law, of which, as of the revealed law, the Pope is the guardian and judge; and hence the Council of the Vatican declares him supreme and infallible in morals no less than in faith. This is the only possible remedy for political atheism, for it makes the Pope supreme under the natural law, from which the state holds, as well as under the revealed law, and subjects to his authority as vicar of Christ the whole moral order, as well as the Christian dogmas and sacraments; and while it gives him no direct power in temporal affairs, it gives him supreme authority to judge of the morality of the acts of temporal princes and governments, as well as of the acts of private individuals, and to subject them to such ecclesiastical discipline as he judges proper or necessary.[1]

---

1. "The Church Above the State," *Brownson's Quarterly Review*, July, 1873, online.

Since Brownson's time, the Church has dropped her practical resistance to the "separation" of Church and state. The basic position of the Church regarding her moral authority in temporal matters, however, has not changed. Although Brownson's ultramontanism may appear extreme, note that he denies the direct power of the Pope in temporal affairs, and limits the Pope's power to the ability to pronounce authoritatively – and therefore in a way that binds individual Catholics – on the moral aspect of matters both public and private. Henri de Lubac, who also made a study of the subject, agrees; he argues that a proper understanding of the Church's tradition rejects the idea that the Church has any effective *juridical* power in temporal matters.[1] What the Church does have, however, is spiritual power in temporal matters.[2]

> Since the supernatural is not separated from nature, and the spiritual is always mixed with the temporal, the Church has eminent authority – always in proportion to the spiritual element present – over everything, without having to step out of her role. If this is not true, then we might as well admit that the Church has no authority over anything, that she can speak only in the abstract. She must not limit herself to outlining absolute principles, to proclaiming doctrine and ethics from "above the fray." When circumstances require it, she must be able to make decisions – that is, either approve or condemn, *hic et nunc* – about concrete activities where doctrine and morality are involved.[3]

In today's context, the Church does not possess a recognized jurisdiction over the state, direct or indirect. This jurisdiction can only be effectively exercised "when a whole nation [is] thoroughly Catholic in spirit, and the force of papal decisions [is] recognized by all as binding in conscience."[4] As Pius IX candidly conceded, "for their execution in the temporal sphere, [these] ecclesiastical ideals depended . . . on the consent and custom of the people, in the absence of which the papacy no longer claims to exercise power and rights that public law and common consent once accorded to the Supreme Judge of Christendom for the common welfare."[5] The judgment of Joseph Cardinal Hergenröther, Church historian and canonist (ap-

---

1. It should be noted that in order to avoid confusion about the limits to the Church's authority, the proposition that "the Church has no direct or indirect temporal power" was condemned by Pope Pius IX in the *Syllabus of Errors* in 1864 (Dz. 1724).

2. Henri de Lubac, "The Authority of the Church in Temporal Matters" and "The Church's Intervention in the Temporal Order," in *Theological Fragments* (San Francisco: Ignatius Press, 1989).

3. De Lubac, "The Authority of the Church in Temporal Matters," *op. cit.*, p. 215.

4. *Catholic Encyclopedia* (henceforth *CE*) (New York: Robert Appleton Company, 1907–1912), s.v. "The Pope."

5. *Discorso agli Accademici di Religione Catholica*, July 20, 1871, quoted in *CE*, s.v. "Papal Arbitration."

personal conscience higher power and the power of the masculine authority

pointed first Cardinal-Prefect of the Vatican Archives by Pope Leo XIII), is the same: "[The Pope's] power [is] not physical or material, but [is] a moral and spiritual power relying upon public opinion for its efficiency."[1] Today the Church admittedly speaks directly to the consciences of the faithful, be they rulers or ruled. As Romano Amerio, a Vatican II *peritus* and expert historian of the Church in modern times, point out, the Church's primary method for exercising her authority in temporal matters – particularly after the "separation" of Church and state that followed upon the liberal revolutions – is by acting upon the consciences of the faithful.[2]

Henri de Lubac stresses, however, that the Church's word to the conscience, in temporal no less than other matters, can be not merely advisory, but issued with binding authority, and in certain grave circumstances accompanied by ecclesial discipline.[3] The Catholic sense of how this process works – i.e., how the Church's pronouncement on temporal matters acts upon the conscience via effective spiritual means – is illustrated by an interesting episode from the 12th century. When King Richard Cœur de Lion (Lionheart) was imprisoned by Leopold, Duke of Austria, in 1192, Queen Eleanor, Richard's mother, appealed to the Pope to take whatever action was necessary to secure the King's release. In one of the Queen's letters, she preempted a possible reply from the Pope which might argue that his jurisdiction extended only to souls and not to bodies (i.e., only to spiritual and not to temporal matters):

> But you will say that this authority is given you over souls, not over bodies. Let it be so; it is sufficient for us that you should bind the souls of those who keep my son chained in a dungeon.

The constant practice of the Church has been to pronounce authoritatively on temporal affairs wherever a sufficiently grave moral or spiritual interest obtains. Traditionally the right to so pronounce has been both delimited and expressed by the notion of "intervention in temporal matters *ratione peccati*," or intervention "for reason of sin." For it is sin that falls under the spiritual jurisdiction of the Church, whether in purely spiritual or in temporal matters.[4]

---

1. *Catholic Church and Christian State* (London: Burns and Oates, 1876), Vol. I, p. 375.

2. *Iota Unum: A Study of the Changes in the Catholic Church in the 20th Century* (Kansas City: Angelus Press, 1992), p. 251: "In a situation where sovereignty is lodged in the whole body of citizens, as it is in most modern regimes, the Church can resist . . . unjust laws by charting a course of action that Catholic citizens should follow in using their political rights, while avoiding any spirit of hatred or sedition."

3. De Lubac, *op. cit.*, pp. 206, 233.

4. Canon 1401 of the current Code is clear on this matter: "1401. The Church has its own and exclusive right to judge: 1° cases which refer to matters which are spiritual or linked

Reviewing the history of this practice, even up to relatively recent times, leaves no doubt that the Holy See considers such pronouncements to be efficacious, at least in the realm of conscience, regardless of whether or not they are accepted as binding by the civil power (and, it should be added, they do not always or necessarily carry with them coercive spiritual measures). In 1729 Pope Benedict XIII declared null and void the Decree of the Parliaments of Paris and Bordeaux which prohibited the office of St. Gregory VII; Pope Gregory XVI did the same in 1833 to the liberal decrees of Dom Pedro of Portugal.[1] Three years later would show Gregory XVI also condemning as invalid the anti-Catholic laws passed by the Spanish Regency.[2] His successors, Blessed Pius IX and St. Pius X, would deal likewise with similar situations, the former declaring null and void certain laws of the Republic of New Granada (1852) and Austria (1862), and the latter doing the same with the French law of Separation (1906).[3]

Furthermore, closer to our own time, Pope Pius XI was faced with the tragic situation of Mexico, a nation almost entirely Catholic but ruled by Masonic leaders. In the 1920s, the Mexican government passed laws restricting Catholic worship, to protest which the Mexican bishops simply suspended all public worship. This state of affairs continued for several years, but Pius XI eventually intervened, declaring as "condemned by God" the laws that infringed against the rights of the Church. Fr. Baierl considers this to be a clear example of a papal exercise of spiritual authority over temporal matters, citing as further examples Pius XI's protest against violations of the Concordat of 1933 by the German Reich and his condemnation of Communism in *Divini Redemptoris*.[4] Pius XI's successors attached significant spiritual penalties to those who supported Communism; although such measures did not affect the temporal order directly, they were no doubt further examples of the Church's willingness to exercise what

---

with the spiritual; 2° . . . whatever contains an element of sin." Canon 1553, part one, of the old Code of Canon Law (1917) is no less clear, and indicates the continuity of the Church's understanding of this issue: "The Church has the inherent and exclusive right to judge: 1° cases which relate to spiritual matters or to temporal matters annexed to spiritual, 2° . . . everything in which there is to be found a *ratio peccati.*"

1. Jacques Maritain, *The Things That Are Not Caesar's* (London: Sheed & Ward, 1928), p. 195.

2. *Ibid.*

3. *Ibid.* Also see Rt. Rev. Joseph J. Baierl, S.T.D., *The Catholic Church and the Modern State: A Study of Their Mutual Juridical Claims*, (Rochester, N.Y.: 1955, St. Bernard's Seminary), p. 88, *Acerbissimum* (1852) of Bl. Pius IX, and *Vehementer Nos* (1906) of St. Pius X.

4. Baierl, *op. cit.*, p. 90. See also *Acerba Animi* (1932) of Pius XI.

she considers her right to bind the consciences of the faithful in temporal matters when necessary.[1]

III. The Church's Authority in War and Peace

"Papal intervention to effect peace," writes John Eppstein in his masterful historical and philosophical treatise, *The Catholic Tradition of the Law of Nations,*

> first undertaken *ratione feudi* [for feudal reasons] at the height of the feudal system, under which many of the Kingdoms of Europe were vassals of the Holy See, were soon made *ratione peccati* [for reason of sin]. *This title to intervene [was] directly derived from the Pope's position as guardian of the Moral Law....* It was expressed in its most authoritative form in the theocracy of Gregory VII. We find it again, long after the disruption of Christendom, in the mouth of a seventeenth century Pope. It is vigorously reasserted by Leo XIII" (emphasis mine).[2]

It should not be surprising that the Church thus claimed the authority to deal authoritatively with matters of war and peace, in view of the idea that the Church possessed the authority to make spiritually binding pronouncements *ratione peccati,* that is, concerning temporal matters that possessed a significant moral component, and in which sin was possibly to be committed. It would be difficult to conceive of a temporal matter admitting of a greater moral dimension than one which presumes to sanction killing in view of a higher end. It would be difficult to conceive of a temporal matter which could involve so much sin as a war erroneously imagined to be just, but which in actuality involved wholesale murder. Thus, we find some of the Church's finest minds not only defending the generic right of the Church to pronounce upon temporal matters where necessary, but also defending the specific right of the Church to pronounce against war, when appropriate to do so.

"This right of arresting hostilities," Eppstein writes elsewhere, "... was extended by Papal as against Imperial apologists to the right of the Pope to

---

1. Amerio, *op. cit.,* p. 255. The Holy Office's decree of June 28, 1949, issued under Pope Pius XII, provided for the excommunication of anyone professing atheist and materialist communism, and condemned anyone who supported the Communist Party. An extension to that decree, promulgated on March 25, 1959, under Pope John XXIII, widened the condemnation to include anyone who voted for the Communist Party or any party that supported it.

2. John Eppstein, *The Catholic Tradition of the Law of Nations* (Washington, D.C.: Catholic Association for International Peace (CAIP), 1935), p. 189. It is interesting to note that this treatise was written at the behest of Prof. James T. Shotwell (a director of the Carnegie Endowment for International Peace and one of the architects of the Kellogg-Briand Pact of 1928) and published under Carnegie Endowment auspices.

forbid war altogether between Christians. This notion was rationalized by the schoolmen and expressed by Vitoria."[1]

As Eppstein points out, Francisco de Vitoria, O.P., (1480–1546), early in the 16th century, declared that

> when princes are at variance with one another about some right of sovereignty and are rushing into war, [the Pope] can act as judge and inquire into the claims of the parties and deliver judgment, a judgment which the princes are bound to respect, lest those numerous spiritual evils should befall which are the inevitable results of a war between Christian princes."[2]

Not long before, Catholic jurist Juan Lopez (1450–1496) of Segovia wrote,

> I doubt not that the Pope could, by pains and censures, prevent every just or doubtfully just war which was not indispensable for self-defense, until the lawfulness of the war had been demonstrated to him; for he has received from God an ordinary power in the spiritual sphere, because of sin: he can exercise it without distinction against all and on all occasions and so intervene in temporal affairs.[3]

The well-known Francisco Suárez, S.J. (1548–1617), for his part, maintained that the

> Supreme Pontiff . . . has the right of examining the cause of war and the power of passing judgment to which the parties are bound to adhere, unless he do a manifest injustice: for this is certainly necessary for the spiritual good of the Church and for properly avoiding infinite evils: wherefore Soto *ad Rom.* 12 says that there is rarely a just war between Christian rulers, because they can have another expeditious means of terminating their common differences.[4]

Elsewhere, Suárez points out that "if the Pope . . . justly issues a prohibition against [a] war in question as being opposed to the spiritual welfare of the Church [he] thereby . . . deprives the prince of all right to make war."[5]

Edward Génicot, S.J. (1856–1900), writing some three hundred years later, confirmed the point made by the great Spanish Scholastics while

---

1. *Ibid.*, p. 190.

2. *De Indis*, II, VI, quoted in Eppstein, *op. cit.*, p. 200.

3. *Tractatus de Bello et Bellatoribus* (1496), quoted in Eppstein, *op. cit.*, p. 163, from Alfred Vanderpol, *Le Droit de Guerre d'après les Théologiens et les Canonistes du Moyen Âge* (Paris: A. Tralin, 1911).

4. *De Caritate*, Disputation XIII (*De Bello*), Sect. II, 5, quoted in Eppstein, pp. 164–5.

5. *De Caritate*, from *On the Three Theological Virtues: Faith, Hope, and Charity* (originally published, Coimbra: Nicolas Carvalho, 1621) in Gwladys L. Williams, *et al.*, trans., *Selections from Three Works* (London: Humphrey Milford, 1944; reprinted, Buffalo: William S. Hein & Co., Inc., 1995), Disputation XIII (*De Bello*), Sect. II, 7, p. 810.

noting the insufficiency of a war conducted for a merely "probable" reason. "If there remains any doubt about the right [to wage war], recourse *must be had* to the arbitration of other rulers *and especially of the Roman Pontiff*" (emphasis mine). Finally, in the section of his treatise that deals with medieval social principles, Cardinal Hergenröther summarizes, in a single concise and interesting statement, the understanding of the issue possessed at the time by the then-Catholic world: "The Church authorities were to decide upon the justice of a war, and many held that without this war was never to be made."[1]

Although several of the above citations dealing with the theoretical claims of the Church refer to war between Catholic rulers, there is clearly no principle of deference to the judgment of civil authorities in matters of war. This will be seen just as clearly below in our review of the practice of the Church, in modern as well as medieval and Renaissance times.

IV. The Church's Practical Judgment upon Matters of War and Peace

The action of the Church in matters of war and peace confirms in practice the theoretical right claimed by her theologians. The first two appendices to Eppstein's book are detailed lists of the "pacific interventions of the Holy See." The first is translated from a chapter in a book by Frédéric Duval (1876–1916), *L'Église et le Droit de Guerre (The Church and the Right of War)*,[2] and deals with the 12th to the 16th centuries. The second is a summary of the major events chronicled by Joseph Müller (b. 1890) in his work, *Das Friedenswerk der Kirche in den letzten drei Jahrhunderten (The Work for Peace by the Church Over the Last Three Centuries)*.[3] Of the first list of events – leaving out the numerous cases of arbitration mentioned and beginning only with the successors of Pope Innocent III – the author notes the instances in which Popes Gregory IX, Boniface VIII, John XXII, Eugenius IV, Pius II, and Paul II issued specific commands, many backed up by strict spiritual penalties, to one or more sovereigns or nations, either commanding the cessation of hostilities, condemning their initiation, or enforcing a truce. "Apart from these authoritative acts," Duval writes, "must be recorded friendly interventions or arbitrations, whether effected at the request of the belligerents or offered spontaneously by the pontiffs."

---

1. Hergenröther, *op. cit.*, Vol. I, p. 277.
2. Paris: Bloud & Gay, 1920.
3. Berlin: Deutsche Verlagsgesellschaft für Politik und Geschichte m. b. h., 1927.

The examples which follow are too numerous to mention. The second appendix, merely summarizing Müller's work, notes 30 instances of papal arbitration or other diplomatic action specifically conducted to arrange a peaceful settlement between parties in (or nearing) armed conflict, or to encourage or support some diplomatic endeavor in favor of more peaceful relations between nations.

An interesting and illustrative episode, occurring during the period dealt with by Müller, involves the activities of David Urquhart (1805–1877) and several groups of bishops in the run-up to the First Vatican Council. Urquhart was a British Anglican diplomat who had become convinced that the best hope for the mitigation of the modern horrors of war was the intervention of the Holy See. Urquhart moved near Rome in 1864 and began to lobby the Catholic hierarchy to establish a body that would clearly promulgate the laws of war and pronounce on the justice or injustice of particular wars between nations. Urquhart was convinced that the Catholic Church held three important advantages that made such a project possible: 1) the Catholic Church could claim to be truly worldwide and transcend the interests of particular nations, 2) the Church had a well-developed canon law in the area of war and a long history of interpreting that law, and 3) the Church had a functioning system of disciplinary measures, such as the withholding of absolution and communion, that could be used to support its judgments. On this last point, Urquhart cited contemporary disciplinary measures against the revolutionary Garibaldians (Italy) and Fenians (Ireland), as well as the earlier example of Bartolomé de las Casas, who traced his own rejection of an unjust war to his being denied absolution by a priest sensitive to the Indians' plight. Urquhart urged the Vatican to establish a "diplomatic college" qualified to rule on whether or not a particular war met just-war criteria. If a war were declared unjust, then absolution would be refused for all killing in that war, and communicant soldiers would be expected to refuse orders.[1]

Pope Pius IX received Urquhart and his wife on several occasions, and referred to him as "nostro Urquhart." Pius IX assured Urquhart of his support for the project, and said, "God has inspired you with very great ideas on the greatest of subjects . . . now the cornerstone has been laid." Pius IX named Cardinal Franchi as his liaison to Urquhart. Urquhart made sig-

---

1. Yoder, John Howard, "David Urquhart: Knight Errant for the Just War Tradition in the Age of Empire," an unpublished "Working Paper" prepared for the Joan B. Kroc Institute for International Peace Studies at the University of Notre Dame, 1993, available at http://www.nd.edu/~theo/jhy/writings/justwar/urquhart.htm.

nificant progress with the bishops of France and Britain, until a draft (or *monitum*) of his proposal – signed by forty bishops, including England's Cardinal Manning – was presented on February 10, 1870, to Pope Pius IX. After lamenting the "intolerable" condition of the world, laboring under the burden and expense of maintaining "huge standing and conscript armies" and forgetful "of law in international affairs" (which, it states, opens "an altogether readier way for the beginning of illegal and unjust wars"), the *Postulata* states that

> serious men experienced in public affairs are of the same opinion as not a few others who are noted for their sanctity and are animated by zeal for religion. They are persuaded that there is an extreme need for a pronouncement in which those parts of the Canon Law, which concern the rights of nations and all those principles which determine whether war is a duty or a crime, should be authoritatively promulgated.[1]

The proposal was accepted for the agenda of the First Vatican Council, with no significant opposition.[2] Meanwhile, the Armenian Catholic bishops approved Urquhart's proposal at their Synod in 1869, and submitted their own *monitum* to Pius IX on March 10, 1870. After discussing the horrors of war and the general failure to heed just-war principles, the bishops conclude that

> a permanent and ceaseless oracle of truth should be able to extend its voice everywhere and to render secure the conscience of all. Therefore this very Synod fears this to be exceedingly necessary and humbly believes that it should be proposed to the ecumenical Council, if it should seem good to you, that a permanent and supreme Tribunal, made up of those of all nations expert in law, be set up before the See of Peter, which might examine and weigh matters of war, whether the mutual relations of societies are in accord with the moral laws of the Christian religion. And let this defender of the Laws of Nations be set up in the name of the See of Peter, whose juridical voice, confirmed by your infallible authority, who are the Vicar of Christ, shall be established as a measure or a rule for the public conscience.[3]

Unfortunately, the proposal was never voted on, due to the untimely breakup of Vatican I. As John Howard Yoder comments, however, "There is little reason to doubt that if the Council had not been broken off by the

---

1. "Postulata respectfully submitted by a number of Bishops to our Most Holy Pope Pius IX and the Most Sacred Vatican Council," February 10, 1870, quoted in Eppstein, *op. cit.*, p. 132.

2. *Ibid.*

3. "Petition of the Armenian Patriarchal Synod to Pope Pius IX," March 10, 1870, appendix to Yoder, *loc. cit.*

outbreak of the Franco-Prussian war, taking account of the momentum led by Cardinals Manning and Beckx, with the Pope's own hand strengthened by the Council's definition on infallibility, the Council would have taken affirmative action on Urquhart's project."[1] There is even less reason to doubt what this particular episode so clearly and conclusively demonstrates: both the Pope and the bishops assumed that the ability to pronounce upon the justice or injustice of a particular war was well within the authority of the Church.

There is today at least one bishop who follows closely in their footsteps; he is on good footing, when he does, for it should be clear by now how consistent his (and his predecessors') position is with the tradition of the Church on this matter. John Botean, the Romanian Catholic bishop of Ohio, wrote a letter on March 7, 2003,[2] to the faithful under his jurisdiction, in which he forbade members of his diocese to participate in or support the war against Iraq. After citing the same passage from the Catechism that Novak and Weigel cite, Bishop Botean comments that

> the nation-state is never the final arbiter or authority for the Catholic of what is moral or for what is good for the salvation of his or her soul. What is legal can be evil and often has been. Jesus Christ and his Church, not the state, are the ultimate informers of conscience for the Catholic. This is why the Church teaches as a norm of conscience the following: "If rulers were to enact unjust laws or take measures contrary to the moral order such arrangements would not be binding in conscience." (Catechism, 1903). She also warns "Blind obedience [to immoral laws] does not suffice to excuse those who carry them out" (Catechism, 2313).

Bishop Botean states that "any direct participation and support of this war against the people of Iraq is objectively grave evil, a matter of mortal sin. . . . With moral certainty I say to you it does not meet even the minimal standards of the Catholic just-war theory." Bishop Botean concludes that any killing in this war "is the moral equivalent of direct participation in an abortion" and he pledges the support of the Church in supporting those whose need to be conscientious objectors to this war may bring them hardship.

Catholics and others may certainly speculate as to the prudence or appropriateness of the Bishop's statement. Insofar as it is based upon clearly accepted doctrine and even further reflects the judgment of the Pope and the general consensus of bishops worldwide, there can be no doubt that

---

1. Yoder, *loc. cit.*
2. Contained in the present volume at pp. 291–294.

the Bishop possesses the right and authority to make such a declaration, and even to bind the consciences of his flock.

V. The Conscience of the Individual Catholic

Catholic and other neoconservative commentators have hastened to assert the right of the individual Catholic to dissent from the judgment of the Pope and bishops on matters of practical judgment, such as the application of the just-war theory in a particular circumstance. In cases of uncertainty within the Church, dissent on matters of practical judgment is indeed possible. One need only cite the cases of Argentina and Rwanda to recognize that the judgments of small groups of bishops in matters of war and peace are not infallible. The problem is that we hear nothing from these commentators, such as Novak and Weigel, about any right to dissent from the judgment of the state when grounds for doing so are sufficiently compelling. In the United States, there is no legal right to selective conscientious objection. The Catholic soldier cannot legally dissent from the President's judgment that a particular war is just. But is this the end of the story for us Catholics? Is this situation morally sufficient? Are we Catholics allowed to dissent once the "call" has been made, and the President has issued his "final judgment" that a war is just?

As Bishop Botean's quotes from the Catechism make clear, the individual Catholic has a grave obligation to inform his or her conscience as to the morality of any given act of war, and not to cede such judgments to the state.[1] Although Novak and Weigel might want to ignore the right of conscientious objection in the case of a war that an individual honestly deems to be unjust, both Vatican II's *Gaudium et Spes* (§79) and the Catechism (2311) recognize that right. In spite of what is often claimed by even competent theologians, the right of the individual soldier to refuse participation in what the individual conscience deems an unjust war has always been recognized and defended by the tradition of the Church.

The teaching of St. Augustine, which lays out the presumption in favor of authority that is typical of the Catholic spirit, is frequently cited to justify the common soldier's giving of the "benefit of the doubt" to the state when the state declares war. To our modern sensibility, St. Augustine's position may seem rather harsh, and overly indulgent of secular authorities:

---

1. See the discussion of conscientious objection by Dr. Peter Chojnowski, on pp. 361–373 of the present volume, for more on this point.—Ed.

The conscience of a soldier [annual soldier] put him up or a higher [important] [primord] secular leader.

LEGITIMATE AUTHORITY AND JUST WARS

[A] just man can justly fight under [the orders of a wicked king] . . . provided he is certain that what he is commanded is not against the command of God, or even when it happens that he is not certain, so that while perhaps the wickedness of the command makes the king a criminal, the duty of obeying proves the soldier guiltless.[1]

This single passage from St. Augustine should not, however, be seen as a complete expression of the Church's traditional position on the issue of war and the soldier's or citizen's individual conscience. On the contrary, it only expresses *one side* of the Church's teaching, which is that in the case of doubt (i.e., as Augustine says, "even when it happens that [the soldier] is not certain"), presumption is in favor of the right and duty to obey the civil authority when it issues a legitimate command, i.e. when it commands its soldiers to make war. This aspect of the question is the one highlighted by today's neocons in the conflict with Iraq. Even if there is some doubt as to the justice of the conflict, the benefit of the doubt should go to the President who proposes to make war and presumably, therefore, is assuring citizens and soldiers of its justice. Their approach here is the same as their approach to the question of whether the Church has the right to make a pronouncement on the legitimacy of a particular war: namely, they expect that *because* the President has made a decision to go to war, the very fact that *he* has made the decision is sufficient to resolve all doubt and to trump any objection raised on moral grounds by the Church.

The problem with this approach insofar as it relates to the pronouncement of the Church has been dealt with: it ignores the right and duty of the Church to judge authoritatively acts of the temporal power, including its decisions to wage war. The problem with the neocon approach insofar as it relates to the question of the soldier's or citizen's conscience is that it ignores the right of a doubtful conscience to seek moral truth over and against the judgment of the state that a particular war should be embarked upon. The neocon position presumes that the state *always* enjoys the benefit of *any* doubt (or worse, that there can be no question of doubt because it is not for the simple, uninformed citizen – who is not privy to classified intelligence – to make a judgment of any kind), rather than recognizing that the presumption of the correctness of the state's decision applies *only in the absence of serious doubt.*

Happily, this truth is and has been maintained by the most respected thinkers of the Church, neocon arguments notwithstanding. St. Robert

---

1. *Against Faustus*, XXII, Ch. 75, quoted in St. Robert Bellarmine, *De Laicis* (New York: Fordham University Press, 1928), p. 72.

Bellarmine (1542–1621), in treating of the need for any war to be embarked upon based on a just cause, points out that soldiers do not sin in an objectively unjust war because "subjects ought to obey their superior, nor should they criticize his commands, but they should rather suppose that their ruler has a good reason."[1] This is the position expressed by St Augustine, noted above, which Bellarmine too cites in his treatise. But Bellarmine's *further* comment is the following: "soldiers do not sin *unless it is plainly evident that the war is unlawful*" (emphasis mine).[2] Here we see that Bellarmine makes an allowance for the judgment of the individual soldier, as he does following his comment that soldiers ought to suppose that their ruler has a good reason: "unless they clearly know the contrary." Francisco de Vitoria is no less clear on the matter: "If a subject is convinced of the injustice of a war, he ought not to serve in it, even on the command of his prince."[3]

Others of the Church's illustrious thinkers were even stricter in their approach. Francisco Suárez quotes Vitoria (in *De Iure Belli*, no. 24) to the effect that senior military leaders, even when not asked for their opinion, are, "in the case of necessity," obligated in charity "to inquire into the justice of [a] war" which is declared or proposed by the sovereign.[4] Elsewhere Suárez notes the stringent positions of two respected theologians who point out that soldiers who have doubts about the justice of a war are "bound to make inquiries in order to dispel those doubts."[5] Of the two, Sylvester Mazzolini (1460–1523), O.P., would allow the soldiers to proceed to war if, after making inquiries, they are unable to resolve their doubts. The second, Pope Adrian VI (1459–1523), "absolutely denies that it is permissible to go to war with such doubts." While Suárez does not himself accept the rigidity of Adrian's position, his gloss on the comments of both Sylvester and Adrian reveals his own conviction that doubts about the justice of a war cannot simply be brushed aside in the name of the state's "benefit of the doubt," but must be dealt with:

> [I]f the arguments showing the war to be unjust were such that the soldiers themselves were unable to give a satisfactory answer, then they would be bound to inquire into the truth.[6]

---

1. Bellarmine, *op. cit.*, p. 72.

2. *Ibid.*

3. Francisco de Vitoria, O.P., *De Iure Belli*, in Ernest Nys, ed., and John Pawley Bate, trans., *De Indis et de Iure Belli Relectiones* (Washington, D.C.: Carnegie Institution, 1917; reprinted, Buffalo: William S. Hein & Co., Inc., 1995), parts V and VI of *Relectiones Theologicae XII* (published previously, Johan Georg Simon, J.U.D., ed., Cologne and Frankfort: August Boetius, 1696), 22, p. 173.

4. Suárez, *op. cit.*, pp. 831–2.

5. *Ibid.*, p. 832.

6. *Ibid.*, p. 833.

VI. The Essential Problem

While the theologians whose writings have been quoted leave some room for the benefit of the doubt to be afforded to the state in the case of a sufficiently inconclusive or debatable argument for or against war, there can be no doubt that they all recognized that the state of the soldier's conscience is a serious matter. For these thinkers, it is not something to be dispensed with simply because the state has made a decision in favor of war. Doubts must be dealt with, and if they are serious enough – or, more to the point, if they lead to a firm conclusion against the justice of a particular war – the soldier or citizen must not, obviously, participate in the proposed war. Suárez is characteristically clear: "common soldiers . . . may go to war when summoned to do so, *provided it is not clear to them that the war is unjust*" (emphasis mine).[1] Vitoria is no less clear:

> Even if the ruler gives the order, a soldier must not put innocent citizens to death and it follows that if a soldier is convinced of the injustice of a war he must not take part in it, for anything that is against a man's conscience is sin.[2]

The individual conscience of the Catholic is indeed important in these matters, but it risks being lost in the neocon shuffle, which elevates the judgment of the state to a binding rule and relegates both the dictates of conscience and the judgment of the Church to mere opinion, "nice to have" but ultimately irrelevant. Indeed, the current problem is not that U.S. Catholics took the opposition to the war by the Pope and the bishops too seriously, regarding it as binding and infallible. The problem is that most Catholics seemed only too willing to overlook the Church's position and in fact regard the state's judgment as binding. At home, a Pew survey found that, asked to name the most important influence on their thinking on the Iraq war, only 10 percent of respondents cited their religious beliefs. Forty-one percent named the media. While the survey did not distinguish between Catholics and non-Catholics, it is not unreasonable to conclude that the Church's position on the war was not taken overly seriously.

To say that Catholics in good conscience may dissent from the Pope and bishops on this matter leaves open the question of what is a good conscience. According to traditional Catholic belief, a good conscience is a well-formed conscience. Moral formation involves becoming a follower of Jesus Christ through the gifts of the Holy Spirit available in the sacraments of the Church and the practices of Christian charity. Though Vatican II's

---

1. *Ibid.*, p. 832.
2. De Vitoria, *op. cit.*, 23, p. 173.

Declaration on Religious Liberty celebrates the freedom of the individual conscience, it adds that

> in forming their consciences the faithful must pay careful attention to the sacred and certain teaching of the Church. For the Catholic Church is by the will of Christ the teacher of truth. It is her duty to proclaim and teach with authority the truth which is Christ and, at the same time, to declare and confirm by her authority the principles of the moral order which spring from human nature itself (§14).

The formation of conscience should be done, insofar as it is possible, in communion with the whole people of God and its pastors. No doubt we should reject the idea of blind obedience to the political whims of individual bishops. But when the Pope and the bishops worldwide unite virtually unanimously in clear and repeated opposition to a war, the Catholic conscience should treat this matter with the utmost seriousness.[1] As Pius XII stated 50 years ago,

> When it is a question of instructions and propositions which the properly constituted shepherds (i.e. the Roman Pontiffs for the whole Church and the bishops for the faithful entrusted to them) publish on matters within the natural law, the faithful must not invoke the saying (which is wont to be employed with respect to opinions of individuals): The strength of the authority is no more than the strength of the arguments.[2]

Pope John Paul II's opinion should count more than Donald Rumsfeld's or Bill O'Reilly's. At the very least, the Catholic should not simply abdicate moral judgment in this matter to leaders of a secular nation-state. On the contrary: the obvious right of the Church to pronounce on particular matters of war in a way that binds the Catholic conscience, along with the Church's clear teaching that, in cases of serious doubt, the rights of conscience must take precedence over the declaration of war by the civil authority – these must, for Catholics, be decisive. And how much more decisive should these two principles be when they work together, i.e., when a clear judgment from the Church is available to form the consciences of the faithful, in a way that frees them from subservience to the decision of the temporal power when that decision is in fact morally wrong.

---

1. The unity of the Church on this issue is very ably captured by Deacon Keith Fournier's piece on pp. 302–314 of the present volume.—Ed.

2. *On the Authority of the Church in Temporal Matters*, an address to cardinals, archbishops, and bishops gathered in Rome for ceremonies honoring the Blessed Virgin, November 2, 1954, §15.

Notwithstanding the clear theoretical teaching of the Church on matters of war, peace, and conscience, and the practical stance taken by the Church regarding the Iraq war, American Catholics and other sincere Christians failed to challenge the claims made by the American government. The problem, I believe, is a fundamental inability of many U.S. Catholics and other Christians to imagine being out of step with the American nation-state. It should not be so difficult to suppose that the gospel does not always magically coincide with American foreign policy, or that Jesus has something to say that is irreconcilable with what Dick Cheney or Richard Perle thinks. Let us imagine that significant numbers of Catholics in the military – not everyone, perhaps, even just 10 percent – agreed with the Pope and the U.S. Conference of Catholic Bishops that this particular war is unjustifiable, and decided to sit it out. Let us imagine that significant numbers of Catholic civilians – again not necessarily everyone – did not agree that the President's judgment was final, and found ways to protest and refuse to support the war effort. Would we be witnessing the Church overstepping the boundaries of its authority, or the dangerous mixing of politics and religion? No. We would be witnessing Catholics recovering their primary loyalty to Christ from the idolatry of the nation-state. And we would be witnessing, for once, the just-war theory being used to limit violence rather than justify it.

THE EDITORS' GLOSS: There was one bishop in the United States who translated discussion of the Iraq war into a practical judgment. That judgment, forbidding members of his flock from participating in it, was expressed in his letter of March 7, 2003, here reproduced.

Many neocon Catholics were outraged that he had the temerity to put his flock in such a difficult situation. As we heard over and over, it is for the government to decide when to go to war. But the Bishop answered this in his letter, as he explained in the remarks (also included here) he made on October 11, 2003, defending his position, for which he received the St. Marcellus award from the Catholic Peace Fellowship.

The best that the senior military churchman, Archbishop Edwin O'Brien, could come up with was, "I do not know what binding force this individual bishop's declaration has"! (He conceded that "it is difficult to justify military action based on just war principles.") Happily for Uncle Sam, he also said that Catholics "can in good conscience follow the direction of their Commander-in-Chief." The intelligent commentary came from canonist Dr. Edward Peters, whose remarks also follow – and they're all the more compelling because he was personally opposed to Botean's position and was a qualified supporter of the war.

The bishop is in good company, though. Governments have long complained of "clerical interference" on the basis of principle, warranted at times to remind nations that the law of God binds them as well as individuals. Charles V of Spain complained to the Dominican prior at Salamanca that renowned theologian Vitoria had taken "excessive liberty" in expressing his opinions regarding the claims made by Spain vis-à-vis the New World. The late John Cardinal O'Connor braced for the same when he questioned the 1999 NATO bombing of Serbia: "It is immoral for a moralist not to ask questions about morality," he wrote. "Such question-asking may be construed by some as a lack of patriotism or a callous indifference to the plight of the refugees and other victims of the Milosevic-reported cruelties." He concluded by saying, "So be it."

One wonders what the neocons would think of the canonized English Bishop St. John Fisher, who, like John Botean, alone among his peers insisted that political forces conform to spiritual realities. In 1533 Fisher even requested of the same Charles V that he invade England to enforce Vatican decrees against his sovereign, Henry VIII. The very thought of it at least puts the fretting over Bishop Botean's decree into some kind of proper perspective.

A Moment of Moral Crisis
. . . .
The Lent 2003 letter of Bishop John Michael Botean

BELOVED BROTHERS AND sisters in Our Lord, Jesus Christ,

Great Lent, which we now begin, is traditionally a time in which we take stock of ourselves, our lives, and the direction in which we are headed. In the common language of the Catholic Church, it is a time for a deep "examination of conscience" as we fast, pray, and otherwise attend to the call for repentance issued by the Church for the forty days before we celebrate the Resurrection of her savior, Jesus Christ.

A serious examination of conscience requires that we recognize that there are times in the life of each Christian when one's faith is seriously and urgently challenged by the events taking place around him or her. Like it or not, these challenges show us just how seriously – or not – we are living our baptismal commitment to Christ. Most of us, most of the time, would prefer to keep our heads in the sand, ostrich-like, than to face truths about ourselves. This is why the Church has found it so vitally necessary to have seasons, such as Lent, during which we must pull our heads out of the sand and take a good, hard look at the world around us and how we are living in it.

We cannot fail, as we examine our consciences, to take into account the most critical challenge presented to our faith in our day: the fact that the United States government is about to initiate a war against the people of Iraq. For Romanian Catholics who are also United States citizens, this raises an immediate and unavoidable moral issue of major importance. Specifically stated, the issue is this: does the killing of human beings in this war constitute murder?

Jesus was violent
God is violent
Michael is violent
man is violent

The fig tree *the temple attack* — *this is no theory*

The Holy Gospels reveal Our Lord, God, and Savior Jesus Christ to be nonviolent. In them, Jesus teaches a Way of life that His disciples are to follow, a Way of nonviolent love of friends and enemies. However, since the latter half of the fourth century, the Church has proposed standards that, if met, would make it morally permissible for Christians to depart from that way in order to engage in war. These standards have come to be known in popular language as the "Catholic just-war theory."

According to this theory, if all of the conditions it specifies are adhered to, the killing that is done in fighting a war may be justifiable and therefore morally allowable. This theory also teaches that if any *one* of the standards is not met, then the killing that occurs is unjust and therefore morally impermissible. Unjust killing is by definition murder. Murder is intrinsically evil and therefore absolutely forbidden, no matter what good may seem to come of it.

The Church teaches that good ends do not justify the use of evil means. The Catechism of the Catholic Church states this principle succinctly: "One may never do evil so that good may result from it" (1789). One contemporary example of this would be abortion. Abortion is intrinsically evil; hence regardless of the good that may seem to issue from it, a Catholic may never participate in it.

Paragraph 2309 of the Catechism of the Catholic Church states: "The strict conditions for legitimate defense by military force require rigorous consideration. *The gravity of such a decision makes it subject to rigorous conditions of moral legitimacy*" (emphasis added). Since war is about the mass infliction of death and suffering on children of God, Christians can enter into it and fight in it only if the war in question strictly meets all the criteria of the just-war theory, and only if these same standards are likewise meticulously observed in the course of fighting the war. Vague, loose, freewheeling, conniving, relaxed interpretations of Catholic just-war theory and its application are morally illegitimate because of "the gravity of such a decision."

"The evaluation of these conditions of the just-war theory for moral legitimacy belongs to the prudential judgment of those who have responsibility for the common good," states the Catechism (2309). However, the nation-state is never the final arbiter or authority for the Catholic of what is moral or for what is good for the salvation of his or her soul. *What is legal can be evil and often has been.* Jesus Christ and His Church, not the state, are the ultimate informers of conscience for the Catholic.

This is why the Church teaches as a norm of conscience the following: "If rulers were to enact unjust laws or take measures contrary to the moral order such arrangements would not be binding in conscience" (Catechism, 1903). She also warns, "Blind obedience [to immoral laws] does not suffice to excuse those who carry them out" (Catechism, 2313). When a moral conflict arises between Church teaching and secular morality, when contradictory moral demands are made upon a Catholic's conscience, he or she "must obey God rather than man" (Acts v:29).

Because such a moment of moral crisis has arisen for us, beloved Romanian Catholics, I must now speak to you as your bishop. Please be aware that I am not speaking to you as a theologian or as a private Christian voicing his opinion, nor by any means am I speaking to you as a political partisan. I am speaking to you solely as your bishop with the authority and responsibility I, though a sinner, have been given as a successor to the Apostles on your behalf. I am speaking to you from the deepest chambers of my conscience as your bishop, appointed by Jesus Christ in His Body, the Church, to help shepherd you to sanctity and to heaven. Never before have I spoken to you in this manner, explicitly exercising the fullness of authority Jesus Christ has given his Apostles "to bind and to loose" (see St. John xx:23), but now "the love of Christ compels" me to do so (2 Corinthians v:14). My love for you makes it a moral imperative that I not allow you, by my silence, to fall into grave evil and its incalculable temporal and eternal consequences.

Humanly speaking, I would much prefer to keep silent. It would be far, far easier for me and my family simply to let events unfold as they will, without commentary or warning on my part. But what kind of shepherd would I be if I, seeing the approach of the wolf, ran away from the sheep (see St. John x:12–14)? My silence would be cowardly and, indeed, sinful. I believe that Christ, Whose flock you are, expects more than silence from me on behalf of the souls committed to my protection and guidance.

Therefore I, by the grace of God and the favor of the Apostolic See Bishop of the Eparchy of St. George in Canton, must declare to you, my people, for the sake of your salvation as well as my own, that any direct participation and support of this war against the people of Iraq is objectively grave evil, a matter of mortal sin. Beyond a reasonable doubt this war is morally incompatible with the Person and Way of Jesus Christ. With moral certainty I say to you it does not meet even the minimal standards of the Catholic just-war theory.

Thus, any killing associated with it is unjustified and, in consequence, unequivocally murder. Direct participation in this war is the moral equivalent of direct participation in an abortion. For the Catholics of the Eparchy of St. George, I hereby authoritatively state that such direct participation is intrinsically and gravely evil and therefore absolutely forbidden.

My people, it is an incontestable Biblical truth that a sin left unnamed will propagate itself with lavish zeal. We must call murder by its right name: murder. God and conscience require nothing less if the face of the earth is to be renewed and if the salvation offered by Our Lord, God, and Savior Jesus Christ is to reach all people, including us. We have no choice before the face of God but to speak unambiguously to the moral situation with which we are confronted and to live according to the Will of Him who gazes at us from the Cross (Catechism 1785).

Let us pray for each other and take care of each other in this spiritually trying time. To this end our Church is wholeheartedly committed to the support of any of our members in the military or government service who may be confronted with situations of legal jeopardy due to their need to be conscientious objectors to this war. Let us also pray in earnest with the Mother of God, who knows what it is to have her Child destroyed before her eyes, that the destruction of families, lives, minds and bodies that war unleashes will not take place.

Finally, my brothers and sisters in Christ, be assured that Our Lord is aware that our "No" to murder and our prayers for peace are our faithful response to His desires. He will remember this forever and ever, and so it is to Him we must now turn, in Him we must now trust.

Amen.

> Sincerely in Christ-God,
> +John Michael
> (Most Reverend)
> John Michael Botean
> a sinner, bishop

15

The Bishop Explains

• • • • • • • • • •

Bishop John Michael Botean

IN THE AUGUST 2003 issue of the Catholic magazine *Crisis,* a letter to the editor appeared under the heading "Why did Orthodox Catholics support the war in Iraq?" The letter was in response to an article published in the May issue which attempted to justify morally the war for Catholics. The letter writer, William Gallagher, begins his reflection this way:

> It seems that the war in Iraq has put the final nail in the coffin of the Catholic Church in America. I say that because so many of the folks who have been decrying the liberal dissent in the Church over the years (and rightly so) have turned into dissenters themselves. I have never seen such evasions and circumlocutions as I am seeing from the so-called orthodox Catholics regarding this war.
>
> The "Guest Column" by Rev. Bryce Sibley ("Bush's Prudential Decision," May, 2003) is a case in point. He says that although "Catholics ought to listen to and respect the voice of the Holy See," it is the President of the United States who has the "ultimate authority to make his prudential judgment and to decide on the justness of a strike against Iraq." Huh? Bishop John M. Botean, the head of the Romanian Catholic eparchy of St. George in Canton, Ohio, puts it better, I think. He argues that "the nation-state is never the final arbiter or authority for the Catholic on what is moral." He stated quite clearly that "any direct participation and support of this war is an objectively grave evil, a matter of mortal sin."
>
> Where were all the other American bishops on this war? The Holy Father said that conditions for a just war had not been met. What part of that statement do the American bishops not understand?

The author of the May article, Rev. Bryce Sibley, then responds to Mr. Gallagher as follows:

> Mr. Gallagher seems befuddled that I or anyone else could claim to be a faithful Catholic and at the same time hold the position that it is President Bush who has the ultimate responsibility and authority to make a prudential decision applying the just-war theory to the specific situation with Iraq.

In response to his doubt, let me once again quote the section of the Catechism of the Catholic Church that deals with just war and legitimate authority: "The evaluation of these conditions for moral legitimacy belongs to the prudential judgment of those who have responsibility for the common good" (Catechism of the Catholic Church, 2309). There is not much more of a retort that I can give.

Fr. Sibley's only "retort that I can give" is something I explicitly anticipated and addressed in my March 2003 pastoral letter in paragraphs eight and nine. Paragraph eight quotes word for word what Fr. Sibley quotes from the Catechism (2309), and then goes on in the remainder of the paragraph, and in paragraph nine, to explain what 2309 means in terms of universally accepted Catholic teaching, and other directly pertinent and controlling sections of the Catechism (1903 and 2313).

Of course, a person or persons "who have responsibility for the common good" have to make a "prudential judgment" to determine if the conditions of the Catholic just-war theory have been met and are being adhered to. But, suppose their judgments result in laws, policies and programs that are going to kill six million Jews or produce other moral abominations? Then what? Is the individual Catholic supposed to follow blindly such a decision by "those who have responsibility for the common good?" In other words, is an individual Catholic in a bureaucracy, or in any other chain of command, morally permitted to follow any course set forth by that bureaucracy or chain of command, so long as such a course is set by those who have the legal authority to do so?

The Catechism emphatically says, "No!" (1903 and 2313). Since the Catechism says no, this means that there are moral standards that must be applied to the choice of whether to follow a law or a course of action designated by political authorities beyond the mere enactment of the law or the political decision to pursue a course of action under the rubric of the "common good." The attempt by some Catholic apologists to legitimize morally the killing of Iraqi people, including Iraqi Catholics, by isolating section 2309 from the rest of the Catechism, and from the Gospel itself, is a disingenuous use of intellect.

It is also telling!

When one raises Stephen Decatur's toast, "My country, right or wrong," to the level of an absolute in moral discourse then, granting the self-evident concupiscence that saturates the politics of every nation-state e.g. the lust for power, wealth, popularity, etc., one has embarked on a road where abominations and atrocities will not just be normalized; they will be divinized as morally in conformity with the Will of God as revealed by Jesus. As the renowned Catholic biblical scholar, the late Rev. John L. McKenzie, wrote, "It is the demonic quality of the state that it desires to be God." The state wants to have the final say as to what is right and what is wrong, what is good and what is evil. The Church, since its beginning, has never granted this level of moral authority to the state over its members. A pinch of incense to Caesar as God might have been the law of the state, but the Church knew that she and her members measured all humanly devised laws against a Higher Law. The history of Christian martyrdom in the early centuries of the Church is proof positive that the Church in no way accepts Decatur's dictum as a moral absolute.

Considering all that has been said, and with immediate and long-range pastoral concern for the spiritual and moral welfare of our Catholic community, especially our Catholic youth, I would propose that it is now imperative that the Catholic leadership in this country unequivocally demand a selective conscientious objector statute be added to the presently existing law. In the past, the U.S. bishops as a body have requested this of the federal government, but they have been shunted aside by calculated congressional- and executive-branch inattention to the issue. However, the time is now upon us when such a law must exist for the protection of those tens of millions of Catholics who presently find it morally acceptable to reject Jesus' teaching of non-violent love of friends and enemies and who are therefore, in conscience, morally subject to the standards of the just-war theory in relationship to state homicide. Blind obedience to political authorities is not an option for the individual Catholic or for the Church (Catechism, 2313).

The Church's insistence that a selective conscientious objection law is mandatory for the protection for those tens of millions of Catholics who are morally formed by the just-war theory is a grave moral imperative that U.S. Catholic leadership must face with ultimate seriousness for the spiritual, moral, psychological, emotional and physical protection of our Catholic youth, today and for all tomorrows. The stakes are infinitely high in this matter.

It has been said that "old men start wars and young men die in them." I am talking about what I consider the most serious challenge facing me as a bishop in the United States. The Catholic youth of this country, I am convinced, need moral and political protection from the power and shrewdness of old men and women who, because of a lifetime spent amid the machinations of nation-state politics and economics, have become desensitized to the reality of what it means to send a young boy or girl to kill and to die on behalf of their elaborate agendas.

If the Church does not protect its youth from the spiritual, moral, psychological, emotional and physical destruction of being forced to kill unjustly – in other words, being forced to commit murder – who will protect them? What is left of the just-war Catholic adolescent's conscience, soul, psyche, emotional structure, etc., if he or she is forced into the situation of being legally ordered to kill another human being (whose killing the Catholic boy or girl believes to be unjust) when such a Catholic boy or girl has no legal recourse by which to say no? Prison, or desertion, or fleeing to another country, or martyrdom, etc., are, of course, options. In fact, they are the only options presently available under U.S. law for Catholic youth who have been formed in and have accepted Catholic just-war theory as a standard of conscience.

Catholic spiritual and pastoral leaders in the United States owe the Catholic youth of the United States a selective conscientious objector law, and we owe it to them now. Whatever resources and whatever strategies are needed to see that such a law comes into existence should be expended and implemented without hesitation and without reserve. All this is said not as a political rallying cry for a selective conscientious objection law. It is said as a cry of the heart on behalf of young Catholic men and women who in the future are going to be entrapped in the wickedness and snares of governmental homicidal violence because they "saw no other choice." Genuine pastoral concern and care for the young people in our Catholic Church demands not leading them into the ordeal of having to choose between murder and martyrdom.

Finally, it must be noted that if the United States Catholic Bishops accepted the nation-state as the final arbiter, for the Catholic, of the morality or immorality of a war, we never would have asked in years past for the inclusion of a selective conscientious objection provision in the selective service law. Again, to present Catholic moral theology as if it accepted Decatur's position as a moral absolute; to present Catholic moral theology as if the state made the final decision for the Catholic about what is moral, what is Holy, what is the way of sanctity, what is the way to eternal life, is to present blatant falsehood as truth. Presenting blatant falsehood as truth is currently the *modus operandi* in many secular circles, but the Catholic Church and its leadership must not allow it to become, by osmosis, the modus operandi of our faith. It is as if some Catholics simply do not want to comprehend intellectually nor integrate morally the witness of Franz

Jaegerstaetter in World War II. But, whether his legalized martyrdom at the hands of a state that insisted it be the final judge of right and wrong, of good and evil, is made visible or downplayed by design, Jaegerstaetter's life and death will forever stand in eternal opposition, indeed in eternal hostility, to "my country right or wrong" as a moral principle in the Catholic Church.

I will close with a quotation from Dostoevsky.

> At some thoughts one stands perplexed, especially at the sight of men's sin, and wonders whether one should use force or humble love. Always decide to use humble love. If you resolve on that once for all, you may subdue the whole world. Loving humility is a mighty force, the strongest of all things. There is nothing else like it.

I submit that humble love can also prevail in a world grown sick, but not sick enough, of fighting, and in a Church grown old through its fear, its infidelity, and its mediocrity!

A Canonist Comments

· · · · · · · · · ·

Edward Peters, J.C.D., J.D.

T HE BISHOP'S STATEMENT clearly invokes, and provokes, fundamental questions of Christian rights and duties because of the following points:[1]

- Eastern Catholics are bound to follow what their bishops declare as teachers of the faith (CCEO 15, §1), though this obligation is qualified by the phrase "conscious of their [the faithful's] own responsibility."

- Individual Eastern bishops are to be regarded as authentic teachers of the faith for those entrusted to their care and the faithful must adhere to that teaching with a "religious obsequium" of soul (CCEO 600). The canon expressly states, however, that individual bishops are not infallible.

- One who disobeys an Eastern bishop can be subject to sanctions for that disobedience (CCEO 1446). Bishop Botean does not threaten canonical sanctions, but warns of "incalculable temporal and eternal consequences" should his letter be ignored.

On the other hand, and in addition to the qualifications already contained in some of the above provisions, we should note that:

- Eastern Catholics have the right to, among other things, make known their opinions on matters pertaining to the good of the

---

1. Citations here are to the 1990 Code of Canons of the Eastern Churches (CCEO) that governs Eastern Catholics.

Church and to make their opinions known to others (CCEO 15, §3). There is no doubt that public statements by Catholic hierarchs on issues related to just-war theory, the duties of citizens toward their nations, and the obligations of Catholics to their bishops, would be legitimate topics of discussion.

- An Eastern bishop who misuses his high office can be subjected to sanctions for that misuse (CCEO 1464, §1).

The eparch's statement is unprecedented for its clarity and starkness; it simply *must* be read to appreciate this point, though fair-minded readers can admit that it is not a peacenik, blame-America-first harangue, but is instead a reasoned (though, I think, wrongly) exercise of conscience. It *cannot* be issued, however, and then forgotten. If Bishop Botean is correct, his argumentation would seem to apply to all Catholics, and only an inexcusable lack of pastoral solicitude on the part of other Eastern and Latin bishops could account for them not following suit immediately. If, on the other hand, Bishop Botean is wrong, then he has placed his faithful in a profound and direct conflict of conscience between their ecclesiastical and civil leaders, which, I suggest, only an inexcusable lack of pastoral solicitude would suffer them to remain in.

Bishop Botean having no superior short of the Holy See, I believe his extraordinary statement must be ratified or rejected by the Holy See without delay (CCEO 1060–1061).

Some have suggested that either the Metropolitan of the Romanians in Romania (CCEO 133 *et alia*), or even the Patriarch of the Byzantines (CCEO 56 *et alia*), might also be called upon to assess Bishop Botean's extreme statement. I think either of these ideas, and perhaps others, is worth considering, cumbersome though they might prove in actual practice. Nevertheless, the Roman Pontiff (CCEO 43) remains the only superior above an eparch unquestionably able on his own authority to address conclusively what, in this case, Bishop Botean (CCEO 178) has imposed as a fundamental question of conscience on thousands of Romanian Catholics in the U.S.

THE EDITORS' GLOSS: Deacon Fournier's piece complements Dr. Cavanaugh's consideration of the Church's authority in the chapter before last. Notwithstanding the refrain of dismissal (reminiscent of *"Mater si, magistra no"*) that came from pro-war Catholics whenever they heard a churchman speak in favor of peace, the fact remains that, universally, the hierarchy of the Church opposed the war, and dismissing the Church's point of view in such a matter is simply not an option. As historian Joseph Cardinal Hergenröther noted, medieval theologians in fact held that "the Church authorities were to decide upon the justice of a war, and many held that, without this, war was never to be made." Canon Law (747, §2) makes the same point: "The Church has the right always and everywhere to proclaim moral principles, even in respect of the social order, and to make judgments about any human matter in so far as this is required by . . . the salvation of souls."

Much of the hate and discontent generated by clerical discussion of war in Iraq revolves around the frequent references to the necessity of working through the UN, comments that not only sincere American patriots but also neocon empire-builders are loath to hear. There are and were more persuasive objections to the war, which it would have been nice to hear more frequently. But, though the UN cannot on its own authority authorize something in contravention of the natural or positive international law (as the chapter 1 postscripts indicate), and its authority comes from an arrangement of positive law and is not otherwise a matter of moral obligation, the fact is that the UN charter's stipulations on war and peace are indeed binding positive laws that signatory nations – like Britain and the U.S. – have committed to. They are therefore binding, or, as the U.S. constitution has it, they are the "law of the land," not less so because they in fact codify the essential, natural-law principles of the just-war doctrine. Which means that the clerical references we heard to the UN are not wholly without substance, and insofar as they formed part of an overall objection on legal and moral grounds to America's march to war, they were valid, and should have been listened to by Catholics. Maintaining instead – as Guimarães does in his book – that papal references to the UN charter were part of a conspiracy to impose a world government upon the United States or undermine its sovereignty is simply infantile. The only kind of sovereignty that churchmen were undermining in opposing the war was America's "right" to conduct itself without regard to law, both man's and God's. And they were correct to do so.

16

Peace Is Still Possible: The Unity of the Church in the Face of the Iraq War

. . . .

Deacon Keith Fournier, Esq.

> "Last night I had the strangest dream I've ever known before . . . I dreamed that all the world agreed to put an end to war . . . I dreamed I saw a mighty room . . . the room was filled with men . . . and the papers they were signing said they'd never fight again. And when the papers were all signed, and a million copies made, they all shook hands and bowed their heads and grateful prayers were prayed . . . and the people in the streets below were dancing round and round . . . while swords and guns and uniforms lay scattered on the ground. . . . Last night I had the strangest dream I've ever known before . . . I dreamed that all the world agreed to put an end to war."
>
> —Ed McCurdy

THE WORDS TO this folk song still echo in my memory. Joan Baez, Johnny Cash and many, many others recorded it and sang it over decades. For the "boomer" generation, it became an anthem, expressing a sincere dream to end war in our lifetime.

Ironically, it is members of this same generation who are now involved in the escalation of war. In fact, some who sang these words seem to be actually championing war as some kind of means to ending hostilities. Unfortunately, peace is still a dream. The world is racked with violence and the war in Iraq not only continues but shows little promise of ending soon. I still cherish that dream as do so many others. I still believe that dreams can become reality when people, and the nations they inhabit, make the right choices.

I am numbered among those who stood in Washington D.C., all those years ago, singing "All we are saying, is give peace a chance." I opposed the War in Southeast Asia. In fact, it was my deep revulsion for the very idea that men and women can ever "settle their differences" through the taking of human life that led me on a journey, searching for another way. That journey eventually brought me home to the Catholic Church.

As a "pro-life, pro-family, pro-freedom, pro-poor and pro-peace Catholic," I have long been troubled by the fact that some of those who walked the same road of conversion as I did, have become the proponents of a so called "preemptive" war with Iraq and seem to have bought the entire notion of "preemptive wars" as a path to peace.

I have often said that I "woke up one morning being called a conservative" because I insisted that the first neighbor in the first home of the entire human race, the child in the womb, must be protected by law and welcomed into the family. The pro-life position has now become associated, by some, with being "conservative" in the strange new world of the twenty-first century and its Orwellian language.

Worse yet is the notion that anyone who expresses a concern for and solidarity with the poor can actually support the killing of the ones whom Mother Teresa rightly called the "poorest of the poor," children in that first home of the entire human race, the womb.

When I watch former favorite performers of mine, those from my old "hippie days," sponsoring concerts to promote the killing of children in the womb as a legal "right," I cringe. What happened to our cry for peace? Unrestricted abortion is the first "preemptive war," and it is being waged against an entire class of persons who cannot even be heard, their cries muffled by the womb. The weapons arrayed against these holy innocents are chemical weapons as well as "surgical strikes." How evil and grotesque it all truly is.

Remembering September 11

On September 11, 2004, I joined the multitudes in reflecting on the "anniversary" of the attack on America. I prayed for peace. As an American, I still feel the utter shock, outrage and deep sorrow for those who lost their lives during this horrible act of barbarism.

This was an appropriate day to reflect on the deeper issues that are raised by such an evil act; and to ask the necessary questions concerning our own responses as a nation to the growing global climate of war. That examination should include a review of our decision to engage in a "preemptive" war in Iraq.

I am not a pacifist, but I have a high regard for those who are. The older I get, the more I am drawn to the simple, clear and prophetic cries of those Christians who have embraced the prophetic stand of the pacifist. However, I believe in self defense and defense of others. I also know that those principles are the foundation of what is called the "just-war" theory and analysis. It is on the basis of that theory that I opposed the preemptive war in Iraq from the beginning. I rejected then – and still reject – any notion of a "preemptive" war as being just.

I am not a "paleo-conservative," a "neoconservative," a "liberal," or a "conservative." I am simply a Catholic who seeks to inform my participation in the social order based upon the social teachings of the Catholic Church. I also believe that it is time to liberate Catholic Social teaching from the exclusive grasp of some American intellectuals who have tried to use it to justify the notion of a "preemptive" war.

There is no doubt that the intellectual framework of what has become the American "neoconservative" movement greatly influenced the decision of this administration to proceed with a "preemptive" war in Iraq. There is a vibrant, powerful subset of prominent Catholics who have embraced this neoconservative position and have developed an "apologetic" that they seek to wrap in "Catholic" clothes. It took me quite a few years to discern what it is that has disturbed me about the analysis and popular political positioning of many of these folks.

First, let me clarify, I am not declaring that they are unfaithful Catholics, nor am I saying they are not influential. In fact, it is their huge influence among the "elites" that has propelled my decision to write frequently about this issue. I am concerned over the continued failure of other thinkers, writers and activists to gain some traction in this vitally important time in American history and particularly on this vital issue.

They are so well positioned they have a significant influence in the current national political administration. These Catholics have apparently billed themselves as representing "Catholics in America." Yet, they do not represent all – or perhaps even most – Catholics on the decision initially to launch this war, including the Pope, most of the Bishops, and numerous of the Faithful from all across the spectrum, from those represented by the *Catholic Worker* to those of the *Wanderer*, along with many, many other Catholics like myself who simply seek to live the fullness of the social teaching of the Catholic Church.

Like the rejection of the tired "political" labels of "left" and "right," we reject the efforts to categorize us with their tired labels as to what kind of Catholic we are. We are simply faithful Catholics, dynamically orthodox, and comfortable in the beauty that is legitimate diversity within the bounds of fidelity to the Vicar of Christ and the Magisterium. Happily, a growing number of all of these Catholics are beginning to speak out and raise the necessary questions about the origins of this war.

I am concerned that the Catholic "neoconservatives" are sometimes casting confusion over just what the Catholic Church really teaches about the human person in society, the principles of economic and social justice, war and peace, and the common good. Their writings are becoming so influential among some emerging young Catholic thinkers that these young leaders actually end up sounding more like these folks than they do the Pope.

There are many emerging faithful Catholics who are fresh thinkers, and who, with other Christians, are seeking to influence the culture by exposing the lies of the contemporary culture of death and building a new culture of life and civilization of love. Many are beginning to question the near captivity that this neocon segment has had on popular Catholic thinking and activism. The neoconservative movement in America, and this subset of Catholic neoconservatives, is not the only voice in popular activism any longer. It is being questioned, and many are realizing that these folks are not as influential as once they may have thought.

For me, it took further graduate theological studies under some brilliant men and women, formed in the full social teaching of the Church, to help me to grasp what I instinctively knew was at best incomplete, if not seriously errant, about some of the neoconservative analyses of contemporary public policy issues. As I engaged in the deeper study of Pope John Paul II's and other Popes' social encyclicals, in totality, I came to understand more fully the incongruity of some of the movement's thought and positions on some vitally important issues. When one actually reads these documents, no one can cast them as "neoconservative."

Additionally, the continual reading of the great classics of Catholic Social Thought, like the works of Belloc, Chesterton, and Ousset, has opened my eyes to the full beauty, continuity and continual relevance of the Social tradition of the Catholic Church. I am deeply grateful for Catholic Social Teaching. I believe that it provides a framework and set of principles that must form the core of all of our efforts in the political, cultural, economic and social arena. And it is not only for Catholics, nor is it "religious" in the sense of only being of interest to "religious" people. It provides a set of principles based upon the natural law, to guide the ordering of human society and the promotion of the common good.

Catholic Social Teaching is a "treasure hidden in the field," which must be rescued from those who seek to use it as a kind of "proof text" to legitimize a pet political theory or economic system in order to try to "make it sound Catholic." We Catholics must always start with Catholic teaching and then inform our thought, rather than using that teaching as a cloak for political, economic or social theories that don't correspond to its correct conceptions of the human person, solidarity, authentic human freedom, economic and social justice, and matters of war and peace.

Our obligation includes rescuing Catholic teaching from those who seek to misuse some of its insights to justify the preemptive war in Iraq. It must continually be offered as a framework in the arena of international policy that can help provide a path to authentic peace in an age where wars seem to be breaking out with a frightening new momentum.

In my ecumenical work, I know that many other Christians, people of faith and people of good will are increasingly looking to Catholics to help lead them in the formation of their worldview. This is particularly true in the wake of the demise of the so-called "religious right" (notwithstanding its purported renaissance with the re-election of President Bush) and the myriad of disillusioned folks who are left in its wake. They hear these "neo-conservative" Catholic proponents of the preemptive action against Iraq and actually think they are hearing the Catholic Church. Unfortunately, in many instances, they are instead hearing the personal views of these men and women dressed up in "Catholic-looking" clothes.

Our Current Challenge

A phrase attributed to Alasdair McIntyre aptly summarizes the atheism of the contemporary West: "The Creed of the English is that there is no God, and it is wise to pray to Him from time to time." Let's be honest, there is little of Christian influence left in the West. This loss of authentic Christian influence left in its wake a virulent form of atheism, one that is hard to discern because it still even uses some of the language of religion. But this contemporary form of "religiosity" is privatized, homogenized and stripped of its power to effect authentic conversion or to influence the social order.

This lack of Christian influence has also fostered indifference toward the growing influence of Islam, which influence must be considered in light of the failure of the missionary work of the Church. Have we in our failure to proclaim and live the Christian faith provided the atmosphere that has allowed Islam to spread? Remember, after all, that while we who are Catholic welcome authentic inter-religious dialogue and co-operation, we clearly profess our belief in the centrality of God's revelation in Jesus Christ and the unicity of Salvation in Him.

Atheism, in all of its expressions, including the current version of a "secularism" that jettisons even the values derived from faith as somehow "religious" and therefore "taboo" or "intolerant," is not the future. It can never satisfy the hunger in the human person or foster the flourishing of the human race. Whence, perhaps, the attraction of Islam?

The greatest "weapons," therefore, that the Church has against the spread of Islam are prayer, evangelization, and courageous missionary activity among Muslims. The struggle we face with Islam is not one between "terror" and "law-abidingness," but one between truth and error. Truth will, eventually, prevail. However, it must be proclaimed in word *and* in deed. The sons and daughters of the Church would be better off using their time, talent, and treasure praying for the conversion of Muslims and developing a faithful and effective missionary approach to them while themselves living truly devout, dynamically orthodox Christian lives.

A Just War?

Frankly, I do not understand why so many neoconservatives who are Catholic continue try to defend the current war with Iraq in its inception as "just" under the so-called "just-war" analysis (*jus ad bellum*). The case for "preemptive" entry into Iraq was examined by the Church and found to lack any moral justification. The decision to engage in this "preemptive war" with Iraq failed to meet the test of clear conditions, commonly referred to as the "just-war" theory, set forth in the Catechism of the Catholic Church (§2309):

> + the damage inflicted by the aggressor on the nation or community of nations must be lasting, grave, and certain;
> + all other means of putting an end to it must have been shown to be impractical or ineffective;
> + there must be serious prospects of success;
> + the use of arms must not produce evils and disorders graver than the evil to be eliminated. The power of modern means of destruction weighs very heavily in evaluating this condition.

The very notion of a "preventive war" is antithetical to this analysis. The determination as to whether any war can be "just"-ified is first rooted in the broader understanding of "self defense." Preventive action is not self-defense. The entry of the United States into Iraq was not an act of "self defense." Neither was it a legitimate "response" or defense against the horror of September 11, 2001.

In spite of what some continue to say, the leaders of the Catholic Church were overwhelming in their unified opposition to beginning the current Iraq war and their assessment of it in light of the "last resort" criteria: they were unanimous in their conviction that no attack was imminent, and that as a result war was far from justifiable. Deep reservations were raised by numerous Bishops' Councils; Cardinal Ratzinger, Prefect of the Congregation for the Doctrine of the Faith; Cardinal Sodano, Vatican Secretary of State; Cardinal Martino, President of the Pontifical Council for Justice and Peace; and most ardently by the Holy Father who clearly stated that not only was war a human failure but that this specific war was unjustified.

Pope John Paul II, as is well known, was unambiguous in his opposition to the war. "Eventual controversies among peoples," he stated at Vatican City, April 6, 2003, "must not be resolved with recourse to arms but, instead, through negotiation." His message was no different on March 25, 2003: "It should be clear by now that war used as an instrument of resolution of conflicts between states was rejected, even before the Charter of the United Nations, by the conscience of the majority of humanity, except in the case of defense against an aggressor. . . . The vast contemporary movement in favor of peace . . . demonstrated this conviction of men of every continent and culture." Nor was it so at his "Address Before Midday Angelus" at St. Peter's Square on March 16, 2003: "There is still time to negotiate; there is still room for peace; it is never too late to come to an understanding and to continue discussions." And in his January 13, 2003, "Address to the Diplomatic Corps," he stated: "War is never just another means that one can choose to employ for settling differences between nations. As the Charter of the United Nations Organization and international law itself remind us, war cannot be decided upon, even when it is a matter of ensuring the common good, except as the very last option and in accordance with very strict conditions."

His leading associates were no less strident. Cardinal Pio Laghi, the Papal Envoy sent specially to meet with the President on March 5, 2003, made this official Statement following the meeting:

> The Holy See maintains that there are still peaceful avenues within the context of the vast patrimony of international law and institutions which exist for

that purpose. A decision regarding the use of military force can only be taken within the framework of the United Nations, but always taking into account the grave consequences of such an armed conflict. . . .

I want to emphasize that there is great unity on this grave matter on the part of the Holy See, the Bishops in the United States, and the Church throughout the world.

The Vatican spokesman, Joaquin Navarro-Valls, stated in an interview with *Catholic News Service*, on March 5, 2003: "[T]he concept of 'preventive war' is not found in the moral principles of Just-War theory – not even if it is authorized by a vote of the United Nations." Archbishop Jean-Louis Tauran, the Vatican Secretary for Relations with States, stated, at a conference at a Rome hospital, February 24, 2003, "A war of aggression would be a crime against peace." Archbishop Celestino Migliore, the Permanent Representative of the Holy See to the United Nations, stated in his address to the UN Security Council of February 20, 2003: "The Holy See is convinced that even though the process of inspection appears somewhat slow, it still remains an effective path." Cardinal Roger Etchegaray, the Envoy of the Holy See to Baghdad and former head of the Pontifical Council for Justice and Peace, said in his interview with *La Repubblica*, February 9, 2003, "War would be a catastrophe in every respect." Cardinal Angelo Sodano, Vatican Secretary of State, in an interview with Italian Reporters, January 29, 2003, said: "We are against the war. That is a moral position, and there's not much that needs to be said about whether (the war) is 'preventive' or 'non-preventive.' It's an ambiguous term. Certainly the war is not defensive." And the September 21, 2002, comment of Cardinal Joseph Ratzinger, Prefect of the Vatican Congregation for the Doctrine of the Faith, was "The concept of a 'preventive war' does not appear in the Catechism of the Catholic Church."

The American Bishops also held the position of the Church on this issue. On February 26, 2003, the Most Reverend Wilton D. Gregory, as President of the United States Conference of Catholic Bishops, wrote:

> Our bishops' conference continues to question the moral legitimacy of any preemptive, unilateral use of military force to overthrow the government of Iraq. . . . Based on the facts that are known, it is difficult to justify resort to war against Iraq, lacking clear and adequate evidence of an imminent attack of a grave nature or Iraq's involvement in the terrorist attacks of September 11.

And this was simply a reassertion of the Conference's position as stated on November 13, 2002, and previously expressed in Bishop Gregory's letter to the President of September 13, 2002:

> Based on the facts that are known to us, we continue to find it difficult to justify the resort to war against Iraq, lacking clear and adequate evidence of an imminent attack of a grave nature.... [R]esort to war, under present circumstances and in light of current public information, would not meet the strict conditions in Catholic teaching for overriding the strong presumption against the use of military force.

This position did not change, even up to the commencement of the war in Iraq. "We stand by the statement of the full body of bishops last November," the Bishop wrote on behalf of the entire Conference on March 19, 2003.

The other nations' Bishops' Conference were no different in their stated positions. Note the following declarations by the bishops from various countries:

Germany: "We approve of the intentions of the international community to put an end to dictatorships. We approve of determined efforts towards a more effective realization of human rights. But we disapprove of policies which aim at achieving these objectives by means of war" (March 13, 2003). And again: "A security policy that advocates preventive war is in contradiction with Catholic teaching and international law . . . " (January 20, 2003).

England and Wales: "It is our moral responsibility to avoid this war unless, *in the face of a grave and imminent threat,* there is no other possible means to achieve the just end of disarming Iraq . . . " (emphasis mine) (November 15, 2003).

France: "To date, the available information does not allow one to affirm that the conditions – as one finds them summarized in the Catechism of the Catholic Church, No. 2309 – are met. . . . [A] military conflict between an Arab country and the United States would . . . deepen the feeling that the great powers use 'two weights, two measures' in enforcing application of UN resolutions in the region" (October 15, 2002).

India: " . . . the remedy for putting an end to . . . terrorist activities and organizations should not be worse than the malady itself, and that is what is feared, namely, a full-scale armed conflict" (February 4, 2003).

Japan: "We are opposed to the use of military power against Iraq" (February 21, 2003).

Korea: "All countries concerned with the danger of war should solve their conflicts through peaceful means. We condemn the logic of power, but support a peaceful solution through dialogue and negotiation" (February 14, 2003).

Pakistan: "We share the concern of our Muslim brethren and all people of good will in expressing their total condemnation of this preemptive strike. . . . [T]his is not a 'war on international terrorism' but rather an outright attack on a sovereign state . . . " (January 16, 2003).

South Africa: "The fight against terrorism cannot be achieved through a war that will inevitably kill hundreds of thousands of innocent people, and terrorise millions more. We strongly believe that one of the main causes for terrorism is the disregard for justified claims of peoples who feel socially, economically and politically excluded, exploited and oppressed" (January 31, 2003).

And Spain: "At the present moment, we have to exhaust all peaceful means to avoid war . . . " (February 19, 2003).

Prudential Judgment?

While the evaluation of when it is ever justified to enter into war does fall to political leaders, they should carefully consider, in the exercise of both prudence and their public office, the Church's interpretation of its own just-war analysis. A consideration of this overwhelmingly consistent opposition to the war by the very institution that has offered the "just-war" analysis should have been a very significant part of that prudence. In actual fact this was not the case.

Ironically and sadly, this omission was partly the result of the strong influence of some Catholics who sought to build a case for the war by misusing this very teaching and obscuring the direction of the Church, insisting – in what really amounts to just belaboring the obvious – that it was all a matter of "prudential judgment." The implication was that in making that prudential judgment our leaders did not have to consider the position of the Church, which is not at all true, especially since matters of war and peace are never merely political issues but profoundly moral ones as well.[1]

I vividly remember the early days of this current Iraq war. Some Catholics who favored the administration's position actually attempted to persuade the Holy See to change its mind concerning its clear opposition to the war, even going so far as to send prominent Catholics to undertake a kind of "lobbying" effort in Rome.

It failed.

---

1. See the substantial and well-argued essay on this subject by Dr. William Cavanaugh on pp. 269–289 of the present volume. —Ed.

Next, some of these "neoconservative" Catholics began to raise arguments against the Church's opposition to the war, relying upon notions that they had assiduously rejected in the past! How odd it seemed to hear some of their number speak of the Church not having "competency" to speak upon such matters. That same line was the buzzword of their opponents in the latter's efforts to reject the Church's opposition to procured abortion and euthanasia. At the time, I felt like asking some of these Catholic pro- ponents of the war a simple question: "If Jesus were in our midst, would He have 'competency' to speak concerning this War?" The answer is clear. Of course! Well, He is in our midst, through His Church. He is still speaking.

Most people, both those who supported the war and those who opposed it, now agree that we cannot abandon the Iraqi people in their great hour of need, though what would constitute "abandonment" is of course open for discussion. The Holy See has clearly and repeatedly expressed its continuing concern for them. However, no accurate review of the position of the Pope or prominent leaders of the Catholic Church prior to the beginning of this war in Iraq can arrive at any conclusion other than this: *they clearly and absolutely opposed it.*

Was the decision to launch a "preemptive strike" against Iraq really the exercise of a "prudential judgment"? Or, was it a *poor decision* masquerading as prudence? Most nations seek to justify their military decisions after the fact. That is not the same thing as following a true Just-War analysis. Though it is obvious that the decision to go to war by legitimate authority is a matter of "prudential judgment," this decision to engage in *this war* was in fact *not prudent at all.*

Conclusion

In an article entitled "Hawks, Doves, and Pope John Paul II," in the August 12, 2002, edition of *America Magazine*, Father Drew Christiansen, S.J., a Senior Fellow of the Woodstock Theological Center at Georgetown University, observed:

> The just-war tradition is fast becoming a contested field of ideas in Catholic circles. At one extreme of this debate are peace activists like members of Pax Christi USA, who do not see any use for the traditional just-war theory. They can conceive of virtually no circumstances that would justify the use of military force.
>
> At the other extreme are the "enablers," especially politically conservative Catholic intellectuals. They form a permissive just-war school that would legitimate most uses of force contemplated by the U.S. government. . . . They are

skeptical, if not scornful, of applying just-war norms to limit the savagery of war.

In this debate, the middle may turn out to be the cutting edge. It is there we find people wrestling with the complexities of Church teaching, rather than simply overthrowing the tradition or using theology to bless war as an instrument of policy.

For example . . . conservatives like John Finnis and Germain Grisez are aiming to fashion a coherent, pro-life moral theology. In doing so, they have developed a more restrictive understanding of what constitutes a just war.

Another broad party in the middle consists of those who take a similarly stringent view of just-war principles. This group speaks of a "presumption" against the use of force and seeks to limit the scale of war by applying just-war criteria restrictively. . . .

John Paul stands at the heart of this debate. . . .

During and after the Persian Gulf War, the Holy Father repeatedly voiced his skepticism of war as a tool of international policy.

An updated and complete Catholic theology of war and peace, following John Paul II, must grapple with an array of components. These include the culture of death, the effects of violence, the usefulness of non-violence as well as just war, the need for justice through development, and the place of forgiveness in peacemaking. By that standard, the stale U.S. debates between pacifists and just warriors, and between less and more stringent just-war types, have very far to go."

I agree.

I still have the dream; I still believe that peace is possible; and I am not alone.

So did – and so does – the Vicar of Christ on earth.

A Higher Law: Conscience, Morality, and the Transcendent Vision

THE EDITORS' GLOSS: In keeping with the President's "you're either with us or against us" diktat, politicians and political commentators tend to focus on whether one supports or opposes America and its aims. The "left" has a reputation (though this is largely caricature) of opposing America's every move, confronting the "America-can-do-no-wrong" crowd with their own "America can do no right." It is these naysayers that Defense Secretary Donald Rumsfeld was responding to when he said recently that he's "not one who gets up every morning . . . looking for ways to prove that America is what's wrong with the world."

But this is another Bush-administration trick of responding to a straw man. Few on even the radical left oppose things merely because they're "American." Many do oppose what America *does* when it fails to account for the rights and aspirations of others (see Michael Scheuer's *Imperial Hubris* on this). Whether or not "America" is what's right or wrong with the world, certain of her *actions* – like the war in Iraq – are wrong in principle and detrimental to a good many people.

What's also wrong is a certain American*ism* (a cause of the myopia that has commentators and politicians assessing opposition to the war in terms of whether people like America or not). It is the contradiction at the heart of the American ideology, reducing much of American politics to a simple will to power. As heir of the French and English Enlightenments, "America" officially maintains that there is no ultimate truth that can be known and agreed upon as a basis for political action. Hilaire Belloc remarked that all political conflict is theological; America's theology is agnosticism, and its handmaiden skepticism. This sad fact explains how much of the world wonders in amazement when America "destroys the village in order to save it," bombs Iraq for "democracy," and sends people to Gitmo in the name of "freedom." If there is no truth or ultimate right and wrong, all bets are off, and the only truth is opposition to those who do cling to a fixed creed. Thus Andrew Sullivan maintains that the terror war is "a war of fundamentalism against faiths of all kinds that are at peace with freedom and modernity," and claims that we are "fighting for the universal principles of our Constitution." As he notes, revealingly, "What is really at issue here is the . . . principle of the separation of politics and religion."

Perhaps Bishop Richard Williamson put it best in his letter of January 2003: "Abandoning God has left a vacuum in the Western nations' lives, which cries out to be turned into a crusade against any enemy of Liberalism, Iraq being merely the present one."

17

Decadent, Belligerent, and Incorrigible
• • • • • • • • •
Prof. John Rao, D.Phil.

O NE OF THE innumerable myths still cherished by most Americans is that the United States is a young country with an embryonic, developing culture. A youthful, evangelical spirit is regularly cited as grounds for its energetic missionary activity on behalf of peace and freedom on the world plane. Understandable juvenile growing pains have often been used as a cover for excusing its past and present violations of natural law. Finally, periodic, sulky retreats into isolationism are frequently attributed to a shocked, childlike reaction to wickedness beyond the comprehension of this endearingly innocent geopolitical neophyte.

But myth, alas, is not always reality. And the sad reality is that the United States of America, founded in the period between 1776 and 1788, is no more representative of a fresh civilization than a unified Italy, independent since 1861, or the federal German Empire emerging ten years thereafter. The American Way is "new" only in the sense that a deadly sore appearing on the skin after a long maturing illness can be said to be new. The fresh sore, in this case, is actually the end result of an old history of decline. It makes a lengthy, snowballing decadence manifest and testifies not to healthy growth and maturation but approaching collapse and death. Yes, America can, perhaps, still move and shake the entire world through bursts of physical energy, as with the imperialist jingoism in which it now so thoughtlessly indulges. But this freneticism also portends impending doom, calling to mind the last, astonishingly vigorous movements of many of the moribund.

Applying such reflections to the Iraq war yields an obvious, ineluctable, though horrifying conclusion: that the conflict in Iraq is the feverishly belligerent act of an old, sick, and dying culture which has nevertheless deceived itself into thinking that it is overflowing with the sap of youth. Rich only in those youthful vices which are aggravated by a fall into second childhood, that dying culture displays an arrogantly juvenile indifference to both the nature and the magnitude of the tragedy the war has provoked. It is, therefore, not only decadent and belligerent but pathetically incorrigible. To appropriate the bitter judgment of Salvian, referring to a Roman Empire about to expire at the hands of problems which it lacked the will to grasp and refused even to recognize as dangers, "it dies and yet it smiles."

It is utterly impossible to understand what is really at play in the Iraqi conflict without devoting a good deal of time coming to grips with the character of the long-term disease from which this old geezer of a culture-in-second-childhood suffers. No mean feat indeed! For that malady involves a maddeningly complex union of two constituent elements: on the one hand, a medley of themes arising from Greco-Roman-Catholic civilization, naturalist philosophy, and heretical theology; and, on the other, the ideology of pluralism. Pluralism serves as the glue "pragmatically" holding together what are otherwise radically opposing world views, and prohibiting "practical" men from "wasting their time" seriously investigating the nature and terminal character of the sickness that it works to spread.

Western society was exposed to this bizarre illness beginning with the simultaneous revival of classicism, heresy and commerce in the High Middle Ages. The early stages of its infection were brilliantly catalogued by the French author Georges de Lagarde, in *La naissance de l'esprit laïque au déclin du Moyen Age*, written in 1934, but, unfortunately, never translated into English. It took many centuries for the disease that he clearly describes to come to full term, only revealing its most nefarious effects once pluralism was given the opportunity to suck the vitality from the most venerable cultures of the globe under the rubric of granting them the life that surpasseth all understanding. Allow me to use this article to explain in broad strokes the character of the two constituent elements of an initially purely Western disorder before returning briefly to the question of how this now plays its role in the current tragedy in the Middle East.

Greco-Roman-Catholic civilization. Orthodox Catholicism affirmed the value of Creation at the hands of a good God, who restated His love for nature, after Adam's sin, through the Incarnation and Christ's offer of Redemption. It drilled into the Western consciousness a religious awareness of the universe as an ordered, meaningful cosmos, one whose various natural and supernatural laws and authorities aided free human persons both in their daily fight against evil as well as in the struggle to perfect their unique individual dignity. In doing so, it called upon and drew the deepest consequences from everything in Greco-Roman culture which might assist Christianity in its labors, with Socratic philosophy taking pride of place at the top of the list. A Greco-Roman-Catholic alliance, emphasizing similar themes and goals, was thus firmly sealed.

Naturalism. Naturalism claims that only purely secular, "natural" tools can be employed to understand the character of this ordered, meaningful cosmos and the means of perfecting the distinct, free, individuals who inhabit it. It brooks no reference to a Catholic Creator God who is a permanent actor in the world of nature, and who offers fallen man a choice for or against supernatural Redemption. Paradoxically, many Christians, by the time of the Renaissance, aided the growth of naturalism. Christianity had brought the nature-affirming teachings of the Greeks and the Romans from out of the academic wilderness into the mainstream of political and social life. It had tried to consign the destructive lessons to which the bulk of the energies of the ancients were devoted to the rubbish heap of history. Enthusiastic Christian Humanists focused overwhelmingly on the positive achievements of the classical world which their own religion had raised to the fore. They so emphasized the intrinsic value of ancient culture as to help encourage a general overestimation of secular man and fallen nature's unaided capabilities. Thus, the admirable engine of nature, which actually needed the fuel of Faith to kick itself into proper motion, was treated as though it were flawless, self-propelling and self-sufficient.

Although the memory and the rhetoric of the Greco-Roman-Catholic alliance continued to exercise a powerful theoretical influence over Western minds and hopes, it was naturalism, in practice, that dominated our culture by the late eighteenth century. Very quickly, however, naturalism's own flaws began to become apparent. It could not keep the concepts of order and freedom in harmony with one another once it refused to recognize the reality of a sinfulness that might potentially wreak havoc with both. After all, if the perfect natural laws of the universe were praised, then the individual "freedom" of the human persons who supposedly could never sinfully disrupt them was reduced to a cipher. Each man became but a cog in a wheel, doomed to perform whatever tasks the Grand Machine of nature marked out for him. If, on the other hand, the unique dignity and "rights" of each sinless, free individual were underlined, then the natural order of the universe had to bend to whatever it was that the human person willed.

Enthusiasts for natural law and order or natural rights and freedom began to part ways. Moreover, to make matters worse, those intent upon rational investigation of the structure of the universe went on to produce a myriad of conflicting mechanical keys to understanding its order. Each of these proclaimed the enslavement of the human mind, soul, body, and will to its inviolable laws. Each was ready to readjust the kinks in the machinery of individual men who refused their assent to "obvious" truth. Each was intent on battling the others to death in constructing a peaceful world of meaning and progress. Meanwhile, those asserting the autonomy of the individual became more and more convinced that the thought and behavioral patterns of human persons were so unique as to justify boundless numbers of contradictory visions of the meaning and style of life. Anarchy was thus introduced into every discipline and discussion of public and private conduct. Social order was critically threatened in consequence.

Heresy, in the form of the ideas of medieval gnostic and millenarian sects, extreme nominalist philosophers, and the initial Protestant reformers, argued against both the value of nature as well as the freedom, dignity and potential perfection of the individuals inhabiting it. Nature, on the macro or micro level, was, for the heretic, the realm of chaos and egotistical struggle, a savage jungle where senseless power ruled supreme. God's realm was, of course, ordered and meaningful, but this could never be approached through the flawed natural tool of human Reason. Entry into its precincts was secured by a supernatural, anti-rational, fideistic (i.e., unexamined) Faith alone. Moreover, redeemed man always remained eternally stained by sin, his presence in Heaven made acceptable only under the cover of Christ's sacrifice, with no personal internal purification and transformation ever taking effect.

Heresy, even though it totally contradicted the secular optimism of naturalism, nevertheless encouraged its tendency to separate all discussion of the wicked world and the depraved individual from dialogue concerning the good and omnipotent God. In ridiculing the absurdity of the hunt for natural laws understanding and controlling what it considered to be essentially uncontrollable, irrational, passionate beings, it also helped explain (and support) the historical degeneration of naturalist society into hopeless confusion. What else could one expect from the cosmos but chaos? "Leave the universe in the gutter where it belongs," as one pious fundamentalist once told me. An orthodox Christian who abandons belief may still possess Reason and, with it, a trampoline from which to leap back even to spiritual wisdom; an anti-rational, fideist heretic who falls from grace has neither God nor nature to support him. And, in fact, many Protestant lands, subject to intense secularization from the 1700s onwards, were left with nothing logical standing between them and an atheistic, absurdist, anarchic vision of existence as a whole. In that vision, the lion does not lie down with the lamb, but necessarily devours him. Secularized ex-Protestants often accepted this dreary secular "truth" with the same irrational, fideist fervor with which they once embraced heretical religious doctrines.

Pluralism is the catalyst for merging together the contradictory themes of these three Western historical influences into a truly irresistible, degenerative, and ultimately globe-trotting disease. On the surface, it merely seems to outline a pragmatic program of peaceful control of the potential for violence emerging from orthodox/heretical divisions and the unraveling of naturalist secular society. What is more, it appears to do so with due deference to all the forces active in the society around it. Hence, like the Greco-Roman-Catholic heritage, pluralism claims to respect both law and freedom. As with embryonic naturalism, however, it also presumes that it must defend these goods without reference to supernatural religion, on the basis of secular constitutional, social, and psychological checks and balances alone. Finally, it does homage to the heretical belief in the total depravity of mankind and the absolute incomprehensibility of a fallen universe for two crucial purposes: to find a peculiarly effective *sinful* tool to harness the divisiveness stemming from any truly serious use of human freedom, and to mock any intellectual effort that might uncover the debasement, contradiction, and ultimate doom emerging from the employment of this instrument in political and social life.

Pluralism ultimately then comes up with the following recipe for protecting endangered order: a) the cynical encouragement of a "multiplication of factions" to make certain that there are so many individuals and groups "freely" active in society that no deeds can ever be strong or significant enough to accomplish – and thereby disturb – social order again; b) promotion of a self-censorship of "divisive" spiritual and intellectual expressions of individuality to the benefit of purely physical, economic initiatives more easily "integrated" into a "pragmatic" social commitment to increased production and consumption. Under this regimen, to take but one example, French-American Catholics would abandon dedication to their dangerously distinct philosophical and religious heritage in exchange for the freedom to open a unique *croissanterie* next to the falafel stand and the sushi bar on Peaceful Pluralist Avenue; and, c) a seizing and unceasing repetition of the traditional Western rhetoric of concern for individual freedom and dignity. This recurring imagery worked forever to associate pluralism with liberty, and to cover over the fact that the latter had, in reality, been stripped of all substantive intellectual and spiritual meaning.

Pluralism's *modus operandi* was suggested by Voltaire, outlined by James Madison in *The Federalist Papers*, and first seriously applied under the threatening conditions provided by an ever more religiously and ethnically diverse nineteenth and early twentieth century America. It has indeed had a truly uncanny history of seducing honest American supporters of the Greco-Roman-Catholic tradition, naturalism, and heresy into thinking that pluralism actually does create a "safe space" of order and security where all of them are free to preach and perfect their various convictions and customs. Amazing as it is to admit, this seduction has continued to be successful even when it has long become crystal clear that honest believers in absolutely anything and everything are required, in practice, to separate all external action from internal thought; that pluralism, its rhetoric notwithstanding, obliges them to live first as schizophrenics, and then as vandals dismantling their own internally "divisive" spiritual and intellectual forum.

How has it carried off a confidence game of such proportions? Through self-deification. Pluralism has made itself an object of worship, its three thematic sources all unwittingly providing it with assistance to allay fears, assuage consciences, cut one another down to size, and prevent any and all discussion of The System's claims to divinity. Pluralism utilizes those who take its pretense of providing freedom and order under the old Greco-Roman-Catholic rhetoric to heart to deny its anti-religious, naturalist character. Such men – conservatives – point with pride to the number of times the word "God" can be discovered in the writings of the founders of its Creed, ignoring the secularist definition that they give to their syncretist and absent Deity. On the other hand, pluralism turns openly to the very naturalists whom conservatives would abhor to insist upon its open-mindedness, scientific rationality, and hatred of hoary, medieval, orthodox religious superstition. Furthermore, it calls upon its legacy of anti-intellectual heretical thought, and uses it to produce a stream of fideistic doctrinal slogans about its obvious glories, to render its battlements untouchable. Pluralism's "fresh, new, vigorous approach to life," contrasted with the "dead end" hopelessness of an evil Old World, is thus presented to be understood by Faith Alone.

That Faith is preached in constitution-thumping revival style, accompanied by a "No Alternative Myth" emphasizing the dreadful consequences rejection of its credal demands would entail. If religious and intellectual divisiveness were not avoided, integration not promoted, and conflict not thereby diffused, the "No Alternative Myth" argues, the world would drown in a tidal wave of bloodshed and genocide. Waving the bloody flag of Fascism, the Second World War, and the Holocaust has proven to be so effective in support of the "No Alternative Myth," that pluralists struggle to make these historical events more current than any truly pressing contemporary news item; more central to the education of youth than basic reading, writing, and arithmetic.

But who is it that actually *has* gained, in practice, from the advance of this mad Western malady? The most committed and consistent criminals. Criminals have no problem working with a vision of nature as a savage jungle and individuals as depraved creatures. Nor are they troubled by the possible contradictions of a world view; why, they never expected life to make rational sense anyway. Moreover, the intelligent among them readily discover just how much pluralism's odd doctrine works to justify their stirring up and then democratically responding to the illicit and exaggerated passions of their fellow men. After all, people like themselves cause no acrimonious spiritual or intellectual debate; they can thus actually claim to contribute to the construction of a peaceful social order. In fact, they can even join pluralism's authorities in working over nobler "disruptive" elements preventing people from getting "what they really want." Strong willed and unscrupulous, they labor more effectively than others to wean men from serious religious, mechanist, or individualist speculations that can trouble daily life. They work to unify them in the common mud of debased human fears and desires. Once they have been permitted to degrade the rest of the population, they can then feel justified in perpetrating the seduction that has responded to its "deepest free, natural wishes." Yes, massive chains stimulating artificial lusts, multinational companies creating genetically altered foods, drug gangs, and mafias may still provoke bloody, unsettling turf wars. Still, whether their respective CEOs understand it or not, all these nevertheless work together for the shared purpose of reducing the bulk of mankind to a universal, low-level, materialist culture, uniform in its drab needs, both licit and illicit. As I noted in an earlier article in the Winter 2002 issue of *Latin Mass Magazine,* referring to nineteenth-century French Catholic critiques of budding pluralist "culture":

> Louis Veuillot's comments regarding a unified, boring culture centered around a base understanding of man and nature appear as germane today as when they were uttered a century and a half ago: "There will no longer be different places or climates, or any curiosity anywhere. . . . Everywhere the same language will be spoken. . . . The old diversity will be a memory of the old liberty. . . . Everything will be done in the image of the main city of the Empire

and of the World" (L. Veuillot, *Mélanges*, Paris, 1933, viii, 369). . . . Pluralism offers the criminal purveyors of passions a chance to tempt good men away from goals that might rock the social boat, and the opportunity to pose as the best representatives of freedom and statesmanlike concern for tranquility as they do so. It gives them *carte blanche* to turn Original Sin into a political and social system, dominated by the greatest sinners, but passed off as something glorious. To paraphrase Chateaubriand, referring to Talleyrand and Fouché, pluralism gives us the spectacle of Liberty and Order walking arm and arm with Vice and Crime.

Only one type of person places a certain obstacle in the path of the ordinary criminals working "competitively" together to build the Drab Society: the pluralist zealot. Remember that pluralism destroys all serious *thought*, but not the kind of heretical, unexamined, fideistic *belief* that it itself relies upon for its own defense. It retains a passion for ideological faith, and thus exalts the zealot, whose life is dedicated to an evangelization which may not always suit the ordinary criminal's basic goals. The ordinary villain or purveyor of passion does not necessarily *believe* in pluralism; he simply finds it eminently useful to the pursuit of his own passions or the plying of his wares. Nevertheless, he is bound by a golden chain to support the fundamentals of the system that gives him this opportunity to pilfer, pervert, and prosper. This means that he has tied himself to the thinkers who invented that system, its basic structure, those who now honestly and zealously believe in it, and the rhetoricians who provide him with the arguments that he uses to justify his own base rapine. In consequence, the ordinary criminal takes on something of the character of the zealot himself, though in a fashion that can, in the long run, be counterproductive to profitable crime.

Similarly, the pluralist zealot does not necessarily *believe* in crime. Nevertheless, his system, and his own uncontrollably passionate pursuit of an irrational vision, encourage it. Furthermore, the criminals that pluralism produces are eminently useful to the zealot. They help him to "evangelize" pluralism in underworld ways that his own personal intellectual inhibitions or continued traditionalist hang-ups might prevent him from pursuing. In consequence, he takes on something of the character of the criminal himself, though in a fashion that can, in the long run, be counterproductive and embarrassing to his honest zealotry.

Disruptions caused by twentieth century ideologies, wars, and global migrations have created a situation wherein a multiplicity of antithetical world views and cultures now exist in the same time and space on a worldwide plane. Imperial America has sought to confront and control the attendant potential for chaos by an application, everywhere, of its own beloved pluralist precepts. Hence, the transformation of the long-festering Western malady into a universal plague promoting the global union of criminality and zealotry, with all its strengths and all its mind-boggling contradictions.

American pluralism has had enormous success in devastating European culture and reducing it to the plaything of capitalist criminals, purveyors of international crime, and pluralist bureaucratic, educational, and artistic zealots. Its greatest European victory came when its two most serious opponents – Roman Catholicism and Marxism-Leninism – almost entirely cracked and self-destructed under its seductive pressures.

One major enemy alone remained to be broken in the years after the Second Vatican Council and the collapse of the Soviet Union if pluralism were to have the opportunity to sing a song of total triumph: the Arab world. Not only was this world dangerous as home to a competing, unexamined, fideistic Faith as effectively irrational as pluralism – Islam; it also hosted fervent opposition to one of the most dangerously criminal forces operating internationally in union with America: the State of Israel. Hence, the need to bestow the blessings of peace and freedom upon Islamic Kingdoms, Emirates, and Republics, and secular Arab nationalist states alike. These, too, had to be taught what liberty and order really meant: nothing more than an eternal shopping spree in a free Supermarket of Criminally Zealous Ideas and Zealously Criminal Merchandise.

Now let us finally return to Iraq and the War on Terrorism that has fraudulently been linked to it. We need do so only briefly. What is it that really lies behind the current conflict? Commitment to the spread of that long-festering Western malady which has already sickened and doomed American culture. What does this specifically mean? That criminal passions fueled the conflict, both those of ordinary villains – the Halliburtons of the world – and of fideist zealots – the gnostic Straussians and neoconservatives, in union with the enthusiasts for the creation of a Greater Israel, and their apocalypse-obsessed, evangelical fellow-travelers. For, once again, the "free society" infected with the Western malady is always one in which the strongest wills of the unrestrainedly passionate predominate. Iraq has been ripped to shreds because its ravaging was willed by strong men who, in a proper social order, would be confined to prison cells or mad houses. Unfortunately, as things now stand, these forces are the ones that silence and abuse the innocent and the sane.

Crooks and zealots favorable to the Iraqi adventure proudly and understandably fly the flag of a pluralism that works so relentlessly to their advantage. An appeal to the all-encompassing pluralist bear hug enables them to abolish the Aristotelian principle of non-contradiction and say anything that they wish in favor of their escapade. It gives them the arguments for claiming, as circumstances dictate, that they are engaged in a crusade for true religion *and* secularism; a struggle for a peaceful, global, multicultural society *and* the protection of Western (religious? naturalist? heretical?) civilization; a battle for universal freedom, justice, and economic opportunity, *but also* for hard-nosed industrial *Realpolitik*, and the victory of masculine martial firmness over soft, feminine, pacifist gullibility. Pluralism's self-deification principle offers the propagandist an obvious retort to those calling up objective, factual evidence to criticize their position. Such critics lack Faith! For Faith alone proves infallibly both the altruism and the pragmatism of the pluralist position in classical, Protestant, "gospel-paradox" fashion. Any appeal to rational discourse is dismissed as illustrating either the lunatic naiveté of the idiot savant or the cynical rejection of Amazing Grace. *Pour comblé de misère*, the "No Alternative Myth" is dredged up to show that the detractor of pluralism is probably a Nazi yearning for the chance to drown the efforts of the paladins of world progress in a bath of blood. Why, his anti-Israeli stance on its own cannot help but prove his National Socialist sympathies.

America, propelled into an unjust conflict in Iraq through the work of these most effective carriers of the Western malady, does, indeed, offer the model of a decadent and belligerent culture. Alas, barring divine intervention, it also appears to be incorrigible in its devotion to the sickness that is killing it, blind to any serious effort fundamentally to reform itself. Why should this be the case? Because, as noted above, old and decadent American culture does indeed display all the characteristics of a second childhood. Thus, it does, in one sense, possess a kind of irresistible "youthful" vigor. Vitality comes, however, in the form of that irreformable attachment to parochial, personal flaws which is all too reminiscent of a juvenile mentality, and all too intensified when compounded by senile dementia. A childlike but senile determination to hold onto and play with toys appears as though it will drive this dying beast until the day of its uncomprehending annihilation.

In this regard, it reminds one of David Hume on his death bed, playing out, before Boswell, that indifference towards the drama of life and the tragedy of death which he had long felt and indulged. How could such a man, convinced as he was that troublesome questions regarding Truth, Goodness, and Beauty might be shaken off by the diversion of a hot bath or a billiard game, be awakened to the magnitude of existence by the mere approach of his own end? How could someone whose embrace of a vision of pointless existence had, in effect, amounted to a life long fling with euthanasia, be taken aback by contemplation of the yawning tomb? He was already dead, long before the actual physical event. Analogously, how could a culture with a lasting dedication to a substanceless intellectual and spiritual life come to terms with the drama of its own sins and imminent doom? On what basis could it build a death-bed conversion?

Hence, despite all the disasters – the turning of "friendly" Shiites into implacable enemies, the excuse given for further oppression of the Palestinian people, the stimulation offered for strengthening of that integral Islam which the Iraqi adventure was supposed to have controlled, and the diversion of attention and resources from *real* dangers to the legitimate security of the United States – the federal government insists on happily maintaining its bear hug with the criminals and zealots and the disease that they carry. As with the belligerent powers in the First World War, much of incorrigible America is digging its feet in the ground for the duration. Pointless, suicidal battle must proceed over the edge and into the abyss. Thus, a recent Bush advertisement gushes over the entry of Iraq and Afghanistan onto the list of "free nations" competing in the Olympic Games, and argues that the sun is shining brighter globally than ever before; that, in every day and in every way, things are getting just a little bit better. The ordinary criminal element that *really* benefits from Iraqi/Afghani "freedom" grows ever more pious in its appeal to pluralist propaganda, and anguished over the unthinkable alternative to the defeat of his altruist position. Similarly, the zealous pluralist becomes more villainous in the lies that he will tolerate about the war and its conduct, and the company that he will keep to defend his program. All in all, it seems that the representatives of both wings of unchained human passion will pursue their work of mutual interaction and obstructionism until their joint destruction. But how many innocent people and how much of civilized society will their incorrigibility bring down with them?

Unfortunately, this unwillingness to correct oneself is no less evident among most of those who are by now upset with an illegitimate conflict, and wish to back away from it. Unlike the great sinners thrown into tragic despair and true repentance who are found in the novels of Dostoyevsky, the little men of pluralist society are incapable of grasping the nature and magnitude of the damage the games that they have played has done, and what this damage requires of them in terms of penance. A true spirit of penitence would involve a thorough-going self-analysis clarifying the terminal character of the Western malady, a massive breast-beating over evils perpetrated, and then a headlong flight from pluralism. However, this is not what one sees in the American confessional. Critics of the war may stop playing the Iraqi War Game, but only to pick up another pluralist-inspired pastime; one thought to be "truer" to the basic goodness of The System. The new game invariably turns out to reflect the same lack of comprehension of the depth of the hole that pluralism leaves in the human heart. It does nothing to remedy the evil that can easily veer back to imperialist adventuring when the mood strikes once more. Thus, to take but one example, many who reject what they recognize to be a foolhardy enterprise in Iraq replace this with a "truly pluralist" effort to dialogue with evangelical Islam, with the purpose of rendering it peacefully substanceless and meaningless. Meanwhile, the number of American converts to Islamic fideism grows by quantum leaps, especially, and dangerously, among the prison population to which a dying culture has nothing more to say or offer. One wonders how long it will be until even those outside the prison gates who are nominally free fill the emptiness of pluralist life with the meat of Islam? If pluralism collapses, it will be a religion of a willful, irrational God, like Islam, that will logically pick up the pieces. For pluralist fideism has trained the entire American public to succumb easily to unexamined faiths in general.

The Western malady has been able to prosper globally chiefly because of pluralism's tremendous success in manipulating rhetoric on its behalf. It is, indeed, a master of murk, confusing honest believers in all manner of opposing ideas that it somehow is truly "on their side"; that it can create one, unified, peaceful society out of many diverging world views, *e pluribus, unum*. But pluralism offers men stones instead of bread. Roman Catholicism provides a substantive unity in Christ out of which a plethora of legitimate natural differences do emerge, and brilliantly so, *ex uno, plures*. Would that Catholics, at least, would cease to be duped by the grotesque caricature of itself that pluralism ultimately is and always will be. Roman Catholic withdrawal of support from this monster would be an impressive and valuable first nail in its coffin. It would give hope to the Iraqi people. It would win us back our own trampled dignity and abused intellects. Most importantly, it would help to prepare us for the inevitable assault on the remnants of Roman Catholic "divisiveness" – apparent in continued pockets of opposition to abortion, homosexuality, and cultural genocide – which is bound to follow from total pluralist victory in Iraq. The ever more frantic criminal and zealot carriers of the Western malady will, by that point, be ready to wipe up any and all counterrevolutionary partisans still active in the Homeland. If die we must, let us adopt a bit of the current jingoist language, and as least go with our boots on.

THE EDITORS' GLOSS: Though much lip service is paid to the just-war doctrine, in order to mean anything it must be applied. As circumstances change, the doctrine must adapt, though not in the sense that the doctrine should be watered-down or modified lest in the passage of time it should fail to account for "new realities," and risk becoming irrelevant (as Michael Novak maintains). On the contrary, the doctrine must, if anything, be expanded and made more profound so as to set proper limits to methods of waging war that were subjects only of science fiction stories just decades ago. The Irish priest Fr. Denis Fahey used to say that "the world should conform to Our Lord, not He to it." In like manner, it is not just-war theory which must adapt to the "new" world, but rather the new world that must submit and respect the limits posed by timeless moral truth.

Dr. Hickson provides a hint of some of the new and frightening realities that just-war doctrine must grapple with. Honesty would compel men and women of good will to admit that a strict and fair reading of just-war doctrine condemns many of these new forms and methods of war. Also condemnable are the huge standing armies and mountains of ordnance and equipment maintained by today's modern nations – our own included – extant not for defense against real threats, but rather supporting postures of mutual, international offense. One need only read the last numbers of the American *National Security Strategy* to see how far we are from taking to heart the dictum of Pius XI, who wrote in a letter of April 7, 1922: "It must not be forgotten that the best guarantee of tranquility is not a forest of bayonets, but mutual confidence and friendship."

C H A P T E R
18

Setting Just Limits to New Methods of Warfare
• • • • • • • • • •
Robert Hickson, USA (ret.), Ph.D.

I N LIGHT OF the history of warfare – both the discovery and development of new armaments and the passionate use of "armed ideologies" – it is a moral certitude that unexpected new combinations of advanced science will be applied technocratically in future forms of war. These new weaponized technologies – in both lethal and non-lethal forms – will also, most probably, be used in police work, peace operations, and "neo-imperial constabulary actions" along the borders of Empire, on the ambiguous frontiers of conflicting and alien civilizations and religious cultures. It will be very difficult to set and keep humane moral limits in such a fevered dialectical context of ideology and technology. The long-developing and self-destructive movement towards "total war" – or what some recent Chinese military thinkers have called "unrestricted warfare" – will take us to the foundations of our existence.

A strategic-minded British general saw this with piercing clarity more than a half-century ago. Almost five years before his death – after a long, active, and reflective life – Major General J.F.C. Fuller (1878–1966) published *The Conduct of War, 1789-1961: A Study of the Impact of the French, Industrial, and Russian Revolutions on War and Its Conduct*.[1] It is a far-sighted and paradigmatic book, which General Fuller himself was inclined to consider as the most important he had written.[2]

It examined the long-growing and destructively cumulative developments in society towards new forms of war – forms that were increasingly unlimited, ambiguous, and intentionally undefined; and, hence, more and

---

1. J. F. C. Fuller, *The Conduct of War, 1789–1961: A Study of the Impact of the French, Industrial, and Russian Revolutions on War and Its Conduct* (New York: Da Capo Press, 1992, first published in 1961).

2. This view was conveyed by General Fuller to his friend and admirer, Brian Holden Reid, author of the book, *J. F. C. Fuller: Military Thinker* (New York: St. Martin's Press, 1987).

more coldly abstract and impersonal and altogether conducive to barbarism and civilizational disaster. Moreover, he saw these great evils growing within the feverish atmosphere and manipulated mass-psychology of "democratic governance," further exacerbated by revolutionary new techniques and purposes of total wars that required the humiliating unconditional surrender of a defeated people. That "absolute surrender" of a whole people (not just of their government) was preparatory to their protracted "re-education" (*Umerziehung* in German). It was as if a defeated criminal nation (*ein Tätervolk*) needed social-engineering or a demiurgic transformation into something "new," which was often then euphemistically called "nation-building."

For example, General Fuller's important Chapter XI, entitled "Soviet Revolutionary Warfare," speaks about the Soviets' deceitful use of "Peace as an Instrument of Revolution." This could also be applied today to new forms of American "Messianic Democracy" and its policies abroad of so-called "creative destruction" and "democratic transformation" abroad.

Based upon the twin premises that there are no technical solutions to moral problems, and that whoever is himself morally and spiritually uprooted tends to uproot others, we shall examine in this essay the moral difficulty of setting and preserving properly proportional limits in the just conduct of modern war.

It is certainly the case that setting *moral* limits is always a profoundly human problem, and so is the keeping of proper limits in war – especially under the stress of war. And here is where the self-understanding provided by the virtues becomes important. For it is a function of the four cardinal virtues – prudence, justice, fortitude, and temperance – to foster wise limits and to develop dispositions or habits of promptness, constancy, and fitting moderation. There are, however, no "techniques" that can be truly substituted for the virtues, which are themselves ordered perfections of common human potentialities (powers or capacities). And the virtues themselves presuppose human free will and voluntariness, and, as a consequence, moral responsibility and moral accountability.

Setting just limits in the matter of going to war (*ad bellum*) and in the matter of the conduct and fitting conclusion of war (*in bello*) is, indeed, a great challenge to our intellectual and moral life, especially amidst the changing conditions and experimental atmosphere of modern science and technology. The French, Industrial, and Bolshevik Revolutions, so keenly analyzed by General Fuller, have disposed us more and more towards "total war." But applied modern science now goes even further.

For example, if a country decides to use, as an offensive weapon, a "computer network attack" against an opponent, what constitutes a legitimate *military* target? Moreover, in long-range "strategic information warfare," what constitutes a licit military target? Can one attack an enemy's financial institutions or stock market? Who is a combatant and who is a noncombatant in the new field of "modern information warfare," which according to an unclassified definition of the U.S. National Security Agency (NSA), entails "disruption, destruction, or deception in information systems"? And how does one know when one is even under attack in "strategic information warfare"? What, indeed, are the "indications and warnings" of an actual or impending assault? What is our criterion of judgment so as to aid our just response according to the principles of discrimination and proportionality?

To shed further light on some of these matters, we may well apply the concept of General Fuller's finely differentiated book, not only thereby to illuminate certain contemporary developments in warfare, but also to anticipate its likely future forms. Just as the science and technology of the Industrial Revolution was resourcefully applied to warfare, so, too, will our own more advanced (and less respectful) culture of science and technology be further applied to war – for example, in the military-strategic application of the "information sciences," and of neuroscience, psycho-neurolinguistics, biotechnology, nanotechnology, micro-encapsulation, and robotics – and *often* in combination or by way of "consilience" (which is the more *technical* concept for "combination" used by Professor E.O. Wilson, the emeritus Harvard sociobiologist). Just imagine how difficult it will be to set and to keep humane, moral limits in the application to warfare of "the Revolution in Molecular Biology," especially when its subtle means of manipulation in genetic engineering are applied against soft economic targets such as crops, livestock, and vulnerable agricultural infrastructure.

Consider, for example, how new methods of direct and *indirect* strategic warfare could be applied, not only against the "soft agricultural targets" of a prosperous and peaceful nation, but also against the illegal drug crops of certain "narco-democracies" and their para-militaries (or well-armed, narco-criminal organizations). To what extent would a camouflaged, subversive attack on the three main illegal drug crops (poppy, coca, marihuana) be a legally and morally permissible form of warfare, even as a new form of *biological* warfare or "biological police work"? Or, would this subtle form of indirect subversion be considered by the "narco-trafficantes" (and their money-launderers) as an act of war – at least an act of economic or financial warfare – that would provoke their reprisals, even their reckless vengeance? For example, what if these foreign "narco-trafficantes" were in turn to attack the United States' geographically concentrated (but not very well protected) veterinary breed stocks of pigs or cattle and the like? If there were such a reprisal, it would certainly be exponentially destructive of the American economy and its international trade.

And let us consider another trenchant example: the ambiguous phenomenon of "bio-remediation." Since bio-remediation is now not only permissible and legal, but also warmly approved, even by the global Green Movement, we may now unexpectedly face a new and dangerous dual-use technology.

Because bio-remediation has greatly helped in environmental clean up and the dissolution of large amounts of normally insoluble trash, we are much less cautious about its potential for misuse. Bio-remediation makes use of very potent and specially engineered micro-organisms, which are very effective in cleaning up the contamination from large oil slicks or spills, as well as in helping to dissolve the almost intractable amount of world trash and other forms of contaminated waste.

However, these same, very potent solvents of trash and of oil spills could also be put to other uses: for example, as an "anti-materièl biological weapon" against private or commercial vehicles, or against buildings or other forms of a society's critical infrastructure. How does one defend against such actual or potential threats? How does one even speak about them without producing what we are purportedly trying to defend against, namely moral paralysis and inaction, or a self-sabotaging sense of futility and despair? These are indeed very difficult matters, which take us to the deeper roots of our common life together in this fragile and vulnerable, and often precarious, world.

The use or abuse of bio-remediation depends upon the intention and the moral purpose of the user. Bio-remediation certainly is an equivocal "dual-use" or "multiple-use" capacity. But how should one – how could one – even legislate against its potential, easily performed, misuse? Indeed, there are no technical solutions to moral problems. And there are no litigious solutions to moral problems. (As the Greek dramatist, Aristophanes, saw many years ago during the tragic Peloponnesian War (431–404 B.C.), a society which primarily relies upon *litigious sanctions alone* is deeply disordered, decadent, and doomed.)

In more concrete terms, let us imagine that the U.S Government had the hostile desire to go after a belligerent foreign leaders's private bank accounts, which are located in a third country that is far away from the one he currently rules. For example, imagine that a Serbian leader had bank accounts on the divided Greco-Turkish island of Cyprus, in neutral Switzerland, and in one or more of the African or Caribbean "offshore islands." Would any of the bank accounts of this leader – or those of any of his close friends – be a proper (i.e., legitimate) military target? Would this not be a special way of influencing this foreign leader (and his friends) in an efficient and "non-bloody" manner, by snatching or destroying their cherished personal (and perhaps ill-gotten) assets? Should the United States be allowed – or allow itself – with or without the permission of its "coalition partners," to use its "special technical operations" and subtle "information warfare tools" against such soft financial targets in a non-cooperative and non-consenting third country? Even in a historically neutral country, like Switzerland, which has very strict bank privacy laws and protections of anonymity?

What are the morally and legally permissible Rules of Engagement (ROE)? And who sets them, and by what authority? For example, if the United States is acting as part of a coalition, who finally establishes the just "rules of engagement" in a *timely* way – and on what grounds? What are the criteria and standards of judgment? Moreover, may one country in the coalition – a more technologically advanced country, for example – take the initiative to operate unilaterally? Or, would going after a foreign leader's civilian bank accounts be, indeed, a "war crime"?

That is to say, may one country's "technological crown jewels," i.e., its special technical operations (STO), be used against an enemy leader's *personal* "crown jewels"? Or is this form of attack another promiscuous opening to "unrestricted warfare," indeed a further development of self-sabotaging "total war"?

Furthermore, if, in waging modern war as part of a coalition of multicultural allies, the United States will soon be legally and politically *required* to establish and sustain interoperability with its less technologically sophisticated partners, what then? Will the U.S. – *should* the U.S. – have to "dim down" and "dumb down" its own sophisticated technological capacities in order to be more co-operative and "inter-operative"? But, if the U.S. "dumbs down," can it then reliably fight with the same precision and combat efficiency, and with the same discriminating care for an enemy's *non-combatant* population and other *non-military* targets? On the premise that "we fight the way we train," how, therefore, should the United States train? Should we train for "coalition warfare" with our more unsophisticated, low-tech, multi-cultural (or multi-religious) partners? However, if we "dumb down" too much, we will then become more un-coordinated, disarticulated, and clumsy, if not effectively paralyzed or catatonic.

But if the U.S. does not "dumb down" its capacities, but, rather, tries to operate most efficiently, humanely, and discriminatingly, it will probably be seen as operating with "arrogant unilateralism" – not only by its enemies, but also by its coalition partners. Indeed, the emerging "American Imperium" will be then regarded more and more as a "rogue superpower" which intends to inflict upon others its own essentially unaccountable ROE; and to claim special immunities from criminal prosecution, for example, at the International Criminal Court. (Indeed, the United States, like China, does not at all endorse, and has emphatically not ratified, the International Criminal Court as it now stands, because of its arguably promiscuous and unbounded claims for retroactive legal jurisdiction in "war crimes" and other acts of purported criminality.)

Under modern conditions of war and peace, moreover, there is an unmistakable "seam" between war and criminality. This was true historically of the relationship – or seam – between piracy and irregular (or unconventional or privateer) naval warfare, as with the British operations against the Spanish Empire. Are "privateers" pirates, or unconventional "special operations forces" of a naval power?

As a contemporary example of this "seam" between war and criminality, let us consider what might happen if the Colombian "narco-trafficantes" are found to be using nuclear submarines, and operating off the coast of California in order to ship their drugs into the Western Hemisphere. What if these nuclear submarines are not operated by Colombian crews, but by foreign mercenary crews (e.g., Russians)? Is this a matter for law-enforcement agencies alone, or is it also a matter of national security, thereby requiring the actual or potential engagement, and the permanent attentiveness, of our armed forces – including our own naval Special Operations Forces?

And there is a further challenge. Given the new missions of the U.S. Northern Command (which includes NORAD – the former North American Aerospace Defense Command – and therefore our Canadian allies, as well as many of our own new "space assets"), to what extent is it permissible for the Commanding Officer of Northern Command (a four-star general or admiral) to conduct military-intelligence operations *within* his own assigned (and presumably legitimate) "Area of Responsibility" (AOR), since most of his AOR is within the continental United States? Can he, for example, legitimately use the National Security Agency (NSA) *domestically*, even with a cover from the FBI?

That is to say, to what extent is such a military commander still restricted by the strict prohibitions of the U.S. Constitution concerning *domestic* military and intelligence operations? And how far should he be limited or hampered in his newly assigned military and counter-terrorist missions? For it is indispensably important to a military commander that he not be "blind" or "deaf" about what is happening in his assigned AOR, especially when he is expected, *and obligated*, to conduct sensitive military operations within that same territorial (or geographical) area. This is a very serious matter. Like reality, it will not go away, even when we stop thinking about it.

There is a further difficulty for a military commander today when faced with the phenomenon of terrorism. To what extent is terrorism itself *an act of war* – indeed, an act of irregular, subversive, "asymmetrical" warfare – as distinct from an *act of criminality?* And what are the military commander's proper ROE, especially on U.S. territory, as in the case of the assigned missions of Northern Command, whose headquarters are in Colorado Springs, Colorado? How is a country to have national security under the conditions of modern technology and travel without becoming an asphyxiating, intrusive police state? Modern criminal syndicates and para-military "terrorist networks," for example, often have very sophisticated encryption systems (as well as deceptive new forms of "stegonography") that, perhaps, only NSA can detect and break!

Setting and keeping just limits in the combat against terrorism is also made difficult by the abstractness and equivocal nonspecificity of the term. Terrorism is certainly much more undefined than, for example, the strategic and psychological method of German warfare known as *"Blitzkrieg."* In World War II, however, it would have been very strange indeed if we had called our intervention a "Global War on *Blitzkrieg.*" So, too, it is strange and confusing to speak now of a "Global War on Terrorism" (GWOT). For terrorism, like *Blitzkrieg*, is a *method* and strategy of warfare – and terrorism itself is a form of political struggle and *psychological* warfare. But, we may ask, how is one ever going to defeat "psychological warfare" or the *method* of "terrorism"? And how will we know we have won – what is our measure of victory? Conversely, how will we know whether we have lost, or whether we even *seem* to be losing? What are our proper criteria and standards of judgment? Furthermore, what *kind* of war is this "war against terrorism"? Carl von Clausewitz profoundly observed that *the most important question* to be soberly asked and honestly answered before one deliberately enters into a war – or after one unexpectedly discovers himself already at war – is, "What is the *kind* of war we are in"? For it is true that if someone is at war with you – even if you don't know it – you're at war! Reality is that which does not go away, even when you stop thinking about it.

So in this purported GWOT, who is the enemy? What are we trying to protect, and why? What can we afford to lose, and how much will it cost us? Furthermore, what is our measure of "cost" – and not just of the *material* cost, but also of the *moral* cost, and the long-term *spiritual* cost?

Moreover, one cannot evaluate the appropriateness of one's means towards a specific and just end when one does not have any clarity about the end itself, or the objective one is pursuing. What, for example, is the specific objective – the specific end – of this GWOT, and what are the most appropriate and well-disciplined *means* towards this end? To what extent, for example, will covert, preemptive, counter-terrorist operations (hence preventative, aggressive "interdictions") further conduce to "total war"?

In the long and articulate Western doctrinal tradition of just war, it is essential and indispensable to have, first of all, clear, specific, and finite aims in order to evaluate whether or not a particular war is morally just. If these aims are undefined, vague, or even intentionally equivocal and ambiguous, then one cannot rationally measure how one's chosen means are conducive to achieving those ends. How can one measure the rightness and the efficacy of one's means for attaining a good end when the end itself is often so suspiciously – even irrationally – undefined? Especially when that end is remote, receding, changing, and very vaguely open-ended? Such a capriciously amorphous end appears to be a method of evasion, and may constitute what the Germans lucidly call *"eine Flucht nach vorne"* ("a fleeing forward"). Such an evasion of hard thinking and clarity is an act of grave irresponsibility, if not also an intrinsic act of irrationality.

It is, in any case, hard to pass the test of a just war, to meet *all* of the criteria. It is even harder to pass the test when the test keeps changing. That is to say, when the criteria themselves are ambiguously and equivocally manipulated, and when we employ the presumptuous and dishonest "shifting-standards" approach, i.e., applying a laxer standard to ourselves, and a stricter standard to others.[1] It is an act of cynicism, indeed, a cyni-

---

1. See the forceful discussion by Noam Chomsky, on pp. 43–59 of the companion to the present volume, *Neo-CONNED! Again*, of the (sadly) all-too-typically American approach to foreign affairs that has employed a dual standard – one for America and one for its enemies – in pursuit of its aims.—Ed.

cal flippancy; and it is always a temptation (an alluring incentive to evil and to consequent disorder) to respond to the stresses of war by saying, with a Machiavellian smirk: "Well, if you can't pass the test, change the test!" Yet it is a temptation to say just that: "If we can't pass the test, we'll change the test." (A temptation wouldn't be a temptation if it weren't attractive!) Our current GWOT has provided an example of, and altogether too much "maneuver room" for, such cynical manipulations of language. And it has led to our self-sabotaging over-extensions of self-deception and blinding intellectual pride, whereby we may soon be further "strutting to our confusion."

For example, by attacking Iraq the U.S. has actually aided Osama bin Laden. If he is still alive (perhaps somewhere in Pakistan or western, Muslim-permeated China), he must be very happy about how the United States took the "bait" and helped him radicalize the Muslim world against us. By our attacking Iraq and removing the regime of the secular Arab Ba'athists, the U.S., it would seem, aided and abetted Osama bin Laden's long-range plans. Indeed, the U.S. has effectively acted as a proxy force – though perhaps unwittingly – to advance the military strategic and grand-strategic plans of bin Laden and his collaborators. The United States' preemptive intrusion into Iraq has fomented a global Islamist insurgency against the United States and its allies. It is now likely that the United States is even more hated and despised in the Muslim world than the Israelis, and we are also perceived to be more vulnerable to attack.

Furthermore, as a result of our "GWOT," in combination with our aggressive war against Iraq and our precarious occupation, the United States is now even more centrifugally over-extended abroad and at home. And we are thereby more multifariously vulnerable to a wide range of "asymmetrical attacks" by way of reprisal and vengeance. The Muslims know that if they do certain things to Israel directly, Israel will turn Mecca and Medina into dust! The Muslim world, however, does not fear such desecrating responses or vengeful reprisals from the United States.

Indeed, the United States is perceived by many in the Muslim world (as well as in China) to be truly weak and incapable of long-range, sustained operations. In Fritz Kraemer's memorable words, the United States is perceived to have the problem of "provocative weakness" – i.e., we are so weak (or are *perceived* to be so weak) that we are provocative to others! Just as China has long called the United States a "Paper Tiger," so, too, we are seen to be a "Rogue Superpower," but *with clay feet.*

Such a vulnerable strategic and moral position, whether actually or only seemingly so, will likely make it more difficult for the United States to set just limits in the conduct of its various wars and expeditionary interventions. Moreover, to the extent that the increasingly secularized, feverishly messianic, but post-Christian and apostate United States wages large-scale "cultural warfare," or engages in the "clash of civilizations," against a growing, global Islamist insurgency, it will be even more difficult for us to set and to keep just limits both in our initiation and in our conduct of war. Many latent religious (or ideological) passions will be inflamed in combination with dangerous new forms of high-technology weapons.

Such a war will likely be a long-range religious war – and not just a "Hundred-Years War" – at least on the Muslim side. And if someone is at war with you – especially if he is in a religious war with you – even if you do not know it, you *are* at war! Remember, reality is that which does not go away even if you stop thinking about it. (Trotsky is supposed to have said: "You might not be interested in war, but war is very interested in you!") An increasingly secularized American political culture, moreover, cannot easily take the measure of foreign religious cultures or "world-views" – an incapacity which might produce very tragic results.

The cultivation of the four traditional cardinal virtues – both intellectual and moral virtues – may at least alleviate the grave intellectual astigmatisms of the United States in its current grand-strategic vulnerability.

Also by way of strategic anticipation, one wise way to set and to keep limits in the conduct of war – whether one consciously chooses to enter into war or finds oneself already at war – is to cultivate the largely forgotten and *often misrepresented* first cardinal virtue of *prudence* (in Latin, *Prudentia*). This indispensable intellectual and moral virtue is rooted in "the knowledge of reality," and no better introduction can be found to it than Josef Pieper's little book, entitled, *Prudence*.[1]

As Dr. Pieper says:

> To begin with, only the prudent man can be brave. Fortitude [i.e., the third cardinal virtue] without prudence is *not* fortitude. . . . To mention fortitude and prudence in the same breath seems in a measure to contradict modern man's notion of prudence and also of fortitude. This is partially due to the fact that current usage does not designate quite the same thing by "prudence" as classical theology understood by *prudentia* [i.e., the virtue of far-sighted, practical wisdom] and *discretio* [i.e., intellectual discernment, tact, and *disciplined* discretion]. *The term "prudence" has come to mean rather the slyness*

1. Richard and Clara Winston, trans., (London: Faber and Faber, Ltd., 1960).

*which permits the cunning and "shrewd" tactician to evade any dangerous risk
to his person, and thus escape injury and even the possibility of injury. To us,
prudence seems to be the false "discretion" and "cool consideration" conjured
up by the coward in order to be able to shirk the test. To "prudence" thus conceived, fortitude seems plainly unwise or stupid* (emphasis mine).[1]

Properly understood, the cardinal virtue of prudence means that *truth
must not be taboo* – no matter where the truth comes from. For the truth
is a "report from reality." The virtue of prudence is *rooted* in "the knowledge of reality," which is then morally converted to "the realization of the
good" – and hence to the realization of the "common good" (the *Bonum
Commune*), which is radically distinct from the mere "public *interest*" or
the "national *interest*." The *good*, as such, is much more inclusive and much
more important than mere interest.

"In truth," says Josef Pieper, "fortitude [especially in a protracted war!]
becomes fortitude only through being 'informed' by prudence."[2] That is
to say, by the specific reality of things, the specific, concrete actualities of
the real situation – without distortion and in proper proportion. True prudence, in its perception of reality, is not distorted by fevered (or messianic)
ideologies or sentimentalities.

Because there is today so much manipulated selectivity, "spin," and
subtle censorship (as well as "self-censorship," which is both fear-driven
and intellectually stunting) in our public discourse about matters of great
moment, the indispensable pre-conditions for truly practical wisdom are
too often not existent. The exercise of the cardinal virtue of prudence is
thereby stunted and stifled. It is a revealing sign, indeed, of the decomposi-
tion of discourse, and the pervasiveness of sophistry, and the subversion
of *Logos* itself.

Others may give us an example of virtue, to inspire our own resilience
and recovery. As a highly intelligent and robustly candid Israeli Jewish author recently said in his book, *Flowers of Galilee: The Collected Essays of
Israel Shamir*, we must strive not only for "the liberation of Palestine" but
also for "a broader goal as well: that of the liberation of Public Discourse."[3]
Shamir also introduces his own central thesis: "These essays attempt to
prove the inherent connection between two liberation movements" (i.e.,

---

1. Josef Pieper, *The Four Cardinal Virtues* (Notre Dame, Indiana: University of Notre
Dame Press, 1966), p. 123; my emphasis added.

2. *Ibid.* To "inform" here means both "to instruct" and "to give inner form to," i.e., "its
specific character as a virtue."

3. Israel Shamir, *Flowers of Galilee* (Tempe, Ariz.: Dandelion Books, 2004), p. ix (from
the author's Introduction).

the liberation of Palestine, and the liberation of Public Discourse from the Lie, from one lie after another[1]). He, like Josef Pieper, strives to attain to and communicate the "knowledge of reality," without lies, without deception, without specious sophistry. The realization of the good – the *true* common good – must be founded upon the knowledge of reality.

Wherever *the truth is taboo*, however, it will be even harder to set and keep just limits in war, especially in view of the alluring and often tempting, advanced methods and technologies of modern warfare. And sometimes – and increasingly so today it would seem – certain truths are *so* taboo, that you even can't say that they're taboo!

But, without our liberation from the lie, without the liberation of public discourse and a deeper respect for the *Logos*, we shall not only *not* set just limits to the new methods and weapons of war, but we shall also painfully perish from the asphyxiation of untruth.

As Alexsander Solzhenitsyn so courageously said, and vividly lived out in his own life, we must "come out from under the rubble," and, even though we can take only one step at a time, "we must not participate in the lie." The lie must not advance because of our co-operation or our negligence. Even if the truth is taboo, we must not be in complicity with the lie.

With respect to war and its moral limits, the burden of proof – the moral and legal *onus probandi* – must be on those who would destroy moral limits, on those who would remove limits or weaken any sense of a just moral limit in war and its aftermath. Truth matters – and so does the sober truth about modern weapons and methods of war, so many of which derive from our advanced sciences, often in "synergistic" combination or "consilience." And their sophisticated technological applications and manipulations also include some very frightening, so-called "non-lethal weapons."[2]

The combination of these new technologies with the intense passions of religious and cultural warfare could easily constitute a very dangerous and self-sabotaging "binary weapon." If other ingredients are added – such as the new materialist ideologies of neuroscience and its applied eugenics of genetic engineering – this "binary weapon" could become a "ternary weapon" or a "quaternary weapon," and therefore prove to be even more

---

1. *Ibid.*

2. See Malcolm Dando, *A New Form of Warfare: The Rise of Non-Lethal Weapons* (Washington, D.C.: Brassey's, 1996); and also Dr. Dando's book for the British Medical Association, entitled *Biotechnology, Weapons, and Humanity* (Amsterdam: Harwood Academic Publishers, 1999), wherein he also discusses race-specific genetic weapons.

intractable and dangerously "self-replicating" – another contribution to the danger of "total war."

After World War II, the French dramatist and philosopher, Gabriel Marcel, wrote a profound little book entitled, *The Decline of Wisdom.* In the year 2004, the decline has gone even further. Given this manifest decline of wisdom on many fronts, it is even more important for us today that our focus be on the matter of limits. And, once again, the burden of proof must be on those who would weaken or remove limits.

A few years ago, I visited a famous biological scientist, in Santa Fe, New Mexico, in order to discuss with him various issues of advanced biological warfare. That man was Dr. Stuart Kaufman, who is also a scholar and theoretician of advanced "complexity theory." He said to me, during our visit, "A signal can easily be turned into a poison." Dr. Kaufman was speaking about the risks of a very steep "slippery slope" – a "biological slippery slope." It includes the danger, at the "nano-scale level," of ungovernable "self-replication," especially in the manipulations of "molecular electronics." And these new nanotechnologies are already being applied in preparation for future forms of warfare – a very dangerous development indeed.

Let the civilian lawmakers and warriors beware!

Let us come out from under the rubble and not live the lie. Let us refuse the sophistical seductions or prohibition of discourse that would deceive us and lure us to cross gravely perilous thresholds – irreversibly.

Modern military officers must have a very high standard of prudence and fortitude. They must not allow truth to be taboo. They must resist the lies and seductive sophistries of their civilian masters and their sometimes-fevered ideologies, which are "mind-forged manacles." They must resist the lies and seductive sophistries that come sometimes even from their own fellow military leaders. And their public accountability must be kept very high, given the easily intractable effects of modern war and its fevered propensities to crack and to break limits; and to do it, often enough, with immoral and reckless abandon.

THE EDITORS' GLOSS: The thought that an inanimate object, such as a weapons system, might be evaluated from a moral standpoint might come as a surprise to some readers. Indeed conservatives are fond of defending the Second Amendment – and rightly, in general terms – by pointing out that "guns don't kill people, people do." Nevertheless, the Catholic church has for centuries sought to lessen the terror of warfare, by imposing truces and seeking to forbid the most awful forms of weaponry, which in and of themselves can be so horrific as to incur the sanction of moral authorities (see Appendix III). Indeed, civilized men in times past lamented the increasing application of technology to the development of weapons, the poets Dante and Ovid being just two.

More recently, the attention of the Church has turned to a moral critique of the entire militarized situation of "armed peace" that prevails in modern times, "preventing" the outbreak of war by assuring the destruction of those embarking upon it. In truth, having the "most powerful military in the world" is nothing to crow about; at best, it's a regrettable necessity. At worst, it's a tremendously inhuman enterprise.

Jesuit philosopher Theodore Meyer put it best a hundred years ago when he wrote: "The material and personal burdens which [the] constant state of armed peace imposes on citizens can only be likened to the burdens of a perpetual war. In other words, it is not sufficiently understood that, whatever the arguments put forward today on the grounds of necessity, this condition of civil society, so far from being in conformity with the requirements of nature itself, *arises rather from a state of moral disease in human society.*" For this reason did a 1931 declaration by three Catholic international-relations societies – approved by Cardinal Bourne of Westminster – urge "Catholics of all nationalities [to] seek by prayer and action to promote an international agreement for the general reduction of the armed forces of the world."

Such was the guidance of the orthodox clergy of several decades ago, and the judgment of unquestionably sound theologians. The fact that the American bishops are the most recent to demand the reduction of armaments and the limitation of weaponry – like the kind that Paul Likoudis discusses in what follows – does not make the message any less true.

CHAPTER
19

The Morality of Weapons Systems
· · · · · · · · · ·
Paul Likoudis

> "[Depleted Uranium (DU)] is more of a problem than we thought
> when it was developed. But it was developed according to standards
> and was thought through very carefully. It turned out, perhaps, to be
> wrong."
>
> —Brent Scowcroft, National Security Adviser to President George H. W. Bush

THE PHOTOGRAPHS ARE gruesome beyond description.[1] They are newborn Iraqi babies, born without heads and limbs, sometimes they are blood red, sometimes black, sometimes covered in an unknown white film, sometimes with gaping holes in their torsos that expose their internal organs.

They are, say doctors in Iraq and international experts from Europe, Japan, and the United States, the result of the United States' heavy use of weapons made of depleted uranium in Gulf War I and Operation Iraqi Freedom, which have left densely populated parts of Iraq a radioactive toxic wasteland, where adult cancer and childhood leukemia rates are soaring.

During a presidential campaign where abortion at home and the American military occupation of Iraq were pivotal issues before the electorate, there ought to have been a serious public discussion on the morality of weapons used in Iraq.

"This is such a serious issue," said Dr. John Hittinger, a professor of philosophy at Sacred Heart Seminary in Detroit and a nationally recognized expert on moral issues related to the military and warfare.

In a recent telephone interview, *The Wanderer* asked Dr. Hittinger, who previously taught at the United States Air Force Academy, if the use of de-

---

1. As of early 2005, the photographs were available at the following URL: http://www.xs4all.nl/~stgvisie/VISIE/extremedeformities.html.

pleted uranium in Iraq (as well as in Bosnia and Afghanistan) constituted a war crime and genocide.

He was reluctant to say it was, explaining that to meet the definition of genocide in international law, one has to establish a "deliberate and systematic intent to eliminate a people."

But, he added, "I don't say that to clear our conscience. We can't hide behind the doctrine of double-effect, or legalisms, and we need to face squarely the indiscriminate effect on Iraqi civilians.

"This has the beginnings of a genocidal effect, so serious questions need to be raised. Although this is not a deliberate, direct, planned attack on the unborn of Iraq, it is such a serious matter because we are attacking the sources of life in Iraqi men and women. There is a potential here for a genocidal effect."

Dr. Hittinger has impeccable Catholic credentials: a *cum laude* graduate of Notre Dame University, he earned his doctorate from the Catholic University of America; he is a former managing editor of the *Review of Metaphysics*; he was the first civilian professor of philosophy at the Air Force Academy; he is writing a book on the morality of warfare; and he is an internationally recognized authority on Aquinas and Jacques Maritain.

He told *The Wanderer* that it "is time for the Catholic bishops and the informed Catholic laity to revisit the whole 'war and peace' issue," which, he said, "is necessary now that the cold war is behind us and a protracted 'war on terrorism' is before us.

"We need a whole new debate and new parties to the debate," he added, "in light of the breakdown of the international system."

A Controversial Issue

The United States' use of depleted uranium weapons has sparked international outrage around the world. After Gulf War I, thousands of returning war veterans claimed exposure to DU weapons was the cause of debilitating illnesses.

The Pentagon has routinely insisted, from then until now, that exposure to DU poses no threat to American soldiers. In a $6 million, five-year study released October 19, the Pentagon again insisted that DU is not radioactive or toxic enough to harm U.S. soldiers.

According to a report by Matthew L. Wald for *The New York Times*, published October 19: "The conclusion, said Dr. Michael E. Kilpatrick, deputy director of the Deployment Health Support Directorate of the Defense Department, is that 'this is a lethal but safe weapons system.'"

But soldiers of Gulf War I, and returning soldiers from Operation Iraqi Freedom, have a different story.

In April 2004, *New York Daily News* reporter Juan Gonzales broke a story on how soldiers from the New York National Guard, recently released from Iraq, tested positive for radiation poisoning. And on September 29, Gonzales reported that one of those soldiers, Gerard Darren Matthew, recently became the new father of a deformed baby girl. Matthew also suffers daily from severe headaches, blurred vision, painful urination, and extreme lethargy, according to this report.

In "Committing a War Crime," Michael Jansen, Middle East reporter for the *Irish Times,* wrote on September 30 about the growing fear throughout the entire region that depleted uranium dust from exploded weapons is spreading far beyond Iraq, into Jordan, Iran, Syria, and Turkey.

DU weapons, reported Jansen,

scatter fine radioactive particles which are carried by the wind and ingested by human beings, animals, and plants. The indestructible particles last forever. Therefore, the areas where DU munitions have been deployed – the Middle East, the northern Indian subcontinent, and the Balkans – have been contaminated with endlessly destructive radioactive dust. . . .

The International Atomic Energy Agency (IAEA) estimated that half a million people would die by the end of the 21st century due to radioactive debris and dust left in Iraq, which makes its way into the rivers, lakes, and seas of the world and the atmosphere which surrounds it.

While Jordan has expressed concern about possible contamination by airborne particles escaping from Israel's nuclear reactor, there is a far greater danger from DU dust blown across the desert from Iraq.

Doug Rokke, ex-director of the U.S. Army's DU project in 1994 and 1995 and a former professor of environmental science at a Florida university, said: "They're using it now, in Fallujah; Baghdad is chockablock with DU – it's all over the place."

An Iraqi doctor specializing in blood disease at one of the capital's universities told this correspondent that thousands of Baghdadis had developed cancer since 1991 and warned that incidence of the disease will rise due to the use of DU munitions during the 2003 war. Dr. Jenan Ali, a senior specialist at the Basra College of Medicine, said that in the decade after the 1991 war there was a 100% rise in child leukemia and a 242% increase in all cancers in the region.

Birth defects are also much higher than normal. Malignancies and defects have also soared in Afghanistan since the 2001 U.S. war, but no statistics are available in that chaotic country.

While the Pentagon uses DU munitions to save the lives of its troops, DU may be killing more than the number who would have died if these munitions had not been deployed. The use of DU in 1991 and 2003 is also considered responsible for malignancies in U.S. veterans and birth defects amongst their children. While only 467 U.S. troops were wounded during the 1991 war, of the nearly 600,000 discharged personnel one-third are receiving disability compensation and another 25,000 cases are pending. The figure does not include those who have died. Amongst the 169,000 veterans of the current conflict, 16% had applied for treatment by July 2004. . . .

According to an August 2002 UN report, the use of DU munitions breaches the Universal Declaration of Human Rights, the UN Charter, the Genocide Convention, the Convention Against Torture, the four Geneva Conventions of 1949, the Conventional Weapons Convention of 1980, and the Hague Conventions of 1899 and 1907.

Just the Facts

One pertinent web site on problems caused by weapons made of depleted uranium is www.idust.net, operated by the International Depleted Uranium Study Team. It contains a library of news reports and editorials from the world's press on the consequences of exposure to DU weapons. Others are part of the University of Wisconsin's depleted uranium project, www.uwec.edu/grossmzc/belowmc.html, and www.citizen-soldier.org; they document the illnesses of Gulf War I and Operation Iraqi Freedom veterans and the Pentagon's refusal to acknowledge veterans' illnesses. The Deerfield, Mass.-based Traprock Peace Center (www.traprockpeace.org) has an extensive library on DU-related media reports and scientific and legal studies.

The following historical information on the use of DU weapons is taken directly from citizen-soldier.org:

> The American and British militaries first used DU weapons during Operation Desert Storm in the Persian Gulf in 1991. Army and Marine M1A1 Abrams main battle tanks fired 120mm rounds that each contained 10.5 pounds of depleted uranium. The M1 and M60 model tanks fired a 105 mm round with 8.5 pounds of DU in each shell. The Pentagon later estimated that 14,000 such rounds were expended during the war; 7,000 were fired in Saudi Arabia during target practice, 4,000 were used against Iraqi forces, and another 3,000 were consumed by fires or other accidents.
>
> Another 940,000 30mm DU rounds were fired by A-10 "Warthog" jets in support of their "tank killing" operations during the brief war. All told, the Pentagon has estimated that 320 tons of depleted uranium was fired by U.S. and U.K. units. As of today, not an ounce of this toxic residue has been removed by either the U.S. or any other agency.
>
> Months before the Gulf War, the Army's Armament, Munitions, and Chemical Command published the following warning: "Following combat, the

condition of the battlefield and the long-term health risks to natives [sic] and combat veterans may become issues in the acceptability of the continued use of DU for military applications." The report added that DU has been "linked to cancer when exposures are internal. . . . "

[T]he Army is clearly aware that environmental concerns could eventually undermine support for these dangerous weapons. Not long after the Gulf War ended, an Army colonel stationed at the Los Alamos National Labs wrote to a subordinate: "There continues to be concern regarding the impact of DU on the environment. If no one makes the case for the effectiveness of DU in battle, DU rounds may become politically unacceptable and be deleted from the arsenal." His memo ends with the following: "I believe that we should keep this sensitive issue in mind when 'after action' reports are written."

In the first years after the Gulf War, thousands of vets began to experience some chronic health problems and many of them sought evaluation and treatment at either VA medical centers or military hospitals. They reported some or all of the following symptoms: neurological problems, chronic skin rashes, respiratory problems, chronic flu-like symptoms including severe body aches, immune system disorders, severe fatigue, joint pain, gynecological infection, bleeding gums and lesions, and unexplained rapid weight loss.

Eventually, about 186,000 Gulf vets were examined medically at a VA or military medical facility. Virtually all who reported health problems were eventually told that they suffered from "undiagnosed illness." Very few have received disability payments for service-connected illness. Despite the large number of sick veterans, the Army surgeon general continued to tell Congress and other investigators that only a tiny number of these cases (where vets had been struck with DU shrapnel) could be attributed to depleted uranium exposure.

The Toll on the Unborn

A handful of American reporters have tried to alert the American public to DU, including *The Chicago Tribune*'s Robert C. Koehler, who in a March 25, 2004, report, headlined, "Silent Genocide," wrote:

This will not be easy to read, especially if you've projected evil out of your own heart, into some cave in Afghanistan or a spider hole in Iraq, reduced the age-old question it inspires to this one: how can we bomb it off the face of the earth? Before the damage we inflict grows greater, before history's judgment gets worse, before we contaminate the whole world – even before we vote in the next election – we must stop what we're doing. We must stop now.

It's time to listen for a moment not to defense analysts, briefing officers, pols or pundits, but to people like Jooma Khan, a grandfather who lives in a village in Laghman Province, in northeastern Afghanistan. Surely he deserves 30 seconds of our undivided attention.

"When I saw my deformed grandson," he told an interviewer in March of 2003, "I realized that my hopes of the future have vanished for good. [This is] different from the hopelessness of the Russian barbarism, even though at that time I lost my older son Shafiqullah. This time, however, I know we are part of the invisible genocide brought on us by America, a silent death from which I know we will not escape."

We're waging war-plus in Afghanistan and Iraq – in effect, nuclear war, with our widespread use of depleted-uranium-tipped shells and missiles. . . .

And DU dust is everywhere. A minimum of 500 or 600 tons now litter Afghanistan, and several times that amount are spread across Iraq. In terms of global atmospheric pollution, we've already released the equivalent of 400,000 Nagasaki bombs. . . . The numbers are overwhelming, but the potential horrors only get worse. DU dust does more than wreak havoc on the immune systems of those who breathe or touch it; the substance also alters one's genetic code. . . .

This ghastly toll on the unborn – on the future – has led investigators to coin the term "silent genocide."

www.albasrah.net

www.informationclearinghouse.info

THE EDITORS' GLOSS: In the run-up to the 2004 presidential election, some liberal Catholics in Pennsylvania were sporting bumper stickers that read "Life Does Not End at Birth." The slogan was no less true because those spreading the message were not particularly orthodox on other subjects of serious interest to Catholics.

The reason for their campaign was clear. Certain clergy in the United States were intimating at the time that Catholics should consider themselves obligated to cast their votes for George W., because he was (it was imagined) sound on "abortion," while the area in which he was weak – the war – was a matter for disagreement among reasonable men.

As Dr. Vance points out, echoing not only Joe Sobran but also the great Counter-Reformation Catechism of the Council of Trent, killing in an unjust war is murder. The fact that men can licitly take part in wars which are doubtfully just or unjust (when the burden of responsibility falls on the government because it is responsible for resolving questions of subtlety), and that men can and do disagree even about wars that are obviously unjust, doesn't change that fact one iota.

Nevertheless, the "good men can disagree" line is horribly abused in order to get folks off the hook of condemning the American aggression in Iraq. "Good men disagree" about abortion (ever hear of a sincere but erroneous conscience?). That doesn't mean that someone who knows abortion is wrong can take part in one because *other* well-intentioned people don't recognize its evil. When "good men disagree" about a particular war (and not war in general), the question to be asked is not what kind of *excuse* that disagreement offers to men *unwilling* to oppose it if clearly unjust, but what kind of *obligation* it places upon those who see it as such. Whether or not that obligation is comfortable and convenient makes it no less obligatory. After all, the Cross was inconvenient and uncomfortable for Our Lord. But He did what He knew had to be done. Shouldn't we who are His followers at least attempt to do the same?

CHAPTER
20

Christian Killers?
· · · · · · · · ·
Laurence M. Vance, Ph.D.

THERE IS NO doubt that many of the soldiers responsible for the recent death and destruction in Fallujah are Christians. And there is no doubt that many Americans who call for more death and destruction in Iraq and elsewhere are Christians as well.

Christian killers.

The phrase should be a contradiction in terms. If someone referred to Christian adulterers, Christian drug addicts, Christian prostitutes, Christian pimps, Christian gangsta rappers, or Christian acid rockers, most Christians would get extremely perplexed looks on their faces. But when Christians in the military continue killing for the State, and Christians not in the military call for more killing in the name of the State, many Christians don't even raise an eyebrow.

In some respects, this is the fault of religious "leaders." Christians in the pew are in many cases just blindly following their pastors, priests, elders, and ministers who, instead of preaching the Gospel, are preaching the same pro-war politics their congregation hears on the Sean Hannity radio show, or else they are not denouncing the debacle in Iraq for what it is: unscriptural, immoral, and unconstitutional. Conservative religious leaders are in some cases nothing more than cheerleaders for George Bush and the Republican Party.

But even if a Christian hears nothing but pro-war propaganda from the pulpit, it is still no excuse, for Christians have access to the truth if they will just put forth the effort to look for it. They have a Bible they can read for themselves. They have the example of some principled Christian leaders who have opposed the debacle in Iraq from the beginning. They have an abundance of alternative news sources to receive information from besides the pro-war propaganda they get from the FOX "War" Channel and the *"War" Street Journal*. It is unfortunate that some Christians won't read anything unless it was written by some other Christian they know and usually agree with. God forbid that they should read something by someone outside of their denomination, circle, or "camp" – or even worse, someone they consider to be only a nominal Christian or not a Christian at all.

To justify their consent or silence, and to keep their congregations in line, Christian leaders repeat to their parishioners the mantra of "obey the powers that be," a loose paraphrase of Romans xiii:1, as if that somehow means that they should blindly follow whatever the President or the government says, and even worse, that it overturns the commandment "Thou shalt not kill" (Exodus xx:13; Deuteronomy v:17), which is repeated in the New Testament (St. Matthew xix:18; Romans xiii:9). The way some Christians repeat the "obey the powers that be" mantra, one would think that they would slit their own mothers' throats if the State told them to do so.

Under what circumstances, then, is a Christian justified in or excused for killing another human being? Is it ever alright for a Christian to be a "killer"? As I see it, there are four circumstances under which a Christian could justifiably kill or be excused for killing: capital punishment, self-defense, accidents, and "just" wars.

A Christian who lawfully carried out capital punishment would not be committing murder. Although the subject of capital punishment is sometimes hotly debated, the Bible sanctions it before the law (Genesis ix:6), under the law (Numbers xxxv:16–21, 30–31), and under the New Testament (Acts xxv:11; Romans xiii:4). For more on the death penalty see Walter Block.

No one, Christian or otherwise, would fault a man for killing another man in self-defense. Only the most diehard pacifist would refuse to act in self-defense if he were attacked. This would have to include the protection of one's family as well, for if the Bible condemns a Christian for not providing for his own house (1 Timothy x:8), how could a Christian not ensure the protection of his family's life by whatever means necessary?

Accidents happen, and sometimes someone is tragically killed. This does not make the perpetrator a murderer. The Jews were commanded in the Old Testament to establish cities of refuge (Numbers xxxv:6, 11–15) to which someone might flee that killed his neighbor unawares or ignorantly (Numbers xxxv:11; Deuteronomy xix:4–5).

Most Christians would wholeheartedly agree with these first three propositions. The problem is with war; specifically, the fact that all wars are not created equal. The vast majority of wars in the world's history have been destructive, unjust, and immoral. What constitutes a just war is a question I have answered in my essay "Christianity and War." Obviously, an aggressive, preemptive war against a country with no navy or air force, an economy in ruins after a decade of sanctions, and that was no threat to the United States is not a just war.

A Christian fighting for the U.S. Government in Iraq doesn't fall under any of the circumstances described above.

After Bush launched his nebulous "war on terrorism" by having Afghanistan bombed back to the Stone Age supposedly to rid the world of Osama bin Laden, al-Qaeda, and the Taliban, he announced to the world his "axis of evil" and went to war against Iraq to – depending on what day it was – rid the world of the evil Saddam Hussein, or because Iraq violated UN resolutions, or to destroy Iraq's supposed stockpiles of weapons of mass destruction, or because of the perceived connection between al-Qaeda and Iraq, or to liberate the Iraqi people, or to bring democracy to Iraq.

Christians who support or remain silent about Bush's "war against terrorism" are terribly inconsistent. If the State were to say: "Here Christian, put on this uniform, take this gun, go to your hometown, and kill your father," Christians would recoil in horror and refuse to obey the State. But if the State were to say: "Here Christian, put on this uniform, take this gun, go to Iraq, and kill someone else's father," I am afraid that many Christians would reply, "When does my plane leave?"

Why is it that the Christian who would not do the former has no qualms about doing the latter?

Christians who voted for George W. Bush (even if it is true that he was in fact the lesser of two evils – a dubious proposition), or make excuses for his invasion of Iraq, are supporting a man with blood on his hands (Iraqi blood and American blood). The fact that the President himself never killed anyone is irrelevant – Adolf Hitler never gassed a single Jew.

What, then, is a Christian to do? What should any citizen do? Even though it is no longer posted in the public schools, most people know the answer: "Thou shalt not kill" (Exodus xx:13). Stop killing or supporting or making excuses for those who do. Quit ignoring the fact that the United States has a global empire of troops and bases that inevitably leads to more killing. Realize that it is the interventionist foreign policy of the United States that is the main reason why the world hates us. Acknowledge that the reason more countries don't hate us is because we bribe them with foreign aid – after the money is first confiscated from U.S. taxpayers.

[handwritten margin note: this same absolute right applies to taxes shall not steal]

It is true that the Bible commands the Christian: "Submit yourselves to every ordinance of man for the Lord's sake" (1 Peter ii:13). It is also true that it says: "Let every soul be subject unto the higher powers" (Romans xiii:1). But it doesn't take a seminary education to see that this doesn't trump the commandment: "Thou shalt not kill." To know when to submit and when to be in subjection, we have some relevant biblical examples to go by – two in the Old Testament book of Daniel and two in the New Testament book of Acts.

In Daniel chapter 3, we read that King Nebuchadnezzar "made an image of gold, whose height was threescore cubits, and the breadth thereof six cubits: he set it up in the plain of Dura, in the province of Babylon" (Daniel iii:1). It was then decreed that when the music started, everyone was to "fall down and worship the golden image that Nebuchadnezzar the king hath set up" (Daniel iii:5). The penalty for non-compliance was to be "cast into the midst of a burning fiery furnace" (Daniel iii:6). It was then charged that Shadrach, Meshach, and Abednego would not worship the golden image (Daniel iii:12). When brought before the king and threatened with being cast into the furnace, Shadrach, Meshach, and Abednego answered the king: "If it be so, our God whom we serve is able to deliver us from the burning fiery furnace, and he will deliver us out of thine hand, O king. But if not, be it known unto thee, O king, that we will not serve thy gods, nor worship the golden image which thou hast set up" (Daniel iii:17–18). Although Nebuchadnezzar did cast them into the furnace, and God did deliver them, the point is that these three Hebrews did not submit and were not subject to King Nebuchadnezzar.

In Daniel chapter 6, we read that King Darius made a decree that "whosoever shall ask a petition of any God or man for thirty days," except from the king, "shall be cast into the den of lions" (Daniel vi:7). But "when Daniel knew that the writing was signed, he went into his house; and his windows being open in his chamber toward Jerusalem, he kneeled upon his knees three times a day, and prayed, and gave thanks before his God, as he did aforetime" (Daniel vi:10). For his disobedience, Daniel was cast into the den of lions, but God delivered him. The point, however, is that Daniel did not submit and was not subject to King Darius.

In Acts chapter 4, the Apostles Peter and John were imprisoned by the leaders of the Jews and then brought before them and commanded "not to speak at all nor teach in the name of Jesus" (Acts iv:18). But instead of submitting and being in subjection, they replied: "Whether it be right in the sight of God to hearken unto you more than unto God, judge ye. For we cannot but speak the things which we have seen and heard" (Acts iv:19-20). They even prayed for boldness to continue speaking (Acts iv:29).

In Acts chapter 5, some apostles were put in prison by order of the high priest (Acts v:17–18). They were freed by an angel and ordered to "stand and speak in the temple to the people all the words of this life" (Acts v:20). These apostles were then brought before the leaders of the Jews and asked: "Did not we straitly command you that ye should not teach in this name? And, behold, ye have filled Jerusalem with your doctrine, and intend to bring this man's blood upon us" (Acts v:28). But rather than apologizing and submitting and being subject to them, the apostles replied: "We ought to obey God rather than men" (Acts v:29).

To say, as some Christians do, that because "The LORD is a man of war" (Exodus xv:3), and God allows wars between nations, that it is honorable for Christians to participate enthusiastically in U.S. wars of aggression is about the most profound demonstration of biblical ignorance that one could manifest.

Perhaps I should close by saying that I have never advocated, nor am I now advocating, nor do I intend to advocate in the future, any armed resistance to the government or any aggression against the government in any way. The pen is mightier than the sword. "The weapons of our warfare are not carnal" (2 Corinthians x:4). However, as Thomas Jefferson said in the Declaration of Independence:

> We hold these truths to be self-evident, that all men are created equal, that they are endowed by their Creator with certain unalienable rights, that among these are life, liberty and the pursuit of happiness. That to secure these rights, governments are instituted among men, deriving their just powers from the consent of the governed. That whenever any form of government becomes destructive to these ends, it is the right of the people to alter or to abolish it, and to institute new government, laying its foundation on such principles and organizing its powers in such form, as to them shall seem most likely to effect their safety and happiness. Prudence, indeed, will dictate that governments long established should not be changed for light and transient causes; and accordingly all experience hath shown that mankind are more disposed to suffer, while evils are sufferable, than to right themselves by abolishing the forms to which they are accustomed. But when a long train of abuses and usurpations, pursuing invariably the same object evinces a design to reduce them under absolute despotism, it is their right, it is their duty, to throw off such government, and to provide new guards for their future security.

And, as even Abraham Lincoln said (long before his invasion of the Southern states):

> Any people anywhere, being inclined and having the power, have the right to rise up and shake off the existing government, and form a new one that suits them better. This is a most valuable, a most sacred right – a right which we hope and believe is to liberate the world.

What is a Christian – or anyone – going to do when he faces God at the Judgment and has to give an account of his actions? Suppose he is asked a simple question: "Why did you kill those people defending their homes in Iraq?" And suppose he replied: "Because the U.S. government told me to." What do you suppose would be the Lord's reaction to such a reply? But what else could a man say? He could not say that the United States was under attack. He could not say that Iraq was a threat to the United States. He could not say that he was protecting his family. He could not say that he was protecting his property. He could not even legitimately say that he was protecting himself, since he was in fact a trespasser on someone else's property intending to do the owner great bodily harm.

"Cursed be he that taketh reward to slay an innocent person. And all the people shall say, Amen" (Deuteronomy xxvii:25).

www.albasrah.net

www.islamicdigest.net

THE EDITORS' GLOSS: Many who deny the right of a soldier or sailor to object to a war on the grounds of its injustice do so based on the notion that the government has access to highly classified intelligence, which can convince those with access to it of the justice of a war, while others that have no such access have no grounds for forming a judgment one way or the other. This is, unsurprisingly, the position of Michael Novak, who points out that the governmental authorities "are by the principle of subsidiarity the authorities closest to the facts of the case and – given the nature of war by clandestine terror networks today – privy to highly restricted intelligence."

Interestingly, one of his ideological fellow-travelers, Doug Feith, denied the assertion, though he did so only *after* it was clear that the reason originally adduced in support of going to war – Saddam's possession of WMD – was revealed to have been wrong.

"The strategic rationale for the war," he said to his "alma mater" the American Enterprise Institute on May 4, 2004, "didn't actually hinge on classified information concerning chemical and biological stockpiles . . . . "

He continued: "Intelligence can play a crucial role in operational decision-making. But it should surprise no one that the grandest strategic considerations of statesmen in democratic countries are commonly based on open, rather than secret, information. Such statesmen, after all, would have a hard time arguing that their country should go to war, for example, but the reasons for the war cannot be shared with the public."

A hard time indeed. If such is the case, then it should be equally hard for statesmen's lackeys to deny individuals the right to refuse support to an unjust war on the grounds that "secret information" confirms the war's justice. Or at least one would think that such should be the case in our so-called "democracy."

Is Conscientious Objection a Moral Option?

. . . .

Peter E. Chojnowski, Ph.D.

> "The praise of fortitude depends upon justice."
>
> —St. Thomas Aquinas

I BEGAN WRITING THIS article on October 15, 2004, the day it became known that a 17- member Army Reserve platoon stationed in Iraq refused to go on what they referred to as a "suicide mission" in vehicles which they judged to be "deadlined": inadequately armed and/or protected and hence extremely unsafe. According to calls made to family members back in the United States, the platoon was normally escorted by armed Humvees and helicopters, but did not have that support on the day they refused their orders. The mother of a female member of the platoon said, "They knew there was a 99% chance they were going to get ambushed and fired at. They would have had no way to fight back." For refusing to obey an order, the entire platoon could have faced severe disciplinary action: possibly even dishonorable discharge, forfeiture of pay, and up to five years in confinement, according to military law expert Mark Stevens, Associate Professor of Justice Studies at Wesleyan College in Rocky Mount, North Carolina.[1]

True, this was not a case of refusal to fight in a war on the usual "conscientious" (i.e., moral) grounds, nor a refusal to use methods and techniques of warfare that violate the moral law. However, the event was well-publicized because the media understood that the American people would find such action on the part of American service personnel "shocking," regardless of the motivation. The only reason such an event – an act of prudential judgment for the sake of the self-preservation and the common good of the

---

1. Jeremy Hudson, "Platoon Defies Orders in Iraq," *The Clarion-Ledger*, October 15, 2004, online.

platoon – could be considered shocking is because Americans have been brought up in a climate of Legal Positivism (a theory which holds that the civil law is in no way grounded in nor dependent upon a higher law that can trump the demands of man-made law).

So even *had* it been a case of "conscientious objection" on moral grounds, it still would likely have been considered "shocking." We are simply not used to the idea that moral choice has a serious role to play in matters of warfare. Not only do we accept the idea that the government's (read, the President's) decision to go to war renders that war "just," but we take it as a matter of course that any means necessary can be employed by our country to win a military conflict. For a country that has never "apologized" for the dual horrors of Hiroshima and Nagasaki, the ends certainly justify the means.

So now, when dealing with the question of a person citing his moral objection to war in general, or to a particular war being fought by the United States at a given moment, we are presented with somewhat of a void. Only for those who are standing members of a religious denomination that unequivocally rejects all war and violence is the case fairly clear-cut. For them, the United States government acknowledges their absolute pacifism and does not call upon them to serve. But when it comes to individuals who are not members of such groups, the situation is evidently more clouded. For American Catholics, the situation is downright paradoxical. The hierarchy of the Catholic Church has, on occasion, urged civil resistance (normally in an extremely mitigated and passive form) to certain social and moral evils – think of partial-birth abortion and, in the past, the sale of artificial contraceptives. But for the most part, the message regarding warfare sent out by the bishops, the clergy, military chaplains, and Catholic moral theologians has been one of an almost slavish acceptance of the government's right to call up men for combat regardless of the moral implications of a particular conflict. This is a grave and unique aspect of American Catholic history: the gravest ethical situation confronted by a man in his relationship with other men – whether or not to kill another human being in war – is all too often treated as the one situation where an individual is not allowed to make a moral judgment based upon his conscience's conception of the moral law and its application to a particular military situation.

For some reason, we have come to believe that our "lack of sufficient information" as to the government's rationale for entering into a conflict obviates the need to consult the moral law, the objective facts of the political and military situation, and our own consciences in the matter of the decision to participate in war. Why is it, for instance, that I *must* protest the murder of the unborn in an abortuary – though the government (wrongly) tolerates this practice – yet there is no necessity to consult my conscience and/or the criteria for a just war when I am confronted with the question of whether or not I should show up for military duty, fight in a war, participate in an attack on a civilian center, or endanger myself and those under my command while following the orders of a military superior.

Scholars Examine the Question

With regard to the question of if and how a Catholic (or any person of morality and good-will) can employ his conscience in time of war or military call-up, there was a theologically and philosophically reasoned teaching put forward by the Ethics Committee of the Catholic Association for International Peace. The committee was made up of some of the foremost Catholic intellectual and clerical figures of its time. It included Mgr. John A. Ryan, who served as chairman, and Mgr. Fulton Sheen; along with two Benedictines, a Franciscan, two Jesuits, two Dominicans, and a dozen other clergymen and lay scholars. The committee issued a report in 1941, prior to the United States' involvement in the Second World War, entitled *The Morality of Conscientious Objection to War*.[1] It treats of the moral aspects of conscientious objection for those who do not reject war as intrinsically evil, but who, rather, judge military service in a *particular* conflict, at a *particular* period, or in *certain* situations *to be morally illicit*.

Philosophical and Moral Foundation

The committee begins its report on the moral question of conscientious objection to military call-up or war by pointing out the moral principle that must be the basis for every moral action and every ethical analysis of one's moral situation: "We must obey God rather than men" (Acts v. 28, 29). This truth, so explicitly part of the entire Christian moral tradition, cannot be gainsaid. If God is Creator and we are His creatures, and if the State itself is a creature of the creative will of God, then all men are *obliged* to obey God rather than man, when the laws and stipulations of man contradict the objective moral law of God, as this is understood by an individual man

---

1. See Cyprian Emanuel, O.F.M., Ph.D., and the Committee on Ethics, *The Morality of Conscientious Objection to War* (Washington, D.C.: The Catholic Association for International Peace (CAIP), 1941).

or woman.[1] Thus, if God exists, and He promulgates a moral law for all of His creatures to follow so they may be in conformity with His will and His Providential Plan, we must allow that there will be occasions in which a man or woman will not only have the option of refusing the commands of the State in matters of war, but will be *positively obliged* to resist participation in combat that is unjust and contrary to the moral teaching on war that has been laid down by God through His Church – the only infallible teacher of both the Natural and the Divine Positive Law.

The Scriptural stricture that we must "obey God rather than men" presupposes two underlying moral and metaphysical facts, neither of which can be denied if the conscientious objector's position is to stand. Here we must remember that there is no appeal to a higher authority than that of the State *if* one refuses to acknowledge the existence and authority of God as Master of creation. The radical, autonomous individual who might claim the right to avoid military call-up on other than religious grounds, is in an insoluble dilemma due to his tacit consent to the "social contract" upon which the Liberal State supposedly rests.

The Liberal materialist is caught in a moral and psychological dilemma that the faithful Catholic is not caught in. This is because there are two "foundational principles" that are taken for granted by the Church and its faithful adherents. These principles ground (in an absolute way) not only the thinking regarding "just war" and unjust service in war, but all moral reasoning whatsoever, as well.

The first foundational principle comes from the very essence of man. Man is a free being, whose spiritual soul has mastery over his material body. This soul is undetermined with regard to the many choices that confront it as a moral agent. When any moral agent is confronted with a choice between an action that would be morally evil and one that would be morally good, he has the innate power and physical ability to choose between the two. On the other hand, if man were a mere machine or biologically determined organism, "conscientious objection to certain acts would be as utterly meaningless as, for example, conscientious objection to the operation of the physical laws of condensation and rarefaction."[2] If man has no control over his actions because they are determined by his environment or cultural mentality, there can then be no thought of freely adhering to an "invisible," but higher, law that outweighs the "visible" power of the State.

1. *Ibid.*, p. 5.
2. *Ibid.*, p. 7.

The second foundational principle absolutely excludes from any designation as true conscientious objectors those who reject the existence and providential care of God. It is from God that the moral law is derived, for what St. Thomas Aquinas called the "Eternal Law" is simply the law that is *one* with the Divine Mind and which contains within itself the Providential Plan by which God directs all His creatures to their true and proper ends. The existence of the moral law cannot be separated from the very essence of God; belief in an objective moral law cannot be separated from belief in God, Who, as Master of Heaven and Earth, is the unchanging Source of all inclination and directionality towards an end. The moral law, therefore, properly understood, is objective. Its content is fixed and it does not depend in its general commands upon any kind of subjective feeling or sentiment. According to the committee, "Conscientious objection demands the acknowledgement that morality is not man-made. It demands the conviction that morality has deeper roots than mere personal likes and dislikes, individual emotions, or personal persuasions subjectively arrived at."[1]

Moreover, the traditional Western moral teaching appreciated by the Greeks and systematized by the Scholastics insists upon the fact that the "law" is a thing with its origin in the intellect, not in the will. The Eternal Law is marked in the natures that God has created, which gives us the Natural Law. Therefore, human (civic) law, if it is to have any validity, *must* be a rational derivation and application of the Natural Law, which has its origin in the Divine Mind itself. And unanimous Church tradition holds that a human law that is not derived in some way – no matter how remote – from the Natural Law, does not have the character of law, but rather, has the character of governmentally sanctioned violence. As St. Augustine said, "A law that is not just seems to be no law at all."[2]

Conscience

Rather than being an autonomous source of self-serving "principles" and arbitrary judgments, "conscience is the human intellect – man's spiritual faculty of cognition – insofar as it is the medium by which man comes into the knowledge of the legislator's will . . . [and] applies this law to his individual concrete actions."[3] According to the Ethics Committee, the rela-

---

1. *Ibid.*, pp. 7–8.
2. See St. Thomas Aquinas, *Summa Theologica* (henceforth *ST*), II, i, Q. 96, A. 4. Also, see St. Augustine, *De libero arbitrio*, I, 5 (P.L., 32, 1228).
3. Emanuel, *op. cit.*, p. 9.

tionship of an individual's conscience to the moral law is qualified by four considerations:

> a) Conscience presupposes the existence of the lawgiver as my legitimate superior (God or human legislator), possessing over me the jurisdiction requisite to bind my will in such a manner that I become, in consequence, morally bound to do his bidding as set forth in his law;
>
> b) As soon as the lawgiver has enacted his law and has done his part in bringing it to the notice and knowledge of his subjects, I am strictly obliged to apply all reasonable diligence to learn to know the law, not as I, perhaps, should like to understand it, but according to the true meaning and intent of the legislator;
>
> c) As soon as I have acquainted myself with the law, I become morally bound through the medium of conscience to conform my actions to it, i.e., to do whatever the law commands and to refrain from doing whatever the law forbids;
>
> d) In spite of all good will and requisite diligence on my part – hence, without even a vestige of culpable negligence – it can happen, and does happen, that I remain in complete or partial ignorance of the law or misunderstand its true meaning, with the natural result that my actions are at variance, whether completely or partially, with the aim and will of the lawgiver. I have now what is technically known as an invincibly ignorant conscience. *I am obliged to obey the dictates of such a false conscience just as rigidly as though it were in perfect accord with the law and with the intention and will of the lawgiver* (emphasis mine).[1]

The committee elaborates further on this last point with an admonition explaining why a man is strictly obliged to follow his conscience insofar as he is applying the moral law to his own circumstances with as much moral exactitude and clarity as he can muster: "I am strictly obliged to obey my false conscience, *not because it is false, but because I am convinced in good faith that it is in accordance with the law and, hence, also with the will of the lawgiver* (emphasis mine)."[2]

Conscience and the Common Good

Yet how can it be that anyone who views the moral law as an objective entity (and believes that the common good must override his personal concept of his private good) can uphold the judgments of his own conscience at the expense of the public welfare, as this is conceived by those charged with the governance and protection of the State? This difficulty is easily resolved when viewed from a moral position consonant with the per-

---

1. *Ibid.*, pp. 9–10.
2. *Ibid.*, p. 10.

ennial philosophy of the West. Such a moral position can be called *teleo-logical* (from the Greek word, *telos* or goal). It posits that all natural beings, whether rational or non-rational, are oriented towards an end that will, once attained, fulfill the built-in potential that each being has according to its own specific nature, this nature being called the being's "formal cause." This goal, towards which each being is oriented due to its specific nature, is referred to as the being's "final cause." Here we must consider that each divinely created nature not only possesses a final cause (which gives ratio-nal order and meaning to a being's actions), but all choices of objectively true good in any particular moral act constitute fulfillment of that nature, and more perfectly conforms it to the will and eternal Providential Plan of God the eternal Father.[1]

What we must remember here is that it is not only man who is directed towards a specific end. Institutions, along with all socio-political struc-tures and actions, are also directed towards a specific end as determined by their unique place in the Divine Plan. It is the great political thought of the perennial philosophical tradition that man and all of his institu-tions and socio-political actions are directed towards the glorification of the Divine Creator. Man and the State are part and parcel of the same Divine Plan for the realization of the universal good. In light of this we can say, along with the Ethics Committee, "Whatever is opposed to a higher moral law, no matter what be the name and garb under which it appears, cannot possibly make for true and genuine public welfare."[2] If this is the case, then the question of whether to adhere to the State-determined "common good," or to an honest assessment of the moral law's application in the circumstances of an unjust war, draws this answer: "Whenever the emergency arises and I am compelled to make the choice, I am obliged to choose what actually is, or, at least, what I am honestly convinced is, the true law of morality in preference to what in reality, or at least, according to my honest conviction, is *parading under the false appearance* of the public good (emphasis mine)."[3] This principle relating to the clash between the human and the divine law rejects, on moral grounds, the possibility of Machiavellian statecraft. And rejects the idea that the conscientious objec-tor is choosing his own good – as opposed to the good of the State – when he opts to follow his conscience and refuses to participate in unjust wars or unjust actions in just wars. Can we imagine the historical outcome if more

1. See St. Thomas Aquinas, "Treatise on Law," *ST*, II, i, Q. 93.

2. Emanuel, *op. cit.*, p. 11.

3. *Ibid.*

men were to adhere to the good that their conscience dictates, instead of to the jingoism of modern totalitarian regimes? (I include, here, of course, the liberal totalitarianism that has increasingly marked life in the Western world.)

The commandment "Thou shall not kill" has traditionally been understood to prohibit the taking of innocent life. It imposes upon anyone contemplating the taking of another man's life a grave moral obligation to ensure that the life to be taken is not an "innocent" one. One whose life I am allowed to take is the one who directly threatens my own existence, the existence of my loved ones, or the existence of the civic community. Yet the high standard of Christian morality does not even allow me to *desire* to kill another man; it allows me only to desire to stop him from committing a grave injustice. Christ's law of perfection demands that I love my enemies even as I shoot them. Hatred must be excluded from the battlefield.

If such is the case, there must be standards by which we can judge the moral legitimacy of killing great masses of men in a conflict that is usually termed "a state of war." In an earlier publication by the Catholic Association for International Peace – one cited by the 1941 Ethics Committee report – these standards and conditions are enumerated as follows: a) Defensive warfare alone is justifiable. b) It must be undertaken solely in vindication of a strict right. c) There must be adequate proportion between the violated right and the evils of war. d) Recourse may be had to war only after *all* less drastic measures have proved unavailing. e) There must be reasonable hope of victory. f) War may be initiated by public authority only. g) The right intention must be had on the part of the combatants.[1]

Though all these criteria are relevant in our own day of preemptive strikes and war "justified" by the need to maintain the military and political supremacy of the United States, it is the moral requirement that a war be *defensive* which is the most relevant for our consideration here. Even though the Natural Law does not demand that a just war be fought only within the confines of one's own, invaded country,[2] it does demand that a war launched by competent authority not be *offensive* in nature. An offensive war – a war of aggression or conquest – is one initiated without just and sufficient cause, or merely to injure or destroy a State or for purposes

---

1. *Ibid.*, p. 17, note 8. See Pamphlet No.1 of the CAIP, *International Ethics* (Washington, D.C.: CAIP, 1928), pp. 23–24.

2. CAIP, *op. cit.*, pp. 23–24. Here we find that, "the natural law at times demands that the war be carried into foreign territory. The duty of one state to come to the assistance of another with armed force under certain circumstances is a clear instance."

of enrichment or aggrandizement at the expense of another State. A *defensive* war, on the other hand, is one undertaken in defense of the people, or in the defense or for the recovery of territory or property of the State. A war may be aggressive in the military or strategic sense while it is strictly defensive in the moral sense. However, in a just war, the declaration of war *necessarily presupposes some previous hostile or unjust act on the part of that State against which war is declared.* In this circumstance, the offended State, though the first to declare war (the aggressor in the military sense), is in reality entering upon a defensive war, since it is defending itself against those acts of hostility and injustice that preceded it and brought it about, and still continue in their effects.[1] Here we can see that an action like the Iraq war, which involved *no previous hostile or unjust act* on the part of the State against which war was declared (or, more accurately, simply initiated) must necessarily come under the heading of an unjust aggressive war. Mere dislike for a regime has no justificatory role to play in the moral calculus involved in deciding whether to initiate conflict with a State; especially a conflict that involves the death of civilians and soldiers fighting to uphold the authority of that sovereign State.

As cited in the quotation opening this article, St. Thomas Aquinas insists that without a "just cause" there can be no fortitude. "Man does not expose his life to moral danger, except to maintain justice. Therefore the praise of fortitude depends upon justice."[2] Correspondingly, in his *Book of Duties,* St. Ambrose states that, "Fortitude [the virtue proper to the warrior] without justice is a lever of evil."[3] In this regard it is interesting to note that when St. Thomas emphasizes that lawful combat need be directed by sovereign authority against a enemy that has *actually done* grave harm to the State and the commonweal, he points out that a war may be "unlawful" if specific conditions are not met: a) declaration by a legitimate authority, b) a just cause, and c) an intention that is not "wicked."[4] Notice that *three* conditions are required. Not just the "authority of the ruler," which by itself does not justify the taking up of arms and the killing of another man. Combat in such an unjust war would be objectively sinful; and, objectively speaking, the State which attacked another under these circumstances

---

1. See Cyprian Emanuel, O.F.M., Ph.D., and the Committee on Ethics, *The Ethics of War: A Report of the Ethics Committee* (Washington, D.C.: CAIP, 1932), pp. 6-7.

2. *ST,* II, ii, Q. 123, A. 12, ad 3.

3. St. Ambrose, *De officiis,* I, 35.

4. *ST,* II, ii, Q. 40, A. 1.

would be *required* to uphold a person's *right* to object conscientiously to its war.[1]

In all of the above, we see there are many conditions that must be satisfied before a war can be considered just. So we must be careful to avoid a certain nonchalance with regard to our use of the terms "just" and "war." What we really mean here is that if an act of killing is performed within the context of an unjust war (i.e., one that does not meet *all* the necessary criteria), the man who performs that act (on the side of the unjust aggressor) is objectively guilty of murder, and his act is a crime against the social and the moral order.

The Role of the Citizen

The primary argument on the part of those who acknowledge that a war may be morally unjust, but who oppose the right of conscientious objection to unjust war, is as follows: the criteria for what constitutes a just or unjust war are meant for the moral consideration of the ruler and not for consideration of the ruled who may be called upon to fight. According to this well known position, since the potential conscientious objector cannot have all the intelligence information that is available to the government, he must rely completely upon the government's judgment as to whether or not another nation possesses a real threat. The Ethics Committee asks itself, in this vein,

> But, in instances of serious doubt, does not the responsibility of adjudicating the justice or injustice of the war rest with the war-declaring authorities of the state? May we not, nay more, *must* we not, presume our country to be in the right unless it is evidently in the wrong, and in doubt are we not obliged to obey the commands of our legitimate superiors? Is it not true that the private individual will seldom be in a position to declare the war undoubtedly unjust because of his ignorance of many facts and considerations known frequently only to the country's highest officials?[2]

To these questions the committee answers an "emphatic affirmative." But along with this *theoretical* endorsement of the position that cedes to the state the role of judging the "justice or injustice of war," the Ethics Committee adds a significant caveat:

> [P]rovided the heads of government are believers in God and in their accountability to God for their actions of state, both of peace and of war, and, in

---

1. Emanuel, *Conscientious Objection*, p. 23.
2. *Ibid.*, p. 33.

consequence, are ordinarily wont to give proper conscientious consideration to the moral points involved before resorting to the extreme of war.[1]

To bolster support for their contention, the members of the Ethics Committee adduce, via a lengthy footnote, the testimony of Francisco de Vitoria, O.P., that for a war to be just, it is not always sufficient that "the ruler is convinced that his cause is just . . . ";[2] in other words the civil authority's mere decision and declaration that a war is just is not sufficient to make it so. It is necessary, rather, Vitoria goes on to explain, that the cause itself be examined in the most objective and rigorous way possible, and that numerous unbiased, upright, and judicious men be consulted in assessing the potential war's justice.[3]

This theoretical explanation made (namely, that the government's subjective judgment is not sufficient to guarantee a war's justice, and that there is a need for objective and prudent moral consideration of the justice of a belligerent's cause), the Committee further explains the likelihood of this need being met today. The explanation is worth quoting in full, for it provides a worthwhile "reality check" as to just how much stock one should put, today, in the ability of modern governments to assess the presence or absence of requisite conditions for the justice of a contemplated war.

> When, however, we come to weigh these all-important conditions [that the heads of government believe in God and in their accountability to God for their actions of state, and that they are therefore ordinarily wont to give proper consideration to moral points before resorting to war] in the balance of objective reality at the present time, we discover that they fall lamentably short of verification in very many instances. There are, in the first place, dictators of totalitarian states steeped in the false and pernicious philosophy of state absolutism. They hold and practice the doctrine that the state, being an end in itself, can do no wrong; that the right to declare and to carry on war comes implicitly from the fact of war itself; that it is not necessary to attempt to justify it by the ordinary maxims of morality – it is its own justification.
>
> In a degree, less exaggerated it is true, but nonetheless verily, the absence of the moral emphasis is noticeable in the war deliberations of modern democracies and other forms of constitutional government. Other interests, especially economic, assume importance beyond all adequate proportion. The natural consequence is that moral issues frequently receive but scanty, if any, consideration, or even are deliberately rejected as irrelevant and bothersome

---

1. *Ibid.*, p. 33.

2. *Relectiones Undicem* (2 vols in 1, ed. Alphonsi Muñoz, O.P., Salmanticæ: 1565), I, Relectio V, 20, quoted in Emanuel, *op. cit.*, p. 33. [See also the discussion of this point in the essay by Dr. William Cavanaugh on pp. 269–289 of the present volume.—Ed.]

3. De Vitoria, *op. cit.*, nn. 20, 21, 24, quoted in Emanuel, pp. 33–34.

encumbrances standing in the way of successful statesmanship. After making due allowance for notable exceptions, we find that modern statesmen in many instances either are deliberately blind to the moral phases of peace and war or, because of lack of proper training in matters of morality, are not equal to the task of assigning to God and morality and conscience the place that is theirs by every right in world affairs.

Moreover, we are faced with the fact that in very few, if any, modern wars have the necessary justifying conditions been simultaneously fulfilled, and with the sadder fact that, as a rule, not even has an honest attempt to observe them been made by the nations initiating hostilities. Nor can we close our eyes to the further reality that the state authorities connive at, condone, and., perhaps, even positively countenance, certain practices of war that are undoubtedly direct and flagrant violations of the natural law.

All this cannot but serve to weaken our confidence in the state's willingness and ability to decide correctly the justice or injustice of a war at the present time.[1]

The ultimate conclusion which the Ethics Committee draws from the foregoing, and which bears on our initial question as to the obligation of the citizen to render the benefit of the doubt to the government's determination on the justice of a war, is crystal clear:

> We must conclude, therefore, that until modern statecraft begins to give more serious consideration to the moral element in national and international affairs we cannot with unquestioning assurance rely upon the judgment of the state authorities to allay all doubts concerning the moral issues involved in warfare.[2]

Later on, the authors of the Ethics Committee report go on to cite cases where a man or woman would in fact have a legitimate and morally justifiable right – indeed, an obligation – to refuse service in war. The more obvious moral possibilities cited are: a) because one is honestly and sincerely convinced that the conditions demanded by the natural law as prerequisites for a just war fall short of complete fulfillment in relation to this particular war, or even must necessarily fall short of the verification as regards all wars between civilized states *at the present time;* b) because one has knowledge of certain facts which have a distinct bearing on the morality of this particular war, but which are unknown to the general public; c) be-

---

1. Emanuel, *op. cit.,* p. 35.

2. *Ibid.* [The degree to which this denunciation of modern amoral statecraft applies to the current government of the United States may be gathered from the discussion by Dr. Thomas Ryba of the wholly insufficient moral model used by the Bush administration to conclude upon the alleged justice of the war in Iraq; see pp. 223–244 of the present volume.—Ed.]

cause one, for example the trained moralist or ethicist, in virtue of deeper study and more technical training in matters of morality, clearly and correctly discerns implications and applications that lie concealed from the ordinary lay mind.[1]

What is most critical in the above possible cases is that there are some *obvious* examples of situations in which a man would be *morally obligated* to refrain from all participation in a war which he knew or believed to be unjust. Yet there need only be a few *genuine* and obvious moral situations of conscientious objection in order to legitimize the possibility itself. Participation in a government-mandated war is therefore by no means a moral necessity.

Sometimes Even a Duty, Not Just a Right

We noted at the outset that it is often taken to be the case that the only moral decision a man *cannot* make for himself is the decision as to whether or not to go to war. The conclusion reached by the Ethics Committee's study – a study, it should be remembered, based upon the deliberation of clerics and theologians such as Mgrs. Fulton Sheen and John A. Ryan – rejected that claim. Summarizing its teaching on the question of the morality of conscientious objection, it concludes:

> Practically speaking, the task of deciding the justice or injustice of any particular war devolves upon the conscience of the individual conscript or soldier. It is his conscientious duty to decide, as a matter of concrete fact, whether any particular war is aggressive or defensive, and, if defensive, whether it is justified or unjustified, and, in consequence, whether he is free or obliged or forbidden to participate formally in it, whether he is free or obliged or forbidden to be a conscientious objector.[2]

---

1. *Ibid.*, pp. 16–17.
2. *Ibid.*, p. 39.

THE EDITORS' GLOSS: What follows is a piece that former Army Staff Sgt. Camilo Mejia wrote while he was in prison serving time for desertion. While in prison, he was awarded the St. Marcellus Award (the same one presented to Bishop Botean the following year) by the Catholic Peace Fellowship; this piece served as his "acceptance speech."

As we have noted elsewhere, many, including Catholics, take issue with conscientious objection because it's imagined to be a creature of the left-wing fringe. It's been saddled with overtones of treason and cowardice, and Amnesty International's endorsement has done little to commend the practice to Catholics.

The same individuals who have qualms about soldiers refusing to follow unlawful orders (and what else are orders to fight in an obviously unjust war?) don't seem to balk at the idea of St. Thomas More refusing to "acknowledge the King's title." One is a sign of pacifist weakness, the other a sign of courage and conscience.

The reality is somewhat different. Even before the "curse" of 1960s liberalism descended upon the American populace and even some of the American Catholic clergy, serious and orthodox thinkers were applying the courage of St. Thomas More to the subject of refusal to fight in an unjust war. The statements of Cardinal Ottaviani (Appendix II), the Ethics Committee of the Catholic Association for International Peace (Chapter 21), of which Bishop Fulton Sheen was a member, Fr. Delaney (p. xx), and others, attest to that fact. To these may be added the comments of one Brother Alfred, F.S.C., Ph.D., who wrote, in the April 1939 issue of *Religious Educator*, "if we are morally certain of the injustice of the war we are bound in conscience to abstain from taking part in the hostilities."

He further affirmed that "it is not altogether a pleasant situation to face." Almost presaging the predicament of Mejia and others, he said that "the conscientious objector will have to bear abuse even from fellow Catholics in all probability. The state will not be particularly pleased and may invent more stringent penalties for this 'offense.' But if worse comes to worse, it is better to die for peace than to die in an unjust war; better to obey God and conscience than authority commanding injustice."

His conclusion is one Mejia's detractors would do well to bear in mind.

CHAPTER
22

The Sounds of Conscience
· · · · · · · · · ·
Former Army Staff Sgt. Camilo Mejia

WHEN I FIRST heard about the possibility of war, I said to myself that many unlikely things would have to take place. I felt that without clear evidence of nuclear or chemical weapons, without a clear link between Saddam Hussein and al-Qaeda, that without clear evidence of Iraq posing a threat to us, we would not really invade. I did not feel we had made a case for going to war. But I am a soldier, I am still a soldier, and as good soldiers we are told not to question the reasons for war. We are not supposed to concern ourselves with politics or foreign policies. We fight wars without questioning them.

And, so I began training and preparing for war. But we had still not made a case for war, and I trusted that our leaders would do the right thing and use military force as a last resource. When we deployed to the Middle East in early March 2003, Saddam Hussein was destroying his missiles, the UN weapons inspectors were asking for more time, and many of our allies were opposing the war. I figured we would do a show of force – and for a while I didn't know if there really would be a war. Given the uncertainty, I had hope in my heart that peace could prevail.

But then there was war and I opposed the war, but I was afraid of saying anything. I didn't want to sound like a coward or a traitor. And I knew that soldiers are not supposed to question their governments. I knew of the possibility of severe punishment for refusing to participate in the war – scorn and rejection by my peers, incarceration, even the death penalty. I was terrified of it all.

I was an infantry squad leader in combat – and when your life is in the hands of the man right next to you and his life is in your hands, you suddenly become more than brothers. I didn't want my brothers to think I was a coward or a traitor, and I didn't want to go to prison. I was afraid to stand up and say: I am against this criminal war. I was so afraid to stand up for my beliefs and principles that I chose to take my chances in combat.

The combat situation was very dangerous and we knew that every minute that went by could be the last we ever lived. I started praying to God to let me see my daughter one last time, even if I died right after seeing her. I started praying that my family would not suffer on my account. I started praying for the families of the other soldiers, as they too were suffering.

I felt that we were trapped in a big lie where war itself was the only real enemy, and I started praying for the Iraqi families, asking God to ease their suffering. I asked God to end the war in Iraq, and then I asked God to end every war. And then I realized that my personal prayer had become a prayer for humanity. I realized that in war, through God, I was connected to the rest of humanity.

It was the unfounded reasons for war given by our government that made me oppose the invasion and occupation of Iraq, but it was my own experience in combat that made me oppose every war.

I want to believe that the Iraqi insurgents did not mean to kill their own people. I want to believe that we did not mean to kill the Iraqi people. But the reality was that the innocent were the ones paying the price of this war. I realized that even if the reasons for going to war were politically sound, the loss of human life, the loss of innocent blood, renders every war immoral and unjustifiable.

But it is difficult, if not impossible, to concern oneself with deep questions about the morality of a war, to place oneself in the position to judge the righteousness of an invasion when you are in the middle of a war. Nobody wants to die or see their friends die in a foreign land, far from everything we love, far even from ourselves, from our own humanity. I didn't have the courage to put my weapon down when my life and the lives of my friends were in danger.

Upon my return home for a two-week leave, I had the opportunity to put my thoughts in order. Far from the sounds of machine guns and mortar, it became hard not to listen to what my heart was telling me. I came face to face with my feelings about the war. I came face to face with the memory of each and every one of my actions. I tried to justify my behavior, my being in Iraq in the first place. I realized that I was holding myself accountable for my own behavior.

When the sounds of battle are gone, the sounds of one's conscience take over. And my conscience is the place where I meet with God. I don't need an angel to descend from heaven to tell me what God wants me to do, all

I have to do is listen to my conscience and do what I know in my heart is the right thing.

After being convicted of desertion, during the sentencing phase of my trial, they gave me the opportunity to ask for clemency. I know that I did and said things that put me where I am at this very moment, in prison. But in everything I did, I was following my conscience. To express regret for my actions in exchange for a lighter sentence would be like denying God, and God is my only salvation.

If I were to ask for clemency, it would not be from a military panel, but from God. I would also ask God to have mercy on the souls of those who wrongly convicted me. And, if I am ever to seek forgiveness on this earth, I shall seek forgiveness from the Iraqi people.

According to the Second Vatican Council: conscience is the most secret core and sanctuary of man. There, he is alone with God whose voice echoes in his depths.

Thank you for allowing me to share the voice that still echoes in the depths of my conscience. It is in those depths that I remain a free man.

Thank you and thank God.

THE EDITORS' GLOSS: This mock interview was penned by Eric Gill on September 21, 1939. It was originally published in his autobiography, *Eric Gill* (New York: Devin-Adair Co., 1941, pp. 303–307), and it was prefaced with the following note from the author: "This tract is written in the form of question and answer not because any tribunal is likely to allow a C.O. so much rope but because it is not a mere essay on war and law but is an attempt to answer some of the questions underlying conscientious objection."

Perhaps most notable in Gill's short canned exchange is his recognition of the fact – and it's one which most are loath these days to admit – that one of the paradoxical things about the war and peace question today is the presumption that a government that professes to believe in no fixed vision of right and wrong will nevertheless be capable of passing a judgment upon exactly that in assessing whether it has the right to initiate a war. In Gill's words: "As the legitimately constituted authority, it is to be obeyed, but only when its commands are not immoral. As to whether this or that war be just, such a government cannot judge. Justice is a conception depending upon the acceptance of certain moral and philosophical principles, and no government today is founded upon such acceptance or subject to it." Food for thought, to say the least.

Meanwhile, the English Carmelite Fr. Brocard Sewell offered Gill, in his memoirs (*My Dear Time's Waste*, 1966), this modest tribute: "The Catholic conscientious objector is no longer universally regarded by the clergy as a kind of religious pariah. For this improvement in his position we have to thank Eric Gill and the other PAX pioneers . . . . "

A Tribunal

· · · · · · · · ·

Eric Gill

**ARE YOU** *a conscientious objector?*

A. Yes.

Q. Do you think all use of violence in support of law is wrong?
A. No.

Q. Do you think all war is wrong?
A. In the abstract, no.

Q. Do you think war is wrong today?
A. Yes.

Q. Why?
A. Because the conditions which might justify war are of two kinds – a just cause and just means. Today it is *doubtful* whether the cause is just and *certain* that the means are not.

Q. I see – ends and means. With regard to ends: what right have you to set up as judge against lawfully constituted authority? If the Government judges it right to go to war, by what authority do you judge it to be wrong?
A. There are two sorts of law-giving, positive and negative – things you must do and things you must not. The former are rightly confined to general principles, as: "Thou shalt love the Lord thy God," or "Honour your father and your mother." The latter are rightly confined to particular acts, as "Thou shalt not steal." Positive commands as to particular acts are bad law and are only submitted to for convenience, as when the Government says that every child shall be registered at birth. What the law really means

is that the Government chooses to keep a register and demands the assistance of parents and guardians. But it could, if it chose, keep the register without that assistance; the assistance is convenient but not essential. In general it is true to say that people can justly be forcibly *prevented* from doing certain things but cannot justly be forcibly compelled to do anything. This principle is derived from the facts of nature. You can take a horse to the water but you cannot make him drink. So, in this matter of war we may say: you can take a man to the slaughter but you cannot make him kill. Therefore I say that the Government has the right to demand that we love and honour our country but no right to say: thou shalt kill her enemies. I am not saying that there are no circumstances in which enemies should be killed – there may be or there may not – I am only saying that no government can justly compel a man to take the job of executioner.

Q. Your contention, that the Government cannot compel particular acts, will not "hold water" – what about paying taxes? Cannot the Government justly compel you to pay?

A. Yes, but that's only saying that it can justly take your money, and that, if you refuse to pay, is precisely what they will do. And may I say this: that considering the methods of electioneering and the whole corrupt business of politics today, and, quite apart from the fact that no government even claims to represent all the people, there is no reason why anyone should look up to the government as though it were in any way holy or to be reverenced. It represents the big economic and financial interests of our empire even more than it represents persons. It has no unity of mind upon moral principles – except that its members are almost unanimous in denying that morality has anything to do with economics – and it has therefore no mandate to teach morality or any power to do so. As the legitimately constituted authority it is to be obeyed, but only when its commands are not immoral. As to whether this or that war be just, such a government cannot judge. Justice is a conception depending upon the acceptance of certain moral and philosophical principles and no government today is founded upon such acceptance or subject to it. To ask the Government for a ruling in a matter of justice is like asking the keeper of a cat's home for a ruling on ping-pong. In brief, I hold that the Government has the right, as it has the power, to prevent my doing what it judges to be contrary to the common advantage, but that it has not the right, and it has not the power, to compel me to do what I believe to be wrong or even to do any particular thing, whether wrong or right.

Q. Let us leave all that and let me ask you the old simple question: If a man threatened your wife with a gun, would you not defend her?

A. Why yes, naturally.

Q. Would you use force?

A. Yes, if I could command it. Failing that, the good thing to do would be to get between her and the gun, and then to throw myself upon him and, before he had time to use it, to wrest the awful weapon from his horrid grasp.

Q. Isn't that, in effect, what the country asks you to do – to defend your wife and children and your home?

A. That's how they express it. But, if you will forgive the slang, they "kid" themselves. For where is the parallel? Times have changed. What they ask of me in fact and not "in effect," is not simply to join an army of defence but, in accord with the old saying, "offence is the best defence," to join up in an organization for the destruction of the enemy. But of course no one is deceived (or are you, Sir?) by the talk about only destroying "military objectives." We know very well that immediately airmen start bombing they cannot possibly confine their attention to such. They will bomb whatever they can and particularly any centre of population. "In effect," to borrow your phrase, it is as though, in answer to your question about the man with the gun, I were to answer: yes, I would defend my wife, but I would not give a poker to the baby and rush out of the back door and down the street to my enemy's house and throw vitriol in his wife's face to "break her morale." There are in fact "some things which no fellow should do." I do not believe that "all's fair in love and war." Nobody does really. I don't believe in killing prisoners. I don't believe in killing the wounded. I don't believe in killing children or their mothers or old people or imbeciles. In short, I don't believe in killing the innocent, i.e. the harmless and I don't believe in killing people, whether soldiers or not, who are running away – as we did to the Turks in the last war – that is massacre. And it's no use any longer trying to make out that such things are only done by accident. It is not true and everyone knows it. Do you believe in gouging out the eyes of prisoners or mutilating them to break their morale?

Q. You're here to answer questions, not to ask them.

A. Please ask.

Q. Assuming for the moment that you are right in saying that it is the intention of our commanders to bomb open towns – though I don't admit it and it is grossly insulting to our Government and to our soldiers – even so, are you not compelled to use the same means as our enemy uses?

A. No, of course not. There's no compulsion about it.

Q. *But if we do not, will they not have us at a hopeless disadvantage?*

A. Perhaps – but that's no argument, unless you think it's right to do evil that good may come. History seems to show the contrary even if God's word were insufficient.

Q. *Would you allow the enemy to ride rough-shod over your country?*

A. Not at all. I should, as I said before, attempt to defend it. But I refuse to use evil means to that end. A man may refuse to defend himself but he cannot honourably refuse to defend his wife and children. Nevertheless he can and should refuse to defend them by immoral means. If good means are not sufficient, if, for example, his anti-aircraft guns are not good enough, or his barrages defective, then he must surrender. It cannot be helped. Murdering your enemy's children would be no remedy and you would only stir up hate and lust for revenge.

Q. *Don't you think a man is entitled to defeat the enemy by any means in his power?*

A. No, I do not.

Q. *Are you prepared to take the consequences of your opinions?*

A. Of course I am.

Q. *Will you join the anti-aircraft corps?*

A. Yes, if I am given a written guarantee, which I am allowed to carry about with me always, that I shall not be drafted into the bombing section of the Air Force or into any overseas army of offence.

Q. *That is impossible; for it is not only the home-country that must be defended but also our colonies and dependencies and they cannot be defended, as perhaps England can, by anti-aircraft guns or barrages, but only by attack on the enemy in his own country.*

A. Very well then. I refuse to join even the anti-aircraft defences. But, I repeat, I will join those defences on the condition I have stated. And I should like to add that in taking part in anti-aircraft defence there is no suggestion of any desire to kill enemy airmen, but only to destroy their machines. In the same way one should endeavour to disarm an intending murderer rather than to kill him.

Q. What alternative service will you accept?

A. Broadly speaking, I will do anything which it would be good to do in any case. For example: the land needs tilling and cultivating. It has been shamefully neglected in the interest of our overseas trade – trade conducted by methods and policies which are themselves very largely the cause of this war and others. Then again, if we are to attain to a just peace, a lot of propaganda will be required to stem the natural tide of hatred and anger which war sets flowing. People who can write should be employed to do this work before it is too late. Again: building work. It would be much better to employ C.O.s on slum clearance and rebuilding work than to shoot them or imprison them. They are anxious to serve their country. Let them do so. Unless you shoot them all, they will have to be fed. Let them earn their keep. But do not talk to us about justice and honour. The present war is not due to Hitler's injustice or deceit, heinous though they may seem, but to economic developments and compulsions reaching back over many centuries. And the beam in our own eye is not inconspicuous. We cannot set up as arbiters. Our hands are no cleaner than anyone else's. Therefore I ask for total exemption – that I may serve my country without disservice to God.

The growth of democracy implies that the people shall have a larger share in determining the form, attributions, and policies of the government to which they look for the preservation of order. It should also imply that THE CALM DELIBERATE JUDGMENT OF THE PEOPLE, RATHER THAN THE AIMS OF THE AMBITIOUS FEW, *shall decide whether, in case of international disagreement, war be the only solution. Knowing that the burdens of war will fall most heavily on them, the people will be slower in taking aggressive measures, and, with an adequate sense of what charity and justice require, they will* REFUSE TO BE LED OR DRIVEN INTO CONFLICT BY FALSE REPORT OR SPECIOUS ARGUMENT. RELUCTANCE OF THIS SORT IS ENTIRELY CONSISTENT WITH FIRMNESS FOR RIGHT AND ZEAL FOR NATIONAL HONOR. *If it were developed in every people, it would prove a more effectual restraint than any craft of diplomacy or economic prudence. The wisest economy, in fact, would be exercised by making the principles of charity and justice an essential part of education. Instead of planning destruction, intelligence would then discover new methods of binding the nations together; and the good will which is now doing so much to relieve the distress produced by war, would be so strengthened and directed as to prevent the recurrence of international strife.*

—James Cardinal Gibbons
In his own name and in the name of the
American Hierarchy
Washington, D.C., 1919

SPEAKING WITH AUTHORITY: THE TRUE JUST-WAR DOCTRINE AS A LIGHT FOR OUR TIME

THE EDITORS' GLOSS: This article originally appeared as Chapter III of *The Church and War: A Catholic Study* (New York: P.J.Kenedy and Sons, 1928, pp. 47–92). The entire work bore the *Nihil Obstat* of Thomas McLaughlin, S.T.D., and the *Imprimatur* of Edmond Canon Surmont, Vicar General of Westminster, England.

The Catholics we mentioned earlier (in our gloss on chapter 10), who asserted the justice of the Iraq war, were convinced that, in order to justify an attack on Iraq, "no 'expansion' of traditional moral and legal limits [was] necessary or . . . called for." Such an assertion might persuade individuals unacquainted with the just-war tradition, who wouldn't know what did or did not constitute an expansion of the traditional doctrine. A study of the work by Fr. Stratmann will quickly remedy any such ignorance, and, more importantly, reveal just how wrong these particular Catholics are.

What Stratmann's essay also brings to mind is the serious contribution of Catholics to international law as it is known and understood today. Many are wont to consider Hugo Grotius as the founder of international law, but the fact is somewhat different. The Belgian Ernest Nys, Nobel Peace Prize nominee for 1907, and scholar of international law and arbitration, considered Francis de Vitoria to have been the first to have seriously defined international law. And James Brown Scott, American scholar of international law, president of the Geneva Institute of International Law, and trustee and secretary of the Carnegie Endowment for International Peace declared: "Fray Francisco de Vitoria, Spaniard, Catholic, and Dominican friar, is the true founder of the modern school of international law."

With this kind of powerful endorsement of the Church's thinking on matters of war and peace, even by modern standards, Catholics need feel no qualms about accepting, promoting, and adhering to their patrimony as regards the proper conduct of nations one to another. In this light it also seems all the more disheartening to witness some of them ignoring it in favor of a mess of neoconservative pottage.

Just-War Doctrine:
The Metaphysical and Moral Problem
• • • • • • • • • •

Fr. Franziskus Stratmann, O.P.

W AR IS AN appalling evil. The Prayers of the Church speak of it in the same breath as pestilence and famine, though pestilence and famine are not on the same level as war, because they are nearly always the result of war and because they are not due to human will. War is not only an evil as pestilence and famine are; it is not only blood shedding, but it is the exaltation of every physical, mental and moral evil. That war is an evil, almost everyone, certainly every Christian, must allow, but the majority considers it a necessary evil, to be borne as something that cannot be avoided.

Perhaps one of the sharpest divisions between spiritually and materially minded men is that the materially minded only know *Facts* – riches and poverty, content and discontent, progression and retrogression. For the spiritually minded man, the most ordinary matters of daily life are *Problems* – they make him think of the meaning of Facts. For the one, war is merely an occurrence that comes and goes like pleasure and suffering. The other ponders over the meaning of war, its metaphysical origin, its right or wrong, the possibility or impossibility of its prevention.

A. The Necessity of War

War seems always to have been a normal factor in the world's history. Johann van Bloch[1] writes that although, for civilised countries war is not by any means perpetual, yet taking the world as a whole, from 1496 B.C. till A.D. 1861 there have only been two hundred and twenty-seven years in

---

1. *Der Krieg*, 6 Bände, Bond I, Einl, xi.

which there was no war anywhere – one year of peace to thirteen of war, so that we may say that war is almost the world's normal state.

This state of things cannot be quite independent of the Divine Government. We are faced by the question whether God positively wills war as an element in His ordering of the world. One of the laws of nature given by God is the struggle for existence which must lead to a warlike spirit and it seems that God leads up to war directly, whether by an unmistakable manifestation of His Will or by simply leaving men and circumstances to themselves and using their conduct for the fulfilment of His Desires.

Thus we ask whether this fact of the constant recurrence of war springs from a direct or an indirect law of God.

Undeniably struggle is one of the main conditions of life. Development and destruction are ever allied in the world of nature and of men. Nothing living can escape this conflict. The law runs through the vegetable and animal world up to man. With man as with the rest of creation this law of struggle drives him on, but there is also the lust, even when necessity does not drive him, to try his strength, to use that power which is his birthright. Man is by nature not only a ruler, but also a conqueror. The more alive his spiritual and physical powers are, the more he longs to rise, to increase his influence, improve the conditions of his life, to step forward in every way. All this is quite legitimate and can take place without any failing in duty or any wrong. It can be a sign of natural perfection, even of likeness, to the image of God.

Yet even the unreasoning beasts do not blindly destroy one another. They work together for mutual support and fellowship. And with man likewise the law of conflict must be limited and hedged round by the law of mutual fellowship, of consideration for his fellows, for all the animate and even the inanimate creation. It is even truer to say of man that he is by nature a worker than to say that by the laws of nature he is a fighter. That he is not primarily intended to be a fighter is shown in this, that he is not provided with any natural weapons. He has no horns, or hoof, nor poison in his teeth, nor natural coat of mail. He is primarily equipped to be a worker and is given his *hand*. Nor is it fair that the talents which make man fitted for a life of peaceful labour should be used for war. Is not that against the laws of nature? Must man, who by nature is a peaceful worker and under certain conditions a fighter and ruler and conqueror, be also by nature a warrior? Is it right and fair that because of the original sin of fallen human nature, war is to be a necessity? The result of man's fall is that personal sinfulness, suffering and death have become unavoidable; but it in no way follows that any *particular* sin or result of sin is unavoidable, and therefore neither the sin of war nor the sinful results of war. Unfortunately it is very necessary to emphasise this truth as strongly as possible for we are always being told that war is a law of nature.

The Romans went even farther and maintained that the state of war was the natural state of nations towards each other – that *Pax* was the result of *pacisci*, that Peace was only subjection to the Roman Legions.

Hobbes also taught that war was the natural state and peace only the subjection of special groups bound by an artificial contract. When war breaks out the natural condition is restored; when peace comes again nature for the time is thrust back. We may not hear these very extreme theories today, but we still are told that history teaches the necessity of war. Bismarck said in 1891, "War is a law of nature. It is the struggle for existence in a general form and till men become angels it will not cease." Here we have a mixture of truth and falsehood. Because a thing has happened a million times, it does not become a law of nature. The conclusion is false. It is quite true that as long as mine and thine, man and woman, flesh and spirit exist there will be sin and suffering: human nature being what it is, it is impossible to eliminate them from the world. But does that apply to war?

Supposing there was no war – that war had come to an end forever, should we ask: what has happened to the Divine ordering of the world? If sin and suffering were no more we should say mankind is altered; but if war could never be again, we should say that a particular evil resulting from sin had ceased, as slavery, for instance, has ceased. For centuries the world's greatest thinkers, with Aristotle at their head, considered slavery as part of the Divine unchangeable ordering of the world. Slavery was *man's* work allowed by God, brought about by man's perverted will and ended by man's reformed will. In his Pastoral of 1914 Bishop Casartelli, of Salford, asks why if the nineteenth century did away with slavery the twentieth should not do away with war.

Both slavery and war are incompatible with the solidarity of the nations. As long as the power of the slave owner and the weakness of the slave lasted, so long slavery was looked on as part of the Divine ordering of the world; and so long as the present system of armaments and its result the explosion of war is considered as a necessity for the State, just so long shall we go on hearing that war is part of the Divine economy. God does indeed hold all things in His Hand, and in that sense it is true to say that war is an element in the Divine ordering of the world. Anything so tremendous as a war must play a large part in the counsels of God.

In war God weighs the nations in His Scales and passes judgement on them. But He does not drive man against man in strife by a law of nature or by a direct command.

What is forever necessary so long as man is man, is struggle. That harmony which came originally from God in each man's own nature and in his relation to his fellows was disturbed by the Fall. The flesh is no longer subject, without struggle, to the spirit, and this inner conflict is continued in the outer world. Man must fight for his life and for the necessities of his existence and in this fight man is his neighbour's adversary.

Each individual will is free – one wants this, one that. Freewill leads men, too, to combine in groups and these groups have a common will which differs from the common will of other groups; and so there must be struggle as long as human nature is unchanged.

BUT STRUGGLE IS NOT WAR.

If these groups had no trained and equipped army behind them, what we mean by war would be impossible. That is to say, if justice could take the place of force, and a trial by law the place of carnage. This would certainly make a police force necessary, but then indeed war, *not struggle*, would be driven out of the world.

War in the meantime is a standing example of the perversity of the human ordering of the world when it is allowed by God to work itself out freely.

B. Just and Unjust War

(1) In the Natural Law

If war is looked upon as an ordinary means of struggle, recognised by the law of nations and accepted by the present conditions of society, we ask on what moral grounds it is justified and what are its moral limitations? Just as there is a completely unphilosophical attitude to the metaphysics of war, so there is also an amoral attitude, namely an attitude that takes no heed of the moral side, to the problem of war.

On the boundary line between mere facts and problems stands the theory that the right to make war and the right in war comes simply from the fact of war itself. It is said not to be necessary to justify war by the ordinary maxims of morality, for war bears this justification in itself.

Nietzsche says: "You say that a good cause makes war holy? I tell you, the good war (i.e. the destruction of your enemy) makes everything holy. All those who rejoice in war for its own sake really pay homage to this philosophy."[1]

The other less unscrupulous theory which was common before the Great War, is that war is the blood and iron cure for weakness and idleness. Hegel says that war teaches us the vanity of worldly things, and makes that into reality which had hitherto been only edifying talk.[2] Moltke's saying is well known, "Everlasting Peace is only a dream, not even a beautiful dream, and war is an element in God's Government of the world. It develops in man the noblest virtues, courage and self-denial, love of duty and self-sacrifice. Without war the world would sink into materialism."[3]

The Great War has certainly proved the fallacy of this last opinion. Modern machine warfare may still produce much that is spiritual and good, but its terrible brutality and its imperialistic and capitalistic origin make it far more an orgy of materialism than an influence through punishment, making for something higher and better.

As to the moral justification of war: the morality of an action depends on what is primarily effected by it, not by what its indirect object may have been.

We must put the question then: can war, this awful upheaval, with all its destruction and misery, be in itself permissible? It is clear that its own lawfulness is not the first consideration; it is only the means to an end. And what is that end? It can only be the preservation or restoration of justice. When war is only resorted to as a last means – when every other influence has been tried and has failed – of restoring justice, then it is allowable by natural law.

Justice is the highest good on earth. No material good, no undisturbed possession of this world's goods, neither health nor life itself, is of such high worth and dignity as the guarding of justice. If no home was destroyed, no life lost in war, but justice went unvindicated, it would be shameful.

The fact that war is a destroyer bringing much suffering in its wake would not be sufficient cause to forbid it. When war is waged in the name of outraged justice, then is its work of upheaval holier than any consideration of property or life apart from justice.

---

1. *Thus Sprach Zarathustra.*
2. *Rechtsphilosophie*, 324, Werke, Band VIII.
3. In a letter to Bluntchli, December 11, 1880.

The purely abstract consideration is theoretically unassailable; but we ask ourselves where, in the concrete world of man and nature, war can really be waged in this high and holy way as the servant of justice and as the protector of the moral ordering of the world.

Defensive wars

If, without just cause, one State overruns another, lays waste the land, murders the inhabitants: in a word, treads right and justice under foot, then the State that is attacked has undoubted right to defend itself with armies.

Individuals or nations have the right of defence, and in necessity the right to take their enemy's life to save their own. There is even a deeper principle involved: the shielding of the world's moral order from injustice in the name of God and man. Worse than the attack on human life is the attack on God's order which is destroyed by crime. Where the innocent are saved through the death of the guilty aggressor, the Fifth Commandment is not broken. What is right for the individual is right for the State. If all other means have been tried and have failed, armed defence is justified both in self-defence and in defence of God's moral ordering of the world – God does not will that injustice should go unpunished. The sword must be drawn from the scabbard to resist an unjust attack which can only be opposed by a war of defence.

It will be seen, by the conditions given below, how strongly Catholic moral theology, which in this case only interprets the law of nature, insists that a just cause alone can make a defensive war permissible:

(1) The aggression must be unmistakable. The growth of armaments of other nations is not enough. At the same time it is not indispensable that the enemy should fire the first shot. It suffices that the attack be quite certain – this constitutes the necessity, but –

(2) The defensive must not exceed absolutely necessary defence, for a great war of defence would become unjust if the attacked, when the tide flowed in his favour, attempted more than to make the attacker harmless, since the only ground for allowing war is that the attack of the opponent was unjust.

(3) If justice was on the opposite side – if, for instance, the enemy had gone to war to rectify some great injustice done by the State he is attacking – that State, though on the defensive, would have no right to fight. Justice would forbid any action in opposition – the guilty State must submit to punishment from its adversary.

Now let us ask how often has a war of defence been carried on according to the conditions of the Law of Nature? If these conditions are considered impracticable, does it necessarily follow that they are foolish? Not at all. They are entirely just. What follows then from the fact that man and nature are incapable of waging a simply defensive war? It follows that everyone who has the courage to think the matter out will gravely doubt the practical possibility of such a war as a means to justice.

It is, to begin with, almost impossible to decide who is the original aggressor – whether it is the side which declares war, or that which issues the ultimatum or that which has necessitated the ultimatum. Will any nation acknowledge today, when the feeling of responsibility for the war is very much stronger than formerly, that it was the unjust attacker? Sudden invasions, without any diplomatic announcement, do not take place in these days. No one is now the aggressor in the sense that he could not demonstrate that he was in some degree on the defensive.

In the late war,[1] each State defended or pretended to defend some sacred ideal: Serbia defended herself against absorption by Austria; Russia and Montenegro defended the peoples of their stock; Austria her "Prestige" in the Balkans; Germany her fidelity to her "Nibelungen ideal" (*Nibelungentreue*); England defended the rights of neutrals; Japan the Mongolian interest; France fought to free the annexed provinces from the oppressor; Italy to release her subjected Italian brethren; Armenia for the democratic ideal. Belgium alone fought in self-defence. What Turkey fought for is not apparent, but seemingly she was dragged unwillingly into the fray. These attempts to justify the war by proving it to be purely defensive are so far a move in the right direction in that they show, compared to previous occasions, an increased feeling of the moral responsibility which rests on all Governments in declaring war.

Even if it were proved that a war was strictly defensive, how would the check of the so-called measure of authorised protection really work? What would be practically impossible is the application of punitive justice, the idea being that only one of the fighting parties should bear the punishment resulting from the war and should submit quietly like a boy being punished by his father.

Wars of aggression

It is still more difficult to establish the moral conditions which justify a war of aggression than it is to do so for a defensive war. Theoretically this

---

1. Here and elsewhere the author is referring to World War I.—Ed.

kind of war can also be justified. We have seen that the justification of defensive warfare is based not only on the right of self-defence, but on something deeper still, i.e. the moral order, which cannot be attacked without sinning against law and also against the author of law – Almighty God. An unjust aggressive war not only wrongs the enemy country and its inhabitants, but there are other ways in which one nation fighting against another incurs guilt. Is this guilt to remain unatoned?

So long as there is no super-national tribunal with international powers of punishment there will be no atonement unless the aggrieved State defends itself and calls the aggressor to account. This happens when the war is carried into the aggressor's country and the aggrieved party takes the law into his own hands, in default of an arbitrator, and gets satisfaction. This, since the time of Augustine, has been the tradition of the Catholic Church with regard to the justification of an aggressive war. St. Thomas Aquinas states this clearly,[1] as do Francisco de Vitoria, O.P., and Francisco Suárez, S.J. St. Thomas gives three conditions which make a war just: (1) a declaration of war by the highest authority of the State; (2) a just reason for going to war; and (3) the right object in view.

Lawful authority

The first condition is directed against "the right of the fist" which prevailed in the Middle Ages, by which every little prince or every citizen thought he had the right to make war.

St. Thomas says that private individuals, by whom he means those who have an earthly ruler over them, should seek justice at his hands. And on this is based the justification of war.

It can only be lawful for a State to help itself in this way when there is no power above the State from which it can obtain justice.

An international court, with authority over all States, whose object was to preserve peace would be the lever of Archimedes, whereby the whole world could be raised above war and its miserable substitute of justice. Given the *judicium superioris* of St. Thomas, endowed with the necessary authority and strength, and war as a means of national self-defence is at an end. Till we have this court, he who has the care of any State must protect and defend it from its external enemies and punish them even with the sword. As St. Paul says (Rom. XIII, 4), "Let not the powers that be bear the sword in vain, but they are to be helpers of God and punish evil doers," so also must the rulers defend their trust from outside aggression.

---

1. II, ii, Q. 40.

There is a second point on which the right to make war stands or falls, and in the opinion of many it has fallen! Max Scheler says: "Many consider untenable the Thomistic conception of a punitive war (*bellum punitionis*), but Kant rightly disagrees."[1] And why? "Because between States there is not the relationship of superior to subordinate."[2]

The Scholastics recognise the objection that a Power or a State has no jurisdiction over another State. Cajetan answers that the right of a State to punish its own subjects is undoubted. But foreigners must also submit to punishment if they have sinned against a State because every State must safeguard its own well-being. If a State had not the right to punish foreign peoples and princes, it would be incomplete and imperfect, for tyrants, robbers, murderers, criminals of all kinds, who as citizens of other States have done evil, would avoid all punishment and the national order would be wanting in just the three things which are most important."[3]

Suárez quotes the Old Testament, where God commanded wars for the punishment of guilty nations.[4]

This comparison of a direct command of God must not be taken literally, for it only refers to the State where, according to God's rule, it is "A perfect community." Such a State must of course have rights necessary for its well-being. Does the right to punish the foreign enemy extend to warding off aggressive attacks, i.e. to a war of defence? If this is conceded, how is it reconciled with the Scholastic teaching that the enemy deserving punishment must not defend himself, but accept his chastisement as the act of justice?

This problem of punitive war goes still further. It raises this great question. Can the guilt of the other State be established, and who can establish it? Sometimes of course there is no doubt; but is this generally the case? And yet according to the Scholastics, firstly, undoubted guilt is the only reason for an aggressive war; and secondly, this guilt must be only on the attacking side.

Just ground and just intention

St. Thomas's second requirement for war to be permissible is the "just cause" (*justa causa*). He knows one only: that the attacked have deserved to be attacked because of some fault (*ut scilicet illi, qui impugnantur, prop-*

---

1. *Zum ewigen Frieden*, 6. Präliminarartikel.
2. Scheler, *op. cit.*
3. Cajetan, *Summa S. Thomae*, Comm. il. II, ii, Q. 40.
4. *De Bello*, p. 4.

ter aliquam culpam impugnationem mereantur). St. Thomas quotes St. Augustine, who defines a just war "as the avenging of injustice, when a State or town is to be punished because its inhabitants have been unjust or have neglected rightful restitution."[1] Francisco de Vitoria emphatically requires such deeds of injustice as the one and only justification of a declaration of war.[2] On the authority of St. Augustine, St. Thomas and all the Masters, he says: "Aggressive warfare must have as its object the punishment of unjust dealing. Punishment can only be meted when there has been a fault and an injury to the rights of the aggressor." Also he says: "The Prince has no more authority over foreigners than over his own subjects, but he can use the sword equally against both to punish all unjust deeds. By the law of nature it is murder to kill the innocent."

Clearly from these authorities there must be moral guilt to justify war, and they refer us to St. Paul, who tells us that the Ruler is the helper of God, His avenger of the evil doer.

Vanderpol, in his great work, *La doctrine Scholastique du droit de la Guerre*, considers that it is a great loss to humanity that the Scholastic teaching on war has been in abeyance since the seventeenth century. Commenting on the Pauline text, he says: "A servant of God: he must only punish when God Himself would punish – an avenger of His Wrath. He may punish only those whose actions would call for the wrath of God – those who have done evil. He must never use his power against those who have not sinned."

All moral and religious people who mourn over the light-hearted way in which war is begun will be grateful to Vanderpol for having drawn attention to the teaching of St. Paul and St. Augustine, but he will ask himself whether, in the face of the practical experience of many centuries, these theories are possible. To begin with: what rulers or States in declaring war consider themselves as the helpers of God, the avengers of His Wrath? Therefore, where is the guilt or the guiltlessness? Where is the conflict which on the one side is absolutely just and on the other absolutely unjust? What are the necessary conditions, according to St. Augustine, and the Scholastics? And what do we mean by punishing a whole nation? Is the whole nation ever guilty? And lastly are these just aggressors sure of being only the avengers of the wrath of God, sure that they only right the wrong? Is their just and holy mission sure to triumph and to preserve the true meaning of an aggressive war?

---

1. *Lib. Qualst.*, VI, 10.
2. *De Bello*, I., 3.

These are serious questions to be answered. To the first we may say that it is not necessary for the aggressor to realise that he is in the place of God. Perhaps not for the *results* of his work of punishment; but certainly subjectively, for the sake of the purity of his own conscience and the single-mindedness of the way in which he will carry out his terrible task. Only the General and the Army inspired with something like the Faith of the Israelites of old could let loose so terrible a thing as war in the spirit of God and not of the devil.

And now: where is the guilt and where the guiltlessness? Or is this question of the moral guilt of a just war unimportant? Till the end of the sixteenth century all Catholic Teachers and Theologians held that only the absolutely certain moral guilt of one of the contending parties gave to the other the right to fight. St. Augustine says: "For the wise (the just and the pious) it is the injustice of the opponent's cause which makes a just war."[1] He says again: "In a just war the other side is fighting on the side of sin";[2] and lastly: "The good, if they are really good, do not fight against the good. Those who fight are either the bad against the bad, or the bad against the good, so never good against good, never the defenders of justice against the defenders of justice."[3]

What is to happen if the apportioning of guilt is doubtful? A clear moral rule comes in. In positive doubt nothing must be done. Suárez declares that the State that declares war must have no manner of doubt, the grounds of its rights must be clearer than the day. Mistakes are inexcusable. To declare war is to pass sentence of death, and to do that with a doubting conscience is mortal sin.[4]

Vasquez says that to arrive at certainty, both parties must mutually examine their grounds: not to do so is pure barbarism. But who is to subject his cause to his adversary? Both parties must do so, for no State could be expected to subject itself to its adversary without reciprocity. In these circumstances, where would the proposed war be? Nowhere, for each side would see that each had right on his side and a just war is only conceivable as punishment for injustice: and then each side would acknowledge its faults. (O that the world could think and act with the logic of the Scholastics in their Cloister. The world must! But of that later.)

---

1. *De civ. Dei*, XIX, 7.

2. *Op. cit.*, XIX, 15.

3. *Op. cit.*, XXV, 5.

4. *Schol. Com*, in II, ii, Q. 40, A. 1.

Clearly such a doctrine, strong but not bitter, yet so opposed to military passion and the so-called interests of the State, would be difficult to enforce. The conduct of States and rulers is so different: but would it be impossible to call them before a moral court? Should they be allowed to fight if they acknowledged that there was sufficient right on the enemies' side to make the justice of their cause doubtful?

Suárez is the first who says Yes – that if, after careful examination of the cause of dispute, the prince or ruler considers there is more to be said on his side than on the other, then he is justified in going to war. Suárez applies for the first time the principles of distributive justice to war. With St. Augustine and St. Thomas these principles are applied only to an act of vindictive justice. Suárez teaches that a ruler may go to war knowing that a great deal of right is on the opposite side, but considering that, on the whole, more right is on his side! Here we have the first loosening of the old, strict war morality. The terrors of war are to be let loose because the balance is ever so slightly on the aggressor's side! though even Suárez recommends an umpire. His point of view is most repulsive, for he holds strongly to the punitive character of the aggressor. "The proofs in criminal matters must be sufficient, but if the crime cannot be proved guilt must be presumed."[1]

What becomes of justice when an individual or a nation is sentenced to death on the grounds of probable guilt?

A lively protest was raised against this weakening of the teaching of St. Augustine and the Thomists. Vasquez, in particular, opposed his brother in the Society: "I could never accept such teaching, on the contrary I have always held its dubiousness and believe that it may do great harm to Christianity. That might is right is simply a return to barbarism."[2]

Molina went further.[3] According to him a *material* injustice on the part of those to be attacked justifies a war of aggression. Thus the high character of war as a means of punishment for grave *moral* guilt ceases. It is true of course that in the case of mere national injustice which Molina had in mind, the unjust possession of something belonging to the other State might be a very important consideration for that State. But this unjust possession either can be proved or cannot be proved. If it is proved and the State refused to give up what had been unjustly acquired, then it is morally guilty, and by all the rules of morality may be attacked. If it cannot be

---

1. *De Bello*, 7.

2. *Com. in Summa St. Thomae*, Disp., 64, Cap. 3.

3. *De Justitia et Jure* (Paris, 1602), Tom. 1, Tract II.

proved, then there is not even a material injustice, and war is ruled out. The harm of the war theory lies just in this carelessness in getting direct proof of real injustice. A wrong, an injustice, without moral guilt is a most doubtful thing, and the old school is surely right in insisting on proof of this moral guilt before plunging into the horrors of war. After the strict principles of the old School had been tampered with, excuses for war were made more and more easily. Not all the sixteenth and seventeenth century theologians, however, departed from the more perfect teaching of St. Augustine and St. Thomas. Sylvius in particular (1648) remained true to their principles and says: "When it is a question of imperilling the lives of a mass of men, the safest way must always be chosen. If it is a question of possession, he who is in possession is not bound to give it up, but he must discuss the question with his adversary, he must receive his ambassadors and listen to their propositions." The new School, however, has been active and busy in its teaching. War has been looked upon as a function of commutative justice.

Vanderpol, on the other side, shows how easy it is on such grounds to justify a war undertaken for no just cause, i.e. to keep the so-called balance of power, or to prevent the extension of a neighbouring state. This is all the more important as we find in modern authors no word as to the moral guilt which ought to be punished by war. Things had gone so far that in the nineteenth century Gousset wrote that "war was justified if it were 'necessary' for a nation either to defend it against invasion or to break down any opposition to the exercise of its rights."[1] We ask *what* rights.

How does St. Alfonsus Liguori stand to all these questions? He belongs to the new School and adopts its views – specially those of Busenbaum – but he sympathises with those who consider a declaration of war such a serious matter that it can only be justified if there is no possible doubt as to the justice of the cause. He says "War brings such evils with it – such harm to Religion and to the innocent that in practice it is hardly ever justifiable."[2]

Considering the terrors of modern warfare and their results, and considering also that the Catholic Church *as such* has no defined teaching about war, it is surely permissible to take such a line as to the justifiableness of war as will restrict it as much as possible. This book holds completely to the teaching of St. Augustine and St. Thomas. The deduction we draw from their teaching, that a war of aggression is only allowable when the adversary's guilt is absolutely certain, is that a *just* war of aggression is hardly possible.

---

1. Gousset, *Theol. mor.*, 1845
2. Lib., III, Tract IV, Nh. 404.

The *"justa causa"* must contain two features: moral guilt and certain knowledge of this guilt. A merely judicial or material, i.e., an unconscious guilt, is not enough. It is not an evil deed. Those who commit it are not evil-doers. To declare war on such is forbidden by the laws of nature. Certainly material wrongdoing is to be eliminated from the world, but war is not the means. If we are told that this sets up an unjust state of things, we can truly answer that war does so much more disastrously. Firstly, to go to war on account of a material injustice is immoral and only makes it worse; secondly it is quite uncertain if the injustice will be rectified, and, as a means to the removal of material injustice, war is a failure.

But, before it can be healed, moral guilt requires a cure equal to its enormity. It would be a crime to plunge recklessly into war, even if the fault is proved, without any doubt, to be on the other side. The punishment must be, so far as is possible in earthly justice, in proportion to the moral guilt. For instance, a ruler or ambassador is murdered. This is a great crime committed against some State for political reasons. Should the answer of the injured State be an immediate declaration of war, or even only a short and impossible ultimatum? What are the results? Because one criminal, or group of criminals, commits a crime, millions of innocent people are to be punished in the most terrible ways? Would the real murderers be the sufferers? Supposing even that the injured side wins, is justice appeased when millions of innocent men are slaughtered, others are crippled and maimed for life, women and children are widowed and orphaned, immeasurable property is destroyed? In fact it seems simply the denial of human instincts of right, even though there were no shadow of doubt as to the moral guilt of the conquered State. Instead of a just war would not the following method be better? The State responsible for the political murder should be required to punish the murderer. If this was done adequately there would be no question of war. If not, there should be a referendum of the inhabitants and in modern times the people can practically compel the Government to act as they wish. In this case it would be to insist on the punishment of the murderer and giving such satisfaction as was possible. Only when the majority refused satisfaction, i.e., sided with the murderer, would the question of war be raised as the punishment of moral guilt: and in these circumstances when the country was being dragged into war, the inhabitants would be justified in refusing military service.

But justice also lays a heavy responsibility on the other side before it dares to resort to war. As the meaning of war really is atonement, it must not be entered into unless this object is moderately certain of attainment.

Hence Cajetan and Vitoria maintain that no war must be begun unless the attacking party is morally sure of victory.

The following point deserves particular notice. Vitoria teaches that a town or province has the right of reconquest, and yet, nevertheless, war is forbidden because of its disastrous results. As we have seen, war must only be undertaken in the common interest. For example, if a town can only be retaken at the price of enormous evils, by injuring many other towns, by the murder of countless men, when it would cause enmities amongst Princes, would probably result in further wars, and if it would harm the Church, then the Prince must undoubtedly withdraw from the war, even if its results would include the conversion of the heathen.

For example, suppose the King of France had rights on the Province of Milan, but that war would bring great suffering and distress both to France and to Milan, the King would not be allowed to go to war, as war could only be permitted if it were to benefit both France and Milan. If, on the contrary, it was to injure them it would not be a just war.

> A war is not just, if it is evident that it will do the State more harm than good, even if there is "just cause." The State has only the right to declare war for self-protection, and the defence of itself and its property. If a war must result in its being weakened then the war is unjust, no matter by what King or State it is declared.

The leading thought of his book, the necessity of Unity and mutual consideration in the Mystical Body of Christ, is dealt with by Vitoria as follows: "A Christian Province is part of a State, a State part of the whole world: so if a war benefits one Province or one State, but injures the whole world or Christendom, I consider such a war unjust."

Thus the School of St. Augustine and St. Thomas limits the right of a State to declare war even when the guilt of the opponent is clear. The common conception of national honour does not consider the results of war – commonsense and morality, which differ in many respects from this conception, do consider these results and declare this game of hazard, which is war, immoral, and therefore forbidden even when national honour has been insulted and the enemy refuses satisfaction! Divine and human interests are more important than the interest of the individual State.

Here we have the whole difference between the mediaeval and the modern outlook. Before the Western communities were individualized and rent in pieces, the community interests were in the foreground. National egoism which thinks only of itself, was condemned even where the ideal involved heavy sacrifice. After the individual – and also the individual State – became emancipated from the higher obligation to the community, national individual interest became the chief thing and the supernatural interest of the community at large, a side issue. This does not mean that hitherto there has been no unprincipled self-seeking and trickery in national life, and in the conduct of war, but that there was no moral theory which justified it. The new individualistic morality as opposed to the old morality of solidarity is just the *proton Pseudos* of false, modern culture.

The second *justa causa* is the undeniable assurance of moral guilt. And here let us remember that apart from the actual point at issue, there is the psychological fact to bear in mind that very often the fault exists only in the imagination of the accuser and proceeds from his arrogance, whether it is the individual or the State.

We can see the mote in the eye of another and not the beam in our own. This weighty fact is just as worthy of consideration with regard to the justice of a war as are external circumstances. The Catholic Professor of Moral Theology John Baptist von Hirscher lays much stress on this. "The first question," he writes, in his chapter on war,

> is, has there been a real unjust insult? Pride, greed, over-bearingness, love of power, are often hurt, but there need be no injury to justice in the offence but on the contrary, opposition to oppression and greed of possession, unjust annexation, etc. Powerful nations, too, are often condescending and overbearing to their neighbours and intend to insult them if they offer any opposition. No one is free from guilt and all should remember the saying: do to others as you would they should do to you. If there is real injury, it is for the injured party to complain in a fair and manly, but not offended, manner. If this is not done then the cause must be made public and pleaded before a Court of Nations. Possibly the result of this appeal will be that the wrong will be righted. If not, then the time of necessity and self-help has come. The first step is reprisals – the last step, war.

As regards the "just cause." The old moralists forbid war if it can be found that the unjustly accused side had given great provocation. If the Thomists do not acknowledge a war to be just on both sides, it does not follow that they do not acknowledge a cause of strife that is justifiable on both sides, all they ask is that no doubtful case should lead to war. Right and wrong can be so shared by both sides that humanly speaking it is impossible to apportion the blame.

"Right," Lammasch says,

> is not always on one side and falsehood and mere bluff on the other. Often it is only a question of forcing the original cause of war far enough back. War

may be justifiable from the immediate point of view and unjustifiable if we look further back for the cause. Unless we can unravel the original causes we cannot say whose is the original guilt. State A has wronged State B centuries ago. The bitterness and hate have simmered for ages, and finally State B does something which State A considers a just cause of war.[1]

It may well be said that the State that makes war, never has believed in its own wrong and the right of its adversary. It has always considered that there were justifiable grounds for attack or self-defence. For instance, Mohammedans were convinced of the justice of their Religious wars – Christians equally convinced of their injustice. In modern times we remember the Royal Proclamations on both sides. King William, in 1866, declares:

> Austria will not forget that her Princes once ruled Germany and she will therefore only see in young Prussia an enemy rival instead of an ally, and consider that she must always oppose Prussia because what benefits her harms Austria. An old, unholy jealousy burns fiercely again. Prussia is to be weakened, and dishonoured. Faith is not kept with her. Wherever we in Germany look, we are surrounded by enemies and their war-cry is the humiliation of Prussia. To the last minute I have sought and left open the path to a friendly solution, but Austria does not will it.

The Emperor Franz-Josef, on the same day, issued the following proclamation: "The latest events show unmistakably that Prussia puts Might in the place of Right and therefore this unholy war of German against German is inevitable. I call him who is responsible for it before the judgement Seat of God to answer for all the misery he is bringing on nations and individuals."

And on which side was the *justa causa*? If war broke out now between France and Germany both would be convinced that they had right on their side. Therefore we may be sure that only history – namely a later generation – can possibly judge fairly as to who is responsible for a war. In the excitement of political conflict it would be impossible so to prove the moral guilt of the opponent that no doubt would remain, and yet an absolute certainty is necessary for the justification of war.

St. Thomas's third condition for a just war is a right intention (*intentio recta*). His definition is:

> The intention to further Good and avoid Evil. For, says, St. Augustine, in *De verbis Domini*, "With the true servants of God even wars make for Peace, as they are not undertaken for greed and cruelty but for the sake of Peace, that

---

1. *Volkermond oder Volkerbund*, Haag, 1920.

the wicked may be restrained and the good protected." Therefore it may be that a war is declared by lawful authority and for a just cause and may yet not be justifiable because the intention of those undertaking it is wrong. For what Augustine rightly blames in war, is "the desire to harm, the cruelty of revenge, a vindictive spirit, the rage of self-defence, the lust of power and such like."

It is truly difficult to justify war. For it is to be not only just but quite free from evil intent and ugly passions. Has there ever been a war without the "wish to harm" (*nocendi cupiditas*) or without "the lust of power" (*libido dominandi*), and "such like"?[1]

The right way

Suárez and Bellarmine add a fourth condition to the three of St. Thomas, namely: *debitus modus* – the right way of conducting war.

Victor Cathrein, S.J., defines it in the following terms: "The conduct of the war must be confined within the limits of justice and love."[2] This condition deserves special notice when it is applied to modern warfare.

War comes up every hour against "the limits of love and justice," and it would indeed be difficult to remember them always. But one limitation must surely always be held sacred: the difference between combatants and non-combatants, between armed and unarmed. It is dishonourable to bear arms against those who cannot defend themselves – against old people, women and children, indeed against civilians at all. In fact it is against military law, except in absolutely unavoidable circumstances, i.e., the siege of a town when civilians have to share the soldiers' fate. Their injury is then, even in just war, quite unavoidable; but if done intentionally it becomes a crime crying to Heaven for vengeance.

The whole of Catholic Moral Theology forbids in the strongest terms the injury or killing of unarmed *persons*, with direct intention, and condones it only *per accidens*, namely, when unavoidable. This follows from the old view of war as the punishment of guilt – those carrying arms were considered the guilty – the civil population innocent. This distinction, of course, takes for granted that the soldiers have joined the army to go to the help of their Ruler of their free will, and do not belong to a conscript army, the members of which are really in the position of innocent citizens. The old authorities call those fighting for the unjust cause "guilty," but the non-combatants "innocent"; and they lay down that it is never justifiable to

---

1. II, ii, Q. 40, A. 1.
2. *Moralphilosophie* (Freiburg, 1911), II., S., 744.

kill the innocent by direct intention – *per accidens* is the only justification. Francisco de Vitoria says,

> We must be careful that war does not bring with it greater evils than it is to cure. If a decisive victory depends on the destruction of a fortress or garrison containing a number of innocent, defenceless people, it is not permissible to sacrifice them in order that a lesser number of the guilty should be punished. Let the tares grow with the wheat – lest in pulling up the tares the wheat is pulled up too.

Today the idea of punishing moral guilt is forgotten, but the distinction between innocent and guilty remains: and the newest idea is that even this should be done away with. It is certain that modern military technique no longer takes the distinction into consideration. Poison Gas Warfare is specially directed against the civil population, which is a sufficient proof of its injustice and its criminal murderous character.

Summary

If we consider the conditions which justify a war from the standard of Catholic morality we find that war is almost an impossibility. Defence or restoration of justice are the only justifications for war. As faith in attaining these ends by means of war slowly disappears one also finds that Catholic authors are restricting more and more the occasion when war may be considered permissible.

Hirscher has already taught

> that before the bar of justice and morality only a defensive war that protects inalienable possessions can be justified and that, only after every other means has been tried and has failed. An offensive war between nations is just what robbery, murder and violence are between individuals, but robbery, murder, and violence on what a scale! A war for any subordinate interest, however undeniable the claim may be, is always against the spirit of Christianity. If it concerns possessions which a nation will miss why not let it be? 'Rather suffer wrong gladly' applies to nations as much as to individuals, and wrong suffered for God's sake and for the sake of peace will never bring dishonour.[1]

The exalted Christian ideal that for nations to suffer injustice brings with it no shame is so completely opposed to the standard of modern statecraft, that it is not surprising that in no other book on Moral Theology do we find such teaching. We have to look for the Christian ideal in the teaching of men like Tagore. Certainly Eberle does not acknowledge an aggressive war

---

1. *Die christliche Moral* (Tübingen, 1838), III, 5, 714.

as just. He maintains that the only moral justification of war is necessity – a war, defensive and really preventive.[1] The modern writer, Schulemann, in 1923 says: "On the whole only defensive wars can be just."[2]

Max zu Sachsen explains that "the state should only be allowed to make war when the alternative is to be literally overrun, so that it is compelled to defend itself to avoid destruction."[3] Even if others take a laxer view of an offensive war, all Catholic moralists condemn a war undertaken for any reason short of gross injustice. According to unanimous Catholic teaching, all are unjust when undertaken for national or dynastic interests, from covetousness or lust of conquest (Imperialism or lust of annexation), wars manoeuvred by Cabinets or religious wars, in fact the overwhelming majority of all past wars. Their authors are, perhaps, to be excused, as they acted in the spirit of their surroundings, but they in no way deserve to be honoured by national memorials or extolled in patriotic verse. The verdict of the Christian conscience is quite different. With St. Augustine it calls an unjust war, even of its own country, "a gigantic robbery."

Here we come across the old teaching of St. Augustine and the Thomists, supported by Suárez and Bellarmine, with their four conditions of a just war. It may seem strangely out of place in the world of today, fit only for the Cloister from which it came – so much the worse for the world! During the last centuries the world's conscience has been so darkened and confused by nationalism and militarism that it can no longer grasp any national moral idea. Woe to morality if it capitulate. Morality must not adapt itself to men, but men to morality, even if the accepted point of view has to be broken down. *Fiat justitia pereat mundus*, the world will say scornfully, but no, *Fiat justitia floreat mundus*, we must and we will say. European civilisation has collapsed not because of the war-morality of the Middle Ages, but because of the war-immorality of the new age. If there is to be any improvement the moral anarchy must be overcome which has arisen between different States, from the idea of the absoluteness of the State. The *lex aeterna*, which is above all States and which makes for justice, must once more be the foundation of the State. By the necessary limitation of their rights the nations will not be weakened but, on the contrary, strengthened. The world, civilisation, society, the Church, are all crying out that war may be overcome. A simply sentimental sense of need is not enough and cannot satisfy any thinking man. The ending of war, or at least the possibility of its

---

1. *Krieg und Frieden im Urteil chr. Moral*, S. 8.
2. *Kern aller Philosophie*, S. 138.
3. Max zu Sachsen, *Ratschläge und Mahnungen zum Volks und Menscheitswohl*.

being reduced almost to nothing, must be founded on a clear, thought-out, moral system. We believe that the Augustinian-Thomist theory can render this service to the world and to the Church. Just because it makes war's *raison d'être* so difficult, it is the most practical and useful theory that can be thought out and fits in with the new moral consciousness which has been born of the agony of the World War. The modern conscience asks imperatively for that *judicium superioris*, that tribunal of justice above all State courts and rights of nations, the failure of which alone, according to St. Thomas, justifies war. The modern conscience is occupying itself in an unprecedented manner with the moral guilt of war. That war is the affair only of princes and statesmen is no longer believed. Never has war been so generally considered a crime. Men are asking that the moral guilt should be declared and the guilty sharply punished. Such an attitude was unknown ten years ago, and it is precisely the Augustinian conception of the responsibility of the State. If this guilt can never be established without doubt then so much the better, for there is no cause for war and it must not be declared. The best teaching is that which makes it most difficult to find a ground for war, which always takes the arms out of the hands of one party – and on the Augustinian and Thomist principles in no war are both parties in the right – and gives the citizens a handle to justify them in declining to fight. This was the teaching till the seventeenth century of the Catholic Schools! On one side, a war is always unjust. Augustine says of war that it is a struggle for sin. Cajetan declares that an unjust war is in itself a mortal sin.[1]

"No authority," says Francisco de Vitoria,

> can command the death of the innocent, and in an unjust war the enemies are innocent, therefore it is not permissible to kill them. The ruler who declares such a war is guilty, and not those only who do evil but those also who agree to it, are worthy of death (Rom. L, 32). Even if the ruler gives the order, a soldier must not put innocent citizens to death and it follows that if a soldier is convinced of the injustice of a war he must not take part in it, for anything that is against a man's conscience is sin.[2]

As to the "just cause" the ordinary soldier is probably not able to judge but he can do so as to the "intention," the *intentio recta* – and as to the way the war is conducted, for the *intentio recta* according to St. Thomas consists in seeking good and avoiding evil, and the ordinary citizen can

---

1. Cajetan, *Summula V.*, Bellum.

2. *De jure belli*, II, 2. [Stratmann's citation corresponds to section 20 of the 1917 (reprinted, 1995) edition of *De Iure Belli*. *Vide supra*, p. 226, note 4, for the full citation.—Ed.]

certainly form an opinion on this, especially as to the right way – the *debitus modus*. If this *modus* transgresses the demands of morality, the war, according to St. Thomas, is unjust and the soldiers must not take part in it. Vitoria and others consider that it is not the *duty* of the private soldier to enquire into the justice of a war, but that he has the *right* to do so and Vitoria says: "The injustice may be so flagrant that ignorance can be no excuse, otherwise the unbelievers who followed their leaders into wars against Christians and murdered them would be blameless, or the Roman soldiers who crucified Christ at the command of Pilate."[1] This question of the right of freedom of conscience in taking part in war is a fiercely contended point today, and the question of refusing military service comes up. There may be much that is ignoble, unheroic and materialistic, connected with it; obedience to rightful authority in everything not opposed to the Christian conscience and that is not sinful, is of course a plain duty, but refusing to serve can be justified on the highest Christian principles, specially when the sinfulness of modern warfare is considered. Further, it is extremely dangerous when this modern movement against war threatens to be, like the devils who were driven out by Beelzebub, the prince of the devils, the reckless revolutionising of the masses against lawful authority, and the unchecked rule of individualism. But it is therefore all the more necessary that the protest against the boundless arbitrariness and barbarity of modern war should find an echo where the greatest spiritual and moral power is still enthroned: on the rock of Peter. It must be confessed that the protest against the exaggerated power of the State and military ruthlessness, and the right, in certain cases, to deny obedience to the State, can be confirmed by appealing to Tradition, Holy Writ and to the noblest authorities of the Church teaching and the Church taught.

That classical teaching of peace and justice, which has been formulated by the greatest teachers of the Church, Augustine and Thomas Aquinas, must stand against modern anarchical Pacifism for the thought on which it is grounded was unquestioned till the seventeenth century and belongs to the future as much as to the past.

The following ten points contain the principles which constitute a just war according to St. Augustine, the Thomists, and Francisco de Vitoria:

1. **Gross injustice on the part of one, and only one, of the contending parties.**

---

1. *De jure belli*, I, II. [As above, the citation in this case corresponds to section 26 of the 1917 edition.—Ed.]

2. Gross formal moral guilt on one side – material wrong is not sufficient.

3. Undoubted knowledge of this guilt.

4. That war should only be declared when every means to prevent it have failed.

5. Guilt and punishment must be proportionate. Punishment exceeding the measure of guilt is unjust and not to be allowed.

6. Moral certainty that the side of justice will win.

7. Right intention to further what is good by the war and to shun what is evil.

8. War must be rightly conducted: restrained within the limits of justice and love.

9. Avoidance of unnecessary upheaval of countries not immediately concerned and of the Christian community.

10. Declaration of war by lawful authorised authority exercised in the name of God.

Failing these conditions war is unjust. Whether they have been fulfilled, in the past or in the present, or are likely to be fulfilled in the future, the reader must decide.

Our motto must be, "Backward and forward to St. Augustine and to St. Thomas Aquinas."

(2) In Revelation

(a) In the Old Testament

The examination of natural law with regard to war as a whole reveals much that is unnatural and wrong. The unending and destructive struggle of man and man shows such degeneration as can only be accounted for by the Christian doctrine of the Fall: but even so war is not a necessity. It always has depended on man's freewill and always will. It is only necessary when, how and for so long as man wills it. Man is, therefore, responsible for war. Only as the last resource of justice and under quite exceptional circumstances may the State employ it as the Hand of God to avenge His wrath against evildoers.

Revelation tells us that in certain circumstances and for certain purposes God has Himself put this instrument into the hands of man. The Old Testament speaks of wars undertaken by the Chosen People in the Name of God and carried on at His command. Some critics do not take these passages literally. Max von Sachsen says: "This is the Old Testament language which refers everything that happens to the ordering of God." Origen, who was absolutely opposed to war, considered the Old Testament wars as allegorical and typical – as shadows and pictures of spiritual and moral combats against sin and the powers of darkness, foreshadowing the great fight of Christ and His people against these powers. According to him not even in the Old Testament is there a God of war: "Unless the terrible stories of wars in the Old Testament are to be considered allegorical, the Disciples of the Lord Jesus who came to preach peace, would never have allowed them to be read in Church." On the same grounds Bishop Ulfilas left the war books out of his translation of the Bible, but even if we acknowledge them, and accept as true that God ordered war, it only means that He did so in very exceptional circumstances. It certainly follows that not every war is necessarily immoral and to be condemned, as God cannot approve of anything immoral even to gain the most holy ends. It is possible that something in itself wrong may be ordered by God for some special object, and in that way become right. For instance, a child killed by its father. If God commands such an act, as He did in the case of Abraham and Isaac, simply because it is God's Will, it becomes right and moral. It may be so with the wars of the Old Testament that they were not against the moral law simply because they were undertaken in obedience to the command of God and in exceptional circumstances, but even if these wars were not overruling of God's ordinary laws scriptural justification of war cannot be stretched further than to cover these concrete cases. It is not fair, on account of the biblical wars, to justify war for all time as people are so fond of doing. There is also development in Revelation – religious, moral and cultural progress. Nothing is more untrue than to think that Revelation teaches that the world and mankind are never to develop and that everything is the same for all eternity. The Kingdom of Heaven is like the seed hidden in the ground, but which is ever growing till it becomes the great tree and if mankind as a whole, after the Fall, is ever developing from such lowly beginnings to a higher culture, so also is this the law of the Kingdom of God. He chose one nation for the realisation of His plan for the government of the world. It was to carry out His ideal, to keep monotheism pure and gradually to permeate the whole human race with the moral principles of the Decalogue. For this high object war, in those early days, was necessary as the means whereby to overcome the surrounding nations, sunk in idolatry and wickedness. The object of these wars was to bring these nations into the Theocracy and under the Blessing of the True God – also under the discipline of His yoke, and if the people of Israel wielded the chastening rod of war – they most certainly felt it themselves. The Israelites and the nations surrounding them were to be brought through a hard schooling, through the law of fear and of atoning justice, to a higher dispensation, to a kingdom of peace and love, to the promised reign of Christ the Messiah. Also under the Old Covenant, war had a special ethos. It was the School of God suited to the actual state of human development – the hardships of war braced up a very sensuous nation to physical and moral endurance. It was therefore the judgement of God, a punishment for sin and also an acknowledgment of the True God because the ever-recurring victories of the Chosen People over all their enemies were proof of the divine calling and protection. So it is that the stories and lessons of the Old Testament about the people of God are unique. These wars have a special and sometimes a wonderful character. It can even be said that in them the human leadership was a side issue, a disguise for the immediate acts of God. As we read in the word of God, in Chronicles xxv:8, "If you think that the strength of war is in the armies, God will let you be overcome by your enemies for it is the Lord's to help and to destroy." To refer, then, to the Old Testament wars as a justification for later ones devoid as these are of any religious object, is quite unfair, and it is equally unfair to drag out Old Testament texts to justify the modern war spirit which completely ignores the Christian revelation and development of the New Testament. If the commands of God for justice and a high standard in war really prove anything, the defenders of this thesis can be answered by their own argument: so be it – God's command justifies war. Show me, then, a command of God which justifies war *as it is today*, and I will believe in its righteousness. If you cannot do this, then I must decline to believe, because such a terrible upsetting of all order as modern war brings with it can only be justified by a direct command of God.

This is plainly only an argument *ad hominem* for people who can twist the justification of modern warfare out of the divine commands of the Old Testament.

Would that we could call forth the noble *ethos* and aim which lay beneath the Old Testament wars! That inspired patriotism was truly of divine origin, the war songs were religious songs, for the Israelite the death of the enemies of Jehovah was a sacrificial act. Would any one dare to compare what Benedict XV calls the "suicide" of a modern European war, caused as it is by capitalism, imperialism, and militarism run wild, with the conflicts of the Jewish Theocracy?

Lastly the Old Testament shows something nobler than the theocratic war inspiration. The theocratic theories of peace are far more characteristic – first in their infancy but gradually developing. The most perfect periods of Old Testament conceptions of God were the very earliest and the prophetic, those namely which acknowledged the universal being of God.

These were equally the times of peace and peace theories. God's thoughts were of peace and reconciliation for all nations and peoples. It was during the less perfect times of religious faith and thought that God, on account of the hardheartedness of men, condescended to be the ally of one nation only. The Prophets who were the purest interpreters of the Old Testament spirit were above this standpoint. In the light of their teaching the Old Covenant does not appear as supporting war but as overcoming it.

(b) In the New Testament

When we open the New Testament we are in another world. Coming straight from the Old Testament, and from the warlike spirit of the historical and poetical books, the complete absence of such a spirit strikes us all the more sharply. We hear nothing of war's heroism, the national point of view has disappeared, and instead we leave behind us all this earthly glitter. It seems sometimes as if to Our Lord the State was a *quantité négligeable*, which, of course, had its rights, which must be respected and whose dues must be paid, but which was not to be weighed in the balance with the Kingdom of God. With what self-assurance Our Lord puts Himself above the national customs, how lovingly He welcomes foreigners, foreigners who were repugnant politically and religiously to the Jew. The relation of the Gospel to the State and to armies can only be understood if we take into consideration these hidden matters. In the beginning of the late war a great attempt was made to justify war from the Gospels. In truth Our Lord gave no opinion on war either for or against it. He stands above it. Tax collector or captain, priest or Pharisee, Jew, Samaritan or Roman, man or woman, matters not. He sees only men, their souls and spirits. The profession of a soldier may be good or bad, like anything else, and it is the same with tax gathering, interpreting the law, marriage feasts or carrying the dead to their graves, even with prayer and Sabbath keeping. If military service, with all it involves, serves to preserve order and righteousness, then Our Lord gives it His Blessing. When it leads to outrageous pride, to bullying instead of serving, to oppressing instead of bringing freedom, to devastating instead of protecting, when order and justice are trodden under foot, men and nations hounded one against another, when the life and health of nations are destroyed in the insatiable lust for power and blood, when incredible harm is done to the Kingdom of God, its freedom, its temples, when its souls are trampled down and soiled, then the loving eyes of Christ are turned away and from His sacred lips rings out the terrible sentence "Get thee hence, Satan." It is absurd to compare the horrors of a great war with the military service of the Captain of Capharnaum, and to argue from Our Lord's goodness to him that the infamy of the World War would have His Blessing. It is blasphemous to try and reconcile the Spirit of Christ with the swamp of sin such a war is from its beginning to its end. If we want to keep in Christ's or St. Paul's opinion we must not think of the humble soldier of Capharnaum, or of that other who stood by the Cross, startled and amazed by that great sacrifice; or of Cornelius, the Centurion; but of those politicians and military leaders, the industrial speculators, and the speculators on the Stock Exchange who play with men's bodies as if they were dice. There is a mighty difference between war *and* war, and as we have seen it is almost impossible, without God's special help, for any war to be so conducted that the requirements of justice and morality are satisfied. It must be caused by very great moral guilt, its object must be the furthering of good and avoiding of evil, and it must be so conducted that the limitations of justice and love are never infringed. A war on such a high plane would be holy. We should bow before it in reverence and Christ Himself with the Gospels in His Hand, would bless it. But put war as it is today with its lust of the eye, lust of the flesh, and pride of life before the eyes and heart of Christ! Would He not turn away weeping, with the words: "The world, oh Christendom, oh Mystical Body of which I am the Head, would that thou hadst known the things that belong to thy Peace? But they are hidden from thine eyes." Each case, each individual soldier, each war, Christ judges as to its justice, and certainly His sentence is not less severe than that of the theologians of the Middle Ages. It is impossible to say that Christ acknowledged war as the recognised means of arranging international disputes, nor can we allow that the Christian conscience should be reconciled to war because of its periodical recurrence. When Our Lord speaks of war and rumours of war, referring either to the destruction of Jerusalem or to the end of the world, He does not prophesy that war is to be a regular occurrence in the Christian era. There is no justification for such an idea. Our Lord tells us that wars are accompanied with terror and fear.

In a like manner the Gospel also reckons with the historical fact of sin. We know that we shall sin again and again, yet we are bound to avoid sin, for ourselves individually and also to influence others to avoid it. Just such a duty has the Christian about war. It is the result of sin, but also the cause of far more sins, and in countless cases it is in itself sinful. The mere fact that an evil exists or recurs can never satisfy the Christian conscience.

People even go further and say because of the friendliness of Our Lord Himself, and St. John the Baptist, and St. Paul with soldiers, that the Gospel cannot be the friend of soldiers, and the enemy of war. We might as well say that the Gospel could not be the friend of sinners and the enemy of sin. Christ always makes this difference between person and thing, between sinner and sin. He condemns the sin and pities the sinner. We ourselves are perpetually in the same position. The socialist curses capitalism and blesses the individual capitalist, a pacifist may be the sternest opponent of everything military and yet his dearest friend is a soldier. How can people draw the conclusion that because St. John the Baptist and Our Lord and St. Paul did not insist on soldiers giving up their profession, they approved of war. Do not Christians, priests and religious, come daily in contact with those whose outlook and manner of life they disapprove, without thinking it necessary to expound their errors to them? Christ, St. John and St. Paul do not say a word against their heathen religion to the Roman soldiers – but they do not, therefore, approve of it. The Gospel method of conversion is always tender. Its spirit works slowly, like leaven, in the Jewish and heathen masses, and only looks for error and imperfection to be got rid of very slowly. But in fact this friendly intercourse of Christ and His followers – with *foreign* soldiers (and this should be noticed) – is directly opposed to the war spirit, for it shows us that they were quite free from nationalism.

We must not make the common mistake, made by those who wish to justify war, of pressing the letter, or some illustration, quite unfairly in order to get the meaning we want. Certainly this would be easier for the enemy than for the friend of war. Anything can be "proved" from Scripture. Still, the spirit of the Gospel is plain enough – justice, love, peace, humility. Because that spirit is just, it cannot, in certain circumstances, forbid injustice being met and opposed by force. Radical Pacifism, or the anarchical quietism of Tolstoy, which denies this right to use force, would become a Gospel of thieving and murder if any State adopted it. It is absolutely discredited by the Gospel account of the cleansing of the Temple when Our Lord used physical force to drive out the buyers and sellers, and overthrew the tables of the money changers. He said to those who sold doves: "Make not My Father's House a den of thieves." We are told that His Disciples remembered the text, "The zeal of Thine House has eaten me up" (St. John ii:14–17). Christ's words, "But you shall not withstand evildoers" (St. Matt. v:39) must not be taken as accepting injustice patiently. It is quite true that He forbids the Old Testament's eye for an eye, tooth for a tooth – the idea that we have a *right* to revenge, to the requital of evil with evil. The meaning of His command to Christians is: you must not withstand evil with evil, but, contrariwise as I do, with good. The renunciation of this right of resistance really affects the private individual when he is unjustly accused and suffering is brought on himself alone. It is always a Christian's duty to see that when he defends himself against wrong he does not do wrong himself. If war could be carried on in the spirit of Christ in the Temple, with that consuming zeal for God's Honour, as God's Helper, as the executor of justice on evildoers (Rom. xiii:4; St. Thom. II, II, Q. 40, A. 1), then it would be justified before the judgement bar of the Gospel, but then only.

Common sense tells us that the *just cause* for war must be more than mere *material guilt*. The Gospel idea of justice is a higher and deeper idea than that of the Old Testament. To Christians and therefore to Christian politicians, statesmen, soldiers and generals, Christ says: "Unless your justice exceed the justice of Scribes and Pharisees you cannot enter the Kingdom of Heaven. You have heard that it was said of old 'thou shalt not kill. Whoso killeth shall be in danger of the judgement,' but I say unto you, whoso is angry against his brother, whoso calls him *Raca* is in danger of the judgement, but whoso calls him *thou fool* (one who forgets God, *Gottvergessener*) shall be in danger of Hell fire" (St. Matt. v:20–22).

That is the judgement of Christ. It is deep and stern, and searches the heart and forbids not only the unjust deed, but the unjust feeling.

If this is the Gospel spirit how can we imagine that it gives its approval to war? So far we have only thought of the justice of the Gospel, not its Love, which expects us to love our enemies! Love them always! Before war, during war, after war: "You had heard that it has been said to them of old time, thou shalt love thine enemy, do good to those that hate you, pray for those who despitefully use you and persecute you. For if you only love those who love you, what praise have you? Do not the heathen do likewise? Be ye also perfect as your Father in Heaven is perfect" (St. Matt. v:43).

People who want to be good Christians and also good citizens of this world are perplexed by such words as these – their religious and worldly duties seem in honourable, but painful, conflict. A great breadth of mind and heart is indeed necessary if we are to understand them and their results. All the sects are wanting in this breadth. Their very existence depends on this one-sidedness. Their vision is limited to one side, almost to one word of the Gospel teaching. There is only one truth, generally only part of a truth, in this one-sided view, and therein lies their strength and their weakness. Their strength, because all their thought and striving and tolling is fixed on one point. Their weakness, because they must miss a universal outlook.

Those sects which condemn war always, and under any conditions, see in the Gospel only love and patience and peace, only the Christ who is meek and lowly of Heart and Who suffers wrong willingly. When they are confronted with the stern cleansing of the Temple, they are reduced to some such explanation as this:

> Because the Lord Jesus, when He cleansed the Temple, made a scourge of cords, does not prove that He used it, or that the traders were frightened by it. It was only a manifestation of divine peace to which they had to yield. The scourge may have been used to drive out the cattle (John Horch).

Equally they pass over the solemn warning of St. Paul that the powers that be are ordained by God, for the terror of the evildoers, and that they are not to wield the sword in vain, but are to use it in the Name of God against evildoers. (Rom. xiii:4)

They emphasise the love of the Gospel so much that they forget the justice. The Gospel is wide as God Himself circled with the greatest mercy and the greatest justice, with Heaven and Hell. Justice, strength, sternness, the avoiding and the punishing of wrong must and shall remain. This is the answer to those who so misunderstand the teaching of Christ about Love – even to loving our enemies – and making His Teaching useless in real life, especially in the life of the State.

On the other hand we must not lessen the Gospel command of love, any more than that of justice. Evangelical justice is the application of force, free from any sinful passion, from hate, or love of strife, love of vengeance, or greed of possessions, and except in most rare and unusual cases it falls back on spiritual methods instead of force; and here we must say a word to those who do not really grasp the Gospel spirit. They undervalue its real strength and power. They believe that hardness in life, and of men to each other wins the day over love and spiritual methods. The fate of Christ and the martyrs proves it. The fate of Christ and His true Disciples proves exactly the contrary. Those spiritual weapons of love, handled by Jesus and His followers, are incomparably sharper and more powerful than the arms of any warring power. This or that political kingdom has been set up by the

Those who the word live by
Those who live by the sword die by the sword
JUST-WAR DOCTRINE: THE METAPHYSICAL AND MORAL PROBLEM

sword, and there, surely, through its own sword or the enemy's, it has been by degrees weakened, and at last overcome.

Through the sword, things remain as they were. The benefits that come through the sword are no real benefits which can satisfy man's higher needs, only spirituality and love give us such benefits. They really build up the world, and the progress of true culture (which is something different from civilisation) is only possible when we have the spirit of peace and love.

The path of that spirit is often through suffering, as with Christ and the martyrs, but at last comes triumph, the triumph of the spirit of love.

Unfortunately the politicians of no State have tried the methods of Evangelical justice and love: that State would indeed be the greatest and most wonderful in the world. The ideal may not be realised till the millenium, but the Christian conscience must always have before it the ideal of the justice and the love of Christ even if it is never to be realised.

The over-ruling of wars is assuredly the most urgent need of any really Christian policy. Take any of the causes of war in the course of history and measure them under the Eye of Christ. The provocation may have been great, but would He have authorised the aggrieved State by its declaration of war to send millions of men to their death? Should any king or minister or politician – a Disciple of Christ – decide differently in any *casus belli* to his Master, Christ? This is the only question which concerns Christians. The Christian who has different standards of justice for political and for private life differs from Christ. For Him there is no double standard of justice, no political interest alongside of the religious interest. Politics must be religious. The solution we are seeking is not indeed "Peace at any price," but "Justice at any price." But it is the justice of Christ which pursues murder and any hatred and bitterness unrelentingly. War undertaken for any other object than from zeal for the justice of Christ, which means the moral order announced and exacted by Him, is not to be accepted by the Christian conscience. If this object, which alone is allowable, cannot be attained by the world as it is today, then war loses any right to be, and loses that right far more before the bar of the Gospel than before that of the Law of Nature.

THE EDITORS' GLOSS: What follows is an extract from Cardinal Ottaviani's masterful treatise on the public law of the Church, *Institutiones Juris Publici Ecclesiastici* (Vatican, Polyglot. 3rd Edition, 1947). Specifically it comes from Vol. I (*Jus Publicum Internum*), *Pars I, Titulus iii, Art. 3* (*Relationes societatum perfectarum in statu conflictus*), *Principium 2*, pp. 149-55. The English translation is based principally on that found in the English Dominican magazine *Blackfriars* of September 1949, with corrections and modifications as appropriate.

Cardinal Ottaviani is a man who needs no introduction. Best known for his opposition to the New Order of the Catholic Mass, he is also known as the Council Father at Vatican II who was so concerned about the council's liberal direction that he said, "I pray to God that I may die before the end of the council – in that way I can die a Catholic." His testimony as it concerns just-war doctrine is not, therefore, that of a raving, "left-wing" lunatic. It is rather the considered judgment of a serious, if not intransigent, Catholic theologian and prelate. As Fr. Stratmann noted: "Because of his scholarly accomplishments, as well as his personal standing at the Vatican, Cardinal Ottaviani is in the first place a man of such authority that his opinion cannot be ignored as might that of just any moralist and canonist."

And that opinion runs thus: "modern war is to be altogether forbidden." It is a position that did not weaken as time went on, for those who might suspect he was merely reacting to the horrors of World War II. Even during the Council whose changes he so much feared, he defended his position. "Several council fathers have said that war must be altogether condemned," French peace activist Jean Goss quotes him as saying (in his report on part of Vatican II's work) during the debates on *Gaudium et Spes*. "I fully agree to this." And Tom Cornell, of the New York *Catholic Worker*, related that, though "said to have been the least popular bishop among the council fathers," in the end he "rose to defend Schema XIII [of *Gaudium et Spes*, dealing with war and peace] and to urge its acceptance against the efforts of some American bishops, led by Cardinal Francis Spellman, to weaken the text."

The result speaks volumes, and will be news to most. "Ottaviani was given the longest and loudest ovation of the council, and *Gaudium et Spes* was accepted resoundingly."

Let us both hope and pray that the good Cardinal's legacy will be appreciated and acted upon.

APPENDIX
II

Modern War Is to Be Absolutely Forbidden
· · · · · · · · · ·
Alfredo Cardinal Ottaviani

W HEN TWO SOCIETIES which are only materially distinct from each other come into collision, *neither is to be sacrificed to placate the other, but the interests of each are to be catered for in a rigidly fair manner.*

This principle is based on the fact that these two societies are of equal standing, enjoy therefore identical rights and have neither of them any legal advantage over the other; neither in fact is obliged to waive any of its rights in favor of the other. On this account a balance in no way derogatory to either must be struck as accurately as is possible between the conflicting rights; for example, by dividing up the disputed matter (granted it is divisible) or by making compensation. At times indeed the right claimed on one side may be a putative one only, and that on the other side clearly unimpeachable (objective); or at least one rather than the other side clearly unimpeachable (objective); or at least one rather than the other may have a greater interest at stake or stronger grounds on which to quarrel. But even in situations such as these, peaceful methods of settling the issue must take precedence over all others.

First of all, therefore, every effort should be made *to establish the existence of whatever right is being claimed;* then an attempt should be made to *compose differences* amicably; finally, should this fail, war must not be declared without *first trying out certain coercive measures* which, though of less consequence than war, may be equally effective in the circumstances.[1] These last, indeed, are the only measures to be taken whenever it is clear that they of themselves can effect a settlement, and avoid the disasters of war.

---

1. This is especially the case because the greatest coercive measure – war – cannot be proportionate to the reality of the situation. The lesser measures include breaking off economic and diplomatic relations, reprisals, sanctions, naval blockades, creating buffer zones, threats issued as "ultimatums."

But what of *mediation, arbitration,* or an investigation by an international tribunal? Are not these also possible means? To me, indeed, they seem of so obligatory a nature that they alone are the only justifiable and lawful means of vindicating rights in present times; war is out of the question. It is important, however, to note with regard to this view that this is not the opinion of past centuries: in those days mediation, etc., were not considered the exclusive means of settling disputes between perfect or fully autonomous societies; they were at the most highly commendable from a humanitarian viewpoint.[1] For, granting the concept of the sovereignty of every state, then each state, because of its very independence and perfection, was also possessed of the juridical power of safeguarding its rights even by force of arms. The state, it was held, had ample resources at its disposal with which to uphold its rights in face of an adversary struggling against or simply ignoring the obligations these rights imposed upon him.

Warfare, however, was not to be indulged in merely because one had a *just*[2] and *proportionate* cause with which to justify the action; it also had to be *necessary* to the preservation of the social well being, and withal reasonably assured of success.

The justification of war did not rest, therefore, on the presumption that war was as satisfactory as a duel between two private persons: neither course proves on which side right and reason lie. No, the sole justification of recourse to warfare was on an occasion when there was little hope of appealing to, or – if a disputed right were in question – of getting a decision from an authority higher than the state. War could be used then to compel

---

1. Consequently, people admitted the existence of a moral or personal duty to employ those means for resolving conflict. Cfr., Laurent, *Etude sur l'histoire de l'humanité*, t. XI. A famous example is the intervention of Pope Leo XIII in the dispute between Germany and Spain over the Caroline Islands. Schioppa, *L'arbitrato Pontifico*, Napoli, 1887.

2. The conditions for a justly fought war demand that it be just – not only in an intrinsic sense, but also an extrinsic one. *Intrinsic* to the extent that the cause be morally justifiable – at the very least – subjectively; *extrinsic* to the extent that the conventions recognized in international law are observed while waging the war. We know full well how, practically speaking, modern wars have been started: namely how they have resulted from a pre-existing treaty obligation being superimposed upon natural obligations.
In our age, a great number of nations have voluntarily entered into treaties that limit them to peaceful means for resolving conflict, and these treaties have been ratified before the League of Nations: v. gr. cfr. *Société des Nations, Recueil des Traités*, etc. vol. CXXXIV, 1932–33; *Bulgarie et Norvège, Traité de conciliation, d'arbitrage et de règlement judiciaire*, November 26, 1931 (n. 3081); *Norvège et Portugal, Traité de conciliation, de règlement judiciaire et d'arbitrage*, July 26, 1930 (n. 3097); *Convention pour le règlement pacifique des conflicts internationaux, comme à la Conférence de la Paix, à la Haye*, October 18, 1907, vol. CXXXVI, 1933; *Pacte de non aggression entre Pologne et Union des Républiques soviétistes-socialistes*, July 25, 1932 (n. 3125); *Traité d'arbitrage Etats-Unis d'Amérique et Grèce*, June 19, 1930 (n.3137).

an adversary to make good some infringement of rights – but with the understanding that it was a physical instrument the only concern of which was to keep intact the moral implication of the right infringed.

All war is to be prohibited. All the foregoing reasoning is cogent enough if we confine ourselves to a purely theoretical treatment of warfare. But in practice and in relation to present conditions the principles enunciated do not seem to hold. They were meant, we should remember, to cover warfare of a special kind, that between mercenary armies,[1] and not our *mammoth* warfare which sometimes entails the *total* downfall of the nations at grips with each other; the principles, in fact, cannot be applied in the life of modern nations without doing serious damage to the particular peoples involved, and (leaving aside a question of a defensive war begun, under certain conditions, for the protection of the state from *actual* and unjust aggression) *no state is justified any longer in resorting to warfare when some right has not been given its full due.* Not that we for a moment wish to despise or belittle the theories of the great exponents of Christian international law! That would be unpardonable! The war of their treatises is not the war of our experience. The difference indeed is not even of the purely numerical or mathematical order; it goes much deeper. It affects the very principles governing war. Principles indeed drive from and vary with the nature of things; the difference between war as it was and war as we know it is precisely one of nature.

At the Vatican Council the Fathers intimated to Pope Pius IX their desire that some definite statement be drawn up which might induce men to abandon warfare altogether or at least induce them to conduct their wars according to humanitarian principles. The salvation of certain Christian peoples was the chief cause of their concern; not simply because these peoples were then in the throes of war but "rather because of the horrible disaster" with which they were afflicted as a result of war.[2] War – they were

---

1. It is certainly the case today that enormous harm is done to civilians who are required to perform military service because of compulsory universal conscription; whereas previously those who willingly agreed to serve in the military were entitled to pay.

2. At that time – a time before the enormous war crimes of the twentieth century – the course and effects of compulsory military conscription were described as follows: "The present state of the world has been made unbearable by the vastly elevated numbers of troops – both standing forces and conscripts. People groan under the weight of the expense. An atheistic spirit and a wanton disregard for the laws that pertain to international affairs have paved the way for triggering illegal and unjust wars, or rather for horrible disasters spreading far and wide. This is the reason why the livelihood of the poor is diminished and economic stability is shattered, this is the reason why the human conscience is either utterly disengaged and warped or cruelly wounded, and finally this is why a great number of souls are ruined." Acta et Decreta Sacr. Œcumenici Concilii

gravely troubled to note – was the occasion of disasters, not the least of which was a lowering of moral standards that accompanied and persisted after war and made shipwreck of the faith of so many souls. We in this century have even further cause for concern:

a. On account of the great development of communication in modern times and the desire on the part of nations to extend their interests to all parts of the world, excuses for war are now all too frequent.

b. The disasters which worried the Fathers at the Vatican Council now affect not only soldiers and armies at war but also entire peoples.[1]

c. The extent of the damage done to national assets by aerial warfare, and the dreadful weapons that have been introduced of late, is so great that it leaves both vanquished and victor the poorer for years after.

d. Innocent people, too, are liable to great injury from the weapons in current use: hatred is on that account excited above measure; extremely harsh reprisals are provoked; wars result which flaunt every provision of the *jus gentium,* and are marked by a savagery greater than ever. And what of the period immediately after a war? Does not it also provide an obvious pointer to the enormous and irreparable damage which war, the breeding place of hate and hurt, must do to the morals and manners of nations?

e. In these days, when the world itself has become seemingly shrunken and straitened, the bonds between the nations of the world are so close and exigent that almost the whole world becomes involved once war is declared.

f. A regime may be under the impression that it can engage in a just war with hope of success; but in fact secret weapons can be prepared to such effect nowadays that they, being unforeseen, can upset and utterly thwart all calculations.

These considerations, and many others which might be adduced besides, show that modern wars can never fulfill those conditions which (as we stated earlier on in this essay) govern – *theoretically* – a *just* and *lawful* war.[2] Moreover, no *conceivable* cause could ever be sufficient justification

---

Vaticani, vol. VII, *Collectio Lacensis,* col. 861–866, Friburgi Brisgoviæ, Herder, 1890.

1. This is especially the case because of universal conscription and the requirements placed upon citizens for organizing home defense and resistance; warring parties refuse to distinguish between soldiers and civilians any longer, and consider the whole population as potential targets with no distinction from combatants.

2. "Historically, war is no longer an instrument of justice, and in practice it is the greatest possible violation of charity . . . . We must have the courage to re-examine the modern practice of war, because the theological conditions for a just war are now hardly ever met." Cordovani, *Il Santificatore,* Roma, 1939, p. 490 *sq.*

for the evils, the slaughter, the destruction, the moral and religious up-
heavals which war today entails.

IN PRACTICE, *then, a* DECLARATION *of war will never be justifiable.* A
defensive war even should never be undertaken unless a legitimate authority, with whom the decision rests, shall have both certainty of success and
very solid proofs that the good accruing to the nation from the war will
more than outweigh the untold evils which it will bring on the nation itself,
and on the world in general.[1]

Otherwise the government of peoples would be no better than the reign
of universal disaster, which, as the recent war [World War II—Ed.] has
shown, will claim its victims more from the civilian population than from
the combatant troops. In what way then shall international crises be dealt
with on future occasions? "Discussion and force," says Cicero, "are the
main ways of settling quarrels, the former of which is peculiar to man, the
latter to brute beasts." [2]The former therefore is ever to be preferred; the interests of peace must be our chief concern ever – and it is not the forming
of armies but the formation of minds which will best secure this.

In this formation the weapons of charity, justice and truth shall be:

a. A civil and religious education of nations which so disposes peoples
(and hence the rulers chosen from them) to co-operation and to an honorable recognition and interchange of rights and obligations, that class bitterness, race enmity and imperial competition – than which there is no
better kindling for wars – are entirely eliminated.

b. The setting up of an international body whose pronouncements all
nations and rulers should respect.

c. The inculcation among peoples of a spirit of brotherliness in accord
with gospel principles; as a result each nation will be prepared to place
the good of the whole human brotherhood before its own interests, in the

---

1. "It is the wrongdoing of the opposing party which compels the wise man to wage just
wars; and this wrongdoing, even though it gave rise to no war, would still be a matter of
grief to man because it is man's wrongdoing. Let every one, then, who thinks with pain
on all these great evils, so horrible, so ruthless, acknowledge that this is misery. And
if any one either endures or thinks of them without mental pain, this is a more miserable plight still, for he thinks himself happy because he has lost human feeling." (St.
Augustine, *De civitate Dei,* cap. XIX, trans. Marcus Dods, in *Nicene and Post-Nicene
Fathers,* Series 2, Vol. II, New York: The Christian Literature Publishing Company,
1890.) However, Cordovani, *Il Santificatore,* Roma 1939, p. 490, notes: "A war won today
does not any longer outweigh the damage that arises from having fought it."

2. Cicero, *De Officiis,* I, 1, 11, where he affirms that war could be undertaken: "we must
take recourse to the second (force) only if it is not possible to resort to the first (discussion) . . . . In my opinion, we must always determine to pursue a peace that will not be
open to some future treachery."

manner in which individuals in any republic worthy of the name ought always to contribute to the common good from whatever they themselves possess.

d. To render impossible totalitarian regimes, for they above all else are the turbulent sources from which wars break out.[1]

Moreover, should the representatives of any people (or the people themselves) ever have *conclusive indications* that their rulers are on the point of undertaking a war in which nothing but blood and ruin will be the lot of the nation, they may and should take *just measures* to overthrow that regime.[2]

---

1. With regard to all these things, cfr. *The Allocutions of Pope Pius XII*, broadcast by radio during the years 1939–1944.

2. "The citizen, no less than the people, has the right to be secure in the knowledge that no one can behave injuriously towards him with impunity, and all would have the right to rebel when an evil government really proved to be the cause of intolerable miseries. A revolt against enforced poverty, against the wickedness of a government that undermines the very foundations of the state, against an anarchy that oppresses in the name of liberty, against a tyranny that violates all law and rips life apart in the name of irrational ambition, this revolution would be both legitimate and holy. But it should be those governing who lead the revolt, for the good of the people and the whole human race." M. Cordovani, *Diritti e doveri sociali secondo S. Tommaso*, Roma, 1939, p. 18.

THE EDITORS' GLOSS: This final appendix was originally published as Chapter XXVII of *Iota Unum: A Study of the Changes in the Catholic Church in the 20th Century* (Kansas City: Angelus Press, 1992, pp. 441–452) by the learned Italian Catholic philosopher Romano Amerio. His discussion may shock those Catholics and other "conservatives" who are most accustomed to thinking of an "international society" as a frightful approximation of world government, or as a tool of left-leaning "anti-Americans." If it does shock, we hope it will also provoke and educate.

Most shocking, among much that is valuable and interesting, is perhaps this comment: he exhorts the nations to "climb down from their pretended absolute sovereignties, and realize the Catholic ideal of a community of nations, by subjecting themselves to a supranational authority . . . . "

Some might dismiss this as sheer novelty, but before doing so they would do well to hear Fr. Francisco Suárez, the Jesuit just-war theorist of the late 16th and early 17th century. "It is not to be doubted," he says in *De Potestate Civili*, "that the world is in a certain sense a single community, [and] possesses the right to prescribe equitable and appropriate laws for its members, like those which constitute the law of nations." This is not to say that the Catholic position is one of a vague and cosmopolitan internationalism. But it is one of civility, justice, and even charity, *between* nations, no less than within them. And it is this notion that Catholics and others of good will must grasp if we are to avert another tragedy like the present one in Iraq.

III

A Study of the Development of Church Teaching on Matters of War and Peace

• • • • • • • • •

Prof. Romano Amerio

E VEN THOUGH IT might appear from some episcopal pronouncements and from many of the views voiced among Catholics that there has been a *saltus in aliud*[1] in this area, the change that has occurred in the understanding of war is in fact a coherent development.

Christianity and War

The development in question shows the real meaning of the old adage: what was not a sin can become one, and vice versa. It can become one not because there is a change in the moral law, but in the circumstances that make an action more or less culpable, or altogether inculpable; and because further reflection can lead to a conscientious awareness of new duties. It is part of classical Catholic teaching that circumstances can change the quality of acts. The same act can be virtuous in marriage or culpable in fornication or still more culpable in adultery. To give a modern example, driving a car after having too much to drink used to be a venial sin in the days of empty roads, but it becomes a mortal sin in an age of crowded roads and dangerous traffic. Circumstances can change the moral evaluation that one must make of war, and can render illicit things which were licit and good in the different circumstances of times past.

The absolute condemnation of war is, however, alien to Catholic tradition; the profession of arms is not forbidden in the Gospel, is held to be an honest occupation by the Fathers, and has been followed by Christians, many of the martyr saints being soldiers. War was only regarded as illicit by movements of a Manichean or otherwise heretical stamp. Even the rule of the Franciscan

---

1. "Leap into something different."

tertiaries allows for carrying arms in defense of one's country. The same is true of the whole of Catholic theology from Augustine to Thomas to Taparelli d'Azeglio. When discussing acts that disturb harmony among men, Aquinas describes war in a negative manner, by laying down that it is not always sinful. St. Augustine says[1] the evil of war lies in injustice, not in killing:

> *Quid enim culpatur in bello? An quia moriuntur quandoquidem morituri, ut domentur in pace victuri? Hoc reprehendere timidorum est, non religiosorum. Nocendi cupiditas, ulciscendi crudelitas, implacatus atque implacabilis animus, feritas rebellandi, libido dominandi et si qua similia, haec sunt quae in bello culpantur.*[2]

After declaring that "everyone who violates the rights of others should be put into shaming isolation, under the ban of civilized society," Pius XII forcefully denounced pacifism in his Christmas message of 1949: "The attitude of those who abhor war because of its atrocities but not for its injustice as well, is preparing the way for the aggressor."

War can only be seen as the worst of evils by those who adopt an irreligious view of life, in which the supreme good is not a transcendent goal but rather life itself, and for whom pleasure is the reason for man's existence. War certainly is an evil; the Church lists it with hunger and disease among the scourges from which it wishes men spared. In his encyclical *Praeclara Congratulationis* of 1894, Leo XIII denounces the futility of war and looks forward to an international society of nations and a further development of international law. Benedict XV deplored the "horrendous butchery" and the "suicide of Europe" during the Great War, and denounced its "useless slaughter" in his Note of August 1, 1917.

Pacifism and Peace; Cardinal Poma; Paul VI; John Paul II

The kind of peace the Church supports is not the sort that absolutizes life, but the sort that subjects both peace and war to the demands of justice. By contrast Erasmus of Rotterdam, the most forthright of pacifists, teaches in his *Querela pacis* and his paraphrase of the *Pater Noster,* that "there is no unjust peace that is not preferable to the most just of wars." Absolute

---

1. *Contra Faustum*, 74.

2. *P. L.*, 42, 447. "What is wrong with war? Is it that some men, who are bound to die eventually, die now so that those who are defeated can be governed in peace? To object to that is a sign of men who are cowardly rather than religious. What is wrong in war is an eagerness to cause harm, a cruel vengeance, a remorseless and uncontrollable spirit, a rebellious wildness, a desire to dominate, and other things of that sort."

pacifism has been widely taken up, and can appeal to some supporters in high places. The Archbishop of Milan, Cardinal Poma, says: "Nothing is so opposed to Christianity as war. It is the synthesis of all sins, since in it pride and the unleashing of the baser instincts are combined." An assertion so sweeping and so lacking in historical sense is at odds with centuries of Christian practice, at odds with the canonization of fighting saints such as Joan of Arc, and at odds with the praise of a just war that Paul VI made in a special document issued for the fifth centenary of the death of Scanderbeg.[1] When making a speech that recalled Pius XII's visit to the people of Rome after the bombing of the City in 1943, the same Paul VI described as "stupid" the cry of one young man who shouted: *"Papa, papa, meglio la schiavitù che la guerra! Liberaci dalla guerra!"*[2] Ghandi, great promoter of freedom and peace that he was, comes close to branding pacifism as cowardice:

> It is a noble thing to defend one's welfare, one's honor and one's religion at the point of the sword. It is still nobler to defend them without attempting to harm the evildoers. But it is immoral and dishonorable to abandon one's partner in order to save one's skin by leaving his welfare, his honor and his religion at the mercy of evildoers.

There are indeed statements by Paul VI that assert "the absurdity of modern war" and "the supreme irrationality of war."[3] Then there is John Paul II's statement at Coventry in May 1982: "Today the scope and horror of modern war, whether nuclear or conventional, make war totally unacceptable for resolving disputes and disagreements between nations." Nevertheless, if one examines the terms of the two papal declarations, one sees that they do not depart from the traditional principles of the theology of war and that they constitute one of those developments in moral sensitivity that result from changed circumstances. The legitimacy of war depends on certain conditions: that it be declared by a competent authority; that it be aimed at righting a wrong; that there be a reasonable hope of actually righting the wrong; that it be conducted with due moderation. These conditions reflect an uninterrupted tradition in Catholic scholastic theology, and are recognized, for example, in Article 137 of the "Social Code" drawn up by the International Union of Social Studies founded by Cardinal Mercier.

---

1. Scanderbeg (1403–1467), leader of Albanian Christian resistance to the Turks.
2. R.I., 1971, p. 42. "Pope, Pope, better slavery than war! Free us from war!"
3. *Osservatore Romano*, December 21, 1977.

The Teaching of Vatican II

Vatican II reiterated the legitimacy of a defensive war, condemned offensive wars undertaken as a means of resolving disputes among nations, and absolutely condemned total war, especially of the atomic sort.[1] The council also allows military service by citizens, designed to ensure the safety and freedom of their country, and indeed says that "by fulfilling that duty they contribute effectively to the maintenance of the peace." The right to wage war had to be re-examined from a new point of view because one of the aforementioned conditions no longer applied, and thus the council decreed: "any act of war aimed at the indiscriminate destruction of whole cities or large areas together with their population is a crime against God and man which should be strongly and unhesitatingly condemned." Total war is forbidden even in cases of legitimate self-defense, since that too can become illegitimate through a lack of due moderation. While teaching that a defensive war against an aggressor is legitimate "until such time as an effective international authority equipped with adequate coercive force is constituted," the council teaches that such a war is wrong if it aims at the total destruction of the enemy. Thus, both wars begun offensively to resolve a dispute, and wars of any sort, offensive or defensive, that are fought without due moderation are condemned. But a defensive war conducted with the due restraint is not censured. As can happen with anything affected by circumstances, the moral judgment to be made about war has been changed by the new circumstance that total war has become a possibility.

A suggestion was made at the First Vatican Council to define that *Qui bellum incipiat, anathema sit*[2] but that proposition fails to address the moral aspect of the question since chronological priority in waging war does not determine the moral question involved.

The reason indiscriminate slaughter is condemned is that it alters the nature of war and changes it into something it cannot legitimately be. In the past, nations waged war through the specific actions of a specific organ,

---

1. *Gaudium et Spes*, §§79–80. This condemnation of unrestrained warfare is analogous to the decree against artem illam mortiferam et Deo odibilem ballistariorum et sagittariorum ("the lethal art, hateful to God, of archers and those who operate mangonels") by the Second Council of Lyons under Innocent II in 1139. The condemnations result from the same moral objection to excessive destruction, manifesting itself differently amidst the relativities of history. Such condemnations also show the ineffectiveness of the Church's action in this field; an ineffectiveness also apparent in the banning of war by the pact made in 1919, and again by the Kellog-Briand Pact of 1929, and yet again by the Charter of the United Nations in 1945.

2. "Let whoever begins a war be anathema."

to wit, the army, while in recent times they have waged war with the whole body of society and everything is militarized; there is political war, commercial war, diplomatic war, propaganda war, chemical war, biological war and even meteorological war:[1] on the modern Olympus, Mars has been joined by Minerva, Mercury, and a host of other gods.

Total war was begun in France in 1793 in the form of the *levée en masse*, involving the conscription of men, economic strength and even of minds, through the use of propaganda. The introduction of compulsory conscription, a kind of blood tax, by all modern states signifies the loss of freedom enjoyed by ancient societies, despite the fact that some people consider it a step forward in social equality.[2] It was the result of citizens being bound more closely together by the growing power of a state in the process of becoming a leviathan, in which the individual is merely a cell, and it led to war's losing its specific character. It should however be noted that military doctrine is now moving away from the idea of war as something waged by the whole people and the whole of a nation's resources, and is returning to highly specialized professional armies. The idea of war as the activity of a special group is thus being restored, and bloody deeds are again Mars' peculiar concern. To fight with one arm of the nation rather than with its whole body is more in accordance with the natural law, and brings us back to the situation described by Frederick II of Prussia: "When I make war my people don't realize the fact, because I do it with my soldiers." Nonetheless, at the level of nuclear arms, the whole movement of national life is still oriented towards total war and thus all the organs of society become a single instrument aimed at the total destruction of the enemy. Talleyrand's maxim to the effect that states ought to do as much good as they can in peace and as little evil as they can in war, is overturned by modern war, which turns society into an engine of destruction.

War's Unanswered Questions

War is moral subject to two conditions: that it be just, and just use of force can only occur in the face of aggression; and that it be moderate, and there

---

1. In Geneva in 1977 the USA and the USSR signed a convention renouncing meteorological warfare. During the Vietnam war the United States rendered the Ho Chi Minh trail unusable by dropping fifty thousand containers of silver hydrate and carbon substances to make it rain.

2. Seneca praised the prince who assured such freedom, *Epist.*, LXXIII, 9, and G. Ferrero also praises it in *Discorsi ai sordi*, Milan, 1920. Rosmini, on the other hand, said that compulsory conscription was "the greatest benefit" left to Europe by the Napoleonic Empire, *Filosofia del diritto*, paragraph 2154, National Edition, Vol. XXXIX, p. 1426.

can be no right to war that is not bound to that moderation. We will not go into the theory propounded by Don Luigi Sturzo,[1] namely that wars are not produced by any intrinsic or necessary element in human nature, and are merely a passing stage that can be overcome, like polygamy or slavery. We should note however that the use of force, and therefore the principle of war, is essential to civilized society: namely a society that organizes the community towards achieving the common good by means of law, but which also restrains lawbreakers; and it is in its restraining functions that its primary task admittedly lies, even if we do not agree completely with Hobbes on that point. Hence, if the races of the earth are to climb down from their pretended absolute sovereignties, and realize the Catholic ideal of a community of nations by subjecting themselves to a supranational authority,[2] that authority would have to have an effective power of repressing lawbreakers, that is of making war on any rebel member. In the present imperfectly organized condition of international life, war is legitimate to defend the rights of individual states; in a fully organized community of nations, war would be legitimate to repress attacks on the community as such.

As to the justice of wars, some philosophers, including Cajetan, have held that a nation waging a war of legitimate defense is performing an act of vindicatory justice, so that the just combatant *personam gerit iudicis criminaliter agentis*.[3] Others believe such wars are acts of commutative justice, by which reparation or restitution is sought for a good of which one has been unduly deprived. The question does not have to be decided here. Cajetan's opinion nonetheless harmonizes with the Catholic principle, upheld in the *Syllabus of Errors*,[4] that one should defend the rights of another innocent state under attack, rather than adopt the notion of absolute nonintervention. Because a perfect international organization of society has not yet been established, with the three usual powers, legislative, governmental and judicial, it remains difficult to show that a particular war is just, and difficult to impose some sanction on an unjust warmaker through the operations of a universal tribunal.

Even a just war is always a sad thing, for two reasons. Firstly, because it is a form of fratricide and, if fought among Christians, also a sort of sacrilege, given the sacred character of a baptized man. Secondly, in war the actions

---

1. In *La comunita internazionale e il diritto di guerra* (Paris, 1932).
2. See Vatican II, cited in the previous paragraph.
3. "Plays the part of someone judging a criminal."
4. Proposition No. 62.

of one side cannot be good without those of the opposite side being bad. The defensive war of the side in the right is just, but can only be so if the attacker is unjust. Thus it is that Kant, in his *Zum ewigen Frieden*[1] says that on the day of victory both victors and vanquished should wear mourning; and in Manzoni's *Carmagnola* "homicidal choirs" raise "thanksgivings and hymns that Heaven abhors."

Another unanswered question where wars are concerned is the uncertainty of the outcome even for the party that is in the right. Providence has decreed that earthly goods should *tend* to accompany moral virtue, but this tendency is not enough in any particular case to override the slings and arrows of outrageous fortune. Anyone acquainted with history knows that it is full of fortunate scoundrels and just men who suffer. The numerous instances in which nemesis overtakes the evildoer are not enough to turn the general tendency into a universal law. In the Catholic understanding of things, there are no inbuilt punishments, either individual or collective, that work infallibly; the just man can only look forward to security in the future. The uncertainties of war make the conflict two-edged right to the last, and Mars a faithless god. The outcome can depend on some minute accidental event, within which lurks the permanent power of a single moment.[2]

War is a kind of gambling, since chance plays a large part in it; indeed Manzoni said it should be regarded as gambling at the level of politics. Philologically, warfare and dueling are closely related, *bellum = duellum*. The good aimed at in fighting is itself something essentially obtainable without fighting. The same rational processes that tell us war is a bad thing in itself also tells us how we could obtain the desired good without war.

The chances of war tend to make the strength of the two sides irrelevant. Then again, as Jomini noted, the improvement in weapons that all states so assiduously pursue, only provides an advantage if the other side has not got the weapons in question, as in the case of firearms at Crecy in 1346 and the atomic bomb in Japan in 1945. The acquisition of the same weapons by both sides affords an advantage to neither. Weapons become more expen-

---

1. "Towards an eternal peace."

2. The fortuitous element in a general's fate was recognized by the ancients, who counted felicitas, or fortune, among the endowments of a successful leader, as well as leadership and expertise, and can be seen in the election of Pompey to lead the war against Mithradates (Cicero, *Pro Lege Manilia*). Bonaparte also set great store by fate; of General Mack, whom he defeated at Ulm in 1805, he said: "He is incompetent: worse still he has a bad star."

sive and more lethal, but the outcome still depends on luck and bravery. In a combat of three against three, one side is no more likely to beat the other than in a fight between equal armies numbered by the million.

The Question of Moderation in War; Voltaire; Pius XII; Ultimate Impossibility of Modern War

Moderation is essential to a just war. Even the party in the right is bound to exercise it. Defending oneself to the last by useless sacrifices, when there is no hope of winning, is thus illegitimate.[1]

Whence derives this duty of moderation? Metaphysically, it comes from the principal of sufficient reason, which implies that it is irrational and therefore immoral to perform actions that are superfluous to the end in view. Actions should be directed towards an end, and those that are not are useless; war too must be conducted with a minimum of destruction since its aim is the universal restoration of justice and peace. The total destruction of the enemy is counterproductive of that end and thus illegitimate.

The moral reason for this restraint is even more important. One should never wish moral evil on one's neighbor. Nor should one ever will his physical evil *directly*, but merely as a means to some good, and to the minimum degree necessary. One does not desire war for its own sake, but as a means to a just peace.

Voltaire's opinion, given in his *Des droits de guerre*, to the effect that since war originates in a breakdown of law it cannot be expected to obey any rules, is a perfect justification of total war. It is incompatible with our religion. As G. Gonella argued,[2] a just war fought on moral grounds will naturally be governed by moral principles, including that of due restraint. This is where the difficulty arises. A state that wages war within due limits against an aggressor who observes no limits will often lose the battle and go down before an overpowering evil. A just war will thus be lost precisely because of its justice. A due restraint imposed on the slaughter will rule out the possibility of victory and make even a defensive war illegitimate. Justice includes a due proportion between the damage entailed in upholding some good, and the importance of the good in question. When that proportion between means

---

1. Examples of this are the defense of Stalingrad by General von Paulus during the last war, and the defense of Attu, where all two thousand Japanese holding the island were killed or committed suicide. The Hague Conventions of 1899 and 1907 forbid fighting without quarter and defending to the last man.

2. In *Revue de droit internationale*, 1943, p. 205.

and end is lacking, it can become one's duty to tolerate a lesser injustice in order to avoid a greater. Pius XII teaches explicitly:

> *Il ne suffit pas d'avoir à se défendre contre n'importe quelle injustice pour utiliser la méthode violente de la guerre. Lorsque les dommages entraînés par celle-ci ne sont pas comparables à ceux de l'injustice on peut avoir l'obligation de subir l'injustice.*[1]

The conundrum posed by modern war is clear. On the one hand it is legitimate to defend oneself by waging war; but then one is bound to exercise restraint in doing so, and may therefore be doomed to succumb before an unrestrained assailant. Circumstances can thus make even a defensive war immoral and create an obligation to submit to injustice. There are both ancient and modern examples of this. Pius IX's surrender on September 20, 1870, is a clearly justified instance of such submission; the surrender by King Leopold of Belgium in June 1940 was also legitimate, although it was widely condemned. Should all wars be absolutely forbidden then, on the grounds that in modern circumstances they cannot but be unlimited; and should all defensive acts of war be forbidden, even in their initial stages?

Removal of the Problem of War by an International Confederation

The Second Vatican Council teaches that: "Until a competent international authority equipped with forces adequate to restrain transgressors has been constituted, governments cannot be denied the right of legitimate defense."[2] In a future international society, consisting of a confederation of associated nations that are subject parts of one society rather than sovereign entities, the supreme authority would remove the right of individual nations to enforce justice for themselves, just as a single person's right to procure justice on his own initiative is removed at present by the authority of individual states. The human race should organize itself into a perfected *societas populorum*[3] of the sort that Leo XIII hoped for and that Benedict XV outlined in detail, leaving behind the wild state in which the community

---

1. Speech on October 15, 1953, to the XVI session of the International Office for the Documentation of Military Medicine, in *Discorsi ai medici*, 4th ed., Rome, 1960, p. 307. "The fact that one has to defend oneself against injustice of some sort is not enough to justify using the violent methods of war. When the harm caused by the latter are out of proportion to the harm caused by the injustice, one may have a duty to submit to that injustice."

2. *Gaudium et Spes*, §79.

3. "Society of peoples."

of nations still finds itself, and should thus conform to an ideal traditional in Catholic theology from the medieval thinkers to Suárez, Campanella and Taparelli d'Azeglio. War would of course not be eliminated, but it would be clear that persons who waged war to secure justice on their own account, as if they constituted a sovereign entity, would be acting unjustly and that a war conducted against such groups by the sole sovereign authority would be just. International order and peace can only rest upon the use of force by a supranational authority designed to put down those who act unjustly. Individual states dissolve into anarchy when the authorities have no force at their disposal: international society is no different.[1]

In a message for World Peace Day[2] John Paul II states that a solution to the problem of modern war is only possible through the recognition of a supranational authority, but the Pope envisages the community of nations as an institution for dialogue and negotiation, which it is already, while he says nothing about *force,* which is the backbone of authority. Nor does it seem that the Pope condemns the idea of a defensive war, for if he were to, there would be a *vacatio legis*[3] which would leave the world at the mercy of evildoers. The Pope's words at Coventry do not condemn the type of defensive war allowed by the council, but rather initiatives by those who resort to either nuclear or conventional weapons in order to resolve disagreements unilaterally. On the other hand, any party that is attacked and that defends itself has a perfect right to use force. Nonetheless, the ambiguities remain because of the obligation to observe due restraint.

The duty to attempt to form the human race into a confederation of nations flows from the principle on which the whole of our argument is based, namely the idea of the dependency of dependent being; dependency on human law, on the moral law, or on God. Parts must be considered precisely as parts, not as the whole. States must be reduced to their true states as relative rather than absolute wholes, subjects rather than sovereigns, creatures rather than mini-gods.

---

1. In his *L'azione politica dell'ONU 1946–1974* (Padua, 1983), M. Vismara shows with full documentation that the only clearly successful action by the UN was the solution of the Congo problem, and this was because it was obtained by the use of force; fifteen thousand men were deployed and soon put an end to the secession of Katanga under Tshombe and Kisai under Lumumba. The firm action taken by Hammarskjold, the secretary general, was effective because of the use of an international military force.

2. *Osservatore Romano,* December 21, 1981.

3. "A legal vacuum."

About the Contributors

Bp. Hilarion Capucci is a Greek-Melkite Catholic priest and bishop who was ordained in 1947 and consecrated a bishop in 1965. He served as the Greek-Melkite Patriarchal Vicar of Jerusalem (1965–1974) and Apostolic Visitor of the Greek-Melkites of Western Europe. He was Bishop of Caesarea, Palestine, in exile, until his retirement in 1999. His ministry in later years was extended particularly to Palestinians of the European diaspora, and he has long been an advocate and activist for justice for the Palestinian people of the Holy Land.

George A. Lopez, Ph.D., is Professor of Political Science and Senior Fellow at the Joan B. Kroc Institute for International Peace Studies at the University of Notre Dame. Lopez's research focuses primarily on the problems of State violence and coercion, and gross violations of human rights. He has been published in a variety of law, human-rights, and scientific journals, and has been editor or contributor to five books on repression and state terror. Lopez has served as advisor to a number of organizations involved in human rights, international affairs education, and peace research.

Jude Wanniski is founder and chairman of Polyconomics, Inc. He holds a B.A. in Political Science and an M.S. in Journalism from UCLA. Wanniski was an economist under President Reagan and was an associate editor at *The Wall Street Journal,* where he coined the phrase "supply-side economics." He appears frequently in the broadcast and print media, and also writes weekly commentary for *Polyconomics.com,* where he brings to his audiences a unique mix of experience in journalism, academia, politics, and business.

Marc Bossuyt, Ph.D., J.D., holds degrees from Ghent State University in Belgium (J.D.) and Geneva University in Switzerland (Ph.D.), along with a Diploma of International and Comparative Law of Human Rights from the International Institute of Human Rights, Strasbourg, France, and a Certificate of International Relations from the Bologna Centre of the School of Advanced International Studies of Johns Hopkins University. He has been a professor at Antwerp University, Belgium, since 1977, where he specializes in international law and the law of international organizations, including the international protection of human rights and international humanitarian law. He is frequently invited as a visiting professor by universities in Africa, North America, and Europe. He has held numerous professional positions in Belgium and at the UN, including that of UN Human Rights Officer (1975–77); secretary-general of the Belgian Society of International Law (1978–1990); vice chairman (1986) and chairman (1989) of the UN Commission on Human Rights; vice-president (1990–2000) of the Executive Council of the International Institute of Human Rights at Strasbourg; Belgian Commissioner-General for Refugees and Stateless Persons (1987–97); and (since 1997) judge at the Belgian Court of Arbitration. He is also a member of the editorial staff of the *Revue Belge de Droit International (Belgian Review of International Law)*.

Joy Gordon, Ph.D., J.D., is Associate Professor of Philosophy at Fairfield University. A specialist in political philosophy and international law, she holds a law degree from Boston University School of Law and a doctorate in philosophy from Yale. She has spent several years researching the economic sanctions imposed on Iraq following the first Gulf War, and has become a recognized expert on the subject. She is the author of numerous articles about the ethics of sanctions, and is working on *A Peaceful, Silent, Deadly Remedy: The Ethics of Economic Sanctions*, a book currently under contract with Harvard University Press, . She has been interviewed by various media outlets for her perspective on Iraq sanctions, including the *BBC*, National Public Radio's *Counterspin, Between the Lines*, and *Democracy Now.* She is also a frequent lecturer on sanctions, foreign policy, and international ethics. Her recent presentations include appearances at Brown University's Faculty Seminar and Watson Institute for International Relations, Bryant College, and Brandeis University's International Center for Ethics, Justice, and Public Life.

Patrick J. Buchanan was a senior advisor to three U.S. presidents. He has himself twice sought the Republican nomination for president, and in 2000 was the Reform Party's candidate for the office. A nationally syndicated columnist, Buchanan is a founding member of three of America's foremost public affairs shows, and is the best-selling author of seven books. He is currently a commentator for MSNBC and was founding editor of the bi-weekly magazine *The American Conservative.*

Samuel Francis, Ph.D., R.I.P., held a doctorate in history from the University of North Carolina, Chapel Hill. He was a nationally syndicated columnist as well as editor-in-chief of *Citizens' Informer,* political editor of *Chronicles,* and associate editor for books for the *Occidental Quarterly.* Among other works, he authored *Beautiful Losers: Essays on the Failure of American Conservatism* (University of Missouri Press, 1994), *Revolution from the Middle* (Middle America Press, 1997), *Thinkers of Our Time: James Burnham* (Claridge Press, 1999), and *Ethnopolitics: Immigration, Race, and the American Political Future* (Representative Government Press, 2003). He died unexpectedly in early 2005.

Joe Sobran has been a nationally syndicated columnist since 1979, first with the Los Angeles Times Syndicate, then Universal Press Syndicate, and now with Griffin Internet Syndicate, for which he writes two columns per week. He was senior editor at *National Review* for18 years, and from 1979 to 1991 was a regular commentator for CBS Radio's *Spectrum* series. Sobran is the author of three books, the most recent of which is *Hustler: The Clinton Legacy* (Griffin Communications, 2000).

Charley Reese is a conservative columnist whose articles are distributed three times a week by King Features Syndicate to more than 150 newspapers. He began his career in Florida as a cub reporter, and has honed his craft by reporting everything from sports to politics in jobs ranging from columnist, assistant metro editor, assistant publisher, and editorial board member. He has traveled throughout Europe and the Middle East on assignments, and, among his other awards, has been nominated for the Pulitzer Prize. Reese is the author of four books, including *Great Gods of the Potomac* (Sentinel Star, 1978).

Thomas Fleming, Ph.D., is a classicist, poet, and philosopher who edits *Chronicles: A Magazine of American Culture.* He holds a degree in classics from the University of North Carolina, Chapel Hill, and is the author of several books, including, most recently, *The Morality of Everyday Life* (University of Missouri Press, 2004). Fleming also serves as president of the Rockford Institute, a think tank based in Rockford, Ill., dedicated to the defense of the fundamental institutions of civilization and the renewal of Christendom.

Eric S. Margolis is foreign-affairs editor for CFRB Radio, Toronto, and for the Sun Media Corporation, where he is a regular columnist. He holds a number of degrees, including a B.S.F.S. from the Georgetown School of Foreign Service and an M.B.A. from New York University. His affiliations include the International Institute of Strategic Studies, London; the National Press Club, Washington, D.C.; and the Institute of Regional Studies, Islamabad, Pakistan. Margolis was the recipient of the 1998 South Asian Journalist Association Award.

Wendell Berry is the author of more than 40 books of essays and poetry, and a number of novels. The *New York Review of Books* called him "a Kentucky farmer and writer, and perhaps the greatest moral essayist of our day." A ruralist, he has taught at Stanford, at New York University, and at the University of Kentucky in his home state, where, since 1965, he has worked the 125-acre farm that has been in his family since the early 1800s. Berry is a past fellow of the Guggenheim and Rockefeller Foundations.

Paul Gottfried, Ph.D., is the Horace E. Raffensperger Professor of Humanities at Elizabethtown College and a member of the executive board of the Historical Society. He is also contributing editor for *Chronicles* and *Telos,* and is editor-in-chief of *This World*. In addition to being an Adjunct Scholar at the Ludwig von Mises Institute, Gottfried was a Guggenheim Fellow in 1984 and was recognized by *Who's Who in the World* in 2000. He is author of a long list of papers, articles, reviews, and publications, among the most recent of which is *The Strange Death of European Marxism* (University of Missouri Press, 2004).

Fr. Juan Carlos Iscara entered the seminary of the Society of Saint Pius X (SSPX) in Argentina at the age of 30, and was ordained in 1986 by Archbishop Marcel Lefebvre. He studied history at the Instituto Nacional del Profesorado in Buenos Aires before becoming an assistant priest in 1987 at the SSPX Wanganui Priory in New Zealand. Fr. Iscara later became a professor at the SSPX Seminary in Goulburn, Australia, and superior of the SSPX District of Mexico and Central America. He is currently Professor of Church History and Moral Theology at St. Thomas Aquinas Seminary, Winona, Minn.

Thomas Ryba, Ph.D., is Notre Dame Theologian-in-Residence at the Saint Thomas Aquinas Catholic Center at Purdue University, where he is also Adjunct Professor of Philosophy and Adjunct Professor of Jewish Studies. Ryba holds degrees in the history and literature of religions from Northwestern University. He has authored over 30 articles on theology, philosophical theology, and theories of religion, and in May 2004 became North American editor of the journal *Religion*. He is principal editor of

The Comity and Grace of Method (Northwestern, 2003), and is at work on a book on the thought of John Henry Cardinal Newman.

David Gordon, Ph.D., is a senior fellow of the Ludwig von Mises Institute and editor of *The Von Mises Review*. He is the author of *Resurrecting Marx* (Transaction, 1990) and co-author of *Individualismo metodologico: dalla Scuola austriaca all'anarcho-capitalismo* (Luiss Edizione, 2001). Gordon's numerous articles have appeared in such prestigious journals as *Analysis, Mind, Ethics,* and many others.

James Hanink, Ph.D., is Professor of Philosophy at Loyola Marymount University and is the associate editor of the *New Oxford Review*. He holds degrees from Michigan State University. His academic specialities include the philosophy of religion, ethics, social philosophy, and personalism. He and his wife, Elizabeth, are the parents of five children, and are active in pro-life work.

William T. Cavanaugh, Ph.D., is Associate Professor of Theology at the University of St. Thomas. He holds degrees from the universities of Notre Dame, Cambridge, and Duke. Cavanaugh is the author of *Torture and Eucharist: Theology, Politics, and the Body of Christ* (Oxford: Blackwell, 1998) and *Theopolitical Imagination* (Edinburgh: T. & T. Clark, 2002), both of which have also been published in French by Editions Ad Solem of Geneva. He is also co-editor of *The Blackwell Companion to Political Theology* (Oxford: Blackwell, 2004).

Bp. John Michael Botean is Bishop of the Romanian Eparchy of St. George the Martyr in Canton, Ohio. He was ordained a priest in 1986 after attending St. Fidelis Seminary, and was consecrated a bishop in 1996. He earned an A.B. in Philosophy, *summa cum laude,* at the Catholic University of America. Bishop Botean is Episcopal co-sponsor of the American section of the Society of St. John Chrysostom, member of the Committee on Vocations of the United States Conference of Catholic Bishops, a former staff member at the Pax Christi USA Center on Conscience and War, and a past secretary of Eastern Catholic Associates, an organization of the Eastern Catholic hierarchy in the United States.

Edward Peters, J.D., J.C.D., majored in political science at Saint Louis University, and has a law degree from the University of Missouri School of Law. He earned his licentiate (1988) and doctorate (1991) in Canon Law at the Catholic University of America School of Religious Studies. As a canon lawyer he has served for years in a variety of diocesan and appellate tribunals, and in May, 2001, became a charter member of the faculty of the Institute for Pastoral Theology in Ypsilanti, Mich., teaching canon law, liturgy and sacraments, canonical structures, and ecclesiastical Latin.

Deacon Keith Fournier, Esq., is a Roman Catholic deacon of the Diocese of Richmond, Virginia, who also serves the Greek-Melkite Catholic Church with approval. He is a constitutional lawyer and founding partner of Lentz, Stepanovich, and Fournier, P.L.C. Long active in social, cultural, and political affairs, Fournier has served as a pro-life and pro-family lobbyist, as first Executive Director of the American Center for Law and Justice, and as an advisor to the presidential campaign of Steve Forbes. He is a founder and director of Your Catholic Voice, features editor for *Catholic Online* (www.catholic.org), and founder and president of the Common Good Movement. Fournier holds degrees from the Franciscan University of Steubenville (B.A.), the John Paul II Institute of the Lateran University (M.T.S.), and the University of Pittsburgh (J.D.), and honorary degrees from St. Thomas University (Ll.D.) and the National Clergy Council (D.D.).

John Rao, D.Phil., holds degrees from Drew University and Oxford. He worked for a year with the Intercollegiate Studies Institute before becoming Associate Professor of History at St. John's University in 1979. He is the author of *Americanism and the Collapse of the Church in the United States* (Roman Forum, 1995) and *Removing the Blindfold* (Remnant Press, 1999). Rao is also chairman of the Roman Forum and the Dietrich von Hildebrand Institute, and is president of Una Voce, America.

Robert Hickson, USA (ret.), Ph.D., is a 1964 graduate of the U.S. Military Academy, retired U.S. Army Special Forces officer, and Vietnam War veteran. Following his retirement he served for many years in the intelligence and special-operations communities in varying capacities. His degree is in comparative literature and classics from the University of North Carolina, Chapel Hill, and he is a founding faculty member of Christendom College. Hickson has held professorships at the U.S. Air Force Academy, the Joint Special Operations University at U.S. Special Operations Command, the John. F. Kennedy Special Warfare Center and School, and the Joint Military Intelligence College.

Paul Likoudis is news editor for *The Wanderer,* the oldest independent, lay-edited Catholic newspaper in the United States, founded in 1867. Likoudis began his work for the Catholic press in December 1978, two months after the election of John Paul II.

Laurence M. Vance, Ph.D., holds degrees in history, theology, accounting, and economics. He is a freelance writer, teacher, publisher, and book dealer. He regularly contributes articles and book reviews to both secular and religious periodicals, and is the author of six books and two collections of essays. Vance is a member of the Society of Bible Literature, the Grace Evangelical Society, the International Society of Bible Collectors, and the Ludwig von Mises Institute.

Peter E. Chojnowski, Ph.D., holds degrees from Christendom College and Fordham University. He has taught at a number of colleges and universities, and is currently Instructor in Philosophy at Gonzaga University. Chojnowski is a well-known Catholic thinker and writer who has had over 100 articles, reviews, and books published on topics ranging from education to economics, principally in light of the philosophy of St. Thomas Aquinas, in publications such as *Catholic Family News, The Remnant, The Angelus, Faith and Reason,* and *The Review of Metaphysics.* He lives with his wife and six children in Post Falls, Idaho.

Former Army Staff Sgt. Camilo Mejia emigrated to the U.S. in 1994. He took night classes to finish high school and, in 1995, went to work at a Burger King to help pay for his college education. When the government turned down his request for financial aid, Mejia, then 19, joined the Army. March of 2003 found him an infantry squad leader in Iraq, fighting a war he believed to be morally wrong. On failing to return to his unit following a two-week leave in October 2003, he was convicted of desertion and sent to prison; Amnesty International declared him a Prisoner of Conscience. He completed serving his one-year sentence at Ft. Sill, Ok., on February 15, 2005.

Eric Gill (1882–1940) was an English stone carver, wood engraver, essayist, and typographer. A convert to the Catholic Church, he was, together with G. K. Chesterton, Hilaire Belloc, Fr. Vincent McNabb, and others, a founder of the Distributist movement: an economic and social theory based on Catholic Social Teaching and regarded as a "third way" beyond capitalism and socialism. Gill was also a founder, with other leading Catholics such as Fr. Gerald Vann, O.P., Donald Attwater, and E.I. Watkin, of the Pax movement in England.

Fr. Franziskus Stratmann, O.P. (1883–1971), was a Dominican priest and Thomistic moral philosopher. During World War I he became convinced that war was not the Christian solution to world problems, and spoke out against militarism, war, and its atrocities. He dedicated his life to peace, and his writings, especially *The Church and War* (P. J. Kenedy and Sons, 1928) and *War and Christianity Today* (Newman Press, 1956), made him a key figure in the German Catholic peace movement.

Alfredo Card. Ottaviani (1890–1979) was born in Rome, educated at the Pontifical Roman Seminary there, and ordained a priest in 1916. The list of offices he held is immense, and he was a canonist of wide repute. Standing out in an outstanding career are his elevation to the cardinalate (1953), his appointments as Secretary of the Holy Office (1959) and Prefect of the Congregation of the Doctrine of the Faith (1966), and his election as Titular Archbishop of Berrea, Italy, and corresponding episcopal consecration (1962).

Romano Amerio (1905–1997) was a man of broad and classical erudition. He taught Philosophy, Greek, and Latin at the State Academy of Lugano, Switzerland, from 1928 to 1970. He received degrees in Philosophy (1927) and Philology (1934) from the Catholic University of the Sacred Heart in Milan, Italy, where he also served for many years as an instructor in the history of philosophy. He was an episcopal consultant to the Central Preparatory Commission of Vatican II and was a friend of the late Giuseppe Cardinal Siri (1906–1989) of Genoa.

Acknowledgements

The editors wish to thank the following individuals for kind assistance rendered during the course of our work on *Neo-CONNED!*: Judge Albert C. Walsh (ret.), Dr. Timothy A. Mitchell, Dr. William Fahey, Lindsey Carroll, James Vogel, Ted Schluenderfritz, David Brindle, Phillip M. Runkel, Archivist, Marquette University Libraries, Wm. Kevin Cawley, Archivist and Curator of Manuscripts, Archives of the University of Notre Dame, Malachy R. McCarthy of the Claretians, Daniel McAdams, Christopher McCann, Mark Weber, Muhammad Abu Nasr, Colette Sgambati, Scott Richert, Tom Cornell, Jason Winschel, Ovidiu Marginean, and Maike Buß. This extremely important project was made easier, and its final result better, owing to their support.

We also gratefully acknowledge permission received from the following individuals or organizations for publication of material by the authors indicated in parenthesis: Bishop Bernard Fellay and The Angelus Press (Fr. J. C. Iscara), *Harper's* (Joy Gordon), *Commonweal* (Dr. William Cavanaugh), Shoemaker & Hoard, Publishers (Wendell Berry), *Sign of Peace*, the journal of the Catholic Peace Fellowship (Botean and Mejia), The Angelus Press (Romano Amerio), *The American Conservative* (Patrick Buchanan), *The Wanderer* (Paul Likoudis), and King Features Syndicate (Charley Reese).

Finally, we would like to acknowledge photographer Harvey Finkle, Michael Robert Patterson of www.arlingtoncemetery.net, and the webmasters and staff at www.informationclearinghouse.info, www.robert-fisk.com, www.albasrah.net, and www.islamicdigest.net for the images contained in this volume.

Further Resources

Given that the Iraq war remains tragically ongoing, readers of the *Neo-CONNED!* volumes may wish to continue their studies of the vitally important subjects relating to it. The editors herewith offer a few suggestions for further reading, included among which are also certain of our contributors' other related online and print publications. We do not necessarily endorse the opinions expressed in all the sources listed below. Readers should consult them with discernment.

Catholic reference works on matters of war and peace:

St. Robert Bellarmine, *De Laicis*, Kathleen E. Murphy, Ph.D., trans. (New York: Fordham University Press, 1928).

Catholic Encyclopedia (New York: Robert Appleton Company, 1907–1912; Online Edition Copyright 1999 by Kevin Knight), s.v. "War," at www.newadvent.org.

Rev. Cyprian Emanuel, O.F.M., Ph.D., and the Committee on Ethics,
The Morality of Conscientious Objection to War (Washington, D.C.: CAIP, 1941);
The Ethics of War (Washington, D.C.: CAIP, 1932).

John Eppstein, *The Catholic Tradition of the Law of Nations* (Washington, D.C.: CAIP, 1935).

Charles G. Fenwick, Ph.D., *A Primer of Peace* (Washington, D.C.: CAIP, 1937).

The International Union of Social Sciences, John Eppstein, trans. and ed., *Code of International Ethics* (Westminster, Md.: Newman Press, 1953).

Rev. Harry C. Koenig, S.T.D., ed., *Principles for Peace: Selections from Papal Documents, Leo XIII to Pius XII* (Washington, D.C.: National Catholic Welfare Conference, 1943).

James Brown Scott, *The Catholic Conception of International Law* (Washington, D.C.: Georgetown University Press, 1934);
The Spanish Origin of International Law (Union, N.J.: Lawbook Exchange, 2000).

Franziskus Stratmann, O.P., *The Church and War* (New York: P. J. Kenedy and Sons, 1928);
War and Christianity Today (Westminster, Md.: Newman Press, 1956).

Francisco Suárez, S.J., *De Caritate*, from *On the Three Theological Virtues: Faith, Hope, and Charity* (originally published, Coimbra: Nicolas Carvalho, 1621) in Gwladys L. Williams, et al., trans., *Selections from Three Works* (London: Humphrey Milford, 1944; reprinted, Buffalo: William S. Hein & Co., Inc., 1995), Disputation XIII (*De Bello*).

Francisco de Vitoria, O.P., *De Iure Belli*, in Ernest Nys, ed., and John Pawley Bate, trans., *De Indis et de Iure Belli Relectiones* (Washington, D.C.: Carnegie Institution, 1917; reprinted, Buffalo: William S. Hein & Co., Inc., 1995), parts V and VI of *Relectiones Theologicae XII* (published previously, Johan Georg Simon, J.U.D., ed., Cologne and Frankfort: August Boetius, 1696).

The Archives of the Catholic Association for International Peace (CAIP) at Marquette University are a particularly useful reference for those interested in conducting serious research into the Church's position on war and peace. The CAIP was an association of Catholics founded in 1926 by representatives of the Social Action Department of the National Catholic Welfare Conference (NCWC), the National Council of Catholic Men, and the National Council of Catholic Women, to further the aim of international peace. The "ultimate purpose" of the association (administered as an independent branch of the NCWC's Social Action Department, which served as its secretariat) was "to promote, in conformity with the mind of the Church, the Peace of Christ in the Kingdom of Christ." The association was left by the newly founded U.S. Catholic Conference, reorganized by the American bishops from the NCWC, to go out of existence in 1968. During the CAIP's existence it produced dozens of pamphlets and other publications on topics relating to matters of war and peace. The most outstanding of its publications are indicated in the list above.

Recent and related books by the contributors:

Buchanan: *Where the Right Went Wrong: How Neoconservatives Subverted the Reagan Revolution and Hijacked the Bush Presidency*
The Death of the West: How Dying Populations and Immigrant Invasions Imperil Our Country and Civilization
A Republic, Not an Empire

Fleming: *The Morality of Everyday Life: Rediscovering an Ancient Alternative to the Liberal Tradition*

Margolis: *War at the Top of the World: The Struggle for Afghanistan, Kashmir and Tibet*

Berry: *The New Patriotism Series: Vol. I: In the Presence of Fear: Three Essays for a Changed World; Vol. II: Patriotism and the American Land; Vol. III: Citizens Dissent: Security, Morality, and Leadership in an Age of Terror*
Citizenship Papers

Gottfried: *Multiculturalism and the Politics of Guilt: Towards a Secular Theocracy*

Vance: *Christianity and War and Other Essays Against the Warfare State*

Periodicals (subscription information available on the Internet):

Current Concerns
Culture Wars
Chronicles: A Magazine of American Culture
Houston Catholic Worker

The American Conservative
Occidental Quarterly: A Journal of Western Thought and Opinion
Middle East Policy

Websites:

Antiwar.com
LewRockwell.com
www.arabmonitor.org
www.freearabvoice.org
www.benjaminforiraq.org
www.albasrah.net
www.occupationwatch.org
www.mfso.org
www.vvaw.org
www.ivaw.org
www.bringthemhomenow.org
www.gsfp.org
www.counterpunch.org

www.sandersresearch.com
www.globalsecurity.org
www.oldamericancentury.org
www.iacenter.org
www.tompaine.com
www.tomdispatch.com
www.wanniski.com
www.sobran.com
www.ericmargolis.com
www.prwatch.org
www.robert-fisk.com
www.thornwalker.com/ditch

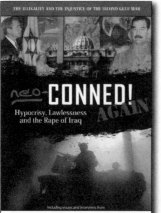